Senator Lenroot
of Wisconsin

Herbert F. Margulies

SENATOR LENROOT
OF WISCONSIN
A Political Biography
1900–1929

University of Missouri Press
Columbia & London, 1977

Library of Congress Cataloging in Publication Data

Margulies, Herbert F
    Senator Lenroot of Wisconsin:
    A Political Biography, 1900–1929

    Bibliography: p. 411
    Includes index.
    1. Lenroot, Irvine Luther, 1869–1949.
    2. Legislators—United States—Biography.
    3. Progressivism (United States politics)
    4. United States—Politics and government—
1901–1953. I. Title.
E748.L573M37 328.73′092′4 [B] 76–52341
ISBN 0–8262–0221–7

To Fran, Karen, Ned, Dan, and Laura

PREFACE

When Irvine L. Lenroot died in January 1949, one event in his eighty-year life was remembered in the obituaries. Lenroot, according to the papers and magazines, was the man chosen by the Republican Senate oligarchs of 1920 as vice-presidential running mate for Warren G. Harding, only to be turned down by the rebellious delegates favoring Calvin Coolidge. But for the unprecedented act of delegate independence, the obituaries noted, Lenroot would have become president on Harding's death in 1923. The reader could presume further that he would have been elected in his own right in 1924, as Coolidge was.

These stories were accurate and their presumptions were reasonable. If they tended to underplay other less sensational aspects of Lenroot's life, they nevertheless did focus on one of the more valid and important might-have-beens in American history. That being so, one may well wonder about this man—what was he like and how different would things have been had the plan of the party bosses not been frustrated.

In some ways, the obituaries, like historians, were unjust to Lenroot, not in what they said but in what they left unsaid. The fact is that Lenroot was a far more important figure than has generally been realized.

There are several reasons he has received less attention than his importance would warrant. One is simply that his private papers did not become available to historians until 1964 and proved small and fragmentary. Lenroot discarded a great amount of correspondence when he left the Senate in 1927 and again when he composed his memoirs in the 1940s.

Other factors are more important. Lenroot's career was intertwined with that of "Old Bob" La Follette. The nature of each of the two, the relationship between them, and the interaction of events upon them provide much of the explanation for Lenroot's undeserved obscurity. Through the early and majority of the years of their association, the two worked together in a close political and personal partnership. La Follette was the senior partner. Fourteen years older than Lenroot, La Follette entered the Wisconsin statehouse as governor when Lenroot first went to the assembly. La Follette had magnificent political talents. An extraordinary public speaker and magnetic personality, La Follette would often ignore political middlemen and would make direct, personal appeal to voters on the basis of some immediate issue. Issues came and went, but the stratagem persisted. Inevitably, for the politicians drawn to La Follette, the glorification of the leader became inseparable from the progressive cause that he represented. Lenroot understood this. Intensely loyal, devoted to the measures La Follette championed, and wedded by long-run if not always short-run self-interest to La Follette's cause, Lenroot, who was in any case neither flamboyant nor a ready mixer in his early days, willingly subordinated himself to La Follette in many ways. This situation persisted at least to 1912 and two unsuccessful presidential tries by La Follette. Gradually, Lenroot developed his own career in the House of Representatives in the years that followed, but he remained a progressive in a state whose progressive leader was still La Follette.

Between 1912 and 1918 the two gradually parted. They separated completely during the war, when Lenroot ran for the Senate in a special election as a champion of loyalty against a candidate closer to La Follette's antiwar view. During 1917 and 1918, Lenroot stood on at least equal ground with La Follette and shared the limelight. With peace, though, the political pendulum in Wisconsin swung decisively toward La Follette. Though Lenroot survived the senatorial election of 1920, his faction in the state was weak and divided. To the outside world, Wisconsin still meant La Follette.

Certain features of Lenroot's style and philosophy would have kept him from the spotlight under any circumstances. He shared a view quite widespread in the age of innocence preceding World War I—a view that some students of the time have called meliorism. That is, he believed in progress, but with the strong qualification that there would be many difficulties and setbacks along the way. The part of the good man was not to seek utopia in his own time, but to give his best effort to making the world a little bit better. Although an idealist in the common sense of the word, Lenroot was intensely practical in his day-to-day activities. Among other things, he appreciated the need for compromise, for the half-a-loaf solution. His skills and personal attributes lent themselves to this approach. Lenroot worked effectively with others. He was, first of all, a master of himself. As ambitious as any, he denied himself glory when to give the credit to another would advance the immediate end; he was uniformly friendly and courteous, though not effusive; he dealt honestly with others and earned their confidence; and he complimented those he dealt with by attributing to them motives as lofty as his own. Thus, many of Lenroot's most important efforts were behind the scenes and he was willing to let them remain so. Furthermore, the course of compromise led to the unspectacular and often unnoticed middle of the road.

During the years of Lenroot's service in the Senate, from 1918 to 1927, he was like a voyageur of old trying to steer a slender craft through narrow channels against treacherous currents. The war produced confusion, anger, suspicion, and extremism. Men and measures were seen as reactionary or radical. The moderate was lost sight of and the odds against Lenroot's efforts were such that his greatest accomplishments would produce little of immediate and visible gain. Thus, the Agricultural Credits Act of 1923, which Lenroot fathered and though a long step forward, was not equal to the massive and unprecedented challenge posed by the postwar agricultural crisis; the St. Lawrence Seaway project, potentially a godsend to the Middle West and West, and advanced over a period of years more strongly by Lenroot than any other national legislator of his time, met such opposition and delay that it was not until after his death and his contribution had been forgotten that the project was undertaken. With some skill, Lenroot helped to steer American adherence to the World Court protocol through the Senate in 1926, after four years of delay by isolationists like William E. Borah, only to have this modest step toward international cooperation blocked when one of America's five reservations proved unacceptable to the member states and nonnegotiable in the United States. For months in 1919 and 1920, Lenroot labored daily as a skillful, tactful leader of the mild reservationists to achieve ratification of the Versailles treaty and entry into the League of Nations, but against obstacles that were too great.

As exemplified above, claims for Lenroot's importance do not depend wholly on a list of triumphs. To a degree, he was important simply because of the prominent role he played in major events, such as the League of Nations fight, irrespective of the outcome. Happily, many of his legislative efforts were more fruitful. As speaker of the Wisconsin assembly, he helped to write and steer through the legislature the major reforms that earned Wisconsin its prominence as a progressive state—the primary election, railroad taxation, and railroad regulation measures were probably the most important of these. Lenroot rapidly achieved a position of leadership in Congress, as he had in the Senate. Elected in 1908, he soon took a leading part among the insurgents in the rules fight, in the overthrow of Speaker Joe Cannon, and in other battles of insurgency, especially in the early formation of the Mann-Elkins Act, which was to strengthen national regulation of railroads. Though a Republican during Woodrow Wilson's Democratic party-oriented administration, Lenroot was a prime mover behind the major conservation legislation of the period. During the war, the administration often depended heavily on Republican rather than Democratic support in the House, and Lenroot was often the man Wilson had to see. Through his career in the House and Senate, though not on the tax and tariff writing committees, Lenroot participated in tariff and tax debates and contributed significant amendments. He was generally considered a likely prospect for Speaker of the next Republican-controlled House of Representatives when, in 1918, he left the House for the Senate, much against his personal inclination.

Though an adroit and thorough legislative draftsman and skilled parliamentarian, Lenroot was not an innovative political philosopher. But, he had deep sincerity, strong logical powers, and was a fine orator. His thought and inclination usually led him toward the possible. As a result, Lenroot was, at certain key points, an important spokesman. In February 1917, for example, in a widely noted speech in Congress, he departed from the views of his colleagues in the Wisconsin delegation and argued for the policy of armed neutrality in the face of renewed submarine warfare by Germany.

Lenroot was often important politically. A very large measure of national attention focused on him in the spring of 1918, when he ran for the Senate in a special primary election. The contest was widely seen as a test of public sentiment toward the war. In this primary election, Lenroot vindicated Wisconsin's then suspect loyalty by defeating La Follette's candidate. Then, in a general election even more widely watched, he upheld the loyalty of the Republican party by defeating Democratic candidate Joseph E. Davies despite the appeals of President Wilson and Vice-President Marshall. This election gave the Republican party just the incentive needed to win control of Congress in November, even after the president made a similar partisan appeal, and Lenroot's vote proved essential to Republican organization of the Senate. The Treaty of Versailles soon came before that body.

While Lenroot merits attention because of his near brush with the presidency and his prominence in a wide range of important events in the years 1901 through 1928, he may be of equal interest for another reason. Study of Lenroot's life offers many insights to reformism in the twentieth century, especially the history of progressive Republicanism. Students of modern reform have been much interested in the relationship between the Progressive movement and later reform movements, such as the New Deal. Thus, some historians have focused attention on the Republican party, the majority party during most of the years between 1897 and 1932, as the main vehicle for progressivism in many of the states and the party of Theodore Roosevelt and of insurgency in the Taft years. In light of the conservative reputation of the Republican administrations of the 1920s and the hostility of most Republicans, including former progressives, to the New Deal of the 1930s, many questions have been asked about progressive Republicanism. How pronounced was the conservative drift? Was it latent in progressive ideology? What events, in particular, evoked it during the post-progressive years? Answers to such questions are elusive and must be sought by close study of a great many men and situations. Lenroot's career and thought offer partial answers to these and related questions.

Partly because of the nature and extent of the materials available, but still more because of the interests of the writer, what follows is a political biography. The purpose is to illuminate and draw lessons from Lenroot's public and political career.

The writer has been helped by more people than can practicably be named. Above all, however, I am grateful to Irvine L. Lenroot's daughter Katharine for unstinting assistance and encouragement.

H. F. M.
Honolulu, Hawaii
October 1975

CONTENTS

I

THE BACKGROUND OF
A LA FOLLETTE MAN

Irvine L. Lenroot was the son of pioneers. His parents were among the first of what was to become a great wave of emigrants who had left Sweden to come to America in the second half of the nineteenth century. In the United States, they chose the new frontier town of Superior, located in northwesternmost Wisconsin at the head of Lake Superior, in which to make their home and fortune and rear their family.

Irvine's father, Lars, the son of a tenant farmer whose own parents had but recently died in the parish poorhouse, was born in 1832 on a farm in Kristianstad County, a province of Skåne. Lars was the fifth of eight children and the fourth son. He was named Lars Larsson but when he became an apprentice to a smith, to avoid confusion with all the other sons of Larses, he changed his surname to Linderoth. It was as Lars Linderoth that, in the summer of 1854, he journeyed to Boston, joining a brother Nils, who had arrived the previous summer. Soon afterwards, he changed his name again to the simpler Lenroot. A year earlier, Fredrika Regina Larsdötter, then eighteen or nineteen years of age and a farmer's daughter from the province of Jönköping, also immigrated to the States, where she met Lars and eventually married him.[1]

Lars and Fredrika probably came mainly for economic reasons. But with their fellow migrants from Sweden, they brought noneconomic values that caused them to love their new home even when it disappointed their hopes for comfort. For them, the United States offered individual liberty and social equality.[2]

1. Katharine Lenroot, "Lars and Fredrika Lenroot—Swedish Pioneers," MS, pp. 1, 3. A copy is on deposit in the Irvine L. Lenroot Papers Addition, Manuscript Division, Library of Congress (hereafter referred to as LC). The Irvine L. Lenroot Papers Addition consists of papers donated subsequent to the initial deposit of Irvine L. Lenroot Papers. Duane Swanson, "The Lars Lenroot Family," enclosed in Katharine Lenroot to the author, 9 October 1969, citing entries in Lars's Swedish prayer book, in the possession of Irvine L. Nichols; Katharine Lenroot to the author, 8 June 1970, referring to emigration papers in her possession; Eric Anderson to Katharine Lenroot, 11 November 1969, enclosed in Katharine Lenroot to the author, 13 February 1970; Katharine Lenroot to the author, 18 October 1971, 19 April 1976.

2. On the traits of Swedish migrants see especially Florence Edith Janson, *The Background of Swedish Immigration, 1840–1930*, pp. 43–46; and George M. Stephenson, "When America Was the Land of Canaan," pp. 237–60.

Religion was important to many of the Swedish migrants, including the Lenroots, and the character of it was of some importance. A strong pietistic, democratic movement swept Sweden in the nineteenth century, directed against the formalism of the state church and social immorality. The earliest Swedish Lutheran pastors to come to America reflected this feeling—they were free, pietistic churchmen and strongly inclined toward temperance. The name *Lutheran* carried great prestige, but the organizers of the Swedish Lutheran church in America received little help from the Church of Sweden or American Lutheran churches. Emigration was a factor in schismatizing many from the church, but for those who remained, like the Lenroots, the pietistic impulse thrived under American conditions. The new Lutheranism rising in America included Sunday school, prayer meetings, and revival meetings.[3]

The Lenroot's first home was on a wilderness farm in Polk County, Wisconsin, three miles from the nearest neighbor. There, in September 1856, Fredrika bore a child, Louis, without any medical assistance.[4]

America was the land of hope and promise to the energetic and enterprising. One need only meet fortune halfway. Word of great opportunities and unlimited prospects in Superior, Wisconsin, spread among the settlements on the St. Croix River. The town had developed rapidly since 1853, when work began on the Sault Ste. Marie Canal, which would link Lake Superior with the other Great Lakes. No less a person than Sen. Stephen A. Douglas of Illinois had said, "A city at the head of Lake Superior has more possibilities for the future than any city on Lake Michigan." Superior was known to have a wonderful harbor. A railroad was already planned to link Superior to the Mississippi and points south. And the place was talked of as an eastern terminus for a transcontinental railroad. The canal, occasioned by the rapid growth in iron and copper mining on Michigan's Upper Peninsula during the forties, was completed in 1855, and the enterprising leaders of Superior had succeeded with the support of the federal government in building two roads to the south. Lars sold one hundred-sixty acres of land for two hundred dollars, and in early summer of 1857, he and his brother Nils, Fredrika, Louis, and the belongings traveled by horse and team and wagon to Superior. The trip took four days.[5]

If the Lenroots had any doubts, what they found in Superior must have been reassuring. Such a place could hardly fail to give fair return for honest

3. George M. Stephenson, *The Religious Aspects of Swedish Immigration: A Study of Immigrant Churches*, pp. 17, 20–21, 24, 26, 147–48, 156, 164.

4. Katharine Lenroot, "Lars and Fredrika Lenroot," p. 12, Lenroot Papers Addition; entry, Lars Lenroot prayer book, enclosed in Katharine Lenroot to the author, 9 October 1969.

5. Attachment to Nelson Thomasson to John C. Spooner, 24 January 1899, Box 27, John C. Spooner Papers, LC; Reginald Mathison Shaw, "Historical Geography of Superior Wisconsin" (Ph.D. diss.), p. 38; excerpt from "Greeting from the City of Superior to the Minnesota Conference of the Scandinavian Lutheran Synod of North America, Feb. 9 to 18, 1892," enclosed in Katharine Lenroot to the author, 9 October 1969; Katharine Lenroot, "Lars and Fredrika Lenroot," pp. 10–11, Lenroot Papers Addition.

labor. By then over fifteen hundred people were there. The harbor was as much as anyone could hope for. Slanting from northwest to southeast, Superior Bay was ten miles long and a half to three quarters of a mile in width.

The possibility of rivalry with Minnesotans on the western shore of St. Louis Bay and Lake Superior seemed remote, when one contrasted the handful of people in what was called Duluth with the bustling numbers at Superior, where 2,500 would be recorded by the end of the summer, and when compared to the sharp granite cliffs of Duluth with the broad, flat acres of Superior, which sloped gently to the harbor, inviting the ships, trains, shops, and factories of the future. Almost immediately, Lars wrote a glowing report to his brother-in-law in Sweden, urging him to come to the States. The John Swensons, along with Lars's mother and his younger brother Swen, set out for Superior, arriving in 1858.[6]

For various complex reasons, the railroad construction on which promoters and settlers had depended was delayed. Superior was still confidently awaiting its railroad when, starting in late August 1857, the possibility of a railroad fell through. As a result, values fell and people moved as swiftly as they had come. That fall, almost everyone left, and the town was reduced to perhaps five hundred. Duluth was abandoned altogether.[7]

Almost a decade later, a visitor found Superior "a desolate looking town of deserted wharves, broken-windowed warehouses, dilapidated shops and dwellings." In 1872 an old-time resident complained that "the dulness [sic] of Superior this year is distressing. In broad day you can stand on the street perhaps 5 minutes, without seeing a soul in sight, up or down. It was never, not even in 1858, 59 or 60, so dull as now." Yet Superior was no livelier eight years later.[8]

Lars Lenroot had built a modest house for his family. He also constructed a blacksmith shop, which was across from the house. There the Lenroots remained through it all. Perhaps they had no good alternative initially. Despite repeated disappointments, the residents who remained boasted of Superior's geographical advantages and talked of new railroad schemes. Lars Lenroot acquired as many town lots as he could.[9]

Superior began to revive in 1881, but it did not grow substantially until

6. Paper by Edward Swenson, Sr., 16 December 1931, in the possession of the author; Swanson, "The Lars Lenroot Family," enclosed in Katharine Lenroot to the author, 9 October 1969.

7. Lillian K. Stewart, *A Pioneer of Old Superior,* p. 189.

8. S. T. Trowbridge, "A Week in Duluth," *Atlantic Monthly* 25:609 (June 1870), quoted in Shaw, "Superior," p. 81; James Bardon to Ethan C. Clarke, 26 July 1872, Box 1, Ethan C. Clarke Family Papers, Minnesota State Historical Society (hereafter referred to as MSHS); *Superior Times,* 21 August 1880, quoted in *Superior Sunday Leader,* 4 October 1891.

9. Helen Marie Wolner, "The History of Superior, Wisconsin, to 1900" (M.A. thesis), pp. 37, 100–101; Frederick Merk, *Economic History of Wisconsin During the Civil War Decade,* Wisconsin Historical Publications, vol. 1, pp. 279, 284; J. H. Beers and Co., *Commemorative Biographical Record of the Upper Lake Region,* pp. 202–3.

1889 when mining, timber, and wheat sustained local commerce, and manufacturing, railroads, and shipping lines served the port, and wealthy land companies developed town lots and commercial property.

Lars supported his family through the years in various ways. He did some smithing for local residents, Chippewa Indian parties, and other transients; he himself tried mining occasionally; later he ran a scow, engaged in timber operations and finally moved into real estate. Through the hard times, the family helped itself to fish, game, and wild fruit, and farmed a little.[10]

The nature of society in Superior and the place of the Lenroots in it in the early days is conjectural. There is some reason to believe that they were on the fringe of a tenuous aristocracy of what might have been termed *the better people.* The term, as applicable to a struggling frontier community in which distinctions of wealth were merely gradations of poverty and pedigree was ludicrously irrelevant, is meant to connote attributes of culture and character prized by the Puritans and their descendants. Certainly, Lars was a leader among the Swedes of whom there were thirty-nine in 1860.[11]

The Lenroots had much in common with the better people among the predominant Yankees. Beyond a basic community of interest and shared experiences and hopes, there were attributes of mind and spirit—a mutual respect for cultural attainment; a shared enthusiasm for America itself and the things it represented—equality, freedom, opportunity, ideals, and virtues that for the descendants of the Puritans were more highly developed and prized on the western frontier than in the more formal towns and cities of the east. The Lenroots shared, also, in strong piety and certain common beliefs that cut across the gap between Calvinist and Lutheran backgrounds, including temperance, hard work, thrift, and charity.

In the year 1857 when the Lenroots came to Superior, a schoolteacher named Irvine Willard Gates arrived with his wife and family. Born in 1822 in Hancock, New Hampshire, where his father and grandfather had farmed, and his father had been a member of the legislature and a justice of the peace, Gates began a lifetime career as a teacher at the age of sixteen. His life in Superior paralleled and intertwined with the life of Lars Lenroot, and after the death of each in 1898, the relationship continued through their sons.

Gates lived on a forty-acre farm seven blocks to the south of the Lenroot home and shop. When school was out, he attended to his farm, which had a barn, garden, and hayfield. He was the chief pillar of the Presbyterian

10. Irvine L. Lenroot, "Memoirs," pp. 3–24, Box 13, Lenroot Papers; Irvine L. Lenroot, MS speech, "Annual Picnic Old Settlers Association, July 24, 1929," Box 9, Lenroot Papers.

11. Wolner, "Superior," p. 14, note 25; John Morrison Barnett, "Annals of the Early Protestant Churches at Superior," *Proceedings of the State Historical Society of Wisconsin, 1907,* pp. 217–43; Clara and Irvine L. Lenroot, "Memories," MS, Lenroot Papers Addition; Harry Ashton in *Superior Telegram,* 26 June 1909. The "Memories" are clearly the work of Clara, written in the 1930s.

church and its Sunday school as well as of the Bible Society and became the first president of the Free Library Board. Politically, he was a Republican.[12]

Gates and Lars Lenroot had a great deal in common, and there was much that each could admire in the other. To a Swedish immigrant, for a man to be at once an intellectual and religious leader and yet be kindly, democratic, pious, and willing to work with his hands must have been impressive. Undoubtedly, Louis Lenroot and his brother Albert attended Gates's school. Beyond that, the connection between the two men during the sixties is suppositional. Did Gates, a leader in a very small community, by representing Puritanism in its loftier, kindlier forms, serve to bridge the gap between *the better people* among Yankee and Swede, and did the Lenroots perceive and appreciate the fact? Perhaps. In any case, when Fredrika gave birth to a third son on 31 January 1869 she and Lars named him after Gates.[13]

In 1876, Irvine Luther Lenroot, almost seven, began at the nearby three-room schoolhouse. His father thought the children would do better in later years if they were enrolled in school at approximately that age. Irvine was prepared for the new challenge. He was a bright boy and his parents had given him preliminary instruction in the alphabet and reading. He was already able to read simple sentences. His mother and father had been in America for sixteen and fifteen years, respectively, when Irvine was born, and they stressed speaking English in the home. And young Irvine heard a native-accent speech among playmates and townfolk. So language posed no problem or embarrassment. Despite their poverty, the Lenroots kept books and an organ in their home and inculcated in the children attitudes suitable to what lay ahead in the future.[14]

No pictures or physical description of the new schoolboy survive. Certainly, though, he was fair of hair and skin, on the slender side, and probably of average height. He was quiet and well mannered, perhaps even shyer than others; but he was curious and adventurous, enjoyed play, was a good athlete, and had a need for achievement and recognition. According to a boyhood fishing companion, he would share his belongings generously.[15]

One might suspect that any second-generation immigrant lad growing up an American might have suffered from insecurity and self-doubt. These traits did sometimes show, but they were secondary and kept well under

---

12. Beers, *Record of the Upper Lake Region*, pp. 7–8; Shaw, "Superior," p. 106; Achille H. Bertrand, "Recollections of Old Superior," (pamphlet), p. 43; Clara Lenroot, "I. W. Gates: The Beloved Teacher," speech, n.d. (Summer 1923), Lenroot Papers Addition; Barnett, "Protestant Churches at Superior," pp. 229–30.

13. Lenroot, "Memoirs," p. 14, Box 13, Lenroot Papers.

14. Ibid., p. 9; Lenroot to Shirley Briesemeister, 24 January 1948, Box 13, Lenroot Papers; Katharine Lenroot, "Lars and Fredrika Lenroot," p. 19, Lenroot Papers Addition.

15. James Hile in *Superior Telegram*, 3–4 August 1918.

control. One emerges from a study of his life impressed with the firmness of his psychological foundations. A number of factors in his early childhood combined to produce this result.

Poverty was no source of shame, for everyone in town was poor. Indeed, his family was somewhat better off than most.

Free sources of amusement abounded; the children had one another, the bay, and the forest all readily available. There were some shops and work places to visit, too. In preschool years, young Irvine spent a lot of his time in his father's blacksmith shop. The place was a mecca for children and grown-ups; it had much the same attraction as Longfellow's celebrated blacksmith shop. The proprietor and host, Irvine could easily see, was not only a man of awesome competence and wisdom, but one who was held in high esteem by young and old alike. Achille H. Bertrand recalled Lars as below medium height, with a beard of the fragile kind, "as was his physical appearance . . . but wielding a blacksmith hammer the major portion of a long and industrious life disillusioned any impression of a delicate constitution." Lars, Bertrand remembered, "was a man of fine intelligence; kept posted on matters of current interest, and loved to discuss them in his dispassionate and logical way." Clara Clough, too, and Irvine himself, remembered Lars as "a shrewd and well informed man." [16]

Years afterwards, Irvine remembered the periodic visits that Chippewa groups made to his father's shop. They marched in single file, "sometimes to get guns and traps repaired but more often to consult with him about their problems in connection with the Government . . . I remember how fascinated I was by the Indian speeches made to father and his replies, wherein he rarely hesitated to find the right word in the Chippewa language." [17]

Irvine's father continued as a leader in the Swedish community. Through him the first Lutheran church was organized, and he served as its officer throughout his lifetime. In Irvine's early boyhood and years after, the church had no regular pastor but occasional services were held by a visiting pastor, who always stayed overnight with the Lenroots.

Irvine's mother had the best traits of those pioneer women who survived and succeeded. She mastered every frontier task and every obligation of hospitality and piety with no loss of spirit or equanimity. Two photographs, taken in the eighties and early nineties, show a small woman, of rounded face, hair parted in the middle and combed back, with ears exposed. The face in the second photograph is heavily lined, with a somewhat determined-looking straight mouth. No letters by her remain, and little was written of her. Clara Clough remembered her as "utterly self-affacing [sic]." Only

16. Lenroot, MS speech, "Annual Picnic Old Settlers Association, July 24, 1929," Box 9, Lenroot Papers; Clara and Irvine L. Lenroot, "Memories," Lenroot Papers Addition; Bertrand, "Recollections," p. 55.

17. Lenroot, "Memoirs," p. 4, Box 13, MS speech, "Annual Picnic Old Settlers Association, July 24, 1929," Box 9, Lenroot Papers.

rarely did an unusual event in her life imprint itself on the memory of her family. One incident remembered occurred in the mid-seventies when a destitute brother of Lars came to Superior looking for work in the woods, and how she worked all night by dim candlelight to make him a pair of blue jeans for the next day. As a result, she supposedly damaged the sight in one eye. Irvine remembered his mother as a deeply religious woman, "devoted and ambitious for her children." She was evidently a woman of compassion and also good sense.[18]

According to the census of 1880, the population of Superior decreased in the seventies, and the immigrants remained as the substantial minority—191 foreign-born persons as compared to 464 people of the native-born populace. The children of Lenroot and of other immigrants were included as natives. The number of Swedes and Norwegians was totaled at 51 by the census taker. Only Canada contributed more—66.[19]

Included in the foreign-born population of Superior and Duluth were many close relatives, aunts and uncles, cousins, and a grandmother. Their presence could only have been comforting rather than constricting for young Irvine.

At about the same time that Irvine started school, he began his lifetime of work. Lars needed all the help his children could give him, partly just to keep things going but partly to take advantage of new opportunities. By the time Irvine was seven or eight, he was responsible for cleaning the barn each day after school, getting in wood, and keeping generally useful until dark. "When I was about twelve years old," he later recalled, "I was taking care of two cows and one horse, and had to take them over to the neighborhood pump every day to water them. The pump was at all times a pretty stiff proposition for a boy of my size, and when I first resumed my duties after an attack of scarlet fever, the task of watering the stock was almost a physical impossibility, but I did it, though the memory of my great weakness still makes me tired!" He also had to do some minor chores in the early morning. School of course occupied much time. And in the haying season, Irvine helped his brothers get in the hay, which Lars grew on his vacant lots. "A two hour play spell on a Saturday afternoon was a great treat." [20] Later he helped with the other family enterprises. Due to the death of an older brother and sister, Albert and Eda, and the birth of Nellie and Arthur, Lenroot's help with chores was of great necessity. In his teens he was a store clerk, peddled milk, helped his father in the cutting and grading of streets

18. Photographs, Box 14, Lenroot Papers; Clara Clough Lenroot, *Long, Long Ago*, p. 60; Katharine Lenroot, "Lars and Fredrika Lenroot," p. 13, Lenroot Papers Addition; Lenroot, "Memoirs," pp. 7, 14–15; Lenroot to Briesemeister, 24 January 1948, Box 13, Lenroot Papers.

19. Bureau of the Census, *Tenth Census of the United States, 1880: Population*, vol. 1 (Washington, D.C., 1883), p. 553.

20. Irvine L. and Clara Lenroot, "Memories," Lenroot Papers Addition; Lenroot, "Memoirs," pp. 21–22, Box 13, Lenroot Papers.

in West Superior, worked as an axman, and did odd jobs at his father's lumber camps.[21]

When at last family fortunes improved, Fredrika seized the chance to send Irvine to the Parsons Business College in Duluth. Lars might have preferred that Irvine continue full time in the prospering timber business, but on this point his wife was very insistent and prevailed. In the fall of 1887, Irvine enrolled for the full business course, including shorthand and typing. Not yet nineteen, he looked ahead to a future as a lawyer and a career in politics. Still, he was glad to help in the lumber camp on weekends and to help with a new house. At this time, or very shortly after, Irvine began to participate in real-estate speculations, acquiring much know-how in the process.[22]

For Lenroot and two classmates, graduation from Parsons Business College was a noteworthy event. Exuberantly, the three young men confided their ambitions for the future. Lenroot said he would go in for honest politics and hoped to become a U.S. senator. A week later, on 7 February 1889, he was glad to start as a stenographer in the law offices of Ross & Dwyer, a prominent Superior firm, at a salary of sixty dollars a month. He continued to live with his family for a time. Nevertheless, his graduation and immediate employment marked the end of his youth and the beginning of his career and his manhood.[23]

Young Lenroot was not physically imposing. Of medium height, perhaps five feet seven, he was at this time and for years afterwards quite slender, weighing about one hundred-thirty pounds. The prominent jaw, strong nose, and piercing brown eyes, though softened somewhat by a well-trimmed mustache that he affected for a few years, seemed better suited to someone of larger frame. Casual acquaintances might have noticed a similar incongruity in his demeanor. Quiet and reserved among them, the result of Scandinavian custom and breeding, some shyness, and a cool intelligence that set him apart from others, he betrayed his nervous energy.[24]

When he launched his stenographic career at the age of twenty, basic habits and attitudes and ideas had already set. Certainly, the lifetime habit

21. Lenroot, "Memoirs," pp. 3–24, Box 13, Lenroot Papers.

22. Ibid., p. 24; Louis Lenroot, Diary, 14, 15, 21, 22, 28 January, 7, 9 July, 5 October 1888, Lenroot Papers Addition; Hulett Merritt to Lenroot, 2 August 1939, Box 3, Lenroot Papers; Lenroot to "Dear Folks," 15 December 1889, to "Dear Father," 14 January 1890, Lenroot Papers Addition.

23. Lenroot's confession of political ambition was recalled in Merritt to Lenroot, 2 August 1939, Box 3, Lenroot Papers. Though Merritt's letter came forty years after the event, his account is probably accurate. No intermediate contacts between them could have caused confusion, and the number involved in the incident was small. The occasion was memorable and the event simple. On the facts of Lenroot's employment see Irvine L. to Nellie Lenroot, 7 February 1892, Lenroot Papers Addition; and Lenroot, "Memoirs," p. 26, Box 13, Lenroot Papers.

24. Photographs, Box 14, Lenroot Papers; interview with John Lenroot, 28 June 1970; interview with Katharine Lenroot, 2 April 1969.

of work was deeply rooted. He had developed it from an early age. Often, the work he had done had been difficult, even painful; often it had been dull, sheer drudgery; frequently it cost him chances to play or to relax. But always it had been necessary. He had unquestioningly played his part in the family's struggle for survival and, in the last years, for some security and comfort. Many of the satisfactions of his early life were from the triumphs of larger responsibility successfully undertaken. So work would continue to be natural and good in itself, and accomplishment would continue to yield satisfaction. And he would continue to seek avenues of usefulness and opportunities for larger responsibility and achievement.

The Puritan upheld work as a godly trait.[25] Irvine Lenroot perhaps also shared this belief. If he did follow the heritage of Puritanism, there is good reason for it.

The descendants of New England fathers had moved to the Midwest and made that section the heartland of latter-day Puritanism, thus affecting Superior.[26]

Perhaps most influential of Superior's latter-day Puritans was Irvine W. Gates. Irvine Lenroot certainly was strongly influenced by this man for whom he was named. Apart from Mrs. A. C. Brown, with whom Irvine studied for about the first three years of his schooling, Gates was his only teacher. There were no grades in the small school but many classes. Under Gates's tutelage, Irvine studied the three Rs, algebra, plane and solid geometry, trigonometry, physics, chemistry, physical geography, ancient and modern history, and zoology. Gates offered Latin also, but Irvine and his parents saw no value in it and he did not study it, to his later regret.

"Mr Gates was a wonderful teacher, highly educated, music loving and deeply religious," Irvine wrote years later. "Each session of the school was opened by his reading a chapter from the Bible followed by a prayer. Then came a period of singing by the school to the accompaniment of a melodeon played by one of the pupils. Each pupil was furnished with a book entitled 'The Song Garden.' I have never had any ear for music, cannot carry a tune, but under Mr. Gates I did learn to read music." [27]

By all accounts, Gates was indeed an exceptional teacher, who made a profound and general impact. Bertrand, in his recollections, singled him out for special attention as a teacher who always gave a student a patient, interested, sympathetic hearing. For violations of rules, Bertrand recalled, Gates thought a firm reprimand was sufficient, administered without anger. Another former student, Clara Clough, felt that Gates was "called" to teach. His chief characteristics were optimism and enthusiasm. "His interest never slackened; his enthusiasm never waned," she remembered. "He entered the schoolhouse each morning with a firm, elastic step, rapped with his ruler upon the desk, and instantly we were alert and attentive. His enthusiasm

25. Milton Viorst, *Fall From Grace: The Republican Party and the Puritan Ethic*, pp. 7–8.
26. Ibid., p. 3.
27. Lenroot, "Memoirs," pp. 14, 16, Box 13, Lenroot Papers.

outlasted the regular hours of school and he made his schoolhouse a social center for the community." [28]

Moral instruction was integral to liberal and classical education in the period. Imparted by a sympathetic teacher like Gates, it was bound to take hold. Gates exerted influence also through the Presbyterian church and Sunday school. The Presbyterian church was something of a community church at which pastors of various denominations frequently preached. The Lutherans had a building but no regular pastor when Irvine was young. In any case, services were in Swedish, then and later. So Irvine attended the Presbyterian church. In 1891 he became a member. Writing of it later, Lenroot added, by way of explanation, that Gates was the leading member of the church.[29]

The mature Lenroot showed in his thought and rhetoric the abiding impact of a latter-day Puritanism, imparted through school and church and all the subtle ways by which the Yankee tamed the West. At a teacher-training school in Marinette in 1923, Lenroot told the graduating class: "While we must protect equality of opportunity, we must also protect the rewards of industry and perseverance. The man who loafs his way through life, doing nothing for society or himself, is usually the man who cries out loudest against the inequality of wealth." Further condemning the radicalism of his time, Lenroot recalled that in his youth Superior "did not have one family possessing the luxuries now at the command of the average man." The new teachers, he said, should teach the youth "that the acquiring of wealth is not the measure of a successful life," and that "there can be no true success without service to one's fellow men, and the greater the service the greater the success." "Nor does wealth bring happiness," he added. While his message was conservative, Lenroot was not taking a laissez-faire position. Still thinking of the radicalism then rampant in the state, he urged that men "must be big enough in mind and heart" that in seeking justice for one group, they be concerned not to do injustice to another. Laborers should deal justly with capital, in short. But by the same token, a capitalist "must realize that he has no more right to drive a hard bargain with labor than labor has to drive a hard bargain with capital." [30]

The speech, typical of his viewpoint in the twenties and differing from his earlier pronouncements as a progressive only in emphasis, embodied many of the doctrines of Puritanism. It contained the familiar association of failure with vice, and by implication success with virtue; it presumed that

28. Bertrand, "Recollections," p. 44; Clara Lenroot, *Long, Long Ago*, p. 60. Gates is praised also in Clara Lenroot, "I. W. Gates," Lenroot Papers Addition; and in Beers, *Record of the Upper Lake Region*, pp. 7–8.

29. Clara Lenroot, "I. W. Gates," Lenroot Papers Addition; Lenroot, MS speech, "Annual Picnic Old Settlers Association, July 24, 1929," Box 9, Lenroot Papers; interview with Katharine Lenroot, 20 November 1968; Katharine Lenroot, editor, Clara Lenroot, Diary, 23 January 1891, Lenroot Papers Addition.

30. *Milwaukee Sentinel*, 15 June 1923.

the pursuit of self-interest, as by the capitalist, is socially productive. Here was the old idea of the "calling," which gave divine sanction for an individual doing what he could do best. To this extent, the speech adhered to the Puritan glorification of work and the pursuit of material blessings. But the Puritans qualified their point. They followed neither Epicurus nor Adam Smith, nor did Lenroot. The Puritans spoke of a "general calling" as well as a "particular calling," the former involving direct service to God and man, as against the indirect service rendered by the man who pursued self-interest. And so Lenroot put material gain in its proper place and commended a life of service. And to the average man, engaged in the particular calling, the Puritan warned that he should be guided by canons of fairness, not the advantage sometimes afforded by the impersonal laws of supply and demand. Indeed, when they had the power, the Puritans legislated to this effect. Lenroot urged the same self-restraint. Privately, he felt despair and a sense of something going wrong when businessmen did not conduct themselves by a standard of morality.

Lenroot's family background, far from posing an alternative to Puritan attitudes toward work, reinforced them. Lutheranism had its version of the idea of a calling. In Sweden, the ministers carefully inculcated in the peasantry respect for work and its attendant virtues as godly. Apart from that, conditions of life were such that survival alone required the acceptance of such values. The Swedish Lutheran ministers also preached a doctrine of resignation and acceptance of one's appointed station in life. The liberal descendants of the Vikings, however, readily dismissed these teachings when given the opportunity. Their latent individualism craved expression. For Lars and Fredrika, the Lutheran church remained the proper one; there could be no other. But they did not object to Irvine's entry into a church and culture that they knew to be basically godly and that would not only sanction but also facilitate his personal advancement. By the 1880s, of course, the Lenroots had been in the west for three decades. As large numbers of Swedish and other immigrants came to Superior and its environs in the late eighties, Lars and Fredrika were glad to help them, but they were no longer as one with them. They were, in part at least, "old settlers."

Lenroot's optimistic attitudes toward work, and other matters, were partly shaped by the frontier conditions of his youth. In early Superior, it was too apparent for argument that progress came from effort and initiative, and that the most successful people were those who contributed most. His own father was a prime example. The urban frontier, as historians of Jacksonianism have stressed, was a capitalist frontier. Even the boom spirit that pervaded Superior, in the early days and after, with all its materialism, selfishness, boastfulness, and tendency toward ethical compromise, contained within itself much that Lenroot could accept and take with him. It was, after all, in the direction of progress, and all would share in the benefits to the extent of their contributions; there was something heartening, too, in the spirit of community generated by the common effort and interest.

Although Lenroot might have been influenced by the hearty spirit of frontier capitalism, he was never wholly captivated by it. He learned as a boy how economic hopes might be frustrated, regardless of one's worth or ability or effort. To a degree, he guarded himself against the land speculation in Superior. In this regard, he acted more cautiously than his father, whose faith in Superior was unquestioning. After his father became land rich, with property valued at about $250,000 Irvine urged him to sell $100,-000 worth of property and put the money into government bonds, then yielding 5 percent interest. Lars would not take the advice, saying nothing was sounder than Superior real estate. Irvine did not take his own advice and lost his own speculative parcels when the depression of 1893 struck Superior. He did not feel too badly about it, he later recalled, "because what I had, other than my home, was the result of real estate speculation." [31] He felt more comfortable when individuals contributed to the development of their community by solid, nonspeculative work, done with respect to the highest standards of honesty, fair play, and social responsibility.

Another body of thought reinforced the lessons of Puritanism and urban frontier capitalism. By the late nineteenth century, stimulated by the Civil War, a rather vague but powerful spirit of patriotism pervaded the north and west especially. Nationalistic symbols—the Constitution, the Founding Fathers, the flag—were honored. There could be no ideological division on the subject, for Americanism embraced all desiderata—individualism, freedom, equality, opportunity, democracy, constitutionalism, Christianity, capitalism, progress. Having settled her own internal problems and preserved the Republic, America was seen now to be proceeding toward fulfillment of her mission to the world. She was developing her economic might and peopling the continent. Whether by example or by the more direct route of economic and religious and military expansion, America would, by fulfilling her own destiny, benefit mankind at large, in the same fashion as did the individual in his particular calling. In this, America was pursuing a destiny foreseen by the earliest Puritans, who looked to the new world as a new Zion, where God's plan would unfold. The western frontier continued as the hotbed of Americanism since colonial times. To Swedish immigrant families, all this was congenial. And so, again, the individual, pursuing his own advantage, if he did so in a moral way, was seen as contributing to a larger good, to the upbuilding of his country.[32]

The economic doctrines of Lenroot's youth, evolving from the Puritan cultural background and the frontier, buttressed by attitudes brought from Sweden and sanctified by an overriding Americanism, dovetailed reasonably well with the standard economic policy of the time, the canons of laissez-faire. During the late nineteenth century, Smithian thought was strongly

31. Lenroot, "Memoirs," p. 33, Box 13, Lenroot Papers.
32. For a good discussion of late nineteenth-century Americanism see Louis Hartz, *The Liberal Tradition in America: An Interpretation of American Political Thought Since the Revolution* (New York, 1955), pp. 203–27.

supported by social Darwinism, popularized in America by the Englishman, Herbert Spencer, and American scholars such as John Fiske and William Graham Sumner. Laissez-faire and social Darwinism joined in justifying the pursuit of self-interest on grounds of social utility. Both, however, if pushed to the extreme, suggested conclusions unacceptable to most Americans. It was all well and good for the fittest to survive, since they contributed most, but Americans could not be callous to the unfit. Thus, Superior newspapers of the nineties, though full of the conventional economic wisdom, made little use of cliches of social Darwinism.[33]

Thus, one might theorize that self-interest, if morally pursued, would be conducive to social good. From this perspective, it was possible to view socialists as preaching a lesser doctrine, one that required people to subordinate their individualism to narrow class interests and to seek their personal advantage at the expense of persons in another class instead of making contributions to society at large. Lenroot increasingly viewed affairs from this relatively conservative perspective, in his later years. But the seeds of progressivism were also present. And the younger Lenroot focused his attention on men and corporations that did not follow the rules of the game, that pursued self-interest dishonestly and by ways inimically alike to the welfare of society and to the opportunities of less powerful individuals.

The economic attitudes of his youth influenced Lenroot not just in his political views but in his personal philosophy. Though, like a good Puritan, he saw the general calling, involving direct service to the community, as the highest way of life, he saw virtue too in the conscientious and honest pursuit of self-interest. In his own life, he set out to combine the two. Though Lenroot knew poverty as a youth, he was never mired in a horizonless culture of poverty. He saw in his father and others an example of enterprise and found ambition and achievement to be unanimously applauded. Naturally enough, he set out to capitalize on his abilities to the fullest. The American dream appeared in various forms, holding out as an ultimate goal wealth or position or recognition for achievement. While never entirely impervious to the first two, his ambition focused largely on the last.

To end at this point would result in an incomplete and distorted description of Irvine. He was, above all else, well bred, in the best sense of the phrase. And he had a penetrating intelligence. Recognition might be won without real achievement, but that would be a sham, a false fame and a shallow success. If choice had to be made, as it sometimes did, the proper course, he knew, was for the accomplishment, the social good, not the fame. He knew, too, the virtues of patience and honor in the pursuit of ambition.

Lenroot began his career as a confirmed Republican. The Scandinavians of the Civil War and post-Civil War era were almost automatically Republicans. To its devotees, the party stood for union, liberty, morality, competence, and progress. Feelings were strong and deep and Lenroot was ex-

33. Kendall Birr, "Social Ideas of Superior Business Men, 1880–1898" (M.A. thesis), p. 267.

posed to Republicanism at a tender age. His father and older brother were ardent Republicans, as were most of his neighbors.[34]

In the fall of 1888, while Irvine was still studying at the business college in Duluth, Clara Clough McCoy, a widow, enrolled. The Cloughs and Lenroots lived within two blocks of one another. As a teenager and later, Clara had visited often in Lars's blacksmith shop and Fredrika's parlor. After the death of James McCoy in November 1886, Clara, who was twelve years older than Irvine, had been his Sunday schoolteacher. The Northern Pacific Railway Company ran a special train between Superior and Duluth, and Irvine and Clara improved their acquaintance during the morning and evening trips to and from Duluth. Despite the disparity in age, they were drawn strongly to one another. On 19 April 1889 they became engaged.[35]

Clara was an extraordinary person. From early childhood, she loved nature and the free play of imagination. At the same time, she was herself highly cultivated, schooled in the conventional arts and graces of the Victorian maiden and in the dogmas of religion and society. Beneath, though, was a loving and pious nature.

The frontier often evoked the best, as well as the worst, in American character. For families like hers, it acted as an abrasive against the barnacles of superficiality, snobbery, and superciliousness that often blighted old families in the more comfortable and regular circumstances of the east.

Clara had a beauty that was of the ageless sort. There was a dreamlike quality to her face, dark complexioned, with almond-shaped eyes, a well-modeled, gentle smile, regular features tending toward roundness, and topped by brown curls. She was more attractive in her early thirties than she had been a decade earlier. She was roughly four inches shorter than Irvine.[36]

Clara was born to Katharine and Solon Huntington Clough on 14 August 1856. The Cloughs were upright, cultured, pious people, of New York state origin. Solon Clough had served as a circuit judge and was a close friend of Sen. John C. Spooner.[37]

34. The Swedish attachment to the Republican party is noted in Paul Kleppner, *The Cross of Culture: A Social Analysis of Midwestern Politics, 1850–1900*, pp. 52, 71, and Richard Jensen, *The Winning of the Midwest: Social and Political Conflict, 1888–1896*, p. 80. Louis's strong attachment to the Republican party is evident in his diary entries for 3 and 6 April 1883, 26 October, 2, 3, 4, 7, 8, 9, 10, 11 November 1888, and 2 April 1889 as summarized in Katharine Lenroot, "Louis John Lenroot," pp. 12–13, Lenroot Papers Addition.

35. Katharine Lenroot, "Lars and Fredrika Lenroot," p. 22, Lenroot Papers Addition; Lenroot, "Memoirs," p. 27, Box 13, Lenroot Papers; Clara Lenroot, Diary, 9 April 1926, Lenroot Papers Addition. Lenroot, in his "Memoirs," makes no mention of the fact that Clara had been his Sunday schoolteacher. This was common knowledge, however, confirmed by Katharine Lenroot in a conversation with the author in June 1969.

36. Interview with Katharine Lenroot, 2 April 1969; photographs, Box 14, Lenroot Papers.

37. Clara Lenroot, *Long, Long Ago*, pp. 2, 16, 35, 64; Beers, *Record of the Upper Lake Region*, p. 121; Supreme Court of Wisconsin, "In Memory of Solon H. Clough," 3 February 1914, Lenroot Papers Addition.

Clara's father, a bearded, spare-looking man, was the unchallenged master of his household. Clara both loved and feared him. Her mother, somewhat delicate in appearance, possessed a gentle sweetness that was rather taken for granted. Both parents were devout Baptists. In Superior, finding no Baptist church, the family joined the First Presbyterian Church.[38] Clara was truly pious and properly respectful of her parents and their authority. But she was more than a dutiful, ornamental daughter of Victorian mould. When she fell in love with James McCoy, her parents opposed the marriage. Clara persisted in her determination, however, and eventually it was the Cloughs who relented.[39] McCoy died of peritonitis in 1886.[40]

Again Clara asserted herself when her parents objected to her marrying Irvine Lenroot, who to them was disgracefully young for her.[41] Eventually after the marriage, her stern father again relented.

The marriage was successful, in the sense that Clara and Irvine were extremely devoted to one another for over half a century, until Clara's death in 1942.

If Lenroot's youthful high-mindedness needed any buttressing, Clara provided it. She always admired her husband extravagantly, was never much of a feminist, and could not compete with him in knowledge of public affairs. So she rarely presumed to advise him, and concurred unreservedly in his opinions on practical matters. One senses that she influenced him nevertheless, by her very presence and outlook on things.

Irvine and Clara had been married in Minneapolis, where he had worked and studied stenography. Soon after Clara's father accepted the marriage, the young couple returned to Superior. Lenroot did stenographic work privately for the city and for the firm of Ross, Dwyer and Smith. When in 1893 the firm's newest member, Charles Smith, was elected judge of the superior court, Lenroot became reporter. He had long hoped to go to the university in Madison to study law, but the onset of severe economic depression and the birth of two daughters, Katharine and Dorothy, in 1891 and 1893 made that impossible. Instead Lenroot read law on his own and took instruction with Judge Smith. In December 1897, he took and passed his bar examination, but he prudently continued as court reporter and in fact kept that job until 1908.[42]

His was a politically minded family and Lenroot was quietly active within

38. Clara Lenroot, *Long, Long Ago*, pp. 24, 28, 37–38; Frank A. Flower, *The Eye of the Northwest: First Annual Report of the Statistician of Superior, Wisconsin*, p. 162.

39. Interview with Katharine Lenroot, 20 November 1968, Belle McCoy to Clara Lenroot, 26 January 1890, Lenroot Papers Addition.

40. Katharine Lenroot to the author, 5 December 1968.

41. Bertha Clough to Clara McCoy, 2 April 1889, Louis Lenroot, Diary, 9, 13 September 1889, Lenroot Papers Addition; *Superior Telegram*, 24 January 1917; Lenroot, "Memoirs," pp. 26–28, Box 13, Lenroot Papers; Lenroot to "Dear Folks," 22 September 1889, Lenroot Papers Addition.

42. Lenroot, "Memoirs," pp. 29–34, Box 13, Lenroot Papers.

the Republican party through the nineties. In 1893 he was chosen head of
the three-member committee from his quiet residential ward and automatically became part of the nine-member city central committee. The following
year he chaired that body. By 1898 he had served long enough, and capably
enough, to warrant election as chairman of the Republican County Committee, his first important office.[43]

There is little direct evidence that is indicative of his attitude on public
questions during the decade. However, members of his family made suggestive comments in 1891 and 1892.

From 1889 to 1893, Superior was a rough-hewn boom town and wide
open. Martin Pattison, a man of wealth but limited education, accommodated to the situation as mayor. But the Lenroots did not approve. When
Pattison was reelected in 1891, Clara thought it "a disgrace to the city." The
following year, when Pattison was overthrown by a group of "Reform
Republicans," Louis called it "a grand victory for the Republicans and good
government," and Lars looked for "a new deal and cleaning out the old
gang." The victory of good government was short lived, however.[44]

In the context of depression a variegated reformism blossomed in Superior. The absentee-owned Superior Water, Light and Power Company
became a target of criticism, for its rates and the quality of its service.
Wealthy men and corporations that withheld taxes while litigating their
legality alienated many people, as did certain trusts, which curtailed local
milling and shipping late in the decade. Waste, political boodle, and governmental inefficiency became less tolerable, particularly when the machine
politicians seemed also to be in league with predatory corporations. To
break the control of bosses, reformers set out to democratize political procedures.[45] The extent and nature of Lenroot's involvement in the reform
movement is not clear, but his sympathy for most phases of it is apparent
in his record as an assemblyman from 1901 to 1906 and his abiding concern
in later years for control of franchised monopolies, fair taxation, stronger
antitrust laws, governmental economy, and, above all, democratization of
government.

Urban reform dovetailed with the statewide effort of Robert M. La Follette
to wrest control of the Republican party and the Wisconsin government
from the dominant organization. In 1891 the diminutive former congressman committed the unpardonable sin of publicly accusing Sen. Philetus
Sawyer, the venerable leader of the Republican party in the state, of at-

43. *Superior Leader,* 28 March 1893, 15, 24, 25 March 1894; *Superior Telegram,* 26 September
1898.

44. Clara Lenroot, Diary, 7 April 1891, Lars to Nellie Lenroot, 8 April 1892, Louis to Nellie
Lenroot, 11 April 1892, Lenroot Papers Addition.

45. See especially David P. Thelen, *The New Citizenship: Origins of Progressivism in Wisconsin,
1885–1900,* pp. 185–201, and Herbert F Margulies, "Progressivism, Patriotism, and Politics:
The Life and Times of Irvine L. Lenroot," MS, located in the Lenroot Papers Addition and
the Manuscript Division, Wisconsin State Historical Society Library (hereafter referred to as
WSHSL), pp. 67–118. This manuscript (hereafter referred to as Margulies, "Lenroot") is a
longer version of the present book.

tempting to bribe him. Three years later he challenged the Republican machine in supporting for governor the congressman from Lenroot's district, Nils Haugen. Lenroot in upholding Haugen, a man who was particularly popular with his fellow Scandinavians, came into La Follette's orbit. When La Follette himself took up the gauntlet in 1896 and 1898 and 1900, he had Lenroot's support.[46]

In supporting La Follette, Lenroot committed himself to nothing very radical by modern standards. "Never in the history of the state was there a more urgent demand for reducing expenditures at the state capitol and in all the state institutions to an economical business basis," La Follette wrote in his widely distributed campaign announcement in 1898. "Now, more than at any other time in recent years, there is urgent necessity for practical, effective legislation justly equalizing the burden of taxation. It is becoming well understood that the man of moderate means pays an undue and disproportionate share of the taxes; that homes and farms and visible personal property are within easy and certain reach of the tax-gatherer, while the bonds and notes and mortgages of many wealthy holders, and the great incomes of many corporations, escape taxation wholly or in part." He went on to write of the tax breaks for sleeping car, express, and trust companies; of railroad passes, lobbying, and the need for anti-pass and corrupt practices legislation; and for measures against trusts. The failure to achieve just and conservative reforms along these lines, he maintained, "proves that an all-powerful influence, hostile to the common interest, controls official action. This is the rule of the political machine manipulated for private interests." The remedy for that, he maintained, was the primary election under an Australian ballot. Reverting to the conservative note on which he began, La Follette assured the people he was not entering to make a factional fight, nor was his a contest against individuals.[47]

In 1900 La Follette and his enemies temporarily compromised their differences and La Follette was nominated for governor.[48] Soon afterwards, the followers of La Follette in Superior agreed on Lenroot as a candidate for the Wisconsin assembly from one of Superior's two districts.

The choice of Lenroot was logical. While willing to bargain with some of the county offices, the La Follette men wanted to put their own people in the legislature, ones they could trust to support La Follette's legislative program. Despite the harmony talk, the Superior leaders foresaw the possibility of factional division over La Follette's main proposals. Some among them may have wanted one of their own for patronage reasons, as well. Lenroot had proved his loyalty and there could be no question of his competence. The choice was reasonable on other grounds, too. His long service to his party and his recognized position within the La Follette faction made

46. Lenroot, "Memoirs," p. 32, Box 13, Lenroot to La Follette, 24 May 1900, Box 3, Lenroot Papers.

47. Robert M. La Follette, "An Address to the Republicans of Wisconsin," 15 July 1898, enclosed in La Follette to "Sir," 18 July 1898, Box 12, Robert M. La Follette Papers, WSHSL.

48. Robert S. Maxwell, *La Follette and the Rise of the Progressives in Wisconsin*, pp. 10–23.

nomination for his first public office a routine, conventional action, one that could cause no raising of eyebrows. As Republicans dominated the district and 1900 was expected to be a Republican year, a candidate who could hold the solid party vote, as one capable of the office and deserving of recognition, met the test of availability. Lenroot's background and his role and that of his family in the community added to his attractiveness. Also, by 1900 the Scandinavian vote loomed large in the Superior electorate, those of Scandinavian birth constituting almost 5,000 out of a total population that had reached 31,091. As La Follette Republicans, for the most part, the Scandinavian element was deserving of recognition and their political representatives made a point of seeking it.[49]

Nominated despite belated opposition from an anti-La Follette man, Lenroot spoke briefly to the delegates during a district convention. "I am a republican and have always belonged to the republican party," he began. "I believe that the interests of the people are best safeguarded by that party and its policy."

"There are two planks in the state platform which I wish particularly to note at this time," he continued. "One is the primary election plank. I believe this to be a most commendable measure, and I pledge before this convention my most hearty support to that measure. The other plank I refer to is that advocating readjustment of the tax laws so that all property will pay its just proportion of taxes. To this, too, I pledge my most hearty support." [50]

On 8 October, before about five hundred people assembled by the "Mac, Teddy and Bob Club," a group of first-time voters, Lenroot spoke at somewhat greater length. His remarks were entirely suitable to a campaign in which Republicans were trying to smooth over internal divisions and present a solid front against the Democrats. Lenroot focused on the national campaign and put forth standard Republican fare, served in a way that made it palatable to the progressive minded. He eschewed all levity, but his words had the ring of earnestness and uplift. While consistent with the needs of the moment, they reflected also Lenroot's own heritage, experience, and convictions. First, addressing the young men present, he spoke of the need for parties and urged all young voters to join one or another party. He advised them to seek only for facts and arguments based on facts. He then responded to points that Democratic presidential nominee William Jennings Bryan had stressed at Superior a week before. On the subject of imperialism, Lenroot flatly denied that an American empire was being built on the ruins of the Republic or that the purpose of a standing army was to suppress workingmen. "When a man tells you that the stars and stripes no

49. Kirby Thomas to Robert La Follette, 21, 31 August 1900, La Follette to George P. Rossman, 17 August 1900, to James A. Frear, 17 August 1900, Box 40, La Follette Papers; *Duluth News Tribune*, 28 June 1900; *Superior Telegram*, 31 August 1900; Bureau of the Census, *Twelfth Census of the United States: Population*, vol. 1 (Washington, D.C., 1901), pp. 646, 800–803.
   50. *Superior Telegram*, 31 August 1900.

longer stand for liberty, use your common sense, and you will then be able to tell that man that the flag we love has never been a symbol of tyranny anywhere. Wherever it has been raised it has raised with it liberty, and law and order." Taking the offensive, he twitted the Democrats for inconsistency and hypocrisy in talking of self-government for the Philippines while taking it from Negroes in the South. In the same vein, instead of denying the seriousness of the trust problem, he acknowledged it but argued that the Democrats had done nothing about trusts during the Cleveland administration and had voted solidly against an antitrust measure in the last session of Congress. Young men, if they study the issues, would enroll in the "Mac, Teddy and Bob Club." Older men would vote "for a continuance of prosperity, will vote for the principle that wherever the flag has been raised it must be respected." [51]

The election proved quieter than most. But crowds gathered on election night wherever returns were available. They quickly learned that the Republicans had swept the county, as they did the state and nation. Lenroot won easily, with 1,966 votes to his Democratic opponent's 1,221.[52]

Lenroot knew that the pinnacle he had reached after ten years of service was modest enough. Certainly he would get no immediate economic benefits. As against the pay of $500 for the biennium plus ten-cent mileage to and from home, he would have to bear the cost of a substitute in his court reporter job. Since he did not want to go to Madison without his family, he would have to meet the expense of lodging for four; and development of a law practice, hardly started yet, would be further delayed. Neither did the office promise great political advancement in the future. Politicians in Superior had developed the habit of passing around the assembly nominations, so no more than a single term was assured.

Whether he knew it or not, Lenroot was far better prepared for accomplishment and recognition in the upcoming session than most who would serve with him. So evident was this that, despite the disadvantages noted, service in the 1901 Wisconsin legislature would prove not an honorific culmination, but a first step toward three decades in state and national politics. He brought to the job ahead youthful enthusiasm and energy, fair mindedness, good manners, and an ego well checked by respect for others. He brought a firm sense for right and wrong but not self-righteousness nor condescension—as a child of immigrants in a frontier community, then in politics in time of depression, he had learned the lessons of morality and practicality. A firm believer in the principles and in the person of the new governor, and fourteen years younger than La Follette, he brought to the session ahead a willingness to follow and, if given a chance, assist the new administration toward attainment of its legislative goals.

51. *Duluth News Tribune,* 9 October 1900; *Superior Telegram,* 8 October 1900, 4 February 1949; "First Political Speech, Superior, Wisconsin, 1900," Box 8, Lenroot Papers.
52. *Duluth News Tribune,* 7, 8 November 1900; *Wisconsin Blue Book,* 1901, p. 387.

II

WISCONSIN BATTLES

The period from 1850 to 1900 was a half century of rapid social and economic change in Wisconsin, which required legislative adjustments. The political system remained archaic throughout, based on intricate, semi-feudal relationships adequate for the equitable disposition of office but not the rational determination of policy; it was unequal to the challenges of an urban, industrial economy and a polyglot society. Great corporations had brought some order to politics, but their despotism was not sufficiently benevolent or enlightened for the purposes of the newly organized dairy-men, the unorganized people of the pine regions, the city people concerned over franchises, or the country folk scrambling for a living and angry that they were paying more than their fair share of taxes.[1]

Momentum for reform had been building since 1895.[2] Republicans took the lead, as Wisconsin seemed to be moving toward modernization.

Even so, and despite the good feeling that characterized the "harmony campaign" of 1900, the La Follette men expected opposition to their main proposals. They wanted to increase railroad taxes, preferably by changing from a license fee to an ad valorem system. The railroads would surely fight anything drastic. The La Follette men considered their primary election proposal even more important—a way of breaking the system of machine-corporation control. To veteran anti-La Follette politicians, the threat of the primary was like prohibition to saloonkeepers. They intimated their purposes by their attention to legislative candidacies and contests in 1900. The fact of a meeting of twelve senators in Milwaukee in advance of the session confirmed suspicions.[3]

Between 17 January and 19 February, Lenroot introduced sixteen meas-ures. Most of them were purely local, and some were made by request, but, generally, all had strong local import. A few were of considerable impor-

---

1. Good interpretations of the origins and character of the progressive movement in Wis-consin are David P. Thelen, *The New Citizenship: Origins of Progressivism in Wisconsin, 1885–1900;* Kenneth Claire Acrea, Jr., "Wisconsin Progressivism: Legislative Response to Social Change, 1891–1909" (Ph.D. diss.); and Roger E. Wyman, "Voting Behavior in the Progressive Era: Wisconsin as a Case Study" (Ph.D. diss.).

2. Acrea, "Wisconsin Progressivism," p. 183.

3. Albert O. Barton, *La Follette's Winning of Wisconsin,* p. 169.

tance for their potential impact in his district or for their larger implications. These fitted well with the administration's reformist program.[4]

Lenroot's first bill was designed to bring Wisconsin's taxation of vessels into uniformity with Minnesota's, so Superior could get more of the business and publicity as a home port. His very stringent antitrust bill attracted much more interest and opposition.[5] Two measures bore on Superior's persistent battle with its franchised utilities. One took the form of a resolution for a constitutional amendment, to increase the debt limit for municipalities like Superior from 5 to 10 percent of assessed valuation, with the stipulation that the additional 5 percent be used only for the purchase or construction of public utilities. His other proposal was for a popular referendum on the granting of all franchises on petition by 10 percent of the voters. Franchises granted by city councils would not be operative for sixty days during which time voters might file such a petition.[6]

In all, six of Lenroot's minor bills were enacted into law. But his municipal ownership resolution failed in the assembly, and his antitrust and franchise bills were defeated in the senate after passing the assembly. Lenroot's major proposals fell victim to the same stalwart opposition that battled against the administration's primary election and railroad taxation bills.[7]

The young and idealistic law school graduate E. Ray Stevens of Madison, assisted by Lenroot with whom he soon became very friendly, worked hard on the primary bill through January and introduced it at the end of the month. Stalwarts responded immediately. Edwin D. Coe, federal pension agent and former Republican state chairman, said that the Republican convention had only "recommended" a primary law. To map strategy for a session-long fight, James G. Monahan, collector of internal revenue in Madison, stalwart Sen. "Long" Jones, Phil Spooner, astute brother of the senator, Assemblyman Philo Orton, chairman of the judiciary committee, and Dan Starkey, a political functionary, met in Madison. They felt sure the bill could not pass the senate that session but wanted to kill it forever. With the opening of public testimony on 12 February, they began to put their plan into effect. Early in the hearing, Monahan delivered a strong and effective

4. *Wisconsin Assembly Journal,* 1901, Index; *Duluth News Tribune,* 11, 15, 17, 18, 24, 26, 28, 29 January, 5 February 1901.

5. The course of these measures may be followed in the *Wisconsin Assembly Journal,* 1901. The vessel tax bill was 21A and the antitrust bill 84A. The journal does not include floor discussion. On the vessel tax bill see the *Milwaukee Journal,* 17, 25 January, 12, 19 February 1901. On the antitrust bill see the *Milwaukee Journal,* 25 January, 4 May 1901; and the *Milwaukee News,* 28 January, 4 May 1901.

6. The resolution for a constitutional amendment was joint resolution 9A; the franchise bill was 47A.

7. *Wisconsin Assembly Journal,* 1901, pp. 1109, 1147, 1182, 1202, 1207, 1227, 1261, 1293, 1323, 1365–66; *Milwaukee News,* 4, 7, 8 May 1901; *Milwaukee Journal,* 4 May 1901; *Wisconsin State Journal,* 4, 7, 10, 14 May 1901; Clara Lenroot to Bertha Clough, 12 May 1901, Box 1, Irvine L. Lenroot Papers; La Follette to Wallace Andrews [*sic*], 4 June 1901, Cor., vol. 2, Robert M. La Follette Papers; *Wisconsin Assembly Journal,* 1901, pp. 302, 368, 406, 419–20, 481.

speech against the primary. Other stalwarts followed his lead during the next two weeks, before the committee and outside. At the same time, the stalwarts, armed with funds probably obtained by Spooner in Milwaukee, furnished free anti-primary supplements to papers through the state. Though they could expect little help from the Scandinavians, who had fought hard for political liberty and readily accepted the primary as fortifying it, they hoped to arouse the more numerous and conservative Germans to their side, calling the measure radical and revolutionary. Above all, they depended on German sensitivity about encroachments on personal liberty, a traditional fear that had been rekindled in the nineties by the Bennett law, which supported the anti-parochial school movement, and was constantly being fanned by temperance agitators. Germans, stalwarts hoped, would agree that the primary posed another threat to personal liberty, freedom of assembly.[8]

La Follette had more to fear from Washington and Milwaukee than Madison. Warned in January that the wealthy Milwaukeean Charles Pfister was dickering for the purchase of the *Milwaukee Sentinel,* which was widely circulated and respected in the state, La Follette tried to induce the aged lumberman Isaac Stephenson, an ally of recent vintage, to head a rival group. Stephenson investigated the matter from a business standpoint but turned it down, perhaps because several lawsuits, including a libel suit by Pfister, went with the property. Pfister, however, his strong determination encouraged during a visit with Senator Spooner in Washington, returned "determined to consumate [*sic*] the deal at almost any cost." Pfister's firmness reinvigorated the Milwaukee utility magnate Henry C. Payne, the national committeeman. "I believe this change in the management of the paper is fraught with great consequences in the politics of Wisconsin," he wrote John Spooner. "All of us will feel more disposed to take an active interest if we feel that the paper is friendly to us. It has been a very discouraging factor as you know, for a long time to those of us who have had to live with it every day." The deal completed by the end of February—after a fruitless interview between the new editor and La Follette—the Republican *Milwaukee Sentinel* took the lead against the new Republican administration. The "solid fellows" out in the state gladly took their places in the ranks.[9]

8. Robert S. Maxwell, *La Follette and the Rise of the Progressives in Wisconsin,* pp. 30–31; Lenroot, "Memoirs," p. 35, Box 13, Lenroot Papers; Monahan to John C. Spooner, 1 February 1901, Box 42, Elisha Keyes to Spooner, 13 February 1901, Box 43, John C. Spooner Papers; A. G. Zimmerman to James A. Stone, 18 February 1901, Box 9, James A. Stone Papers, WSHSL; Allan Fraser Lovejoy, *La Follette and the Establishment of the Direct Primary in Wisconsin, 1890–1904,* p. 61.

9. Isaac Stephenson to La Follette, 25 January 1901, H. A. J. Upham to Stephenson, 28 January 1901, enclosed in Stephenson to La Follette, 29 January 1901, Box 51, La Follette Papers; *Milwaukee Journal,* 1, 15 February 1901; Henry C. Payne to Spooner, 7 February 1901, Box 42, Spooner to Payne, 11 February 1901, Bound Cor., Box 155, Gardner Stickney to Spooner, 8 March 1901, Box 43, Spooner Papers.

La Follette had to build his legislative forces along factional lines, as he had expected. Later called "progressives," at this time his supporters were commonly called either "La Follette men" or "half-breeds," the latter term pairing them with the national faction that had for so long backed James G. Blaine against Roscoe Conkling and his "stalwarts" in Republican battles of the seventies and eighties. More than spoils had been involved and the half-breed-stalwart distinction remained apt in Wisconsin.[10]

Early in the session, Stevens introduced Lenroot into the governor's inner councils. Lenroot, already known to La Follette in a casual way and well endorsed, had shown himself an effective administration backer in the assembly. Consistently loyal to La Follette's program and principles, he had helped in drafting legislation and had shown great aptitude. On the floor, he quickly established himself as a ready debater, despite his youth and inexperience. Always in command of the facts, polite but not easily cowed by old-timers like Orton, he was quick, logical, fair, yet forceful. In due course, the *Wisconsin State Journal,* which balanced precariously between the Republican factions, took note of him. "Among new men are always a few who, by virtue of ability, spring to the front. Assemblyman Lenroot, a smooth-faced, nervously constituted young lawyer of Superior, has early attracted attention." Before the session was half over, Lenroot had established himself as one of the leaders.[11]

La Follette was impressed. In mid-February, the factional battle well underway, he set out to enhance Lenroot's usefulness in the assembly and draw the young man closer to him. Lenroot had clashed with Judge Orton in committee several times. Finally, after Lenroot objected to a provision in one of Orton's own bills and been "turned down pretty hard," Lenroot threatened a floor debate. Speaker George Ray urged against it and told Lenroot that if he would introduce a separate measure covering his objections, he would see that it passed. Orton agreed to the procedure and on 19 February Lenroot introduced his bill. Meanwhile, though, Orton's bill passed both houses and awaited the governor's signature. La Follette sent for Lenroot and said he had heard of his objection to Orton's bill and how he had been turned down, stressing his disappointment and his desire to teach "these fellows" a lesson. Therefore, he proposed to tell them he would not sign their bill until Lenroot's bill passed. By the following day Lenroot's bill had passed under suspension of the rules and La Follette again sent for him. "Lenroot," the young assemblyman proudly quoted the governor in reporting the affair to his sister, "I guess we have taught these fellows a lesson. I want them to understand they have got to reckon with you in the Legislature, and that I am going to stand by you." "Now I have told all this," Irvine explained to Nellie, "just to show you that I stand pretty

10. See especially H. Wayne Morgan, *From Hayes to McKinley: National Party Politics, 1877–1896;* and Richard E. Welch, Jr., *George Frisbee Hoar and the Half-Breed Republicans.*

11. Barton, *Winning of Wisconsin,* p. 235; *Wisconsin State Journal,* 12 March 1901; Clough Gates to Solon Clough, 24 February 1901, Lenroot Papers Addition.

well with the Governor." He added that just the other day La Follette said
he relied on him and Stevens more than any other members in either
house.[12]

Lenroot was soon included in La Follette's inner circle. Years later, no
longer well-disposed toward Lenroot, Belle La Follette, Bob's wife and
herself party to the most critical decisions, noted the traits that helped
Lenroot earn "a foremost place in the 1901 legislature." "He was an able
young lawyer, with political acumen. . . . In our councils, as I remember,
we relied upon him to point out obstacles and state objections rather than
initiate new proposals. However, once enlisted in a cause, he was a fearless
champion, a sagacious and effective lieutenant. He was a ready debater, with
a special gift in bill drafting." She might have added that from the first he
showed great skill as a parliamentarian.[13]

The stalwarts had the makings of a case. Many serious objections could
be brought against the primary election system, especially that it weakened
party government and party responsibility and promoted diffusion of authority and irresponsibility. "I believe the primary election bill if passed as
proposed will break the party to pieces," Spooner wrote Payne. The best
method and level of railroad taxation was not easily determined; cogent
arguments could be adduced on both sides. On the subject of who was the
party-wrecker, who threw the first stone, the stalwarts had some points.
Certainly, in the negotiations leading to the harmony campaign, La Follette
had not prepared the railroad presidents and their political allies for the
strong proposals of his 1901 message. Genuine hard feelings surfaced
among men who felt that they were betrayed by him and that his attacks
were unprovoked—especially when he abandoned the counsel of men like
Emanuel Philipp, the refrigerator car magnate, and when as governor he
encouraged a conspiratorial atmosphere in the capitol.[14]

But Lenroot had no doubts. The politics he had known were unrefined,
unstable. Under the caucus-convention system, powerful corporations,
seeking monopoly privilege, had gained control and had fallen into corruption.[15] Democratization of nominations was patently American and reasonable. Experience in Madison quickly confirmed these verities. From almost
the outset, Lenroot saw federal officeholders politicking against the primary. In late February and early March, he felt the force of the street railway

12. Lenroot, "Memoirs," p. 35, Box 13, Lenroot Papers; Belle and Fola La Follette, *Robert
M. La Follette*, 1 of 2 vols. (New York, 1953), p. 156; Irvine to Nellie Lenroot, 21 February 1901,
Lenroot Papers Addition.

13. Belle and Fola La Follette, *La Follette*, vol. 1, p. 156.

14. Spooner to Payne, 11 February 1901, Bound Cor., Box 155, Spooner Papers; Robert
S. Maxwell, *Emanuel L. Philipp: Wisconsin Stalwart*, p. 35; Barton, *Winning of Wisconsin*, pp. 169–
70; Herbert F. Margulies, *The Decline of the Progressive Movement in Wisconsin, 1890–1920*,
p. 38; Lovejoy, *Direct Primary in Wisconsin*, pp. 61–62, 64, 65, 73–74; *Milwaukee Journal*, 25 March
1901.

15. Irvine L. Lenroot, review of Lovejoy, *Direct Primary in Wisconsin*, *Wisconsin Magazine of
History*, pp. 17–19.

lobby, especially the Milwaukee Electric Railway and Light Company, on his own debt limit and franchise referendum proposals.[16] As the fight on the primary and the railroad tax bills reached critical stages in March and April, Lenroot saw colleagues succumb to bribery and intimidation. He also was approached with an offer of an attorneyship with a railroad. He came to understand that any assemblyman wishing financial improvement could do so by siding with the railroad companies on the tax question. Following a great assembly fight on the primary, a member told Lenroot of overhearing a senator offer an assemblyman five hundred dollars for his vote. Minutes before the first critical vote on railroad taxation, another young assemblyman, seated next to him and through the session a trusted administration supporter, said, "Lenroot, in five minutes I am going to violate my oath of office. It is a question between my honor and my bread and butter, and I propose to vote for my bread and butter." It turned out that railroad lobbyists had threatened to ruin his manufacturing business, and he knew they could do it. Others told him of bribe offers and/or threats.[17]

These episodes strengthened Lenroot's opinion that politics involved a rather simple contest between right and wrong, the honest and the dishonest, the people and the two-headed monster of corrupt machine and corrupting corporation, a view long upheld by La Follette.[18] Midway in the session, even before legislative action on the primary or railroad taxation but after the lobby had fought his own franchise and city debt measures in the assembly, Lenroot prepared a stringent anti-lobby bill in the judiciary committee. The bill would permit the governor, when a bill awaited his signature, to ask the person promoting the measure just how much money had been spent for its passage. Nothing came of this, but in early April Lenroot was successful in warding off an effort to repeal the Corrupt Practices Act, which required candidates to file expense statements.[19] Throughout the session, Lenroot told La Follette what he knew of corruption in the assembly and tried to induce men who were offered bribes to give evidence.

Lenroot could not take the stalwart efforts to minimize the extent of the party's platform commitment seriously, nor could he view talk of compromise as anything but a smoke screen. By contrast, he felt that the administration was struggling to accomplish something, not simply to make political capital, but for improper methods used against it, seemed to have every

16. *Milwaukee News*, 26, 27 February, 1, 12 March 1901.

17. Robert M. La Follette, *La Follette's Autobiography: A Personal Narrative of Political Experiences*, pp. 110, 114–15. Though the book must be used with great caution, the passages cited are corroborated by other material. See especially David Evans, Jr., to Spooner, 3 April 1901, Box 51, Spooner Papers; Evans to La Follette, 7 November 1903, Box 90, Evans to La Follette, 11 May 1901, and memo, n.d. (ca. 11 May 1901), Box 56, La Follette Papers.

18. On La Follette's early thinking see David P. Thelen, *The Early Life of Robert M. La Follette, 1855–1884*, pp. 47–48, 104; and Belle and Fola La Follette, *La Follette*, vol. 1, p. 100.

19. *Milwaukee News*, 8 March, 4 April 1901; *Milwaukee Journal*, 4 April 1901.

prospect of success. La Follette, impressed with Lenroot's commitment as with his energy, ability, and discretion, found him ever more valuable and drew him deeper into his inner circle as the session advanced. After the session was done La Follette let letters out over his signature addressed to "Mr. Lenroot," and it would be some time before the governor mastered his young friend's first name. La Follette had hardly any time or energy for the amenities; but La Follette liked Lenroot, trusted him, and above all, in the 1901 session and for years after, needed him. Lenroot was beginning to fill a deep void left by the death in 1898 of Sam Harper, La Follette's dearest friend, wisest adviser, and most dependable political aid. For a time Gilbert Roe, a former law partner, had taken Harper's place, but Roe had moved to New York City. He continued useful and was in fact on the scene as an insurance company lobbyist during part of the session, but he could not resume his former role of first lieutenant. La Follette did have the advice and friendship and political help of several older men, notably Gen. George Bryant and Nils Haugen, both Madison officeholders now, and A. R. Hall, and Madison attorney Herbert W. Chynoweth. Certainly he knew hundreds of men of all ages glad enough to do his bidding, and he used the services of a number of zealous young men for jobs of minor or middling importance. But what he needed especially was the help of younger yet seasoned men like Lenroot and Stevens—men of ability and character and quickness whose ideals and interests coincided with his own; men whose subordinate place was determined by their age, but who were capable of assuming responsibility.

La Follette was a genial, warm, outgoing person, who could quickly persuade one to join in bonds of fraternity and to become mutually dedicated to lofty purposes. He was also an astute, tough, experienced politician. Unconcerned about money, except as it was necessary for politics, and unsparing of his own energies and health, he easily confirmed the good opinion Lenroot had long since formed of him.[20]

Although Lenroot was impatient for some show of accomplishment, neither he nor La Follette blanched at a fight. During the 1901 session, both preferred defeat to compromise on the basis of unsatisfactory legislation, confident that if platform pledges were not honored, they could get from the people a better set of legislators at the next election. If possible, though, they would avoid that risk. Especially, they wanted a primary law that would apply to legislative and state executive offices and that would be in effect for the elections of November 1902.

They failed. The assembly passed the Stevens bill by a narrow margin, but the senate adopted a very weak alternative, the Hagemeister bill. The administration men in the assembly, Lenroot among them, pushed through a compromise proposal but the senate rejected it. As matters developed,

---

20. The best description of La Follette's background and assessment of his character is Thelen, *Early Life of La Follette.*

the assembly had to choose between the Hagemeister bill and nothing. Lenroot and Stevens preferred the latter, but Speaker Ray supported the Hagemeister bill and it passed, forty-eight to forty-six. Everyone knew La Follette would veto it, though they did not all anticipate the caustic terms he would use.[21]

The history of the railroad tax bill was similar. Massive opposition by the railroad companies resulted in defeat of two alternative bills. But La Follette dramatized the issue when he vetoed a tax on dogs, contrasting the legislature's willingness to tax the poor farmer on his dog with its reluctance to make the railroads pay a fair share. The proposal for a railroad commission, a favorite idea with Assemblyman Hall, a veteran reformer, was also rejected. But this was a measure that the administration forces had not expected to adopt in 1901.[22]

History, faithful to politics, has focused on the great factional issues of the session, the primary, the railroad tax bill, the dramatic messages, vetoes, and counter-resolutions. But the legislature busied itself daily with many other things, some touched only tangentially or not at all by the factional division. Lenroot took an interest in many such matters, in committee and on the floor, thus making himself more prominent and, for those looking back, revealing his attitudes and attributes.

The perennial temperance question emerged in the form of a bill which by narrowly defining "intoxicants" set out to protect "no license" towns from being flooded with strong beer. Lenroot admitted that he was "not wholly ignorant of alcoholic beverages" but consistently voted dry. The measure died in the senate.[23] He opposed a woman suffrage amendment, perhaps to avoid beclouding other issues in the 1902 campaign, but gave strong support to a bill allowing women to vote for county and state school officials, ridiculing the high cost estimates of opponents and defending the measure's constitutionality.[24]

Many issues were moralistic. Though Lenroot, with most of the administration men, usually took the more puritanical side, as on the liquor question and on a gambling bill, he was not fanatical. On a bill regulating divorce procedures, he voted with the minority for an amendment to allow a judge granting a divorce to wave the one year ban on remarriage. He was one of the seven who voted to make incurable insanity grounds for divorce. Such La Follette men as Stevens supported Frank Cady's bill outlawing interra-

21. Ernst C. Meyer, *Nominating Systems: Direct Primaries Versus Conventions in the United States,* pp. 252–53; *Wisconsin State Journal,* 25, 27 April, 3, 11 May 1901; *Milwaukee News,* 15, 24 April, 3 May 1901; *Wisconsin Assembly Journal,* 1901, pp. 1022–24, 1116–18; Belle and Fola La Follette, *La Follette,* vol. 1, p. 144.

22. *Wisconsin Assembly Journal,* 1901, pp. 833, 980–81, 983, 1088; *Milwaukee News,* 28 March, 4, 5, 10, 15, 24 April, 2 May 1901; Maxwell, *Rise of the Progressives,* pp. 35–38; Belle and Fola La Follette, *La Follette,* vol. 1, p. 143.

23. *Wisconsin Assembly Journal,* 1901, pp. 850, 988; *Wisconsin State Journal,* 11 April 1901.

24. *Milwaukee News,* 5, 9, 10 April 1901; *Wisconsin State Journal,* 9, 26, 30 April 1901. No strong campaign preceded the vote on the suffrage amendment.

cial marriage, but Lenroot joined in making the fifty-eight to thirty-three majority against the bill.[25]

He was a practical legislator in personal relations as in affairs requiring compromise. In the last week of the session, he went out of his way to do a favor for George Rossman of Ashland, a judiciary committee colleague and a veteran La Follette man, even though Rossman had shocked the administration by his long speech and then by his votes against the railroad tax bills. Rossman took a temporary leave of absence and wanted a certain measure laid over until his return. Facing objection to his request for delay, Lenroot saved the bill temporarily by moving to table.[26]

When the session ended, powerful conservative Republicans like Amos P. Wilder of the *Wisconsin State Journal* and "Hod" Taylor, assistant secretary of the Treasury, wanted peace—give La Follette a second term, secure Spooner's reelection to the Senate, and eventually the status quo ante would be restored. Meanwhile, La Follette would have no more luck with the next legislature than the last, they felt.[27] But Pfister, supported by party wheel-horses and abetted by the conservative Democratic *Milwaukee Journal,* called for an all-out fight in an editorial in the *Milwaukee Sentinel.* In August, a group of anti-La Follette legislators gathered in Milwaukee and established the "Republican League of Wisconsin." Since it was headquartered on the eleventh floor of a Milwaukee building, it was quickly dubbed the "Eleventh Story League." On 18 August, the league issued a manifesto signed by eighteen senators and forty-one assemblymen, including Speaker Ray and several former La Follette associates, expressing alarm at "the persistent effort to strengthen the executive at the expense of the legislative department of the state." In due course, the league began to flood the state with literature, subsidize the local press, and organize. From the start, the insiders planned to use the respected conservative state senator, John Whitehead, to defeat La Follette in 1902.[28]

La Follette, though fatigued and close to a health collapse at the end of the session, was equally willing to push the fight to a conclusion. Most importantly, he continued his efforts to establish a new paper, the *Milwaukee Free Press,* on a sound basis. In May, persistent wooing of the wealthy Stephenson, principal behind-the-scenes sponsor of the project, elicited a fresh infusion of cash; on 18 June, the paper put out its first issue. La Follette took an equally aggressive stance in his post-session appointments, especially that of the rough-and-tumble politician Henry Overbeck, a Stephenson man, as chief game warden to preside over a corps of deputies soon

25. *Milwaukee News,* 16 April 1901; *Wisconsin Assembly Journal,* 1901, pp. 718, 866.

26. *Milwaukee Journal,* 23 April 1901; *Wisconsin State Journal,* 4 May 1901.

27. Margulies, *The Decline of the Progressive Movement,* p. 61; *Wisconsin State Journal,* 13, 27, May, 4 June 1901; H. A. Taylor to Spooner, 23 May 1901, Box 45, Spooner Papers.

28. Margulies, *The Decline of the Progressive Movement,* p. 61; Barton, *Winning of Wisconsin,* p. 183; Henry Fink to Spooner, 27 May 1901, Box 45, Spooner Papers.

notorious more for pursuing voters than poachers. These, along with a corps of oil inspectors, became the bone and sinew of La Follette's machinery.[29]

Lenroot returned to Superior at one with La Follette, ready to press the fight and confident of victory. He understood that he was now the leader of the La Follette men in the northwesternmost counties.

In September, Superior was jolted at news of the assassination of President William McKinley by an anarchist. Lenroot spoke at a memorial service held by a Swedish church group. "That hideous monster, anarchy, must and shall be stamped out of this country at once and forever . . . punishment, swift and sure will come to whoever advocates the tearing down of our government and institutions which have cost so much in blood, and suffering and hardship, to establish and maintain." There are very few anarchists among Scandinavians, he went on.

> We love liberty, but we also believe in law. . . . The right of free speech does not mean that an individual may say what he chooses, regardless of the consequences, any more than liberty means the right to do as one chooses, regardless of consequences. No man has the right to advocate the killing of another, and one who does so advocate should be punished just as surely as if he committed the act.

Lenroot went on to condemn vilification of men in high office, to speak of McKinley's high character, and to defend his expansionist policy as bringing "the blessings of civilization and Christianity to millions of human beings who have lived in darkness and ignorance." He concluded on a religious note.[30]

Deplorable as it was, the assassination of McKinley quickened the pace of the Progressive movement, by bringing Theodore Roosevelt to the presidency. In Wisconsin, the members of the La Follette faction of the Republican party were already active in advancing that movement, and they would, in turn, be advanced as a result of it.

When Lenroot visited Madison in early January, he found the faction's financial problems unresolved. By early February, though, Stephenson had been brought around, the *Free Press* subscription campaign was well underway, and prospects looked better. In good health and spirits, La Follette assured Hall that "we are going to win this contest, hands down, Albert, and I *know* it. We will simply pulverize the Eleventh Story aggregation before many months roll by." La Follette was counting on expanding the circulation of the *Free Press* through a weekly issue. His main hope, however,

29. Theodore Kronshage to La Follette, 11 May 1901, La Follette to Stephenson, 14 May 1901, Kronshage to La Follette, 14 May 1901, Stephenson to La Follette, 16 May 1901, Box 56, La Follette to Kronshage, 28 May 1901, Personal Cor., vol. 2, Kronshage to La Follette, 14 June 1901, Box 58, La Follette Papers; Belle and Fola La Follette, *La Follette*, vol. 1, p. 147; *Milwaukee News,* 5 February 1901; Lovejoy, *Direct Primary in Wisconsin,* p. 69, note 52.

30. MS speech, "Memorial Service Mission Church, Superior, 1901," Box 8, Lenroot Papers.

lay with a projected *Voters' Handbook* that would tell his side of the story in detail, to be published by the *Free Press* and distributed to virtually every Republican household in the state. While in Madison, Lenroot enlisted to aid these projects. Most important, he agreed to write an article for the *Handbook* on the history of the railroad taxation bills in the 1901 legislature, to be printed in the form of a letter to the *Free Press* over his signature. Two others, Hall and David Evans, Jr., a down-to-earth G.A.R. veteran who had been shocked by the 1901 proceedings, agreed to write similar accounts on other subjects.[31]

Back in Superior, Lenroot organized the *Free Press* circulation drive, wrote the article, and even provided fifteen dollars for postal distribution of the *Handbook* in Douglas County. The article, which came to occupy eight pages of the one hundred forty-four-page booklet, reviewed the railroad taxation issue from the creation of a tax commission in 1897; referred to the Republican platform of 1900; recited the history of the license fee and ad valorem bills, noting that all who spoke against these measures later joined the Eleventh Story League; and laid special stress on lobbying and corruption. By these charges, Lenroot marked himself a target for great and continuing abuse. However, La Follette on receipt of the draft complimented him and took the occasion to address him as "Dear Irvine." [32]

Publication of the *Handbook* was delayed somewhat, but administration fortunes surged nevertheless. On 10 February, the *Free Press* carried a six-column story by John Hannan irrefutably exposing the heavy-handed tactics of the Eleventh Story League in buying the editorial columns of newspapers through the state. The impact proved far greater than anticipated as a talking point, arresting the drift of papers away from La Follette. On 19 March, La Follette began to campaign, making speeches in which he stressed the issues of the primary and railroad taxation, both of which proved popular. Finally in May, the *Handbook* came out, combining a defense of La Follette's record with attacks on the "bolters league," whose members were listed prominently in the front and noted later as speaking and voting against the primary and railroad taxation bills.

Superior became a major battleground. At stake was the delegation to the state convention and the legislative nominations. Lenroot, as La Follette's acknowledged local representative, as chairman of the Republican County

31. Clara Lenroot to Mrs. Solon Clough, 13 January 1901, Lenroot Papers Addition; La Follette to Hall, 4 February 1902, Box 65, La Follette Papers; Lenroot to La Follette, 5 March 1902, Box 3, Lenroot Papers; La Follette to Evans, Jr., 8 February 1902, Box 65, La Follette Papers.

32. Lenroot to George E. Bryant, 24 February 1902, Box 65, La Follette Papers; Lenroot to La Follette, 5 March 1902, Box 3, Lenroot Papers; Lenroot to H. P. Myrick, 2 April 1902, Box 7, Albert O. Barton Papers, WSHSL; "Voters' Handbook, 1902: The Truth About the Governor, the Legislature, Taxation, and Primary Elections," (Milwaukee, 1902), pp. 41–47; "Public Record of Irvine Lenroot," (Superior, Wis.), n.d. (1906), Box 5, Lenroot Papers; La Follette to Lenroot, 8 March 1902, Personal Cor., vol. 7, La Follette Papers.

Committee, and as candidate for renomination, took the lead for the administration.

With trouble enough ahead Lenroot hoped to avoid unnecessary fights. When Madison leaders warned that Congressman John Jenkins's postmasters were hostile and should be neutralized in some way, as by mounting a campaign against Jenkins's renomination, Lenroot discussed the situation with Kirby Thomas, the local postmaster. He then reassured young Rogers, La Follette's clerk, that the danger was slight. Though there was some local opposition to Jenkins, the La Follette people did not as a group participate. In late May, the matter was steered to a harmonious conclusion as the nominating convention chose Jenkins again and in their resolutions avoided state issues. For the larger cause in Superior, the outcome preserved intact the tenuous lines between the La Follette men on the one hand and the *Superior Telegram* and the postmaster's office on the other.[33]

Lenroot was cautious too on the Spooner issue. The senator had written that he would not seek reelection, but most men thought he could be persuaded. Spooner was esteemed among voters of all factions as an orator, constitutionalist, and man of influence. He had special claims in Superior, based on investments. Lenroot knew that of Spooner's representatives in Superior, railroad attorney Solon Perrin and officeholder Tom Mills were beyond redemption, but that John T. Murphy, publisher of the powerful *Superior Telegram,* might be dealt with. Since Spooner professed a hands-off policy in state politics, Murphy retained some maneuverability. Prone to salvage rather than to abandon, Lenroot continued to respect Spooner's attainments, shared his views on foreign policy, and perhaps hoped that in the future the senator might adhere more strictly to the neutrality that he professed. Also, of course, he had strong family reasons not to oppose the close friend of Clara's beloved father. His actions in April and May cannot be documented, but since by the power of appointment he controlled the local La Follette machinery, we may presume that the big meeting of June 2 reflected his thinking in denouncing the use of Spooner's name by the Eleventh Story League and declaring that "in Senator Spooner all citizens of the state have a common justifiable pride." At the congressional convention days earlier, no Douglas County man objected to a resolution complimenting Spooner and Sen. Joseph Quarles. And during June, Lenroot repeatedly declared himself for Spooner's reelection.[34]

Stalwarts in Superior nevertheless made a strong fight. Whitehead was

33. Alfred T. Rogers to A. R. Hall, 18 February 1902, Box 65, to Henry S. Comstock, 26 February 1902, to Lenroot, 29 February 1902, to James Frear, 29 February 1902, Bound Cor., Box 6, Lenroot to Rogers, 7 March 1902, Box 66, La Follette Papers; *Duluth News Tribune,* 21–24, 31 May 1902.

34. Ibid., 2 June, 31 May 1902, Frear to La Follette, 31 May 1902, Box 70, La Follette Papers. Lenroot's pledges are mentioned in J. T. Murphy to Spooner, 8 July 1902, Box 55, Spooner Papers.

hopelessly weak, but they induced former Gov. Edward Scofield, a substantial property owner and employer locally, to come to town and to offer his name; they raised doubts about La Follette's intentions regarding Spooner; and they used money liberally.[35] In mid-June, Clara wrote her mother in California that in the past week railroad companies had put two thousand dollars in the hands of stalwarts "and as a consequence, every thief and boodler in the city is anti-La Follette, and every newspaper ranting against the administration." Pfister "practically placed his account at the disposal of the counties which need to draw," Willet Spooner wrote his father, and downstate stalwarts hoped for victory in Douglas.[36]

Lenroot, though busy with a court transcript, redoubled his political efforts in face of the challenge. It was not self-interest that moved him, in Clara's biased but perceptive view. "He is by nature an ardent partisan, and is tremendously in earnest in his efforts for La Follette, and realizes the responsibility of being the recognized La Follette leader in Douglas County, the chairman of the Republican County Committee, and all that." [37] Lenroot summoned and then deployed all possible help from outside, but most of the work remained to be done locally.[38] Lenroot helped perfect the La Follette organization and, in the last furious week, plunged headlong into the campaign of public speeches. He charged that money had been used in the last legislature not only to defeat railroad taxation but also the primary and said the fight on the primary was instigated by railroad companies as part of a scheme to defeat higher taxation.[39]

At last it was done. Polls opened at 5 P.M. on 1 July, for three-and-a-half hours. Approximately at 11 P.M. Lenroot wired the results to La Follette. "In the hardest fight ever put up in this city we carried every ward but one." [40] The following day, the two assembly district conventions met at the city hall. Each district elected a delegation instructed for La Follette. The first chose Lenroot as chairman of the delegation and adopted a resolution calling for the reelection of Spooner.[41] In the immediate aftermath,

35. Elisha Keyes to Spooner, 19 June 1902, Box 54, Spooner Papers; *Duluth News Tribune*, 20 June 1902; Homer Fowler to Spooner, 26 June 1902, Box 54, Spooner Papers; W. H. Crumpton to J. C. Harper, 10 June 1902, Lenroot to La Follette, 20 June 1902, D. E. Roberts to Harper, 21 June 1902, Box 71, Fred Eward to "Dear Sir," 24 June 1902, A. C. Titus to La Follette, 25 June 1902, Box 55, La Follette Papers; *Duluth News Tribune*, 21 June 1902.

36. Clara Lenroot to Mrs. S. J. Clough, 17 June 1902, Lenroot Papers Addition; Katharine Lenroot to the author, 25 June 1971; Willet to Spooner, 19 June 1902, Keyes to Spooner, 23 June 1902, Box 54, Spooner Papers.

37. Clara Lenroot to Mrs. S. J. Clough, 15 June 1902, Lenroot Papers Addition.

38. *Duluth News Tribune*, 1 July 1902; Lenroot to La Follette, 20 June 1902, L. N. Qualey to Rogers 30 June 1902, Box 72, Rogers to Lenroot, 28 June 1902, Bound Cor., vol. 9, La Follette Papers; *Duluth News Tribune*, 26, 28 June 1902; Lenroot to La Follette, 11 June 1902, Box 72, Murphy to Lenroot, 25 June 1902, La Follette to C. M. O'Hare, 25 June 1902, Bound Cor., vol. 9, La Follette Papers.

39. *Duluth News Tribune*, 25 June 1902.

40. Ibid., 2 July 1902; Lenroot to La Follette, 1 July 1902, Box 73, La Follette Papers.

41. *Duluth News Tribune*, 3 July 1902.

half-breed leaders gave Lenroot chief credit for the victory and he was named chairman for the full Douglas delegation.[42]

Lenroot realized that only a preliminary victory had been won. Proper handling of the Spooner question remained the key for himself and for the larger cause. Due to the scheduling of the senatorial district convention for 23 July, the latest the assembly conventions could meet was 22 July. With little time left, Lenroot mended his fences before leaving for the state convention in Madison. Above all, he went out of his way to record himself for Spooner; then he called on Murphy to ask for his support and pledged to vote for Spooner if returned to the assembly. Though Murphy had earlier hoped to encompass Lenroot's defeat, he now saw little prospect of doing so and was convinced that Lenroot was sincere. He asked Spooner to accept the Lenroot situation as the best that could be done under the circumstances.[43]

By the time the Republican convention met on 16 July in Madison, La Follette's renomination was assured. The knotty Spooner problem remained, though. With his own situation still uncertain but not alarming, Lenroot went to Madison on 12 July to discuss strategy and above all to urge a resolution strongly favorable to Spooner. A great many La Follette men, especially those running for office that year, shared Lenroot's view, but a strong segment agreed with Haugen that "before any Spooner resolutions are passed the convention will want to know whether he will permit his name to be used to elect members of the legislature that will refuse to be bound by the platform." [44] La Follette disclaimed interest in the senatorship and allowed other men to fight it out. He was of two minds. He did not want to make things unduly difficult for allies like Lenroot; he understood the expediency of an outright endorsement, and pressure from the ambitious Stephenson to overthrow Spooner had abated. On the other hand, La Follette had little use for Spooner, and he knew that Spooner Republicans defecting from him might be replaced by "fair minded" Democrats at the polls.[45]

For two days, Lenroot and others fought for a firm, unqualified call for Spooner's reelection. The anti-Spooner men were taken aback but soon

42. Kirby Thomas to La Follette, 3 July 1902, Titus to La Follette, 5 July 1902, Box 73, La Follette Papers.

43. Lenroot to Harper, 3 July 1902, Box 73, La Follette Papers; *Duluth News Tribune*, 9, 10 July 1902; Harry H. Grace to Spooner, 9 October 1902, Box 56, Murphy to Spooner, 8 July 1902, Box 55, Spooner Papers. Murphy's earlier hostility to Lenroot's candidacy is indicated in Murphy to Spooner, 4 March 1902, Box 50, Spooner Papers. Perrin had also hoped to defeat Lenroot and probably still did. Perrin to Spooner, 21 April 1902, Box 52, Spooner Papers.

44. Nils P. Haugen to Rock Flint, 9 July 1902, Letterbooks, vol. 13, Nils P. Haugen Papers, WSHSL.

45. Stephenson to La Follette, 1 July 1902, Box 76, La Follette Papers. La Follette's concern to win Democratic votes is made clear in La Follette to A. T. Rogers, n.d. (Summer 1902), and 2 September 1902, Box 103, Series B, La Follette Family Collection (hereafter referred to as La Follette FC), LC.

rejoined with the demand "If we endorse Spooner, he must endorse us." [46]
The resulting resolution, adopted by the convention after an unconditional
one failed, was embarrassing to Lenroot and others but was the best they
could get and Lenroot agreed to it. The resolution said:

> We especially commend the official career of Hon. John C. Spooner. We again
> express our regret for his announced determination not to serve the state another
> term in the senate and should he now find it possible to reconsider this decision
> and express his willingness to stand as a candidate in harmony with the sentiments,
> and in support of the platform principles here adopted . . . and for the election
> of a legislature favorable to their enactment into law, his decision would meet with
> the general approval of Republicans everywhere.[47]

The response around the state was immediate and angry. To stalwarts
and moderates, the plank seemed a petty and vindictive blow.

Despite all that he had done before, Lenroot returned home to find
opposition for the assembly nomination because of the Spooner issue. With
just days remaining before the caucuses, he quickly launched a new round
of public and private pledges and explanations, again persuading Murphy
of his sincerity as well as his strength. He told of his role at the convention
and said he would vote for Spooner whether Spooner withdrew his letter
or not. Ostensibly satisfied, the more formidable of his two opponents
withdrew.[48]

Lenroot carried every ward but the populous fourth at the 21 July caucuses. Had he lost the fifth as well, he would have been defeated. As it was,
the convention gave him a unanimous nomination the following day, then
passed strong resolutions endorsing Spooner, La Follette, the national administration, and La Follette's measures.[49]

Suddenly, in the first week of October, Lenroot's political career was
threatened. He learned that local stalwarts, working with the Democrats,
planned to put a stalwart Republican, James P. McDonald, into the race
against him as the Democratic nominee. The La Follette men had given no
fresh provocation. Although they were in control in Superior, they continued to support Spooner and to seek unity for the campaign. Following
the state convention, La Follette had not overtly pushed an offensive against
Spooner and in fact praised him in his opening speech.[50]

Lenroot and others saw Perrin as instigator of the move. Perrin, in addition to being Spooner's best friend and chief political representative locally,

46. *Duluth News Tribune*, 18 July 1902; *Wisconsin State Journal*, 14 July 1902.

47. Dorothy Ganfield Fowler, *John Coit Spooner: Defender of Presidents*, p. 296.

48. Murphy to Spooner, 21 July 1902, Box 55, Spooner Papers; *Duluth News Tribune*, 18, 19
July 1902; J. B. French to the Republicans of the First Assembly District of Douglas County,
19 July 1902, Box 2, Lenroot Papers.

49. *Duluth News Tribune*, 22, 23 July 1902.

50. Elisha Keyes to John C. Spooner, 12 September 1902, John Hicks to Spooner, 3 October
1902, Willet to Spooner, 2 October 1902, Keyes to Spooner, 3 October 1902, Box 56, Spooner
Papers.

was also counsel for the Omaha lines, a subsidiary of the Chicago and Northwestern, whose agents continued to oppose La Follette and his forces. Lenroot was widely recognized as a key La Follette leader. Stevens and Hall had declined to run again and Lenroot was being spoken of as the prospective speaker of the assembly. But, as Lenroot realized, his purely urban district was not entirely safe in an off-year.[51]

Lenroot thought that Senator Spooner, who was at his home in Madison, held the key to the situation. Though Lenroot and Spooner were acquainted and Spooner recognized their special relationship due to the Clough family, Lenroot did not feel that he could approach the senator directly.[52] He turned instead to two mutual friends, Hiram Hayes and Harry H. Grace, who were associated more with the stalwarts than the La Follette faction and men of wealth, position, and sound judgment. Both attorneys wrote to Spooner in Lenroot's behalf.[53]

Spooner replied immediately. He disclaimed all knowledge of the McDonald candidacy, protested his esteem for Lenroot as "a man of more than ordinary ability, and a man of sincerity," but declined to intervene against McDonald until he had talked with Perrin, who was to visit him in a few days. Hayes or Grace, or perhaps both, told Lenroot of Spooner's response. In any case, Lenroot called on Murphy on the morning of 11 October; the two conferred for an hour. Lenroot took up a suggestion from Murphy and said he would like to see Spooner to allay any suspicions of him that Perrin might have induced. But he was unwilling to do so unless Spooner first indicated a disposition to see him. Murphy could give no such assurances but offered to call Spooner, and Lenroot was to return later for the results. That afternoon, Murphy reported that he could not reach Spooner but urged Lenroot to go to Madison. Lenroot would not. Instead, he presented his views to Murphy, who passed them on to Spooner. "He says he thinks he can win out in any event and of course says he will be for you in any event, but he is afraid the fight here will result in fights all over the state and that there will be reprisals from one side and the other and that there is great danger of the election of a Democratic majority whether La Follette is elected or not. He says he appreciates the fact that if McDonald is taken out of the way now that it will be largely done by your friends and that he will have to thank you for it anyway, but I could not get him to go to Madison without some intimation from you that you would like to see him." Murphy again sided with Lenroot. "I sincerely believe that Lenroot is a pretty fair Spooner man

51. H. H. Grace to John Spooner, 7 October 1902, Hiram Hayes to Spooner, 5 October 1902, Box 56, Spooner to Grace, 9 October 1902, General Cor., Box 168, John T. Murphy to Spooner, 11 October 1902, Box 56, Spooner Papers. Soon after he agreed to permit use of his name, Perrin recommended McDonald to Spooner for a federal job. W. A. Jones to Spooner, 11 November 1902, Box 57, Spooner Papers.

52. Spooner to Lenroot, 2 October 1902, Box 4, Lenroot Papers. Spooner was responding to a minor civil service recommendation.

53. Hiram Hayes to Spooner, 5 October 1902; H. H. Grace to Spooner, 7 October 1902, Box 56, Spooner Papers.

and that he is disposed to advise the La Follette people throughout the state, so far as he can make suggestions at Madison, to let you alone." [54] Four days later, McDonald told a reporter that he was still in the race, but two days later he withdrew. Spooner had acted. The Democrats substituted a token nominee, and a minor stalwart with no general backing persisted, but the main crisis was over.[55]

Lenroot had no special reasons to worry as he prepared for his campaigning in the week preceding the election. Then, he found everything in doubt again. On the morning of 26 October, newspapers reported that after La Follette had finished his set speech at Appleton, which included the usual praise for Senator Spooner, he was asked about his attitude toward "the unconditional reelection" of the senator. Baited by this reference to the conditional terms of the platform endorsement, La Follette had responded:

> I am for the success and for the principles of the republican party as laid down, and the day and the hour that Senator Spooner raises his voice for the principles of the republican party, as laid down in the state platform, I will raise my voice for his re-election to the United States Senate, because I then can do so in conformity with the platform of my party.[56]

Appalled, Lenroot immediately wrote to Spooner. Without referring to La Follette's statement, he thanked the senator for McDonald's withdrawal and added, "It may not be out of place to say to you personally what I have always said publicly, that if elected to the legislature I shall vote to return you to the Senate regardless of whether you are a candidate or not. Some of your friends here have apparently tried to drive me into an attitude of opposition to your return, but they have not succeeded." [57] These same friends of Spooner came to Lenroot to complain of La Follette's statement and to warn against the local results unless the fresh threat to Spooner were withdrawn. Lenroot promptly wrote to La Follette or his secretary.[58]

The La Follette men in Superior did their best in reconciling the matter, and Lenroot took his place among the speakers. He had prepared a twenty-eight-page manuscript from which he drew according to the occasion. He stressed equal taxation, including taxation of street railways and primary elections.[59] Following his discussion of the railroad taxation question, Lenroot concluded that in the 1901 legislature fair measures were beaten not by good argument but by money, promises of position, or railroad mileage, and by threats of political extinction and business ruin. Such persuasion would be successful again, he warned, "unless the people will see to it that

54. Murphy to Spooner, 11 October 1902, Box 56, Spooner Papers.

55. *Duluth News Tribune,* 15, 17 October 1902; Lenroot to Spooner, 26 October 1902, Box 57, Spooner Papers; Spooner to Lenroot, 8 November 1902, Box 5, Lenroot Papers.

56. Barton, *Winning of Wisconsin,* p. 222.

57. Lenroot to Spooner, 26 October 1902, Box 57, Spooner Papers. Spooner replied that he had never doubted Lenroot's friendship. Spooner to Lenroot, 8 November 1902, Box 4, Lenroot Papers.

58. Murphy to Lenroot, 28 October 1902, Bound Cor., vol. 11, La Follette Papers.

59. *Duluth News Tribune,* 28 October, 1 November 1902.

their representatives are men of character, are men who will shun the whisperings of the tempter, and through all of the villainy and corruption and baseness surrounding them, will still be able to hear the still small voice of conscience, men who will stand up and say to these corruptionists, say to them, I am a free man, an American citizen, and I represent free men and American citizens and I defy you." With such men, not only the people's interests but also the legitimate interests of the railroads would be safe. Companies "will not be sandbagged and forced to resort to bribery and corruption to secure fair treatment." Finally, he made it clear that he did not regard all those in opposition in 1901 as dishonest; many had merely been misled.[60] Ultimately, then, the greatest challenge was not so much the business of adapting institutions to a changed economy and society; that had to be done, to be sure, but determining success or failure in that would be the outcome in the age-old battle between men and within men, between good and evil. If human character could meet the challenges, all other problems might be dealt with.

On the whole the campaign was quieter and more decorous than those of the past, and the people liked it better that way. Even so, the sparseness of the turnout on election day came as a surprise. For Lenroot and the La Follette men, it made no great difference. La Follette carried Superior by a wider margin than did Congressman Jenkins. Lenroot had a closer call but not frighteningly so. He polled 1,178 votes to 899 for the Democrat and 113 for the independent Republican.[61] Soon, returns from around the state showed that La Follette had won reelection by a plurality of almost 50,000. Subsequent analysis indicated that substantial stalwart cutting and nonvoting had been largely compensated by as many as thirty thousand Democrats voting for La Follette.[62] The remainder of the Republican state ticket won election too, and the Republicans retained control of both houses of the legislature.

A bitter undercurrent of recrimination mingled with the cheers in the aftermath of the 1902 election. Stalwarts and moderates remained angry over La Follette's statement. La Follette men charged stalwarts with cutting the ticket and blamed Spooner for it; Spooner in turn blamed La Follette for disrupting the party, saw himself as having saved some semblance of unity, and bitterly resented all imputations to the contrary.[63]

"The grey wolves are hunting the ranges. They are out for blood. May the good God give us health and strength for the hard fighting that is still ahead," La Follette wrote to Hall. He thought the stalwarts would try to

60. MS, campaign speech, no title, n.d. (1902), Box 5, Lenroot Papers.
61. *Duluth News Tribune*, 2–6 November 1902; *Wisconsin Blue Book*, 1903, pp. 400, 594.
62. Barton, *Winning of Wisconsin*, p. 230.
63. John Hicks to John C. Spooner, 27 October 1902, Box 57, Spooner to George Brumder, 7 November 1902, to John Hicks, 8 November 1902, Bound Cor., Box 169, John Whitehead to Spooner, 11 December 1902, Dan B. Starkey to Spooner, 16 December 1902, Box 58, Spooner Papers.

control both houses and would kill everything possible in the assembly "and charge the senate with responsibility only in the matter of primary election law deficiencies." As against that, La Follette urged that "everything should be passed through the Assembly and left to the Senate to maul to pieces, if they are so determined." Above all, the assembly must be organized in friendly hands and the primary and tax bills must be passed there unamended.[64]

Initially, the stalwarts acted cautiously, pending the reelection of Spooner to the Senate. But they were active enough, and suspect enough, to stir the La Follette men to painstaking preparations for the new session. La Follette himself may have had special reasons for concern, additional to all the statewide considerations. Through Roe, he was trying to develop a favorable reputation among eastern Republicans. Financial and political help in the Wisconsin struggle may have been La Follette's concern, but perhaps La Follette thought also of his future presidential prospects.[65]

First order of business was choice of a speaker of the assembly. After an inconclusive half-breed conference at Minneapolis, La Follette hinted to supporters that he preferred Lenroot to Cady.[66] Ray remained to contest with Lenroot for the office, but the half-breeds controlled the assembly caucus and Lenroot was duly nominated and elected. Soon after, before substantive issues could again disrupt the Republican party, Spooner was reelected to the Senate.

On 15 January, the second day of the session, Governor La Follette came before the legislature to deliver his message. The document, which was of unprecedented length and required three hours to read, heavily stressed the need for primary election legislation, for ad valorem taxation of railroads as well as public service corporations, and especially, for a strong railroad commission. The governor presented exhaustive statistics to show that Wisconsin people were paying from 28 to 40 percent more in freight rates for the same length of haul on the same commodities than their neighbors in Iowa and Illinois, where commissions regulated rates. La Follette called also for control of lobbying and other reforms that had failed in 1901.[67]

In the days that followed, Lenroot finalized committee assignments,

64. La Follette to A. R. Hall, 9 December 1902, Bound Cor., vol. 12, Jerre Murphy to C. O. Marsh, 1 December 1902, vol. 11, La Follette to Gilbert E. Roe, 15 December 1902, to C. W. Bowren, 10 December 1902, vol. 12, La Follette Papers.

65. Roe to La Follette, 1 November 1902, Box 78, La Follette Papers.

66. Lenroot to James A. Stone, 14 November 1902, Box 11, Stone Papers; to La Follette, 30 November 1902, Box 79, Jerre Murphy to C. O. Marsh, 1 December 1902, Bound Cor., vol. 11, J. A. Henry to A. T. Rogers, 19 December 1902, Box 80, Rogers to Henry, 20 December 1902, Cor., vol. 12, La Follette to John W. Thomas, 12 November 1902, Cor., vol. 11 (making a point of Lenroot's attendance at the Minneapolis meeting), La Follette Papers; M. P. Rindlaub to John C. Spooner, 18 November 1902, Box 57, Spooner Papers; *Milwaukee News*, 18, 19, 24 November 1902.

67. Barton, *Winning of Wisconsin*, pp. 235–36; Belle and Fola La Follette, *La Follette*, vol. 1, p. 157; *Wisconsin Assembly Journal*, 1903, pp. 21–114.

which he announced when the assembly reconvened on 20 January. The task, which was largely his, though done in consultation with La Follette, was important and delicate. Lenroot performed it well. He honored experienced members such as Ray and Ira Bradford but made sure that half-breeds controlled the key committees. Stevens and Hall were not back, but in able and aggressive James Frear and the young, studious Herman Ekern Lenroot found worthy replacements.[68]

Relations with the La Follettes quickly became personal. Lenroot lunched with the governor almost daily at the executive residence. He "felt free to enter any sanctum at any time" and to advise La Follette on all policy questions.[69] The entire family often visited the La Follettes. At this time, Katharine was twelve and Dorothy ten, while La Follette's boys, Robert and Philip, were eight and six. Mary at that time was four, while Fola was mainly an offstage presence, a legendary actress of twenty-one. Clara, witty, artistic, gracious, youthful and gay in spirit, profoundly devoted to nature, and of about the same age as Belle and Robert La Follette, gained their affection and admiration, which she reciprocated. Belle La Follette, a law graduate, was far more political than Clara in her interests, but the whole La Follette family had a flair for the dramatic, enjoyed group readings and the little plays and masquerades of the children, and came to appreciate Clara as a poet among them.[70] A firm bedrock of Victorian morality underlay the pleasures of all the Lenroots and La Follettes and gave them the comfortable knowledge that they stood together on common ground.

If Lenroot had entertained self-doubts about the speakership, they were soon gone and he was enjoying his work, though hopelessly busy. Though not on the privileges and elections committee, it was Lenroot who drafted the primary election bill. Lenroot busied himself preparing other legislation as well. To sister Nellie, he admitted regret that he could not indulge in the public stages of the process and would get none of the credit but philosophized that he should be satisfied because "as Schley said at Santiago, 'There is glory enough for all.' " He found some consolation in the comforts of the speaker's office, stenographers, and "attendants eager to obey my slightest wish." [71] A *Duluth News Tribune* reporter judged him equal to his new responsibilities:

> The casual observer who sees Mr. I. L. Lenroot seated in the speaker's chair is impressed with the youthful appearance of the man occupying the position

68. Ibid., pp. 139–40.

69. Lenroot, "Memoirs," p. 39, Box 13, Lenroot Papers; Barton, *Winning of Wisconsin,* p. 264; "I. L. L. to Dear Governor," n.d. (April 1903), Box 92, memo on bond legislation, written by Lenroot on speaker's stationery, n.d. (April 1903), Box 85, La Follette Papers.

70. Lenroot, "Memoirs," p. 39, Box 13, Lenroot Papers; Irvine to Nellie Lenroot, 25 January 1903, Fola La Follette to Clara Lenroot, 6 April 1938, Lenroot Papers Addition; Columbia Oral History Projects, Social Security Project, Katharine Lenroot, 2 February 1965; Belle and Fola La Follette, *La Follette,* vol. 1, p. 195.

71. *Milwaukee News,* 30 January 1903; Irvine to Nellie Lenroot, 25 January 1903, Lenroot Papers Addition.

picked out for him by the governor. Mr. Lenroot is certainly boyish in appearance, but there the similarity ends. When he speaks, one notices that he has not the voice of a youth, but that it is powerful and far-reaching. Mr. Lenroot's decisions are made promptly, except where he is forced to ask Mr. Ray for his opinion, and are announced so that they can be heard all over the chamber.[72]

In truth, he had an aptitude for the speakership. He easily mastered parliamentary intricacies, had a nimble mind, and was by nature fair. Often, he mediated disputes in his private office when his colleagues seemed at loggerheads. A veteran political reporter of many sessions later wrote to Katharine that Lenroot "was the finest presiding officer I ever saw in action—and I have seen many." [73]

The primary election bill was uncompromising. It covered all state and legislative offices, proposed to limit primary campaign expenditures, and provided for counting of second-choice votes, as La Follette had proposed, so that divided half-breeds would not lose to united stalwarts having a plurality but no majority. As in 1901, the bill called for open primaries. The recent election had reminded the administration how useful Democratic votes might be.[74]

La Follette men held that the subject had already been thoroughly discussed, so Lenroot helped to rush the bill through the assembly to put the pressure squarely on wavering senators. In the process, the administration showed that it had about a two to one ratio of strength in the assembly.[75]

The half-breeds presented the stalwarts with a difficult situation. The primary measure as passed in the assembly was intolerable, especially to Senator Spooner and those closest to him. "If the bill goes through as passed by the Assembly," his brother Phil wrote to him, "the next legislature will send La Follette to the Senate. That being almost an acknowledged fact, nothing that we can honorably do should be left undone to defeat it in the Senate." The prospect of La Follette becoming his colleague was personally distasteful beyond measure to the senator, quite apart from patronage implications.[76] But the stalwarts had to consider the railroad questions, too. The administration would push hard for its popular taxation measure. Though La Follette became involved in the regulation idea at a later stage, he made clear in his message that he would go all out on this issue too.[77]

72. *Duluth News Tribune,* 25 January 1903.

73. A. B. Cargill to Katharine Lenroot, 28 January 1949, Box 1, Lenroot Papers; his mediatory role is exemplified in the *Milwaukee News,* 25 March 1903.

74. Lenroot, review of Lovejoy, *Direct Primary in Wisconsin,* pp. 219–21.

75. Barton, *Winning of Wisconsin,* p. 237; Herman Ekern to Lily Ekern, 4 February 1903, Box 2, Herman L. Ekern Papers, WSHSL; *Wisconsin Assembly Journal,* 1903, pp. 180, 185, 190–91, 204–5, 206–10; *Wisconsin State Journal,* 31 January, 3 February 1903.

76. Phil to John Spooner, 11 February 1903, Box 61, Spooner Papers.

77. Background on this issue is available in Stanley P. Caine, "Railroad Regulation in Wisconsin, 1903–1910: An Assessment of a Progressive Reform" (Ph.D. diss.), pp. 6–26. While I have used Caine's dissertation, the reader may find his book, *The Myth of a Progressive Reform:*

Both measures were of course obnoxious to the railroads and their powerful lobby, which, with the cooperation of big manufacturers, became active in Madison, Milwaukee, and elsewhere.[78] Stalwart politicians would have to help block the railroad measures. But each of the administration's three major proposals was popular with large segments of the electorate.[79] For stalwarts to use their thin senate margin to block all three would be difficult at best and politically jeopardizing even if accomplished.

At the outset stalwarts focused their attention on the primary. Confused and in some disarray, they settled on a strategy of delay, while beseeching Senator Spooner to use his influence in the fight. Spooner would not leave Washington while Congress was in session, but after many conferences agreed that Congressman Joseph Babcock should take charge in Madison with power to act in his name. The congressman arrived in mid-March, just in time to brace the wavering lines in the senate and to effect passage there of a compromise proposed by Spooner. The primary would be used for municipal and county offices, but the people would decide as to legislative, congressional, and state offices in a November 1904 referendum. Spooner, Quarles, and most of the congressmen pledged to stump against it, and stalwarts thought it could be defeated; moreover, the delay would give stalwarts another chance to regain control through the caucus-convention machinery.[80]

The administration continued to hope to put popular measures through the assembly and thus bring maximum pressure on the senators, some of whom were pressurable. After some delay in the Tax Commission, an ad valorem tax bill finally cleared the assembly on 6 March. Though its adoption was unanimous, and some such tax legislation was now certain, in light of the latest tax commission report and the nature of public sentiment, half-breeds knew they would still have to fight the senate for the kind of bill they wanted, one that would take immediate effect and would not exclude bonds as a basis of taxation.[81]

Railroad Regulation in Wisconsin, more useful. Early agitation by the *Free Press* suggests that La Follette in part responded to pressure from the owners of that paper. Caine notes (p. 18) that E. P. Bacon's Milwaukee railroad reformers owned a minority interest. It may be significant, too, that Isaac Stephenson also had shown an interest in the question, through one of his close associates. E. A. Edmonds to La Follette, 19 February 1901, Box 52, La Follette Papers.

78. Barton, *Winning of Wisconsin,* p. 256; Caine, "Railroad Regulation in Wisconsin," p. 32; Lovejoy, *Direct Primary in Wisconsin,* p. 34.

79. The *Wisconsin State Journal,* an adversary of the administration, noted the popularity of the rate commission issue, 21 January 1903. It had been agitated by A. R. Hall since 1891, then by the commercial people in Milwaukee, and was much discussed in the press in late 1902. Caine, "Railroad Regulation in Wisconsin," pp. 7–25.

80. Elisha Keyes to John C. Spooner, 11 March 1903, J. W. Babcock to "My Dear Senator" (Quarles), 19 March 1903, to Spooner, 26 March 1903, Edwin D. Coe to Spooner, 27 March 1903, Box 62, Spooner Papers; Lovejoy, *Direct Primary in Wisconsin,* pp. 80–81.

81. La Follette to N. S. Gilson, 3 February 1903, Bound Cor., vol. 13, La Follette Papers; Barton, *Winning of Wisconsin,* pp. 242–45; Maxwell, *Rise of the Progressives,* pp. 50–52.

Already, a bitter fight had begun over La Follette's plan for a railroad commission. Transportation representatives denounced La Follette's statistics as inaccurate and the whole scheme as potentially disastrous to railroads and shippers.[82] This was a subject in which Lenroot was deeply interested. Perhaps he was drawn to it because of its similarity to the local rate-control issues that had for years bothered reformers in Superior; or perhaps it was of Hall's influence on him and his admiration for Hall; or maybe it was that he saw in the railroad lobby the ultimate source of corruption and bad government. In any case, before the session, he had corresponded with George H. D. Johnson, the younger partner of Edward P. Bacon, who was Milwaukee's venerable champion of federal and state rate regulation, a grain merchant, and head of commercial organizations that had been agitating for federal regulation for many years. Lenroot was fortunate in his associations, for in Johnson, Bacon, and Robert Eliot, also of Milwaukee, he had made contact with the experts.[83] On 6 March, the day the railroad tax bill cleared the assembly, the Committee on Railroads reported a preliminary proposal as a basis for beginning the fight in earnest.[84]

By the end of March, factional feeling was such that when a minor senate resolution providing for additional legislative help came up, the assembly postponed action on it in retaliation for senate delay on the primary bill. Even the visit of President Theodore Roosevelt to Madison did little to reunite Republicans.[85]

After the senate finally acted, the assembly rejected its primary election bill and for almost two months neither set of conferees yielded anything. Meanwhile, the battle shifted to the railroad questions. The railroad companies, prepared to compromise on the tax question and to mollify the public and their own beleaguered legislative friends, mounted on all-out attack on the commission scheme. The administration, though not really hopeful of immediate victory, willingly made a battle royal of it, to pave the way for a commission law in the future, and to better the chances for the tax bill, and to build a campaign issue. The railroad lobby set out to kill the measure in the assembly, since the stalwart senators were chafed at all the demands on them.[86]

In the early stages of the battle of 1903, the companies were in the forefront. The initial commission bill, introduced on 6 March, reflected confusion as to goals and strategy among the proponents. Though in due course the measure was improved in committee, the railroads retained their initial advantage.[87]

Assuming some commission, there were three basic issues—should the

82. Ibid., p. 52.
83. George H. D. Johnson to La Follette, 30 December 1902, Box 80, La Follette Papers; Caine, "Railroad Regulation in Wisconsin," pp. 9–29.
84. Ibid., p. 35.
85. *Winsconsin State Journal*, 26 May 1903; Barton, *Winning of Wisconsin*, p. 256.
86. *Duluth News Tribune*, 3 May 1903; *Wisconsin State Journal*, 2 May 1903.
87. Caine, "Railroad Regulation in Wisconsin," pp. 42–60.

commissioners be appointed or elected?; should the commission have power to initiate rate changes, or simply review them?; and what allowance should be made for "special rates"? Lenroot, familiar with the subject, probably acted as intermediary between the committee and the Milwaukee experts in refining the bill. Certainly, he approved the results. As amended in committee, the bill called for an appointive commission, so that nonpartisanship and expertise might be secured. Reformers feared, also, that if the commission were elective, the railroads would successfully focus all their authority in securing men favorable to themselves. The amended measure, unlike the earlier version, gave the commission power to initiate rates. And it specified that "special rates" would be permissible.[88]

Politicians, newsmen, lobbyists, and businessmen strongly attacked the bill through March and April. The railroads induced manufacturers to petition, write, and finally appear in person against the bill. La Follette, Lenroot, and others charged the railroads with coercion, but it is evident that many manufacturers felt that they benefited from current rate structures and feared inflexible schedules decreed by a commission.

As the measure reached a critical stage, La Follette surprised his adversaries in a bold effort to regain the initiative. He sent the legislature a special message asking that the state bank examiner be given power to scrutinize the books of the railroad companies to see if they were paying their fair license fees. Coming during a period of national concern over rebating, the message, implying that railroads as well as shippers were benefiting from the system, was well timed.[89] It greatly improved chances for the commission bill to be voted on in the assembly on 30 April. On 28 April, La Follette struck again, this time with a long message directly on the commission bill, again presenting elaborate rate comparisons but now adding a scathing attack on railroad lobbyists. Arguing that higher railroad taxes would surely bring higher railroad rates, he urged that the commission be given power to fix maximum rates.[90] In debate two days later, Lenroot was fully conversant with the intricacies and nuances of La Follette's argument; he had surely helped in writing the message.

The shippers returned in protest in such numbers that they could be accommodated only in the senate chamber. There, on the night of 29 April, over one hundred-fifty shippers, claiming to represent many more back home, prepared a carefully worded protest to the assembly. They laid special stress on the importance of commodity, group and concentration rates —carefully developed over time—and charged that the clause approving special rates could not be effective within an act that banned the granting of any preference or advantage to one locality over another.[91]

---

88. Ibid., pp. 49–53. On the role of the Milwaukee experts see especially Robert Eliot to Robert La Follette, 4 June 1903, Box 86, La Follette Papers, and E. P. Bacon to John C. Spooner, 10 October 1904, Box 72, Spooner Papers.
89. Caine, "Railroad Regulation in Wisconsin," p. 54.
90. Ibid., pp. 55–56.
91. Ibid., pp. 56–57; Barton, *Winning of Wisconsin*, pp. 249–50.

Great crowds assembled for the showdown as the measure came up as a special order the following morning. Senator Spooner lent the opposition the moral support of his presence in the city. Early votes showed the administration in a minority, but no decisive action occurred until the assembly reconvened from a recess that night. By then, Cady, looked upon as a leader for the bill, had startled observers with a lengthy speech in opposition. Edward LeRoy offered a compromise and the administration's last hope, a referendum on the bill at the April 1904 elections. Though Frear, Andrew Dahl, and others spoke for the measure, Lenroot had foreseen the need to take a hand and had prepared himself. Having turned over the chair to a trustworthy half-breed, Lenroot took the floor for the bill in what turned out to be a high point of the contest, delivering what the La Follette ladies, who were rooting in the gallery, called a "dramatic and brilliant argument" that "held his hearers spellbound." [92] He probably knew that the battle at hand was lost but hoped to prepare the ground for another test under more auspicious circumstances, before the voters in the 1904 election. A stenographer recorded his remarks, which were soon safely ensconced in the governor's office.[93]

Lenroot offered evidence that many manufacturers had been coerced by railroads to oppose the bill. He also pointed out that the bill did not ban all preferences to localities but only undue preference; he distinguished between the present bill and a commission bill of the seventies that had failed; he charged that large manufacturers had received special favors. The heart of the matter, he said, was blatant corruption.[94]

At long last, the assembly voted and rejected the LeRoy amendment, with a vote of thirty-seven to fifty-six. It went on to reject the amended bill and to approve Ray's motion to indefinitely postpone the original measure. So ended the battle for that session.[95]

Railroad men and stalwarts celebrated at the Park Hotel, but in truth their victory came at a fearful price.[96] In the last stages of the contest the political tide shifted toward the half-breeds, and in the days that followed the administration pushed the bandwagon relentlessly. Recognizing the political need for some railroad legislation, the railroads agreed to a compromise on the tax bill. The senate conferees withdrew their insistence on the exemption of bonds from taxation and the assemblymen agreed to postpone application of the ad valorem system for a year.[97] Of course, the railroads

92. Katharine Lenroot, "Memorandum of conversation with Fola La Follette on March 30, April 2, 1969," in author's possession.

93. MS, speech by Lenroot, n. d. (1903), Box 86, La Follette Papers; the *Duluth News Tribune* quickly noted that the governor's message of 28 April and Lenroot's speech made it clear that the administration would make the rate bill a major issue in 1904. *Duluth News Tribune,* 3 May 1903.

94. MS, speech by Lenroot, n.d. (1903), Box 86, La Follette Papers.

95. *Wisconsin Assembly Journal,* 1903, pp. 1005–8.

96. John M. Whitehead to Amos P. Wilder, 4 October 1902, Box 1, John M. Whitehead Papers, WSHSL.

97. Barton, *Winning of Wisconsin,* pp. 242–45.

knew that they might delay the system further with a court challenge and also pass on higher taxes to shippers. Nevertheless, for the administration, the passage of this bill, which was so bitterly fought in 1901, represented a major achievement.

The great question of the primary remained. Senators delayed matters in conference. But Speaker Lenroot told the assembly that final adjournment would not be taken until the matter had been settled. At last a compromise was reached in the assembly, and after Lenroot conferred with Whitehead the senate accepted it. All phases of the primary would be put before the voters in a referendum in November 1904.

The bill was thoroughgoing in its application, though it omitted the second-choice vote and the features of corrupt practices. The half-breeds had the bill and received credit for it. The stalwarts were relieved of the annoying charge of obstructionism and were comforted in the knowledge that the bill would not take immediate effect, and indeed, if their political hopes were fulfilled, might never become operative.[98]

Through the session, but especially at the end, Lenroot gave much attention to economy efforts. The importance of economy in La Follette's program and in the thinking of La Follette's constituency has rarely been fully appreciated. Economy was, however, stressed by the governor, in his messages and speeches and in a number of vetoes. In late May, La Follette urged general appropriation legislation in the future, decrying the existing piecemeal system. Meanwhile, he urged legislators to look closely at every appropriation.[99] Lenroot, believing in economy and appreciating its political wisdom, and as half-breed leader in the assembly, fought for reductions but consistently found himself in a minority, even among half-breeds. On one occasion he was on the losing side of a seventy-two to three vote. He did, however, support additional appropriations for the university.[100]

After the acrimonious session, Lenroot returned to Superior more than ever committed to the faction and the fight. But he was unsure what he should do and therefore unhappy. He had reached a personal crossroad, but the direction signs pointed confusingly. Lenroot wanted to go to Congress, and he made no bones about it. But so did Frear of the same district. Either of them would be strong in his home county, but to defeat Jenkins each would need the support of a united La Follette organization in the congressional district. For both to run was suicidal. But it was difficult for La Follette to choose between them, especially since several other half-breeds also had aspirations.[101]

98. *Wisconsin Assembly Journal*, 1903, pp. 708–9, 902–11, 1323, 1350–52; *Wisconsin State Journal*, 15, 19, 20 May 1903; *Duluth News Tribune*, 16, 20, 29 May 1903.

99. *Wisconsin Assembly Journal*, 1903, pp. 1201–2.

100. Ibid., pp. 336–38, 345, 397–98, 1038, 1182–83, 1206–7, 1220–23, 1287.

101. A. R. Hall to James Frear, 31 May 1903, 10 November 1904, Box 61, Series B, La Follette FC.

For the Lenroots, their personal status in Superior was humiliating. Now, more than ever, they sensed the incongruity between their position and their poverty. The children were getting older, so were Irvine and Clara, while in pecuniary terms the family was retrogressing, with no clear prospect for better things ahead. For the present, Irvine had to resume his court reporter position in order to gain some minimum security. The townsfolk could not but note, with compassion or satisfaction, the disparity between Lenroot's status and income, especially since he was of the best local pioneer Scandinavian stock, and by marriage related to the Yankee elite, and when considering what would be expected ordinarily of the position of assembly speaker and political power.

A congressional bid would offer an immediate solution that accorded with Lenroot's lifelong ambitions and with his talents. The pay of a congressman, $5,000, combined with travel allowances, would permit the Lenroots to live if not lavishly, at least with dignity. Though redistricted in 1902, the new eleventh was substantially the same as the old tenth, where a tradition of long tenure gave some security. With La Follette sentiment high and the district strongly Scandinavian, especially Swedish, Lenroot had natural advantages that made him a logical half-breed candidate. Should he succeed, moreover, he might reasonably look forward to being joined in Washington soon by La Follette, coming to replace Quarles in the Senate, and of the two continuing to work in tandem on what they already saw as a national fight.

Yet Lenroot could not afford to try it and fail, for the hurt it would do to La Follette's statewide campaign and his own future. He did not want to act selfishly nor to seem to, and he wanted to be sure of his ground before taking any step. All these considerations, joined with the immediate feelings of humiliation, entered into his reply when, a week after they had parted in Madison, La Follette wrote, as he had already writen Frear, advising against a precipitous congressional candidacy announcement, "to the end that misunderstanding and possible friction may be avoided." With unaccustomed petulence, Lenroot rejoined: "When I come home here and find my business demoralized and practically gone, and no money in sight, I feel that I ought to leave politics alone, at least until such time as I can better afford to engage in it, and for that reason, if no other I shall be very slow in coming to a conclusion." [102]

After some months, Lenroot put aside congressional ambitions for the time and decided to run again for the assembly.[103] With somewhat less grace, Frear also withdrew in favor of a state senate bid.

102. La Follette to James Frear, 3 June 1903, Box 61, Series B, La Follette FC; La Follette to Lenroot, 8 June 1903, Box 3, Lenroot Papers; Lenroot to La Follette, 11 June 1903, Box 87, La Follette to Lenroot, 24 June 1903, Bound Cor., vol. 14, La Follette to Lenroot, 1 August 1903, Box 88, La Follette Papers.

103. Lenroot to Frear, 16 January 1904, Box 2, Lenroot Papers; Frear to Nils P. Haugen, 21 January 1904, Lenroot to Haugen, 29 January 1904, Box 52, Haugen Papers.

The team was set, with La Follette already showing the way. Starting on 29 January, he began an intensive campaign of speeches that enthused audiences and wavering politicians and gave direction to the statewide campaign. His main theme was the same as it had been at the county fairs, the railroad commission issue. He continued to use elaborate statistics, which were applicable to the immediate locale. Finally, in April, his administration released the first results of its examination of railroad books, indicating that the four major railroad companies had failed to report $1,700,000 in gross earnings.[104]

During this round of speeches, La Follette immeasurably increased the emotional intensity of the fight by intervening in legislative and senatorial contests. Professing not to deal in personalities, he resorted to a recital of the legislative record. This otherwise dull document took on vibrant life as La Follette, sometimes in the presence of the offending legislator and his embarrassed neighbors, first told about a measure, then read from the record the vote of the local man.[105]

Lenroot had himself been doing a great deal of public speaking, ever since the end of the legislative session. In May, at a Madison dinner honoring Scandinavian members of the legislature, Lenroot voiced an idea common among half-breeds—that the force of wealth and power, bent on taking away the rights and privileges of the people, inadvertently gave life to a counterforce. Then he expressed an opinion less commonly heard among Wisconsin reformers of the time. La Follette was content to contrast "the people" with the "special interests" and let it go at that. Lenroot took a different tack, similar to the ideas of President Roosevelt. The counterforce evoked by the special interests, Lenroot warned, "if not properly guarded, if it is not directed by the hand of wisdom, will grow and grow until stung with the wrongs of the people, real and imaginary, it will sweep on in a work of destruction to such an extent that not only will that for which it was called into being be destroyed, (but) the very foundations of our civil institutions may be attacked and seriously menaced." Scandinavians, he continued, are well fitted to occupy middle ground, to save the country "on the one hand from becoming a Populistic and revolutionary government, and on the other hand, from being dominated in its policies by corporate influences. We are conservative as a race, but we also believe in the right of the people to govern themselves. We believe in liberty, we believe in justice; justice to the poor, and justice to the rich."[106] Lenroot knew his Scandinavians and spoke as one. He spoke, also, as a Republican who had lived through the era of populism; he spoke as an American patriot, inured to the idea of America as a land of ample and equal opportunity; and he spoke as a

104. Barton, *Winning of Wisconsin,* p. 335; Caine, "Railroad Regulation in Wisconsin," pp. 76, 83; Belle and Fola La Follette, *La Follette,* vol. 1, p. 170.

105. La Follette, *Autobiography,* pp. 142–43; Belle and Fola La Follette, *La Follette,* vol. 1, p. 172.

106. MS speech, "Madison, Wis., 1903," (May), Box 10, Lenroot Papers.

cautious man and a politician, drawn magnetically to the middle of the road.[107]

Lenroot delivered a significant address on Labor Day at Superior. His views, as expressed then, were appropriate alike to a rising young leader of the progressive movement and to a man who in the circumstances of the 1920s would be classed as a conservative. Addressing himself to the relations between labor and capital, Lenroot said each was necessary to the other. Labor is entitled to a living wage "which should always be first considered in the cost of production, then the other elements." Capital is entitled to a fair return, determinable on the basis of the risks involved. Anything above a fair return belongs equally to labor and capital.

To meet combination of capital, labor must combine. Lenroot favored unions. "But we must remember," he cautioned his audience of laborers, "that the acts and deeds of union labor must be measured by the same standard as the acts of corporate wealth."

Characteristically, Lenroot presumed that a disinterested, honorable, involved citizenry should and would act as the ultimate arbiter between capital and labor; it would be a moral, concerned, educated populace, thinking and acting without reference to class ties or other narrowly selfish interest.[108]

After mid-January, his own congressional ambitions shelved, Lenroot gave all his spare time to La Follette's statewide battle. By then, the fight was desperate and the outcome doubtful. Stalwarts were supporting two men formerly associated with La Follette and not yet identified as against him, each a veteran in politics with personal sources of strength. Emil Baensch of German extraction, formerly lieutenant governor, was the man Spooner induced to run. Samuel A. Cook, a lumberman whom La Follette had backed for the Senate in 1898, came in on his own. The stalwarts planned to pool the strength of the two at the convention. In charge of the stalwart campaign was the astute and experienced Babcock, chairman of the National Republican Congressional Campaign Committee. He was assisted by the shrewd and influential Philipp and in the later stages the equally wily Phil Spooner.[109] With Senators Spooner and Quarles quietly committed, and most congressmen presumed friendly or at the least neutral, the officeholders could be counted on. And in a presidential year, those who deplored faction and yearned for unity and lived by the standards of party regularity had reason to follow what seemed the federal lead. Thus, fence

107. On Scandinavian thinking in the Wisconsin Progressive movement see especially Jorgen Weibull, "The Wisconsin Progressives, 1900–1914," pp. 191–221. Lenroot expressed his opinion elsewhere, to good effect, according to John Hannan. MS speech, "Ladysmith, May 30, 1903," MS speech, "Graduating Class, Matt Carpenter School, 17 June 1903," Box 8, Hannan to Lenroot, 6 June 1903, Box 2, Lenroot Papers.

108. MS speech, "Labor Day address, Superior, Sept. 7, 1903," Box 8, Lenroot Papers.

109. Barton, *Winning of Wisconsin*, p. 296.

sitters like publishers Wilder and Murphy aligned themselves against La Follette. Above all, in December the railroads met several of La Follette's best arguments; they cut rates and the Northwestern retired its conspicuous lobbyist Merritt C. Ring.[110]

As part of his own fight for survival, La Follette undertook to cause the defeat of Congressman Babcock in his bid for renomination. He called on Lenroot to help. "You will greatly dishearten us if you refuse. Don't back up now, Irving [sic]," La Follette wrote. Lenroot replied immediately. "I don't feel myself that I can be very effective in the Third District, for I have never been accustomed to attacking individuals, and it goes very much against the grain for me to do so. However I think Babcock should be attacked, and vigorously so, and I shall be glad to be of any service that I can." Babcock, apart from antagonizing the La Follette men by his political actions in the state, was reputed to have misused his position as chairman of the House Committee on the District of Columbia to make a fortune.[111]

Lenroot prepared a twenty-three-page manuscript, then went south into the third district for a week.[112] He omitted the distinctions that marked his speeches earlier in the year. The issue, which as made over the past six years, was clear, he said. "It was the public service corporations and politicians against the people." The love of money had increased along with material prosperity, and public office had become "merely an opportunity for public plunder." But logic required Lenroot to go beyond appeal to the self-interest of the people, since Babcock's friends had a strong case when they boasted of all he did and could do for the district. So, as before, he appealed to the best in people, to their high mindedness, their disinterestedness.

After attacking Babcock for his work against the primary in 1903, Lenroot began criticizing the "harmony" theme. He blamed the stalwarts for disharmony, for not adhering to the party platform and the public interest. By that argument, Lenroot continued to reconcile factionalism with partisanship, a combination that he found personally and politically congenial. But the argument was not wholly realistic, and Lenroot knew it. Perhaps, in addition, he foresaw circumstances when he and his friends might have to cut themselves adrift from the anchor of Republicanism. Therefore, he added that he would rather see his party defeated and disrupted than victorious only to serve the public service corporations.[113]

Despite the speeches of Lenroot, Frear, and others; and the use of a

110. Caine, "Railroad Regulation in Wisconsin," p. 80. Correspondence in the Spooner Papers for the period is especially illuminating.

111. La Follette to Lenroot, 2 February 1904, Box 3, Lenroot Papers; Lenroot to La Follette, 4 February 1904, Box 94, La Follette Papers; Lenroot, "Memoirs," pp. 35–36, Box 13, Lenroot Papers. Lenroot here writes of a Baraboo anti-Babcock speech as occurring in 1902; in fact, it was 1906.

112. *Duluth News Tribune,* 11 February 1904; Lenroot to John Hannan, 19 February 1904, Box 94, La Follette Papers.

113. MS speech, no title, n.d. (February 1903), Box 5, Lenroot Papers.

handbook that documented Babcock's perfidy; and the stratagem of advancing favorite sons in each county, time to organize was limited, and Babcock controlled the situation. In swift succession, starting on 16 February, the caucuses sided with Babcock.

In the course of the stalwart's statewide campaign, Lenroot met opposition to his own renomination. He survived the challenge, however, and also helped to secure his own and neighboring counties for La Follette.[114]

It became evident weeks before 18 May that control of the state convention would depend on a number of disputed delegations. Regarding many of the contests as spurious, the La Follette men were aware that through the State Central Committee they would control the initial rolls, but that the contests would be brought to the floor. Anticipating parliamentary trickery as prelude to the possible use of force to take over the convention, La Follette's friends in Madison set out to forestall their enemies. The presiding officer, they knew, must not only be favorable to them but be a man of force, thoroughly conversant with parliamentary rules, quick thinking, and decisive; they expected that they would need no special favors, only scrupulous, competent fairness, so the stalwarts would have no excuse for a takeover or a bolt. It was for the State Central Committee, headed by old General Bryant, to name the man. In early April, before the situation reached a critical stage, Bryant wrote La Follette that he wanted to honor Hall with the post. Though Hall was a skilled parliamentarian, La Follette evidently thought him inadequate in other ways and discreetly ignored Bryant's letter.[115] A week before the convention, Lenroot met with others of the inner circle to complete plans. At that meeting, he was decided on for temporary and permanent chairman of the convention.[116]

The La Follette men did not leave things at that but made elaborate physical preparations. When on convention day the stalwarts, who were marching four abreast from the opera house, reached the university gymnasium, they found the place looking more like a penal institution than the site of a Republican state convention. Burly guards checked the credentials of each delegate, who was then led single file through a passage lined with barbed wire to a small side entrance. Inside, a heavily guarded wire fence separated delegates from observers, many of these contesting delegates. Other guards stood at the front, protecting Bryant, Lenroot, and the gavel.[117]

114. Margulies, "Lenroot," pp. 221–25.

115. George E. Bryant to La Follette, 7 April 1904, Box 97, La Follette Papers. The letter is marked at the top "no. ans."; perhaps La Follette thought it better to state his objections personally.

116. *Wisconsin State Journal*, 12 May 1904; Lenroot, "Memoirs," p. 41, Box 13, Lenroot Papers.

117. Barton, *Winning of Wisconsin*, pp. 348–49; Lenroot, "Memoirs," p. 42, Box 13, Lenroot Papers.

Everything went according to schedule at the outset. Finally, after the tedious roll call, Bryant announced that the State Central Committee had selected Lenroot for temporary chairman.

Though Lenroot had not been chosen primarily for his speaking talents, he delivered a very creditable address, which was praised at the time by the hostile *Wisconsin State Journal* as on the whole "a great speech" and later favorably recalled by La Follette partisans who in the intervening years had become hostile. Albert O. Barton called it "a ringing, militant effort, in strong defense of the administration." [118]

One could sense an atmosphere of tension, but no violence occurred, although Lenroot had to intervene with one of the guards to allow a stalwart to recover his hat from under a front-row seat.[119]

The major test of strength between the rivals came on a parliamentary question. As presiding officer, Lenroot naturally became involved from the first. Acting as attorney and as political emissary, he continued to argue the question in the months that followed. The State Central Committee had certified the original roll of delegates, judging the many contests. Not until the convention had been temporarily organized, with Lenroot as temporary chairman, were the stalwarts able to effectively challenge the makeup of the convention. But following Lenroot's speech, a heated debate ensued regarding the temporary rolls. Marvin Rosenberry for the stalwarts contended that all those whose credentials had been signed by the party chairmen and secretaries in their counties should be seated. Indeed, the State Central Committee had originally required only this in its official call and had not added that the credentials also be signed by the chairmen and secretaries of the conventions that chose the delegates, nor that it would retain the prerogative to go beyond all credentials in search of the facts in cases of dispute. In practice, the State Central Committee had gone beyond the specific terms of its call in deciding contests. Within the State Central Committee, stalwarts had acquiesced in the procedure but now, on the floor, they challenged it.[120]

After much heated debate, punctuated by hisses and groans, E. R. Hicks, the floor manager for Cook, made a strong plea for harmony. He ended it, though, by moving "that those persons be entitled to vote upon this question who hold certificates of election to this convention signed by the chairman and secretary of the county committees as the law required and that this convention herewith have submitted to it in detail every controverted judgment upon what shall be done without the vote of anybody interested." The motion in effect supported the view of the stalwarts and if sustained would have given the stalwarts voting control. Levi Bancroft,

---

118. *Wisconsin State Journal,* 18 May 1904; Barton, *Winning of Wisconsin,* p. 353. See also Belle and Fola La Follette, *La Follette,* vol. 1, p. 176.

119. Lenroot, "Memoirs," p. 42, Box 13, Lenroot Papers.

120. Barton, *Winning of Wisconsin,* p. 355.

the La Follette leader in this debate, made a point of order against the motion. Lenroot sustained the point and cited a similar ruling at the 1892 national convention. In effect, Lenroot in his ruling was judging the procedural question itself, the nub of the issue. Hicks appealed from the chair and brought on the test vote. It showed that no unforeseen wave of defection had occurred and that the La Follette men controlled by almost a hundred votes. One by one now, each contest was voted on. For the record, a stalwart leader entered a protest after each ballot. The contests disposed of, a half-breed moved that the temporary organization be made permanent. Those who disputed the legal status of the convention could not compromise themselves by further participation, so at this point Malcolm Jeffris invited "all anti-third term delegates . . . to meet in caucus at the Fuller opera house at 8 o'clock tonight." Amidst further tumult, while the unhappy delegates supporting Cook sat stolid and silent, the much larger contingent of Baensch delegates paraded out. As Jeffris was about to leave, he commented, "I protest that this convention is not legally organized."

Hicks delivered another plea for harmony and for delay, but the majority pushed ahead to make the temporary organization permanent. The Cook delegates, with about one hundred-thirty votes, stayed on, thus helping to legitimize the proceedings. Finally, the convention adjourned for the night, leaving a guard posted to defend the gymnasium.[121]

That evening, the stalwarts met at the opera house, which was rented weeks before for such a contingency, and they fervently established themselves as a rival convention. That done, they too adjourned for the night.[122]

The next day, their ardor unabated, the stalwarts put on a show that easily rivaled the performance at the gymnasium where the delegates renominated La Follette and adopted a strong platform. With the two senators present, two former governors, several congressmen, and other dignitaries, the opera house gathering had every appearance of being a Republican state convention. That afternoon, Baensch appeared on stage to announce his withdrawal, paving the way for the nomination of Cook, whose delegates and support seemed essential to the cause. Following Cook's nomination, the convention adopted a platform that opposed the primary and called for a railway commission that would be chosen at spring elections. The convention reached its peak of enthusiasm when a stalwart leader escorted onto the stage Senators Spooner and Quarles and former Governors Upham and Scofield. Each in turn, and some others too, pledged support for the nominees and platform of that convention, as the delegates repeatedly yelled the name of Spooner. Spooner's speech was easily the most notable; he called the fight a battle for no selfish purpose but for representative government itself.[123]

For the moment, the half-breeds had the upper hand. But the battle was

121. Ibid., pp. 356–61.
122. Ibid., p. 362.
123. Barton, *Winning of Wisconsin,* pp. 362–66.

just begun, and after the last trains had taken the lesser lights from Madison, Lenroot joined La Follette and some others in the inner recesses of the executive offices to plan strategy.[124] The immediate goal was national recognition by the party and the president through seating of the convention's delegate choices at the Republican National Convention in Chicago.

Politicians and observers naturally speculated about a compromise by which the delegates from each convention would be seated and given half a vote apiece. President Roosevelt and his close advisers might welcome that approach, to avoid an embarrassing convention fight and subsequent division in the state.[125] Most La Follette men, exultant over their recent triumph, had little sympathy for compromise. Lenroot shared the fighting mood, though he realized that Spooner, Quarles, Babcock, and Payne would have great influence on the president. He considered his convention ruling correct and the gymnasium convention the legitimate one; it was a simple question of right or wrong on which there could and should be no temporizing.[126] Feeling no need for any, he allowed a reporter to quote him as saying, "Senator Spooner is an able man. So was Jefferson Davis. Davis was guilty of treason to the state; Spooner is guilty of treason to the party. Neither his services to the state, nor his services to his party, will save him from condemnation, more than did the services of Jefferson Davis before he attempted to create a new republic." [127] Strongly advocating a no-compromise position, Lenroot proposed to pressure national party leaders with the threat that if the Spooner men were recognized at the convention, La Follette Republicans might leave it to the Spooner faction to carry the state for the national ticket in November.[128]

While still in Madison, Lenroot agreed to go east with some others to present the half-breed case. First he returned to Superior briefly where he was pleased to find that the position of the half-breeds was not weakened despite the stalwart bolt. A few days later, he was back in Madison for final conferences and by 30 May was in Washington, D. C., ready to meet President Roosevelt the following morning.[129]

Lenroot served as spokesman. He stressed the regularity of the gymnasium convention. Roosevelt was friendly but noncommittal, saying that he had followed the Wisconsin contest closely, was much impressed by Lenroot's comments, but that Spooner was an important and influential man who, as head of the rival delegation, could not be lightly disregarded. Roosevelt, keen to the dangers of an open fight, suggested that before

124. Ibid., p. 371; *Duluth News Tribune,* 22 May 1904.

125. H. A. Taylor to John C. Spooner, 21 May 1904, Box 70, Spooner Papers; *Duluth News Tribune,* 23 May 1904.

126. Lenroot to Herbert W. Chynoweth, 24 May 1904, Box 102, La Follette Papers.

127. *Duluth News Tribune,* 23 May 1904.

128. Lenroot to Chynoweth, 24 May 1904, Box 102, La Follette Papers.

129. Lenroot to La Follette, 24, 27 May 1904, Walter Houser to La Follette, 30 May 1904, Box 102, La Follette Papers.

returning to Wisconsin the group should see Sen. Nelson Aldrich of Rhode Island, the Senate majority leader. He arranged the interview for them, which was to take place in New York the following day. Lenroot and Secretary of State Walter Houser were deputized to see Aldrich, while the others in the delegation went on to Chicago to settle the technicalities of the contest for seating.[130] The presidential interview encouraged the Wisconsin men, and that evening Houser sent a wire to Madison: "We are pleased with trip." [131]

Aldrich, though a notorious reactionary, was an astute politician. After Lenroot had stated the legalisms of the case for about twenty minutes, Aldrich bluntly stopped him, saying he had little interest in that aspect of it but would like to see the matter compromised, especially since Lenroot had said the La Follette delegates would support Roosevelt. He promised to see Spooner about it. Going further, he arranged that Houser and Lenroot meet with William E. Chandler back in Washington.[132]

Chandler, sixty-nine and semiretired, could never really retire from politics. Widely connected, an astute Republican, and a senior statesman, he had in the past been a strong advocate of Negro rights, the architect of a Republican strategy based on that idea, and a powerful member of the Blaine, half-breed faction. Fourteen years a senator from New Hampshire, Chandler lost his seat in 1900 and blamed the railroads for it. He was predisposed toward sympathy for La Follette and his cause and anxious to do his party another service by arranging a compromise, which he saw as the most the La Follette men could hope for.[133]

Again, it was Lenroot who did the talking. Chandler listened attentively. After the Wisconsin men left for home, he took up their cause. Days later,

130. Lenroot, "Memoirs," pp. 44–45, Box 13, F. S. Wood to Lenroot, 30 June 1925, Box 4, Lenroot Papers. Lenroot's account of the meeting with Roosevelt, later incorporated in his "Memoirs," is attached to this letter. Chynoweth to Lenroot, 31 May 1904, W. D. Connor to Chynoweth, 30 May 1904, Box 102, La Follette Papers.

131. Houser to John Hannan, 31 May 1904, Box 102, La Follette Papers. Belle La Follette and A. O. Barton, hostile to Roosevelt at the time of writing, later described the interview with him as unsatisfactory. Belle and Fola La Follette, *La Follette,* vol. 1, p. 179; Barton, *Winning of Wisconsin,* p. 380. In his autobiography, Robert La Follette did not mention that he had even permitted a group to present his case to Roosevelt.

132. Lenroot, "Memoirs," p. 45, Box 13, Lenroot Papers. That it was Nelson Aldrich who directed Lenroot and Houser to Chandler is indicated in Chandler to Aldrich, 2, 4 June 1904, vol. 143, William E. Chandler Papers, LC, and is the view of Chandler's biographer. Leon Burr Richardson, *William E. Chandler: Republican* (New York, 1940), pp. 652–53. In 1946, Lenroot recalled only that Aldrich received him and Houser coldly. Fowler, *Spooner,* p. 304.

133. On Chandler, in addition to the Richardson biography, see Vincent de Santis, *Republicans Face the Southern Question: The New Departure, 1877–1897* (Baltimore, Md., 1959); and Stanley Hirshson, *Farewell to the Bloody Shirt: Northern Republicans and the Southern Negro, 1877–1893* (Bloomington, Ill., 1962). Chandler's animus toward railroads is indicated in Chandler to John C. Spooner, 13 September 1900, Box 39, and Spooner to Henry C. Payne, 4 July 1904, Bound Cor., Box 179, Spooner Papers. Chandler expressed sympathy for what La Follette represented and urged compromise in Chandler to Aldrich, 4 June 1904, vol. 143, Chandler Papers.

complimenting Lenroot on his clear and concise oral presentation of the case, he urged him to supply something in writing.[134] Though Lenroot, in tandem with Houser, continued to reject compromise, he supplied a thirteen-page manuscript. Lenroot's covering letter was adroit in tone, conciliatory instead of stubborn, yet yielding nothing of substance. Commenting on Chandler's suggestion of a division of delegates, he wrote, "We are sincerely anxious for the re-election of President Roosevelt, for we realize that he and Gov. La Follette stand squarely upon the same platform. If there was the slightest doubt as to our position, the legality of our convention, if there was room for legitimate argument even, I would think that your proposition would receive very serious consideration." But under the circumstances, the only course open was to submit the contest to the national convention and let it decide. "If justice is done," he concluded, showing a bit of the flag, "there need be no fears of the result in Wisconsin as to President Roosevelt." [135]

Chandler did what he could and remained optimistic to the last. But Roosevelt finally decided in favor of Spooner and the Republican National Committee ratified the judgment. La Follette then chose to present the matter to the voters rather than the Credentials Committee.[136]

During the first week of July, Irvine and Clara, with Frear and some others, visited the St. Louis World's Fair as guests of the La Follettes. The governor dedicated the Wisconsin building.[137] While there, Lenroot and La Follette mixed politics with pleasure. Over a three-day period they told their side of the story to the celebrated muckraking journalist Lincoln Steffens, who was preparing an article on Wisconsin for *McClure's Magazine*. Weeks later, Steffens visited Lenroot at Superior. Lenroot told all he knew of bribery by the opposition and referred Steffens to others who could add

134. Chandler to Lenroot, 5 June 1904, vol. 143, Chandler Papers.

135. Lenroot to Chandler, 10 June 1904, see also Chandler to Houser, 5 June 1904, to Henry Cabot Lodge, 5 June 1904, and Houser to Chandler, 8 June 1904, vol. 143, Chandler Papers. Lenroot received a copy of Houser's rather blunt reply to Chandler before completing his own letter, filed in Box 1, Lenroot Papers.

136. Chandler to Roosevelt, 15 June 1904, Henry Cabot Lodge to Chandler, 8 June 1904, Chandler to Lodge, 9 June 1904, Lodge to Chandler, 13 June 1904, Chandler to Whitelaw Reid, 12, 13, 14 June 1904, George G. Hill to Chandler, 15 June 1904, Chandler to Reid, 18 June 1904, vol. 143, Chandler to La Follette, 15 March 1905, vol. 145, Chandler Papers. Lodge to George von L. Meyer, 13 June 1904, George von L. Meyer Papers, MHS; Hill to Chandler, 15, 16 June 1904, vol. 143, Chandler Papers; "Memorandum by G. G. Hill," n.d., Nelson Aldrich Papers, cited in Nathaniel Wright Stephenson, *Nelson W. Aldrich: A Leader in American Politics* (New York, 1930), p. 460, note 26; Chandler to H. P. Myrick, 22 October 1904, vol. 144, Chandler Papers. Of the secondary literature covering the convention test the best account is Fowler, *Spooner*, pp. 304–7. For Roosevelt's attitude see Roosevelt to Nicholas Murray Butler, 21 May 1904, to William Edward Cramer, 23 May 1904, to Henry Cabot Lodge, 13 June 1904, in Elting Morison et al., eds., *The Letters of Theodore Roosevelt*, vol. 4 of 8 vols. (Cambridge, Mass., 1951–1954), pp. 802, 805, 833. See also Horace S. and Marion G. Merrill, *The Republican Command, 1897–1913*, pp. 184–86; Barton, *Winning of Wisconsin*, pp. 388–91; La Follette, *Autobiography*, p. 141.

137. Lenroot, "Memoirs," p. 41, Box 13, Lenroot Papers; *Duluth News Tribune*, 6, 7 July 1904.

detail on that subject.[138] Steffens's article hit like a bombshell at the end of September.[139]

Though La Follette men planned to go ahead in any case, they were much concerned how the state supreme court would decide the contest between the rival conventions for the Republican place on the ballot. La Follette figured to win whatever the ruling, but the rest of the state ticket and the legislature were less sure. To make what proved a tortuous legal test, La Follette named Lenroot to a four-man team of attorneys headed by Chynoweth. Roe did preliminary work on the case in July, as did Lenroot; in August, Lenroot made final preparations; in September, he helped present the case in court and before the State Central Committee. Belle La Follette evidently thought well of his work, for she commented to the astute and experienced Roe in whom the La Follettes had the greatest confidence that "he works something as you do." Through unforeseen delays, the court was unable to render a verdict until 5 October. Finally, by a three to one vote, it ruled for La Follette. The decision did not end the political fight, but it heartened the half-breeds greatly and demoralized the stalwarts.[140]

The stalwarts could no longer hope for national help, and their leader, Spooner, dispirited at the turn of events, felt he had to take himself almost entirely out of the campaign. The death of Payne weakened them further.[141]

Even so, a bitter, uncompromising campaign lay ahead. Samuel Cook withdrew and former Governor Scofield took his place. But stalwarts had already started moving into coalition with the conservative Democrats, who dominated their party in the state. The stalwarts would support former Gov. George Peck while, depending on local circumstances, Democrats might back stalwart congressional or legislative candidates. The railroad companies remained as concerned as ever, in many cases taking the lead. For their part, the half-breeds had long since coalesced with progressive Democrats who accepted La Follette especially and in some cases other half-breed Republicans.

138. Belle and Fola La Follette, *La Follette*, vol. 1, pp. 181–83; La Follette to Gilbert Roe, 27 July 1904, Bound Cor., vol. 21, La Follette Papers; Lincoln Steffens, "Enemies of the Republic: Wisconsin," *McClure's Magazine* 23:6 (October 1904): 563–79. For the Lenroot reference see the reprint of the article in Robert S. Maxwell, ed., *La Follette: Great Lives Observed* (Englewood Cliffs, N. J., 1969), pp. 88–111.

139. Belle and Fola La Follette, *La Follette*, vol. 1, p. 185; La Follette to Steffens, 14 November 1904, Bound Cor., vol. 23, La Follette Papers; Houser to William Chandler, 28 September 1904, vol. 144, Chandler Papers.

140. Lenroot, "Memoirs," p. 46, Box 13, Lenroot Papers; La Follette to Gilbert Roe, 27 July 1904, Belle La Follette to Roe, 27 August 1904, Box 4, Series H, La Follette FC; Barton, *Winning of Wisconsin*, pp. 402–7.

141. Spooner to B. W. Howe, 14 October 1904, to Louis A. Pradt, 16 October 1904, Bound Cor., Box 180, Spooner Papers. The national decision against the stalwarts followed immediately the Wisconsin court decision. William Loeb, Jr., to George B. Cortelyou, 6 October 1904, Cortelyou to Loeb, 6 October 1904, Box 35, George B. Cortelyou Papers, LC; Theodore Roosevelt to Cortelyou, 6 October 1904, enclosed in Loeb to Chandler, 6 October 1904, vol. 144, Chandler Papers.

Though he faced opposition, in mid-October Lenroot went on a two-week campaign trip at his own expense.[142] As a matter of tactics he had warned La Follette against committing himself to an appointive railroad commission, preferring to leave it to the legislature to accomplish that, but he himself went on record for a stronger railroad commission than the railroads or their political allies wanted, one that would have "power to give relief without . . . the aid and consent of any railroad corporation." [143]

Lenroot began to speak for himself on the night of 2 November and continued nightly through the fifth. For the most part, he adhered to safe themes, which he developed competently. Four days before the election, though, on learning that Spooner was coming and realizing that Spooner's speech would occur too late for reply, he took the attack to the senator.

Anticipating Spooner's themes and methods, Lenroot said that the campaign was not about the tariff, free silver, the Philippines, or imperialism; "it is a question of whether our government shall be one of, by and for the people, or one ruled by the great corporations." That, he said, was not just the issue in the state but nationally. Roosevelt, the greatest president since Lincoln, "cannot be controlled by the corporations." He explained his own vote for Spooner as in the interest of harmony. Now he was sorry he so voted. Brushing aside earlier distinctions, Lenroot attempted to link Spooner to the railroads and the corrupt fight against La Follette's measures. "Spooner will tell you Monday night, with tears in his eyes, while his voice breaks with emotion, how much he regrets the fight in the Republican party of Wisconsin and the condition of affairs in this state. I want to tell you that no one man is more to blame for that condition than Senator Spooner himself," Lenroot said. "For the last four years in the assembly at Madison, scenes have been enacted which were a disgrace to the fair name of the state. When measures came up which affected the railroads and other corporations, corruption and bribery were on every hand and in those scenes the followers of Senator Spooner played a prominent role."

Partisanship had been moved aside through the campaign by both sides, but in praising Roosevelt and defending the legitimacy of the Madison convention and the court decision, Lenroot draped himself in the robes of Republicanism. He concluded on that note, warning voters not be fooled by the name National Republican party on the ballot. Spooner and probably Scofield would vote for Peck, the Democrat.[144]

As things turned out, the speech made little difference. Well before com-

142. Lenroot to Chandler, 14 October 1904, vol. 144, Chandler Papers; *Duluth News Tribune*, 17, 19, 25 October, 1 November 1904, John A. Malone to E. F. Dithmar, 20 October 1904, Box 13, Stone Papers.

143. Lenroot to Chynoweth, 23 September 1904, Box 107, La Follette Papers; *Milwaukee Free Press*, 29 October 1904, cited in Caine, "Railroad Regulation in Wisconsin," p. 88, note 50.

144. *Duluth News Tribune*, 4 November 1904.

plete returns were in, the La Follette men in Douglas County knew they had won a sweeping victory. Lenroot had been expected to win, but his large majority was surprising. Final returns showed Lenroot with 1,659 votes to 717 for John Hobe and 181 for Henry Parks, the social democrat. Other local La Follette men won easy victories too. The primary was approved overwhelmingly. La Follette carried the city and county by large pluralities, though he trailed Roosevelt by almost 800 votes in the county.[145]

The story was somewhat similar throughout the state. The primary won overwhelming approval. La Follette carried the state by about 50,000 votes but trailed the rest of the ticket; even the candidate for treasurer, seen as a friend of the conservatives, led him. La Follette trailed Roosevelt by over 100,000 votes.

But since there had been doubt of the overall outcome and since the battle had been so hard fought, half-breeds took satisfaction in the major results— the victory of La Follette and the primary and election of a legislature likely to be friendlier than before. In Washington, Chandler rejoiced at the news of La Follette's victory. He immediately wrote to the editor of the *Milwaukee Free Press,* which he had been receiving daily, "The President having declined to be a candidate in 1908 I name Robert M. La Follette for President. . . . He will be the natural and worthy successor of Theodore Roosevelt." A bit more circumspectly, La Follette, writing Steffens to tell him how much his article had helped, added that this was but the beginning of a glorious fight in which Steffens would continue to have a great part.[146]

Assured of reelection as speaker, Lenroot gave attention to the senatorial question much in advance of the new legislative session. He wanted to send La Follette to Washington, D. C., and the governor was anxious to mount the national stage. But there were difficulties. While running for governor, La Follette had said he would not be a candidate; he must first finish his work in Wisconsin. In December La Follette backtracked, but two conditions remained: He would not seek the office, and his legislative program must be accomplished. Meanwhile, other candidates, some of them half-breeds, had entered the lists. But in advance of La Follette's second statement, Stephenson gave him the impression that he would not himself be a candidate, for fear of embarrassing charges of his free use of money in his 1899 bid for the office. The door was open to La Follette, but it was up to Lenroot to take the lead for him.[147]

To meet La Follette's requirement that his program be achieved, above all a strong railroad commission bill, Lenroot engineered an extraordinary coup. He put to the caucus of Republican assemblymen resolutions to exclude from the caucus those who would not adhere to the party's platform

145. Ibid., 9 November 1904; *Wisconsin Blue Book,* 1905, pp. 268, 316, 465, 510.
146. Chandler to H. O. *[sic]* Myrick, 9 November 1904, vol. 144, Chandler Papers; La Follette to Steffens, 14 November 1904, Bound Cor., vol. 23, La Follette Papers.
147. Margulies, "Lenroot," pp. 247–57.

pledges. The resolutions passed after an acrimonious debate. Fourteen stalwarts walked out, but the next day even they returned to vote for Lenroot for speaker.[148]

Soon afterwards, Lenroot convened a secret meeting of about six of the most trustworthy La Follette men. He told them that if they tried to elect La Follette as senator, they could expect no help from La Follette, but that he, Lenroot, nevertheless thought it could and should be done. They all agreed. Lenroot then suggested that each of them discuss it confidentially with other members in whom they had faith; he proposed that the group meet again the next night and that each one try to bring two others. The following evening, fifteen or twenty men gathered and talked enthusiastically of their prospects. They agreed to try the plan again. The next meeting also was successful; it showed, Lenroot later recalled, that they lacked only one vote of a majority in the Republican caucus of the two houses. The group adjourned subject to Lenroot's call.[149]

Before Lenroot could proceed further, he encountered a new difficulty. Stephenson, whose financial help would be as important to La Follette in the future as it had been in the past, let the governor know that though he would not himself mount a campaign, he wanted to be senator and expected La Follette to get the office for him. It fell to Lenroot to dissuade the venerable lumberman. At a conference in Milwaukee, he told Stephenson and his aides that the eight or ten stalwart votes Stephenson thought he could get would cost more in half-breed defections. Further, he claimed that neither Stephenson nor any of the other avowed candidates could win—only La Follette could be elected. Finally, according to Stephenson's embittered recollection, "Lenroot and some others . . . proposed that La Follette be elected and that, in the meantime, they canvass the legislature to ascertain whether a sufficient number of votes could be obtained to elect me, in which event La Follette would decline the office and I would go to Washington instead." [150]

The meeting ended without even a firm agreement on that, and Lenroot returned to Madison with unabated enthusiasm for his task, being free to continue his efforts for La Follette in the knowledge that almost certainly the governor would not have to decline; he was not bound to make the eleventh-hour canvass for Stephenson, and in any case he knew half-breeds

---

148. Irvine to Clara Lenroot, 10 January 1905, Lenroot Papers Addition. Evidently written after the caucus, the letter was not finished until at least the twelfth, following La Follette's speech to the legislature. A. O. Barton, "1905 Organization of Legislature," Box 7, Barton Papers; Herman Ekern to B. M. Sletteland, 13 January 1905, to H. A. Anderson, 12 January 1905, Box 3, Ekern Papers. Ekern discussed the relationship of the caucus action to the senatorship. He claimed a role in preparation of the resolutions. *Wisconsin State Journal,* 11 January 1905; *Wisconsin Assembly Journal,* 1905, pp. 9–10.

149. Lenroot, "Memoirs," pp. 46–47. Though recollections are suspect, the preceding account squares with all known facts.

150. Isaac Stephenson, *Recollections of a Long Life, 1829–1915,* p. 227; John Hannan to Lenroot, 5 December 1906, Box 2, Lenroot Papers.

would balk at being asked to vote for a man whose only qualification was his great wealth. Stephenson and his lieutenants were not happy with the situation, but it was the best they could do so they accepted it as their only hope and sent their assemblymen friends into the decisive half-breed caucus on the evening of the nineteenth.[151]

Lenroot's immediate problem was to secure the additional vote needed to nominate La Follette. He thought he knew the man and how to get him. In his "Memoirs," he called the man "Cook," but there was no man named Cook at that session and another member John A. Fridd had characteristics attributed to "Cook." [152] The caucus took place in a large room with chairs along the walls. Lenroot arranged it so that the key member, who was pledged to Judge Charles Webb, sat at the end of one row. When all were seated, Lenroot asked each of the forty-eight present to express himself, "starting with the man at the end of the line of chairs along the opposite wall farthest from Cook." As each one rose and spoke with enthusiasm for La Follette, "Cook" grew visibly nervous and embarrassed. Finally, when his turn came, he arose and, speaking with some difficulty, asked whether it would be all right if he met his pledge to Judge Webb by voting for him on the first ballot and then switching to La Follette. Lenroot, knowing Webb could not succeed on the first ballot, readily assented.[153]

Confident of victory and with La Follette's private approval, his friends had already called a full Republican caucus to meet on the evening of Monday, 23 January.[154] Counting on a number of half-breed senators to supplement the main corps from the assembly, they felt sure of the fifty-seven votes needed in the caucus. Congressman Henry Cooper withdrew, but Webb, Congressman Esch, and Senator Quarles remained on stage and many heard Stephenson stirring fitfully in the wings. Since none of the half-breed hopefuls could afford to antagonize La Follette, some who voted for him on the nineteenth actually favored other candidates. Many of them continued to think that La Follette wanted only a complimentary nomination, or an election that he might decline. Between 19 January and 23 January, the confusion as to La Follette's intentions grew. Thus, at the 23 January caucus, even Quarles, hoping La Follette would not accept and forlornly counting on some half-breed votes when the real test came, threw

151. *Milwaukee News,* 20 January 1905.

152. Lenroot, "Memoirs," p. 48, Box 13, Lenroot Papers; *Wisconsin Blue Book,* 1905, p. 1123; *Duluth News Tribune,* 20 January 1905.

153. Lenroot, "Memoirs," p. 48, Box 13, Lenroot Papers. Newspaper accounts indicate that two of the forty-eight expressed themselves as for Webb but otherwise support Lenroot's account. *Wisconsin State Journal,* 20 January 1905; *Duluth News Tribune,* 20 January 1905; *Milwaukee News,* 20 January 1905.

154. Memo, n.d. (January 1905), Box 116, La Follette Papers. The memo, probably written by Lenroot, outlined the pros and cons of having a full caucus, in which stalwarts might participate, as against taking the senatorial question to the legislature in open-joint session without a prior caucus. It asked for La Follette's decision.

four of his votes to La Follette. Sixty-five Republicans out of the one hundred-seven present voted for the governor. His election the following day was assured.[155]

The large margin of La Follette's victory in the Republican caucus brings into question the importance of the single Webb vote that Lenroot later described as so important. At the time, though, between 19 and 23 January, every delegate was being counted. Winter Everett of the *Milwaukee News* thought La Follette was one vote short. On the basis of their count, La Follette men freely predicted victory. The action of Quarles in throwing four of his votes to La Follette indicates that these claims were generally accepted, so for La Follette's rivals, the only hope lay in his declination. It may well be, then, that Lenroot did not exaggerate the importance of that single second-choice pledge. Quite apart from that, Lenroot had gone far toward accomplishing La Follette's election when he established a La Follette caucus of forty-eight assemblymen, forty-six of whom agreed to vote for La Follette on the first ballot.[156]

La Follette accepted but conditionally. He said to the legislature "if there should appear any conflict in the obligation I entered into when I took the oath of office as governor, and that of United States senator-elect, then I shall ask you to receive it from me and place it in other hands of your own choosing. The selection of United States senator is your prerogative and will, of course, be preserved by you." [157] One thing was clear. He would continue as governor through most or all of the session.

For Lenroot, as for La Follette, the job immediately at hand was to write and secure the major reforms—above all an effective railroad regulation act. The task was invigorating. In the wake of the 1904 election, administration leaders had more legislative and popular support than ever before. Obstacles remained, but the session was unprecedentedly productive. Before the members went home, they had enacted measures on railroad regulation,

155. Reflecting the varied opinion as to La Follette's course see *Wisconsin State Journal*, 23, 25 January 1905; *Duluth News Tribune*, 24 January 1905; Herman Ekern to B. M. Sletteland, 22 January 1905, Box 3, Ekern Papers; Elisha Keyes to John C. Spooner, 25 January 1905, Box 74, Spooner Papers. The possibility of Stephenson becoming the new senator, in alliance with La Follette, is suggested in *Duluth News Tribune*, 19 January 1905; *Milwaukee News*, 19, 20, 24 January 1905; and Joe Quarles to Spooner, 19 January 1905, Box 74, Spooner Papers. But Wallace Andrew and Lenroot denied any deal. *Duluth News Tribune*, 21 January 1905. Without attribution, they predicted La Follette would accept, and privately Lenroot told George Hudnall he would accept if his legislation were passed by 4 March. *Duluth News Tribune*, 22, 24 January 1905.

156. *Milwaukee News*, 21 January 1905. After the 19 January caucus, the La Follette men not only claimed victory publicly but also privately. *Duluth News Tribune*, 20 January 1905; Herman Ekern to B. M. Sletteland, 22 January 1905, Box 3, Ekern Papers; James Stone to James W. Shaw, 23 January 1905, Box 14, Stone Papers.

157. *Journal of the Senate*, 1905, p. 173, cited in Belle and Fola La Follette, *La Follette*, vol. 1, p. 189.

civil service, lobbying, and many other things. Lenroot delighted in taking an active and important part.

The administration men, aware of their weak position in the senate, moved slowly during the first months of the session. But the course of their ambitions could not but lead them into more conflict before long. However, the character of the senate did not change, so men like Lenroot, and Frear, in the senate, had to give long, patient effort, bargain hard, and finally accept compromise.

The railroad commission bill was the keystone of the administration's program. The key senator with respect to the commission bill was a rather eccentric moderate named William Hatton. Forty-eight years old, tall, spare, handsome, very wealthy, taciturn but tough and brilliant, a bachelor lumberman of abstemious habits, Hatton chaired the railroad committee. Popular and respected in all quarters and in the absence of firm administration control in the senate, Hatton went his own way.[158] Unhappily for the administration, Hatton's views were decidedly more moderate than those of La Follette, Lenroot, or many of the experts who had advised them. The historian of the subject speculates that Hatton's outlook was that of a lumberman fearful of the disruption of good relations with the railroads.[159]

In the protracted negotiations and maneuverings that preceded enactment of a law, Lenroot took the lead for the administration. Having studied the question earlier, he supplied the governor with material for his message and drew the administration bill along the lines of the strong Texas law. Lenroot wanted a commission that would have authority to establish not just maximum but absolute rates and one that would act on its own initiative, not just on complaints from shippers.[160] Hatton introduced the administration bill in the senate, but he had no part in drafting it nor any intention of reporting it from his committee.[161]

The opponents of the administration's bill offered a weaker alternative, one which would allow commission rate interference only on complaint of a shipper and one which differed from Lenroot's bill in other significant ways. La Follette and Lenroot tried to build support for their measure but were unsuccessful. With Hatton more sympathetic to the weaker plan than to the bill that bore his name, the administration found by late March that it would have to compromise.[162]

Lenroot, representing the assembly, worked with Hatton and George

158. Caine, "Railroad Regulation in Wisconsin," p. 113.

159. Ibid., pp. 114–15.

160. *Duluth News Tribune*, 8, 11 February 1905; *Wisconsin State Journal*, 11 February 1905; Caine, "Railroad Regulation in Wisconsin," pp. 101–5.

161. Ibid., pp. 104–5, 109–10, 113–14.

162. Robert Eliot to Lenroot, 23 February 1905, John Barnes to La Follette, 25 February 1905, E. A. Edmonds to La Follette, 25 February 1905, Box 117, La Follette Papers; La Follette to Lenroot, 25 February 1906, Box 3, Lenroot Papers; Lenroot to William E. Chandler, 25 March 1905, vol. 145, William E. Chandler Papers; *Wisconsin State Journal*, 14 March 1905; Caine, "Railroad Regulation in Wisconsin," pp. 105–9, 111, 116–18.

Hudnall of Superior, who was on the senate railroad committee, toward a compromise. Lenroot retained some bargaining power. The assembly had already passed a two-cent fare bill, and if no satisfactory commission bill eventuated, the two-cent bill, anathema to the railroad companies, seemed likely to pass the senate. Lenroot and the assembly also retained power to hold up bills in which senators of every stripe were interested. Lenroot was therefore able to effect a compromise, which was promptly reported to the assembly from its railroad committee. In some ways it was premature, for Hatton and Hudnall could promise nothing as to senate action. But considering the fragmented state of the senate and the endorsement stalwarts had gotten from federal appointments, Lenroot evidently judged it essential to make an immediate show of progress, willingness to compromise, and the ability of assembly and senate half-breeds to work together.[163]

The new bill took from the commission its original ratemaking power and added explicit reassurances regarding commodity and other special rates. However, it left the commission with authority to investigate and revise rates that were found unreasonable or discriminatory. While yielding a little in regard to court review, the bill left the commission's position strong and appointive. As a result, the fate of the bill remained doubtful during the first weeks of April.[164]

On 11 April, Lenroot took the floor in the liveliest debate of the session, which was witnessed by Belle La Follette and others, to defend the new bill against a weaker substitute and, more particularly, against an amendment to make the commission elective. He argued that the railroads would find it easy to elect a commission favorable to themselves. Lenroot's forces held against both the amendment and substitute bill, by votes of thirty-four to fifty-seven and twenty-two to sixty-nine. The main measure then passed, eight-one to ten.[165]

Orchestrated with threats and displays of power, over a month of negotiation ensued. Senators, half-breed, stalwart, and Democrat, entered into the power equation; Philipp, Pfister, and Babcock participated in the bill drafting. Behind the scenes, Lenroot acted as liaison with and spokesman for both the administration and the assembly. By the nature of the power situation, the bill that finally came to the senate for action on 18 May was weaker than the one passed in the assembly five weeks earlier but was nevertheless acceptable to the administration. To the very last, the result in the senate was not certain, and Lenroot armed Hudnall, who was more

163. *Wisconsin State Journal,* 23, 27 March 1905; *Duluth News Tribune,* 23, 24, 31 March, 3 April 1905; Caine, "Railroad Regulation in Wisconsin," pp. 118–19.

164. Caine, "Railroad Regulation in Wisconsin," pp. 119–20; *Wisconsin State Journal,* 27 March 1905; *Duluth News Tribune,* 6 April 1905; Emil Baensch to John Spooner, 4 April 1905, Elisha Keyes to Spooner, 10 April 1905, Box 76, Spooner Papers; James O. Davidson to J. D. Stuart, 6 April 1905, James O. Davidson Papers, Letterbooks, WSHSL.

165. *Wisconsin State Journal,* 11 April 1905; *Duluth News Tribune,* 12 April 1905; *Wisconsin Assembly Journal,* 1905, pp. 1021–25.

orator than debater, with points to be used against Whitehead's prospective amendments and arguments. After seven hours of debate during which the senate rejected several weakening amendments, the bill passed. Asked for his reaction, Lenroot said "just tell them that I smiled." He went on to say, "I think we have the best bill of its kind in the country. . . . The most eminent authorities on the subject have all examined the measure and all pronounce it an excellent one. I also consider it a great personal victory for the governor, who has now won everything for which he contended." In short order, the assembly concurred in the senate's bill and sent it on to the governor.[166]

Hall, dying of Bright's disease, rejoiced at the news of the senate action, undoubtedly seeing in it the fulfillment of his own unremitting effort, begun in 1891. He congratulated La Follette on the outcome as meeting all his promises, so that now he could take his seat in the U. S. Senate "where other important duties await you." The more matter-of-factly political Houser reacted in the same way. Calling the measure the strongest of the kind to pass any state legislature, he felt that "there is scarcely any doubt now but that Governor La Follette will take his seat as senator." Other reformers, including some who had closely studied the legislation, wrote La Follette in the same vein, while John R. Commons praised it in *Review of Reviews.*[167]

Even after all the compromises had been made, much of substance remained. At first glance, it seemed to half-breeds that the law gave the commission power to initiate investigations of rate inequities as well as to act on complaints. This power, they felt, made the commission a dynamic body, able to help the small man not just serve the large shipper. The court review provisions—more restrictive than the half-breeds wanted them to be—compared favorably with the provisions Congress enacted the following year for interstate commerce and also opened the way for stays in the application of a commission-set rate, which was pending appeal from a circuit court to the Supreme Court.[168] In providing for appointment rather than election of commissioners, the half-breeds won an important victory.

The bill, however, had serious faults, including some potentially dangerous ambiguities. Senate confirmation was required for commissioners, a veto power very promptly invoked by the senate. The courts remained a potent safety valve for railroads persistent enough to use all the opportunities opened to them by the act. At best, the commission would have difficulty determining a fair basis for rates, as La Follette recognized when he belat-

166. Caine, "Railroad Regulation in Wisconsin," pp. 121–31, 150, 152; *Wisconsin State Journal,* 18, 19 April, 5, 9, 16 May 1905; *Duluth News Tribune,* 20 April, 6, 19, 22 May 1905; La Follette to Lenroot, 25 February 1906, Box 3, Lenroot Papers; *Wisconsin State Journal,* 19 May 1905; *Wisconsin Assembly Journal,* 1905, pp. 1755–57, 1842, 1864.

167. A. R. Hall to La Follette, 19 May 1905, Box 121, La Follette Papers; Walter Houser to Chandler, 20 May 1905, vol. 146, Chandler Papers; David Evans, Jr., to La Follette, 20 May 1905, R. M. Bashford to La Follette, 20 May 1905, La Follette Papers.

168. Caine, "Railroad Regulation in Wisconsin," pp. 121, 196–97.

edly and vainly urged the legislature to let the commission control the issuance of stocks and bonds, so that future capitalization would reflect true value and thus make Tax Commission valuation of railroad property easier. The bill's provisions for special rates made ratemaking yet more difficult for the Railroad Commission. The most serious difficulty with the bill, perhaps, was that the commission's powers to handle complaints were more clearly and broadly expressed than its powers to initiate investigations. The ambiguity left the measure vulnerable to narrowing construction. And in some rather specific ways, as, for example, power over long- and short-haul discriminations, the bill was restrictive.[169]

La Follette took some time before signing the bill. Finally, when he signed it, he attached a memo explaining that though he saw the deficiencies in the measure, he thought it the best act possible under the circumstances. He was right. Much would depend, though, on how the commission construed the measure and what the legislature might later add to clarify the ambiguities and fill in the gaps.

Despite the bitterness and length of the fight over railroad regulation, the final vote in each house was lopsidedly favorable. For varying, sometimes contrasting reasons, partisan and factional ranks closed to form a common chorus in praise of the measure and those who had accomplished it. The one most praised of the legislators was William Hatton, and historians have generally echoed the contemporary judgment. Lenroot's role was largely ignored, then and afterwards. Of the many reasons why Hatton is called the father of the rate bill, the single most important one is that the senate, not the assembly, posed the chief obstacle to legislation; Hatton took the lead in negotiating a compromise acceptable to a majority of senators, to the railroads and shippers, to himself, and to the assembly as well. Without his patient and skilled diplomacy, and keen instinct for just the proper wording and just the right balance between strong and weak provisions, the bill might never have been approved in 1905. In this sense, Hatton is responsible for the new law. However, insofar as the bill represented progress toward better regulation of railroads, it is Lenroot more than any other who merited the credit among the legislators, as the draftsman of the assembly's bill and the negotiator who achieved for his side as much as the circumstances would permit.

Of course, "credit" need not be universally accepted as the right word. Judgment is in part subjective. Some may view the law as excessively lax, while others could consider it overly restrictive. Whatever one's judgment, Lenroot's large role is clear.

Though the commission bill was the most prominent and important legislation enacted in 1905, the legislature also adopted other reforms. Lenroot

169. Ibid., pp. 121, 124, 149, 197, 223; *Wisconsin Assembly Journal,* 1905, pp. 1852–56; *Wisconsin State Journal,* 10 June 1905.

took a leading role in drafting and passing many of them. A number of measures that Lenroot sponsored or supported failed to pass, but some of these are noteworthy as an indication of the direction of his interests.

Lenroot gave a good deal of attention to economic legislation. He introduced, and probably drafted, an employer's liability bill. He continued to be keenly interested in the trust problem, with little success. He backed La Follette's pioneering recommendations for more careful allocation of water-power sites to corporations and exaction of fees for dam privileges. The bill failed in the senate, but Lenroot's later interest in the subject perhaps dates to this time. Lenroot continued attentive to economy, though he remained liberal in respect to university appropriations.[170]

For Lenroot, honesty in government, rooted in a concerned and moral citizenry, was the foundation on which social and economic life was built. He gave support and much attention to measures designed to purify politics. Some of the measures that Lenroot backed, such as initiative, referendum, and recall, depended for their effectiveness on the direct actions of the people. Others, like civil service and anti-lobby restrictions, did not. Lenroot withheld support from only one political reform measure, to extend suffrage to women in city, village, and town matters. He gave his fullest attention and support to a recall bill that he himself drafted and defended with some eloquence on the floor of the assembly. Applicable to aldermen, the bill was timely, coming in the wake of scandals in Milwaukee. In passing the assembly, the bill did better than the initiative, referendum, and woman suffrage all of which suffered because social democrats sponsored them. Lenroot's recall bill failed in the senate, however.[171]

Civil service and anti-lobby legislation passed. Lenroot, for some time concerned about lobbying, gave particular attention to that subject. "The great majority of lobbyists are criminals, whose occupation is to destroy the manhood and the integrity of the legislator," Lenroot asserted. "They are paid and maintained at legislative sessions to prey upon the members by developing their weaknesses and their vices. And this is as persistent and systematic a manner as that by which the wide awake merchant promotes the sales of his wares." Lenroot acknowledged that argument before committee could be useful but urged that lobbyists be restricted to that and be forbidden the right to solicit the votes of individual members. Both houses agreed to a bill along the lines advocated by La Follette and defended by Lenroot.[172]

170. *Duluth News Tribune*, 15 February 1905; *Wisconsin Assembly Journal*, 1905, pp. 358, 641, 688–89, 1047, 1050–54, 1558, 1744, 1937; "Voters' Handbook—1906," Box 5, Lenroot Papers.
171. On Lenroot's role in the recall bill see the *Wisconsin State Journal*, 16, 17, 21 March 1905; *Duluth News Tribune*, 17, 29 March, 6, 20 May 1905; "Voters' Handbook—1906," Box 5, Lenroot Papers; for his votes on other political legislation see the *Wisconsin Assembly Journal*, 1905, pp. 819, 893, 1204–5, 1212. The point about social democratic sponsorship working against the initiative and referendum is made in the *Wisconsin State Journal*, 18 March 1905. And a socialist also sponsored the woman suffrage bill.
172. MS, "The Legislative Lobby, I. L. Lenroot, Speaker, Wisconsin Assembly," n.d., Box 92, La Follette Papers; *Wisconsin State Journal*, 15 June 1905.

A legislature that reflected the strength of the La Follette movement was bound to give more than an ordinary measure of attention to moral, or social issues, considering the nature of La Follette's appeal, the segments of the electorate with whom he was popular, and the kind of men he drew into politics.[173] An anti-cigarette bill, which had failed in the previous session, passed easily this time and was signed into law. A safety-valve provision permitted users to send out of state to feed their habit. Temperance proposals, in a great variety of forms, were more hotly disputed through the session. Lenroot supported most of these measures and was among the more active in backing a local option bill. This and most similar bills failed, but the legislature did enact a law prohibiting saloons within three hundred feet of any school.[174]

Before La Follette would resign as governor, he wanted to satisfy himself as to the succession. He had little confidence in Lt. Gov. James O. Davidson, a man of limited education and not noted for forcefulness or ability. State Chairman W. D. Connor did not lack these qualities, but his progressivism was suspect. In preference to these or others, La Follette chose Lenroot. Though perhaps flattered, Lenroot did not leap to the bait. He much preferred a congressional bid and doubted that he could win the nomination for governor. La Follette was not easily dissuaded, however, and after Lenroot was assured of support by the Norwegian-language newspaper *Skandinaven*, he acceded to La Follette's wishes. There were many factors involved in the failure of preempting the nomination for him, such as the refusal of Davidson and Connor to make way; the objections of Milwaukee reformers who were under the leadership of District Attorney Francis E. McGovern and who thought that Lenroot would only weaken the ticket; and the withholding of support of the *Milwaukee Free Press* by Stephenson.[175]

Belatedly, La Follette realized that Stephenson still coveted the senatorship. He decided to make an all-out effort to give it to him. If it could be accomplished, he, La Follette, would continue as governor through 1906 instead of giving Davidson a foothold in that office, and, therefore, the transfer of power to Lenroot would be easier. With Stephenson's help La Follette could move directly on the presidency in 1908 or, failing that, take the next Senate vacancy in 1909. Accordingly, La Follette called a special session, ostensibly to improve the railroad commission law and effect other legislation.[176]

The gambit failed. A news leak, the speculation about the political pur-

173. Ibid., 4 April 1905.

174. Ibid., 18 April, 13, 14 June 1905; *Wisconsin Assembly Journal*, 1905, pp. 1050–56. The history of the major temperance bills in the assembly, including Lenroot's favorable votes, may be followed in the *Wisconsin State Journal*, 22, 23 March, 12, 14, 18, 25, 26, 27, 29 April, 16 May 1905; and the *Wisconsin Assembly Journal*, 1905, pp. 1120, 1197–1201, 1206, 1218, 1230–32, 1455–56.

175. Margulies, "Lenroot," pp. 284–301.

176. Herbert F. Margulies, "Robert M. La Follette Goes to the Senate, 1905," pp. 214–25.

poses of the special session, and word of conferences between La Follette's
secretary, Hannan, and Stephenson men in Milwaukee, destroyed the
secrecy so essential to development of a surprise, snowballing movement
for Stephenson.[177] Some began to talk of other candidates, Davidson men
expressed anger that their friend was to be shut out of the executive office,
and admirers of La Follette pressured him not to give up his Senate opportunity.[178] Nevertheless, La Follette played the game to the very end, as he
had to do.

The members proved unreceptive. La Follette delayed matters to the last,
and after the two houses organized during the afternoon of 4 December
and after the assembly reelected Lenroot speaker without contest, the governor decided to spend the night in final efforts at persuasion instead of
delivering his message. He found the cause hopeless. Stalwarts had decided
not to cooperate, nor would the backers of Davidson or Connor or Hatton.
And some of La Follette's best friends argued that the plan was unwise or
impossible.[179]

The following day, after reading the legislature his message from the
printed text, La Follette pulled from his pocket another document. Reading
carefully, La Follette explained his delay on various grounds, then said that
he would, during or immediately after the session, submit his resignation
as governor and take up his Senate duties in Washington.[180]

The *Wisconsin State Journal* soon observed contentedly that "the hopeless-
ness of the Lenroot boom . . . has given the owner of the boom, as well
as its wet nurse, a drawn and haggard look." [181] Lenroot was now committed
to the governorship, but he had failed to preempt the nomination before
La Follette's departure, and prospects of success were dim.

Viewed in broader perspective, Lenroot's situation was far from bleak.
He had come a long way since 1900. In the assembly, he had both demonstrated and developed ability as a bill draftsman, parliamentarian and
debater, and had played an important part in enactment of major reform
legislation. His earlier progressive inclinations fortified by fresh experience,
he had earned a place just behind La Follette among half-breed Republicans, and he had seen that faction gain control in state politics. Whether
he realized it or not, Lenroot was well prepared and well positioned for a
long and fruitful career at the national level, whatever the outcome of the
gubernatorial contest.

177. *Milwaukee News*, 23, 24, 25, 27, 28 November 1905; *Wisconsin State Journal*, 23 November
1905; *Duluth News Tribune*, 26 November 1905; Thomas W. Braheny to John C. Spooner, 29
November 1905, Box 78, Spooner Papers.

178. *Milwaukee News*, 28 November 1905.

179. Ibid., 5, 6, 18 December 1905; Braheny to Spooner, 29 December 1905, Box 78, Elisha
Keyes to Spooner, 5 December 1905, Box 79, Spooner Papers.

180. *Wisconsin Assembly Journal*, Special sess., 1905, pp. 51–52.

181. *Wisconsin State Journal*, 8 December 1905.

III

TO WASHINGTON
AND INSURGENCY

"We are not going to reach enough people to win this fight," Lenroot wrote his wife in mid-August 1906. "I judge that by the large number of men who come to me after my meetings saying they had been for Davidson but after hearing me were for me. With that general condition and in view of the fact that we can reach only a small portion of the people it don't look very encouraging." [1] His pessimism was warranted. The Milwaukee reformers had remained aloof, as did Isaac Stephenson. James O. Davidson had made a strong appeal on the basis of political precedent—he had been a loyal half-breed and was the incumbent governor. His fellow Norwegians, twice as numerous as the Swedes, had rallied to him. W. D. Connor had joined him as candidate for lieutenant governor, and had made quiet deals for stalwart help. Half-breeds were confused and many followed Davidson's bandwagon. [2]

Ready for defeat, after the returns were in Lenroot admitted to La Follette that "we got a harder drubbing than I looked for." He lost by a vote of 109,583 to 61,178. [3]

With no public office at hand, other than his court reporter post, Lenroot had to plan for the future. La Follette took the occasion to present a "business proposition" to him. La Follette had recently formed a new law firm with his former clerk, Alfred T. Rogers. Now the two proposed that Lenroot move to Madison and join the firm. La Follette would do no work, but his name would bring in business; Rogers liked Lenroot very much and was most anxious that he accept. The partners promised Lenroot bright and well-assured prospects for a lucrative practice. [4]

Clara had made many friends in Madison and enjoyed the city; she urged Irvine to take the offer. But he hesitated. In mid-October he went to Madi-

1. Irvine to Clara Lenroot, 18 August, 1 September 1906, Box 1, Irvine L. Lenroot Papers.

2. Padraic C. Kennedy, "Lenroot, La Follette and the Campaign of 1906," pp. 163–74; Herbert F. Margulies, *The Decline of the Progressive Movement in Wisconsin, 1890–1920*, pp. 83–99.

3. Lenroot to La Follette, 10 September 1906, Box 138, Robert M. La Follette Papers; *Wisconsin Blue Book*, 1907, p. 389.

4. Lenroot, "Memoirs," pp. 59–60, Box 13, Lenroot Papers; Rogers to Gilbert Roe, 5 October 1906, Box 4, Series H, Robert M. La Follette FC.

son to talk the matter over with La Follette, Rogers, and others. La Follette and Rogers pressed Lenroot hard; but Lenroot insisted on further consideration. Home a few days later, Lenroot heard from Rogers immediately, again urging acceptance.[5] Finally, he wrote Rogers his answer. He admitted all the advantages, which were many and weighty. Yet he declined. Against the plan, he explained, was the uncertainty of getting business before his own finances were exhausted, and the fact that the Madison bar was abler than that of Superior, while Superior's long-term economic prospects exceeded Madison's. The main reason, though, was his attachment to Superior. "Here my life has been lived. In some degree it is a part of the city. For me to cut loose from it all, I feel that my judgment should be so well settled as to cause me no serious misgivings." [6]

Lenroot had other reasons for declining, which he finally confessed to La Follette when they met in Madison later that week. If he located in Madison as La Follette's partner, he would inevitably be seen as La Follette's political representative and would be constantly drawn away from his law practice. He would remain uncomfortably divided between business and politics, at a time of life when he felt it essential to decide between the two. By remaining in Superior, he could very soon make a clear-cut decision, "either to quit politics except in a very minor way, or run for Congress in the next election," knowing that the congressional salary, in process of being raised from $5,000 to $7,500, would allow him to support his family adequately.[7]

These last reasons, not recorded in contemporary correspondence but only in Lenroot's recollections years later, meshed well with the patently sincere explanation Lenroot had given Rogers. Taken together, they reflected two very strong urges—one was to speedily get out of the embarrassing situation of being a personage in politics and a nobody in economic life. Equally important, Lenroot wanted to control his own destiny. This he could do in Superior, either in law or in politics. But in Madison, he would seem and be La Follette's subordinate. Intellectually and emotionally, he remained committed to La Follette and the causes La Follette represented; politically, to the extent that he continued in politics, he would remain on La Follette's team; personally, he would continue to be La Follette's faithful friend. In tangible ways, nothing would be changed, and his would still be the subordinate place. Yet, rooted and based at home, he would be the willing ally, not the dependent servant; he would be his own man.

Lenroot settled into living a life in Superior once again, ready to accept political opportunity whenever it might come. He hardly expected that it would turn up so soon as it did, however, and in so attractive a form. On late Sunday, 3 March, with the expiration of the Fifty-ninth Congress, Sena-

5. Lenroot, "Memoirs," p. 60, Box 13, Irvine to Clara Lenroot, 14 October 1906, Box 1, Rogers to Lenroot, 18 October 1906, Box 4, Lenroot Papers.

6. Lenroot to Rogers, 22 October 1906, Box 4, Lenroot Papers.

7. Lenroot, "Memoirs," p. 61, Box 13, Lenroot Papers.

tor Spooner announced to the press his resignation, which would be effective 1 May. Though the announcement startled all but a few, politicians speculated less about Spooner's motives than about the larger consequences of his action. Although the seventy-eight-year-old Stephenson immediately announced his candidacy for the two-year term, friends of Lenroot around the state wired messages to him, urging him to run. More important, Rogers phoned encouraging news from Madison and requested that he come there immediately. A number of legislators, probably headed by Lenroot's friend Herman Ekern, had come in to tell him they could not support Stephenson and wanted Lenroot. These men evidently did not relish the charges that would fly if they were forced to vote robot-like to pay off La Follette's debts with a place in the U. S. Senate. La Follette, foreseeing this difficulty and the opposition Stephenson's candidacy would evoke from many quarters, had called Rogers from Washington—Lenroot by this time was informed—and had made it clear that though he would support Stephenson, he doubted that the old man could win and hoped Lenroot would enter the race. Privately, La Follette evidently felt that if Lenroot could not win, he could be relied on to hold a substantial group, and those the most faithful, who might later be switched to Stephenson.[8]

By late Tuesday Lenroot had thought the matter through and was determined to set out in full pursuit of the prize, but by a circuitous route that would permit a graceful retreat in case of need. "I think that probably Stephenson stands the best chance at present, but if he cannot rally sufficient support I believe I would stand an excellent chance," he wrote a supporter. "I take it that Cooper, Esch and Hatton will also be candidates. The more the better for the present. . . . If I should go in now, the whole field would be against me, for in going over the list of members I could probably lead in number of votes, but still a ways from a majority." [9]

La Follette's commitment to Stephenson was known to insiders, rumored in the papers, and claimed by Stephenson backers. Though in fact La Follette wanted Stephenson promptly elected and feared the consequences if he were not, many doubted his sincerity by the time Lenroot reached Madi-

8. The wires to Lenroot were not preserved. However, on 4 March James A. Stone wrote Andrew Dahl: ". . . get our fellows to crystallize sentiment upon Lenroot, if possible." A day later Dahl replied from Madison, Wis., that he was not sure Lenroot could win, but hoped he might, and was sure "nothing would please our boys better." He felt, too, that "it would meet with the approval of the junior Senator. . . ." Stone to Dahl, 4 March 1907, Dahl to Stone, 5 March 1907, Box 16, James A. Stone Papers. Lenroot told in his "Memoirs" of Rogers's phone call. Though he telescoped events, it is clear that Rogers called on 4 or 5 March. On La Follette's thoughts, see Belle and Fola La Follette, *La Follette,* vol. 1, pp. 228–29; and Robert to Belle La Follette, 4 March 1907, Box 6, Series A, La Follette FC. Regarding Spooner's resignation see Dorothy Ganfield Fowler, *John Coit Spooner: Defender of Presidents,* pp. 369–70; and the *Wisconsin State Journal,* 4 March 1907. Spooner stressed the need to provide for his family financially.

9. Lenroot to Edwin J. Gross, 5 March 1907, Edwin J. Gross Papers, Box 1, WSHSL. In business matters, William Hatton spelled his name "Hatten."

son. Laid up with the grippe in Washington and committed to a long out-of-state lecture tour, La Follette could not bring full personal pressure to bear; recent experience made him leary of giving orders from afar. Lenroot himself judged that La Follette would not return to Madison at all during the contest. Most of those he talked with thought La Follette's support of Stephenson would actually benefit Lenroot.[10] Having received indirect encouragement from La Follette at the outset and aware that even if he did not run, half-breeds would not immediately coalesce behind Stephenson but would support local favorites like Congressmen Cooper and Esch, Senator Hatton or others, Lenroot had no second thought about his candidacy as it might relate to the larger cause and the feelings and interests of La Follette.

Lenroot soon found himself in an embarrassing position. Though strong, he could not get a majority among Republican legislators. But to withdraw would open him to the charge of serving as cat's-paw for La Follette. He tried to meet the difficulty and keep half-breed ranks in order by agreement among the candidates to abide by the decision of a half-breed conference, but Esch's forces blocked anything binding. Finally, with his resources gone and prospects looking dim, Lenroot withdrew. Soon, to his embarrassment, Stephenson was elected. To make matters worse, the old man emerged from the long fight embittered at La Follette for failing to deliver the election more promptly; he felt under no obligation to confine himself to the short term, despite early pledges.[11]

In 1906 at La Follette's request, Lenroot had spoken before influential reform groups in New York and Kansas, telling of Wisconsin's recent accomplishments, and by implication, those of La Follette. In 1907 and 1908, as the tempo of presidential politics increased, Lenroot again campaigned for La Follette outside Wisconsin and assisted him with national legislation. But he resisted the senator when La Follette urged him to compete with Stephenson in the 1908 preferential senatorial primary. He could not match Stephenson's money and in a presidential year could not expect much money from others. Early on, Lenroot made it clear that he would at long last try for the congressional nomination against John Jenkins.[12]

His fighting spirit was perhaps buoyed by confidence in the outcome. Men in the district wrote to him with encouragement; and when a group of half-breed leaders of the eleventh district gathered in Superior in late Feb-

---

10. Irvine to Clara Lenroot, 7 March 1907, Box 1, Lenroot Papers; Belle to Josie Siebecker, 10 March 1907, Box 5, Series A, La Follette FC. This letter is quoted in Belle and Fola La Follette, *La Follette,* vol. 1, p. 229. *Wisconsin State Journal,* 5, 7, 8, 11 March 1907; Elisha Keyes to John C. Spooner, 8 March 1907, Box 90, Spooner Papers.
11. Margulies, "Lenroot," pp. 348–61; Isaac Stephenson, *Recollections of a Long Life, 1829–1915,* p. 101.
12. Margulies, "Lenroot," pp. 365–77.

ruary, ostensibly to finalize the choice of district convention delegate candidates, they all agreed that Lenroot's chances were good.[13]

Under other circumstances, the confidence shown by Lenroot and his friends would have been inconceivable. The sixty-five-year-old Jenkins had served fourteen years in the House of Representatives. A friend of the Speaker and chairman of the judiciary committee, he was privileged above others to secure patronage and pork, benefit manufacturers, and get special legislation for his fellow Civil War veterans. There was reason to believe that he would have a large campaign fund and he had overwhelming newspaper support in the district. His home base, Chippewa Falls, though smaller than Superior, was in the more populous southern part of the sprawling district. Jenkins had tacked skillfully with Wisconsin politics and had met a half-breed challenge in 1906 by carrying ten of thirteen counties and 62 percent of the primary vote.[14]

Under the special circumstances of 1908, many of Jenkins's strong points served only to accentuate his major weakness, his close association with "Boss Cannon," the reactionary Speaker of the House. Continuing to move with the country, President Roosevelt threw his great popularity behind the progressive cause and progressive measures in his State and the Union message of 3 December 1907, urging greater control over business, curbs on the labor injunction, physical valuation of railroads, tariff reductions after the next election, but prior to that elimination of tariffs on wood pulp and newsprint, postal savings, and an employers liability law for federal employees. Opposed to virtually all of these measures, Joseph Cannon carefully deployed his forces in the key committees, renewed his own vigil at the legislative Thermopylae, the rules committee, and proceeded to block everything. For measures like the anti-injunction bill and the Littlefield Interstate Commerce Liquor Bill, an Anti-Saloon League measure, Jenkins's judiciary committee served as Cannon's "legislative crematory." Roosevelt renewed his requests at the end of January and later in the spring, but in the House his messages met with scant courtesy. On 5 February 1908, freshman Congressman John M. Nelson of Wisconsin lashed out against Cannon's arbitrary powers, and before the session closed over two dozen Republican members promised to join the Democrats to change the rules by which Cannon governed. The Democrats had happily joined the attack, in preparation for the coming election. Newspaper publishers, anxious for reduced newsprint costs, complained of the "paper trust" and against Cannon. When Cannon's rules committee killed bills for Appalachian and White

13. Lenroot to Nils P. Haugen, 7 February 1908, Box 55, Nils P. Haugen Papers; to James A. Stone, 22 February 1908, Box 17, Stone Papers; Ekern to La Follette, 24 February 1908, Box 147, D. C. Coolidge to Ray J. Nye, 6 February 1908, Box 146, La Follette Papers.

14. Robert Griffith, "Prelude to Insurgency: Irvine L. Lenroot and the Republican Primary of 1908," pp. 16–28. Griffith notes Jenkins's popularity with the G.A.R. The support of the newspapers for Jenkins was due as much to patronage for the publishers as to any other factor. Jenkins's geographical advantage is noted by Clough Gates, *Superior Telegram*, 4 February 1949.

Mountain forest reserves, *Collier's* and *The Outlook* leaped to the attack, raising the conservation issue against the Speaker. So unpopular had Cannon become by summertime, with so many powerful groups, and with the public at large, that the Democrats made him a prime issue in their campaign and the Republican presidential nominee urged that Cannon not be sent west to campaign.[15]

Lenroot set out to capitalize on Jenkins's association with Cannon. By polarizing the issue as between progressivism and Cannonism and by mobilizing discontent to the fullest, he hoped to override the incumbent's many advantages. The district had been a La Follette stronghold for years—it was not merely rural, but poor, and in its southern part well organized by a pro-half-breed farm organization, the Wisconsin Society of Equity. The Scandinavian element was strong and the Swedes heavily concentrated in the district. And La Follette leaders were numerous throughout it. Labor, centered in Superior, was relatively well organized and could be aroused over Jenkins's recent role in killing the anti-injunction bill. "Between 1902 and 1907," an economic historian has written, "three cases brought American labor leaders to the verge of panic." As of 1908 Samuel Gompers was under contempt proceedings for violating an injunction, and he was leading the A.F.L. into political activism against those who would construe unions as falling under the definitions of the Sherman Anti-trust Act and would restrain their activities by injunction.[16] Jenkins could expect financial help from brewers, but in the district "drys" outnumbered "wets" and their leaders, locally and nationally, were a quietly active lot who were out to beat the congressman.[17]

Lenroot had long been confident that he would win in the eleventh district. In 1908, his chances were good. He was already well acquainted with most half-breed leaders in the thirteen counties, as a result of his work in the legislature, his statewide campaign in 1906, and periodic missions for La Follette in the northwest. The leaders, and many of the voters, already associated him with La Follette; and he had something of a reputation in his own right. His Swedish ancestry would be an asset, though he knew he would have to court the Norwegians. The positions he would take and would

15. Blair Bolles, *Tyrant from Illinois: Uncle Joe Cannon's Experiment with Personal Power*, pp. 90–101, 112, 113–19, 122, 144; William Rea Gwinn, *Uncle Joe Cannon, Archfoe of Insurgency: A History of the Rise and Fall of Cannonism*, pp. 148–49, 153–54; George E. Mowry, *The Era of Theodore Roosevelt, 1900–1912*, pp. 220–25; Kenneth Hechler, *Insurgency: Personality and Politics of the Taft Era*, p. 43.

16. Griffith, "Prelude to Insurgency," pp. 19–25. Griffith quite properly stresses the importance for Lenroot of "Cannonism" as a unifying theme. For a convenient summary of percentages of Swedes and Norwegians in the counties in the district see Jorgen Weibull, "The Wisconsin Progressives, 1900–1914," p. 195. The labor cases are referred to in Edward C. Kirkland, *A History of American Economic Life*, rev. ed. (New York, 1951), p. 552. See also Philip Taft, *Organized Labor in American History* (New York, 1964), p. 218; and Marc Karson, *American Labor Unions and Politics, 1900–1918*, pp. 42–66.

17. Bolles, *Tyrant from Illinois*, p. 144.

expound with vigor and conviction would be well received, he knew, especially among farmers. And the people could still be counted on to turn out for a well-timed and advertised political speech, for want of any better amusement. A speaking campaign would not be costly, and his friends had already promised to raise a thousand dollars and his brother Louis to loan five hundred. Superior, though remote at the northern tip of the district, was, however, a fine base, with its strong tradition of support for local men and its population of approximately forty thousand.[18] In Superior, Lenroot would have the help of a numerous and able group of volunteers. He had the support of key labor leaders and of John T. Murphy and his *Superior Telegram.* Though regarded as something of a radical elsewhere, in his hometown Lenroot was better known as a man of upright character and good family. Such a man, seen as deserving and also as a possible winner, could come close to unifying Superior and Douglas County. In addition, Lenroot knew he could count on help from outside—from Haugen and Ekern among the Norwegians and also from La Follette.[19]

Lenroot campaigned quietly after January and actively from May into September. In his stock campaign speech, he called for downward revision of the tariff, antitrust legislation, stricter control of railroads, including physical valuation as a basis for ratemaking, conservation, federal aid for rural road construction, controls on stock watering, and curbs on the use of labor injunctions. He read the roll call on Jenkins, associating him with the conservative leadership in Congress, and pledged that if elected he would vote against Cannon for Speaker. Cannon, with helpers like Sereno Payne and Jenkins and senators like Nelson Aldrich and Joseph Foraker, stood in the way of "representative government," he said.[20]

During the congressional campaign, Lenroot charged Jenkins with overstating his services to the district, denied the congressman's countercharge that he misrepresented Jenkins's record or himself promised post-office appointments to supporters, and challenged Jenkins to debate. On a somewhat loftier note, Lenroot disputed Jenkins's strict constructionism, which the congressman had consistently put forth against federal antitrust and road legislation. To Jenkins's accusation that he was no Republican, Lenroot replied that he was a Roosevelt Republican and more truly representative of the mass of Republicans in the country than Jenkins. He reiterated and emphasized his attack on "Boss Cannon," who increasingly served to symbolize the forces that subverted true representative government. Happily for Lenroot, the anti-Cannon theme was not only logically but politically basic, since those less concerned than he about representative govern-

18. Lenroot, "Memoirs," p. 64, Box 13, Lenroot Papers.

19. Hayden M. Pickering, a volunteer in the 1908 campaign, wrote in 1969 that the Lenroot family was well thought of in Superior and that Lenroot won in 1908 "mostly because he was such an upright man and his opponent was beginning to lose favor." Pickering to the author, 11 February 1969.

20. Griffith, "Prelude to Insurgency," p. 19.

ment could see in Cannonism the obstacle to more prosaic ends, such as lower prices through tariff reduction, good roads, lower railroad rates, stronger labor unions, or communities protected by temperance legislation.[21]

Jenkins, who was neither a witty talker nor a classical orator, wisely declined to debate.[22] Lenroot was still not an orator of the old school. But times had changed. By 1900, as Clough Gates later put it, "the campaign was a crusade and the speaker who could not dish out the facts in large and pertinent doses failed to hold and impress the crowd. It was in just such a situation that Lenroot shown." Of the 1908 campaign Gates wrote, "An avid reader and deep student of public questions, he had the ability to marshal his arguments in convincing fashion. And his vigorous platform delivery and sonorous voice carried conviction both in their earnestness and their eloquence. To follow him through a discourse that often ran through an hour and more was both education and entertainment." [23]

Lenroot's early confidence was well placed. He won the primary election by a vote of 17,284 to 11,003 for Jenkins. He carried the rural areas with 65 percent of the vote, against 54 percent in towns and cities of 1,500 or more.[24]

In this staunchly Republican district, election in November posed no problem. Nevertheless, he felt his campaign obligations and met them. In his general election speech, Lenroot carefully showed that the Republican party was more progressive than the Democratic party. On trusts, the record of the Democrats was poor, he said, while the Republicans had put legislation on the books and launched the major prosecutions. Though William Jennings Bryan called for more democracy, his party was controlled by bosses from the Southern courthouses and halls of Tammany. With respect to labor legislation, the record of Republican-controlled states easily surpassed that of Democratic states. Bryan, he admitted, was a progressive Democrat, but as president he would be ineffective, hamstrung by the Southern aristocrats who controlled the party. Nor was Bryan a constructive statesman—witness his earlier free silver vagaries and his more recent advocacy of nationalization of railroads. William Howard Taft, by contrast, was not only progressive but constructive. In that connection, Lenroot took occasion to talk of Roosevelt, who had chosen Taft, and to say, as he had said before, that with all his faults, Roosevelt "has been the greatest President we have had since Lincoln." [25]

La Follette also supported Taft, as being more progressive than his party's platform but gave him unsolicited advice regarding physical valuation

21. Ibid.; MS, "Speech made by Hon. I. L. Lenroot at Superior, Wisconsin, July 29th, 1908," Box 5, Lenroot to John J. Jenkins, 21 July 1908, Box 2, Lenroot, "Memoirs," p. 64, Box 13, Lenroot Papers; *Superior Telegram*, 30 July 1908.

22. *Duluth News Tribune*, 6 November 1904.

23. *Superior Telegram*, 4 February 1949.

24. Griffith, "Prelude to Insurgency," p. 27.

25. MS speech, "Election Campaign 1908, Speech for the Ticket," Box 5, Lenroot Papers.

and disclosed that he would soon launch a national weekly magazine, an ominous piece of news for whichever candidate won the presidency.[26]

In the eleventh district, all went well. Lenroot carried every county and defeated "Silver Joe" Konkel by a vote of 30,104 to 10,467. A social democrat drew 1,117 votes.[27] Most of the other elections that day came out as Lenroot had hoped. Though the Democrats made gains around the country, Taft was elected president, backed by a Republican Congress, and the party retained full control of the executive and legislative branches in Wisconsin. Progressive sentiment evidenced itself on a bipartisan basis.[28]

The bad weather that marred Taft's inauguration was a harbinger of political storms to come. Indeed, even as he assumed the presidency, Taft was already started on the course that would ultimately lead to his own political ruin and the breakup of his party. During the four years of his presidency, he would, by all too human political errors, make the situation worse. On balance, though, he was to be more the victim of overwhelming circumstance than the cause of his own downfall and his party's division.

By the time Lenroot reached Washington for the inauguration and the start of the Sixty-first Congress, the insurgent movement within the Republican party was well underway. Anxious to join, for Lenroot the fight against Speaker Cannon and the seemingly autocratic House rules was the first and most important order of business. In February, he had been alerted to the plans of the insurgents and had pledged his support.[29]

The rise of progressive sentiment was a national phenomenon in these years, as La Follette and Lenroot were well aware. In the South, it was expressed through the Democratic party; in two-party states, it resulted in Democratic gains in each election from 1906 through 1912; but in the one-party Republican states of the north-central region—Wisconsin, Minnesota, Iowa, Kansas, Nebraska, and the Dakotas—the battle was fought and won within the Republican party. With the development of progressive Republicanism in these states, some of the congressmen found it expedient, or feasible, to rebel against conservative domination of the House and against "Boss Cannon" and the rules he used. The rebellion was muted in advance of the 1908 elections, but with those done, national anti-Cannon feeling concretely evidenced, and reinforcements on the way, Republican insurgents made an open though unavailing fight in the second session of the Sixtieth Congress.

26. Belle and Fola La Follette, *La Follette,* vol. 1, p. 262; La Follette to Taft, 17 July, 12 October 1908, Box 103, Series B, La Follette FC; E. J. Jones to La Follette, 2 November 1908, Box 153, La Follette Papers. Isaac Stephenson had parted company from La Follette in running for the long term in the Senate, and the *Free Press* was, therefore, unhelpful to La Follette. However, La Follette's projected magazine was to be more than a replacement for the *Free Press* in Wisconsin politics. It had been talked of for some time and from the first had been seen as serving a national mission.

27. *Wisconsin Blue Book,* 1909, p. 469.

28. Mowry, *Era of Theodore Roosevelt,* p. 231.

29. Lenroot to Victor Murdock, 16 February 1908, Box 22, Victor Murdock Papers, LC.

Despite Taft's victory over Bryan, his party's majority in the House was reduced to a modest forty-seven—219–172—as the new Congress prepared to meet in special session to act on the tariff. And on the Republican side, there would be more insurgents than before and fewer standpatters. Champ Clark's secretary tried to pressure the insurgent Republicans to get them to vote for the Democratic leader as against Cannon.[30] Though by that time, the insurgents had abandoned hope of defeating Cannon with one of their own men, neither Lenroot nor any of the rest would go so far as to vote for a Democrat. However, on the question of changing the rules, the insurgents hoped to renew their coalition with the Democrats. If all the Democrats held firm, only twenty-four Republican votes would suffice to leave the Speaker with less power. Even if a few Democrats defected, the rules changes might still be accomplished.[31] Under the circumstances, Congressman William McKinley's pre-inaugural reception for new members was a less successful social icebreaker than similar parties of the past.

It was at this reception that Lenroot was first introduced to Speaker Cannon. The young congressman found before him a slender, white-whiskered man of seventy-three whose perpetual tilted cigar, shredded messily across his lips and smoldering fitfully at the end, contributed to a studied folksiness that had helped him to remain in Congress since 1873 except for a single term. Cannon fixed Lenroot with knowing, cold blue eyes, then turned to the crowd, and said, "as mild mannered man as ever scuttled a ship or cut a throat." [32]

Cannon knew he was in trouble and on 9 March, six days before House action, he, together with Aldrich and the venerable Payne, the chairmen who would have charge of the tariff bill in the two Houses, called on President Taft. Months earlier, Taft had thought of fighting Cannon's reelection. But Roosevelt and Root cautioned against it and Taft's own inquiries showed that Cannon could not be ousted, so he had reconsidered. Now Cannon asked more of him—that he exert himself against any changes in the rules. Taft understood the three men to promise support for tariff reduction in return; in any case, these were the men who held the fate of the tariff bill in their hands. The president therefore yielded.[33]

30. Wallace D. Bassford to Edward E. Higgins, 8 March 1909 (two letters), 9 March 1909, Box 23, Murdock Papers.

31. Hechler, *Insurgency*, p. 50.

32. Mark Sullivan, *Our Times: The United States, 1900–1925*, vol. 4, pp. 374–77; James E. Watson, *As I Knew Them: Memoirs of James E. Watson*, pp. 92–93; George E. Mowry, *Theodore Roosevelt and the Progressive Movement*, p. 41; John M. Nelson, typed fragment of speech, n.d. (ca. 1910), Box 16, John M. Nelson Papers, WSHSL; Lenroot, "Memoirs," p. 65, Box 13, Lenroot Papers.

33. Stanley D. Solvick, "William Howard Taft and the Insurgents," pp. 279–95, 280–81; Stanley D. Solvick, "William Howard Taft and Cannonism," vol. 48, pp. 48–58; Gwinn, *Cannon*, pp. 159–61; Henry F. Pringle, *The Life and Times of William Howard Taft*, vol. 1, pp. 402–6; Mowry, *Era of Theodore Roosevelt*, pp. 238–41; Paolo E. Coletta, *The Presidency of William Howard Taft*, p. 59; Hechler, *Insurgency*, pp. 51–53.

A few days later Taft backed off and sought a compromise by which the rules battle might be postponed until the regular session in December, after action on the tariff. The Iowa insurgents wanted something of the sort, but most of their colleagues balked, as did Cannon and his friends.[34] As each side girded for battle, the new president found himself opposed to a determined group that, though a minority in Congress, was engaging in an effort already popular in the country.

On Thursday, 11 March, Lenroot met with his insurgent colleagues to plan for the rules fight that would ensue when the special session convened on Monday. Lenroot was only one of two freshmen in the Wisconsin delegation of ten Republicans and one Democrat, but in the context of insurgency he was by tacit understanding one of the leaders from the first. Some of the Wisconsin congressmen came to the fight reluctantly; others had only local standing within the La Follette movement and not much experience in the House. The stately Henry A. Cooper was an established figure in the House who had represented La Follette there and taken his place among the insurgents earlier; John M. Nelson, elected from La Follette's own district in 1906, had been an ardent La Follette worker in Madison since college days in the nineties; he too had been an insurgent from the start and now acted as liaison to the Democrats. But as La Follette's most trusted lieutenant and the conqueror of Jenkins on the issue of Cannonism, Lenroot outranked even these two men, though he was not the sort to provoke jealousies and disunity by asserting claims of rank.

The caucus gave Lenroot opportunity to meet and see in action the insurgent leaders. Best known was Victor Murdock, a pugnacious, loquacious, and burly red-haired journalist from Kansas. More astute and important than Murdock, though quieter, was George Norris of Nebraska, a late convert to reform but a man with a fine mind and "a streak of patience that was part of his combative equipment." [35] Augustus Peabody Gardner of Massachusetts, the blue blooded son-in-law of Sen. Henry Cabot Lodge and a strong supporter of Taft, was far more conservative than his insurgent colleagues but strong in his indignation against the unfairness of Cannon and the rules. Steadiest of the leaders, the one most regretfully lost to Cannon and his friends, was Edmund H. Madison of Kansas.

The insurgents, who included a number of sturdy individualists, disagreed on a strategy for unified action on the related questions of entering the party caucus and supporting the caucus's preordained choice for

34. Hechler, *Insurgency*, p. 53.

35. On Murdock see Sullivan, *Our Times*, vol. 4, p. 373; Thomas Dreier, *Heroes of Insurgency* (Boston, 1910), pp. 125–37; and Hechler, *Insurgency*, pp. 37–38. The literature on Norris is abundant. See especially Richard Lowitt, *George W. Norris: The Making of a Progressive, 1861–1912* (hereafter referred to as *Norris*), vol. 1; and Richard Lowitt, *George W. Norris: The Persistence of a Progressive, 1913–1933*. The quotation about Norris is from Sullivan, *Our Times*, vol. 4, p. 381. Gardner's importance is obvious in Hechler, *Insurgency*, pp. 50, 69, 196, 207. His background is described briefly in Augustus Peabody Gardner, *Some Letters of Augustus Peabody Gardner*, pp. xi–xiii.

Speaker. They did agree on the most important matter, however—to join
with the Democrats in support of a new set of rules that would take from
the Speaker his power to appoint all members of committees and deny him
control of the Committee on Rules. Lenroot acted with the majority of the
Wisconsin delegation and the insurgent bloc in boycotting the party caucus
altogether.[36]

True to his promises, Lenroot, with eleven other Republicans, voted
against Cannon when the new Congress organized on 15 March. Most of
the insurgent leaders voted for Cannon, to emphasize the point that their
fight was not personal but against the autocratic rules.[37]

While Cannon's election had been presumed, the outcome of the rules
fight was not. To the dismay of the reform coalition, Cannon won again.
He had influenced, with a variety of promises, the votes of twenty-three
Democrats.[38]

The outcome of the rules fight shocked the country, and as a result,
anti-Cannon sentiment increased. But Lenroot and the other insurgents,
aware that they were not likely to have another chance to change the
rules or unseat Cannon until the next Congress, quickly turned their attention to the intricacies of the tariff bill, which Payne introduced on 17
March.[39]

Though the bill occasioned some bitter debates in the House, where it
began its legislative course, the main factional battle did not come until it
reached the Senate in mid-April. Chairman Payne, who had spent twenty-
five of his sixty-two years in Congress, a college graduate and a lawyer,
whom Norris acknowledged to be "a man of very high character, exceptionally well posted upon tariff legislation," had conducted extensive hearings
from 10 November to Christmas Eve; then, in company with the Republicans on his ways and means committee, he had laboriously prepared a bill
that was surprisingly satisfactory to insurgents.[40]

Grounds for complaint did exist, and the north-central bloc led successful
attacks on certain schedules. Sectional resentment against the east in general and particularly the New England area spurred the attacks. Reductions
were all well and good, western insurgents felt, but why should raw materials produced in the west, such as hides, be put on the free list while eastern-

36. Hechler, *Insurgency,* pp. 55–57.

37. Ibid., p. 56; *Congressional Record,* 61st Cong., 1st sess., 1901, vol. 44, pt. 1, p. 18 (hereafter
referred to as *CR* 61:1).

38. Hechler, *Insurgency,* pp. 56–57; *CR* 61:1, pp. 21–54.

39. Hechler, *Insurgency,* p. 63; Sidney Ratner, *American Taxation: Its History as a Social Force
in Democracy,* p. 270.

40. Oscar Underwood, *Drifting Sands of Party Politics* (New York, 1931 [1928]), p. 163; George
W. Norris, *Fighting Liberal: The Autobiography of George W. Norris,* pp. 113–14; Hechler, *Insurgency,*
pp. 94–99; Frank W. Taussig, *The Tariff History of the United States,* 6th ed., pp. 367–68, 371,
373, 393; Ratner, *American Taxation,* pp. 270–71; Richard C. Baker, *The Tariff Under Roosevelt
and Taft,* pp. 76–81.

ers using the hides to manufacture boots and shoes continued to have high protection? [41]

Lenroot adhered to the custom that new members should not speak, but he gave the bill careful study, for his own use and La Follette's. While the bill was still in the House, the senator began preparations for the fight that lay ahead in the upper chamber, and Lenroot spent nearly every evening at the La Follette home, studying the House bill and the eight volumes of hearings with La Follette.[42]

Most of the few record votes on the Payne bill came on Friday, 9 April, just before final action. In these, Lenroot, like most of his insurgent colleagues, supported reduction in the lumber schedules, a higher rate for barley, and some protection for hides.[43] Though his side won only on the barley schedule, the outcome of these votes made little difference so far as his vote on the bill itself was concerned. Indeed, the day before the final vote he had secured permission to have remarks extended in the Record indicating how he would vote and why. When the House finally emerged from the Committee of the Whole House on the afternoon of the ninth, Lenroot, acting with the other insurgents, helped his party defeat Clark's motion to recommit the bill to committee with instructions; then he voted with his party to approve the Payne bill and to send it to the Senate.[44]

As Lenroot explained it, the bill, though not in conformity with the party platform, had been improved in the House and in its final version was better than the existing Dingley tariff law, a supremely protectionist measure passed in 1897. But he warned that if the bill that came back from the Senate were not better than the existing law, he would vote against it. In passing, he concluded from his study of the bill and the hearings that a Tariff Commission was badly needed to gather in a scientific way the information on which tariff legislation should be based.[45]

Lenroot had planned to go home to Superior following House action on the Payne bill and while the Senate was working on its version of the new tariff law. But La Follette persuaded him to remain, live at his home for the time, and help the senator prepare his tariff speeches.[46]

41. Jerome Martin Clubb, "Congressional Opponents of Reform, 1901–1913" (Ph.D. diss.), p. 119; Hechler, *Insurgency,* p. 96; Miles Poindexter to Bartlett Sinclair, 27 October 1909, File 14, Series 1, Miles Poindexter Papers, University of Virginia Library.

42. Lenroot, "Memoirs," p. 67, Box 13, Lenroot Papers; Hechler, *Insurgency,* p. 101; *CR* 61:1, Appendix, pp. 33–34. The last citation refers to remarks that Lenroot had extended in the Record, which indicate that he studied the Hearings.

43. *CR* 61:1, pp. 1293–98.

44. Ibid., p. 1301. Only one Republican, Richard Austin of Tennessee, voted with the Democrats against the bill.

45. Ibid., Appendix, pp. 33–34. Lenroot never revised his remarks for the Record, so the source is reliable. Earl Godwin in the *Milwaukee Sentinel,* 29 December 1916. Internal evidence substantiates Godwin's report.

46. Lenroot, "Memoirs," p. 67, Box 13, Lenroot Papers.

Lenroot saw the opportunity that was at hand. Aldrich would seek a hyper-protectionist bill. La Follette would have Republican allies in a fight against it. He would either better the bill or win the country's admiration in trying.

The battle that ensued is justly famous. The insurgents failed to defeat the Aldrich bill, but they made it odious. When the vote came on 8 July, ten Republicans deserted their party on the issue. President Taft held largely aloof from the battle at this stage, disappointing the insurgents. He, in turn, was already impatient with most of them.[47]

Between 12 July and 30 July, President Taft battled with the high protectionists Aldrich and Cannon handpicked for the conference committee. He got the committee to put hides on the free list and won reductions on gloves, hosiery, lumber, and several other products, as well as coal, iron ore, pig iron, scrap iron, and steel. These concessions, reluctantly granted, were mere tokens in the context of the entire bill. Taft worked well but within narrowly limited possibilities, and his veto threats carried little credibility. Furthermore, the changes on hides and lumber offended westerners, especially since most eastern manufactured goods retained the higher rates won in the House or Senate bills. Nevertheless, Taft felt pleased with the reductions he had secured and proud of his efforts. In any case, the bill reported from conference was the Republican tariff bill he had promised.[48]

La Follette, Lenroot, and the more extreme insurgents did not share Taft's pride of parentage; nor did they believe that further attacks on the bill, even to the extent of defeating the conference report, would weaken the party. Unlike the president, they considered the bill thoroughly bad and thought some of its makers still worse.

The bill was distinctly vulnerable. The weak Tariff Board of the Payne bill had been further emasculated in conference, and the fight for an inheritance or an income tax had been lost, though the standpatters, seeing little danger, had agreed to present to the states a constitutional amendment on the income tax. The newspaper publishers had not gotten free pulp and print paper, and many of them denounced the bill as a fraud. Thus, the bolder insurgents were in a strong position to fight to the end. Although public attention had focused on the long and bitter fight in the Senate, it was the House that was the more likely to reject the conference report.

47. See especially Mowry, *The Progressive Movement*, pp. 42–63; Mowry, *Era of Theodore Roosevelt*, pp. 231–48; Hechler, *Insurgency*, pp. 95–116; Coletta, *William Howard Taft*, pp. 1–20, 61–71; Henry F. Pringle, *The Life and Times of William Howard Taft*, vol. 1, pp. 414–36; Claude G. Bowers, *Beveridge and the Progressive Era*, pp. 333–51; Ratner, *American Taxation*, pp. 273–74, 278.

48. See especially Baker, *Roosevelt and Taft*, pp. 96–97; Lewis L. Gould, "Western Range Senators and the Payne-Aldrich Tariff," pp. 49–56; Ratner, *American Taxation*, pp. 278–79; Gwinn, *Cannon*, pp. 181–83; Paul DeWitt Hasbrouck, *Party Government in the House of Representatives*, p. 50; Bowers, *Beveridge*, pp. 361–66; Mowry, *The Progressive Movement*, p. 63; Howard W. Allen, "Miles Poindexter: A Political Biography" (Ph.D. diss.), p. 73; Pringle, *The Life and Times*, vol. 1, pp. 436–41; Coletta, *William Howard Taft*, pp. 69, 71; Stanley D. Solvick, "William Howard Taft and the Payne-Aldrich Tariff," pp. 424–42.

While the administration applied pressure to secure adoption of the report, some insurgent senators lobbied on the House floor against the report. The key vote came on a motion to recommit. By just five votes it failed—186 to 191. Then the conference report was approved by a larger margin—195 to 183. On both tests, Lenroot and two other Wisconsin insurgents, Nelson and William Cary, voted against the leadership.[49]

Hoping not merely to pass the bill but to prevent party schism, in the last days of the contest President Taft conferred with those Senate insurgents he still hoped to redeem. Three of the ten insurgent senators yielded, but La Follette and six others persisted in their opposition. On 5 August, after three more days of battle, the Senate approved the bill—47 to 31—and sent it to the president, who signed it the same day.[50]

Though in late May Lenroot still hoped that President Taft would honor La Follette's patronage requests,[51] and though the insurgents of the House and Senate scrupulously avoided direct public condemnation of the president during the course of the 1909 legislative battles,[52] by the end of the session Lenroot surely foresaw at least the strong possibility of an open break between the insurgents and the president. He had good reason to expect that in short order he would personally feel the president's wrath and have occasion to publicly respond, since Taft pointedly refused to consider census-taker recommendations until Congress finished action on the tariff bill.[53]

After Congress adjourned, public suspicion of the president, which was stimulated initially by his role in the Cannon and Payne-Aldrich contests, grew dramatically. On the last day of the session Cannon, like some irrepressible albatross bent on embarrassing Taft, stripped insurgents Fowler, Gardner, and Cooper of their chairmanships and punished other insurgents with lowly committee assignments. The first public intimations of the great Ballinger-Pinchot fight of 1910 came on 9 August when at an Irrigation Congress at Spokane the two men, one Taft's secretary of interior and successor to the popular Rooseveltian James R. Garfield, the other the head of the Forest Service and a well-known favorite of Roosevelt, spoke in markedly different terms about conservation. And then another Roosevelt-

49. George M. Fisk, "The Payne Aldrich Tariff," *Political Science Quarterly* 25 (March 1910):42, cited in Monroe Lee Billington, *Thomas P. Gore: The Blind Senator from Oklahoma*, p. 31; Thomas R. Ross, *Jonathan Prentice Dolliver: A Study in Political Integrity and Independence*, p. 31; Hechler, *Insurgency*, pp. 135, 141; Bowers, *Beveridge*, pp. 362–63; Sullivan, *Our Times*, vol. 4, p. 363; Pringle, *The Life and Times*, vol. 1, p. 442; *CR* 61:1, 1909, vol. 44, pt. 5, pp. 4753-55.

50. Bowers, *Beveridge*, pp. 363–64; Mowry, *The Progressive Movement*, p. 63; Hechler, *Insurgency*, pp. 139–41; Baker, *Roosevelt and Taft*, pp. 99–100.

51. William J. McElroy to Herman Ekern, 29 May 1909, Box 6, Ekern Papers.

52. Mowry, *The Progressive Movement*, p. 66; Robert to Belle La Follette, 25 July 1909, Box 8, Series A, La Follette FC.

53. Robert M. La Follette, *La Follette's Autobiography: A Personal Narrative of Political Experiences*, p. 194; Robert to Belle La Follette, 28 July 1909, Box 8, Series A, La Follette FC.

ian, Dr. Harvey W. Wiley, hero of the pure food campaign, was denounced by his superior, Secretary of Agriculture James Wilson. In response to these charged events, Taft gave no public intimation of anything but approval for the positions taken by Cannon, Ballinger, and Wilson. *La Follette's Weekly Magazine,* already critical of Taft for his opinions and decisions on the tariff problem, on 21 August attacked the conservation question in a lead editorial. While not condemning Taft directly, the editorial and the related article said that the people must take sides and asserted that "Pinchot is trying to carry forward the Roosevelt policy." After Louis Glavis brought serious charges against Richard Ballinger in connection with the leasing of Alaskan coal lands, *La Follette's Weekly Magazine* associated itself with Glavis and indicated that Taft was on trial. Later in the month, the magazine took note of Taft's statement vindicating Ballinger.[54]

Taft, blissfully overoptimistic, went on a national tour in September to clear up all misapprehensions. He succeeded only in confirming reformers in their suspicions.[55] Taft began his tour in Boston by praising Aldrich for his leadership abilities and public spirit. Three days later, on 17 September, after visiting the Wisconsin State Fair at Milwaukee and making several speeches in the state, the president went on to Winona, Minnesota, to help standpat Congressman James Tawney. There he delivered his ill-fated judgment on the Payne-Aldrich Act—it was "the best tariff bill that the Republican party has ever passed and therefore the best bill that has been passed at all." [56] Interest in the tariff had declined, but Taft's remark evoked much criticism in the nation's press.[57]

Just hours before the speech in Winona, Lenroot, who was in Milwaukee at the time, served as spokesman for the state of Wisconsin in presenting Taft an elegant "golf stick" made of Wisconsin bird's-eye maple. By the time Lenroot returned to Superior, after joining in political conferences at the fair, Taft had given his unpopular judgment of the new tariff law. Meanwhile, an announcement was made in Washington that Lester B. Dresser would be supervisor of census in the Eleventh Congressional District of Wisconsin (in accordance with instructions Taft had given three weeks earlier that the recommendations of Lenroot, Cary, and Nelson were to be ignored). Asked by a *Superior Telegram* reporter for his comment, Lenroot did not equivocate. "President Taft publicly stated that he desired for those

---

54. Mowry, *The Progressive Movement,* pp. 66–68; Gwinn, *Cannon,* p. 184; Hechler, *Insurgency,* pp. 154–56; *La Follette's Weekly Magazine* 1:25 (26 June 1909):3–4; *La Follette's Weekly Magazine* 1:28 (17 July 1909):6–7; *La Follette's Weekly Magazine* 1:33 (21 August 1909):3, 14–15; *La Follette's Weekly Magazine* 1:36 (11 September 1909):13–14; *La Follette's Weekly Magazine* 1:38 (25 September 1909):14. Gardner had been deprived of his chairmanship at his own request, so that his loyalty to the insurgents would remain unquestioned, but this fact was not widely known at the time. Gwinn, *Cannon,* p. 209.

55. Mowry, *The Progressive Movement,* pp. 68–69.

56. Ibid., p. 70.

57. David Detzer, "The Politics of the Payne-Aldrich Tariff of 1909" (Ph.D. diss.), pp. 217, 223.

positions men of the highest character and ability; men who had not been active politicians, and who would not use the office for political purposes," Lenroot said. He had recommended such a man, the former superintendent of schools for Pierce County. Dresser, by contrast, had dispensed money for Stephenson during the 1908 senatorial primary while a member of the State Board of Control, had traveled at the state's expense, and had disqualified himself for the census post under Taft's terms. He declined to discuss it further, except to say, "I shall continue to represent the people of the Eleventh district, opposing Cannonism and Aldrichism, regardless of the fact that such cause evidently will result in an attempt to use the federal patronage of the district to punish me." For the record, Lenroot proceeded to lodge a complaint with the director of the census, elaborating on what he had said to the *Superior Telegram* and indicating that in justice to himself he had publicly disclaimed responsibility for the Dresser appointment. Lenroot's letter caused a small flurry in Washington, but it was too late to rectify the error. In effect, Lenroot had converted a political loss into a political gain.[58]

Within the week, Lenroot had a chance to review the situation with La Follette when the senator came north with Sens. Moses Clapp and Carroll Page to investigate conditions on Wisconsin Indian reservations. Both men understood what needed to be done because of the most recent events, and both had already started doing it. If Lenroot drew blood in his public statement on the census-taker question, he did so by a calculatedly defensive parry. His war was on "Cannonism and Aldrichism," not the president. If the president chose to punish him for that, it was none of his doing. *La Follette's Weekly Magazine,* meanwhile, criticized the president's speech in Winona and noted that it had been delivered to help Cannon's lieutenant James Tawney. Yet the following week, in renewing the conservation battle in defense of Roosevelt's policies, the lead editorial focused on the need for a new secretary of interior and disclaimed doubt about Taft's sincerity in affirming his faithfulness to Roosevelt's policies. In its next issue, the editors of the magazine reiterated their political position.[59] La Follette chafed at the self-imposed constraints but steeled himself to live with them for a while longer, sure that Taft would soon permit him a freer hand.[60]

The direction of all this was unmistakable—an assault on the president himself behind the stout shield marked "Roosevelt." Yet, on the subjects of the tariff and party regularity Taft had joined the battle with the "progressives," as erstwhile half-breed Republicans and reform Democrats were now

58. William Howard Taft to Charles Nagel, 23 August 1909, Presidential Letterbook 6, Series 8, Lenroot to E. Dana Durand, 20 September 1909, enclosed in Durand to Taft, 8 October 1909, Nagel to Taft, 8 October 1909, File 3, Series 5, William Howard Taft Papers, LC; *Superior Telegram*, 20 September 1909.

59. *La Follette's Weekly Magazine* 1:38 (25 September 1909):3–4; *La Follette's Weekly Magazine* 1:39 (2 October 1909):3; *La Follette's Weekly Magazine* 1:40 (9 October 1909):3–4.

60. Robert to Belle La Follette, 25 October 1909, Box 8, Series A, La Follette FC.

being called. Lenroot, no more than La Follette, would or could draw back. But it was still a time for caution.

After talking with La Follette, Lenroot went first to Minneapolis to speak for Senator Clapp; then to Spokane, to help his congressional friend Miles Poindexter prepare for a 1910 senatorial race. Talking to a Saturday lunch club group at Minneapolis, "The clean-cut, eloquent congressman was in good speaking form," a reporter observed. Armed with the tariff tables, Lenroot set out to show that considering the "jokers" in the Payne-Aldrich Act, it was an upward not a downward revision. He attacked the idea of "party solidarity" recently voiced by Taft but went on to discuss the idea and the tariff question, with reference not to Taft but to Cannon.[61]

Days later Lenroot was in Spokane, which was the hometown of Poindexter, whom Lenroot regarded as "one of the strongest and best men in the House." President Taft had just been in the city when Lenroot arrived, and an interviewer cornered the Wisconsin congressman and asked him to comment on the president's speeches. Taft had been mildly critical of those who voted against the tariff bill, he said, but these men represented their constituents in so doing—in the Mississippi Valley, he pointed out, sentiment ran heavily against the bill, since living costs would rise because of it. On most things the president had said during his tour, Lenroot was in hearty agreement. He praised his stand in favor of conservation but ventured that "he will not get very far . . . with Ballinger in the Cabinet. My sympathies are all with Pinchot in the Ballinger-Pinchot dispute." With respect to Cannon, Lenroot was less equivocal. "Uncle Joe" would never be elected Speaker again.[62]

By 1 December, when Lenroot started back to the capital for the regular session, the conservation issue had come further to the fore, as *Collier's* sensationalized the charges made against Ballinger by Louis Glavis, who was earlier dismissed by Taft as chief of the Field Division of the Interior Department. *La Follette's Weekly Magazine* pictured Glavis on its cover and gave full and favorable publicity to his accusations.[63]

While willing enough to continue the rules fight, most House insurgents, like their Senate counterparts, were not anxious to break with President Taft nor in other ways put their Republicanism in question.[64] Lenroot, working in close tandem with La Follette, now took a bolder position, as did Poindexter and a few other insurgents. Already disillusioned with Taft, a victim of his patronage lash, and sensing his vulnerability, La Follette used the occasion of Taft's message to Congress to make his first direct attack on the

61. *Minneapolis Tribune,* 26 September 1909.

62. Robert to Belle La Follette, 25 October 1909, Box 8, Series A, La Follette FC; *Spokane Spokesman-Review,* 1 October 1909.

63. Mowry, *Era of Theodore Roosevelt,* p. 254; *La Follette's Weekly Magazine* 1:46 (20 November 1909):3, 8–9, 12.

64. This became apparent in the House in late December and January; senatorial feelings are indicated in Bowers, *Beveridge,* pp. 369–73.

president in the 18 December issue of his magazine. La Follette argued, among other things, that Taft was not carrying out the policies of Roosevelt.[65] Days later Lenroot took advanced ground in an interview with the *New York Evening Post.* The substantive view that he expressed was not especially radical, nor did Lenroot go beyond positions he had taken in Wisconsin politics. But he strayed further from the anchor of Republicanism than was entirely safe; and between the lines Lenroot called for a movement to replace Taft with La Follette in 1912.[66]

Home briefly for the holidays, Lenroot warned the La Follette club that reelection of the senator in 1910 could not be presumed. Millions of dollars would be used to defeat him. "The two men most thoroughly hated by special interests today are Robert La Follette and Theodore Roosevelt. Roosevelt is in Africa, and they wish La Follette was there."

Lenroot went on to describe the Washington scene as he viewed it. "One who has never sat in the national capitol and watched the proceedings of both houses day after day, can little realize what an awful farce it is for the people to believe that they are properly represented there. No place upon earth contains more hypocrisy and deceit than is found in the national capitol." He did not charge all standpatters with being corrupt. But "they believe that the rights of property are greater than the rights of men and that organized wealth can do no wrong." In any case, whether through corrupt or only misguided representatives, special interests got what they wanted. Against them stood La Follette, the leader of the insurgents, whose every act in the Senate had been in the public interest, a man marked for political extinction.[67]

While calculated to arouse enthusiasm and some healthful anxiety, Lenroot's speech clearly reflected sincere belief. Though called a radical, he was no more radical than he had ever been. Lenroot did not advocate socialism, or any advanced form of welfarism; he deplored class conflict or anything approaching it. In one sense he was radical, however, as he had been during the earlier Wisconsin battles—in his view of how extensive and serious was the menace to honest, representative government and in the willingness to go as far as he had to in this fight between right and wrong.

Back in Washington after the holidays, this time accompanied by Clara, Katharine, and Dorothy, Lenroot quickly rejoined La Follette in the developing national fight for control of the Republican party. La Follette took the lead in organizing progressive senators and friendly newsmen for mutual aid in the 1910 elections when he, Albert Beveridge, and others would be up for reelection. Taft's quixotic patronage policies and public displays of support for Cannon and Aldrich, combined with the fact that the standpatters were already organizing to purge the party of insurgents

65. La Follette, *Autobiography*, pp. 190–95, 204; *La Follette's Weekly Magazine* 1:50 (18 December 1909):3–4.
66. *New York Evening Post*, 21 December 1909.
67. *Superior Telegram*, 31 December 1909.

in the 1910 nominating primaries and conventions, paved the way for the ostensibly defensive alliance, which La Follette successfully promoted during a dinner at his home on 12 January.[68]

Social bonds increasingly reinforced the political ties between Lenroot and La Follette as Belle La Follette took the Lenroot ladies in hand in this—their debut in Washington society. Lenroot had secured quarters at an apartment hotel that was physically comfortable but socially cold. Clara, Katharine, and Dorothy welcomed the frequent and friendly attentions of the La Follettes and their children, enjoyed the often gay atmosphere of the large La Follette home—about a mile from their own rooms—and gladly took the opportunities that the La Follettes created to expand their list of acquaintances and their knowledge of the city. On Thursday afternoons, Clara helped Belle La Follette "receive," with the assistance of Katharine and Dorothy.[69]

By 7 January, Lenroot was already working very hard and feeling quite tired.[70] Undoubtedly, he was spending much of his time studying the railroad question on which the president had asked Congress to act and also researching other issues, possibly for La Follette's use as well as his own. In addition to these legislative matters and the ordinary chores of a congressman, Lenroot gave close attention to the politics of insurgency in the House of Representatives.

Few anticipated any chance to renew the rules fight until the next Congress, when suddenly the burgeoning conservation battle offered House insurgents a vehicle for immediate action on one aspect of the rules question. On 5 January, the House insurgents, allied with the Democrats, scored their first victory over Cannon in connection with establishment of a joint committee to investigate the conservation dispute. Twenty-six insurgents joined the Democrats to form a majority and the House approved Norris's surprise amendment by a vote of 149 to 146. The amendment stated that the House members of the committee be chosen by the House itself not the Speaker. For once, Cannon had been caught off guard. Thirty conservative Republicans were absent when the Norris amendment was passed.[71]

68. Mowry, *The Progressive Movement,* pp. 67–73, 89; Claude E. Barfield, "The Democratic Party in Congress, 1909–1913" (Ph.D. diss.), p. 48; Miles Poindexter to O. C. Moore, 13 January 1910, cited in Hechler, *Insurgency,* p. 64. The insurgents probably misconstrued Taft's intentions at this time. See Solvick, "Taft and the Insurgents," pp. 48–58.

69. Columbia Oral History Projects, Social Security Project, Katharine Lenroot, 2 February 1965, Irvine Lenroot, "Memoirs," p. 69, Box 13, Dorothy Lenroot, "Date Book for 1910," Box 17, Lenroot Papers; Katharine Lenroot to Nellie Nichols, 7 January 1910, Clara Lenroot to Nellie Nichols, 16 January 1910, Katharine Lenroot to Nellie Nichols, 22 January 1910, Lenroot Papers Addition; interview with Katharine Lenroot, 2 April 1969.

70. Katharine Lenroot to Nellie Nichols, 7 January 1910, Lenroot Papers Addition.

71. Lowitt, *Norris,* vol. 1, p. 159. Not all insurgents had been forewarned either, and the matter had not been taken up in their conferences. Augustus P. Gardner to E. E. Gaylord, 11 January 1910, Gardner, *Letters,* pp. 56–57. Quite possibly Norris got the idea just days before offering his amendment from Norman Hapgood of *Collier's,* who on 31 December proposed such an amendment in a letter to Victor Murdock, Box 22, Murdock Papers.

Although the insurgent action was directed against Cannon and the rules, not Taft, in the heated atmosphere of the day the distinction was not easily maintained. Now that the House had the power to choose its investigators, insurgents, in the exercise of that authority, would in effect have to vote for or against the president.

In the days that followed, the insurgents became divided but were determined to act together. Lenroot, who attended every insurgent meeting for which minutes survive, recognized the need for concerted action, even at the cost of compromise, but within these limits he consistently urged the more radical course.[72]

Starting with a meeting on the night after their victory on the Norris amendment, the insurgents gathered at least three times within five days. They readily agreed to insist on the right to name one of the four House Republican members and that neither Payne nor Dalzell be on the committee. But the more cautious or conservative wanted to emphasize their regularity, by working with the president and through the Republican caucus on the makeup of the committee. The bolder or more radical among them emphasized continuing cooperation with the Democrats, especially as to the choice of the two House Democrats for the committee, and argued against entering a binding Republican caucus. At the second of the three meetings, Lenroot spoke strongly against entering the caucus, urging a conference instead. When the group delayed making a definite decision until a committee of three held discussions with Taft, the House Republican leadership, and the Democratic leaders, Lenroot quickly expressed the sense of the meeting, that the insurgents should at least not pledge themselves to enter the caucus in advance of definite agreement with the Republican leaders. Two days later, the committee reported to a gathering of fourteen insurgents that it had met with the president and secured an agreement as to the four Republicans, one of whom would be insurgent Madison. Nelson did not record the comments of the fourteen members, each of whom spoke, but his minutes show that a number, surely Lenroot among them, wanted it understood that satisfactory arrangements be made with the Democrats. Everis Hayes of California, who was the head of the negotiators, told the others to leave that to him. Between 14 and 19 January, Republicans confirmed their agreement as to insurgent representation on the committee and all the insurgents entered the caucus.[73] At the caucus, the regulars quickly carried through with respect to Madison and the other three Republicans.

Even before the start of the investigation, Poindexter predicted a sharp clash with the president over railroad legislation, conservation, postal sav-

72. The minutes were kept by John M. Nelson, Box 16, Nelson Papers.

73. Lowitt, *Norris,* vol. 1, pp. 159–60; Nelson, minutes, insurgent meetings, 8, 10, 12 January 1910, Box 16, Nelson Papers; *CR* 61:2, 1910, vol. 45, pt. 1, p. 838. For the view of one of the more conservative insurgents see Augustus P. Gardner to E. E. Gaylord, 11 January 1910, in Gardner, *Letters,* pp. 56–63.

ings, and limitation on injunctions in labor disputes. The president, he wrote, had taken progressive positions on those issues initially but was in process of receding from them.[74]

The clash Poindexter foresaw was in the making, chiefly on the railroad question. Undoubtedly, though, it was exacerbated as a result of the conservation investigation. The Republican senatorial contingent on the committee was predisposed in favor of the administration and Ballinger's exoneration was a foregone and, therefore, unsensational conclusion. The verdict of the press and magazines, rendered and reiterated daily and weekly for almost four months, was very different and far more consequential. While the administration presented its case ineptly, Louis D. Brandeis, already famous as the "people's attorney," was indefatigable and brilliant in developing and presenting his side, as attorney for Glavis. Though he proved no dishonesty, he did show that Ballinger was not a conservationist of the Roosevelt stamp. He established the connection between the Cunningham claimants and the Morgan-Guggenheim Syndicate. Most damaging of all, he showed that the document on which Taft based his judgment for Ballinger and against Glavis had been predated and that Taft had in fact made his decision in advance of the evidence. Administrative behavior in this matter, and in others associated with the case, was explicable but not in practice explicated.[75]

The fact that in January Taft had been forced to fire Pinchot for publicly siding with Glavis further weakened the president, for the dynamic Pinchot remained associated in the public mind with his friend Roosevelt and with conservation.

During the winter months, Lenroot was involved in unfriendly analysis of the administration's postal savings bill and its still more important railroad bill.[76] Then suddenly and unexpectedly in mid-March and mid-session, the House insurgents again were fighting the battle of the rules.

On 16 March, Congressman Edgar Crumpacker of Indiana called up an amendment to the census bill. Democrat John Fitzgerald objected that it was out of order, but Cannon ruled it privileged, since the Constitution provides for taking the census. Some Republicans joined the Democrats in challenging and overriding his ruling. When Crumpacker called it up the next day, however, the House reversed itself and decided that it was in order, as Cannon had ruled. Norris voted against the ruling on each occasion, but soon he saw the opening Cannon had given him. After some jockeying for recognition, he secured the floor to offer his own resolution

74. Poindexter to Henry C. Campbell, 7 February 1910, File 27, Series 1, Poindexter Papers.
75. Alpheus T. Mason, *Brandeis: A Free Man's Life*, pp. 254–82; Alpheus T. Mason, *Bureaucracy Convicts Itself: The Ballinger-Pinchot Controversy of 1910;* Mowry, *Era of Theodore Roosevelt*, p. 255; Elmo R. Richardson, *The Politics of Conservation: Crusades and Controversies, 1897–1913*, pp. 65–79; Pringle, *The Life and Times*, vol. 1, pp. 510–13; James Penick, Jr., *Progressive Politics and Conservation: the Ballinger-Pinchot Affair*, pp. 144–64.
76. Lenroot to C. H. Crownhart, 4 March 1910, Box 2, Lenroot Papers.

"privileged by the Constitution." To the consternation of Cannon and his
close associates, it turned out to be the rules changes that the insurgents
had formulated in December and January and that Norris had been waiting
for an opportune time to present them. On one test preceding Norris's
resolution, forty-two Republicans voted against Cannon; some of them undoubtedly were influenced by the growing criticism of "near insurgents."
As Dalzell immediately raised a point of order against the Norris resolution,
he, Cannon, and the other regular leaders foresaw the trouble ahead of
them.[77]

Cannon realized that if he ruled immediately on Dalzell's point of order
his ruling would be appealed and might be overridden, after which the
resolution would come to a vote and might well pass. Unsure of the attitude
of some Democrats and aware that many of his own supporters were absent
for St. Patrick's Day festivities, he stalled for time. Instead of ruling, he asked
for debate on the point of order, which was his parliamentary prerogative,
meanwhile calling up reinforcements.[78]

Washingtonians, including Clara Lenroot and Katharine, hurried to the
House galleries that afternoon. They heard debate but saw no vote taken.
Even the debate dwindled in interest as the session dragged on through the
evening and into the early morning. The midnight trains brought only seven
regular Republicans, who were matched by six insurgents and Democrats,
so Cannon continued to withhold his ruling. Most Cannonites left the chamber, not only for rest but to break the quorum. But the insurgent and
Democratic allies, fearing any breach in their lines and sensing that dramati-
zation of the fight would be to their advantage, rebuffed efforts to adjourn
or recess; they stayed on and pressed the sergeant at arms to bring in
absentees under call of the House. Lenroot entered debate for the first time
in his House career soon after four in the morning and again an hour later,
in each case citing from *Hinds' Precedents* to buttress a parliamentary point.
He won out the second instance in which he argued that contrary to the view
of the chair, additional officers might be employed to fetch absent members.
Soon after this Lenroot left, either for a brief rest or to negotiate. Cannon
had quit the chamber long since, but offstage he sent for his clever young
helper of previous sessions, James E. Watson of Indiana, and prepared for
the battle ahead.[79]

At about breakfast time, while members visited good-naturedly on the
floor, twenty-four insurgents gathered in Gardner's office to exchange reports and plot strategy, with Hayes presiding. Nelson's minutes are some-

77. Hechler, *Insurgency*, pp. 66–69; *Chicago Record-Herald*, 17 March 1910; *Washington Herald*,
17 March 1910; *Chicago Tribune*, 17 March 1910.

78. Gwinn, *Cannon*, p. 208; Hechler, *Insurgency*, pp. 69–70; Barfield, "Democratic Party in
Congress," p. 56; Lowitt, *Norris*, vol. 1, p. 171.

79. Dorothy Lenroot, "Date Book for 1910," 14 April 1910, Box 17, Lenroot Papers; *CR*
61:2, pp. 3393–94, 3398–99; Champ Clark, *My Quarter Century in Politics*, vol. 2, p. 276; Watson,
As I Knew Them, p. 119; Bolles, *Tyrant from Illinois*, pp. 55–56; *Chicago Record-Herald*, 18 March
1910; *Washington Herald*, 18 March 1910.

what garbled but indicate that Norris spoke first, saying that two regular leaders had come to him, Hayes, and Lenroot, to propose a compromise. Hayes then told of a second interview at which the warring Republicans discussed details of a compromise. But Norris reported that the proposals of the regulars did not jibe with what the Democrats would agree to. To this point, the discussion turned on the total number of persons who should serve on the rules committee and how they should be divided between the parties. These were details that, as events soon showed, could be ironed out easily among the three groups—the insurgent Republicans, regular or standpat Republicans, and Democrats. But Murdock raised the stickier question, urging that the Speaker be "expressly prohibited" from membership on the committee. Gardner called for a tentative vote and "Lenroot moved that it is (the) sense of (the) meeting that (the) speaker should be prohibited." Others urged acceptance of what some regulars were already privately suggesting—that Cannon should quit the rules committee by agreement among Republicans, rather than by any formal rules change. Finally the insurgents voted and discovered that the vote was evenly divided. At this, James Good of Iowa moved that a steering committee consisting of Hayes, Gardner, Charles Davis, and Lenroot "be authorized to confer with both Regulars and Democrats and report back." The motion carried and the insurgents recessed until two in the afternoon, when the negotiators would report. In practice, Norris acted in place of Davis in most or all of the conferences that followed. The insurgent bargainers were all able, adroit men. The team had a representative character, too, with Lenroot acting for the more radical element.[80]

While the spectators waited vainly through the morning and into the afternoon for something to happen on the House floor, Lenroot and his colleagues held several meetings with Cannon's lieutenants, with Democrats Clark and Oscar Underwood, and with their own supporters. Lenroot, for the radical insurgents, insisted on Cannon's immediate removal from the rules committee as a minimal demand and preferably the specific exclusion of the Speaker by House rule. He was spared an embarrassing break with the other insurgents by the fact that the Democrats, who were indispensable to insurgent hopes, supported the radical insurgent demands, while Cannon's friends could not yield anything more than Cannon's removal at the end of the term, and even on this they had to be highly tentative. At an impasse by late afternoon, the insurgents held firm, confident that they and the Democrats had a majority. But Tawney, still hopeful of compromise, moved postponement until the following day, and the House approved the motion by a vote of 163 to 151.[81]

80. Dorothy Lenroot, "Date Book for 1910," 14 April 1910, Box 17, Lenroot Papers; Lowitt, *Norris*, vol. 1, pp. 174–75; *Washington Evening Star*, 18 March 1910; Nelson, minutes, insurgent meetings, 18 March 1910, Box 16, Nelson Papers; *Chicago Tribune*, 19 March 1910.

81. Lowitt, *Norris*, vol. 1, pp. 174–76; Nelson, minutes, insurgent meetings, second meeting (18 March 1910), Box 16, Nelson Papers; *Washington Herald*, 20 March 1910; Gwinn, *Cannon*, pp. 210–11; Hechler, *Insurgency*, pp. 70–71.

The hopes of the regulars rested on two possibilities, neither of which materialized. The regular leaders knew that moderate Republicans were getting strong pressure from home to act against Cannon; this they hoped to counter by bringing President Taft to the Speaker's aid. However the president, then en route from Chicago to Rochester, New York, declined to intercede.[82] The other possibility to which Tawney, Dalzell, Payne, James R. Mann, and Cannon's other friends clung, was the hope that Cannon would agree to major concessions. But "Uncle Joe," firm, tough, and admirable through the whole trying episode, instead gave explicit instructions to his representatives that they were not to yield anything so far as his membership on the rules committee was concerned.[83] Thus, when Lenroot, with the other three insurgent negotiators, met the regulars on the morning of Saturday, 19 March, in advance of the climactic session, he quickly found, perhaps to his relief, that the regulars came empty-handed. The insurgents offered no concessions and after the fruitless conference Lenroot and Norris predicted victory on the House floor. Mann ruefully agreed.[84]

Meanwhile, Clark, the minority leader, had surprised Norris with the news that the Democrats could not support his resolution but insisted on their own, which had been prepared by Underwood of Alabama, already the intellectual leader of the House Democracy. The Democrats preferred a rules committee of ten rather than fifteen and rejected Norris's idea of geographical representation on the committee, substituting a simple six-four party representation ratio. Norris, though still preferring his own scheme, agreed to the Democratic plan but insisted that he present it. Since the Democratic plan, like Norris's, specifically excluded the Speaker from membership on the rules committee, it met the demands of Lenroot and the radical insurgents and the whole insurgent group accepted it. Neither plan denied the Speaker his power to appoint committee members.[85]

When Congress met at noon, spectators and participants all knew that Cannon was defeated. As expected, Cannon finally ruled and his ruling was overridden. Nevertheless, before Norris's new resolution came to a vote, some members proposed that Cannon be allowed to remain on the rules committee until the end of the session. The proposal, which was strenuously resisted by Lenroot during the insurgent meetings and negotiations, came from a near insurgent from South Dakota, Eben W. Martin, who in the course of the debate on the Norris resolution indicated that he would offer an amendment that would incorporate all parts of the Norris resolution

82. *Chicago Record-Herald,* 19 March 1910; Gwinn, *Cannon,* pp. 203–5, 211–12; Solvick, "Taft and Cannonism," p. 58.

83. Hechler, *Insurgency,* p. 71; L. White Busbey, *Uncle Joe Cannon,* pp. 255–56; Gwinn, *Cannon,* pp. 212–13.

84. Hechler, *Insurgency,* pp. 71–72.

85. Clark, *Quarter Century in Politics,* vol. 2, p. 277; Nelson, minutes, insurgent meetings, March (1910), Box 16, Nelson Papers. This fragment is not entirely clear. It indicates that Lenroot urged the group to support Norris in his decision; the proposal was rejected after some discussion, but a motion made by Norris, unspecified, was unanimously approved. Probably it was to accept the Democratic proposal.

except for the immediate exclusion of Cannon from the committee. Either
by prior arrangement or on the spot, Lenroot got from Norris five minutes
of the hour controlled by the Nebraskan. He used less than that. First,
Lenroot made it clear what Martin was proposing. Then he asserted his
belief that just as in the future no Speaker should be a member of the rules
committee, so too "the present Speaker ought not to be a member of that
committee," a remark that evoked applause from Democrats and insurgents.
He concluded by commenting on the feature of the fight that engaged the
most widespread and deepest attention, saying:

> The adoption of the pending resolution will do much to insure a Republican
> majority in the next Congress. We should remember that the Republican party
> is not confined within the walls of this Capitol, does not depend on its so-called
> leaders, but upon the men upon our farms, in our shops throughout this land,
> in the rank and file of the Republican party and that rank and file desire that this
> body be made a representative body.

The Democrats knew that Lenroot exaggerated, that the Republican party
could not and would not immediately transform itself or its image, and that
their own party would gain the advantage at the next elections. But Republicans were aware that Lenroot was at least partly right—that public sentiment
lay with insurgency and those who joined it had the best chance for political
survival in the immediate future. Thus, insurgent ranks not only held but
increased, as forty-three Republicans joined the Democrats in approving the
Norris resolution by a vote of 191 to 156.[86]

Content with his victory, Norris promptly moved for adjournment.
Calmly, Speaker Cannon asked that the House first permit him to make a
brief statement, and Norris agreed to withhold his motion. Facing packed
galleries and crowded corridors, in firm but measured tones, Cannon proceeded to lecture his adversaries on the virtues of majority rule and the need
for leadership and party discipline to make such rule effective. Noting that
a new majority had evidently come into existence—made up of Democrats
and some Republicans—he briefly considered the idea that he should resign
as Speaker. This he declined to do because of the delay entailed in choosing
a new Speaker, and his continuing responsibility to effect legislation, and
because—here his voice rose in intensity and volume—"the Speaker is not
conscious of having done any political wrong." Cannon, already the object
of sympathy and admiration, brought the regular Republicans to their feet
in wild applause. After a few minutes, the wily Speaker resumed the speech
Watson had written for him. Though he could not in good conscience
himself resign, he challenged "the real majority . . . to have the courage

86. Lowitt, *Norris,* vol. 1, pp. 174–79; *CR* 61:2, 1910, vol. 45, pt. 3, pp. 3430–31; Hechler,
Insurgency, p. 72; *Chicago Tribune,* 20 March 1910; *Washington Herald,* 20 March 1910. Some
sources put the total of the insurgents at forty-two on the final vote but the *Chicago Tribune*
lists forty-three. Historian John D. Baker sees the anti-Cannon effort of the insurgents as a
defensive political move, in anticipation of the 1910 elections. John D. Baker, "The Character
of the Congressional Revolution of 1910," pp. 679–91.

of its convictions" and offer a motion "to vacate the office of Speaker and choose a new Speaker." Believing in majority rule, he said, he would welcome such a motion.[87]

Cannon's speech immediately confused the Democrats. They also were in great discord when Albert Burleson of Texas, who had anticipated Cannon's action, brought forth the resolution Cannon invited. Burleson and his supporters wanted to keep the issue of Cannonism alive, but other Democrats feared that his motion would fail, or if it succeeded would leave the party in the impossible position of having to run the House without a real majority, and that in any case it would seem petty. Cannon anticipated all this, but as his speech and his actions over the previous several years showed, he was even more interested in putting a halt to the insurgent Republicans. The major reason Cannon refused any basic compromise throughout the rules fight, even against the advice of his close friends, was to drive the insurgents out of the Republican party. To him an election, even his own, was far less important than control of the party. From that standpoint, compromise with insurgency was self-defeating. And so he had forced the insurgents to vote with the Democrats on the rules, and now he would make them do it again on the speakership itself, or else back down. Everyone understood the situation. The moderate insurgents and the near insurgents became nervous because of the prospect, while the regulars chortled as Burleson refused to be dissuaded but shouted for recognition, which Cannon willingly gave him despite the counter-efforts of Norris and Democrat Swagar Sherley to bring immediate adjournment. Happily for the less radical insurgents, as soon as Burleson won parliamentary standing for his resolution that the office of Speaker be declared vacant, Norris began to move among them to argue against the motion from the standpoint of high principle. He stressed the idea, as he had before and would again in his later explanations, that the fight was over principle not personalities and that the distinction should not be blurred by seeming vengefulness against Cannon. Just as busily, but with less success, Murdock reminded his colleagues that they had all condemned Cannon as an autocrat and some had called him a tool of special interests. To draw back now, Murdock said, was the rankest hypocrisy and cowardice.[88]

---

87. Lowitt, *Norris*, vol. 1, p. 180; Watson, *As I Knew Them*, pp. 119–22; Hechler, *Insurgency*, pp. 74–75. Watson's account of the incident in his book is not reliable and must be used with caution, but a contemporary report in the *Washington Times*, 21 March 1910, supports the fact of his role.

88. Busbey, *Uncle Joe Cannon*, pp. 267–68; *Chicago Record-Herald*, 20 March 1910; *Chicago Tribune*, 20 March 1910; Hechler, *Insurgency*, pp. 74–77; J. D. Cannon to C. D. Norton, 21 July 1910, Taft Papers, cited in Norman M. Wilensky, *Conservatives in the Progressive Era: The Taft Republicans of 1912*, p. 6; Wilensky, *Conservatives in the Progressive Era*, pp. 5–6; James Holt, *Congressional Insurgents and the Party System, 1909–1916*, pp. 20–23, 25–28; George W. Norris to Harry A. Foster, 25 March 1910, to J. J. McCarthy, 1 April 1910, Box 53, George W. Norris Additional Correspondence, George W. Norris Papers, LC; Lowitt, *Norris*, vol. 1, pp. 178–79, 181; *Washington Herald*, 20 March 1910.

Most of the Democrats voted with Burleson, but only nine insurgents broke party ranks; the motion was defeated by 192 to 155. Lenroot was one of the nine. While Cannon, who had yielded the chair to Payne and left the chamber during the vote, now held court among his friends on the House floor, the dissidents filed out. Lenroot was quickly collared by a reporter, to whom he explained his vote. "I have always believed that the presiding officer of the House should not be Joseph G. Cannon," Lenroot said. "I have voted consistently today, that is all." A few days later, on learning that his course had met with strong approval at home, from the standpoint of both national and party interest, Lenroot wrote: "I could not see, and do not yet see how any insurgent who has taken the position that Cannon is practically a public enemy, could fail to vote to depose him however much he might dislike to be put against that proposition." [89]

Though Lenroot years later claimed that the rules fight "put an end to the power of the speaker theretofore exercised and made him merely a presiding officer," [90] at the time he wrote a friend, "between us, I do not think that anything substantial has been gained by the fight. Cannon controls this new Committee on Rules just as effectively as if he were a member of it, and there is danger that the country will believe that the fight is over when it really should be just beginning." [91]

Poindexter took a more sanguine view, stressing "the new spirit in the conduct of . . . affairs," and *La Follette's Weekly Magazine* said that at least the victory had strengthened the morale of the "progressive organization." Historians later agreed with that judgment, while acknowledging that substantively, little had been accomplished.[92]

In early 1910, the press and public gave attention to the Cannon fight and the Ballinger-Pinchot investigation. But the chief legislative matter before the Congress, and a matter of vast importance, was the railroad bill.

On 7 January President Taft sent Congress a special message calling for a new law and specifying the main provisions he had in mind. Three days later Congressman Charles E. Townsend of Michigan introduced the administration's bill in the House, and the Committee on Interstate Commerce began hearings almost immediately.

Railroads and shippers, for different reasons, had for several years pushed for new legislation. Theodore Roosevelt had advocated a number of reforms, and Taft, true to Roosevelt and the party platform and not particu-

89. *CR* 61:2, 1910, vol. 45, pt. 3, p. 3438; *Washington Herald*, 20 March 1910; *Chicago Tribune*, 20 March 1910; *Chicago Record-Herald*, 20 March 1910; W. R. Foley to Lenroot, 23 March 1910, Lenroot to Foley, 24 March 1910, Box 2, Lenroot Papers.

90. Lenroot, "Memoirs," p. 72, Box 13, Lenroot Papers.

91. Lenroot to Charles Crownhart, 24 March 1910, Box 2, Lenroot Papers.

92. Poindexter to C. M. Miller, 24 March 1910, cited in Hechler, *Insurgency*, p. 81; to A. D. Sloan, 30 March 1910, File 23, Series 1, Poindexter Papers; *La Follette's Weekly Magazine* 2:12 (March 1910):3; Barfield, "Democratic Party in Congress," p. 64; Hechler, *Insurgency*, pp. 81–82.

larly sympathetic to the railroads, had promised reforms during his 1908 campaign. Now he was determined to fulfill his promise. Aware of the power the railroad companies could exert and of the fact that the road officials themselves wanted some new legislation, chiefly to protect themselves from unfriendly state action and to permit rate agreements, Taft in 1909 undertook to secure their cooperation in preparation of the bill and their agreement not to fight it. This agreement he and Attorney General Wickersham, who was chief administration architect of the bill, achieved. Nevertheless, the measure that Taft advocated and Townsend introduced embodied a number of features that the companies did not favor, especially the paragraphs vesting in the Interstate Commerce Commission the power to initiate new rate changes instead of acting only after complaint from a shipper. All things considered, the president regarded his railroad proposals as progressive. The choice of Townsend to act as sponsor for the bill in the House emphasized the point, since Townsend had led in the fight for better railroad regulation during the Roosevelt years, had cooperated with the insurgents in the rules fights, and was already a candidate for the Senate in opposition to standpatter Julius Burrows. In working through Townsend, moreover, Taft was protecting his bill from the taint of Cannonism, which attached to the chairman of the House Committee on Interstate Commerce, Mann of Illinois. John J. Esch, a moderate and an expert on railroad legislation, hailed the bill as highly progressive.[93]

The first point in Taft's message, and nearest his heart, was for a new federal court, a Commerce Court, whose special business would be to hear appeals from the Interstate Commerce Commission. This court, Taft felt, would expedite the decisionmaking process and would relieve the commission of judicial functions. Next, the president recommended legalization of rate agreements, subject to commission approval. More to the taste of shippers, he then proposed allowing the I.C.C. to initiate rate inquiries, and that the I.C.C. be permitted to stay a rate change for sixty days. In very qualified form, he proposed that the shipper be allowed to choose the route his goods would take. Then he urged that railroads be forbidden to acquire the stock of competitive roads, or to issue stocks or bonds at less than par value. Finally, he asked that the I.C.C. be given power to prescribe safety appliances for the railroads.[94]

Despite the president's hopes and efforts, many insurgents reacted to his message and to the administration bill with suspicion and very soon with hostility. Previous experience made some insurgents skeptical of any policy

---

93. Mowry, *Era of Theodore Roosevelt*, p. 260; Gabriel Kolko, *Railroads and Regulation, 1877–1916* (Princeton, 1965), pp. 177–82; clipping, *Chicago Post*, 10 January 1910, Scrapbooks, vol. 30, James R. Mann Papers, LC; Esch to W. B. Tscharmer, 13 January 1910, to Elbert F. Baldwin, 13 January 1910, vol. 21, John J. Esch Papers, Letterbooks, WSHSL. Due to the death of his son, Esch did not have the opportunity to play a large role in the events that ensued.

94. Kolko, *Railroads and Regulation*, pp. 184–85; John Esch to Elbert F. Baldwin, 13 January 1910, vol. 21, Esch Letterbooks.

proposed by Taft. Newspaper reports on the role of railroad executives in framing the bill and the support of Senator Aldrich for it reinforced doubts. Viewing the bill with that attitude, already predisposed to regard the courts as enemies to progressive legislation, and equally antagonistic to measures that might weaken competition and the protections of the Sherman Anti-trust Act, these insurgents quickly imputed sinister meaning to provisions for the Commerce Court, for rate agreements, and for mergers, among other things. The backing of organizations such as the National Live Stock Association and of their own constituents encouraged western insurgents to raise early objection. With little difficulty, they readily discovered sins of omission as well as commission in the bill, including the absence of a physical valuation provision or of a long- and short-haul section.[95] Parting company with many of their eastern allies of the rules fight, the House insurgents who attacked the administration's measure were called "progressives."

In Mann, the progressives found an unlikely but very useful ally during the first stages of the fight. No friend to rules reform, personally loyal to Speaker Cannon, and seen as Cannon's prospective successor, Mann was in his seventh term in Congress from the heterogeneous Hyde Park district of Chicago. Occasionally he wandered from the reservation, as in voting against the Payne-Aldrich tariff. When he did so, it was for his own reasons, and he remained a regular. Mann was by inclination and ability a leader, and Cannon, appreciating his talents, accepted him on his own terms. In this Cannon was wise, for Mann was a valuable friend who might have been a dangerous enemy. Eschewing highballs and poker parties in favor of the library, Mann made himself master of an incredible number of bills and of parliamentary procedure. With little concern for the sensibilities of others, he manifested his knowledge in floor debate without stint and was almost always right. Fifty-three years old, Mann was at the height of his powers. Even before the president delivered his message, Mann introduced his own bill, serving notice that he proposed to be the author and producer of the next railroa l legislation, the plans of Taft, Wickersham, Townsend, and the railroad executives to the contrary notwithstanding.[96]

Wickersham kept in touch with Mann while negotiating with the railroad representatives, but he ignored Mann's advice in including the Commerce Court proposal in his bill. Mann did not make that mistake in drafting his own bill. He hewed closer to the progressive line also in including a long- and short-haul provision in his bill, as well as more stringent protections against mergers, rate agreements, and stock watering. Though a loyal parti-

95. Mowry, *The Progressive Movement*, pp. 95–96; Holt, *Congressional Insurgents*, p. 34; Kolko, *Railroads and Regulation*, p. 187.

96. Gwinn, *Cannon*, pp. 158–59, 194–95, 203, 241–42; clippings, *Baltimore News*, 22 December 1910, Scrapbook 14, *New York Sun*, 4 April 1911, Scrapbook 15, Mann Papers; Clark, *Quarter Century in Politics*, vol. 2, p. 342; clippings, *Chicago Post*, 10 January 1910, *Chicago Record-Herald*, 5 January 1910, Scrapbook 30, Mann Papers.

san, Mann was no hidebound reactionary. Like Cannon, he did not ignore the talk of reform in the Midwest and in the halls of Congress, but unlike the Speaker, he proposed to accommodate to it in pursuit of party and national interest. Twenty years Cannon's junior, Mann perhaps also considered self-interest to a greater degree than did his friend from Danville. Thus, in January and February, the country witnessed a Cannon lieutenant taking up the cause of progressivism to improve a measure that the administration offered as the capstone of its progressive program. With the help of the Democrats, by early March Mann had won virtually all he sought, except for elimination of the Commerce Court. Satisfied, he reversed his field and exercised his prerogative as chairman to attach his own name to the bill and direct its progress through the House, thus disappointing Townsend and his Michigan friends but guaranteeing to the administration vigorous, capable, and untiring advocacy for what it was still pleased to consider its own measure.[97]

Mann's task in the House was greatly complicated by events outside. In the Senate, the imperious majority leader, Aldrich, insisted that the Wickersham bill be reported as written. Albert Cummins of Iowa and Clapp of Minnesota joined the Democrats in a stinging minority report, and in March Cummins led the progressive Republicans in denunciation of the bill and insistence on over a hundred amendments. Meanwhile, presidential patience grew thin. Taft took patronage from some Republicans and let the rest know that he would regard the railroad bill as a test of regularity and would join in fighting the renomination of those who opposed it.[98] Taft soon yielded to realities, the more easily for the fact that through the work of Mann the "administration" bill in the House already differed markedly from the Senate version. But meanwhile the damage had been done, not only in the Senate but also in the House. As of March, the country could see rather clear-cut factional lines within the Republican party, and the president had permitted himself to be identified with the less popular side. Within limits, the progressive Republicans in the House, mainly from the West, were politically free to attack the Mann bill when it came from committee, despite the president's ill-considered threats.

Taft defeated Mann in committee on the Commerce Court question. The court provision was approved by a ten-to-eight vote after the president talked with six members at the White House. But his victory was costly.

97. Mowry, *The Progressive Movement*, pp. 94–95, citing correspondence between Mann and Wickersham in the Mann Papers; Kolko, *Railroads and Regulation*, p. 190; clippings, *Chicago Record-Herald*, 5 January 1910, *Chicago Inter Ocean*, 27 February 1910, Scrapbook 30, Mann Papers; Miles Poindexter to J. B. Campbell, 9 March 1910, File 27, Series 1, Poindexter Papers; clippings, *Carthage Missouri Press*, 28 March 1910, *Philadelphia Record*, 28 March 1910, *Sault Ste. Marie News*, 11 April 1910, *Chicago Examiner*, 7 March 1910, Scrapbook 30, Mann Papers.

98. Ralph M. Sayre, "Albert Baird Cummins and the Progressive Movement in Iowa" (Ph.D. diss.), pp. 367–68; Mowry, *The Progressive Movement*, pp. 97–99.

Aside from the unpopularity of the provision and the discredit it lent to the rest, its inclusion made the bill a measure to appropriate money, which had to be taken up section by section for debate and amendment. Even before the Cannon fight, the leadership was too weak to pressure for a rule limiting debate.[99] Quite a few progressive Republicans found the measure unsatisfactory in one or several particulars. Anxious to work with the Democrats but not to be swallowed by them, they were glad to find their own leader in Lenroot.

Though not sure until debate actually started that he would be able to get the floor, Lenroot prepared to participate by closely studying the president's message, the Townsend bill, a second version of that bill offered by the administration in mid-February, the printed hearings, and other related matter. The Wisconsin experience and the studies he had made for La Follette equipped him to understand the highly technical subject.[100]

Mann called up his bill on 12 April. Six days after debate opened, Lenroot was established as the leader in the House among the Republican critics of the bill with a speech that occupied over an hour, won him a good deal of applause during its delivery and praise afterwards, and that served as focus for much of the debate in the days that followed.[101] Lenroot's greatest difficulty with respect to this speech was in securing the time to deliver it. He had to negotiate with the Democrats before Mann, in charge for the Republicans, would give him the time he wanted.[102]

Lenroot secured the floor at about nine in the evening on Monday, 18 April for his first set speech. He must have been nervous, but he permitted a few interruptions for questions, chiefly barbed ones by Mann, and fielded these coolheadedly.[103]

Lenroot began by discussing the genesis of the bill, emphasizing and illustrating the key role played by railroad men, and the suspicious fact that the major railroad companies did not oppose it in the hearings. The result was inevitable and sinister. Referring to the 17 February bill, Lenroot said, "For every public right secured by that bill there could be found a special privilege granted the railroads and the special privileges compared to the public benefits as mountains to molehills." [104] The bill was later greatly improved in committee, Lenroot acknowledged, and he congratulated the members on it. However, it retained serious faults, which he ascribed to the

99. Clippings, *Chicago Tribune*, 1 March 1910, *Chicago Inter Ocean*, 29 March 1910, Scrapbook 30, Mann Papers.

100. He expressed his uncertainty about getting time in Lenroot to Charles Crownhart, 4 March 1910, Box 2, Lenroot Papers; his preparation is evident in his speeches and debate.

101. *CR* 61:2, 1910, vol. 45, pt. 5, pp. 4946–51; clippings, *Milwaukee Journal*, 19 April 1910, *Milwaukee Sentinel*, 19 April 1910, Box 18, Lenroot Papers. The *Milwaukee Journal* quoted Norris and Hayes in praise of his speech. That summer, *La Follette's Weekly Magazine* quoted from it. *La Follette's Weekly Magazine* 2:31 (6 August 1910):8.

102. Lenroot, "Memoirs," pp. 69–70, Box 13, Lenroot Papers.

103. *CR* 61:2, 1910, vol. 45, pt. 5, p. 4950.

104. Ibid., p. 4946.

fact that the committee members had not been fully independent in their actions. He hoped the House would be.

Lenroot listed six major benefits in the bill, then five "special privileges granted to railroads." Provisions creating the Commerce Court he placed in neither category but judged them "unnecessary, uncalled for, and an unjustifiable expense that ought not to be imposed upon the public." He declined to spend time on the benefits but went directly to the objectionable features of the Mann bill, which he hoped would later be removed by amendment. They were:

1. Authorizing the most flagrant watering of stock in certain cases.
2. The privilege of going before the commerce court and securing a determination in advance as to whether certain action proposed by it is unlawful and stopping the Government from thereafter ever raising any question as to such transaction.
3. Permitting the making of traffic agreements now prohibited by the present law, and relieving such agreements from the condemnation of the Sherman antitrust act.
4. Denial of shipper of any control over actions in the commerce court in which they are interested.
5. Permitting injunctions against the orders of the Interstate Commerce Commission in certain cases without notice and hearings.[105]

Lenroot discussed each of these objections in some detail. For present purposes, it is sufficient to note Lenroot's major concerns and presuppositions. Two of Lenroot's objections reflected popular distrust of the courts as bastions of conservatism; one resulted from the then current feeling that the Interstate Commerce Commission was more likely to protect shippers and consumers than was the attorney general. Lenroot's attention to stock watering, which was considerable and involved a number of separate paragraphs in the bill, reflected not simply concern for stockholders but more important the fact that stocks and bonds constituted the major basis for rate regulation, and watering resulted in excessive rates, by establishing fictitious value as basis for "fair return." Finally, Lenroot's attack on traffic agreements and his solicitude for the Sherman Anti-trust Act reflected a long-felt belief in competition, dating to Wisconsin days. His feeling was typical for the time. Although the railroad industry was one in which unrestricted competition did not always conduce to efficiency, reformers like Lenroot, schooled to the perfidy of railroad executives and their love of monopoly privilege, shied from anything that might reduce the protections of shippers and travelers.

Near the end of his speech, Lenroot noted certain desirable reforms absent from the Mann bill. Of these, he greatly stressed physical valuation of railroad property as essential to ratemaking, a Wisconsin reform with which La Follette was already strongly identified. He concluded by reiterat-

105. Ibid., p. 4947.

ing his appeal for such amendments as would make the bill a good one. To that end, he said, "the wishes of any other department of this government ought not to control our action." [106]

Through the remainder of the week, Lenroot defended the points he had made in his speech, or in one instance correcting a misstatement, while joining others in bringing up new questions and arguments about the Commerce Court and the merger provisions. In the evenings, he met in his office with like-minded insurgents to prepare amendments. The practice continued through the weeks in which the bill was on the floor.[107]

When members began consideration of the separate sections in the last week of April, they found themselves closely divided. But by the time they were done 10 May, Lenroot and his insurgent colleagues, working with most of the Democrats, had won most of what they requested. They failed to eliminate the Commerce Court, but they did modify the method by which judges would be selected and limited the court's injunctive powers. They brought telephone and telegraph under I.C.C. jurisdiction and killed the rate agreement and merger sections. Although physical valuation of railroad property stood no chance of surviving the joint conference, they advanced the idea, a favorite of La Follette, by writing it into their bill.

Meanwhile, events had taken an unforeseen turn in the Senate. There, the early intransigence of the president, Wickersham, and Aldrich boomeranged starting in mid-March, when Cummins began his assaults, especially on the Commerce Court and the role played by the attorney general in preparing the bill. In April, La Follette pitched in with heavy and personal blows, turning on the disgraceful story of the growth of the New York, New Haven, and Hartford railroad monopoly and the fact that at the eleventh hour Wickersham had discontinued antitrust proceedings against the company. Regulars like Lodge were embarrassed by the bill and Stephen Elkins, who was head of the committee that reported it, was an uninspired leader at best and not at all enthused at again serving as cat's paw for Aldrich. By early May, it was clear that Aldrich had lost control to a coalition of Democrats and progressive Republicans. Finally, the cool and experienced Aldrich reformed his lines by promising the Democrats statehood for New Mexico and Arizona, presumed Democratic bastions. By then, however, the original measure had been substantially changed, first by the regulars and Wickersham, to meet some of Cummins's arguments, then on the Senate floor. When it finally passed the Senate on 3 June, even La Follette supported it.[108]

106. *CR* 61:2, 1910, vol. 45, pt. 5, p. 4951.

107. Ibid., pp. 5000–5001, 5145–48, 5193; *CR* 62:3, p. 2875.

108. Kolko, *Railroads and Regulation,* pp. 190–91; Mowry, *The Progressive Movement,* pp. 99–102; clipping, *Detroit Times,* 14 March 1910, Scrapbook 30, Mann Papers, commenting on Elkins's attitude; Hechler, *Insurgency,* pp. 163–75. Elkins's 1909 complaints against Aldrich are noted in Mowry, *The Progressive Movement,* p. 60. On the course of the bill in the Senate see also John Braeman, *Albert J. Beveridge: American Nationalist,* pp. 177–81; and Sayre, "Cummins," pp. 352, 360–64, 370–77.

While the Senate was still considering the bill and before anything final was done with it, the railroads of the west announced rate increases to take effect on midnight of 31 May. With just hours to spare, the Justice Department secured an injunction against the increases, under the Sherman Antitrust Act. On 6 June, the railroad heads, after much discussion, agreed to a compromise with the president under which they would not raise rates until the new law had passed and the I.C.C. had new powers to judge the reasonableness of the increases.[109]

In the few days between Senate passage of the Elkins bill and the presidential agreement with the railroads, progressive Republicans in the House planned their next step. Lenroot spoke for them when on 7 June the House took up the Senate's bill. Undoubtedly he was equally prominent in their preliminary deliberations. The bills adopted by the two Houses differed in many respects; each bill contained "progressive" features absent in the other. To enact all of them required a conference committee. But Lenroot and his friends suspected that a conference might have the opposite result —to eliminate the best provisions from each bill. Lenroot, encouraged by Senate progressives, decided to secure at least part of the features rather than risk all of them, by having the House concur in the Senate bill instead of nonconcurring and asking for a conference. Mann objected to such talk, perhaps partly because he had greater confidence in what might be accomplished in conference, partly because of justifiable pride in his own work and exaggerated appreciation of it as compared to the hodgepodge Senate bill, and perhaps also because only through a conference report would his own name be attached to the landmark legislation. After heated debate, Mann won by a vote of 162 to 156.[110]

Matters worked out satisfactorily for the reformers. Congressmen and senators were anxious to go home and thus susceptible to the kind of pressure that senators like Joseph Bristow of Kansas were already applying. Armed with the power to filibuster, intransigent progressive Republicans warned Aldrich and Elkins that if the conference report proved materially worse than the Senate bill, they could expect to remain in Washington through the summer before it would be adopted. Beyond that, Elkins, unhappy with Aldrich, had for some time encouraged Mann in the development of his House bill. With victory in sight and his adversaries in disarray, the masterful Mann, no less imperious and egotistical than Aldrich and considerably better informed about the legislation at hand, took a strong position in the conference committee and got his way.[111]

Historians have followed the contemporary judgments, regarding the bill as an important reform, though differing as to whether the administration

109. Kolko, *Railroads and Regulation*, p. 191; Pringle, *The Life and Times*, vol. 1, p. 524.

110. Clippings, *Chicago Inter Ocean*, 5 June, 25 April 1910, *Chicago News*, 6 June 1910, Scrapbook 30, Mann Papers.

111. Hechler, *Insurgency*, pp. 176–77; clippings, *Detroit Times*, 14 March 1910, *Kansas City Times*, 15 June 1910, *Racine Journal*, 25 June 1910, *Chicago Tribune*, 14 June 1910, Scrapbook 30, Mann Papers.

or the progressives deserve most of the credit.[112] Another view, however, is that the legislation reflected outdated concerns and was untimely, inhibiting the railroads in their effort to rebuild and expand to meet the heavy demand of the twentieth century.[113] Never during his career would Lenroot wholly accept this judgment, for he always attributed some of the railroads' trouble to fraud and mismanagement, but by 1919 he did take a more sympathetic view toward the problems of the carriers.

The other administration measures enacted in June were affected by the ambiguity experienced over the Mann-Elkins Act. Afterwards, Taft boasted of his accomplishments, which were achieved despite the obstructionism of some progressive Republicans, while the more radical of these congratulated themselves for converting bad proposals into acceptable measures, or criticized the administration for its failures. Taft's very mild anti-injunction proposal came to nothing—it would not have satisfied organized labor in any case—but Congress did adopt a postal savings law and several conservation measures and did continue the Tariff Board with a liberal appropriation, among other things.[114] With respect to conservation, Congress authorized the withdrawal of land from public entry and passed a new General Dams Act that, under rather narrowly defined circumstances, permitted the government to charge a fee for private use of waterpower sites. In each case, the administration and the Pinchot coterie clashed during the course of the legislation and neither side gained full satisfaction.[115] Taft and the progressive Republicans agreed to continue the Tariff Board, which was made possible by the Payne-Aldrich tariff law, and to broaden its functions, but standpatters steered the measure into a parliamentary cul-de-sac in the House and then yielded only a life-continuing appropriation but without giving the board any general powers or permanent status.[116]

From the first, Lenroot gave particular attention to the postal savings bill and by the end of the session, when it reached the stage of final action, he

112. Pringle, defending Taft, and Hechler and Mowry, stressing the contribution of the progressives, judged the Mann-Elkins Act as a significant reform. Kolko, in *Railroads and Regulation*, writing from a more radical perspective, minimized the gap between the parties and the significance of the reforms worked. But for a convincing refutation to Kolko's view see Robert W. Harbison, "Railroads and Regulation, 1877–1916: Conspiracy or Public Interest?," pp. 230–42. Harbison argues that, contrary to Kolko, the railroad industry was at the time oligopolistic or monopolistic in each market situation, and that some public price regulation was essential to the public interest.

113. Albro Martin, *Enterprise Denied: Origins of the Decline of American Railroads, 1897–1917*, pp. 354–55.

114. Pringle, *The Life and Times*, vol. 2, p. 620, and vol. 1, pp. 519–29; Gwinn, *Cannon*, p. 224.

115. Samuel P. Hays, *Conservation and the Gospel of Efficiency: The Progressive Conservation Movement, 1890–1920*, pp. 162–65.

116. Clippings, *Washington Times*, 11, 14 April 1910, *Chicago Journal*, 10 May 1910, Scrapbook 30, *Chicago Tribune*, 24 May 1910, Scrapbook 14, Mann Papers; Lenroot to Finley G. Gray, 13 August 1910, Box 2, Lenroot Papers; *CR* 61:3, 1911, vol. 46, pt. 2, p. 1671; Braeman, *Beveridge*, pp. 181–83.

was prepared to speak on it. Through the combination of caucus action and an illiberal rule he was sidetracked and had no influence on the outcome.[117]

Through the winter of 1910 and into the spring, Lenroot served as alter ego for La Follette in communicating with Wisconsin leaders about the summer primary campaign. For himself and the senator, he tried to harmonize differences as to candidates for the various state offices so that progressives would not be divided in the primaries. So far as possible, he tried also to get agreement on candidates who would be both capable and strong. Yet he held back from the twin hazards of outright dictation on the one hand or sanctioning of a general nominating conference on the other. The first, he and La Follette knew, would be denounced as bossism, while the other would seem like the very convention system that La Follette had so long condemned but without the legal safeguards of the old system.

Lenroot failed in one instance with respect to the state ticket. The Wisconsin leaders committed themselves to the candidacy of Frank Tucker for attorney general, an aggressive political war-horse but undistinguished as an attorney. In connection with the controversy over Tucker, Lenroot made a comment to Rogers that is noteworthy. He argued that for the progressive movement to endure in the state and retain the confidence of the people, "our next progressive step must center . . . in the office of attorney general. We have nearly all of the legislation that the situation demands. The next important step is enforcing the law." The comment is interesting in light of the fact that much of the legislation later considered part of the "Wisconsin Idea," especially laws relating to labor and urban problems, was not enacted until 1911.[118]

Home in Superior on 28 June, Lenroot was so fatigued that he had to cancel plans to attend Rogers's wedding in order to rest for a few days. Very soon, he felt restored enough to resume service in La Follette's campaign. First he stood in for the senator as the main speaker at Chetek, Wisconsin, and took the occasion to confer with Crownhart of Superior, La Follette's manager; then, after fulfilling a few other speaking engagements in the district, he set forth on a Chautauqua tour to raise money for the La Follette campaign. He had talked with La Follette before accepting the Chautauqua offer and both judged that Lenroot would be more useful raising money than making political speeches in Wisconsin so early in the campaign. However he declined August bookings and recommended Norris instead.[119]

When the primary campaign heated up, Lenroot spoke widely in his

117. Margulies, "Lenroot," pp. 476–79.
118. Lenroot to A. T. Rogers, 30 March 1910, Box 4, Lenroot Papers; Margulies, *The Decline of the Progressive Movement*, pp. 130–36.
119. Lenroot to Crownhart, 23, 28 June 1910, Box 158, Crownhart to George E. Scott, 5 July 1910, Box 159, La Follette Papers; Lenroot to Crownhart, 5 April 1910, Box 2, to Keith Vawter, 21, 28 March 1910, Box 4, Lenroot, "Memoirs," p. 72, Box 13, Lenroot Papers. Crownhart later wrote of Lenroot's "liberal contribution." Crownhart to Wallace Andrew, 22 August 1910, Box 163, La Follette Papers.

district and for a week outside it, for La Follette and three progressive congressmen. He was highly effective. A Rhinelander school superintendent reported to Crownhart that Lenroot "pleased the people mightily by his fairness. He has improved much in the last four years and makes a powerful but pleasant address." At Delavan, Wisconsin, in the First Congressional District Lenroot substituted for La Follette, he spoke to a Chautauqua assembly about "Progressive Republicanism." The *Milwaukee News* the next day reported it "a surprise because of its masterly character" and said that Milwaukeeans who heard Lenroot's speech declared it "one of the greatest political speeches ever delivered in the state." The man who arranged the meeting wrote with equal enthusiasm to Crownhart. Crownhart himself urged Edward E. Browne to schedule Lenroot as fully as possible during the day of Lenroot's meeting at Waupaca. "He is doing the very best kind of work," Crownhart wrote, "never in better trim and never made as good a speech as he is making in this campaign." [120]

Although no one remarked on it, Lenroot's appearance perhaps added to his effectiveness at this time. At forty-one, he no longer looked the slender, raw-boned youth. With his strong, regular features smoothed by additional flesh, he had become strikingly handsome in a way that lent a sense of maturity and force to his vigorous sincerity and determination.

Lenroot made essentially the same speech through the campaign, starting at the Sons of Norway hall in Superior on 12 August and ending with a Labor Day address in the town of Washburn on 5 September. His speech was well calculated to exploit the popular features of the progressive position and to meet the strategy of the opposition. His opponents understood the popularity of progressivism and therefore put forth as candidates men formerly associated with La Follette in many cases, pledged to control corporations, conserve resources, and the like; they offered themselves as the true defenders of the progressive policies of Taft and Roosevelt, whom they linked together.[121] As against this, Lenroot set out to show that the fight was just like those of the past—"every trust, monopoly and great railway is trying its best to defeat La Follette." He reviewed the battles for railroad taxation and regulation and the primary and noted that those who had opposed La Follette before were leading the opposition now. Lenroot was willing to let his opponents use Taft's name, but he went out of his way to differentiate between Taft and Roosevelt. "They talk of Taft and following out the policies of Roosevelt when every last one of them was glad when

120. F. A. Harrison to Crownhart, 19 August 1910, Box 162, La Follette Papers; *Wisconsin State Journal*, 20 August 1910; clippings, *Milwaukee News*, 19 August 1910, *Beloit News*, 19 August 1910, Box 18, Lenroot Papers; Maurice Morrissey to Crownhart, n.d. (August 1910), Box 156, La Follette Papers; Henry A. Cooper to Lenroot, 12 September 1910, Box 1, Lenroot Papers; Crownhart to E. E. Browne, 19 August 1910, Box 156, La Follette Papers.

121. Margulies, "Issues and Politics of Wisconsin Progressivism, 1906–1920" (Ph. D. diss.), pp. 143–44. See the Edward Fairchild ad in the *Wisconsin State Journal*, 12 August 1910, for an example of stalwart propaganda.

Roosevelt took that trip to Africa and sorry when he returned," Lenroot said. When the progressives fought the administration, it was to defend Roosevelt's policies. Lenroot reviewed Taft's position on the tariff bill, and his well-remembered Winona speech, and talked of insurgency in Congress. The insurgents lost a few post offices for their efforts, but they at least stopped repeal of the Sherman law, he said.[122]

At Delavan, Lenroot met arguments about the need for party and for party discipline, defending those who sometimes voted with the Democrats. Party means less than before, he said; one must put patriotism ahead of party. But in practice the Republican party remained the best hope for the future, so he would fight within the party to make it right. Back in Superior, and finally at Washburn, he put forth the same theme. While insurgents had opposed the president in some things, he explained, it was only because the president did not live up to the Republican platform in full.[123]

To the voting public, the issues were clear-cut, as in the great days of the half-breeds earlier in the decade. Educated to the dichotomy between people and corporations, men and money, Wisconsin people assimilated national news, reinforced later by campaign rhetoric, within these well-developed categories of thought. For most voters, higher living costs gave point to the tariff issue, in particular, and more generally to the distinction among governmental leaders between the friends and the enemies of the people. La Follette succeeded in maintaining his place in the first group. His opponents attacked these simplicities with a different stereotype, of Taft as the constructive progressive and La Follette the demagogic spoiler. In Wisconsin, as throughout insurgent country, this use of Taft's name did not work. With all his geniality, the president had never gained the people's love and trust in his own right—from the first, he had been accepted on the certification of Roosevelt. But in an intra-party squabble in New York that summer, and in late August on the stump in the west, Roosevelt appeared to the country as the friend of the progressives and the enemy of Taft; just days before Wisconsin's primary, at Osawatomie, Kansas, Roosevelt gave the most radical speech of his career. On his way home, he tried to redress the balance somewhat, to reunify the party. But he could not conceal his own differences with Taft, personal as well as political.[124]

Lenroot expected the progressives to win, but as he got the early returns on the night of 6 September and the following morning and reviewed the fuller results three days later, he experienced pleasant surprise at the magnitude of the victory. La Follette led the way, appropriately enough, winning over Cook by a vote of 142,978 to 40,791. McGovern, the gubernatorial candidate, and the La Follette men on the state ticket won nomination by

122. *Duluth News Tribune,* 13 August 1910.

123. *Wisconsin State Journal,* 12 August 1910; *Duluth News Tribune,* 31 August 1910; MS speech, "Labor Day Address, Washburn, September 5, 1910," Box 8, Lenroot Papers.

124. Margulies, "Issues and Politics of Wisconsin Progressivism," pp. 162–67; Mowry, *The Progressive Movement,* pp. 134–51.

lesser but satisfactory margins. And pro-La Follette legislative candidates won most of their primary contests. Charles Starkweather's campaign against Lenroot had never caught on, yet the congressman must have been gratified at his own margin of victory, finally reported at 19,028 to 3,654. In rural and heavily Swedish-populated (Burnett and Polk) counties, Lenroot's combined total was 2,163 to 130 for Starkweather. He carried every ward of his home city and won there by 1,870 to 553.[125]

News from other states was equally gratifying. Of the forty-one Republican incumbent congressmen defeated for renomination, only one was an insurgent. In the main, the losers gave way to avowed progressives. All the progressive senators survived, while standpatter Burrows lost to Townsend in Michigan, and progressives Poindexter, John Works, and Asle Gronna won nominations in Washington, California, and North Dakota. The fact that Aldrich and his co-worker Eugene Hale had retired was good news too. Only James R. Garfield's defeat for the gubernatorial nomination in Ohio blemished the political picture. For Lenroot, the results around the nation increased greatly the importance of events in Wisconsin. La Follette expressed his own faith and caught the mood of his followers when he told the platform convention on 28 September that Wisconsin was pilot to the nation. "A great campaign is on," he said, "not for our state alone, but all the states of the country, and for our great country itself." [126]

General election results encouraged Lenroot further. He was not himself opposed by the Democrats and he defeated his social democratic rival by 19,224 to 2,473. The state ticket won easily against a divided Democracy and his progressive Republican congressional colleagues won out. News from around the country confirmed what the primary elections results had forecast—the Democrats made substantial gains but so did progressive Republicans, both at the expense of the regular Republicans. The Democrats won a sufficient margin of control in the House to govern without insurgent help, but in the Senate, where the Republicans retained control, the progressive Republicans, numbering perhaps fourteen, held the balance of power.[127] Political as well as legislative prospects looked promising.

125. *Duluth News Tribune,* 31 August 1910; Lenroot to La Follette, 10 September 1910, Box 64, Series B, La Follette FC; Belle and Fola La Follette, *La Follette,* vol. 1, p. 306; La Follette to Gifford Pinchot, n.d. (September 1910), Box 165, La Follette Papers; *Duluth News Tribune,* 7, 20 September 1910; Lenroot to La Follette, 7 September 1910, Box 164, to Crownhart, 10 September 1910, Box 165, La Follette Papers; to La Follette, 10 September 1910, Box 64, Series B, La Follette FC.

126. *Duluth News Tribune,* 11, 15 September 1910; Mowry, *The Progressive Movement,* pp. 128–30; *Duluth News Tribune,* 29 September 1910.

127. Arthur S. Link, *Woodrow Wilson and the Progressive Era, 1900–1917,* p. 7; Mowry, *The Progressive Movement,* p. 164; Clubb, "Congressional Opponents," pp. 230, 232.

IV

PRESIDENTIAL POLITICS

Lenroot and La Follette traveled to Washington for the brief period of the "lame duck" session of Congress preceding the holiday recess. Undoubtedly, they talked of the new national progressive organization that La Follette, with others, had been planning. The organization would advance not only the progressive movement but La Follette's presidential candidacy, the senator confided to friends. With that in mind, he felt some need for haste, for it was already agreed that the reformers should push for various direct democracy measures in the state legislatures and one of these would create presidential primaries. Such a measure, La Follette felt, "will go far to decide the next presidential nomination." [1]

Arriving in Washington, La Follette entered into a whirl of conferences with politicians, journalists, and men of wealth. Within the month, he had cash from Charles R. Crane of Chicago and promises of more, for the organization and for his magazine, from Crane, Rudolph Spreckels and William Kent of California, and E. Clarence Jones, a New York banker. [2] Even sooner, La Follette let himself be persuaded by his progressive Republican colleagues that the organization must be a Republican one; they argued that if it were not, they could not go into it, lest they invite certain defeat in their home states. In explaining the matter to the independent-minded Louis Brandeis, La Follette implied that he would himself have preferred a "non-partisan title," and he used the words "at this time" in connection with the Republican affiliation.

---

1. La Follette to E. Clarence Jones, 30 December 1910, Box 105, Series B, Robert M. La Follette FC. The letters indicating La Follette's presidential ambition and the relationship of the projected organization to that include La Follette to A. T. Rogers, 14 December 1910, to Rudolph Spreckels, 26 December 1910, to E. Clarence Jones, 30 December 1910, to George Loftus, 30 December 1910, to Lenroot, 30 December 1910, to Frank Harrison, 31 December 1910, Box 105, Series B, La Follette FC. *La Follette's Weekly Magazine* urged the presidential primary editorially. *La Follette's Weekly Magazine* 3:1 (7 January 1911):3.

2. La Follette to Rogers, 14 December 1910, to Charles R. Crane, 19 December 1910, 3 January 1911, to Jones, 30 December 1910, Box 105, Series B, La Follette FC. Though Jones backed out, within seven months Crane gave the organization $5,000, Spreckels and Kent gave $1,000 each, and another thousand was given by three others, one of them Louis D. Brandeis. Expenses were light. Account book of the National Progressive Republican League, Jonathan Bourne, Jr., Papers, cited in Albert H. Pike, Jr., "Jonathan Bourne, Jr., Progressive" (Ph.D. diss.), p. 199.

A similar uncertainty, as to which man might emerge as the challenger to Taft for the 1912 Republican nomination, allowed La Follette to include in his group all those who for one reason or another wanted a more popular and progressive candidate than Taft. Some of these, notably Gifford Pinchot and James R. Garfield, were erstwhile Roosevelt men, and they perhaps hoped that eventually the former president would himself agree to contest for the nomination. But La Follette knew that among the more ardent progressive leaders Roosevelt had been somewhat discredited by his ineffectual attempt in the fall of 1910 to ride both Republican horses. And Roosevelt was disinclined to contest with an incumbent president, his own protégé, for the nomination, especially since the Democrats were likely to win the election.[3] The senator knew that in November Roosevelt had spoken of La Follette in friendly terms.[4] He also knew that it would be to his advantage and that of the progressive movement if he could form his organization and make his nomination fight in the name of Rooseveltian policies and with the support of Roosevelt's admirers, and perhaps even Roosevelt himself. Roosevelt would have to be watched. But for the present, La Follette had nothing to gain and much to lose by courting division among progressives. If to leave open the possibility that Roosevelt might ultimately be the candidate was risky, it was a chance La Follette had to take. Beyond a doubt Lenroot favored a broad coalition, and he may have urged La Follette to advance his own candidacy in a way that would not antagonize Roosevelt or his supporters.

For reasons of his own, Roosevelt played La Follette's game to a very large extent. While he would not join the progressive Republican organization, he encouraged the progressives in their general program, not only privately but in his *Outlook* magazine editorials. And he indicated that he did not want to oppose Taft.[5] Until November 1911, Roosevelt thought that the best outcome for the party was for Taft to be nominated. Taft would be defeated and then the warring factions, chastened, would rebuild along moderate progressive lines. At that time, he would come again to the fore. This was the view that guided him through most of 1911, in maintaining relations with the administration while at the same time keeping on friendly terms with the progressives.[6]

In the distance lay hazards and uncertainties; but as of December 1910 La Follette's course was well marked. In Congress and through the new organization, he had to take the lead in drawing clear lines between progressives and the administration and in building progressive political strength in the states. Privately believing that his own nomination on the Republican ticket was not only the most desirable outcome but also a possibility, it

3. Robert M. La Follette, *La Follette's Autobiography: A Personal Narrative of Political Experiences*, p. 215.
4. Belle and Fola La Follette, *La Follette*, vol. 1, p. 312.
5. Ibid., pp. 319–20.
6. George E. Mowry, *Theodore Roosevelt and the Progressive Movement*, pp. 174–82.

behooved him to discreetly advance his candidacy under cover of the larger, more general effort. At stake, La Follette felt, was far more than personal power and glory. Though he had reason to exaggerate to the wealthy Spreckels, one cannot doubt his sincerity when he wrote: "With this progressive organization assured, we stand at the threshold (of) the greatest political movement recorded in the last half century of the history of our country—in some respects the greatest, the most important, since the organization of the government." [7]

"For obvious reasons," as La Follette explained to several friends, he could not take an office in the organization he was spearheading, but Lenroot could and did, as a member of the executive committee—the only Wisconsin man designated for a leadership position. In the ensuing months, Lenroot served the cause with speeches and as liaison with La Follette's Wisconsin friends and his national allies. Although he did not realize it, one of the ideas he voiced would result in future trouble. He praised Roosevelt. Roosevelt had sometimes compromised too much in matters of legislation, he felt, but still "he has been one of the greatest powers for good that our country has known. He has awakened the public conscience of America, and because of what he has wrought politics today are upon a higher level . . . and brains and honesty are commencing to count for more than money and cunning." [8] La Follette was playing up to Roosevelt at this time, but privately he distrusted him; Lenroot truly admired the Roughrider.

Lenroot reserved most of his time for legislation. In the politically charged atmosphere of 1911, inevitably these legislative matters related closely to the ambitions of the progressive Republicans. At the same time, the causes Lenroot gave himself to merited attention in their own right. Since Wisconsin days, Lenroot, with La Follette, had taken a keen interest in conservation questions. In 1907, and again in 1909, La Follette had introduced comprehensive legislation to protect federal coal lands. During the Ballinger-Pinchot investigation, public attention focused on the government's coal lands in Alaska. In the Sixty-first Congress, Congressman Frank Mondell of Wyoming, chairman of the public lands committee, introduced a bill to provide procedures for the leasing of these lands. Pinchot and the other leaders of the National Conservation Association favored the principle of leasing but suspected the bill because of its source. Mondell consistently stressed the view of the rights of states and opposed the growth of federal authority over the public domain, and especially the authority of the Forestry Bureau. When the Pinchot group analyzed Mondell's bill, they found it undesirable in several respects. As Pinchot interpreted it, any claimants, whether fraudulent or not, would have preference to lease; also, lessees of coal lands would also have full surface rights and thus reap a windfall

7. La Follette to Spreckels, 26 December 1910, Box 105, Series B, La Follette FC.
8. MS speech, "Progressive Republican League," n.d., Box 8, Irvine L. Lenroot Papers.

if a town developed; the royalties to the government he judged inadequate; and the establishment of an upper instead of a lower limit on royalties he found indefensible.[9] In the House, Lenroot watched over the course of the bill for the conservationists and engaged in debate with Mondell.[10] More unusual in the relationship of a congressman and a lobbying organization, Lenroot made a careful analysis of correspondence bearing on the Cunningham Alaskan coal claims produced in the Ballinger-Pinchot investigation and provided his findings to the Pinchot group.[11] Victorious against the Mondell bill in late February, it was natural that when a similar conservation question arose within the week, Pinchot should turn to Lenroot for assistance, especially since they were collaborating in the National Progressive Republican League and for La Follette.[12] The Alaska question remained to be settled in a subsequent Congress.

During the "lame duck" session of the Sixty-first Congress, Lenroot gave more attention to the tariff commission bill than any other. The notion of making tariffs on the basis of scientific findings rather than logrolling appealed to him strongly, as it did to the general public and to leaders in the business community. In December, Lenroot testified for the measure, and in January and February he spoke for it before the National Tariff Commission Association, as well as in the House. Old Guard Republicans were skeptical, as were most Democrats, but administration and popular pressure was sufficient to bring favorable House action. The Senate delayed until the last day of the session, however, and amidst much parliamentary confusion and widespread suspicion of chicanery, the Senate bill died in the House. Lenroot salvaged some political capital by blaming Joseph Cannon in the pages of *La Follette's Weekly Magazine*.[13]

The new Congress convened in special session a month later to act on the president's proposed tariff reciprocity agreement with Canada. It had earlier passed the House but died in the Senate.

When the insurgents met on the afternoon of 3 April, in advance of the Republican caucus that night and the opening of the Congress the following day, they confronted a radically changed situation. Not only was their party about to assume minority status, but more important, just two days earlier

9. Gifford Pinchot to Lyman Abbott, 25 February 1911, Box 139, Gifford Pinchot Papers, LC. (Not to be confused with the Amos Pinchot Papers, LC. Pinchot Papers is referred to the papers of Gifford Pinchot.)

10. Lenroot to Philip P. Wells, 31 January, 27 February 1911, Box 1819, Pinchot Papers; *CR* 61:3, 1911, vol. 46, pt. 3, p. 2097; *CR* 61:3, 1911, vol. 46, pt. 4, pp. 3233–36.

11. "Parallel of Correspondence of Hon. R. A. Ballinger . . . with Mr. George W. Perkins . . . Mr. R. H. Thomas and Hon. Miles C. Moore . . . with comments thereon, relating to the Cunningham coal claims. Prepared by Hon. E. [*sic*] L. Lenroot, February 7, 1911," Box 1745, Pinchot Papers.

12. Pinchot to Lenroot, 1 March 1911, Box 1819, Pinchot Papers.

13. Herbert F. Margulies, "Progressivism, Patriotism, and Politics: The Life and Times of Irvine L. Lenroot," pp. 516–26.

Cannon confirmed the rumors that he would not be a candidate for Speaker, and now it was clear that James R. Mann would be the minority leader. In thus abandoning the fight to continue as party leader, Cannon yielded to the inevitable, since in the wake of a letter by Nicholas Longworth opposing his reelection, many Republican candidates for Congress pledged themselves against him and seventy-seven of these had won election. Perhaps even more important in Cannon's mind was the desire not to stand in the way of Mann, his loyal but ambitious friend.[14]

Prior to the insurgent conference, some progressives let it be understood that Mann was acceptable to them. They did not have the votes to elect one of their own, and Mann, though an important helper of Cannon on the floor and not in sympathy with the rules changes, claimed to be a progressive. Though Mann was abrasive in debate, Norris regarded him as scrupulously fair. In his favor, too, was the fact that he was an indefatigable worker and master parliamentarian—"the greatest . . . of his or any other period," according to Fiorello La Guardia. With the Democrats about to use their control of the House to launch a full program and a drive toward the presidency, all Republicans could see the advantage of having someone of the sort as watchdog in the House.[15]

It is not clear how far Lenroot and the more radical progressives wanted to go in the direction of independent action. Certainly, though, they wanted to solidify the progressive faction to the extent that it would act cohesively in advancing a candidate for Speaker on the House floor and a legislative program through the session. In accordance with well-developed insurgent ideology as well as the practical necessities, they hoped the members of this faction would agree to go only into party conferences but not into binding caucuses, including the one scheduled for that night. At the progressive conference, Lenroot moved to create a committee of five to work up a plan for permanent organization, and the chairman, probably Hayes or Gardner, named as members Lenroot, Madison, Solomon Prouty of Iowa, Norris, and William Kent of California. Another new member, Abraham Lafferty of Oregon, pressed the group to nominate a progressive candidate for Speaker. Implicit in this proposal, of course, was the idea that the group should stay out of the party caucus. But respected leaders like Madison and

14. Clippings, *Chicago Tribune*, 1 April 1911, *Chicago News*, 29 March 1911, *Chicago Tribune*, 26 March 1911, Scrapbook 15, *New York Herald*, 20 August 1910, *Chicago Post*, 20 August 1910, Scrapbook 14, James R. Mann Papers.

15. Clippings, *Chicago News*, 29 March 1911, Scrapbook 15, *New York Herald*, 20 August 1910, Scrapbook 14, Mann Papers; Blair Bolles, *Tyrant from Illinois: Uncle Joe Cannon's Experiment with Personal Power*, pp. 57–58, 187; Elizabeth Kent, *William Kent, Independent: A Biography*, pp. 106, 113–14; Richard Lowitt, *George W. Norris: The Making of a Progressive, 1861–1912*, vol. 1, pp. 207–8; Fiorello H. La Guardia, *The Making of an Insurgent: An Autobiography* (New York, 1961 [1948]), p. 135; *New York Times*, 5 April 1911. John Nance Garner later called Mann the most useful legislator he had ever known. Bascom N. Timmons, *Garner of Texas: A Personal History*, p. 111.

Norris spoke up for accepting in good grace the inevitable Mann, though as a matter of principle Norris would not enter the caucus. Under the circumstances, any sort of cohesion seemed impossible except on the basis of compromise. Thus, after a prolonged meeting, the insurgents agreed to continue to advocate progressive policies in connection with the tariff, expenditures, and popular government, but to go their separate ways with respect to the caucus that night and the House vote the following day. Also, either because some of them objected or all did, they agreed to reject a Democratic offer of separate and fair treatment with respect to committee assignments; they would take their assignments through the Republican party. Those who proposed to enter the caucus prepared to fight to have these assignments made by a committee instead of the party leader, but they were ready to accept the caucus decision whatever it might be.[16]

At least seventeen progressives, Lenroot among them, stayed away from the caucus. The insurgents who went joined in Mann's unanimous nomination as candidate for Speaker but engaged in over two hours of debate as to who should make committee assignments. Losing this battle, some of them felt disgruntled. But the regulars deferred to them in small ways, as in choosing Nathan Kendall of Iowa as secretary of the caucus. More important, Mann began to develop the spirit of community against the common enemy in attacking the Democrats for their decision to increase the membership on fifteen committees without increasing the number assigned to the Republicans.[17]

The following day, Lenroot and fifteen others voted for Cooper for Speaker and Cooper voted for Norris.[18] But the Democrats took the spotlight, as their three-time presidential nominee William Jennings Bryan and presidential prospect Judson Harmon, the newly elected governor of Ohio, came onto the House floor to celebrate the great day, and the new Speaker, Champ Clark, himself a likely presidential nominee, put forth the party's program for the session.[19] The following day, Robert L. Henry of Texas, chairman designate of the rules committee, proposed a new set of rules fashioned by the Democrats. The new rules embodied one significant reform carried over from the Cannon fight—that committee members be elected by the House instead of appointed by the Speaker. Other rules changes were either insignificant or self-serving. And Henry moved that the motion to adopt the rules be subject to only a single blanket amendment and that debate be limited to four hours. Lenroot, Norris, Mann, Cannon, and other Republicans denounced the procedure as "gag rule." Lenroot

16. John M. Nelson, minutes, insurgent meetings, fragment, n.d., Box 16, John M. Nelson Papers; *Chicago Tribune,* 4 April 1911. Henry Rainey referred to the Democratic offer in debate with Lenroot. *CR* 62:1, 1911, vol. 47, pt. 2, p. 1289.

17. Clipping, *New York Herald,* 3 April 1911, Scrapbook 15, Mann Papers; *New York Times,* 4 April 1911.

18. *CR* 62:1, 1911, vol. 47, pt. 1, pp. 1, 6.

19. *New York Times,* 5 April 1911.

and Norris attacked the Democrats for relying on their caucus to decide all important questions, thus depriving members of their proper freedom.[20]

At the end of the week, the new minority leader held a series of formal and informal conferences with party members, including Lenroot, Cooper, Nelson, Madison, Good, and Gilbert Haugen of Iowa. "When the erstwhile insurgents left Mr. Mann's headquarters yesterday," a reporter observed, "they looked very much set up and spoke in the gentlest and kindest way of the new minority leader." On the other hand, after Cannon called to find out what was going on, he emerged "not so happy." That night, Mann announced that he would treat all Republicans alike, not punishing those who had stayed out of the caucus and had voted against him.[21] True to his word, Mann promptly named Lenroot and Madison to the rules committee, along with regulars John Dalzell and William Wilson, gave Norris the judiciary committee assignment he had for years cherished, and otherwise treated the insurgents well.[22]

Under the circumstances, Lenroot's course was clear, and it coincided with his inclinations. He would remain aloof from party caucuses, would advance a progressive legislative program, and would vote with the Democrats when the merits of the case warranted, regardless of the position Mann or the president might take. In that way, he would act constructively and independently, as he believed proper, and at the same time would help La Follette to maintain the vital distinction between the Republican factions. But he would join his party in criticizing the Democrats from a progressive standpoint, as on the continuing questions of caucus rule and "gag rule"; and he would work with Mann to the extent possible. Thus, he would steer the progressive insurrection toward capture of the Republican party rather than out of the party and would contribute to the weakening of the Democracy in exact proportion to its unworthiness.

Lenroot did not enjoy his second term in Congress nearly so well as his first. The special session proved typical of what lay ahead. During the special session Lenroot participated in all the major questions before Congress, and some of the minor ones, and helped to prepare legislation on important issues not up for immediate action. Yet as final adjournment approached he wrote in discouragement to Clara: "This whole session will go through with practically nothing accomplished." [23] By talent and inclination the constructive legislator, he could not act but only react during the Sixty-second Congress, with little chance to bring measurable improvement.

20. Clipping, *Chicago Inter Ocean*, 6 April 1911, Scrapbook 15, Mann Papers; Lowitt, *Norris*, vol. 1, p. 209; Paul DeWitt Hasbrouck, *Party Government in the House of Representatives*, pp. 11–13; *New York Times*, 6 April 1911; *CR* 62:1, 1911, vol. 47, pt. 1, p. 72.

21. Clippings, *Washington Herald*, 8 April 1911, *Chicago Inter Ocean*, 8 April 1911, Scrapbook 15, Mann Papers.

22. Alfred Lief, *Democracy's Norris: The Biography of a Lonely Crusader*, p. 116; clipping, *Chicago Tribune*, 12 April 1911, Scrapbook 15, Mann Papers; *CR* 62:1, 1911, vol. 47, pt. 1, pp. 161–62.

23. Irvine to Clara Lenroot, 10 August 1911, Box 1, Lenroot Papers.

The tariff and trust issues remained paramount. With respect to the first, President Taft still wanted Canadian reciprocity in a form that Lenroot found discriminatory against the American farmer, but with Democratic allies Taft had the votes. The Democrats, for their part, wanted to pass certain new duty-free tariff schedules separate from reciprocity, courting vetoes that would yield votes for themselves but nothing for the consumer.[24] Investigation of several trusts held out promise, and Lenroot gave time to resolutions of this sort and to the framing of an antitrust bill. But from the first day of the session, the Democrats made it clear that they would make all major decisions in caucus, so Lenroot, despite the fact of his place on the rules committee and his ability in all phases of the legislative process, could contribute less than he would have liked. Nor could he unify the polyglot and independent insurgents so that the Republican party would be more progressive. They divided on the great tariff questions, and when they came together it was usually under the party banner and to fight at the command of the adroit Mann against the aggressive Democrats. Despite all this, Lenroot did the best he could, trying to advance the public interest as he saw it and playing his part in the political game too.

Passage of reciprocity in the Democratic House was a foregone conclusion. But a liberal rule gave Lenroot opportunity to deliver a full-dress speech for which he began to prepare himself while home in March. He discovered in Superior very strong sentiment among businessmen in favor of the treaty, which gave him additional motive to make a strong speech that might be published for distribution in his district. Beyond these considerations, the simple merits of the question as Lenroot viewed it moved him to take a large role.[25]

Given an hour by Dalzell, and later an additional ten minutes, on Monday, 17 April, Lenroot stated his position. Republicans are protectionists, he said. Alluding to insurgent opposition to Payne-Aldrich rates, he explained that from the progressive Republican standpoint reductions were needed only on trust-made goods. For the rest, competition behind tariff barriers would provide ample consumer protection. Then, moving from defense to the offense, Lenroot called for a consistent policy, applicable to all. If protection was to be the national policy, it should include the farmer, but if there was to be free trade in farm products, then manufactured goods should also go unprotected. Lenroot contended that the cost of production of wheat, hay, oats, and flaxseed was higher in the United States than in Canada, due to the higher costs of land and labor and lower yields per acre.

Lenroot took dead aim at the major weakness in the Democrats' case. The party leaders had said they would take care of agriculture by reducing rates on the products farmers bought in separate legislation. But if they had the

24. Kenneth Hechler, *Insurgency: Personalities and Politics of the Taft Era*, pp. 188–91.
25. "Reciprocity with Canada, Speech of Irvine L. Lenroot of Wisconsin in House of Representatives, Monday, April 17, 1911," Box 8, Lenroot Papers; *Superior Telegram*, 18, 26 September 1911; Lenroot to Nellie Nichols, 23 April 1911, Irvine L. Lenroot Papers Addition.

farmer's interests at heart and were not just making political capital, why not introduce these reductions as amendments to the reciprocity bill? It would not endanger Canadian acceptance, he pointed out, since Canada would benefit. "Your hope," Lenroot said, "is that you can pass that free list bill through this House, and that it will be vetoed by President Taft," which was an accurate statement of the case.

There remained the question of the high cost of living, the prime economic complaint of the time. Reciprocity would not reduce it, Lenroot argued. "The people do not eat cattle upon the hoof, that are admitted free. They do eat beef, which will have a tariff of 1¼ cents a pound. The price of beef to the consumer will not be reduced." The only gainer would be the "Beef Trust," which would increase dividends on watered stock. And other products would also be affected, Lenroot claimed.[26]

Impervious to criticism, except the long-standing charge that they could not work together and could not govern, the House Democratic machine moved smoothly along on its predetermined course. Clark, the new Speaker, affable, agreeable, "grappled men to him with hooks of affection," according to a colleague, but attempted no dictatorship. A group of chairmen divided power among themselves, and the hard-headed John Fitzgerald of Brooklyn doubled as expert on finance and master parliamentarian. Unobtrusively, by virtue of commanding ability reinforced by his strategic position as floor leader and chairman of the committee-making committee of the House, ways and means, Oscar Underwood of Alabama provided overall direction. As the tariff measures of the day came from his committee, Underwood was able to push his party's program without hitch or embarrassment.[27]

With reciprocity passed on to the Senate, Underwood reported out his farmers' free list bill, to admit duty free about a hundred items that farmers bought but did not sell. Lenroot was committed to support the measure, on the basis of fair play, but first he joined in arguing for a broad interpretation of the rules, supported amendments to add additional items to the free list, and offered some such amendments himself. Though he lost on all counts, he voted for the bill, as did twenty-three other Republicans, mainly north-central progressives.[28]

26. *CR* 62:1, 1911, vol. 47, pt. 1, pp. 340–46.

27. James E. Watson, *As I Knew Them: Memoirs of James E. Watson*, p. 174; comments on Fitzgerald by Champ Clark, in *My Quarter Century of American Politics*, vol. 2, pp. 341–42. See also Medill McCormick to Sir Horace Plunkett, 13 September 1917, Hanna McCormick Family Papers, Joseph Medill McCormick Papers, Box 2, LC (hereafter cited as McCormick Papers). Underwood's role is noted in Geroge B. Galloway, *History of the House of Representatives*, p. 108; Charles R. Atkinson, "The Committee on Rules and the Overthrow of Speaker Cannon" (Ph.D. diss.), p. 129; DeAlva Stanwood Alexander, *History and Procedure of the House of Representatives*, pp. 133–35; and James S. Fleming, "Re-Establishing Leadership in the House of Representatives: The Case of Oscar W. Underwood," pp. 234–50.

28. *CR* 62:1, 1911, vol. 47, pt. 2, pp. 1089–90, 1099, 1115, 1121; Hechler, *Insurgency*, p. 188; clipping, *Chicago Inter Ocean*, 9 May 1911, Scrapbook 16, Mann Papers.

Lenroot was able to act somewhat more constructively on the trust question. On 4 May, he was named the minority member of a three-man subcommittee of the Committee on Rules to redraft a resolution calling for House investigation of antitrust violations by the "Sugar Trust," one of the more noxious and highly publicized of the trusts. Perhaps because of preoccupation with the tariff issue, the Democrats had not yet developed a detailed party program with respect to this sort of investigation, so the subcommittee came to agreement and the full committee reported the resolution for the sugar trust investigation unanimously. On the floor, Lenroot joined in defending and defining the resolution. He gave it the broadest possible construction so far as the power of the select committee to investigate prices and costs abroad was concerned.[29]

Before the House completed action on the sugar trust investigation, the Supreme Court on 15 May gave its long-awaited decision in the Standard Oil case. Though the Court formally sustained the government and ordered the dissolution of the trust, it permitted large constituent parts of Standard Oil to continue as before, as long as they acted separately from one another. The majority took the occasion to affirm the "rule of reason," that not all combinations in restraint of trade were illegal but only those that were unreasonable, or contrary to the public interest. To men like La Follette, who was present when the Court rendered its opinion, sinister implications were immediately apparent. Two weeks later, when the Court applied the test in holding that the American Tobacco Company, while in violation of the law, need only reorganize rather than dissolve, it confirmed earlier fears.[30]

In connection with his presidential candidacy, La Follette in March took the first steps toward development of a progressive economic program, to go with the political program of the National Progressive Republican League.[31] Solutions to the problems posed by bigness in business and by monopoly figured to be central in his program in any case. The Supreme Court's Standard Oil decision made it imperative, from the standpoint of the national welfare and of his own candidacy, that he proceed forcefully to develop and put forth a concrete antitrust proposal. The day after the Court's decision, La Follette wired a message to Louis Brandeis in Boston that he should come at once. On 18 May and again on the nineteenth, Brandeis, Lenroot, Pinchot, and a number of others discussed the possibilities of plugging the loopholes in the Sherman Anti-trust Act and at the same time updating it in the light of economic developments over the previous two decades. The group deputized Brandeis, Lenroot, and Francis Heney

29. Record Group 233, "Committee on Rules, Minutes," 62d Cong., 1st sess., 4 May 1911, National Archives (hereafter referred to as NA); *CR* 62:1, 1911, vol. 47, pt. 2, pp. 1146–47.

30. Alfred H. Kelly and Winfred A. Harbison, *The American Constitution: Its Origin and Development*, pp. 608–9; Belle and Fola La Follette, *La Follette*, vol. 1, p. 336.

31. Walter Weyl to La Follette, 22 March, 14 September 1911, Box 70, Series B, La Follette FC.

to draft legislation embodying their thought and the three attorneys set to work immediately. Very soon they put a draft in La Follette's hands. On 23 May, Brandeis and Lenroot each sent La Follette second-thought revisions, Brandeis's involving phraseology, mainly, but Lenroot's of a substantive nature. Lenroot proposed to make explicit the prohibition against accepting rebates from common carriers. Also, he was now more convinced than ever "that there should be a conclusive presumption of unreasonable restraint of trade whenever it is shown that more than a fixed percentage of the business of the country is controlled by a combination. . . ." He was aware that in some lines, 40 percent or even 50 percent of the market might reasonably be controlled by a single firm, but in such cases, he argued, the firm would be protected since before the section became applicable restraint of trade would have to be shown. Finally, he pointed out that the bill did not include a provision strengthening the penalty clause of the existing law, thus "making the punishment fine and imprisonment and fixing a minimum as well as a maximum." The House was taking a temporary adjournment that day, but he promised to think more about it while home and perhaps write again.[32]

Brandeis promptly revised the bill in light of Lenroot's first criticism but argued against the other two. Missing Lenroot's point somewhat, he asserted that to make "control of a certain percentage of the business conclusive of unreasonableness" was tempting but dangerous—it would work inequities in some cases and in others permit excessive control. As to the penalties, he agreed that imprisonment was the only effective remedy but feared that judges and prosecutors would balk, so the stronger penalty would result in fewer prosecutions and convictions. Though Brandeis submitted his criticisms to Lenroot as well as La Follette, Lenroot, at the time, was physically unable to work further on the legislation. Recognizing the need for speedy action, Lenroot urged La Follette to introduce the bill as it was. He promised to try to do more on the subject and soon submitted a rather technical question of construction. Probably Lenroot worked on it further and discussed it with La Follette in late July and early August. When the senator introduced it just before adjournment in August and the beginning of a critical political drive, the bill included the fixed penalties idea for which Lenroot had contended. Lenroot introduced the same bill in December with some refinements and in January, with the help of Brandeis, revised it again. Lenroot nevertheless regarded antitrust as something less than the whole solution to the problem of trusts and bigness. But he appreciated the importance of a strong antitrust law as one part of a larger program that would involve forceful regulation. And with progressives like Woodrow Wilson, among others, he saw the moral aspects of the question as fundamental and, therefore, consistently stressed the idea of judging and

32. Belle and Fola La Follette, *La Follette*, vol. 1, p. 337; Brandeis to Moses Clapp, 22 June 1911, enclosed in Brandeis to La Follette, 22 June 1911, Brandeis to La Follette, 23 May 1911, Box 66, Lenroot to La Follette, 23 May 1911, Box 68, Series B, La Follette FC.

punishing the wealthy wrongdoer by the same standards and in the same fashion as the "common criminal." [33]

When Lenroot returned to Washington in July, the House had not resumed real activity. In any case, the prospect for constructive action was dim, and Lenroot proposed to undertake only one major piece of legislative work, a speech on the Democratic tariff reduction bill on cotton goods. At the La Follette home in the evenings, he occupied himself with the wool and woolens bill and speeches the senator wanted to give. Also, he became involved in political conferences.[34] La Follette's other friends were optimistic and sometimes ebullient, particularly after the senator, working with Underwood, secured adoption of a bill lowering wool schedules, a piece of constructive legislation that belied the charge that La Follette was wholly destructive. But for reasons unstated, Lenroot was by this time deeply skeptical of La Follette's presidential prospects.[35]

Some of his reasons for being pessimistic and sorry about the whole situation are apparent. Even after La Follette's coup on the woolens bill, such good friends of La Follette as Sen. Joseph Bristow and William E. Chandler held out little hope. Progressives explained Taft's advantage as resulting from control of the party machinery, but Chandler further noted that the program of the National Progressive Republican League, still the front for La Follette, lacked appeal in the east, even among reformers. La Follette remained suspect among easterners, whose attitude was reinforced by his vocal opposition to reciprocity.[36]

La Follette had some time to overcome the widespread suspicion of him, but in this pre-radio, pre-television era, and in the face of a generally hostile press, La Follette could not hope to personally reach more than a fraction of the voting public, even with the most intensive speaking campaign. He would need an elaborate national organization to systematically and repeatedly reach the voters with literature and speeches. But, in many states he had only a few dependable contacts, and in some states none at all. Even

33. Brandeis to La Follette, 26 May 1911, Box 66, Lenroot to La Follette, 10, 28 June 1911, Box 68, Series B, La Follette FC; Belle and Fola La Follette, *La Follette,* vol. 1, p. 245; "Hearings before Senate Committee on Interstate Commerce, 1911. Control of Corporations, Report and Hearings, 1911–1913," vol. 1, p. 1146, La Follette Papers; "House Hearings of the Judiciary Committee on Trust Legislation, 1912," Serial No. 1, pp. 104–5, 129–30, typewritten copies submitted by Fola La Follette to Irvine L. Lenroot, 2 April 1938, and marked "correct, I. L. L.," Box 73, Series E, Lenroot to La Follette, 1 November 1911, Box 68, Series B, La Follette FC.

34. Irvine to Clara Lenroot, 23, 25, 27, 29, 30 July, 2 August 1911, Box 1, Lenroot Papers.

35. Irvine to Clara Lenroot, 22 July 1911, Box 1, Lenroot Papers; Hechler, *Insurgency,* p. 185; Ray Stannard Baker notebooks, 27 July 1911, Box 122, Series 2, Ray Stannard Baker Papers, LC; Amos Pinchot to James W. Pinchot, 31 July 1911, Box 9, Amos Pinchot Papers, LC; Irvine to Clara Lenroot, 29, 30 July 1911, Box 1, Lenroot Papers.

36. James Holt, *Congressional Insurgents and the Party System, 1909–1916,* pp. 50–51; William E. Chandler, memorandum, 1 August 1911, enclosed in Chandler to La Follette, 31 July 1911, vol. 161, William E. Chandler Papers; Mowry, *The Progressive Movement,* p. 181.

if the existing nucleus of support had been stronger, the overriding need would have been the same—for money in large amounts. The sums contributed and pledged were hopelessly inadequate to the task.

Two weeks at his new summer cottage on the Brule River, east of Superior, restored Lenroot in body and spirit. While probably still not sanguine about La Follette's prospects, he drew encouragement from signs of fundamental progress in American society. "A few years ago politics were conducted upon a low plane of place and profit. Today nearly every political question is also a moral question, and is so being fought out," he told a church group. The people, Lenroot felt, were awakening as from a long sleep and were coming to use their God-given powers of reason to discern and advance the common good.[37]

Through the late summer and fall of 1911, Walter Houser, in behalf of La Follette at Washington headquarters, sent out copy to supportive newspapers, gave interviews to capital writers, and corresponded with leaders around the nation. John Hannan was much in evidence too, and Medill McCormick kept "flitting about." McCormick's involvement reflected the fact that Roosevelt remained on the sidelines, while La Follette persisted in a strategy of calculated ambiguity. As a member of the family that owned the *Chicago Tribune*, McCormick had been for a time editor and publisher of that paper. Encouraged by his able and energetic suffragette wife Ruth, the daughter of Mark Hanna, McCormick now gave his own considerable energy and talent to reform politics. Though sincerely favorable to La Follette, McCormick continued to admire Roosevelt above all men.[38]

Houser and the others remained and operated in the background of the National Progressive Republican League, and Houser told newsmen that the league was "not in favor of Senator La Follette personally but was designed to bring about the nomination of a progressive republican on the national ticket next year." The league would "control the republican national convention and defeat Taft's efforts for renomination." In Madison, *La Follette's Weekly Magazine* expressed a similar view.[39]

The common-front strategy was very satisfactory to Lenroot, for in addition to being La Follette's only chance for success, it left the door open for unification behind Roosevelt or some other progressive should La Follette's candidacy flounder.

It was with these understandings that Lenroot resumed activity for La Follette early in September, as speaker, organizer, and alter ego for the

37. MS speech, "Pilgrim Church," n.d. (29 September 1911), Box 10, Lenroot Papers; *Superior Telegram,* 28, 30 September 1911.

38. Medill McCormick to James W. Morisson, 30 November 1923, Box 6, McCormick Papers.

39. *Wisconsin State Journal,* 4 September 1911; *La Follette's Weekly Magazine* 3:36 (9 September 1911):15. Officially, Houser was chairman of the Progressive Republican Campaign Committee. The *Wisconsin State Journal* had become an ardent supporter of La Follette, under the editorship of Richard Lloyd Jones.

senator at Midwestern political conferences, while La Follette remained in Washington to complete his autobiography.[40] Wherever he spoke, Lenroot "treated Roosevelt as a Progressive . . . ."[41]

At a two-day Chicago conference in mid-October, Lenroot was one of many speakers. He played a more important role behind-the-scenes. Public and private attention focused on James R. Garfield. More than even Gifford Pinchot, who was not present in any case because of an Alaska trip, Garfield, Roosevelt's friend and secretary of interior, was the spokesman for Roosevelt, whom he had visited the week before. Lenroot, with Houser and Senator Clapp, represented La Follette in prolonged discussions with Garfield about the wisdom of the conference, flatly endorsing La Follette for president. Also, Lenroot worked with Garfield in making the final revisions of the resolutions.[42]

Garfield, backed by some others, argued against any endorsement and was in favor of a favorite-son strategy. Lenroot, Houser, and Clapp resisted, and Garfield finally yielded somewhat but with the understanding that the endorsement was only a recommendation, not a pledge. Garfield was more successful with respect to resolutions, and on this subject he had Lenroot's full support. In addition to commending presidential primaries, the gathering resolved for "affirmative legislative enactment" to give "great business enterprises" definite rules of conduct and to end the "present state of uncertainty. . . . It is worse than idle," the resolution said, "to leave the question of whether great business enterprises are legal or not merely to judicial determination. . . . We seek constructive legislation and not destructive litigation." Afterwards, Lenroot urged this Rooseveltian approach on La Follette, as a supplement to their antitrust bill.[43]

Lenroot's ideas were not offensive to La Follette, whatever fault he may have found in friendly references to Garfield and Roosevelt. La Follette was aware of the need for elaboration of his economic program with respect to big business. But of more pressing concern to him in early December, when Lenroot came back to Washington, was Roosevelt.

Hearing the encouraging reports, but uninformed or deaf to discouraging news, La Follette judged in late October that he could win the nomination if Roosevelt "didn't mess things up." He attributed the burgeoning Roose-

40. *Wisconsin State Journal,* 15 September 1911.

41. Lenroot to Gilbert Roe, 26 February 1912, Box 4, Series H, La Follette FC.

42. *Chicago Tribune,* 16, 17 October 1911; *Wisconsin State Journal,* 12, 16, 17 October 1911; Belle and Fola La Follette, *La Follette,* vol. 1, pp. 353–54; John Hannan to La Follette, 16 October 1911, Box 106, Series B, La Follette FC; Garfield to Theodore Roosevelt, 17 October 1911, Box 117, James R. Garfield Papers, LC; *New York Times,* 17 October 1911.

43. Garfield to Amos Pinchot, 28 September 1911, Box 117, to Gaillard Hunt, 20 October 1911, Box 115, to "Dear Mama," 22 October 1911, Box 30, Garfield Papers; Jack T. Thompson, "James R. Garfield: the Career of a Rooseveltian Progressive, 1895–1915" (Ph.D. diss.), p. 225; Garfield to Roosevelt, 17 October 1911, Box 117, to La Follette, 18 October 1911, Box 116, Garfield Papers; *La Follette's Weekly Magazine* 3:44 (28 October 1911):6–7; Lenroot to La Follette, 1 November 1911, Box 68, Series B, La Follette FC.

velt sentiment to the machinations of the Old Guard, scurrying from Taft's sinking ship.[44] In this last feeling he was partly correct, but he ignored the basic political reality of the Roosevelt boom, which was the confidence of the public in Roosevelt. Whatever the source, the Roosevelt movement had to be conjured with, especially after Ray Stannard Baker wrote from New York that he had seen Roosevelt and was now convinced that "if the demand is loud and long enough, and if the prospects seem right, that he will certainly jump into the game. He thinks Taft's prospects are gone, he evidently thinks you cannot command enough strength to be nominated— therefore—!" La Follette was confirmed in his suspicions and saw himself being used as a stalking-horse. Repelled by the role, he authorized Houser to call a conference to consider the idea of writing Roosevelt the letter that had been contemplated for several weeks.[45]

On 11 December, La Follette met at his home with Clapp, Lenroot, Kent, Crane, Brandeis, Houser, McCormick, Gilson Gardner, and the Pinchot brothers. The idea of a letter to Roosevelt met with general favor, and La Follette, though uncertain about it, authorized preparation of several drafts. He asked Lenroot to prepare one, probably the one presented as La Follette's own when the group met again at the Pinchot home the following morning. The letter would have told Roosevelt that unless he positively refused to permit use of his name, La Follette would withdraw; if Roosevelt were willing to take the nomination if tendered, La Follette would help him, the organization would be maintained, and the work would go on, for Roosevelt. The group conferred late into the afternoon. Finally, La Follette, mistrusting Roosevelt and acting on advice from Gilbert Roe, declined to send any letter. After the meeting, as Lenroot and La Follette walked home, La Follette expressed himself more fully against Roosevelt as reason for not risking the contingent pledge that he would have to make to force a declaration from Roosevelt. Lenroot argued that the risk was worth taking, not because Roosevelt would surely offer the statement hoped for, but on the grounds that " 'if Roosevelt should become President, he would not betray the Progressive cause.' " [46]

That evening Gifford Pinchot called on La Follette to say that after the meeting he, Gardner, and McCormick had conferred and decided to notify him that should a break occur between La Follette and Roosevelt, they would have to side with Roosevelt. Though Pinchot reiterated his judgment that Roosevelt was not a candidate and expressed his hope that Roosevelt

44. Belle and Fola La Follette, *La Follette*, vol. 1, pp. 356–59.

45. Ibid., pp. 363–65.

46. Amos Pinchot, *The History of the Progressive Party, 1912–1916*, p. 131; Belle and Fola La Follette, *La Follette*, vol. 1, p. 365; Lenroot to La Follette, 27 February 1912, Box 3, "Proposed letter from La Follette to Roosevelt, Dec. 1911 . . .," Box 5, Lenroot, "Memoirs," pp. 85–86, Box 13, Lenroot Papers; press release, "Given in Calif., May 7, 1912," (by Gifford Pinchot), Box 1947, Pinchot Papers; Amos Pinchot to Hiram Johnson, 30 March 1912, Box 11, Amos Pinchot Papers; Lenroot to Fola La Follette, 30 April 1938, cited in Belle and Fola La Follette, *La Follette*, vol. 1, p. 365.

would eventually support La Follette, the event served only to fortify La Follette in his developing suspicion of the Rooseveltians in his own ranks and of Roosevelt himself.[47]

Each new day brought La Follette some new evidence of conspiracy. La Follette had been willing enough to play up to Roosevelt so long as there was a good prospect of securing his support or at the least unifying the Rooseveltians behind himself. Now, however, the situation seemed to have reversed itself—La Follette thought that Roosevelt and his friends were trying to maintain a common front with La Follette in order to advance Roosevelt. Thus, when Gifford Pinchot, after conferring with Roosevelt, phoned to urge that Houser and Lenroot come to New York to meet Roosevelt, Gardner, and himself at the home of Amos Pinchot, La Follette refused to let his manager Houser go, in order to avoid giving the public the impression he was working with Roosevelt. Instead, he asked "Billy" Kent, who shared his opinion of Roosevelt, to accompany Lenroot, and he wired Houser, who was in Boston, warning him not to attend.[48]

Over luncheon that Sunday, Roosevelt charmed his guests with stories of his recent trip. Afterwards, during a prolonged but pleasant discussion, Roosevelt stated his position. He was keenly disappointed with Taft and hoped he could be beaten for renomination. He was not himself a candidate but would not publicly declare that in case he should become one. For if it developed that La Follette could not win and he could, he might feel obligated to run. He urged that La Follette go ahead with his campaign, but that if some states preferred to elect Roosevelt delegates there would be no friction, for only by progressive unity could Taft be beaten. Lenroot brought to Roosevelt's attention the danger that both he and La Follette would be listed in the North Dakota primaries. But Roosevelt said probably an agreement could be reached for delegates to be for him as second choice.[49] Lenroot and Kent obviously approved, for Pinchot recorded in his diary that night that nothing spectacular had occurred, but there was agreement that the La Follette men should "keep in close touch" with Roosevelt, and harmony should be maintained. A week later Pinchot, alluding to the 1 January progressive convention in Ohio, wrote Garfield that the 17 December conference had resulted admirably and there was no longer a danger "that the progressives will get their wires crossed, however the result at the convention may come out." [50]

47. Belle and Fola La Follette, *La Follette*, vol. 1, p. 366; La Follette, *Autobiography*, pp. 231–33; "1911: A Chronology of La Follette Candidacy . . .," Box 1947, Pinchot Papers.

48. Belle and Fola La Follette, *La Follette*, vol. 1, pp. 367–68; La Follette to Lenroot, 1 March 1912, Box 3, Lenroot Papers.

49. Lenroot, "Memoirs," pp. 77–79, Box 13, La Follette to Lenroot, 1 March 1912, Box 3, Lenroot Papers. Roosevelt gave a similar account in a letter to Frank Munsey designed for public use. *Wisconsin State Journal*, 6 March 1912.

50. M. Nelson McGeary, *Gifford Pinchot: Forester-Politician*, p. 219; Pinchot to Garfield, 27 December 1911 (dictated 24 December), Box 117, Garfield Papers.

Following their afternoon with Roosevelt, Lenroot, Kent, and Gardner returned to Washington to report to La Follette. They expressed their pleasure over the conference and all three seemed to La Follette "elated" at Roosevelt's response regarding North Dakota. La Follette, in turn, said he was pleased when told that Roosevelt wanted no conflict between progressives, but he also rejected the idea of further conferences to avoid involvement with Roosevelt in any way. After Kent and Gardner left, Lenroot said more. He judged that Roosevelt wanted to be a candidate, if only he could be sure of winning not only the nomination but also the election. But Lenroot argued that it was to La Follette's interest to work in harmony with Roosevelt; he would get enough delegates to hold the balance of power at the national convention, and eventually Roosevelt would throw his support to La Follette in order to defeat Taft. More than that, however, and surely even less pleasing to La Follette, Lenroot reminded his friend that "the most important matter was to defeat Taft and that we should not lose sight of that fact." [51]

A day or two after that meeting, Lenroot gave La Follette suggestions for the stock campaign speech that La Follette, after much costly delay, would finally begin to deliver, starting on 27 December. Lenroot urged La Follette to stress his moderateness—that he would help honest business, whether large or small. He still saw the trust question as the main one and emphasized regulation, even to the extent of price control, as a necessary supplement to antitrust.[52]

La Follette did give prime attention to the trust question. However, he attacked price regulation (which he noted had been suggested by the pro-Roosevelt president of U.S. Steel), but favored a commission to investigate and act against unfair competition and to supervise such "reasonable restraint of trade" as was needed against "the abuses of excessive or cutthroat competition." [53] The influence of Brandeis was more apparent than that of Lenroot.

Before La Follette's trip, which would start in Ohio, Lenroot pressed on La Follette his view that Roosevelt was a dependable progressive and that progressive unity was essential. He urged acceptance of Garfield's plan for Ohio, to oppose Taft with an uninstructed delegate slate. La Follette disagreed on all counts. Beyond that, the physically and mentally strained senator, who was at the time dismayed, bewildered, and suspicious because of the turn of events, undoubtedly found distasteful such advice from his own adviser. As others argued with him for the Garfield strategy and quoted

51. La Follette, *Autobiography,* pp. 235–37; Lenroot to La Follette, 27 February 1912, La Follette to Lenroot, 1 March 1912, Box 3, Lenroot, "Memoirs," p. 79, Box 13, Lenroot Papers.

52. "Suggestions for La Follette's Speech," n.d. (December 1911), Box 5, Lenroot Papers. Lenroot referred to a Tariff Board report that would be forthcoming in a few days. The Board reported to Taft on 20 December. *Wisconsin State Journal,* 20 December 1911.

53. *Wisconsin State Journal,* 27 December 1911.

Lenroot as favoring it, his displeasure grew, the more so, perhaps, for the fact that he could not readily vent it.[54]

Lenroot dealt with La Follette on this important question as he habitually dealt with all men. He imputed the highest of motives to La Follette and spoke his own mind frankly. This method had usually achieved for Lenroot more than any other approach could have. Now it proved hopelessly wrong. Nor did it make much difference that, as Lenroot later protested, he acted for La Follette only when asked by the senator, and in strategy conferences with La Follette supporters he always insisted that the senator's wishes be followed, even when he disagreed with La Follette.[55]

It is not clear whether or not Lenroot sensed a change in La Follette's attitude toward him in December. In January, though, after La Follette experienced what he construed as betrayal in Ohio, Michigan, and his own Washington headquarters, Lenroot found him disinclined to discuss politics and felt himself under suspicion.[56]

La Follette's health became an important, though intricate, factor in the political situation and in his relations with Lenroot. La Follette worked hard and steadily through the summer and fall. As his campaign lagged, and money troubles persisted, the psychological pressure on him mounted.[57] By 26 December, on the eve of his brief campaign trip, Houser told the Pinchots, Kent, and McCormick that La Follette should withdraw while he still had some strength and before his reputation was damaged but thought him so worn out mentally and physically that it would be hard to get him to do the right thing.[58] La Follette returned from his trip very tired, but a few days later Belle thought that he had snapped back nicely. However, in retrospect Fola noted that "without any vacation or rest he took up his work again." [59] In late February, looking back on the previous two months, La Follette commented on the strain he had been under. According to him, it was not so much the work that cost him sleep and caused anxiety, "as the heartbreaking struggle with certain professed friends." [60]

Lenroot was consistently solicitous for La Follette's health; for a year he

54. Lenroot to La Follette, 27 February 1912, La Follette to Lenroot, 1 March 1912, Box 3, Lenroot Papers. La Follette's physical condition was talked of by Houser at a 26 December meeting of progressive leaders. Amos Pinchot to Hiram Johnson, 30 March 1912, Box 11, Amos Pinchot Papers.

55. Lenroot to La Follette, 27 February 1912, Box 3, Lenroot Papers.

56. Martin L. Fausold, *Gifford Pinchot: Bull Moose Progressive*, pp. 72–73; clipping, *Columbus Citizen*, 1 January 1912, Box 1947, Pinchot Papers; Belle and Fola La Follette, *La Follette*, vol. 1, pp. 378–83; La Follette, *Autobiography*, pp. 237–38; Lenroot to Herman L. Ekern, 27 February 1912, Box 2, Lenroot Papers; to Gilbert Roe, 26 February 1912, Box 4, Series H, La Follette FC.

57. La Follette to A. T. Rogers, 13 February 1912, Box 107, Series B, La Follette FC.

58. Amos Pinchot to Hiram Johnson, 30 March 1912, Box 11, Amos Pinchot Papers.

59. Belle and Fola La Follette, *La Follette*, vol. 1, p. 381.

60. La Follette to E. Clarence Jones, 19 February 1912, to Charles A. Lindbergh, 20 February 1912, Box 107, Series B, La Follette FC; Belle and Fola La Follette, *La Follette*, vol. 1, p. 394.

and others had urged the senator to ease up. Now in January, foreseeing the impending breakdown, Lenroot intensified his pleas. Mounting evidence that Roosevelt would take up La Follette's standard figured logically, if tacitly, in Lenroot's argument, and he did not conceal his continuing faith in Roosevelt. But while La Follette could still distinguish between Lenroot on the one hand and those who gave first allegiance to Roosevelt on the other, all such arguments seemed only to serve Roosevelt's game. And the condition of his nerves made him unable to view the situation objectively.[61]

With La Follette still weak and the Roosevelt movement blooming, Gifford Pinchot and Houser, especially, felt the need to bring La Follette to some sort of accommodation with Roosevelt. When a dinner with La Follette on 14 January was unsuccessful, Pinchot called a meeting of La Follette and his aides and contributors for 19 January. It also failed. Lenroot spoke for cooperation with the Rooseveltians in the delegate contest, but La Follette refused. Since Charles Crane, the major contributor, had not been present, and the Roosevelt movement was moving on inexorably, the Pinchot brothers, abetted by Houser and others, called another meeting of contributors for 28 January, which was unknown to La Follette.[62]

On Sunday morning of 28 January, Lenroot went to the conference of contributors, expecting to attend another meeting that night and again the next morning. Clara, writing of it to Katharine, judged the meetings of such importance that she dare not say more in a letter.[63] Nothing decisive happened that day, except perhaps that the Rooseveltians, led by Gifford Pinchot, prepared the ground for a showdown the following day. For some reason, the conferees did not gather on 29 January until early afternoon, by which time the House was in session. Lenroot could not get to La Follette headquarters until almost five, despite frequent phone calls, as he had to remain at the Capitol for completion of three critical roll-call votes. By the time he reached the meeting, the majority had agreed to suggest to La Follette two alternatives—that he withdraw in favor of Roosevelt "with reservations as to differences of opinion, and continue to stump" or that he withdraw "but not in favor of anybody, leaving the individuals of the group to take what course they choose." [64] Though Lenroot had little time to participate in the discussion, he almost certainly favored the idea and may have helped to formulate the alternatives the day before.

61. *Wisconsin State Journal,* 7, 18 February 1912, reporting on arguments put to La Follette by Lenroot and others and on a letter from Lenroot to a Madisonian. Lenroot, "Memoirs," p. 83, Box 13, Lenroot Papers.

62. McGeary, *Gifford Pinchot,* pp. 219–20; La Follette, *Autobiography,* p. 252; Leo Joseph Bocage, "The Public Career of Charles R. Crane" (Ph.D. diss.), pp. 84–85; Belle and Fola La Follette, *La Follette,* vol. 1, p. 391. Bocage puts the date as 28 January; other secondary sources at the twenty-ninth. Bocage is correct, though as it turned out the main meeting occurred on the twenty-ninth.

63. Clara to Katharine Lenroot, 28 January 1912, Lenroot Papers Addition.

64. Lenroot to La Follette, 27 February 1912, Box 3, Lenroot Papers; *CR* 62:2, 1911, vol. 47, pt. 2, pp. 1485–1509; La Follette, *Autobiography,* pp. 254–55.

La Follette came to the conference minutes after Lenroot but remained in the outer room so as not to inhibit discussion. Shortly before five, La Follette was called to the phone and asked to comment on a story in the *Chicago Daily News* that a conference was preparing his statement of withdrawal. La Follette immediately called Houser out of the conference room and drafted a statement for him to issue, denying the report and declaring that he would remain a candidate "until the gavel falls in the convention announcing the nominee." He would campaign in every state for delegates pledged to his principles and candidacy "first, last, and all the time." He then called out Crane, Crane's secretary Walter Rogers, and his friend Charles Merriam, and submitted the statement for their approval. Crane, whose promise of $5,000 a month until the convention made him the key man, looked over the statement, handed it back to Houser, and said quietly, "I think that statement is all right." Thus, with their support, La Follette went with the others into the conference room where he forced the issue with Gifford Pinchot, who then left with his unhappy brother, Gardner, and McCormick.[65]

Disputing Gifford Pinchot's later contention that most of those present favored his withdrawal, the senator noted in a supplement to his autobiographical series that after the Pinchots, Gardner, and McCormick departed, Lenroot, Kent, Crane, Merriam "and all of the others" (Brandeis, Angus McSween of the *Philadelphia North American,* Heney, Hannan, and Houser) promised him that they would support him to the end. Both Pinchot and La Follette were correct. The other members of the conference, besides those who apparently were unsupportive of La Follette, generally favored La Follette's withdrawal but, along with Lenroot, agreed to abide by his decision, thus promising to stay with him.[66]

Though La Follette later found it useful to include Lenroot among the loyalists, at the time he thought less kindly of him—as favoring combination with Roosevelt and as one of those who on 29 January asked him to withdraw. La Follette was unaware that Lenroot had arrived late at the conference and remembered that Lenroot had been promoting coalition and thus, as he now viewed things, had been undermining his cause.[67] La Follette realized that Lenroot felt obligated to accept La Follette's judgment regarding the presidency even though it conflicted with his own. And La Follette was glad to have Lenroot's continued support, if for no other reason than that a break with his first lieutenant would look bad. But his confidence in and patience with Lenroot lessened as of 29 January.

65. La Follette, *Autobiography,* pp. 255–56.
66. Ibid., p. 256; statement by Walter Houser, no title, n.d. (ca. 5 April 1912), Box 71, Series B, La Follette FC; Amos Pinchot, *History of the Progressive Party,* p. 134; McGeary, *Gifford Pinchot,* p. 222; Belle and Fola La Follette, *La Follette,* vol. 1, p. 398.
67. La Follette to Lenroot, 26 February 1912, Lenroot to La Follette, 27 February 1912, Box 3, Lenroot Papers.

Perhaps Lenroot would now have reduced his role in the La Follette campaign if he could have. But on 1 February, the executive committee of La Follette's Wisconsin presidential organization met and ratified a decision that Lenroot had reluctantly agreed to earlier on La Follette's insistence—that he be one of the candidates for delegate at large to the national convention and head the delegation.[68] In any case, loyalty to La Follette and the progressive cause, and the personal need to reconcile the two, impelled him to remain active. There was another motive, too. Though Lenroot felt La Follette's increasing coolness, yet he knew that under the circumstances he more than any other might move his friend toward a less destructive course. Houser and Hannan could not, Roe and Belle would not.[69]

On 2 February, Lenroot saw the situation worsen. The occasion was an important banquet sponsored by the Periodical Publishers Association and attended by six hundred distinguished people—publishers, writers, newsmen, and politicians chiefly. Lenroot went to Philadelphia to hear La Follette, who with Gov. Woodrow Wilson of New Jersey was the principal speaker. Arriving late, Lenroot phoned La Follette's room but was told that he was resting, so he did not see La Follette until he appeared late in the evening, at the end of Wilson's graceful address. Accounts differ as to what happened and why, except that all agree La Follette performed disastrously and seemed to be the victim of a breakdown. According to Lenroot's later account, with the first few sentences he knew "something was wrong. La Follette at once took a very belligerent tone and at times his voice rose almost to a shriek. He had a prepared manuscript before him and at one point he mislaid the sheets. Without appearing to realize it he repeated about three pages of the speech." La Follette droned on and lost the attention of his audience, and Lenroot told publisher S. S. McClure, publisher-Congressman James Cox, and others at his table and adjoining ones that this was not the real La Follette. He explained that Mary La Follette's throat operation (actually scheduled for the following day but put at that day by Lenroot in his "Memoirs") had unnerved the senator. To Cox, Lenroot was "the most brokenhearted man I ever saw." La Follette continued until nearly one o'clock, when the audience began mock applause at the end of nearly every sentence. Finally, La Follette put down his offensive manuscript (which the newspaper editors, guests of the publishers, took to be a belligerent indictment of them) and said that if they would stop their clapping, he would stop speaking, but he would not stop until they did. "Inside of a few seconds one could have heard a pin drop in that large room. La Follette

68. Herman L. Ekern to Robert La Follette, 1 February 1912, Box 105, Series J, La Follette FC; MS, speech for La Follette presidential delegates, no title, n.d. (March 1912), Box 5, Lenroot, "Memoirs," p. 84, Box 13, Lenroot Papers.

69. Roe shared La Follette's outlook. See for instance Norman Hapgood to Roe, 2 January 1912, Box 4, Series H, La Follette FC; Belle's attitude was obvious especially after 2 February, after her husband suffered a physical breakdown.

gathered up his sheets of manuscript and left the room without another word. The dinner then adjourned," after some harsh closing words by the master of ceremonies, Don Seitz.[70]

Lenroot rushed to La Follette's hotel room. Hannan met him at the door and said La Follette was sick in the bathroom and that Lenroot had better not see him. He explained that La Follette "had counted on beginning his speech about ten-thirty, that he had had no dinner and wouldn't eat anything; that about ten o'clock he began drinking whiskey to brace him up for his speech; that this coming on an hour later than he expected he continued drinking until, when finally called on he had had seven or eight drinks, all on an empty stomach." Fola La Follette uncovered no such sequence of drinks, but only one, and attributed his poor performance to fatigue and acute indigestion, along with a number of more or less accidental circumstances.[71]

Later, La Follette sought to minimize the matter, but at the time and immediately afterwards he took it very seriously, as did all who had heard him or had read of it. Lenroot left Philadelphia for Washington at about two-thirty and the following morning, on his way to the Capitol, stopped at La Follette's to see how he was. Nellie Dunn told Lenroot the senator was sleeping. She was unaware of what had happened except that it was something terrible, for that morning she had heard a groaning in the drawing room, rushed in, and found La Follette moaning. Asked what was the matter, he had said, "Oh! I am ruined, I am ruined." She pressed him for particulars and, as Lenroot recalled her account, La Follette replied, "I can't tell you, ask Uncle Irvine, he will tell you." La Follette recovered sufficiently to compose a form letter of explanation in answer to those who might write in sympathy. To John S. Phillips, publisher of the *American,* he wrote, "It took nerve to greet me as you did Friday night—or rather Saturday morning. While sorry you were there, I appreciate your coming up under the circumstances." [72]

La Follette spent that day and part of the next at the hospital where Mary underwent surgery. Then, having canceled his speaking engagements, he began to get some of the rest that he and Belle now realized he needed so badly. Politics would not wait, and with La Follette apparently inaccessible Lenroot, Houser, Hannan, Clapp, Bourne, Bristow, and a few others held a series of conferences to decide what to do and what to tell the newspapers. All the conferees agreed that La Follette must withdraw. The only question

70. Lenroot, "Memoirs," p. 81, Box 13, Lenroot Papers; James M. Cox, *Journey Through My Years,* p. 65; Belle and Fola La Follette, *La Follette,* vol. 1, pp. 398–405.

71. Lenroot, "Memoirs," pp. 81–82, Box 13, Lenroot Papers; Belle and Fola La Follette, *La Follette,* vol. 1, p. 401. George Middleton, Fola's husband, later recalled Lenroot already being in the room when La Follette arrived. Belle and Fola La Follette, *La Follette,* vol. 1, p. 404.

72. Lenroot, "Memoirs," p. 82, Box 13, Lenroot Papers; draft letter, n.d., La Follette to John S. Phillips, 4 February 1912, Box 107, Series B, La Follette FC.

was as to how—how to word the statement; how far to go toward suggesting Roosevelt as an alternative; whether to act for La Follette in the emergency; or secure his consent; and if the latter, how to approach him. Finally a lengthy statement of withdrawal was prepared for submission to La Follette. Soon after, La Follette himself appeared at the headquarters. He was shown the statement and, as Lenroot recalled it, was willing to sign but wanted Belle to agree to it first. Either La Follette himself or the conferees asked Lenroot, Houser, and Hannan to see Belle with the statement.[73]

Lenroot was the one to present the unpleasant matter to Belle. Backed by Houser and Hannan, he argued that La Follette had not been well for some time, that he had been working slowly and accomplishing little. He may or may not have added that La Follette looked far from well and was nervous and irritable. Then he handed her the statement announcing that due to the need for a long rest shielded from strain, La Follette was withdrawing from the race, unless Wisconsin wished to name him. Belle, furious before she even looked at the statement, now read it and handed it back to Lenroot. Protective of La Follette, she declared, " 'Irvine, I would rather see Bob in his coffin than have him sign that paper.' " With that she walked from the room, leaving the three men to find their own way out.[74]

The following day, Belle told part of the story in a letter to Roe. She presumed from all that had been said that La Follette must have made a very bad impression in Philadelphia. Yet "the way Hannan & Lenroot and Houser have been willing to make a funeral of it, rouses my ire." They bemoaned his slowness and the like, she said, and of the three Lenroot "is particularly aggravating along this line." The statement they had submitted would have given the country the impression that La Follette "was a wreck for all time." In this crisis, she felt, "it is you and Alf who are needed here or men like you—if there are any." [75]

In effect, Belle encouraged La Follette to revert to the simplistic treachery explanation that he had been developing. That night he drafted a statement and required Houser to issue it, saying that he would take a few weeks rest but would not retire from the campaign, that he would make an aggressive contest for the nomination and for a strong platform. At the same time, he offered a sort of local option to supporters in states in which he could not campaign and whose primaries were coming up soon. Actually, the statement was rather equivocal and subject to several constructions. But to Roe

73. Belle and Fola La Follette, *La Follette*, vol. 1, pp. 404, 410–18; *Wisconsin State Journal*, 5, 7 February, 30 April 1912; Lenroot, "Memoirs," p. 83, Box 13, Lenroot Papers. Lenroot's account in his "Memoirs" confuses the 29 January and 5 February conferences; however, Hannan's recollection substantiates portions of the above.

74. Belle La Follette to Gilbert Roe, 6 February 1912, cited in Belle and Fola La Follette, *La Follette*, vol. 1, pp. 411–12; Lenroot, "Memoirs," p. 83, Box 13, A. M. Brayton to Lenroot, 10 January 1944, Lenroot to Brayton, 24 January 1944, Box 1, Lenroot Papers. See also Nils P. Haugen to J. M. Winterbotham, 20 May 1929, Box 64, Nils P. Haugen Papers.

75. Belle La Follette to Gilbert Roe, 6 February 1912, cited in Belle and Fola La Follette, *La Follette*, vol. 1, pp. 411–12.

and to his sister, La Follette made it clear that he was in the race to stay and would make no deals with Roosevelt.[76]

Lenroot would not accommodate in silence to La Follette's rapidly hardening attitude. La Follette remained nervous and edgy, was more hostile than ever toward Roosevelt and Gifford Pinchot, and showed no willingness to listen patiently to Lenroot's counsel of cooperation—it was no easy thing to cross him. But the obstacles in his way made it imperative that Lenroot persist. In his view, to remain passive in this situation would be a great disservice to the progressive movement. Furthermore, if La Follette continued in the direction he was headed, Lenroot would find himself in an intolerable situation—forced to either break with La Follette, more or less openly, or to abandon his own convictions and separate himself from the mainstream of the progressive movement. He had to speak up.

A seeming breach of relations resulted. It is not clear precisely how or when it occurred. Almost certainly, it was within the period between 13 and 15 February. Lenroot and La Follette quarreled over Roosevelt; Lenroot protesting La Follette's intimations that he would attack Roosevelt from the stump. Lenroot may also have taken up Pinchot's cause, either before or on 15 January, when La Follette had Pinchot turned away from his house and then informed that he would have no contact with him through the remainder of the campaign.[77]

Lenroot's stomach, always his most vulnerable part, gave way under the emotional strain. Clara called Nellie Dunn at the La Follettes to get the name of the specialist who had treated the senator. La Follette was within earshot, and when he heard the message came to the phone and, as Clara described it to her daughters, "with all his old-time affection and concern asked all about papa, and was generally *nice*." This was probably on 16 January. Late on Saturday morning of 17 January, Clara called at the La Follette's. She met a cordial reception and was taken to Fola's room where Fola and her mother had been talking; Belle invited the Lenroots to Sunday dinner and Clara promptly accepted.[78] That Sunday, the senator seemed to Clara "sad and broken when his face is in repose," and he was silent much of the time, but even so she found the evening pleasant. Young Phil, the more extroverted of the two La Follette boys, appeared in costume before dinner, setting a relaxed tone. Later Mrs. Elizabeth Evans and La Follette read aloud. Bobby picked up the Lenroots and later drove them home, asking to be remembered to the girls. "Altogether," Clara immediately

76. Belle La Follette to Frances Squire Potter, 15 February 1912, cited in Belle and Fola La Follette, *La Follette*, vol. 1, p. 408; *New York Times*, 6 February 1912; Robert La Follette to Jo (Mrs. Robert Siebecker), 5 February 1912, to Roe, 6 February 1912, cited in Belle and Fola La Follette, *La Follette*, vol. 1, pp. 412–13.

77. Lenroot, "Memoirs," pp. 83–84, Box 13, Lenroot Papers; McGeary, *Gifford Pinchot*, p. 224. The above explanation of the breach is supported by Lenroot and La Follette correspondence between 21 February and 1 March, cited below.

78. Clara to Katharine and Dorothy Lenroot, 18 February 1912, Lenroot Papers Addition.

wrote Katharine and Dorothy, "the evening's experience has been a very curious and unexpected ending, or perhaps only interlude, to the recent acute situation." [79]

The rapprochement quickly proved an interlude, not an ending. Clara had evidently missed something in the after-dinner conversation. Irvine could not talk about it while Bobby took them home and perhaps was brooding about it while Clara finished her letter. But La Follette had said that if there were a choice between Taft and Roosevelt, he would prefer Taft. Lenroot had not wanted to argue the matter on the spot, but he was deeply disturbed and realized that he was now at the crossroad he had been struggling to avoid.[80]

After discussing the matter with Clara, Lenroot decided what he must do. Pressed for time, since delegate nomination papers would be circulated in Wisconsin starting 26 February, and failing in efforts to see La Follette, Lenroot sent La Follette a message via Hannan. He would not be willing to go on the delegation if La Follette made any attack on Roosevelt; further, as La Follette promptly reported it to Roe and Rogers, Lenroot would not serve "unless it were understood that in the event Wisconsin had the deciding vote as between Taft and Roosevelt, the delegation would leave me and support Roosevelt." La Follette replied immediately through Hannan. If Lenroot thought that for La Follette to contrast his own record with Roosevelt's was an attack on Roosevelt, "then he must understand that Roosevelt was to be attacked." And La Follette would expect delegates pledged to him to stay with him "to the end." [81]

On Sunday, 25 February, Lenroot, anxious to talk it out, went to La Follette's home. He found the family, except for La Follette, at the breakfast table and chatted with them briefly. Lenroot assumed La Follette did not want to see him when Belle, rather snappishly, and perhaps Fola, volunteered that the senator was busy, and, therefore, he left.[82] Thus balked, Lenroot wrote La Follette a letter. Viewed as a whole, its purpose is clear. Lenroot despaired of converting La Follette, would not himself yield, and so wanted to get off the delegation with as little bad feeling or bad effect as possible.

He declared his willingness to withdraw if La Follette wished and proceeded to make it clear why La Follette should wish it. Lenroot reiterated that as between Taft and Roosevelt, he favored Roosevelt. Though he felt

79. Ibid.
80. Lenroot, "Memoirs," p. 84, Box 13, Lenroot Papers. Lenroot states that the dinner was on 22 February. But La Follette's correspondence indicates that Lenroot misdated it. See next note.
81. Lenroot to La Follette, 26 February 1912, Box 3, Lenroot Papers; La Follette to Gilbert Roe, 21 February 1912, to A. T. Rogers, 22 February 1912, Box 107, Series B, La Follette FC.
82. Lenroot to Herman L. Ekern, 27 February 1912, Box 2, Lenroot, "Memoirs," p. 85, Box 13, Lenroot Papers; Lenroot to Gilbert Roe, 26 February 1912, Box 4, Series H, La Follette FC.

the Wisconsin delegation should stay with La Follette to the finish in most conceivable circumstances, in the event of a deadlock, with Wisconsin holding the balance of power and only Roosevelt able to beat Taft, then he thought the delegation should switch to Roosevelt. "Inasmuch as many Wisconsin papers are saying that your delegates would be for Taft for second choice," he went on, "if you propose to raise any issue with Roosevelt I should deem it necessary to make my position known as being for second choice rather than Taft." He reminded La Follette that their friends would start circulating nominating petitions the next day and offered to wire a message to Ekern, announcing his withdrawal. He would still back the delegation and speak for it in Wisconsin, if he were needed and could get away.

Expediency dictated going along, Lenroot continued, "but like you I have the success of the Progressive movement at heart and I cannot in good conscience approve of a course which in my judgment is sure to retard it and destroy your leadership for the future." Lenroot concluded with reassurances of his "deep and abiding affection" for La Follette and the hope that in time they would again be in agreement on important questions. Even if asked to withdraw, he would remain at La Follette's service in other matters.[83]

Lenroot explained his course further to Roe, who had been summoned to the scene by La Follette and had written Lenroot a letter while on the train back to New York. To go to the convention as a La Follette delegate after silently acquiescing while La Follette attacked Roosevelt "would be to stultify myself." Although this, together with the question of second-choice vote, was sufficient to explain the purpose of his offer to withdraw, he added a more personal note. "My first thought in the letter," Lenroot explained to Roe, "was that with his changed attitude toward me it was only fair to him to give him an opportunity to substitute someone else in my place." [84]

Neither Roe nor La Follette took Lenroot's action in good grace, and both men misconstrued his purpose. Roe, who perhaps imparted his suspicions to La Follette before leaving Washington, wrote to Lenroot: "If you can depart from the ordinary attitude of loyal delegate now its only because you have *waited* till possibly La Follette can not afford at so late a day—within 20 days of the most important primaries—to have your defection announced." In replying to Lenroot, La Follette vented his long suppressed anger and suspicion. He lumped Lenroot with the hated Pinchot and Gardner, who had favored his combination with Roosevelt and then on 29 Janu-

83. Lenroot to La Follette, 26 February 1912 (25 February), Box 3, Lenroot Papers. This letter and Lenroot's of 27 February were evidently not preserved by La Follette. The author could not find them in the La Follette FC, and Fola La Follette knew of them only through La Follette's letter to Lenroot of 1 March. Belle and Fola La Follette, *La Follette,* vol. 1, p. 424, note 37. Internal evidence indicates that Lenroot misdated the letter by a day.

84. La Follette to Roe, 22 February 1912, Box 4, Series H, La Follette FC; Roe to Lenroot, 26 February 1912, Box 3, Lenroot Papers; Lenroot to Roe, 26 February 1912 (27 February), Box 4, Series H, La Follette FC, and Box 4 in Lenroot Papers.

ary his withdrawal, had undermined his organization and caused him an ordeal following his speaking trip "such as I have never but once before experienced in my life." Then he again rejected the conditions Lenroot had set forth as necessary for his continuance on the delegation. "The progressive principles are great moral issues," he wrote. "No distinction can be drawn in morals between a compromise on principles and a compromise on a candidate who has always been willing to compromise principles." [85]

La Follette alerted Rogers to the likely need for a substitute on the delegation and later wired a telegram to Ekern, expressing his unwillingness to have any delegates who would name a second choice, as something that would "be heralded all over the country as a surrender of my candidacy." He penned an editorial for the cover of his magazine, making clear his purpose to move ahead without compromise or combination.[86]

Backing up La Follette, Ekern, Rogers, and three others wired a statement to Lenroot: "We believe second choice statement unwise and absolutely unnecessary. To attempt change delegation now will align you and McGovern against La Follette and disrupt all our forces here." (Gov. Francis McGovern was known to admire Roosevelt.) Rogers wired Lenroot that he and Crownhart, who had state business in Washington, would be there in a few days and asked him to withhold any decision or announcement until then. Ekern and Rogers informed La Follette of these actions.[87]

Lenroot wanted conciliation but not at the cost of either his convictions or career. He wrote to Roe that Rogers and Crownhart were on the way and that he would withhold action until they arrived. Lenroot did, however, give Ekern advance warning not to expect too much, wiring, "senator insists on conditions I cannot accede to. I do not wish to create trouble but see no other way than to withdraw from delegation for that seems to be his wish." To make his own position better known among Wisconsin friends, he wrote Ekern his side of the story, included copies of his letter to La Follette of 25 January and the letter he had written that day, which he frankly admitted was for the record. He made it clear that he was personally inclined to withdraw but would leave the decision "to you boys and the Senator." If withdrawal was their decision, he would minimize the damage in his statement to the press, saying nothing of the differences that impelled it, "unless compelled from self protection." And he would speak in Wisconsin, if the leaders wished.[88]

85. Roe to Lenroot, 26 February 1912, La Follette to Lenroot, 26 February 1912, Box 3, Lenroot Papers.

86. La Follette to Rogers, 22 February 1912, Box 107, Series B, La Follette FC; to Lenroot, 26 February 1912, Box 3, Lenroot Papers; to Ekern, 26 February 1912, Box 105, Series J, La Follette FC; *La Follette's Weekly Magazine* 4:9 (2 March 1912), cover.

87. Ekern, Rogers, John Blaine, George Beedle, Dahl to Lenroot, Box 3, A. T. Rogers to Lenroot, 27 February 1912, Box 4, Lenroot Papers; *Wisconsin State Journal*, 1 March 1912; Ekern to La Follette, 26 February 1912, Box 11, Herman L. Ekern Papers; Rogers to La Follette, 27 February 1912, Box 107, Series B, La Follette FC.

88. Lenroot to Roe, 26 February 1912 (27 February), Box 4, to Ekern, 27 February 1912, Box 3, to Ekern, 27 February 1912, Box 2, Lenroot Papers.

Lenroot's second letter to La Follette was a five-page, single-spaced document in which he set out to disabuse La Follette of some of his apparent misconceptions but also to put in documentary form a full exposition and defense of his position. As Lenroot knew, the letter could not possibly influence La Follette's course vis à vis Roosevelt. And to the extent that his letter was for the apparent purpose of establishing a record, for possible later use, its conciliatory passages were compromised.

Lenroot said he was sorry not to be able to talk the matter over, but La Follette seemed unwilling. Then he reviewed recent political history. He noted that La Follette had initially expressed willingness to back Roosevelt if he came out on a progressive platform, that he had Lenroot draft a letter to Roosevelt offering his support if he would be a candidate, and that La Follette had been pleased when Lenroot came back from his visit with Roosevelt to say that the former president wanted no conflict between progressives. It soon became evident to Lenroot that such unity was essential, for without it not only would Taft be nominated but "the progressive movement in the states would be seriously retarded." Therefore, Lenroot had urged unity, and La Follette had resisted it. They had differed on Roosevelt, and Lenroot remained "sure that the progressive movement would be much safer in his hands than in those of Mr. Taft." He was aware that Roosevelt's record as president "was very unsatisfactory in many respects," but Woodrow Wilson was only a recent convert, yet praised by La Follette in his Philadelphia speech. Why not the same treatment for Roosevelt?

Lenroot denied that he had been party to any written proposal on 29 January, as La Follette had suggested, explaining that he had arrived late, just before La Follette himself. He had not suggested that La Follette withdraw "until it became apparent that you would not cooperate with other Progressives and that your nomination was improbable." He had not undermined La Follette's organization, as the senator had implied, went into no conference except at the invitation of La Follette or Houser, and though he gave his honest convictions, as he assumed La Follette wanted, he had always advised respecting La Follette's wishes, as Houser and Hannan could tell him.

Turning to his responsibilities as a delegate, he reiterated his view that for Wisconsin to stay neutral as between Taft and Roosevelt, "permitting Taft to be nominated, if she could prevent it, would be . . . lowering the political standard." He complained that their years together warranted a response "in a spirit in which my letter was written to you," but accepting the present situation, he was transmitting copies of their correspondence to Ekern and telling him that he would have to speak for Roosevelt if he stayed on the delegation and if La Follette attacked Roosevelt. He judged that "the boys" were exaggerating the impact of his withdrawal but would leave the decision to them and La Follette. If not on the delegation, he could still in good conscience speak for La Follette even if he did attack Roosevelt, for the progressive cause would be best served if La Follette, not Taft, won in Wisconsin. And if he went off the delegation, his statement would be circumspect.[89]

La Follette responded on 1 March with a ten-page, single-spaced letter. Like Lenroot, he was clearly not bent on persuasion. Prepared like a lawyer's brief, La Follette's letter took up and refuted the points Lenroot had made, yielding only where necessary and ignoring the matter that was irrelevant or embarrassing to the case.

Lenroot's letter required a written reply, La Follette wrote. Lenroot had ample opportunity to see him and need not have sent his alternatives with Hannan, especially within forty-eight hours of dining at La Follette's home. La Follette summarized the response he had sent via Hannan, stressing that he proposed not to attack Roosevelt personally but only review his record. Then La Follette expressed his view of Roosevelt—he had accomplished some good in what he had said and written but failed to do things. The time had come for action, but Roosevelt had never shown constructive or fixed economic principles; he had not been a student of such problems and would therefore compromise them when he thought it expedient, thus "blurring, smearing and confusing the issue."

Passing over earlier overtures to Roosevelt, La Follette pointed out that the projected December letter had simply been designed to force Roosevelt into the open. Then he went to the heart of the issue. Lenroot slurred a vital distinction in saying that " 'the progressive movement' would be much safer in his (Roosevelt's) hands than in those of Mr. Taft.' " The progressive movement "has not been in Mr. Taft's hands since he has been President," La Follette wrote. "It would not be in his hands if by any misfortune he were again President." But if Roosevelt became president he would keep command of progressive forces, yet "satisfy the steel trust and other great interests,"—made obvious by George Perkins's current support of him—"a large section of Wall Street," and various machine politicians. The success of the progressive movement in the states could hardly be promoted by dealing with such men. He thought Taft should be beaten, he wrote later in the letter. But "I am not willing . . . to demoralize and prostitute the progressive movement to beat him, for this is an unnecessary sacrifice." He did not explain what made it unnecessary but simply went on to say that in any case it is not right to sacrifice principle for "a cheap victory in a single campaign."

La Follette rehearsed the matter of Lenroot's interview with Roosevelt in December, stating for the record what Lenroot reported and what he replied. He backed off a bit regarding the 29 January meeting in denying that he had suggested "that you at that time, or any other time aided to undermine my organization here." But he pointed out that Lenroot's support for a combination in Ohio and elsewhere had helped others "to carry

89. Lenroot to La Follette, 27 March 1912, Box 3, Lenroot Papers.

out their schemes," for the conspirators "were continually quoting you as being in agreement with them and using our close personal relations, with my friends here, and out in the field to weaken me." Such an alliance would have been a confession of weakness and demoralizing to the surprisingly strong forces La Follette had developed after the Chicago conference and his brief tour.

Nowhere in the letter did La Follette take notice of Lenroot's offer to help in the campaign or in other ways, or of Lenroot's hope for close cooperation between them in the future.[90]

For La Follette, compromise on Lenroot's terms was out of the question, as he made publicly clear in another front-cover editorial. On 24 February, Roosevelt had made his candidacy official. Now, after referring to Roosevelt by name, La Follette said he would have to "discuss the records of candidates as well as the remedies proposed by them." That record, La Follette concluded, may be more important "than his present declarations." Such a discussion "cannot be distorted into an attack upon the candidate." [91]

After 18 February, Lenroot had given up hope that La Follette would change his mind. He simply wanted to get off the delegation with the least possible rancor. The proprieties required that La Follette and/or his Wisconsin managers make the decision, so he had put it to them in a contingent way, indicating the conditions under which he would continue. Roe and La Follette misconstrued his intention, thinking he was trying to force La Follette to change course, so they attacked his "second choice" idea and prepared for a public controversy with him. Lenroot awaited the arrival of Rogers and Crownhart, and also Roe, who was asked by Rogers to return to Washington, as an opportunity to dispel misunderstandings and effect his initial purpose.[92]

La Follette, Roe, Rogers, and Crownhart hoped for more, but they all foresaw that they might have to settle for less than surrender from Lenroot. Crownhart and Rogers, by their very presence at the 5 March meeting, helped to reestablish the old atmosphere of friendship, confidence, and lofty purpose among the men of the "inner circle." Lenroot had to resist every argument against his second-choice position, which he did, but he also had ample opportunity to talk in a reasonable and cooperative way and thus lay the ground for an amicable separation. There could be no other outcome, and after the conference Rogers wired state Sen. John Blaine, who now headed the La Follette organization in Wisconsin, that La Follette and Lenroot agreed that Lenroot be replaced on the delegate slate. With the matter settled, the La Follettes had the Lenroots to dinner, but chaperoned by the Wisconsin visitors.[93]

Belle wrote her friend Elizabeth Evans:

90. La Follette to Lenroot, 1 March 1912, Box 3, Lenroot Papers.
91. *La Follette's Weekly Magazine* 4:10 (9 March 1912), cover.
92. Rogers to Roe, 26 February 1912, Box 4, Roe to La Follette, 29 February 1912, Box 7, Series H, La Follette FC.
93. *Superior Telegram*, 11 March 1912.

Nothing that has happened has been so hard for me. We have managed to keep the personal relation but I realize that Bob and Irvine can never be the same to each other as before. It is a relief to have the matter decided. I think Bob feels better than for some time. He has realized that Lenroot disapproved of his course and was in full sympathy with Pinchot, Kent and the rest in leaving him. This has worked on Bob and while he has accepted Lenroot's criticism in the friendly spirit it was made, now that Lenroot has made the issue and they have agreed to disagree Bob feels the decks are cleared and whatever delegates he has from Wisconsin will know what they stand for.[94]

Afterwards, without modifying his views or his position, Lenroot did what he could to help La Follette, to sustain the personal relationship, and to preserve his own strength in the district and as a leader of the progressives in the state. To explain his withdrawal he wrote a few friends, then issued a statement:

Senator La Follette and I have differed as to certain matters unnecessary to discuss at this time. I have been very close to La Follette for years. If a delegate to the convention, many would regard me as his spokesman there. It would be unfair to Senator La Follette under all the circumstances for me to take positions in the convention with which he is not in accord. It will relieve both the senator and myself from embarrassment if I am not a candidate. I expect to make a number of speeches for the La Follette delegation if the campaign committee deems it necessary.[95]

The La Follette men in Wisconsin responded confusedly and then with some criticism of Lenroot. But Crownhart and others played down the break and Lenroot did his part when he spoke in the state for La Follette.[96]

Though triumphant only in Wisconsin and North Dakota, La Follette conducted a vigorous and bitter campaign, directed more against Roosevelt than Taft. His duty in Wisconsin done, Lenroot held unhappily aloof. He did, however, advise Ekern as to the platform. And in a final effort to avoid potential disaster, he wrote Ekern:

I think the most serious problem that is going to confront the Wisconsin and North Dakota delegates is as to what action should be taken in case of a bolt by the Roosevelt people. If Taft steals the Convention as it is now quite apparent to me he intends to do, to stay in his convention would be disastrous from every stand-point, unless a sufficient number of Roosevelt delegates remain in the Convention so that it is apparent that it is the legal regular Republican Convention notwithstanding the presence of stolen delegates. There is going to be a most serious problem and the action taken there may mean the success or defeat of the party and the progressive cause in Wisconsin next November. I am sure that you

94. Belle La Follette to Elizabeth Evans, 5 March 1912, cited in Belle and Fola La Follette, *La Follette*, vol. 1, p. 424.

95. *Superior Telegram*, 7 March 1912; *Wisconsin State Journal*, 8 March 1912.

96. *Wisconsin State Journal*, 7, 9, 25, 27 March 1912; *Superior Telegram*, 8, 9, 11, 28 March 1912; Herman L. Ekern to Charles Ingram, 13 March 1912, Ingram to Ekern, 15 March 1912, Ekern to Lenroot, 18 March 1912, Lenroot to Ekern, 20 March 1912, Box 12, Ekern Papers.

and others will not overlook the seriousness of this and canvass the matter very carefully.[97]

At the Chicago convention and afterwards, some of what Lenroot had feared occurred. La Follette preferred the nomination of Taft to Roosevelt, and when the Roosevelt leaders supported Wisconsin's McGovern for temporary chairman, he tried to get McGovern to withdraw. Supported by eleven of Wisconsin's twenty-six delegates, McGovern refused and in the highlight of the turbulent convention Houser took the platform to repudiate the nomination as being without La Follette's consent. "We make no deals with Roosevelt. We make no trades with Taft." [98] Defeated on the temporary chairmanship by a vote of 552 to 502, and on other key tests by similar margins, Roosevelt finally yielded to the urging of many of his ardent backers and agreed to a bolt, on the slogan "Thou Shalt Not Steal." La Follette advised his delegates to stay in the convention through the nomination of Taft and they did.[99] But Roosevelt rallied his forces for a third party effort, which with the support of a host of well-known progressives including the Pinchots, Garfield, Hiram Johnson, Judge Ben Lindsey, Poindexter, and George L. Record, and men of wealth like George Perkins and Frank Munsey, might be potent.

Yet, for a number of reasons, progressive Republicanism as a national phenomenon seemed to have a good chance to survive. At the Republican convention, a minority of Roosevelt delegates—107—voted on the presidential nomination and in so doing signified their intention to remain in the party. Their action, with that of the La Follette delegates from North Dakota and Wisconsin, lent a certain legitimacy to the convention and made it clear that Roosevelt would be heading a new party, not one that had any claim to the name *Republican.* Roosevelt at first welcomed the votes of Republican electors, but when ridiculed about it, gave up the effort. When at Baltimore at the end of June the Democrats nominated Woodrow Wilson, a progressive, they contributed some welcome ambiguity to the choice facing progressive Republicans. In the months that followed, it became clear that while Roosevelt would have widespread support among leaders and voters, in the strongest insurgent areas most progressive politicians would not give up their grip on the Republican label and machinery despite Roosevelt's angry comments about them. They had good reason to expect that after the 1912 fight was done, the Rooseveltians, lacking a base in public office, would drift back to the party and resume the progressive fight within it.[100]

97. Lenroot to Ekern, 10 June 1912, Box 12, Ekern Papers.

98. La Follette to A. T. Rogers, 9 June 1912, Box 107, Series B, La Follette FC; Herbert F. Margulies, *The Decline of the Progressive Movement in Wisconsin, 1890–1920*, pp. 107–21.

99. Mowry, *The Progressive Movement*, pp. 247–53; La Follette to John Hannan, 22 June 1912, Box 107, Series B, La Follette FC.

100. Mowry, *The Progressive Movement*, pp. 253, 256–57, 258–59; Holt, *Congressional Insurgents*, pp. 64–72.

In Wisconsin, progressive Republican lines held firm and strong. Though La Follette subtly hinted to the voters that they should vote for Wilson, he also countered Roosevelt sentiment by stressing the importance of remaining Republican.[101]

Wisconsin's progressive Republicans benefited from a new law providing for a separate ballot for presidential voting. Most important of all, in the face of a strong challenge from conservative Democrats, La Follette postponed his confrontation with McGovern for a later time and supported the governor in his bid for renomination. McGovern, in turn, tried to persuade the leaders of Roosevelt's new Progressive party that they should not put up state and congressional candidates against the progressive Republicans.[102] And progressive Republicans could again count on help from "fair minded" Democrats, unhappy with their own state ticket and pleased at La Follette's support of Wilson.

Lenroot found opportunity during the summer to review the political situation locally as well as nationally and to ponder his course. By 31 August, if not before, he had made his decision, which he explained in a letter to Sen. Joseph Dixon of Montana, who had taken charge of Roosevelt's campaign.

Lenroot would not join the new party. He felt strongly that the Moosers should not put a state ticket into the field, since it would give the state government to "the Reactionaries," and the progressive movement had achieved success in Wisconsin through the Republican party. Feeling that way and as a candidate on the Republican ticket, he could not participate "in the new movement." However, he would not support Taft, "as I consider the circumstances of his nomination were such that no party obligation is entailed upon any Republican to support him." Characteristically, Lenroot had probed his own motives and was sensitive on the subject. "In forming my conclusions as to my own course," he assured Dixon (and himself), "I do not think I have been influenced by any personal element in the case for conditions in my district are such that it is reasonably certain that I can be elected no matter what course may be taken." [103]

At Ashland, Wisconsin, on the night of 21 October, Lenroot made public his rather complex and equivocal position on the presidency and the new party. It was as he had indicated in his letter to Senator Dixon but fleshed out somewhat. With regard to the new party, Lenroot readily acknowledged that Roosevelt had been the choice of the rank and file Republicans, and

---

101. *La Follette's Weekly Magazine* 4:28 (13 July 1912):4, 9; *La Follette's Weekly Magazine* 4:33 (17 August 1912):3–5; *La Follette's Weekly Magazine* 3:35 (31 August 1912):7; *La Follette's Weekly Magazine* 4:30 (27 July 1912), cover; La Follette to John Hannan, 22 June 1912, to Rudolph Spreckels, 12 July 1912, Box 107, Rogers to La Follette, Box 27, Series B, Belle to Robert La Follette, 25 June 1912, to Charles La Follette, 27 July 1912, Box 11, Robert to "Bobbie" La Follette, 8 July 1912, Box 12, Series A, La Follette FC.

102. *Wisconsin State Journal,* 6 July, 11, 17, 25, 27 September 1912.

103. Lenroot to Joseph Dixon, 31 August 1912, Box 2, Lenroot Papers.

he admitted that it might be best for progressive Republicans to join the new party, "even at the sacrifice of progress in the states temporarily." But such a step should not be lightly undertaken, for in contrast to the Southern Bourbon-Northern boss-dominated Democratic party, the Republican party had provided a sturdy vehicle for progressivism and even now, after the Rooseveltian bolt, remained progressive at the core. Before abandoning it, progressives should be certain that "the new general is not only competent, self-sacrificing and patriotic, but constructive in statesmanship." He hoped that Roosevelt met the test but said "my doubts are greater than they were at the time of the Chicago Convention." Added to his record on bossism as president was Roosevelt's current stance that only those in his party could call themselves progressives.

Having gone that far, Lenroot would not go further. If Roosevelt persisted in fighting for progressive principles, he might consider joining the Progressive party. For the present, he would remain a Republican. Yet Republicans, under the peculiar circumstances of the campaign, might feel free to vote for any of the three major presidential candidates without being disloyal to their party. Instead of specifically endorsing any of the three, Lenroot proposed to discuss the record of each on the major contemporary issues. Roosevelt faired best under Lenroot's scrutiny. Taft failed most tests, of course, and Wilson he found wanting on the tariff commission question and in his reluctance to use the power of government for progressive ends.[104]

During the campaign, Lenroot discreetly hosted Gifford Pinchot when he came to Superior for Roosevelt and tried to supply Pinchot with some campaign material he had requested. Pinchot in turn gave Lenroot high praise for his conservation services, in his Superior speech. Afterwards, Roosevelt showed some understanding of Lenroot's position and looked to him as one of the progressive Republican congressmen who might be profitably persuaded.[105] Lenroot returned to La Follette's circle. But neither man could forget what happened, nor could La Follette's lesser lieutenants. And insofar as Lenroot remained sympathetic to Roosevelt and open to the possibility of joining the new party, his position was far from La Follette's. The situation was awkward for all concerned. *La Follette's Weekly Magazine* mentioned Lenroot in a friendly way in August, but Lenroot took no part in factional politicking at the state fair, or the platform convention in September, or in strategy conferences in October or November. Lenroot's absence connoted an important change in the direction of his career. At the state convention, moreover, word began to circulate that contrary

104. MS speech, no title, n.d. (October 1912), Box 5, Lenroot Papers; *Superior Telegram*, 22 October 1912.

105. Pinchot to Lenroot, 6, 10 October 1912, Lenroot to Pinchot, 2 October 1912, Box 154, Pinchot Papers; *Wisconsin Blue Book*, 1913, p. 269; *Superior Telegram*, 9 October 1912; Elting Morison et al., eds., *Letters of Theodore Roosevelt* (Cambridge, Mass., 1954), vol. 7, p. 715, note 2.

to earlier understandings, La Follette's choice for the Senate in 1914 would be Lt. Gov. Tom Morris, not Lenroot.[106]

In a campaign speech at Superior, La Follette fully praised Lenroot. "There has been no such man in the house of representatives in twenty-five years," the senator said. "He is the one man without exception who can take the floor, and from the minute he says 'Mr. Speaker,' you can hear a pin drop. Superior has greater cause for pride in having sent a leader of the progressive republicans to congress than has any other congressional district in the union. And I know that Superior will keep on sending him until the progressive element has control there and then you will have the honor of furnishing the speaker of the house of representatives." [107] But of course if Lenroot were to become Speaker, he could not be La Follette's colleague in the Senate.

About a month later, after Lenroot's reelection landslide, Irvine and Clara returned to Washington. La Follette, traveling with his family on the same train, came into Lenroot's car to speak to him about the senatorship. La Follette said, in substance, that if Lenroot wanted to run for the Senate he was entitled to his support and would get it. At the end of the month, after Nellie read a disquieting newspaper report about the relations between her brother and La Follette, Irvine was glad to reassure his sister with news of La Follette's offer. Yet, while he had not come to a final decision, he thought he would not accept.[108] He did not.

Coming as the fulfillment of an obligation, La Follette's offer conveyed little enthusiasm on the senator's part. And Lenroot could not easily forget the trying experience of the past year. To serve as La Follette's junior senator in the Senate was asking for trouble, especially since Lenroot continued to disagree with La Follette on important subjects such as the tariff and Roosevelt. And it was not as though Lenroot lacked alternatives. The new party ran well in his district and posed a problem for the future. Yet his House seat was reasonably secure, and service in the House offered widening opportunities for achievement and recognition. As a congressman, moreover, he might continue to act cooperatively, if not so closely, with La Follette and to exert influence in Wisconsin too.[109]

Since Lenroot always looked for the best, he probably did not admit to himself how fully his own situation had changed. But he acted in the knowledge that it had changed to a significant degree, and in this fact he was realistic. As Belle La Follette had said, things could never be the same again.

106. *La Follette's Weekly Magazine* 4:32 (10 August 1912):12; *Wisconsin State Journal*, 10, 11, 17, 18 September, 2 October, 27 November 1912; *Superior Telegram*, 19 September 1912.

107. *Superior Telegram*, 25 October 1912.

108. *Superior Telegram*, 28 November 1912; *Wisconsin State Journal*, 24, 29 November 1912; Lenroot to Nellie Nichols, 27 December 1912, Lenroot Papers Addition; *Superior Telegram*, 23 December 1912; Lenroot, "Memoirs," p. 98, Box 13, Lenroot Papers.

109. Lenroot to Richard Lloyd Jones, 16 October 1914, Box 3, Lenroot, "Memoirs," p. 98, Box 13, Lenroot Papers.

V

A PROGRESSIVE REPUBLICAN
IN A DEMOCRATIC HOUSE

If the partial break with La Follette caused Lenroot to focus more of his attention on the work of Congress, it is also true that one cause of the painful separation was the fact that Lenroot had already become primarily a national progressive concerned especially with the work of the House of Representatives and with the needs and opinions of its members. During some of the most critical moments in the political drama of 1911 and 1912, Lenroot had been offstage—his time and attention devoted to House business. His activity in the House warrants attention.

In the second session of the Sixty-second Congress, which began in December 1911, Lenroot encountered some of the same obstacles as in the first. Again, the Democrats attempted to control matters through their caucus and by the use of illiberal rules. As the 1912 elections approached, politics intruded on legislation to an extraordinary degree. Since control remained divided between the Democrats in the House, and the Republicans in the Senate and the executive branch, the overall effect of these political considerations was to make more difficult the enactment of sound legislation.

Democratic tactics, though not surprising, remained disappointing. But in the issue of caucus domination and "gag rule," Lenroot found a cause worthy of his constant attention. If progress was small, it was not absent altogether. The magnitude of the issues, from his standpoint, justified and made meaningful his extensive efforts in the rules committee and on the floor, especially since the Democrats were still in process of developing procedural precedents.

Lenroot was not himself unaffected by political considerations in this election year. Progressivism continued in the ascendancy. Yet to Lenroot the Democrats were unprogressive. Meanwhile, despite the bitter struggles involving Taft, Roosevelt, and La Follette, progressivism gained strength in the Republican party. Under those circumstances, it was a service to attack Democrats from a progressive standpoint, for their tactics and their policies. Such attacks figured to weaken the undeserving Democrats while helping in the promising process of casting Republicanism in the progressive mold.

Nor was Lenroot excluded from legislative achievement. In some instances, he found it possible to play on the Democrats' political concerns to bring them to what he saw as the progressive course. Also, legislative accomplishment might be negative as well as positive; in practice, it was easier to stop bad legislation than to achieve good legislation. Meanwhile, through the education of the public and the legislators that accompanied delaying action, the way for betterment was prepared.

Progressive Republicans no longer met as a group, but they remained distinguishable from the rest. By virtue of the variety, quality, and consistency of his action on the floor and in the rules committee, Lenroot became, with George Norris, an unofficial leader and spokesman for the faction.

In retrospect, one sees another and more interesting change—not in Lenroot's position but in his political attitude. Lenroot had come to Congress in 1909 with some well-formed reservations about the Democratic party. But he had never served in a legislative body controlled by the Democrats until April 1911. His suspicion and hostility toward that party increased measurably during the special session. In the second session of the same Congress, Lenroot's attitude further hardened. At the same time and for a variety of reasons, his relationship with regular Republicans improved. The second point should not be exaggerated, for this was just the beginning of a long slow process.

Progressive and conservative Republicans differed on many questions through the session, but in only one instance did they take their quarrel to center stage. In September 1911, insurgent Congressman Madison died suddenly of heart failure. James R. Mann named another Kansas Republican but a regular, Philip B. Campbell, to replace him on the rules committee. On 11 January, when the appointment came to the House floor, George Norris nominated Victor Murdock, arguing that Madison should be succeeded by someone of like mind and that the procedure of appointment by the minority leader was improper.

Twenty-six insurgents voted for Murdock, along with eighty-one Democrats, but Mann held most Republicans and with help from Oscar Underwood's supporters among the Democrats carried the vote for Campbell by a vote of 167 to 109. Lenroot voted for Murdock, but he took no part in the debate, as befitted a member of the rules committee.[1]

After that, Lenroot agreed with Mann on most questions. The omnipresent minority leader was an invaluable ally against the Democrats in the battle of the rules question. And he was helpful, too, on substantive matters, especially on most conservation questions. In this last area of question Mann acted in harmony with the Taft administration, which, through Secretary of Interior Walter Fisher and Secretary of War Henry L. Stimson, took

1. Clipping, *Chicago Record-Herald*, 12 January 1912, Scrapbook 16, James R. Mann Papers; Paul DeWitt Hasbrouck, *Party Government in the House of Representatives*, pp. 45–46; Richard Lowitt, *George W. Norris: The Making of a Progressive, 1861–1912*, vol. 1, pp. 223–24; *CR* 62:2, 1912, vol. 48, pt. 1, pp. 864–65.

positions that were in most cases quite satisfactory to Gifford Pinchot and his conservationist associates.

Lenroot found himself in harmony with the administration on such questions and on others, including support for the Tariff Board and for certain recommendations made by the board. Beyond that, Taft provided no major occasions for attack, for after the reciprocity fiasco he did not enter into any new coalitions with the Democrats and did not advance any controversial proposals. Perhaps the most important law generated by Congress during the session was the establishment of the parcel-post system, and this Taft advocated and willingly signed, as he did on the bills calling for a children's bureau, for the eight-hour day on federally contracted projects, and other mildly progressive measures. In the Congress in 1912 Taft, like the stand-patters, was the object of only ritualistic attacks by progressive Republicans.

While for Lenroot occasion for conflict with fellow Republicans diminished, circumstances made a series of clashes with the Democrats inevitable. The victory in 1910 and subsequent Republican division made the Democrats wary. As they moved toward the presidency and control of both Houses of Congress, they remained aware of their own reputation for divisiveness and incapacity. In reality, the party was deeply divided along many lines, so generous use of the caucus and resort to illiberal rules was imperative to progressive leaders like Robert Henry as to conservatives like Oscar Underwood.[2]

Lenroot was the natural leader of those in opposition to government by caucus and "gag rule." Mann would help, because it was to the party's advantage and he enjoyed twitting his rivals for going back on their professions in the Cannon fight. But he was not moved by conviction and was inhibited by his own commitment to party rule and to leadership. Norris felt no such inhibitions and in fact joined Lenroot in most of his clashes with the Democrats. But Norris was not a member of the rules committee; thus, he was not constantly involved with rules questions. As the lone progressive Republican on the committee, it was natural that Lenroot should take the lead. And he was more than willing to do so. Political reform remained basic, in his view. Moreover, the battle to liberalize procedures was a personal struggle to gain for himself larger opportunity to influence legislation on the House floor, then and thereafter.

Lenroot's running battle with the Democrats that session began on 27 January in connection with the first of the Democratic tariff measures to reach the floor—the metals schedule. He entered only lightly into the merits of the bill, instead protesting that individual members had been given hardly any time to consider it.[3]

Less than a week later, Lenroot again took on the Democrats, unsuccessfully, when they downgraded the priority of the discharge calendar, a reform

2. See especially Stanley Coben, *A. Mitchell Palmer: Politician,* pp. 42–44. See also Harold B. Hinton, *Cordell Hull: A Biography,* pp. 125–26.

3. *CR* 62:2, 1912, vol. 48, pt. 2, p. 1416.

they themselves had initiated earlier by which members could wrest a bill from a committee and put it on the regular calendar. Soon afterwards, he resumed his attack on rule by caucus, in connection with Democratic action to limit the extent of the "money trust" investigation.[4]

On two occasions, in April and May, Lenroot criticized the Democrats for incorporating substantive legislation in appropriation bills. By this device, he noted, they avoided roll-call votes.[5]

In connection with an anti-injunction bill brought to the floor on 14 May, Lenroot criticized a rule providing three hours of general debate. A vote for the rule is a vote against the right to offer amendments, he said, and he proposed instead one hour of general debate and two hours devoted to amendments and debate under the five minute rule by which in effect a member might speak five minutes on an amendment. As he had done before, he quoted their words back to Democratic leaders Clark, Underwood, and Fitzgerald. Since the bill was only four pages long, he found no justification for a rule that prevented amendment, except for one substantive motion. Rules committee chairman Robert Henry would not defend the rule but got to what he saw as the nub of the matter; if amendable, Republicans "would devour everything in the bill that is good. . . . This legislation has been agreed to by those who really favor it, and they think it is of the best character obtainable at this time, and therefore the previous questions should be adopted and the rule passed." The rule was passed by a vote of 174 to 99.[6] Two months later, in debate on another illiberal rule to govern debate on a second labor injunction bill, Lenroot had a chance to meet the argument. Though he favored the bill, he feared the precedent, predicting that in the future Democrats would "use these precedents for bad bills as well as good ones." Affirming that "there is more real consideration of legislation in this House in one hour under the five minute rule than there is in one week under general debate," Lenroot asked Henry: "Have you not sufficient confidence in your own majority to trust your own membership upon that side of the House to support your bill as coming from the committee?"[7] Of course Henry did not, though he preferred not saying so.

In part, Lenroot played out a well-understood political game with the Democrats. But his purpose was more than partisan advantage. A note of sincerity and despair rings through his closing words on the injunction bill rule: "Ever since I have been a Member of this House I have fought against gag rules when the Republicans were in the majority, and I propose to fight against them so long as I remain a Member of the House of Representatives. What has come over the Democratic membership of this House—everyone of you? At the last session of Congress you were fighting the very things for which you are voting now. . . . I shall not take further time." Lenroot

4. Ibid., pp. 1685–90, 2387–89, 5339–40, 5342.
5. Ibid., pp. 4993–96, 5893–96.
6. *CR* 62:2, 1912, vol. 48, pt. 7, pp. 6410–14.
7. Ibid., p. 8719.

finished by saying, "I have discussed this same question over and over again. I do not expect it to have any effect now, and I am inclined to think that for the present at least we must say of the Democratic majority as was said of old, 'Ephraim is joined to his idols. Let him alone.' " [8]

Lenroot's public words expressed his private judgment. In late May, he wrote Ekern that the session had accomplished little. "The Democratic House upon great public questions, such as the trust question, is just as bad as the House was under Cannonism," he felt. "The interests control the principal committees to fully as great an extent as they ever did. Tariff legislation is enacted for politics only, the Democrats deliberately framing their bills in order to invite a veto from the President." [9] Lenroot considered Underwood a reactionary and regarded Clark as living in the past, though "absolutely honest" and one who would not knowingly align with special interests.[10]

Lenroot found consolation in evidence that "the days of the Stand-patters are numbered." "One by one they are going out of the Senate," he wrote Ekern, "and you see Crane has announced his retirement." [11] He might have added that John Dalzell, ranking Republican on the House rules committee, had failed to be renominated. Following the Republican National Convention, progressive Republicans in the Senate patched up the differences caused by the La Follette-Roosevelt fight and the belated candidacy of Cummins. Cummins took the lead in promoting cooperation. La Follette would not forgive and forget so far as Cummins was concerned, but he too wanted unity and late in July accomplished it, on the wool and cotton tariff bills. Taft's forces, anxious to fortify their progressive flank in the wake of the Rooseveltian defection, offered encouraging concessions, as by giving La Follette a vacated place on the interstate commerce committee, an assignment he had always wanted.[12]

To the extent that Lenroot became disenchanted with the Democrats during the second session, it was as much the result of tariff battles as anything else. Like the Democrats, Lenroot favored downward revision, and occasionally during the session he voted for Democratic bills. But more often he found himself at odds with the Democrats, judging their approach to tariffmaking parochial, political, unscientific, and wrong minded. From the beginning, when the majority on Underwood's ways and means committee voted to indefinitely postpone consideration of Sereno Payne's bill to make permanent the Tariff Board, Lenroot knew that the Democrats meant to ignore the board's recommendations, then let it die for want of an appro-

8. Ibid.

9. Irvine L. Lenroot to Herman L. Ekern, 29 May 1912, Box 12, Herman L. Ekern Papers.

10. *Superior Telegram*, 29 June 1912.

11. Lenroot to Ekern, 29 May 1912, Box 12, Ekern Papers. On standpat decline see Horace S. and Marion G. Merrill, *The Republican Command, 1897–1913*.

12. Albert Cummins to La Follette, 1 July 1912, Box 71, La Follette to Charles R. Crane, 21 August 1912, Box 107, Series B, Robert M. La Follette FC; *Wisconsin State Journal*, 8 August 1912.

priation. Soon he realized that, using their control of the House to fullest political advantage, they proposed to pass protective bills designed to please Southern constituents, or bills drawn along lines of free trade or revenue only. Not only did Lenroot disapprove the tariff principles of the Democrats, but he deplored their seeming preference for political gain instead of legislative accomplishment—most of their tariff bills were popular with the public but impossible to pass through the Senate or have signed by the president. So it turned out, despite Lenroot's efforts.

But there was more than frustrated hopes and political reprisal. Lenroot found ways of making himself useful. A biographer's comment about Cordell Hull, one of the more capable and constructive Democrats in the House, can also be applied to Lenroot: "He learned that most members of the House . . . are glad enough to endorse desirable moves but few of them are thoughtful or industrious enough to conceive or execute them." Another of Lenroot's Democratic colleagues, John Nance Garner, after years of service in the House, remarked: "Most times when men sit down around a legislative conference table to work out a solution of matters of vital concern to their country they forget to what political party they belong. . . . Men who have known how to compromise intelligently have rendered great service to their country." [13]

Lenroot had occasion to attack the rules voted by the majority of the Committee on Rules, but more often than not the committee worked harmoniously and he willingly took his share of the heavy work load. In one instance he defended on the floor action taken by the Democratic majority on the committee.[14]

When subjects of consuming public interest arose, members offered resolutions calling for special investigations. It fell to the Committee on Rules to report such resolutions or not, and in that connection to hold preliminary hearings. In the conduct of these, Lenroot was free to participate as fully as he cared to. In connection with the celebrated strike of textile mills in Lawrence, Massachusetts, the committee hearings themselves constituted a full investigation. No legislation resulted, but the hearings contributed to the further development of public sentiment favorable to the workers, most of them immigrant women and children. Although the revolutionary Industrial Workers of the World led the strike, Lenroot, with most of the committee, sympathized with the workers. In his questioning, he did more than his share in bringing out the facts with respect to low wages, intolerable living and working conditions, and the actions of local authorities in preventing the removal of children from Lawrence during the strike.[15]

Lenroot tried to keep himself updated on all legislation coming before

13. Hinton, *Cordell Hull: A Biography*, p. 127; Bascom N. Timmons, *Garner of Texas: A Personal History*, p. 111.

14. Record Group 233, "Committee on Rules, Minutes," NA; *CR* 62:2, 1912, vol. 48, pt. 7, p. 9254. See also the several hearings held by the committee.

15. U.S., House of Representatives, Committee on Rules, *Hearings: The Strike at Lawrence, Mass.*, vol. 62, p. 2.

the House. Painstakingly, he made a digest of all bills on which he might care to speak, as they were reported, and briefed himself further on these.[16] As a result, on a number of subjects, great and small, he was able to hold his own in debate and to offer amendments. Often the number of members on the floor was relatively small, enhancing the importance of those who attended and especially those who participated.

Lenroot held progressive ground in debate on workmen's compensation legislation, parcel post, the bill establishing ground rules for the operation of the Panama Canal, the amendment on direct election of senators, and another proposed constitutional change to eliminate the "lame duck" session of Congress.[17] Through the session, he continued to be interested in antitrust and contributed what he could to the burgeoning movement to strengthen the Sherman Act. On the House floor, in addition to agitating for a thorough investigation of the "money trust," he spoke for a "coal trust" investigation focusing on conditions in the upper Great Lakes region, where his own constituents continued to complain. In the rules committee, Lenroot participated in questioning witnesses in connection with proposed investigations of the "shipping trust" and International Harvester Corporation. The Democrats chose not to legislate on antitrust during that Congress, but the bill he had worked on with Brandeis was reported "in substance" in the House and became a starting point for future Democratic efforts.[18]

The questions on conservation were less encumbered by partisan constraints than were topics of comparable importance. Members of the House divided along shifting ideological and geographical lines, depending on the specific issue. For these reasons, Lenroot exerted considerable influence through the years of Democratic rule.

Lenroot continued to work closely with Gifford Pinchot and his associates in the National Conservation Association, especially Overton Price and Harry Slattery. The latter, though still in his twenties, was well on his way toward becoming a "super lobbyist for conservation legislation." [19] When Pinchot and La Follette parted company, Lenroot sympathized with the former, personally and politically, and continued as one of the two principal Republican advocates of Pinchot's views in the House.

The other was William Kent. Brought together with Kent not only by Pinchot, Kent's old friend, but by La Follette, Lenroot found an ardent co-worker who was quickly becoming a devoted friend.[20]

16. *CR* 65:3, 1919, vol. 57, pt. 3, p. 2600.
17. *CR* 62:2, 1911, vol. 48, pt. 1, pp. 395–96; 1912, vol. 48, pt. 5, pp. 4993–96; 1912, vol. 48, pt. 6, pp. 5646–48; 1912, vol. 48, pt. 7, pp. 6354–55, 6927; 1912, vol. 48, pt. 8, p. 7524.
18. Ibid., pp. 9084–86; U.S., House of Representatives, Committee on Rules, *Hearings: Investigation of Shipping Trust* and *Hearings: International Harvester Company;* Louis D. Brandeis to Robert La Follette, 26 July 1912, Box 71, Series B, La Follette FC.
19. M. Nelson McGeary, *Gifford Pinchot: Forester—Politician,* p. 198.
20. Katharine Lenroot to the author, 26 November 1968.

As a legislator, Kent had his limitations. Intense in debate, he spoke slowly for a minute or two, then bolted out his words. Even his wife acknowledged that he was no orator. Many thought him without influence by virtue of his independence.[21] But he was serious, energetic and intelligent, and unconcerned for personal glory. Sharing common interests, ideals, and views with Lenroot, he developed great admiration for Lenroot's legislative talents, considered him in fact "the biggest man in the House," and followed his lead in many things.[22] Conservationist Judson King later called Lenroot "William Kent's close friend, hardest co-worker and wisest adviser." [23] The two complemented one another well.

Several conservation issues arose during the session. One related to Alaska. By the time Congress met, the administration, through Secretary Fisher, had committed itself to a policy of leasing rather than sale of valuable mineral lands and construction by the government of a railway into some of the coal fields. With prospects bright but unwilling to rely wholly on the administration, Pinchot, in advance of the session, submitted an Alaska bill to La Follette, who turned it over to Lenroot when the congressman reached Washington. Lenroot reviewed the bill, discussed changes with Pinchot, then submitted the revised bill to Pinchot and La Follette. The bill (actually a comprehensive amendment) dealt mainly with the new railroad project. Lenroot's contribution is not entirely clear, except that he enlarged the scope of the section to provide for construction of wharves at the terminals and included a provision empowering the I.C.C. to fix rates. Nothing came of the legislation that session, due in part to differences between Attorney General Wickersham and Chairman Reed Smoot of the Senate Committee on Public Lands. But the groundwork had been laid for settlement of the question on progressive terms in the next administration.[24]

During the session, Lenroot contributed to one notable conservationist success in regard to waterpower. The issue was complex and of increasing importance, as the nation moved into the age of electricity and as public utility companies sought waterpower rights on navigable streams in national forests and on other public lands. Gifford Pinchot, while chief forester, had established a reasonably satisfactory system for the lands under his control, involving the issuance of permits for specified periods, under regulated conditions and with an annual charge. He wished to fortify and improve the system by general legislation and to extend the same system to other public

21. Clipping, *Chicago Post*, 25 November 1914, Scrapbook 21, Mann Papers; Elizabeth Kent, *William Kent, Independent: A Biography*, pp. 247, 369.

22. So reported publisher E. W. Scripps in conversation with Lenroot. Irvine to Clara Lenroot, 28 June 1914, Box 1, Irvine L. Lenroot Papers. See also Kent's statement in the *Milwaukee Sentinel*, 27 March 1918.

23. Elizabeth Kent, *William Kent*, p. 328. That the words are King's is indicated on page 310.

24. McGeary, *Gifford Pinchot*, p. 210; *La Follette's Weekly Magazine* 3:46 (18 November 1911): 4–5, 15; *La Follette's Weekly Magazine* 4:3 (20 January 1912):13; *La Follette's Weekly Magazine* 4:7 (17 February 1912):13; Lenroot to Pinchot, 8 December 1911, Box 144, Harry Slattery to Pinchot, 9 December 1911, Box 148, Gifford Pinchot Papers.

lands that were under the control of the Interior Department and to navigable streams, which fell under the purview of the secretary of war. The utility
companies were not prepared to accept the system without a fight, wanting
not only irrevocable permits, which Pinchot favored, but unlimited permits
without fee to which he objected.[25] Such was the situation when in December 1911, the House Committee on Public Lands reported a seemingly
minor bill sponsored by Democratic congressman John E. Raker of California, which would give right of way over a small parcel of land in Mono
National Forest to the Hydro-electric Company of California.

On 5 January, James R. Mann successfully raised parliamentary objection
to bringing the bill up from the private-bill calendar. The following day the
National Conservation Association threw the spotlight on the measure with
a statement denouncing it. Pinchot and his associates were prone to exaggerate, but in this instance they had a very strong case. They pointed out
that for more than two years the company had been contesting the right
of the government to regulate use of lands within national forests. The
Agriculture Department, parent of the Forest Service, offered use of the
land, which was only 3,800 feet, under standard conditions, but the company declined the offer and proceeded to dig a ditch across the land and
lay a pipeline. The company claimed right to the land on the basis of mining
claims and construction of a road along the route of the pipeline. A master
in chancery detected fraud and rejected the company's contentions. At this
point, the company turned to Congress to seek an irrevocable permit. Although the amount of land was not great, the conservationists felt the
precedent important. "The company is attempting by appeal to Congress
to establish the right of water power companies to take and use for their
own purposes what National Forest land they please," the association argued. "Under the law at present only revocable permits can be given to
water power companies in the National Forests," the statement explained.
Furthermore, "under these permits great development has taken place, but
they are objected to by the companies, and properly so. Permits should be
given for a definite time, and should be irrevocable except for breach of
contract, and legislation to that effect would have been secured long ago
if the companies had not insisted on being given the rights they need in
perpetuity and for nothing." Pinchot's group concluded that there was
strong hope for a satisfactory law that session but not if the Raker bill
passed.[26]

Lenroot took an immediate interest in the matter, and the association
supplied him with material. On his own, Lenroot solicited the written views
of a Wisconsin man, Norman G. Torrison, perhaps because Torrison called

25. Jerome G. Kerwin, *Federal Water-Power Legislation*, pp. 143–53; McGeary, *Gifford Pinchot*,
p. 203; Samuel P. Hays, *Conservation and the Gospel of Efficiency: The Progressive Conservation Movement, 1890–1920*, pp. 74–81.

26. *CR* 62:2, 1912, vol. 48, pt. 1, pp. 682–84; "National Conservation Association," 6
January 1912, Box 2050, Pinchot Papers.

on him in behalf of the bill. He submitted Torrison's statement to Pinchot's men for a point-by-point response. Lenroot, satisfied that a Chicago lumber company active in his district sent Torrison or some other Wisconsin man to influence him, concluded that the bill was more important than its proponents pretended.[27]

Pinchot's men lobbied extensively among potentially friendly congressmen, to sustain the interest their January statement aroused. When the bill came to the floor for action on 6 March, the proponents denied Lenroot's contention that it was among the major bills of the session, but they could not diminish its notoriety. Time lapsing, the bill went over a week. The following Wednesday, Charles E. Pickett of Iowa, an insurgent put on the public lands committee by Mann, made the principal speech in opposition. Lenroot and Democrat Asbury Lever of South Carolina made the other major opposition speeches. Lenroot noted the extensive lobbying effort in the bill's favor as evidence that it represented the entering wedge. Turning to the bill itself, he called it the most unjust bill presented to the House since he had been in Congress and demonstrated the point with reference to the fraudulent effort to get a right of way. Lenroot made it clear that he favored general legislation that would do away with revocable permits and would authorize the secretaries of agriculture and of interior to give permits with fixed tenure and under reasonable regulation. But proponents of this exception were opposing such general legislation. Viewing the matter as a simple moral question, Lenroot pulled no punches but persistently asserted that Raker had known of things he had denied knowing about.[28]

Debate ended soon afterwards and Democrat Ollie James of Kentucky, to kill the bill as swiftly as possible, moved to strike out the enacting clause. The motion carried with a vote of 98 to 27 and so ended the Raker bill.[29]

The shadow of Woodrow Wilson hung over the Capitol during the third session of the Sixty-second Congress. The president-elect would certainly call a special session of the next Congress in which his party would have control in both branches. He would take the lead in resolving the great legislative questions of the day—trust policy, tariffs, a new system of money and banking. In what way, by what means, and with what success remained to be seen. The Democratic chiefs were content to wait, taking up the great supply bills, and leaving other matters for the next administration to settle.

Lenroot chafed at the policy of calculated inaction. Not only was it offen-

27. (Overton Price?) to Lenroot, 8 January 1912, Price to Lenroot, 18 February 1912, Box 1819, Norman G. Torrison to Lenroot, 6 February 1912, Box 1867, Pinchot Papers; *CR* 62:2, 1912, vol. 48, pt. 4, p. 3275.

28. Harry Slattery to Gifford Pinchot, 23 July 1912, Box 158, Pinchot Papers; *CR* 62:2, 1912, vol. 48, pt. 4, p. 3260; James R. Mann to Walter L. Fisher, 22 June 1911, Box 14, Walter L. Fisher Papers, LC.

29. *CR* 62:2, 1912, vol. 48, pt. 4, p. 3288.

sive in itself, but it carried ominous implications for the future. Clark, Underwood, Fitzgerald, and their counterparts in the Senate delayed matters on the premise that in the next Congress legislation could and would be written by the Democratic party.

In the rules committee and on the floor, Lenroot defended a policy of legislative action in the "lame duck" session. The major questions at issue—immigration regulation and limitations on the shipment of liquor—cut across party lines, so the example of effective action, if it could be taken, figured to be all the more salutary. To make it possible, Lenroot defended a somewhat more restrictive rule governing the immigration bill than some members wanted. He charged that members calling for consideration of the Senate bill in advance of the House substitute wanted simply to take advantage of its length to filibuster against any action. He had always favored liberalization of rules "to secure consideration, deliberation, and action." But when a rule "instead of expediting deliberation and action is proposed to be used by the opponents of a bill in a filibuster to prevent action, I am for curtailing such rules to the same extent as I am for liberalizing them where necessary," he told the House.[30]

Both measures were considered and adopted, each with Lenroot's support. The president objected to the literacy test in the immigration bill and vetoed it, and his veto was sustained. But a presidential veto of the Webb bill to restrict shipment of liquor into dry states was overridden. Taft raised constitutional objections, but Lenroot argued that, contrary to Taft's view, the Congress might well leave it to the courts to make the constitutional determination.[31]

Lenroot debated one other major bill during the session. At the very outset, the Committee on Interstate and Foreign Commerce reported a bill for physical valuation of railroads, a measure urged by the Interstate Commerce Commission since 1903 and by La Follette since 1906. Lenroot of course supported the measure, whose general purpose had passed beyond the stage of controversy, but he found fault with some of the wording. His points were sound and well expounded, but in the absence of Chairman William Adamson, Thetus Sims, in charge of the bill, declined to accept changes. One of Lenroot's perfecting amendments passed, but his main one failed.[32] However, in the Senate La Follette was given control of the bill and he brought in professors John R. Commons and Edward W. Bemis to fashion the measure. When finished, it met Lenroot's objections and was approved not only in the Senate but in the House.[33]

On balance, Congress did more than many people had expected when the "lame duck" session began. Yet the greatest issues remained for the new administration to deal with, just as the Democratic leaders in Congress had

30. *CR* 62:3, 1912, vol. 49, pt. 1, p. 656.
31. Ibid., pp. 4445–46.
32. Ibid., pp. 51–53, 68–72.
33. Claude E. Barfield, "The Democratic Party in Congress, 1909–1913" (Ph.D. diss.), pp. 410–14; Belle and Fola La Follette, *La Follette,* vol. 1, pp. 455–57.

planned. On 4 March, the new president was inaugurated. His first words must have impressed Lenroot favorably, though we have no record of his reaction. Wilson said:

> This is not a day of triumph; it is a day of dedication. Here muster, not the forces of party, but the forces of humanity. Men's hearts wait upon us; men's lives hang in the balance; men's hopes call upon us to say what we will do. Who shall live up to the great trust? Who dare fail to try? I summon all patriotic, forward-looking men, to my side. God helping me, I will not fail them, if they will but counsel and sustain me! [34]

Lenroot was more than willing to respond to the summons. But to what extent he would be welcome and what guidance the new president would give toward the solution of the great problems, this he did not know.

In advance of the anticipated special session, which in fact Wilson soon called for 7 April, Lenroot took Clara on an ocean voyage to inspect the almost completed Panama Canal, part of a group of sixty congressmen and their families.[35] Back by the end of March, Lenroot gave immediate attention to politics. Much more than at the start of most administrations and congresses, the people and their political leaders had a sense of starting fresh. Aware of the hazards and the opportunities, Lenroot was certain of his course, perhaps because he was exhilarated a little in a situation in which he might influence events significantly.

Due to the Democratic election sweep in November, one hundred-fourteen freshmen Democrats contributed to the aura of newness in the House, replacing the familiar members such as "Uncle Joe" Cannon, John Dalzell, and Nick Longworth.[36]

The Democrats were more significant for their numbers than their personalities. The party had unquestioned control of the House, with 290 members of the total 435. With a working majority in the Senate, the party had simultaneous control in both branches of Congress for only the third time since the Civil War and the first time since 1895.[37] Only during Grover Cleveland's second administration had the Democrats controlled the presidency at the same time as Congress in the post-Civil War era.

While progressive Republicans like Lenroot might cooperate with the Democrats to one degree or another, they would certainly not amalgamate with them.[38] And for those who had survived the 1912 holocaust, the Democrats, taken by themselves, constituted no great electoral threat in the future. Of more immediate concern to Lenroot was the relationship he and other progressive Republicans should establish with the Moosers and the

34. Quoted in Arthur S. Link, *Wilson: The New Freedom*, pp. 58–59.
35. Lenroot, "Memoirs," p. 94, Box 13, Lenroot Papers; Kent, *William Kent*, p. 252.
36. Link, *The New Freedom*, p. 148.
37. Howard Scott Greenlee, "The Republican Party in Division and Reunion, 1913–1920" (Ph.D. diss.), p. 16.
38. For elaboration see James Holt, *Congressional Insurgents and the Party System, 1909–1916*, pp. 83–84.

regular Republicans. Personal considerations were involved, but beyond that, the future of progressivism was at stake.

The Moosers were not in a very strong position. Though Roosevelt had run well, not many officeholders joined the party and few new men won state or local office on the party ticket. In December, a smoldering feud among the leaders flared; in February, Frank Munsey, who was with George Perkins the party's main financial backer, called for reconciliation with the Republicans. But Roosevelt and his lieutenants disclaimed any such idea. To establish the party's permanency, they hoped to enlist as large a group of congressmen as possible to identify themselves as Progressives. Roosevelt proposed cooperation between the Moosers and "near-Progressives" like Lenroot and Kent, "with the idea that they may ultimately join us," but implicit in the situation was the threat to progressive Republicans that if they stayed in the Republican party they would meet serious opposition from the Progressives at the next election.[39] By the time Lenroot reached New York, the Progressives had made significant advances. They had induced Murdock to join them and to become their floor leader. And they had secured from a willing Underwood agreement to recognize the Progressives with important committee assignments if they would recognize themselves as a party and act independently of their progenitors, the Republicans.[40]

Supported by Kent, Sydney Anderson of Minnesota, and Henry T. Helgesen of North Dakota, Lenroot dealt the Progressive drive what the *New York Times* described as "its first serious setback," in a statement to the press. At the same time, by implication Lenroot suggested the relationship he would try to establish with the regular Republicans. Lenroot said:

> I regard it as very unfortunate that there should be any division among progressives in the House at this time. It may be good personal politics for third party Progressives and for some men who were elected as Republican progressives to take such a position at this time, but there is no statesmanship about it. As far as can now be foreseen . . . progressives of all political parties will be called on to assist and co-operate with President Wilson in his progressive policies, and new complications relating only to party politics can only injure the progressive cause.

Then Lenroot pointed out that personal honor as well as public interest required him to hold aloof from the Moosers, "having been elected upon the Republican ticket and having made use of the Republican organization to secure my nomination and election. . . . The time for me to have joined the Progressive Party was before the election, and to have kept off the Republican ticket. Having failed to do so, I feel in honor bound to act with the Republican Party for the present." [41]

39. George E. Mowry, *Theodore Roosevelt and the Progressive Movement*, pp. 284–86; Theodore Roosevelt to William H. Hinebaugh, 19 March 1913, vol. 95, Series 2, Theodore Roosevelt Papers, LC; clipping, *Washington Times*, 19 March 1913, Scrapbook 17, Mann Papers.

40. William H. Hinebaugh to Roosevelt, 17 March 1913, Box 245, Series 1, Roosevelt Papers.

41. *New York Times*, 27 March 1913; clipping, *Chicago Record-Herald*, 27 March 1913, *St. Paul Pioneer*, 8 April 1913, Scrapbook 17, Mann Papers; *Superior Telegram*, 28, 31 March 1913.

Though Lenroot and Kent (whom newsmen quoted more briefly) stressed the idea of staying free to support Wilson's policies, the practical thrust of their proposal was that the insurgents should move into a loose working relationship with the regular Republicans. Though newspaper accounts differ as to the extent of their commitment as of 26 March, it is clear that Lenroot and his friends intended at least to vote for Mann for Speaker. After a brief trip to Madison and Superior, Lenroot went to Washington a week in advance of the special session and set to work organizing a conference of progressive Republicans, all of whom had been invited to join the Moosers.[42]

While the insurgents were no more inclined to join the Moosers than they had been during the campaign, they needed some good arguments as well as the support of their colleagues. The matter of entering the Republican caucus and supporting the inevitable caucus choice for Speaker and party leader, Mann, was more ticklish. The question was based on insurgent ideology and tradition. The group, in standing for the rights of individual representatives, had rejected binding caucuses. Some had criticized the practice of the party leader choosing committee members. Just two years before, seventeen Republicans refused to vote for Mann for Speaker, and at least that number stayed out of the caucus. Those insurgents who attended battled unsuccessfully over committee selection procedures.

Now Lenroot, who had been among the more radical insurgents in 1911, took the lead, first in organizing the insurgents as a group separate from the Moosers, and as an extension of that, bringing them more fully into the party fold than before.[43] Undoubtedly, he turned to his task by negotiating with Mann and bringing to his insurgent colleagues satisfactory assurances. Lenroot was also able to offer his own well-considered arguments, along with the assurance that individual insurgents would be far from alone in withstanding the pressure and blandishments of the Moosers.

By 5 April, the job was done. A large number of insurgents, having stayed away from the Progressive caucus, gathered in Anderson's office and decided to attend the Republican caucus that night, with the understanding among themselves that they would not be bound to caucus action on legislative matters. A small group of insurgents refused to attend the caucus but the rest went, joined in supporting Mann for Speaker and party leader, and contributed their share to the display of harmony and party fervor. Mann, in turn, promised that anyone voting for him did so with the understanding that he would not be bound on matters of legislation. Two days later, all the insurgents but seven voted for Mann. Of the seven dissidents, only Charles Lindbergh voted for Murdock, and even he declined to otherwise affiliate himself with the Progressives. Eighteen members voted for Murdock, mainly new ones, and nine of them were from Pennsylvania and Illinois. Except for Lindbergh of Minnesota and the non-voting Murdock,

42. *New York Times*, 27 March 1913; clippings, *Chicago Record-Herald*, 17 March 1913, *St. Paul Pioneer*, 8 April 1913, Scrapbook 17, Mann Papers; *Superior Telegram*, 28, 31 March 1913.
43. Clipping, *St. Paul Pioneer*, 8 April 1913, Scrapbook 17, Mann Papers.

no one from the heartland of insurgency, the Dakotas, Kansas, Nebraska, Iowa, Minnesota, or Wisconsin, supported the Progressive candidate.[44]

Minnesotans Anderson, Charles Davis, and James Monahan gave newsmen an explanation of what had happened. In so doing, they implicitly suggested Lenroot's reasoning with himself and with them and indicated the nature of his negotiations with Mann. According to them, the creation of a new party, which was accorded separate recognition, caused insurgents to face a question they had not really met in previous congresses—whether or not they were Republicans. Deciding that they had been so elected, it followed that they should support the party's candidate for Speaker while remaining unbound on legislation. Mann had given assurances as to the last. And he had always treated the progressive wing fairly and had himself voted right on key questions.[45]

These explanations were only partial. The day after the party caucus it was rumored, for example, that as a result of their attendance several of the leading insurgents were scheduled for good committee assignments. When specific predictions proved correct, the appointments evidenced the existence of at least tacit understandings prior to the caucus.[46] These understandings, if they existed, were not narrowly conceived, for Nelson and Cooper, neither of whom voted for Mann, were among the insurgents favorably recognized. Lenroot, yielding the ranking position on the rules committee to Campbell while remaining a member, was permitted to trade patents for public lands, thus replacing the defeated Pickett as the ranking Republican on that committee. Mann also named Kent to the lands committee.[47]

Another consideration was this: If they were to risk opposition from the Moosers at the polls in 1914, progressive Republicans might need to draw the full Republican vote. They could not afford to leave their Republicanism in question. This point, as true for Lenroot as for the others, was something he did not have to point out to anyone.

Although the Republicans had suffered a resounding defeat in the election and many members in its progressive faction had joined the new party, the prospect of making the Republican party the vehicle for progressivism seemed bright to Lenroot and to those he persuaded. Standpatters, coming mainly from two party states, had fallen in great number; but progressives from the Republican heartland had survived almost unscathed, protected by their own progressivism and by the Republican traditions of their dis-

44. *CR* 63:1, 1913, vol. 50, pt. 1, p. 64; clippings, *Chicago Inter Ocean*, 6 April 1913, *St. Paul Pioneer*, 8 April 1913, Scrapbook 17, Mann Papers.

45. Clippings, *Chicago Inter Ocean*, 6 April 1913, *St. Paul Pioneer*, 8 April 1913, Scrapbook 17, Mann Papers.

46. Clippings, *Washington Post*, 6 April 1913, *Cincinnati Enquirer*, 6 April 1913, *St. Paul Pioneer*, 8 April 1913, Scrapbook 17, *Chicago Inter Ocean*, 1 June 1913, Scrapbook 20, Mann Papers.

47. Clipping, *Chicago Inter Ocean*, 1 June 1913, Scrapbook 20, Mann Papers. Though Kent ran as an independent, he voted for Mann for Speaker.

tricts.[48] If one presumed any future for the new Progressive party, progressive Republicanism might not grow. But already the new party showed signs of an early demise.

Old Guard leaders remained in control of party machinery outside of Congress and in it. Some of these men had accepted inevitable defeat at the polls in preference to nominating Roosevelt; they were unlikely to yield much in the future.[49] On the other hand, concessions had been made not only during the election campaign but also afterwards in the Senate and in the House.[50] And certainly Mann was not one of those who proposed to drive anyone away.

Lenroot was able to be quite definite immediately after his return from Panama because he understood Mann's situation and purposes. The minority leader's personal and public ambitions coincided. He wanted to retain his position and eventually become Speaker. And, as a thorough partisan, he wanted to unite Republicans and direct their energies against the Democrats. These things he had made clear during the Sixty-second Congress. In pursuance of these ends, Mann had to make substantial concessions to the insurgents and could do so at a relatively small cost. In a hopeless minority in the House, the Republicans would have little direct effect on legislation. And now that Taft was gone from the White House, the Republicans had no partisan obligations to the president. They had less need, therefore, for a party position on most issues—apart from the traditional tariff question. Indeed, in the absence of one they could turn their diversities to advantage, by shelling the Democrats from several vantage points. Some standpatters would object to the recognition of insurgents, as Anderson noted in thanking Mann for his assignment to ways and means, but that was something the crusty leader could live with.[51]

In the long run, the new system of coexistence could not last; one faction or the other would have to gain dominance. For the time being, however, this agreement was mutually convenient. To Lenroot and his colleagues, this alternative was the safest and most satisfactory. To have joined a new party that was on the road to extinction would have been foolhardy; yet, while that party existed, to have formed still another splinter group that would be neither inside nor outside the Republican party would have been so useless as to appear ridiculous. Inevitably, the members of a faction of that sort would have been drawn either toward the new party or back into the old one, but on unfavorable terms. To avoid these hazards, it was necessary to find a solution immediately, and this Mann offered. The terms

48. Holt, *Congressional Insurgents*, pp. 70–71.

49. Norman M. Wilensky, *Conservatives in the Progressive Era: The Taft Republicans of 1912*, pp. 70–75; Greenlee, "Republican Party in Division and Reunion," p. 8.

50. La Follette and Cummins were named to the steering committee and La Follette's program for the short session had been adopted. *La Follette's Weekly Magazine* 5:8 (22 February 1913):8.

51. Anderson to Mann, 11 April 1913, Scrapbook 17, Mann Papers.

were eminently satisfactory, as Lenroot knew they would be. He and his cohorts retained their freedom to vote with the Democrats when they pleased, to disassociate themselves from other Republicans if they liked, even to join the Progressive party at a later date if it proved more vital than seemed probable. Beyond that, the recognition that progressive Republicans would receive accorded with Lenroot's conception of the true character of the Republican party and of its future, when the will of the "rank and file" was finally reflected by its leaders. The outcome accorded also with Lenroot's sense of honor, his desire to be honorable and seem honorable; he would act as a Republican, having run as one. And as a Wisconsin progressive of the La Follette faction, Lenroot had special reasons for gratification.

Lenroot was still of the La Follette faction. During the period of the "lame duck" session from December to March, the two men and their families amended their personal and political relationship to the extent possible.[52] It was necessarily a superficial piece of work, easily punctured. Perhaps for that very reason, Lenroot was solicitous to develop it and cautious not to impair it.

The renewal of friendship was made possible not by sudden abandonment of independent judgment on Lenroot's part but by a convergence of interest and outlook. It was La Follette's situation that had changed. With his presidential hopes smashed, in the summer of 1912 La Follette rejoiced when he found himself able to resume his old role of insurgent leader in the Senate. In order to oppose Roosevelt and to defend his faction in Wisconsin, he emphasized his Republicanism and argued that the Republican party represented the best hope for progressivism, and La Follette worked along this course without sacrificing his freedom. For the time being, his role was that of constructive statesman, who was concerned for sound legislation and for the advancement of his party along progressive lines.[53]

Lenroot had good reason to work with La Follette—to do so gratified his sense of loyalty and enhanced his effectiveness in Congress and in Wisconsin. Such cooperation, however, required Lenroot to eschew the Bull Moose heresy. Therefore, he needed a viable alternative, and he found it in the

---

52. Evidences of their cooperation on legislation can be seen in La Follette to Gilbert Roe, 14 January 1913, and Lenroot to Gil Roe, 17 February 1913, Box 5, Series H, La Follette FC; that Lenroot worked with La Follette on political matters of Wisconsin is made clear in Lenroot to Ekern, 24 January 1913, Ekern to Lenroot, 3 February 1913, and 21 April 1913, Box 13, Ekern Papers; and Otto Bosshard to La Follette, 2 September 1913, Box 73, Series B, La Follette FC; the personal relationship is indicated in the fact that when Mary La Follette had scarlet fever, Phil was lodged briefly with the Lenroots. Belle La Follette to Mrs. R. G. Siebecker, 28 February 1913, Box 12, Series A, La Follette FC. Lenroot later recalled that he and Clara were frequent dinner guests at the La Follettes, though always when others were present. Lenroot, "Memoirs," pp. 97–98, Box 13, Lenroot Papers.

53. *La Follette's Weekly Magazine* 5:14 (5 April 1913):1; *La Follette's Weekly Magazine* 5:8 (22 February 1913):8.

Republican party. Were he not already inclined toward that alternative for other reasons, the La Follette attachment would not have been sufficient to move him. But under the circumstances, concern for that relationship may have influenced his thinking.

For Lenroot to remain in the Republican party on acceptable terms, that is, with relative freedom of action and with some reasonable prospect that the party would swing toward progressivism, it was essential that the other progressive Republicans join him. For that reason, in deciding his own course, he automatically committed himself to try to persuade his colleagues. In practice, that meant taking the lead. Norris was gone to the Senate, Murdock defected, and Cooper and Nelson were not sympathetic. But Lenroot would have been the leader in any case. Respected for his character and clarity of thought, he was trusted. As a progressive whose credentials were unimpeachable, he lent confidence to moderate men when he counseled moderation and his own respect for the integrity of others helped him as a negotiator.

However qualified to mediate, Lenroot could not have accomplished his purpose had circumstances been materially different. But arrangements are not made by circumstances, and without Lenroot's initiative and his mediating talents, the result might have been different.

During the next month, as the House acted on the Democratic tariff bill, Lenroot had no trouble being at once a progressive and a Republican. Without departing from progressive principles, he and his friends found themselves on common ground with the regular Republicans. With the Democrats and Progressives they were often at odds, and occasionally feeling ran high. Since such an alignment vindicated the decision the progressive Republicans made at the start of the session, one can assume that Lenroot and some of the others encouraged it. Nevertheless, the day-to-day experience of harmony with the regulars and hostility toward the Democrats and Progressives were bound to leave an imprint on the thought and feelings of men like Lenroot.

Party lines were so clearly drawn, at least as between the two major parties, because the issue was the tariff. By tradition, each party had a position to defend, irrespective of factional affiliation. Had the Republicans been framing the bill, Lenroot and Anderson would have found it impossible to agree with arch protectionists like Joseph Fordney or J. Hampton Moore. But under present circumstances such differences were academic —all Republicans could agree that a bill fashioned in accordance with Democratic principles was unacceptable. And no binding caucus was necessary to secure that degree of consensus among Republicans.

Lenroot and his progressive Republican friends differed sharply with the Democrats on matters other than tariff rates, such as the questions in which their progressivism more than their Republicanism came into play. Some had hoped that the new president would act through a progressive coalition.

But Woodrow Wilson found it expedient to rely on Democrats of whatever faction, to the extent possible.[54] In the House, the Democrats were sufficiently numerous to effect his tariff purposes. Lenroot and his friends would be allowed no part in writing the measure. Onto the system of caucus domination, which was offensive to the insurgents, Wilson superimposed presidential "dictation." [55]

Wilson's plan became quickly clear. Prior to the session, the Democrats on the ways and means committee had completed preparation of the bill, but Wilson demanded further downward revisions and the committee Democrats complied. When Congress convened, Underwood immediately introduced his bill, and the president, appearing in person before a joint session of Congress, commended tariff cuts as removing special privilege. Between 9 April and 19 April, the Underwood bill got the only real consideration it would receive by any large number of House members, as the Democratic caucus acted on it section by section. Surviving that unscathed, with only thirteen Democrats asking to be excused from adherence to the caucus decisions because of pledges to their constituents, the Democrats were ready for the formalities in the House. On 22 April, the ways and means committee reported the bill to the House, where Underwood happily operated the legislative steamroller.[56] He capitalized on the caucus decision that most committee assignments would not be made until later in the session.

While the Democrats were reviewing the Underwood bill in caucus, the insurgents were organizing a united Republican opposition along lines that were progressive but acceptable to conservatives. At a public caucus on 1 April, Republicans strongly criticized the Underwood bill. The moderate insurgent Horace Towner of Iowa also attacked the president for interference in a tariff measure, saying that under the Constitution the House had the authority to originate revenue bills. The president, with the great patronage at his disposal, should not make recommendations to the House on such a measure, Towner argued. With little difficulty, those present agreed that amendments to the wool and cotton schedules should be drafted, along with an amendment for a Tariff Board or Commission. At the next meeting on 18 April, the participants decided in favor of the stronger word "commission" and also that future caucuses should be open, in contrast to those of the Democrats. Regulars Martin Madden and Mann spoke in favor of an open caucus. In practice, since the party was not united on other questions, members had no further occasion to caucus during the session.[57]

54. Link, *The New Freedom*, pp. 152–75.

55. For a full discussion of Democratic tactics and Republican response see Elston Edward Roady, "Party Regularity in the Sixty-Third Congress" (Ph.D. diss.).

56. Link, *The New Freedom*, pp. 179–81.

57. Clippings, *Chicago Inter Ocean*, 12 April 1913, *Chicago Tribune*, 12 April 1913, *Washington Post*, 12 April 1913, *Washington Herald*, 12 April 1913, *Chicago Inter Ocean*, 18 April 1913, Scrapbook 17, Mann Papers; Greenlee, "Republican Party in Division and Reunion," p. 58.

The day before the House began debate on the tariff bill, Lenroot excoriated the Democrats for the rule they offered to govern consideration of two large appropriations bills. He felt the rule to be more drastic than any other in his experience, since it sharply limited debate and gave no power to amend except for one recommittal motion. It was based on a Republican precedent from the Fifty-fifth Congress, and Lenroot read the names of Democrats—Adamson, Clark, and Underwood among them—who had voted against it in that Congress.[58]

A week later with the Underwood tariff bill under consideration, Lenroot took up the other abiding procedural question that so concerned the insurgents—the matter of caucus rule. After some debate between the two, Lenroot asked Underwood: "If an amendment is presented which appeals to a Democrat who is not a member of the Ways and Means Committee, is he at liberty to vote for it?" "He has appointed his agents, and his agents are acting for him," Underwood answered.[59]

Though no immediate accomplishments were in prospect, Lenroot continued to be involved in debate. Apart from the motive of scoring political points against the Democrats, Lenroot perhaps felt that his efforts might contribute to the ultimate triumph of the causes he espoused, particularly a Tariff Commission and equitable wool and cotton schedules.[60]

To further the cause of a Tariff Commission, Lenroot reintroduced his bill, and caused to be printed as a House document an article by William Culbertson. On that issue the Democrats were on the defensive, and Lenroot helped Mann in an unsuccessful effort to force a record vote. While not withdrawing his earlier charges against Cannon in the heated partisan debate over which side had killed the Tariff Commission bill in the last days of the Sixty-first Congress, Lenroot put much of the blame on John Fitzgerald and other Democrats.[61]

If Lenroot and his friends were pleased to be able to act with the regular Republicans against the Democrats on the tariff question, it was partly because of the Progressives. Having been forced by the Moosers to choose and having chosen the Republican party, the progressive Republicans needed to justify their decision. Looking toward the future from a personal standpoint and in terms of the future of progressivism, as they conceived it, they needed to find in the Republican party a satisfactory home.

If they were to succeed, the progressive Republicans had to lure the Progressives back to their party. The converse was also true. But to accomplish the purpose, each now tried to discredit the other. Lenroot and the

58. *CR* 63:1, 1913, vol. 50, pt. 1, pp. 295–96.
59. Ibid., p. 752.
60. Ibid., pp. 767, 888, 1006, 1046, 1058, 1233, 1365.
61. William S. Culbertson, Diary, 7, 29 April 1913, Box 3, William S. Culbertson Papers, LC; J. C. Halls to Culbertson, 28 May 1913, Box 11, Culbertson Papers; *CR* 63:1, 1913, vol. 50, pt. 1, pp. 286–87, 767; 1913, vol. 50, pt. 2, pp. 1233, 1326; clippings, *Chicago Tribune,* 8 May 1913, *Washington Post,* 30 April 1913, Scrapbook 17, Mann Papers.

progressive Republicans naturally found in Mann and his helper William Humphrey of Washington willing allies.

The inexperienced, independent-minded Progressives were disunited on the tariff bill, as Humphrey noted. On 3 May, Lenroot took the trouble during a speech on the woolens schedule to remark on Murdock's silence, contrasting it with the forthright position he had taken on the wool bill two years earlier.[62] That night, tariff expert Culbertson dined with Murdock and found him "restless under the 'kidding' he is getting on the floor of the House." Murdock worried that he was not clever enough " 'to put it over' on the other fellow." Culbertson judged that "his great ambition now seems to be cleverness in rejoinder." [63] At the next meeting of the House, Murdock replied to Humphrey's charge that the Progressives were divided among themselves. Though his remarks betrayed more ardor than wit, his counterattack evoked laughter and great cheers from the Democrats. Murdock charged that the Republican party was itself divided in four parts. First, there were arch-protectionist standpatters like Fordney and Moore; the second group, for whom he reserved most of his venom, was headed by Mann, who was "the chief sneerer of the Republican aggregation" and who was inclined toward the first group but held back because of the third; the third group was composed of "some other members of the Republican party who have been in the past progressive. Just where they are now I do not know." He singled out Lenroot as one of them. "Where is Mr. Lenroot and what is he? Is he a Republican? I doubt it. Is he a Progressive? He is not. (Applause on the Democratic side.) Is he a standpatter? I do not know. It seems that the impression is abroad up in Wisconsin that he is a Democrat. (Cries of "No!" on the Democratic side)." Murdock then read a letter published in the *Superior Telegram* in which a local Bull Moose leader wrote that his group had been led to believe Lenroot with them but had long since learned the truth. At this point, Murdock defined the fourth group, which was made up largely or exclusively of Pennsylvanians who had won election on Progressive and Republican tickets and in Congress aligned with the latter.[64]

Lenroot did not respond, but Mann continued his severe attacks. Four days later, however, after Murdock spoke on a Tariff Commission amendment he had just introduced, Lenroot secured the floor and began:

> Mr. Chairman, during this session of Congress there have not been many things with which I have been able to be in accord with the gentleman from Kansas, and

62. *CR* 63:1, 1913, vol. 50, pt. 2, p. 1046.

63. William S. Culbertson, Diary, 3 May 1913, Box 3, Culbertson Papers.

64. *Wisconsin State Journal*, 5 May 1913; *CR* 63:1, 1913, vol. 50, pt. 2, p. 1121. Although Murdock and Lenroot continued to jibe at one another through the remainder of the Congress, the good-humored Murdock, soon after his term ended, told an audience in Superior, Wis., that Lenroot was "one of the really great men in the United States, an honest, fearless champion of the rights of the people," one of the few in Congress always on the job. *Superior Telegram*, 15 April 1915.

so I am especially glad that upon this proposition he and I are in accord in a great many particulars, for I find that this tariff commission bill introduced by him, representing the Progressive Party, has been copied almost verbatim—at least three fourths of it—from a bill introduced by me on the first day of this session, and also introduced by me at the last session of Congress.

Murdock in effect admitted the charge but countered by suggesting that Lenroot's bill went much further than Payne's, which Lenroot was now supporting. "In detail, but not so far as the powers conferred upon the commission is concerned," Lenroot replied. Then he noted that Murdock's bill included two original features, both of which he proceeded to criticize in expert fashion.[65]

The following day, despite the efforts of Roosevelt, journalist J. C. O'Laughlin, and others, the representatives of the Progressive party exposed their division by their votes—four of them breaking rank to vote for the Underwood bill on final passage, as contrasted to only two from the much more numerous Republicans. Lenroot voted with his party, first to recommit, then in opposition to the bill.[66]

To the extent that the Progressive party had less allure in May than in March, the Republican party was the more attractive to Lenroot and other progressive Republicans. At the same time, Lenroot found other reasons to judge his decision for the Republicans a correct one. Starting in November 1912, Cummins spearheaded a drive to reorganize the Republican party's machinery, especially by cutting Southern representation at national conventions. Cummins and others talked of a special convention for the fall of 1913 to accomplish this and related reforms. Although some regular Republican leaders feared any such convention, they were in no position to resist all reform if they hoped to win Bull Moose voters back to the party. To generate pressure and publicity, Cummins called a conference of progressive Republicans to meet at Chicago on 10 May. Three days in advance of that gathering, Charles Hilles called a meeting of the Executive Committee of the Republican National Committee to meet in New York on 24 May to consider party reorganization and Southern representation. Escorting Clara home following the tariff vote in the House, Lenroot did not stay on in Chicago for the conference, though he went there on the same train as Cummins and Sens. Coe Crawford and Lawrence Sherman and perhaps conferred with them en route. Several of Lenroot's friends, including Sydney Anderson and James Good, came to the conference. As of mid-May, it was not clear how much would be accomplished, but it was

65. *CR* 63:1, 1913, vol. 50, pt. 2, pp. 1325–26. Murdock's bill was drafted under the auspices of the party's legislative reference bureau by attorney Donald Richberg of Chicago. William Draper Lewis to Theodore Roosevelt, 4 April 1913, Box 246, Series 1, Roosevelt Papers; and also in the Richberg folder, Box 45, Victor Murdock Papers.

66. Mowry, *The Progressive Movement*, p. 287; clipping, *Chicago Record-Herald*, 9 May 1913, Scrapbook 17, Mann Papers; J. C. O'Laughlin to Roosevelt, 23 March 1913, Box 245, Series 1, Roosevelt Papers; *CR* 63:1, 1913, vol. 50, pt. 2, pp. 1386–87.

apparent that the party was moving in what Lenroot considered the right direction.[67]

On 22 May, Lenroot made a quick trip to Minneapolis where he spoke at a banquet and conference of progressive Republicans of the northwest, Congressmen Anderson and Monahan and Senator Gronna among them. Lenroot attacked the Underwood tariff bill and defended progressive Republicans for their stand against it. The conferees talked of party reorganization but formulated no definite plans.[68] Lenroot was unable to do more on that subject for the time being, but he undoubtedly felt encouraged and in a way vindicated at favorable news. On 24 May, the Executive Committee of the Republican National Committee agreed to the progressives' demand that Southern convention representation be reduced. Whether this should be done by the Republican National Committee itself or by the special convention that the progressives wanted remained undecided, and as the special session of Congress lingered it became obvious that no convention could be held in 1913. However, through the summer progressive Republicans met regularly and talked optimistically of a convention in 1914, which is what Lenroot and La Follette had advocated from the first.[69]

Meanwhile, the House progressive Republicans exacted an important concession from the leadership with the choice of one of their own, Frank Woods of Iowa, as chairman of the Republican Congressional Campaign Committee, replacing William McKinley of Illinois, who had been defeated for reelection in 1912. The meaning of Woods's selection was lessened somewhat, however, with the simultaneous agreement that the committee would focus on national propaganda instead of aid to individual candidates.[70]

Lenroot was not pleased that the Democrats persisted in the use of the caucus and even held committee meetings in secret in development of the Federal Reserve bill. But Sydney Anderson's response surely gratified him. In the midst of floor debate on the bill, Anderson stunned the House by submitting his resignation from the ways and means committee in protest against Democratic tactics. Anderson then bitterly attacked partisan consideration of the tariff and currency bills, likening the Democratic system of legislating to Cannonism. Anderson employed another image, that of the holding company, showing that, as with a holding company, a minority

67. Holt, *Congressional Insurgents*, pp. 99–100; Ralph Mills Sayre, "Albert Baird Cummins and the Progressive Movement in Iowa," p. 429; Greenlee, "Republican Party in Division and Reunion," pp. 58–61; *Chicago Tribune*, 11 May 1913. Lenroot would have attended the conference if he had wanted to. He probably deferred to the feelings of La Follette, who disapproved of the conference and wanted a convention not in the fall but the following spring. La Follette best indicated his reasons in La Follette to A. T. Rogers, 25 June 1913, Box 108, Series B, La Follette FC.

68. *Superior Telegram*, 23 May 1913.

69. Greenlee, "Republican Party in Division and Reunion," pp. 62–65; Gerald D. McKnight, "A Party Against Itself—The Grand Old Party in the New Freedom Era, 1913–1916" (Ph.D. diss.), pp. 94–96.

70. Greenlee, "Republican Party in Division and Reunion," p. 88.

interest was sufficient to control in the House. Furthermore, he demonstrated that the fourteen Southern states sent enough representatives to Congress to control through the caucus, and that Southerners held all but one major committee chairmanship, while by contrast ". . . one hundred and forty-one congressional districts are wholly unrepresented." [71] The following day, Republicans of every faction associated themselves with Anderson's charges.

Having taken a similar line himself, Lenroot well understood the political implication of Anderson's position. The sectional argument was a traditional bridge that united all Republicans. Its basis was economic as well as sentimental, so it persisted beyond the lifetime of Civil War veterans. But to progressive Republicans, it had special significance. If, as men like Anderson and Lenroot contended, the Democratic party was dominated by its Southern Bourbons, with their antique doctrines of states' rights and minimal government and their practical antipathy to measures that would raise the cost of labor or would interfere with resource development, then their opponents, the Republicans, were potentially at least the party of progress. Thus, the sectional argument served not only partisan but factional ends, emphasizing the progressive character of the Republican party. Anderson's restatement of the insurgent case against caucus domination, quite apart from the sectional aspect, had the same effect, that is, rallying Republicans on the basis of progressive arguments. When the progressive Republicans in the Senate, who were led by Cummins, went further and attacked President Wilson for dictatorial behavior, they contributed to the cause.[72]

When the currency bill reached the House floor on 9 September, it encountered strong Republican opposition from Mann and insurgents Everis Hayes, Frank Woods, and Charles Lindbergh of the banking and currency committee. But Lenroot concluded that the benefits far outweighed the disadvantages and felt that the measure was of the greatest importance to the national economy. He thought that the complex new system of banking and currency would be responsive to the changing currency and credit needs of the economy, within the course of a year or the period of a business cycle. He also thought the effect of the bill would be to decentralize control and to disperse bank reserves and felt that minor changes that might be effected by the Senate could eliminate the danger that a single administration could gain complete control of the Federal Reserve Board. On 18 September, Lenroot, with twenty-three other Republicans, joined the majority in voting for the bill.[73]

Lenroot did not remain for the final vote on the tariff bill but arranged

71. Ibid., p. 30; *Superior Telegram*, 12, 16 September 1913.

72. Sayre, "Cummins," pp. 427–28. For the extent of Republican criticism of Democratic tactics see also Roady, "Party Regularity."

73. Greenlee, "Republican Party in Division and Reunion," pp. 27, 34; McKnight, "A Party Against Itself," pp. 36–38; *Superior Telegram*, 30 October 1913; clipping, *Chicago Inter Ocean*, 19 September 1913, Scrapbook 20, Mann Papers; Holt, *Congressional Insurgents*, pp. 107–8.

to be paired against it. In so doing, he accommodated Mann, who wanted a solid front on this party issue. But he differed with La Follette, who participated in consideration of the bill through the long summer months, was taken into Democratic councils and earned for himself a place on the conference committee over the protests of Republican senators.[74]

There is no evidence to indicate that their differences on the tariff either signified or caused any breach between Lenroot and La Follette. They had disagreed on the tariff question for some time, and each understood the other's position.

On 1 December, Congress began a session that lasted almost eleven months. Before it was done, Congress had acted on various measures such as the money question, antitrust, immigration, appropriations, conservation, foreign relations, and much else. Due to a recurrent illness of Dorothy in 1914, Lenroot took leave of absence to help care for her in late April, July, and in the early part of October, thus missing over three months of the session. But while he was on hand, Lenroot was exceedingly active and productive.

He immediately became involved in hearings before the rules committee and the public lands committee. However, the only major legislation on which the House acted before the Christmas recess was the conference report on the Federal Reserve bill.

Back in Washington after the holidays, Lenroot became active on many fronts. He approached each separate measure from a progressive standpoint.

During the rules committee hearings in December 1913, Lenroot supported a proposal for an investigation by the Committee on Mines and Mining into labor disputes that had brought violence and death in Colorado and Michigan. The sponsors thought an investigation would help the coal and copper miners by publicizing the conditions that produced the walkouts and the repression that followed. Neither William J. McDonald of Michigan nor Edward Keating of Colorado was a lawyer, and Lenroot found their resolutions technically defective, but at a hearing he offered suggestions by which their proposals could be improved, chiefly by inserting references to interstate commerce as constitutional justification.[75]

When a Senate bill sponsored by La Follette for the eight-hour day for women in the District of Columbia reached the House floor, Lenroot went to the brink of parliamentary propriety in denouncing a new member for offering a patently unconstitutional amendment to include men under the bill's protections.[76]

In mid-April, Lenroot spoke less personally but with equal vehemence in favor of an amendment by James Good to increase the appropriation

74. *Superior Telegram*, 6, 10 September 1913.

75. U.S., House of Representatives, Committee on Rules, *Hearings: Industrial Disputes in Colorado and Michigan*, 10, 17 December 1913.

76. *CR* 63:2, 1914, vol. 51, pt. 4, p. 3415.

for the recently created Children's Bureau to $139,000, for an investigation of infant mortality and dangerous occupations. Prudently, the House overrode the appropriations committee and voted for the Children's Bureau.[77]

In line with the thinking of organized labor, of many sociologists, social workers, and most of his party members, Lenroot continued to favor curbs on immigration, through use of a literacy test. Undoubtedly he felt the nation was oversupplied with cheap labor. Perhaps, also, he shared the widespread fears for American institutions, on the grounds that the great mass of "new immigrants" who had been coming in ever-growing numbers from southern and eastern Europe since the mid-eighties were not easily assimilated. But he successfully offered amendments to protect the rights of aliens and to ensure that those fleeing religious persecution were exempted from the literacy test.[78]

While no enemy to regulation, Lenroot also remained deeply attached to the idea of antitrust. Trust-busting lay at the heart of Wilson's New Freedom, and the president fully supported the development of a bill that was reasonably acceptable to Lenroot. Although the Democrats made a party measure of it by binding caucus action, the leaders were willing to consider amendments that might perfect the wording.[79]

Already something of an expert on the subject, Lenroot participated in debate on several provisions when the bill reached the floor in late May. In general, he supported efforts to broaden the application of antitrust and to strengthen the enforcement mechanism. In that connection, he offered an important amendment that the committee accepted, as embodying the purposes of the House better than the language initially proposed. Widespread sentiment existed in the House for punishment of corporation officers whose actions contributed to violations by their companies. The wording Lenroot offered accomplished the purpose.[80]

Meanwhile, President Wilson had changed his mind about antitrust. He concluded that it was impossible to anticipate in legislation all the forms monopolistic practice might take, and he felt the Rooseveltian idea, which called for the establishment of a regulatory commission to maintain fair competition, to be more useful than antitrust prosecution. During the summer, the Senate, supported by the president, fashioned a strong Federal Trade Commission bill. The antitrust measure, which was allowed to drift, emerged in much weakened form. Lenroot's amendment, however, survived the conference and became part of the Clayton Anti-Trust Act. Lenroot undoubtedly supported the Federal Trade Commission bill when it passed the House without a record vote on 10 September. Had he been present a month later when the watered-down Clayton bill returned to the House,

77. Ibid., pp. 6794, 6810, 6812–13.
78. Ibid., pp. 2696–97, 2707, 2783, 2786, 2820–25.
79. Link, *The New Freedom*, pp. 423–27.
80. *CR* 63:2, 1914, vol. 51, pt. 10, pp. 9493, 9550, 9581–82, 9606, 9680–81.

he might well have joined the eighteen Republicans who switched to the opposition, for he later criticized the weakened measure.[81]

From 3 December through 5 December, Lenroot, with his colleagues on the rules committee, heard testimony on a resolution to create a special House committee on woman suffrage, paralleling a similar committee recently created by the Senate. In his questioning, Lenroot gave no intimation where he stood respecting a woman-suffrage amendment to the Constitution, which the suffragists wanted, but later he made it clear that while he favored woman suffrage, he preferred that it be accomplished by state action. However, he did not believe in suppressing the issue, which he knew would be the result if the matter were left to the judiciary committee. Failing in the rules committee, Lenroot raised the issue on the House floor. He charged the Democrats with using their caucus to deny suffragists a chance to be heard by a committee of Congress.[82] This was not the last time in the session that Lenroot condemned the Democrats for undemocratic procedures.[83] Indeed, the theme was one to which Lenroot reverted through the years of Democratic control, as the Democrats remained unchanging in their ways.

His attacks naturally opened Lenroot to the charge of partisanship. He strongly denied this charge. In the course of his defense he said:

> I have supported your President and my President. Upon all matters of foreign policy we have supported him as loyally as you have, even though questioning the wisdom of some of his policies, believing that upon such matters it was more important that he had a united country behind him than any close scrutiny of the particular wisdom of a particular policy.[84]

Later, in two instances, he matched action to word. In the first instance, involving repeal of the tolls exemption to American coastwise shipping in the Panama Canal, Lenroot differed with most of his party, with many progressive Republicans in the House, and with La Follette. He differed with La Follette again when, by voice and vote, he backed the president in sending armed forces into Mexico, ostensibly to avenge an insult to the nation and secure full recognition of American rights.[85]

The impact of Lenroot's contributions on the canal tolls and Mexican issues was modest. But in another area in which he worked with Democrats on a nonpartisan basis, he had very considerable effect. This was the broad

81. Link, *The New Freedom*, pp. 433–44; U.S., *Statutes at Large*, 38 Statutes, pt. 1, p. 736; Greenlee, "Republican Party in Division and Reunion," p. 39; *Superior Telegram*, 30 October 1914.

82. U.S., House of Representatives, Committee on Rules, *Hearings: Committee on Woman Suffrage*, 3, 4, 5 December 1913; Record Group 233, "Committee on Rules, Minutes," 63d Cong., 2d sess., 24 January 1914; *CR* 63:2, 1914, vol. 51, pt. 3, pp. 2895–96; *La Follette's Weekly Magazine* 6:7 (14 February 1914):4.

83. *CR* 63:2, 1914, vol. 51, pt. 3, pp. 15642, 15804, 5563–64.

84. Ibid., p. 15642.

85. Herbert F. Margulies, "Progressivism, Patriotism, and Politics: The Life and Times of Irvine L. Lenroot," pp. 707–12.

field of land and resource development and the questions of conservation. The matter was of no small importance. A historian of the progressive era has written that "progressivism's achievements in conservation were by all odds its greatest." [86]

Lenroot had been active and productive in conservation matters from his first term in Congress, but in 1914, through a combination of factors, he emerged as a dominant figure in the House on all such questions. Part of the explanation relates to the Democrats.

During their 1912 campaign in the western states, the Democrats took an ambiguous position with a large states' rights component, in deference to dominant local sentiment. But Wilson, whether out of devotion to progressivism or for fear of incurring the wrath of conservationists and the fate of Taft, determined at the outset of his administration to resist the pressure of those who wanted a lands policy that was generous to private users. Initially, he offered the job of secretary of interior to Newton D. Baker, progressive mayor of Cleveland. When Baker declined, he gave the post to Franklin K. Lane, a member of the Interstate Commerce Commission, who though a Californian, was acceptable to conservationists.[87] Genial, imaginative, and able, Lane managed to please both sides during his first two years as secretary. He showed his concern to improve procedures and encourage resource development, and he welcomed the cooperation of state officials. At the same time, he adhered to Garfield's broad view of the department's jurisdiction and was equally ready to use federal authority against monopoly.[88] In practice, Lane took the initiative on conservation legislation and worked closely with conservationists in Congress. Wilson gave him timely support.[89]

The chairman of the Committee on Public Lands, Scott Ferris of Oklahoma, and the second-ranking Democrat, James M. Graham of Illinois, were staunch friends of conservation. In Congress since 1907, Ferris turned thirty-six in 1913 when he became committee chairman. Formerly a homesteader and lawyer practicing before the federal land office, Ferris sought the chairmanship with the claim that he would not be subject to constituent pressure on matters before the lands committee, since his state had no public lands, only Indian lands.[90]

In the committee, as in the House, the states' rights view was well repre-

86. Grant McConnell, *Private Power and American Democracy* (New York, 1966), excerpted in David M. Kennedy, ed., *Progressivism: The Critical Issues* (Boston, 1971), p. 125.

87. Elmo R. Richardson, *Politics of Conservation: Crusades and Controversies*, pp. 146–47; Link, *The New Freedom*, pp. 16–18.

88. Richardson, *Politics of Conservation*, pp. 151–55.

89. Lane to Benjamin Ide Wheeler, 13 March 1914, to Frederic J. Lane, 27 April 1914, to William R. Wheeler, 6 June 1914, to Lawrence F. Abbott, 12 January 1915, in Anne Wintermute Lane and Louise Herrick Wall, eds., *The Letters of Franklin K. Lane: Personal and Political* (Boston and New York, 1922), pp. 147, 150–51, 153, 161–62; Slattery to Pinchot, 6 June 1914, Box 181, Pinchot Papers.

90. Ferris to Oscar Underwood, 18 December 1912, Box 25, Francis Burton Harrison Papers, LC.

sented among Democrats as among Republicans. Western members inclined toward that outlook regarded the committee as of key importance to their constituents and made strong efforts to get on it.[91] Edward Taylor of Colorado was the most important of those men who succeeded.

Given the division within their party, neither Ferris nor Secretary Lane could afford to take a purely partisan approach in the development and enactment of legislation. Beyond that, the lands committee and the House traditionally acted in a relatively nonpartisan way on conservation questions. The fact that division occurred on geographical more than partisan lines offers partial explanation. However, it would not be accurate to overemphasize conflict. The committee and the House acted unanimously on many questions. It was the only feasible approach in dealing with the many urgent claims of particular groups or localities requiring legislative remedy. And even on major questions, it was to everyone's advantage to achieve consensus if at all possible, for without it success in the Senate and House became problematic.

Under all these circumstances, Lenroot, as ranking Republican on the committee, had ample scope for his energies. He could participate as fully as he cared to in the preparation of legislation, and Ferris welcomed his help on the House floor too. Most committee members took only a casual interest in most proceedings—they were content to allow their leaders to represent them and their party. In effect, then, Lenroot became "Mr. Republican" on conservation matters during the Sixty-third Congress and in the congresses that followed. He was glad to have help from "Billy" Kent, and to a lesser extent Progressive Charles M. Thomson on the committee, and from Mann on the floor. But Lenroot became responsible for the leadership and for drafting many of the bills. He knew the value of specialization, had no fear of hard work, and appreciated the importance of the subject and the possibilities for accomplishment, so he welcomed the responsibilities now available to him. Realizing the importance of precedent, he did not confine his attentions to the major bills.

The administration program, embodied in Lane's first annual report in December 1913, consisted of five major bills. Lane called for a government-built and -operated railroad system in Alaska; a bill for leasing Alaskan coal lands; a new reclamation act; a leasing system to open and develop coal, oil, phosphate, and potash deposits on public lands; and a scheme to lease and develop waterpower sites on public lands.[92] Lenroot played little or no part in passage of the reclamation act, but his role was central to House action on the other four measures.

The first bill to reach the floor was the Alaska railroad measure. The bill, introduced during the first session, was considered in the Committee on Territories of which Lenroot was not a member, but on the floor it was taken

91. See for example Edward T. Taylor to Francis Burton Harrison, 28 February 1911, Box 25, Harrison Papers.

92. Keith Waldemar Olson, "Franklin K. Lane: A Biography" (Ph.D. diss.), p. 124.

up on successive calendar Wednesdays (when committees could report directly to the House) without restriction on debate or on amendment, from mid-December until final passage on 6 March. Since the lands committee had jurisdiction over the companion measure for leasing Alaska coal lands, he had good reason to interest himself in the railroad bill and to update his information on the subject, which had concerned him for several years. Ferris and Graham also participated in debate, the former a member of the territories committee and one of two committee members opposed to the bill.

Wilson's endorsement of an Alaskan railroad bill in his State of the Union message carried great weight. Besides that, the Alaskan settlers, impatient for access to the public coal lands that had been withheld from entry since November 1906, were reconciled to conservationist demands. Northwesterners looked to trading opportunities, while other Americans saw in Alaska a source of inexpensive coal for the Pacific fleet and consumers everywhere. Yet the bill had its opponents in both parties. More important than the self-interested were those who regarded Alaska as a hopeless wasteland and deplored the idea of spending $35 million to build into its frozen interior. Some of these and others were wary also of what they regarded as a dangerous socialistic precedent.[93] As the House began consideration of the bill in December, prospects for passage were good, but the possibility of crippling amendment could not be discounted.

On 17 December, after an introduction by William C. Houston, committee chairman, and a speech in opposition by Fordney, Lenroot delivered the fullest defense of the bill that the House would hear. His main concern was to have cheap coal for the American consumer; secondary to that was the hope of opening fresh opportunity for independent coal operators and farmers. The chief obstacle, in his view, was the Alaska Syndicate, comprised of the Morgan and Guggenheim interests, which he believed had conspired to gain control of Alaska's vast resources not only by such fraudulent claims as Pinchot and Glavis had complained of, but still more, by monopolizing the railroads. Lenroot used most of his hour to show from testimony before the Senate and House committees that the three existing railroads were controlled by the Syndicate and that it proposed to keep out competition.[94]

The Senate was first to pass an Alaska railroad bill, and its bill became the vehicle for House action. When in February the House got to the amendment stage, Lenroot again took an active part. He exerted his influence against limiting the line to the two coastal coal fields, against putting the government in a position of dependence on the private companies for terminal or other facilities, and against exorbitant payments to these companies in the event the president chose to buy them out in whole or part

93. Ernest Gruening, *The State of Alaska* (New York, 1968), pp. 130, 177–88.
94. *CR* 63:2, 1913, vol. 51, pt. 1, pp. 1091–96.

instead of building an entirely new line.[95] Partly through his influence, his side won in the voting on most amendments.

One of Lenroot's comments during debate on amendments clarified his view on the socialism question. He argued that it was not at issue, "because the people of the United States own all of the property in Alaska. We are practically in the same position with reference to Alaska that the directors of a private corporation are in with reference to their duty to the property owned by the stockholders of that corporation. It is their duty to administer that property for the best interests of the stockholders." Lenroot opposed government ownership and operation of railroads, "generally speaking . . . expecially so long as the Democratic Party shall be in power and takes the attitude that it now does with reference to the civil-service question. . . . If it shall ever come—and I am one of those who believe that it may not be far distant—it can only be successful if we shall have a civil service that is honestly administered, and that shall be taken out of politics entirely." [96]

Passage of the Alaska railroad bill almost guaranteed action on some kind of bill on the leasing of Alaska coal lands that session, for members could hardly justify the heavy expenditure if the coal lands were not opened. But on what terms?

During the five days of hearings, Lenroot took the leading part among the questioners. His major consideration throughout was to plug loopholes that might allow the Morgan-Guggenheim group to gain validation for the thirty-three notorious "Cunningham claims," either directly or by indirection. He proposed a number of amendments and won their approval in committee.[97]

The bill was unanimously reported on 9 March and passed in the House. In the Senate, Western and Southern senators pushed through a substitute that was much less satisfactory to conservationists. The Senate version gave claimants preferential leasing rights, set a very low maximum royalty figure—five cents a ton—and opened the door wide to court review. Lenroot could do little to avert the Senate's action. But he felt that the Senate bill "would practically turn over Alaska to the Guggenheim crowd," and determined that as a member of the joint conference with Ferris and Graham, he would resist the Senate provisions even if it meant killing the bill for the session. Ferris and Graham agreed to stand firm with him on that ground.[98]

The House conferees decided to trigger a "publicity back-fire" from Harry Slattery, who complied. It had immediate effect and helped Secretary

95. Ibid., pp. 3345–48, 3359–61, 3614, 3617–21.
96. Ibid., p. 3346.
97. U.S., House of Representatives, Committee on Public Lands, *Hearings: Alaska Coal Leasing Bill,* 17, 23, 24, 25, 26 February 1914; U.S., House of Representatives, *Leasing of Coal Lands in Alaska, H. R. 14233,* House Report 352, 63d Cong., 2d sess.
98. Harry Slattery to Gifford Pinchot, 16 October 1914, Box 181, Pinchot Papers; Lenroot to William Kent, 30 September 1914, Box 32, William Kent Papers, Yale University.

Lane in his efforts with Democratic senators in the conference, Henry Myers of Montana and Key Pittman of Nevada. Meanwhile, Lenroot "stiffened Ferris and Graham" to hold firm. Finally, the two senators backed down, isolating their Republican colleague, Reed Smoot of Utah. For complex reasons, a second joint conference later proved necessary, but the bill emerged as the conservationists wanted it.[99]

The Alaska railroad and coal lands leasing laws had disappointingly modest results. Delays in construction, due in part to the world war, prevented completion of the railroad until 1923. This, in turn, slowed coal development, except for the coal that was produced for the construction operation itself. Coal shipped via the Panama Canal, competition from the burgeoning California oil fields, and the gradual phasing out of coal for naval vessels all discouraged private capital.[100]

Indirectly, the Alaska coal lands bill had an important and useful effect. It gave further impetus to the slow and difficult process by which the nation developed a sound leasing system applicable to the entire public domain, some seven hundred million acres, including all public lands in Alaska except the coal lands.

Few denied the need for legislation. There was no law to govern potash and phosphate lands. In the absence of adequate legislation, President Roosevelt withdrew sixty-four million acres of coal land in 1906. And the old placer mining law was utterly inappropriate to govern disposition of oil lands, the most important and controverted of the government's mineral lands. Under that law, land might be acquired in fee for $2.50 an acre by one who discovered oil and proceeded to develop it. Oil men, in California especially, raced to make discoveries and perfect claims, irrespective of demand. Having obtained a claim, they were forced to produce at full capacity lest their neighbor drain the oil first. Overproduction and waste was the inevitable result. Partly in response to this situation, sentiment for leasing developed, to enable the government to improve conditions. Pending new legislation, in September 1909, President Taft withdrew over three million acres of oil land from entry, mainly in California, and in 1910 he authorized further withdrawals. Meanwhile, as fear for the nation's oil supplies arose and the navy came to use more oil, the idea grew of setting aside some of the public oil lands for the navy. In 1912, the president set aside sixty-eight thousand acres in California as naval oil reserves. Taft's withdrawals, part of a larger policy of withdrawal and reclassification of public land, were the necessary precondition for revision of public land law. The legislative situation was vastly complicated, however, by the clamor of oil

99. Slattery to Pinchot, 16 October 1914, Box 181, Pinchot Papers; Lenroot to William Kent, 10 October 1914, Box 32, Kent Papers; to Slattery, 10, 23 October 1914, Box 1824, Slattery to Pinchot, 15 October 1914, Box 181, Lenroot to Slattery, 23 October 1914, Box 1824, press release, 15 October 1914, enclosed in Slattery to Pinchot, 16 October 1914, Box 181, Pinchot Papers; Gruening, *Alaska,* p. 188.

100. Olson, "Franklin K. Lane," p. 137; Gruening, *Alaska,* pp. 225–26, 537.

men with a welter of claims and counterclaims under the placer law or other, less applicable land laws. Even after the withdrawals, individuals and companies continued to go on the public land, disputing the legality of the withdrawals. From a practical standpoint, the desire of claimants to secure legislative relief conflicted with general leasing legislation.[101]

Lenroot was not involved in the initial drafting of the mineral lands leasing bill, which was done in the Interior Department, but thereafter, in the hearings, the committee meetings, and on the floor, he acted as partner with Ferris in its development. "These are non-partisan measures," Secretary Lane wrote of the leasing and the waterpower bills. "They have been drafted in consultation with Republicans and Progressives, as well as Democrats." [102]

During the hearings, early in the spring of 1914, Lenroot indicated his main concerns. He wanted a workable system that would permit development, and he wanted to do justice to claimants. But he made it his special business to block loopholes that would benefit fraudulent claimants or advance monopoly. He resisted, especially, the strong states' rights drive spearheaded by a Conference of Western Governors in Denver.[103]

To cope with the problem of the claimants, Ferris and Lenroot agreed with the western representatives on a separate bill that would permit claimants innocent of fraud whose claims antedated 3 July 1910 (when the withdrawals assumed full legal status) to exchange their patent claims for leases. But they insisted on three amendments—to leave discretion with the secretary of interior respecting exchange requests, to allow the secretary to set terms and conditions for such leases (except that the royalty was not to exceed one-eighth of oil and gas production), and to reduce the maximum acreage from 2,560 to 640.[104]

The westerners, in turn, with the exception of Edward Taylor of Colorado, the extreme states' righter, reluctantly yielded to Ferris and Lenroot and their allies on the major provisions of the leasing bill. Doubtless the Democrats among them were reluctant to oppose the administration; and all of them knew that the conservationists could control the situation on the floor of the House. Later, as the House neared conclusion of debate on the bill, Lenroot was able to call it "as perfect a measure as the committee could devise." [105]

The oil and gas section of the Ferris bill authorized the secretary of

101. Link, *The New Freedom*, p. 132; Olson, "Franklin K. Lane," pp. 176–80; J. Leonard Bates, *The Origins of Teapot Dome: Progressives, Parties and Petroleum, 1909–1921*, pp. 17–32; John Ise, *The United States Oil Policy*, pp. 291–323, 332.

102. Franklin K. Lane to Lawrence F. Abbott, 12 January 1915, cited in Lane and Wall, *Letters of Franklin K. Lane*, pp. 161–62.

103. U.S., House of Representatives, Committee on Public Lands, *Hearings: Exploration for, and Disposition of Oil, Gas, Etc.*, 63:2, 23 March, 3, 21, 23 April 1914.

104. U.S., House of Representatives, Committee on Public Lands, *Oil or Gas Lands, H. R. 695; CR* 63:2, 1914, vol. 51, pt. 15, pp. 15412–15.

105. *CR* 63:2, 1914, vol. 51, pt. 15, p. 15542.

interior to grant the right to prospect on not more than 640 acres of public lands if within ten miles of a producing well or not more than 2,560 acres if outside that limit. In either case, discoverers might patent a quarter of the land as their reward and the government might then offer the remainder for lease on a highest bid basis for twenty years, with preferential rights to renewal for another ten years. In his report, Ferris explained that these provisions would work against monopolization, which could occur under the placer system, would allow for orderly development in accordance with conservationist principles, and would permit the government to reserve land for itself.[106]

The relief bill was first to reach the floor on 1 September. Despite the committee amendments and the support of Secretary Lane, it had encountered conservationist objections, chiefly on the ground that it would honor legally dubious claims and that the maximum royalty was insufficient. Its proponents were willing to make concessions when the bill was called up from the unanimous consent calendar, but Mann killed it with an objection.[107] So the issue remained to be dealt with in the general leasing bill ten days later.

The conservationists controlled the situation throughout the two weeks of debate and the amendment on the leasing bill. Lenroot and Ferris worked closely together and secured the amendments they wanted, sponsored mainly by themselves or Mann. Just as systematically, they argued against and rejected the amendments submitted by Mondell, who formerly was the chairman of the lands committee but no longer a member. Although occasionally they found themselves opposed to a member of the committee, for the most part Lenroot and Ferris continued to have the reluctant support of the westerners. Lenroot and Ferris in turn agreed to a relief amendment, but with their original committee amendments added, plus an additional one fixing minimum royalty at 10 percent.[108] Finally, on 23 September, the House approved the bill largely as they wanted it, without a record vote.

The bill faced a very uncertain prospect in the Senate, where the sparsely populated western states were much stronger proportionally than in the House. Scholars have judged that the Ferris bill was less than perfect in any case. Among other deficiencies, the maximum acreage specified for patent

106. U.S., House of Representatives, Committee on Public Lands, *Exploration for and Disposition of Coal, Oil, Gas Etc., H. R. 668.*

107. Bates, *Origins of Teapot Dome,* pp. 48–50; *CR* 63:2, 1914, vol. 51, pt. 14, pp. 14557–58. During Lenroot's absence in May, Kent had written him warning against the bill and suggested that he wire Ferris reserving the right to object. Kent to Lenroot, 15 May 1914, Box 32, Kent Papers. Evidently Lenroot did not share Kent's alarm and did not wish to destroy the near unanimity of the committee on the leasing bill, for five days later Congressman Church reported the relief bill for the whole committee.

108. *CR* 63:2, 1914, vol. 51, pt. 15, pp. 15412–16; Ise, *United States Oil Policy,* pp. 327–32. For one instance of the Ferris-Lenroot alliance at work see the remarks of Ferris on p. 15430 in which he notes that Lenroot had approved an amendment he proposed and that Lenroot had dealt directly with the Interior Department on the subject.

or lease was insufficient for conditions in the plains states and even for portions of the California fields. But the leasing principle, which opened the possibility of orderly management of mineral resources, was sound. Its adoption by the House as a basis for mineral disposition was no small achievement.[109]

The most important legislation Lenroot dealt with from his vantage point on the lands committee related to waterpower. Although his committee could report only with respect to waterpower on the public lands, questions of overlapping jurisdiction gave members of the lands committee a right to be heard on the general dam legislation developed in the War Department and in William Adamson's Committee on Interstate and Foreign Commerce.

During debate on the Adamson bill, Lenroot made clear his general approach to the subject. As he had done before, he denied the common charge that conservationists proposed to "lock up" resources. "Conservationists believe in development of all of our natural resources for the greatest benefit of all our people with the smallest amount of waste that is practicable. We do not believe they should be used to make a few men rich without resulting benefits to the great mass of our people. We do not take the position that the men who with brains and capital develop these resources should not be amply rewarded, but, on the contrary, insist that they receive encouragement and protection to the fullest extent not inconsistent with the public interest." But he could not share the view, which he attributed to Judge Adamson, that public resources "should be surrendered to any private interest that will develop them." That policy had contributed more than any other single cause to the development of trusts and monopolies, Lenroot argued. He talked of Standard Oil, and the "Anthracite Coal Trust," and a Steel Trust based on control of iron ore.

Lenroot regarded waterpower as the most important of all natural resources. "Unless we retain control of this, the only resource that cannot be destroyed, the time will come where the owners of the water powers will absolutely dominate all of the industries of the Nation," he warned. In his view, the bills reported by the lands committee showed the way by which development might occur without sacrifice of public control. But if that reconciliation were not accomplished in the pending bill, "then better a thousand times defeat the bill entirely and say to the people of the country that we can better afford to let our waters flow untrammeled to the sea a few years longer than pass a bill denying to them and future generations any control over the most valuable resource which we possess." [110]

Lenroot had good reason to take an uncompromising position. In 1913, the conservationists won two preliminary battles, first in the Supreme Court,

109. For criticisms see Ise, *United States Oil Policy*, pp. 328–32; and Bates, *Origins of Teapot Dome*, pp. 51–53. Bates notes that the problems of the naval reserves were given scant attention, but that Lenroot recognized the distinctiveness of the reserves.

110. *CR* 63:2, 1914, vol. 51, pt. 12, pp. 12333–34.

then at the National Conservation Congress. In the Chandler-Dunbar case, the Court invalidated the legal doctrine that potential waterpower belonged to the riparian owner and upheld national control of waterpower rights in navigable waters. In November, Gifford Pinchot turned the tables on the power lobby, which for a time was in control of the conservation congress, and won a sweeping resolution endorsing his conservationist position.[111] Then Secretary Lane gave vigorous backing in the development of a conservationist bill covering the public domain.[112] Under the existing system, power companies had to receive special congressional authorization for a project, and this requirement had become a difficult proposition. And on the public lands, companies were subject to revocable leases, thus making it hard to raise capital.[113] Although the companies and their mainly Southern and Western allies were reluctant to accept conservationist terms, if the latter held firm in the House, eventually they would have to.

In April 1913, anticipating the possibility of action that year, Lenroot secured from Pinchot's headquarters new materials on the waterpower question. The administration chose not to discuss the issue during the first session, but after Ferris introduced an administration bill in March 1914, the lands committee held extensive hearings. During these meetings, Lenroot had opportunity not only to advance his ideas but also to refine them, prepare himself for the battle that was ahead, and to put the bill into final and satisfactory form.[114]

Through the winter and early spring, Washingtonians speculated on what kind of bill Judge Adamson would report. On 24 June, he provided his answer and, joined by Underwood, announced that his bill had the support of the president. Three days later, after the conservationists had reviewed the bill, Kent, whose progressive reputation, independent status, and pro-administration votes gave him entrée, wrote in warning and protest to Wilson. In his letter, Kent raised several of the issues that especially concerned his faction. Reminding Wilson that Secretary Lane had provided the first draft for the Ferris waterpower bill, he used that bill as a model against which to measure the Adamson bill. "In the Ferris bill," Kent wrote, "we acted on the supposition that it is our duty to use the leverage of Government ownership of land, and power of control over it, so as to protect the public to the last degree. We cast aside the theory that we would be doing our full duty if we merely obtained a pitiful revenue on present value of Government property, which latter thought is frankly embodied in the

111. Judson King, *The Conservation Fight From Theodore Roosevelt to the Tennessee Valley Authority*, p. 73; Kerwin, *Water-Power Legislation*, pp. 161–70.

112. Olson, "Franklin K. Lane," pp. 164–67.

113. Link, *The New Freedom*, p. 129.

114. Harry Slattery to Lenroot, 17 April 1913, Box 1824, Pinchot Papers; Kent, *William Kent*, p. 329; Gifford Pinchot, quoted in the *Milwaukee Sentinel*, 30 October 1920; Pinchot to Lenroot, 8 May 1914, Box 176, Pinchot Papers; William Kent to Lenroot, 20 May 1914, Box 32, Kent Papers.

Adamson bill . . . I consider the Adamson bill the worst piece of legislation that has come before the House." Kent then reminded the president of the Chandler-Dunbar decision and suggested that since the constitutional question had been resolved in favor of the federal government it would be "a betrayal of trust for us to accept the narrower view, and to permit practically uncontrolled grants, and grants unlimited as to time, to be made under the guise of aiding navigation." [115]

One of the objections of the conservationists to the Adamson bill was that it extended the powers of the secretary of war, under whom the Army Corps of Engineers worked, to control navigable streams in the public domain, at the expense of the secretary of interior particularly, and to a lesser extent the secretary of agriculture, in whose department the Bureau of Foresty was sheltered. Experience with the several bureaus and departments caused the conservationists to be alarmed at the proposed change. On the surface, it was possible to ignore the substantive overtones and view this feature of the dispute as a simple jurisdictional question as between the departments and also the several congressional committees. Hastened by embarrassing newspaper comment and after a long conference with Adamson, Wilson realized that it was on the technical level that contending members of the party could most gracefully compromise their differences. On that basis, he set out to restore harmony by bringing together Lane, Secretary of War Lindley Garrison, and Chairmen Ferris and Adamson.[116]

Almost immediately, Wilson was told that the conflict could not be resolved within the group, so on the morning of 30 June, hours before debate on the Adamson bill was to begin, he sent Lenroot a message, inviting him to the White House conference that evening. He invited also Frederick Stevens of Minnesota, ranking Republican on Adamson's committee. The conference marked the beginning of almost three weeks of negotiations, while the House suspended formal consideration of the Adamson bill. First, however, in initial debate on the bill, conservationists announced their dissatisfaction. Lenroot contributed a few barbed questions and comments and attacked the bill in a newspaper interview.[117]

In the absence of the president, the White House meeting developed into a fruitless debate between Lane and Garrison. Home at midnight, Lenroot wrote to Clara, who was in Superior with Dorothy. The conferees had scheduled another meeting for the following night, but "as I gave out a pretty warm interview on the bill this afternoon I don't know as I will go. I expect to speak on the bill Thursday." [118] He changed his mind, however,

115. Kent to Wilson, 27 June 1914, Box 111, Series 2, Woodrow Wilson Papers, LC.

116. Clipping, *Washington Times*, 30 June 1914, enclosed in Harry Slattery to Gifford Pinchot, 30 June 1914, Box 181, Pinchot Papers; Wilson to William Kent, 29 June 1914, Adamson to Wilson, 29 June 1914, Box 111, Series 2, Wilson Papers.

117. Irvine to Clara Lenroot, 30 June 1914, Box 1, Lenroot Papers; King, *Conservation Fight*, p. 46; Harry Slattery to Gifford Pinchot, Box 181, Pinchot Papers; *CR* 63:2, pp. 11413–32.

118. Lane to Wilson, 1 July 1914, Box 111, Series 2, Wilson Papers; Irvine to Clara Lenroot, 30 June 1914, Box 1, Lenroot Papers.

probably because he found that debate would not proceed pending some prior agreement.

Wilson mediated the next White House conference, but tentative agreements soon collapsed.[119] Feeling that the president meant well but was hazy on the subject, Lenroot, Kent, and Ferris met with him privately on 13 July.[120] The following night in a long and sometimes heated discussion, the conservationists won most of their points as Wilson, assuming a judicial role, ruled in their favor most of the time. "The result is," Lenroot wrote Clara the following morning, "that speech I had prepared with so much care, and had been waiting so long to deliver, had to go into the wastebasket . . ., for now an agreement is reached it wouldn't fit at all, for its purpose was to bring about the same result that has now been reached." Lenroot thought a floor fight would have accomplished as much, "and I would have gotten some glory out of it, while now I won't get a bit, except those at the different conferences know the part I have taken but after all getting results is the thing, and not the credit for getting them." He still expected to speak on the bill, "but all the ginger is taken out by the agreement." [121]

On 18 July, the House resumed debate on the bill, with Lenroot the first and principal speaker. He described the bad features of the bill as originally drawn but noted the substantial improvements that would be made by the White House amendments and judged that these would remove "most of the serious objections to the bill." But Lenroot commented also on the deficiencies that remained and that should be corrected by additional amendment. Later that day, Ferris took much the same position.[122]

Three of the four White House amendments related directly to the jurisdictional questions. The substantive gain, from a conservationist standpoint, was to maintain the jurisdiction of the Interior and Agriculture departments over waterpower projects on the public lands; to protect the stringent regulations in existing legislation and permits of dams; and to leave discretionary to the secretary of war the charge that might be fixed for public land required by power companies, instead of fixing a very small charge, as in the original bill. The other amendment ensured that grants would not be perpetual.[123] An unstated benefit of the compromise was removal of jurisdictional obstacles to adoption of the Ferris bill. Since an estimated 72 percent of undeveloped hydroelectric power was on the public

119. Lane to Wilson, 1 July 1914, Kent to Wilson, 2 July 1914, Lindley L. Garrison, "Memorandum with respect to a conference held at the White House on the evening of July 1, 1914 . . .," 2 July 1914, Adamson to Wilson, 2 July 1914, to Garrison, 2 July 1914, Kent to Wilson, 2, 3 July 1914, Box 111, Series 2, Wilson Papers.

120. Slattery to Pinchot, 11 July 1914, Box 181, Pinchot Papers; Lindley L. Garrison to Lane, 10 July 1914, Lane to Wilson, 11 July 1914, Box 112, Series 2, Wilson Papers; Irvine to Clara Lenroot, 13 July 1914, Box 1, Lenroot Papers.

121. Irvine to Clara Lenroot, 15 July 1914, Box 1, Lenroot Papers.

122. CR 63:2, 1914, vol. 51, pt. 12, pp. 12328–34; 1914, vol. 51, pt. 13, pp. 12775–77.

123. Scott Ferris to Woodrow Wilson, 16 July 1914, Box 112, Series 2, Wilson Papers; CR 63:2, 1914, vol. 51, pt. 12, pp. 12330–31.

lands, the settlement of the jurisdictional questions to the satisfaction of the conservationists was an important accomplishment.[124]

Because the White House conferences focused so largely on jurisdictional questions, neither Lenroot nor Ferris felt bound to support the Adamson bill without further amendments. They and Kent used as a standard of judgment provisions in the Ferris bill. In his speech of 18 July, Lenroot proposed additional amendments relating especially to the recapture and renegotiation rights of the government on the expiration of a franchise.

To his surprise, perhaps, Lenroot allied with a group that demanded very extensive amendment. Headed by Democrat Swagar Sherley of Louisville in the House and Gifford Pinchot's man Harry Slattery outside, these opponents of the Adamson bill did not place so great a value on the White House agreements as did the lands committee members or Secretary Lane. Sharing Lenroot's concern about the recapture provision, they wanted also an annual federal charge for the franchise right and federal regulation of intrastate electric rates if the states failed to afford adequate protection to the consumer. Lenroot, Ferris, and Kent disagreed as to the importance of these matters but held to the general viewpoint of the Sherley-Slattery group and had no compunctions against falling in with them in an extended effort to amend the bill. Chairman Adamson, who had insisted throughout that the conferences relate only to jurisdictional subjects, could not charge bad faith.[125]

On 25 July, after securing adoption of four of his own amendments, Lenroot gave support to Sherley's amendment for annual charges, readjustable by the secretary of war after twenty years and every ten years thereafter. Wanting both development and low cost electricity, Lenroot thought that in most cases it would be inadvisable to use the power but agreed that it was important to affirm the right to make such charges, a right that Underwood and others denied.[126] The following day, with Sherley's test amendment still before the House, Gifford Pinchot weighed in with a public statement backing the Sherley forces. President Wilson, by contrast, after endorsing the Adamson bill as revised in the White House conferences, turned to other things, leaving Adamson and Underwood to fend for themselves in the hostile House. On 28 July, the conservationists won a sweeping victory with the adoption of Sherley's amendment by a vote of 143 to 45. They went on to revise the recapture clause and to write in other amendments. When the House voted final approval on 4 August, Adamson voted against the bill, while Slattery expressed pleasure over it.[127]

124. Clipping, *Christian Science Monitor*, 21 July 1914, Box 181, Pinchot Papers; Scott Ferris in *CR* 63:2, 1914, vol. 51, pt. 13, p. 12776; Kerwin, *Water-Power Legislation*, p. 173.

125. Clipping, *Christian Science Monitor*, 21 July 1914; "Gifford Pinchot statement on water power bill, July 26, 1914," Slattery to Pinchot, 22, 23 July 1914, Box 181, Pinchot Papers; Adamson to Joseph Tumulty, 13 July 1914, Box 112, Series 2, Wilson Papers.

126. *CR* 63:2, 1914, vol. 51, pt. 13, pp. 12751–54, 12765, 12768–69.

127. Kerwin, *Water-Power Legislation*, pp. 181–82; King, *Conservation Fight*, pp. 46–47; Slattery to Pinchot, 5, 7 August 1914, Box 181, Pinchot Papers.

The executive secretary of the National Popular Government League, Judson King, later credited Lenroot with a leading role in remodeling the bill on the floor. The earlier and no less important changes at the White House conference were also due in part to his influence. Although the House bill, which King judged "a fairly good conservation measure," went to almost sure death in the Senate, its adoption represented for the conservationists an auspicious beginning of what would be a prolonged battle.[128]

The same could be said for the Ferris bill, which cleared the House on 24 August. Again, Lenroot deserves a share of the credit for his work in the committee and at the White House conferences.

Through the long months of the session, Lenroot drew closer to La Follette. Time restored to some extent the mutual confidence that had been nearly destroyed in 1912.

When war broke out in Europe during the summer, Lenroot and La Follette differed in ways that would prove significant. Years later, Lenroot wrote a historian that from the first he feared the effects of a German victory, while La Follette "from the very beginning sympathized with Germany." There is no contemporary evidence to substantiate Lenroot's recollection of his own initial attitude, but in September 1914, he did greet news of some German defeats as holding out hope for an early peace. As to La Follette, he was correct. Writing in late August to his son Phil, then in Europe, La Follette reported that:

> Bob (Jr.) and I just at this time are for the Germans—because everybody is against them and they are so in the minority. Of course I wanted to see the French take back that patch of country they lost in 1870. But when Great Britain jumped in and then pulled in the Jap—it was too much for my proclivity to fight with the underdog. I dont [sic] want to see Germany carved up by the Russians. Of course if the kaiser cleans up the whole . . . lot in a month—I am going to reserve the right to get on the other side and root for the underdog again—But I dont [sic] much expect to have that put up to me. This is just for you and the bunch.

La Follette was also solicitous for the good opinion of German-Americans in Wisconsin and glad when his convictions permitted him to write editorials that would "please our German friends." [129] By contrast, as he soon made clear, Lenroot feared the inflammatory effect of homeland sympathies and deplored policies and appeals likely to increase divisiveness.

For the moment, however, their differing attitudes toward the war had no practical import. Both men hoped for an early end to the war and wanted to avoid American involvement. While not anti-English, Lenroot did think it wise for the United States to assert her rights, so when England created

128. King, *Conservation Fight*, p. 46.

129. Lenroot to Wallace Sayre, 15 February 1930, Box 4, to Clara and Dorothy Lenroot, 13 September 1914, Box 1, Lenroot Papers; Robert to Phil La Follette, 28 August 1914, to Belle La Follette, 15 October 1914, Box 15, Series A, La Follette FC. Regarding La Follette's concern for German-American opinion see also La Follette to Herman Ekern, 16 November 1914, Box 16, Ekern Papers.

a war zone in the North sea and mined it, he joined with others in filing a protest with the State Department.[130] Not until the issues of submarine warfare and preparedness had come to the front in 1915 and 1916 did Lenroot differ with La Follette over the war.

Lenroot's role in Wisconsin politics was chiefly as adviser to and representative of La Follette. Progressive disunity and a conservative backlash against spending and bureaucracy threatened to cost the progressives the governorship. Key La Follette men urged the senator to save the situation by running for the nomination. Lenroot advised against it, and La Follette rejected the idea. But when his old enemy Emanuel Philipp won the prize, La Follette thought seriously of running as an independent. Again Lenroot opposed the idea. La Follette might nevertheless have run had his health permitted. Instead, he supported the independent candidacy of state Sen. John Blaine. In this Lenroot could not agree, thinking Blaine's cause hopeless and that the candidacy would discredit progressives and weaken those among them who were running for office.[131]

The election results held no great surprises for Lenroot. On the positive side, from his standpoint, he won reelection by a vote of 15,834 to 6,746 for the Democrat and 1,580 for the social democrat.[132] Francis McGovern for whom Lenroot had no regard lost his Senate bid to progressive Democrat Paul Husting. Nationally, Republicans scored handsomely against the Democrats and Progressives. The Bull Moosers' total vote fell under two million, as against over six million two years before, and they elected only one member to Congress. The Republicans reduced the Democratic majority in the House from seventy-three to twenty-five and scored impressive gains in state contests as well. They could reasonably expect to win in 1916, especially if the Progressives returned to the fold.[133] Since Lenroot still viewed the Republican party as the most likely vehicle for progressivism, that was a welcome prospect.

On the negative side, as Lenroot had foreseen the electorate showed itself in a conservative mood. In Wisconsin, Blaine polled only 32,940 votes, as against 119,567 for John Karel and 140,835 for Philipp, the new governor. And Wisconsin voters decisively rejected progressive constitutional amendment proposals for initiative, referendum, woman suffrage, and other reforms.[134] Nationally, while progressive Republicans held their own, the party gains were made by conservative Republicans. "Uncle Joe" Cannon headed the impressive list of standpatters who would be returning to Washington after a two-year absence.

Yet Lenroot shared many of the complaints lodged by conservative Republicans against the Democrats, as on the tariff question. And much

---

130. *Superior Telegram,* 19 March 1917.
131. Margulies, "Lenroot," pp. 736–42.
132. *Wisconsin Blue Book,* 1915, p. 232.
133. Link, *The New Freedom,* p. 468.
134. Herbert F. Margulies, *Decline of the Progressive Movement in Wisconsin, 1890–1920,* p. 158.

could happen to change the national mood before the new Congress would convene in December 1915. In any case, neither nationally nor in his own district or the districts of his insurgent friends was there a viable alternative to the Republican party. The Bull Moosers were reeling toward oblivion while the Bourbon Democrats stood stronger than ever with the defeat of some of their northern colleagues.

Although Lenroot would remain concerned about politics, in the years immediately ahead overseas events would push other considerations to the fore. Lenroot, with others, would have to wrestle with the question of war or peace, the need to reconcile peace with national interest and honor, and the intricate problem of molding international policy in a nation of diverse ethnic background.

VI

DECISION FOR WAR

In December, the Lenroots returned to Washington. Soon Katharine came on and established herself near her parents, having passed an examination for a position with the Children's Bureau. Dorothy, recently married to Paul Black, continued in poor health, but her parents hoped that when the couple moved to California the change in climate would help her.[1]

Quickly active, Lenroot succeeded through the rules committee to have the House consider the constitutional amendments for woman suffrage and prohibition. In the case of woman suffrage, the committee vote was four to three, with Martin Foster of Illinois deserting his fellow Democrats to vote for Lenroot's motion.[2]

No one could ignore the powerful and, in the case of woman suffrage, clamorous lobby favoring the two amendments. And Lenroot sympathized with the purposes of each. Nevertheless, although he supported adoption of the rules permitting their consideration, he felt impelled to vote against both amendments. The prohibition amendment came up first, on 22 December, and Lenroot explained why he would vote against it. Acknowledging the truth of all the charges against John Barleycorn, Lenroot said that "whether prohibition is practicable and desirable is not the question before us now. . . . In my mind there are but two questions for us to consider—first, is the present state of public opinion upon this question such as would justify the Congress of the United States in submitting this amendment, and, second, is the question one which ought to be the subject of Federal jurisdiction?" His answer to both questions was no.[3]

Neither amendment secured a two-thirds majority, but proponents felt that progress had been made. The prohibition amendment got a simple majority by a vote of 197 to 190, and the suffrage amendment, though defeated by a vote of 174 to 204, had at least been brought to a vote.

1. Clara Lenroot to Nellie Nichols, 10 December 1914, Irvine L. Lenroot Papers Addition; Columbia University Oral History Projects, Social Security Project, Katharine Lenroot, 2 February 1965; Clara Lenroot to Nellie Nichols, 29 January 1915, Lenroot Papers Addition; Irvine to Clara Lenroot, 18 February 1915, Box 1, Irvine L. Lenroot Papers.

2. Record Group 233, "Committee on Rules, Minutes," 63d Cong., 3d sess., 12 December 1914.

3. *CR* 63:3, 1914, vol. 52, pt. 1, pp. 504–5; 1915, vol. 52, pt. 2, pp. 1412–13.

Both issues were politically dangerous. But Lenroot had long since explained his views to the president of the Wisconsin Woman Suffrage Association, Mrs. Henry M. Youmans, and had helped the suffrage cause in the rules committee and by speaking for enfranchisement in Wisconsin. Now Mrs. Youmans came to his defense with an interview praising him for his honesty of purpose and for being a good suffragist despite his speech and vote. "If Mr. Lenroot had been influenced by political considerations," she said, "he would have voted for suffrage because his district is the strongest suffrage center in the state." [4]

Though they gave no interviews, the politically sophisticated leaders of the Anti-Saloon League surely continued to think of Lenroot as a friend.

Lenroot was active throughout the session, in committee and on the floor, in dealing with minor legislation relating to the public lands.[5] In advance of the session, the president hoped to push through the Senate the major pending measures, the waterpower and leasing bills, and he stressed conservation questions in his message of 8 December. But when two Senate committees fashioned measures that were unacceptable to conservationists, Wilson let the legislation die for the session.[6] Lenroot joined with Harry Slattery, Scott Ferris, Senator Norris, and others in a concerted effort to win administration support, but by the end of January, despite the help of Lane, he knew the most that could be gotten was a stalemate. Meanwhile, he prepared for the next session by gathering new material.[7]

Lenroot's one significant legislative triumph during the session came on 19 January on a conservation question that involved him in conflict with powerful Democratic leaders headed by Oscar Underwood. At issue was an item in the legislation on rivers and harbors, stating that survey work be done prior to dam construction at Muscle Shoals. A thirty-seven mile stretch of the Tennessee River in northern Alabama, Muscle Shoals was ideal for waterpower development. First in a running debate, then in a twenty minute set speech, Lenroot contended that the proposed dams were not mainly for navigable purposes and what was really involved was not the survey, which was to provide Congress with additional information, but a waterpower scheme that would benefit the Hydro-Electric Power Company, and the

4. Clipping, *Milwaukee Free Press*, 14 January 1915, Box 15, Lenroot Papers.

5. U.S., House of Representatives, Committee on Public Lands, *Hearings: Rocky Mountain National Park*, 23 December 1914, *Hearings: Imperial Valley*, 23 December 1914, *Hearings: Legalizing Conveyances on Certain Railroads in Nevada*, 63d Cong., 3d sess., 27 February 1915; *CR* 63:3, 1914, vol. 52, pt. 1, p. 445; 1915, vol. 52, pt. 2, p. 1805; 1915, vol. 52, pt. 3, pp. 2796–99; 1915, vol. 52, pt. 5, p. 4540; 1915, vol. 52, pt. 6, pp. 5478, 5487.

6. Ray Stannard Baker notebooks, 17 September 1914, Box 122, Series 2, Ray Stannard Baker Papers; Arthur S. Link, *Wilson: The Struggle for Neutrality, 1914–1915*, p. 138; Harry Slattery to Gifford Pinchot, 26 January, 15 March 1915, Box 189, Gifford Pinchot Papers.

7. "Report of the Secretary . . . National Conservation Association . . . January 19, 1916," Box 148, James R. Garfield Papers; Slattery to Lenroot, 16 January 1915, Lenroot to Slattery, 18 January 1915, Slattery to Lenroot, 28 January 1915, Lenroot to Slattery, 30 January 1915, Slattery to Lenroot, 3 February 1915, Box 1831, Pinchot Papers.

money was to be used to actually start the project. If Congress appropriated the $150,000, it would commit itself to an ultimate expenditure of over $18 million, the estimated cost of the total dam project, this at a time of fiscal embarrassment, he argued. The project would benefit a monopolistic company, itself linked with the nationwide power trust, with inadequate recompense to the government or protection for the consumer. And a matter of this sort should not be considered as part of a rivers and harbors bill, whose items are rarely given the close study reserved for power schemes, he said. In a final statement Lenroot, who controlled the time for his side, sustained the points he had made earlier and warned, pointedly, that "if this item remains in the bill it will open up a discussion in another place that when the 4th day of March comes this river and harbor bill will still be pending and not become a law." It was probably this warning along with the hazard of political embarrassment about the money commitment that led members to do what they had not done in years—delete an item from a rivers and harbors bill. The vote was 77 to 62. Except for Martin Foster, Lenroot's aides in debate were all Republicans, chiefly Mann and Horace Towner and earlier James Frear, who was beginning a personal war on the whole system of rivers and harbors legislation.[8]

With the end of the Sixty-third Congress, Lenroot joined Clara in Madison where the two saw Dorothy and her husband off for their new home at Los Gatos, California. While in Madison, Lenroot spoke to the Saturday Lunch Club on "Neutrality and the Position of the United States." He took the opportunity to explain his opinion on several major questions—the proposal to place an embargo on shipments of arms and munitions to belligerents and the related issues of neutral rights. At the start of the short session, German-Americans and others had brought heavy pressure for an arms embargo and Lenroot had committed himself to it in the abstract, in response to a petition from Superior. But he agreed with administration supporters who did not want to raise the question in the House, and it never reached the floor for a vote, although in the Senate it was voted on and tabled—51 to 36.[9] In February, the international situation became more serious. Germany announced a submarine blockade of the British Isles against which even neutral vessels would not be safe from destruction without warning, since the British misused neutral flags. President Wilson declared that the United States would hold Germany to a "strict accountability" for the loss of American ships and lives. It was in this situation that Lenroot now renewed his adherence to the embargo idea. But he admitted grave doubts and stipulated a number of important qualifications, some of them relating to neutral rights.

8. Jerome G. Kerwin, *Federal Water-Power Legislation*, pp. 266–67; *CR* 63:3, 1915, vol. 52, pt. 2, pp. 1860–74; *La Follette's Magazine* 7:4 (April 1915) :7.

9. *Superior Telegram*, 7 January 1915; *Milwaukee Sentinel*, 27 March 1918. The *Milwaukee Sentinel* reported a campaign speech by Lenroot in which he told of his opposition to reporting an embargo bill. Lenroot misdated the event by a year, as he did two related events.

Lenroot noted that the United States government could not legitimately ship arms to belligerents while maintaining neutrality, but he emphasized the fact that it was not a violation to permit private parties to do so. But "neither would it be a violation of our neutrality under international law if we choose to stop it. . . . It is our absolute right to deal with this question as we choose," he said. Apart from the legalities, "the question of an embargo can be, and usually is, placed upon humanitarian grounds, though it is not always evident that such is the controlling motive of its supporters. It is said that we occupy a very inconsistent attitude when we set aside a day of prayer for peace and then go on permitting the sale of the means of destruction of human life to those at war," he continued. "This has appealed to me very strongly and at the time of the Mexican embargo, I took the position that we ought to adopt a general policy that we would not permit the shipment of arms and munitions of war to any belligerent. I am still inclined to that opinion, but much can be said on the other side of the question." If the leading nations adopted an embargo policy, Lenroot explained, it would force many others to manufacture and keep constantly on hand arms and munitions, thus in turn, providing an incentive to "raise a military establishment prepared to use them."

In the course of his speech, Lenroot stressed the importance of giving the president full support in his foreign policies, even if not in full agreement with him. "We must give the world to understand that we are a united America, that in every effort made by President Wilson to secure our rights without involving us in the conflict, we stand back of him regardless of the land of our birth, and that whatever our sympathies may be, we are first of all American citizens."

On the subject of submarines, Lenroot admitted that changed conditions and methods of warfare modify international law, and that a strong argument could be made that the old rules, requiring warning and provision for the safety of passengers and crew, could not be applied to submarine warfare. Nevertheless, he judged that the old rules remained applicable, "for any other theory is unhumanitarian and means the destruction of lives not participating in any way in the war." [10]

Back in Superior in April, Lenroot again spoke on neutrality, before a Normal School assembly. On 28 March, a German submarine had sunk the British liner *Falaba* and one American died. The president was still formulating his response when Lenroot spoke. Again, Lenroot stressed the duty to "stand by President Wilson because he is doing everything he can to prevent the United States from becoming involved in the present war." The first loyalty of each citizen is to the United States, he reiterated.

After describing international law as related to the rights of neutrals, Lenroot concluded that both sides were violating American rights.

What are we going to do about it? Violations of international law are not personal affronts to us. We ought to wait until the war is over and then make the belligerent

10. *Superior Telegram,* 13 March 1915.

nations pay for damage done to our commerce. I would rather see all our ships stripped from the oceans than to have the United States become involved in the war. We would for fifty years have to pay more each year on the debt arising from such a war than all our present commerce with the belligerents amounts to. All our foreign commerce ought not to weigh one feather's weight against American lives.[11]

Lenroot's postulates were clear, if not necessarily consistent. The United States must avoid war, and it must do so by following the lead of the president to the extent feasible. The polyglot character of Lenroot's own constituency made this a matter of simple political prudence. Swedish-Americans, partly due to traditional fear of Russia and admiration for Germany as a land of high culture and defense against Catholicism, tended toward a policy of neutrality heavily tinged with pro-Germanism.[12] The Norwegian element sympathized with the neutral interests of the home country, while the German-Americans leaned strongly toward the fatherland. The Irish were divided, but those of French and English and Polish and old Yankee stock tended toward a more belligerent policy as against Germany.[13]

What was true of Lenroot's district was true in varying degrees of his state and nation. The possibilities for explosive division were apparent and frightening. For Lenroot, the goal of unity transcended personal expediency—it was a matter of the very highest purpose and principle.

Lenroot had special reasons to feel the need for unity. In frontier days and boomer days, he had learned to deplore petty divisiveness and to value social cohesion. The lesson was perhaps especially real to one who in his person bridged the cultural gap between natives and immigrants. Moreover, Lenroot saw social harmony as conducing to every sort of progress. This it did partly because people working in harmony with one another were acting either unselfishly or in accordance with enlightened self-interest. That people should be true to their best selves was itself deeply desirable, from Lenroot's standpoint. Thus, harmony, or unity, was for Lenroot not just a means, but in part an end in itself.

Talk of patriotism, of putting the nation's interest above that of a mother country, contributed to unity and to that extent served a useful purpose. But for Lenroot such talk was itself more than an expedient, even toward an unselfish end. In his youth, Lenroot had been nurtured in veneration for

11. Ibid., 9 April 1915.

12. Finis Herbert Capps, *From Isolationism to Involvement: The Swedish Immigrant Press in America, 1914–1945,* pp. xi, 31; George M. Stephenson, "The Attitude of the Swedish-Americans Toward the World War," pp. 70–94. On the ethnic composition of Lenroot's district see Jorgen Weibull, "The Wisconsin Progressives, 1900–1914," pp. 195, 197.

13. News reports in the *Superior Telegram* for 1915 and 1916 support the above generalizations with respect to Superior, Wis., and Douglas County. On Polish-American opinion see Louis S. Gerson, *The Hyphenate in Recent American Politics and Diplomacy* (Lawrence, 1964), pp. 63, 68–72; and Louis S. Gerson, *Woodrow Wilson and the Rebirth of Poland* (New Haven, Conn., 1953).

America and her institutions, the lessons of school and society strongly reinforced by his parents.

The goal of unity, by no means new in Lenroot's thinking, was to persist into the period of American involvement in the war and even beyond. It would ramify on his domestic thought and action, as what under other circumstances would have been progressive goals were subtly transformed in his thinking into means toward consensus.

Lenroot had to struggle with a major difficulty, however, then and later. National interest, objectively determined, might diverge from the broad path of unity and political expediency. He would have to discern that interest and, to the extent possible, lead others toward his own perception, to minimize the damage to consensus. At the moment, he was not himself entirely clear respecting the main issues of policy—an embargo, defense of neutral rights, preparedness. His study of these subjects showed them to be complex. And swiftly changing circumstances made dogmatism untenable.

During the months between congresses, America's international situation approached crisis. On 7 May 1915, a German submarine sank without warning the British liner *Lusitania*. The count of deaths totaled 1,198, including 124 Americans. When Congress met in December, the administration was still negotiating with Germany for suitable guarantees. The shock of the *Lusitania* sinking along with other incidents augmented by irritation over heavy-handed propaganda by German-American groups, made the public more receptive than before to the warnings of the preparedness advocates. The near anarchic situation in Mexico, resulting in the loss of American life and property and the commitment of troops to border patrol, contributed to preparedness sentiment. During the summer of 1915, President Wilson himself swung to the preparedness side, and on 7 December he presented a detailed program before a joint session of the new Congress.

Although public feeling against Germany had been heightened by revelations of "sabotage, intrigue, and plotting against American neutrality," anti-preparedness feeling was strong in the country, and congressmen responded coolly to Wilson's speech. Along with those who objected to specific features of Wilson's program for development of the army and navy, a powerful group of Democrats in the House opposed preparedness in any form. A group of about thirty admirers of William Jennings Bryan, who in June resigned as secretary of state and then took to the stump, depended on help from the new majority leader, Claude Kitchin of North Carolina, and from many midwestern Republicans.[14]

How Lenroot reacted we do not know. In August, while on the Chautauqua circuit, he told an interviewer that the loss of human life could not be ignored and that Americans should be safe wherever they are when comply-

---

14. Arthur S. Link, *Wilson: Confusions and Crises, 1915–1916*, pp. 26–33. Oscar Underwood, formerly majority leader, had been elected to the Senate.

ing with international law. In November, when asked about national defense by a *Superior Telegram* reporter, he replied noncommittally, saying he approached the subject with an open mind and would make no decision until he had heard both sides in Washington. He volunteered, though, that the government was not getting full value for its defense dollar.[15] Whatever his attitude, Lenroot had no occasion for action on preparedness until the army bill reached the House floor late in March. Meanwhile, he opposed taking up an arms embargo proposal on the grounds that the propaganda for it was designed to help Germany.[16]

During January and February, while committees labored over the army and navy bills, the House considered a variety of domestic questions. The lands committee was quickly ready with two major bills, which were modified only slightly from measures it had drawn in the previous Congress. As before, partisanship played no great part and Chairman Scott Ferris continued to welcome Lenroot's help in committee and on the floor. If anything, the partnership between the two was stronger than before, partly because, with the departure from Congress of James Graham, the position of second-ranking Democrat on the committee fell to Edward Taylor of Colorado, who deplored the leasing idea.

On 5 January, Ferris called up the first lands bill, for leasing waterpower sites on public lands. Opponents of the leasing principle carried on a strong campaign through 1915, culminating in a conference at Portland, Oregon, in September. But Pinchot's lobby counterattacked effectively; Lane held firm, and Ferris and Lenroot felt they could again hold the House for a strong bill, whatever might happen later in the Senate.[17] After Ferris explained the provisions of the bill, Lenroot, in a systematic, effective, and factual manner, set out to answer in advance the common objections of westerners.

As the House, in Committee of the Whole, considered the separate provisions of the bill, Lenroot spoke for the committee in accepting or rejecting amendments and meeting arguments.[18] Despite attacks by westerners, on 11 January the bill went to the Senate largely as the committee had reported it.

The following day, Ferris brought forth the mineral lands leasing bill. Even more than in the previous Congress, the question of relief for claimants hung over the bill. In February 1915, the Supreme Court had upheld the legality of the government's withdrawals of 1909 and 1910. Attorney General Thomas Gregory then stepped up efforts to recapture oil lands, especially on California naval reserve land, causing alarm among California

15. *Superior Telegram*, 16 August, 6, 27 November 1915.
16. *Milwaukee Sentinel*, 27 March 1918.
17. Keith Waldeman Olson, "Franklin K. Lane: A Biography," p. 169; clipping, *Washington Evening Star*, 5 November 1915, attached to Harry Slattery to Gifford Pinchot, 13 November 1915, Slattery to Pinchot, 13 December 1915, Box 188, Pinchot Papers.
18. *CR* 64:1, 1916, vol. 53, pt. 1, pp. 555–56, 680–93, 732–38, 742–43.

oil men. At the same time, a fierce battle was developing within the administration, pitting Secretary Lane against Secretary of the Navy Josephus Daniels. Lane wished to uphold the decisions of the commissioner of the land office approving for patent thirteen of seventeen claims by the Honolulu Oil Company, in the heart of Naval Petroleum Reserve No. 2. Daniels objected and won delay while Attorney General Gregory investigated the matter. The uncertainties and hazards surrounding administrative action caused all claimants to look to Congress for relief.[19]

Ferris, Lenroot, and Kent continued to view the claims controversy primarily as a complication to the establishment of an equitable system for the development of mineral wealth on the public domain. The new bill embodied their efforts to clear the deck of outstanding claims in a fair way. It included the relief proviso of the 1914 bill, and it excluded the naval reserves from the bill's provisions. Adhering to the position of the Interior Department, the Ferris bill pleased neither the claimants nor the Navy Department. It was, at least, satisfactory to the small number of representatives in attendance, despite the fact of a minority report by Taylor and three others and the objections of Frank Mondell. In four days, Lenroot and Ferris, who were assisted by Mann, succeeded in passing the bill through the House without serious amendment.[20]

The Senate took no action on the two Ferris bills that session. Senate committees fashioned substitutes, but each gave way for a time to legislation more politically urgent and to the major preparedness bills. After the party conventions in June, the cross fire of opposing views prevented any action at all. But Secretary Lane, caught in the cross fire, partly due to the redoubts of Gifford Pinchot, hoped for final action in the second session.[21]

With two major bills disposed of for the time being, Lenroot gave close attention to a variety of other domestic questions being considered in the House or in committee, while continuing to look after a variety of constituent matters before administrative agencies. On the floor, in connection with a Hawaii utility franchise bill, Lenroot questioned the provision that called for a general court review of actions taken by the public utility commission. In an able eight-minute speech, he defended the constitutionality of a

19. Gerald T. White, *Formative Years in the Far West: A History of Standard Oil Company of California and Predecessors Through 1919*, p. 444; J. Leonard Bates, *The Origins of Teapot Dome: Progressives, Parties and Petroleum, 1909–1921*, pp. 64–70.

20. *CR* 64:1, 1916, vol. 53, pt. 1, pp. 990–91, 1041–46; 1916, vol. 53, pt. 2, pp. 1089–92, 1114–16, 1122–25; Bates, *Origins of Teapot Dome*, pp. 63–64; White, *Formative Years*, pp. 445–46.

21. On the waterpower bill see especially Franklin K. Lane to Woodrow Wilson, 20 April 1916, John W. Kern to Wilson, 30 April 1916, Lane to Wilson, 27 June 1916, Wilson to Lane, 29 June 1916, Folder 1888, Series 4, Woodrow Wilson Papers; Gifford Pinchot to William Hard, 25 April 1916, Box 194, Harry Slattery to Pinchot, 23 May, 31 August 1916, Box 197, Pinchot Papers; Pinchot to James R. Garfield, 15 November 1916, Box 148, Garfield Papers. On the leasing bill see especially Olson, "Franklin K. Lane," pp. 178–84; White, *Formative Years*, pp. 447–49; and Bates, *Origins of Teapot Dome*, pp. 72–73, 83–87.

proposed bill on child labor, as a legitimate exercise of the commerce power. In both instances, Lenroot took standard progressive positions that had become habitual with him. But on a rural roads bill, Lenroot differed with his progressive colleagues, except Kent, and led the opposition on grounds of economy, though he approved the purpose of the bill.[22]

In an era still innocent of Keynesian economics and welfare spending, Lenroot's deep concern for thrift was no anachronism. He had expressed it as a leader in the Wisconsin legislature and, more recently, had sympathized with his constituents' complaints over heavy state spending and taxing. An activist and nationalist, and for many purposes a loose constructionist, the broadened governmental role that he long favored was regulatory, and the increased expenditures involved were not great. Lenroot was not fanatical on the subject. As he said in his speech, he had long favored federal aid for road construction, and he supported moderately higher spending in other areas too. But he was always concerned that public money be honestly and efficiently spent and that governmental spending should not be burdensome to taxpayers. With the coming of the New Deal in the 1930s, those who insisted on economy and balanced budgets seemed hardly progressive. But in 1916, Lenroot was in the progressive mainstream.

On another issue that had interested him for a long time, the administration reversed itself, opening the way to what Lenroot hoped would be constructive legislation. In order to blunt Republican attacks, win over Progressives, and meet the demands of businessmen who feared postwar threats to the nation's international trade from Europe and Japan, Woodrow Wilson endorsed the tariff commission idea in a letter of 24 January to Kitchin. Despite Kitchin's lack of enthusiasm for the idea, it immediately became a part of an administration program fashioned in a series of conferences that week, and on 1 February Henry T. Rainey, second-ranking Democrat on ways and means, introduced a bill drafted in the Treasury Department.[23]

Lenroot, who had introduced two tariff commission bills earlier that session, inspected the administration bill closely. He approved most of its contents, especially appointment features that would minimize partisanship on the commission. But, on the other hand, he found several features that he judged weak and also dangerous to the bill's prospects. Lenroot might have viewed the matter from the standpoint of partisan or personal advantage, in which case he would have reserved his criticisms for future use on the House floor and the campaign stump. Instead, he pointed them out in some detail to William Kent, who still had the president's favor and who,

22. *CR* 64:1, 1916, vol. 53, pt. 2, pp. 1265, 1476, 1536–37, 1584.

23. Link, *Confusions and Crises,* pp. 321, 341–44; Joseph Frederick Kenkel, "The Tariff Commission Movement: The Search for a Nonpartisan Solution of the Tariff Question" (Ph.D. diss.), pp. 103–4; William S. Culbertson, "The Legislative History of the Law Creating the United States Federal Tariff Commission," Box 134, William S. Culbertson Papers.

in turn, passed them on to Wilson.[24] One of Lenroot's suggestions was embodied in the final version of the bill when it passed the House in July, as part of a new revenue law.[25]

The great questions of the day related to war and peace, which were complex, changing elements of great importance. Lenroot approached them conscientiously but warily. He knew, when the session began, that he would have to come to some definite decisions when the army and navy bills reached the House floor. But events conspired to thrust the great international questions before Congress and before the rules committee sooner than he had expected and in a surprising and unwelcome form.

The issue of Americans traveling on belligerent ships was raised dramatically by the *Lusitania* incident. The matter seemed on course toward settlement when on 10 February 1916 Germany announced that she was ordering submarines to attack all armed belligerent merchant ships without warning. In January, President Wilson and Secretary of State Robert Lansing attempted to settle the problem of how submarines were to cope with armed merchant ships by suggesting to Allied governments not to arm their vessels. But when Britain reacted negatively, Wilson, to avoid damage to mediation efforts being promoted by Col. Edward House, drew back from the idea. Now, due to Germany's announcement, Lansing gave the press the government's new position. The United States would not insist on changing the rules if its January modus vivendi proposal were rejected by the Allies. It might let the German campaign take effect without further action. What the government would do if American life were lost when a submarine sank an armed merchantman without warning would depend on many things, including the character of the ship's weapons, whether defensive or offensive. In Congress, the subtleties of Lansing's statement were widely missed; many thought he had committed the government to defend the right of its citizens to travel on all armed merchantmen. Jeff McLemore of Texas promptly introduced a resolution asking the president to warn Americans to stay off the armed vessels of belligerents, and in the Senate, Thomas Gore of Oklahoma agitated for bills he had introduced along the same lines. The president met with three congressional leaders but neglected to clarify Lansing's meaning or discuss the mediation efforts that were in process. Instead, he adopted a hard line and urged against adoption of the McLemore resolution. Members in the Capitol became worried, and key Democratic leaders were determined to force the issue with the president. Wilson, in turn, began to plan his resistance carefully. He knew that the adoption of the warning resolution would weaken his standing with the Allied and German governments and with his own people. This goodwill, not the principle underlying the warning resolution, was the important

24. *CR* 64:1, 1915, vol. 53, pt. 1, pp. 186, 436; Kent to Wilson, 23 February 1916, File 180, Series 4, Wilson Papers.

25. *CR* 64:1, 1916, vol. 53, pt. 11, p. 10672.

thing. Indeed, he and Lansing had contemplated a warning resolution not long before.[26]

Struggling to keep control of the situation, Wilson seized on a letter from Sen. William Stone of Missouri as occasion for a public reply, which was published on 25 February. Asserting the duty to protect American rights, the hurriedly composed letter gave an impression of inflexibility. A conference with congressional leaders Clark, Kitchin, and Henry Flood, chairman of the House Committee on Foreign Affairs, served only to reinforce that impression. But the president's letter, arguing that unity behind him was needed to prevent war, did rally many to his cause, which Postmaster General Burleson pressed among congressional friends. A clarifying statement by Lansing on 26 February, that the administration would support the right of Americans to travel on armed merchant ships but only if their arms were defensive strengthened the president further, and McLemore said he would not urge a vote until Wilson could negotiate with Germany. At this point, the administration received new threats from Germany and Wilson decided to force the issue in Congress, to disabuse the Germans of the idea that his hands were tied by Congress. On 29 February, he startled Congress with a letter to Edward Pou, acting chairman of the House rules committee, asking for an early vote on the McLemore resolution.[27]

There was a good deal of confusion as well as heated discussion among House leaders, relating in part to the parliamentary status of the resolution, which was before the foreign-affairs committee. Thus, the House delayed and the Senate acted first, on a parallel resolution by Gore. But Senate action proved ambiguous, as at the last moment Gore reversed the sense of his own resolution; public and administration attention therefore shifted again to the House. By this time, the administration had a clear plan. It did not really want a vote on a simple warning resolution, which would have been embarrassingly popular with the Congress and the country. The McLemore resolution was a better vehicle, for it contained much more than a simple warning. Even Kitchin disliked it, for it seemed too pro-German and unnecessarily disrespectful of the president. But though the Wilsonians prevented any modifications in the resolution, even when McLemore requested it before the rules committee, they did not want a straight vote on it. What they wanted was a vote on a motion to table the McLemore resolution, as the safest way to secure the desired vote of confidence.[28]

Either because he unjustly suspected the Democrats on the rules committee or because he saw the need for Republican help on the floor in the face

26. Link, *Confusions and Crises*, pp. 99, 142–46, 163, 167–71.

27. Ibid., pp. 172–78, 188–89; Edward Keating, *The Gentleman From Colorado: A Memoir*, p. 415; *Washington Post*, 1 March 1916.

28. *Washington Post*, 1–6 March 1916; Monroe Lee Billington, *Thomas P. Gore: The Blind Senator from Oklahoma*, pp. 70–77; Alex M. Arnett, *Claude Kitchin and the Wilson War Policies*, pp. 174, 177–78.

of a divided Democracy, and also in advance of rules committee and floor action, Wilson summoned Lenroot and William Bennet of New York to the White House. Lenroot, aware of the purpose of the conference and of the proper course, came prepared for the occasion. As he later recalled it, Wilson knew they planned to vote against reporting the McLemore resolution, but if reported, they intended to vote against tabling. Surprisingly, Wilson talked of Austria, providing what Bennet later recalled as "inmost secrets." According to Lenroot's later recollections, he also argued that if the resolution passed, or was not tabled by the House, the country would be forced closer to war. Lenroot responded by bringing forth an issue of the *Congressional Record* containing a copy of Lansing's modus vivendi note to Great Britain. He pointed to Lansing's statement that the right of American citizens to protection when on a belligerent merchant ship was doubtful. Wilson studied it for a minute or two and then said it was the first he had heard of the statement. If he tried to explain the dramatic change of position, which is unlikely, it made no impression on Lenroot and Bennet. Lenroot told waiting reporters the Republicans would not bring party considerations into the matter, then proceeded with Bennet to the meeting of the rules committee, where the two unsuccessfully opposed the motion to report the McLemore resolution, whose accompanying report from the foreign-relations committee recommended tabling.[29]

After word of the rules committee's action filtered through the House —even though the House was not scheduled to act on the rule and resolution until the following day, 7 March—debate broke out on the floor late that afternoon and continued for more than an hour, filling the House galleries with spectators. Augustus P. Gardner began the debate and called for a straight vote on a warning resolution, which he ardently opposed. But it was Mann and Lenroot who voiced the more widespread Republican position, as it had been developing in the foreign-affairs committee and in the House. After Henry Flood and Swagar Sherley defined the issue as testing whether Congress would sustain the president or Germany, Lenroot said, "Mr. Chairman, Germany or any other belligerent nation is interested in the attitude of this House only in one respect, and that is how far will the House of Representatives and the Congress of the United States go in sustaining the President. And we have only one constitutional duty to perform in that respect, and that is the making of a declaration of war.

"Now, Mr. Chairman," he continued, "I am not prepared . . . to decide that question now. I am not willing to vote to sustain the President of the United States to the extent of war upon this question nor ready to vote that under certain circumstances I would not so vote; and so, Mr. Chairman,

29. *Washington Evening Star*, 6 March 1916; *New York Times*, 7 March 1916; Columbia University Oral History Project, interview, "The Reminiscences of William S. Bennet," p. 147; Lenroot to Fola La Follette, 27 March 1939, Box 3, Lenroot, "Memoirs," pp. 114–15, Box 13, Lenroot Papers.

when the proposition comes before the House to-morrow I shall vote against the rule bringing up the matter for consideration, as I voted against it in the committee to-day, because I want to keep myself free and untrammeled to vote upon that question when the question properly comes before the House. (Applause.) Those who are in favor of declaring war if Germany will not yield will, of course, vote to adopt the rule and table the resolution." Lenroot went on to say that if the president wants the advice of the House, let him ask for it. "But until that time comes," he concluded, "this House ought not to commit itself either for or against war, ought not to commit itself upon these very grave problems, but ought to leave them where they now are, in the hands of the President of the United States." [30]

For the Republican party, whose eastern and midwestern wings harbored the extremes of opinion on foreign policy, congressional inaction made good political sense, as Lenroot, Mann, and others knew very well. Beyond that, though, the divisions in the Republican party in Congress reflected division among the people in the country and in Lenroot's own district. From the standpoint of domestic tranquility, congressional inaction and acquiescence in presidential leadership seemed the patriotic course. The difficulty was, however, that the president demanded congressional support for a particular line of policy and one to which Lenroot could not in conscience subscribe. Furthermore, the specific action demanded—tabling —was itself a form of congressional noninterference in presidential leadership, according to the foreign-affairs committee's report.[31] From a practical standpoint, once the resolution cleared the rules committee, the possibility of complete inaction was foreclosed, and Lenroot's words better reflected what he wished might have been done, or left undone, than what he now hoped would be done.

The fallback position of the Republicans, in what was becoming an increasingly partisan matter, was already clear—to offer members the prospect of voting on a simple warning resolution if they would vote down the previous question on the rule and open the way to alternatives to the McLemore resolution. Observers predicted that the critical vote would be close, especially when they considered such factors as the balanced reactions in the House to the 6 March speeches; the meeting of Bryan with supporters that day; and the calling in of absentees by worried Democrats.[32]

Visitors gathered into the galleries and corridors the next day, for what promised and proved to be a dramatic session. In the House, the atmosphere was heated and tense from the start and continued so through the seven hours of debate and voting. Only once, when Mann announced that it was Champ Clark's sixty-sixth birthday, did the tension break for a time, as members clapped and cheered for five minutes and Clark responded appropriately.

30. *CR* 64:1, 1916, vol. 53, pt. 4, p. 3643.
31. *Washington Post,* 4 March 1916.
32. Ibid., 7 March 1916; *New York Times,* 7 March 1916.

Pou of North Carolina, recovering from an illness and speaking slowly, began the debate, denying gossip that the president wanted war. "All the imps of hell never devised a more infamous lie. No President save Lincoln ever went through what Woodrow Wilson has suffered in twelve months to avoid war." Then Philip Campbell, controlling the time for the opposition to the rule, explained very simply where he stood. If the previous question were voted down, he would offer a substitute by which the House could vote directly on the simple warning. He made it clear he would favor adoption of such a resolution, which he had drafted. After short but spirited speeches by Pat Harrison of Mississippi, Gardner, Bennet, and James Cantrill of Kentucky, it was Lenroot's turn, for seven minutes. He used his time to explain the parliamentary situation, warning members that they could not vote for the previous question and later be able to say they favored a resolution of warning but had no opportunity to vote on it. "The responsibility is upon you. If you are not willing to commit yourselves to a declaration of war against Germany if it does not see fit to yield to the demands of the administration, the responsibility is upon you now to vote against the previous question, to permit an amendment to this rule, to permit the House to express its real convictions upon this question, so that the President of the United States may know upon what he can rely." The applause that followed was the greatest accorded to any of the speakers to that time but was largely confined to the Republican side, foreshadowing the outcome on the vote, which came after five more short speeches, the last a rousing appeal by Finis J. Garrett to support the president. With Fitzgerald, Kitchin, and Dorsey Shackleford (considered the leader of the pro-warning Democrats) voting for the previous question, it carried by a vote of 256 to 160. Except for a smattering of extreme Bryanites, Democratic lines held firm and fifty-three eastern Republicans more than made up for the twenty-one defecting Democrats. Key Democrats would have led their many willing followers for a simple warning on a bipartisan basis, but they were unwilling to align themselves behind Republican leadership against the president. Even Bryan had muted his appeal.[33]

The vote on the rule was 271 to 137. Then, the House began debate on tabling the McLemore resolution. Only the magnitude of the vote to table remained in doubt, but members continued to give close attention to the debate. Lenroot, who had avoided commenting on the substantive issues in his earlier remarks, secured five minutes to do so now. He pointed to Lansing's note of 18 January to the Allied powers referring to doubtful rights and then asked "shall we say by voting to table the McLemore resolution that that right is now so clear and unquestioned that this House, if called upon, will be ready to vote for a declaration of war against Germany

---

33. *Washington Evening Star*, 7 March 1916; *New York Times*, 7, 8 March 1916; *CR* 64:1, 1916, vol. 53, pt. 4, pp. 3688–99.

in case an American citizen loses his life upon one of these armed merchant vessels?" He would vote against tabling, "because if it is not tabled there will then be an opportunity to amend it . . . giving the House an opportunity to vote for a simple resolution of warning, and thereby give notice to your President and to my President that in the opinion of this House that right is not so clear, is not so unquestioned, as to justify this country in going to war for a violation of it." The possibility of amending was theoretical not practical. The practical reality was that under the rule the House could not, in Committee of the Whole, alter the obnoxious resolution before the vote on tabling. With the practical situation remaining inflexible, the House tabled the McLemore resolution, early that evening, by a vote of 276 to 142. Ninety-three Republicans voted with most of the Democrats, while thirty-three Democrats, one hundred-two Republicans, and some others voted against tabling. The bulk of the opposition to tabling came from the Midwest, especially from midwestern Republicans. The large German population in the area was but one of several factors at work there.[34]

Eleven days later, the army reorganization bill was called up in the House, the first of the preparedness bills to reach the floor. It was a very moderate measure, which would increase the regular army from 100,000 to 140,000 men and would bring the National Guard under the control of the War Department, and it had the united support of the administration and the Democrats. The president had initially hoped for much more, but because of strong opposition he abandoned Secretary Garrison's idea of a "Continental Army" (a volunteer national reserve) as an alternative to the federalized National Guard and then accepted Garrison's resignation. The speeches he gave while on tour, in which he presented preparedness as helpful to peace and useful in securing American rights not just against German violations but English, contributed to a favorable public opinion. Preparedness sentiment was stirred further when the deteriorating Mexican situation climaxed on 9 March as Francisco Villa shot up a town in New Mexico and Brig. Gen. John J. Pershing was ordered into Mexico with an American column to capture him, the beginning of a vain effort lasting eleven months.[35]

The key votes came on 23 March on Republican amendments. The most important, by Julius Kahn of California, ranking Republican on military affairs, would increase the army to 220,000 men instead of just 140,000 as in the Hay bill. The House voted down Kahn's amendment. In supporting

---

34. *CR* 64:1, 1916, vol. 53, pt. 4, pp. 3699–3700, 3709; *Washington Post*, 8 March 1916; Meyer J. Nathan, "The Presidential Election of 1916 in the Middle West" (Ph.D. diss.), pp. 19–20; John Milton Cooper, Jr., *The Vanity of Power: American Isolationism and the First World War, 1914–1917*, pp. 113–15.

35. Link, *Confusions and Crises*, pp. 45–53, 327–29; Frederic L. Paxson, *American Democracy and the World War: Pre-War Years, 1913–1917*, vol. 1, pp. 294, 299–300.

the amendment, Lenroot differed with many insurgent colleagues and with Mann.[36] He offered no explanation in debate.

The following day the international situation took a grave turn, when Germany torpedoed without warning an unarmed British steamer, the *Sussex*. Four Americans were injured. The explanation given by the German government was unacceptable, thus increasing the anger of Americans. After considerable delay, on 18 April the State Department dispatched a note to Germany threatening a break in diplomatic relations, which in turn would lead directly to war, unless Germany would observe the rules of cruiser warfare in her use of submarines.[37]

During the *Sussex* crisis, the Senate passed the Chamberlain bill, increasing the army to 250,000 men, authorizing a national reserve army of 261,-000, and federalizing the National Guard while increasing its authorized strength to 280,000. Conferees soon settled their differences and the president signed the bill. It called for a regular army of 206,169, but expandable to 254,000 men, on presidential order. It also increased the authorized strength of the National Guard to 425,000 men, but dropped the Senate's reserve army plan.[38]

Gardner, Roosevelt, and the leaders of the National Security League condemned the Hay-Chamberlain Act as a fake. Anti-preparedness people, on the other hand, felt reasonably content with the result, as they moved into round two.[39]

After keeping the bill in committee for four months, as their national convention approached, the Democrats finally settled their differences and brought out a navy bill. The administration yielded on its five-year building program, agreed to accept five battle cruisers in place of new battleships, and made other concessions, in return for which the "little navy" men accepted a larger one-year program than they really wanted. The Republicans on the committee, while going along with the one-year format, considered the level of appropriations inadequate and prepared an elaborate amendment for significant increases. Lenroot supported the Republican alternative, although, as it turned out, eighteen westerners, mainly insurgents, did not. During general debate, he explained his position briefly.

> In the past I have been for a small Navy, . . . because up to the beginning of this European war neither the power that had the first nor the power that had the second navy was in such a position that there was any possibility of our expecting trouble from them. It was not even a remote possibility so long as each was

36. Nathan, "Presidential Election of 1916," p. 23; Howard Scott Greenlee, "Republican Party in Division and Reunion, 1913–1920," pp. 116–17; *CR* 64:1, 1916, vol. 53, pt. 5, pp. 4728–29.

37. Link, *Confusions and Crises*, pp. 228–55.

38. Ibid., pp. 327, 331, 332.

39. Ibid., p. 332; Nathan, "Presidential Election of 1916," p. 19.

watching the other and had to reckon upon the other's aggression upon it if there was trouble with us. This European war has changed that situation. We can not now tell what the condition will be with reference to the balance of power in Europe when this war is over. If either side crushes the other and absolutely dominates the situation, then we may need a Navy that is equal to the best in the world.[40]

Under those circumstances, Lenroot went on to say, "it is our duty to make the utmost preparation possible at this time, not as a naval policy for the future, for we are not in any position to fix our future naval policy now until we know what conditions are abroad, but we should take every precaution possible to prepare for the conditions that may flow from the European war, and that is to build such dreadnaughts and battle cruisers as it is possible to build with our present yards and facilities, and to build them just as quickly as possible." In support of the Republican program, he was willing to vote for two battleships and six battle cruisers and preferred that construction of all eight capital ships be started immediately rather than four that year and four the next.[41]

On 2 June, the Republican program lost in the House by a vote of 189 to 183 and the compromise program of the Democrats was accepted. That Lenroot was not simply rationalizing to accommodate party interest became evident later. After each party in national convention endorsed a strong navy, the president, dissatisfied with the House bill, persuaded Democrats in the House to accept a much stronger Senate bill that telescoped much of his original five-year program into three years.[42] Mann urged Republican support for the committee report, and on the final vote of 283 to 51, only 15 Republicans broke ranks. But Lenroot was one of them, on the basis of the argument he had presented in May. If the sixteen authorized capital ships could be built immediately, he would vote for them, but they could not. And the bill did not even contemplate that. He argued that naval policy for the future could not be set at the present, but only if the outcome of the war were known. The only reason for not leaving the matter to the next Congress, or the one after that, Lenroot charged, "is to use the sentiment that is now pervading the country for a very large Navy." [43]

So ended Lenroot's involvement in preparedness and in questions on foreign policy for the session. He had made clear that he was against interventionism or expansionism and was unwilling to risk war over "doubtful legal rights." At the same time, he supported army and navy increases to a great extent, much to the disapproval of House Democrats and many

40. Harold and Margaret Sprout, *The Rise of American Naval Power, 1776–1918*, pp. 332–33; Link, *Confusions and Crises*, pp. 334–35; *CR* 64:1, 1916, vol. 53, pt. 9, p. 8895.

41. *CR* 64:1, 1916, vol. 53, pt. 9, p. 8895.

42. Henry Cabot Lodge emphasized the extent of the change wrought by the Senate and took partial credit for it. Lodge to Lord Charnwood, 24 January 1924, Henry Cabot Lodge Papers. The boxes are not numbered but are organized chronologically.

43. *CR* 64:1, 1916, vol. 53, pt. 13, p. 12868.

Republican insurgents. Undoubtedly, he was gratified when he could act with House Republicans or, less frequently, with La Follette. Perhaps, though, he was more interested in supporting policies that were moderate and reasonable and, by virtue of that, most likely to command respect among a divided people, in his own district and in the nation.

Although Lenroot gave the questions of defense and diplomacy the attention their gravity warranted, they occupied only a portion of his time. He was not expert in them, nor a member of one of the key committees reporting the bills. Not surprisingly, then, after the great preparedness measures reached the House floor, Lenroot continued to focus on other legislation. As the conventions approached and partisanship increased, Lenroot stood with his party without embarrassment. But some of the issues were nonpartisan in nature, so more to his liking.

In the conflict over waterpower development on navigable streams, he was able to exert some influence. On 8 March, the Senate adopted the Shields bill to which conservationists objected, claiming that it provided inadequate compensation to the government and what amounted to an indefinite lease on power sites. Wilson was in a position to influence the House, but he was wary of making a mistake. "The matter is giving me a good deal of anxiety," he wrote Lane and concluded that "it is much better to do nothing about the use of water power than to do the wrong thing." He wrote Kent for publication implying that he might veto the Shields bill and, despite objections from John Shields, did nothing to dispel the impression. Lenroot, in turn, worked behind the scenes in the House and on 22 May he was able to assure Pinchot that "we have the matter in such shape now that there is no possibility of the Senate Bill either going through the House in its present form, or that it will come out (of) conference embodying in any material way, views contrary to those which we have been fighting for." Chairman Adamson promised to make no final agreement in conference without first submitting it to Lenroot, Mann, Sherley, Foster, and perhaps a few others. Pinchot's public agitation and Kent's prodding of the administration may have reinforced the agreement, with the result that the issue carried over into the next session.[44]

Early in June, Republican members began drifting off to their party's national convention in Chicago or, as in Lenroot's case, home. For reasons unknown, Lenroot and La Follette had quietly drifted apart somewhat after 1914. Probably their divergence on foreign policy questions was chiefly responsible. In any case, while not breaking with his long-time friend and colleague, nor repudiating his candidacy, Lenroot had declined to run for

44. Lane to Wilson, 2 March 1916, Wilson to Lane, 9 March 1916, Box 142, Series 2, Shields to Wilson, 10 May 1916, Wilson to Shields, 18 May 1916, Folder 1888, Series 4, Wilson Papers; Lenroot to Pinchot, 22 May 1916, Box 1831, Pinchot Papers; *CR* 64:2, 1917, vol. 54, pt. 4, p. 3695; Harry Slattery to Pinchot, 22 August, 19 July 1916, Box 197, Kent to Newton D. Baker, 21 July 1916, Box 1831, Pinchot Papers.

district delegate on a slate pledged to La Follette.[45] But though he found
it expedient not to be too close to the convention proceedings, he did take
an interest in the outcome. When in late April one of the progressive
delegates from Wisconsin, James A. Stone, asked his advice as to candidates
after La Follette released him, Lenroot responded confidentially, indicating
his preference. After dismissing the chances for La Follette and Cummins
as nil, Lenroot wrote, "Of all the possibilities, I believe that Hughes is the
most desirable from every standpoint. We do not know that he will accept
but it is my best judgment that he would. If Hughes is out of it and political
conditions in June are as they now exist, I think Roosevelt is the most
formidable candidate. I think, however, his nomination would be most unfortunate and I do not think he would be elected unless we should be
engaged in war ourselves." Roosevelt had become outspokenly belligerent
in his foreign policy statements against Germany. Lenroot went on to consider the other possibilities but judged the nominee would be Charles Evans
Hughes or Roosevelt.[46] Lenroot stopped briefly in Chicago on 5 June, then
he went on to Superior and the Brule. In Superior, he expressed hope for
Hughes's nomination.[47]

In this he was gratified. Among his reasons for favoring Hughes, undoubtedly, was the prospect that the Progressives would find him acceptable and
would return to the Republican party. As he had foreseen and predicted
in his interview with the *Superior Telegram,* the Bull Moosers agreed to support Hughes by the end of the month, after first nominating Roosevelt
conditionally. Although he made no public comment about the Republican
platform, Lenroot probably found it reasonably satisfactory too. It was not
a rousing progressive document and was adopted over the objection of the
La Follette delegates. But Henry Cabot Lodge, chief designer of the platform, wanted party unity, reconciliation with the Progressives, and victory
in the election, and fashioned it accordingly. The platform muted its criticism of Wilson's progressive legislation and was vague on problems of
foreign policy and the hyphenated American. It called for conservation,
rural credits and extended free delivery, an end to abuse of civil service,
and other measures satisfactory to Lenroot.[48]

Aware of the critical importance of Progressive support, candidate

45. *Superior Telegram,* 17 November 1914; Lenroot to Nellie Nichols, 6, 21 February 1916,
Lenroot Papers Addition; Herbert F. Margulies, "Progressivism, Patriotism, and Politics: The
Life and Times of Irvine L. Lenroot," pp. 783–86.

46. Stone to Lenroot, 21 April 1916, Lenroot to Stone, 27 April 1916, Box 21, James A.
Stone Papers.

47. *Superior Telegram,* 6 June 1916.

48. Nathan, "Presidential Election of 1916," pp. 36–38; Alan Rolf Havig, "The Poverty of
Insurgency: The Movement to Progressivize the Republican Party, 1916–1924" (Ph.D. diss.),
pp. 21–22; Nicholas Murray Butler, *Across the Busy Years: Recollections and Reflections,* vol. 1, p.
256; George H. Mayer, *The Republican Party, 1854–1966* (London and New York, 1967), p. 342;
Gerald D. McKnight, "A Party Against Itself—The Grand Old Party in the New Freedom Era,
1913–1916" (Ph.D. diss.), p. 303.

Hughes held aloof from Old Guard domination in preparing for the campaign. He put in his own man as national chairman, set up a special campaign committee of seventeen, including six Moosers, and put a Roosevelt Republican, Alvin T. Hert, in charge of western headquarters in Chicago. Some of the more radical Progressives would not follow Roosevelt back to the Republican party, and William Kent became national chairman of the Woodrow Wilson Independent League. But on the whole the situation was quite tolerable from a progressive Republican standpoint.[49]

While home Lenroot further improved his standing with the drys when, replying to a W.C.T.U. petition, he wrote that as a result of his observations in Superior during a battle on liquor the previous spring and in North Dakota during the summer, he was reviewing his position on prohibition by constitutional amendment, "with a view of changing my position upon this question, if I can reconcile such action with certain general principles which I believe should govern the submission of all federal constitutional amendments." In any case, he assured the ladies, as a member of the rules committee he would do all he could to get another vote in the House.[50] Although dry gains in the district were only moderate that spring, and the wets continued strong where there were substantial numbers of workers and/or Germans, Lenroot's stand helped politically, for he had more supporters to lose among the drys than among the wets.

On the war issues, his moderate and in some ways noncommittal position served him well, not offensive enough to bring concerted reprisal. The *Superior Telegram* took a position somewhat more belligerent than his but offered no criticism of him. On the contrary, the paper gave Lenroot consistently good publicity in its news columns, in effect emphasizing his importance as a national figure. The *Superior Telegram*, serving the same diverse constituency as Lenroot, shared his concern for unity.[51]

By mid-August, Lenroot knew he would have only token opposition for renomination. But once back in Washington for the last weeks of the session, he found himself in an atmosphere frothy with politics. As debate became increasingly partisan with each day, Lenroot joined in on the Republican side. On 31 August, in connection with a bill to promote shipping by means of exemption from antitrust, Lenroot took the opportunity to chide the Democrats for their inactivity on the antitrust front. Their platform made no mention of trusts, and they had failed to dissolve any, he said.[52]

49. Greenlee, "Republican Party in Division and Reunion," p. 173; McKnight, "A Party Against Itself," pp. 315–18; Havig, "Poverty of Insurgency," pp. 21–22, 87; George E. Mowry, *Theodore Roosevelt and the Progressive Movement,* pp. 357–60; Elizabeth Kent, *William Kent, Independent: A Biography,* p. 286; Nathan, "Presidential Election of 1916," pp. 40–41, 120; *Superior Telegram,* 24 June 1916.
50. *Superior Telegram,* 3 February 1916.
51. Ibid., 18 November, 9, 11, 13, 31 December 1915, 1, 6, 7, 8, 17, 21, 25, 31 January, 2, 12 February, 1, 6, 7, 15, 16, 30 March, 5 April, 5, 6, 9, 10, 31 May, 16 June 1916.
52. *CR* 64:1, 1916, vol. 53, pt. 13, p. 13535.

The following day, in debate on the rule governing the momentous Adamson bill, Lenroot criticized the president. The bill, hastily prepared because of Wilson's urging and to avert an imminent and potentially disastrous national railroad strike, mandated the eight-hour day and maintenance of wages for eight hours at the existing level of ten hours, with overtime to be compensated at the rate of eight hours, pending the report of a commission. Lenroot told the House he would vote for the bill "because with the emergency which exists we have the choice of voting blindly to-day, surrendering our right to have facts to form a judgment upon the merits of the proposition, or having a strike that in its effect and results will be equal to war in the suffering that will follow." His vote did not commit him in favor of the principles involved in the bill. Were it an hours law, Lenroot made clear, he would be for it. But as everyone knew, it was really a disguised wage law, and on the merits of that he had no present basis for judgment. Lenroot criticized the president on various grounds—for preventing a settlement by his intervention in the dispute and for not seeking fundamental remedial legislation early in the session. What Lenroot had in mind, he made clear, was legislation to prohibit such strikes "prior to some careful impartial investigation." He was frank to admit that he changed his mind.

> During all the years I have been in public life . . . I have fought, as best I could to establish the principle that railway managers have an obligation to the public and that the public have an interest in the conduct of the railroads. I have never believed that it would be necessary for the Congress of the United States to consider the proposition of whether or not the men who work upon the railroads do not likewise have an obligation to the public (applause on the Republican side), and whether or not legislation is necessary to regulate to some degree their conduct as well as the conduct of the managers themselves.[53]

With the end of the session, Lenroot returned to Wisconsin. As anticipated, he had won renomination on 5 September with ease. La Follette, too, had defeated his stalwart opponent by a wide margin. But Governor Philipp, whose administration had been surprisingly moderate, won renomination against the still divided progressives and his forces gained slightly in legislative contests. Conservatives did well in the economy-conscious north and, according to one estimate, twelve of fifteen legislative nominees from Lenroot's district inclined toward the governor. Philipp's control of the platform convention and the State Central Committee was assured.[54]

The *Superior Telegram* drew the obvious lesson from the primary results. With conservative and progressive factions evenly balanced, it behooved

53. Ibid., pp. 13582–83; Arthur S. Link, *Wilson: Campaigns for Progressivism and Peace, 1916–1917*, pp. 83–91.
54. Herbert F. Margulies, *The Decline of the Progressive Movement in Wisconsin, 1890–1920*, pp. 187–89; *Superior Telegram*, 6, 7, 8, 13 September 1916.

each to make special efforts toward harmony. Continuance of the fight would beget reprisal and prove self-defeating. And the national ticket in the state would stand in jeopardy. Understanding the situation in the same way, Lenroot delivered appropriate remarks at a banquet in which he and Philipp were the guest speakers, in connection with a new hospital at Ladysmith, Rusk County, Wisconsin. He said it was good for political opponents to get together on something on which they can agree. It was especially important to transcend political differences at that point in history, he went on, for in a time of bestiality abroad, Americans needed a higher patriotism, a deeper brotherhood and charity, upholding civilization.[55]

While a great many other Republicans of both factions found Hughes's candidacy a unifying vehicle for local purposes, Lenroot approached the matter from the other direction—he would do what was correct in order to benefit Hughes and the Republican party nationally. In mid-September, instead of attending the state fair and the platform convention downstate, Lenroot spoke at a number of county fairs in his district. Then, as the campaign moved into its decisive stage, he spoke under the auspices of the National Committee in Indiana and Nebraska, before stumping his own district. To Clara, he reported that it would be a close contest for Hughes in Wisconsin.[56]

The greatest blow to the factional truce and to the Hughes campaign in Wisconsin came from La Follette, who steadfastly declined to mention the presidential candidate in his speeches and in effect supported Wilson. It would have been awkward for La Follette to have supported Hughes while defending his own record on the Underwood tariff and the Adamson Act. Besides, Hughes opposed La Follette's Seamen's Act. And Wilson pleased La Follette with the appointment of Brandeis to the Supreme Court and by holding off from war with Mexico during a spring crisis. The senator's failure to support Hughes figured to cost him some Republican votes, but these he could more than make up from the Democrats. He had been led to believe that the national administration would not seek to defeat him, and it did not. Even his Democratic opponent, William Wolfe, who was concerned for Wilson's success, urged against a presidential endorsement.[57]

Despite La Follette, Hughes carried Wisconsin by approximately 30,000 votes. But late returns from California gave the presidency to Wilson. Len-

55. *Superior Telegram*, 6 September 1916; MS speech, "Banquet Ladysmith Sept. 12, 1916," Box 8, Lenroot Papers.

56. Lenroot to E. J. Gross, 28 November 1916, Box 1, Edwin J. Gross Papers, WSHSL; *Superior Telegram*, 14 September, 4, 24, 25, 28, 31 October, 1 November 1916; Lenroot, "Memoirs," p. 119, Box 13, J. R. McCarl to Lenroot, 3 October 1916, Box 3, Irvine to Clara Lenroot, 1 November 1916, Box 1, Lenroot Papers.

57. Charles Crownhart to J. W. Pryor, 24 October 1916, to T. M. Thomas, 25 October 1916, Box 110, Series B, Robert M. La Follette FC; Gilson Gardner in *Superior Telegram*, 18 October 1916; William Wolfe to Joseph E. Davies, 31 October 1916, Wilson Papers, cited in Nathan, "Presidential Election of 1916," p. 119; *Superior Telegram*, 27 October 1916.

root won his usual sweeping victory by a vote of 22,570 to 8,726 for Democratic wheelhorse George Cooper and 2,252 for socialist Henry Parks.[58] La Follette, too, was easily reelected, along with Philipp. The Republicans carried all eleven congressional districts in Wisconsin and made gains elsewhere in the country, but it was not immediately clear whether they would have enough votes to organize the House. That would depend, in part, on some contested elections and also on how six minor party members voted.

Lenroot's reaction to the results was mixed. He was deeply disappointed over the defeat of Hughes. Although the Wisconsin result had nothing to do with it, La Follette's role in the campaign aggravated and embarrassed him. Years later, he recalled that the breach between himself and the senator that had been opened in 1912 "widened in 1916 over the unwillingness of La Follette to affirmatively declare himself for Hughes for President in that campaign." [59]

But word that the Republicans might organize the next House was of interest to him. [60] There was a distinctly personal side to the matter, for speculation in Milwaukee, which was soon echoed in Washington, had it that if the Republicans controlled, Lenroot would be his party's choice for Speaker or floor leader.[61]

The second session of the Sixty-fourth Congress began on 5 December; the belligerents had reached a stage of desperation, when Germany might, at any time, discard the rules of cruiser warfare in an all-out submarine campaign to cut the supply lines to England. Until 31 January 1917, however, she still remained faithful to the *Sussex* pledge, and progressive Republicans like Lenroot, anxious that the United States remain at peace, focused attention on domestic matters.

Lenroot took the initiative in resuming friendly relations with La Follette. The day after La Follette's return to Washington, Lenroot called on him at his office and the two talked of their families. The senator had left his at Maple Bluff, Wisconsin, for the short session, and the Lenroots soon invited him for Sunday dinner, together with Congressman Edward Browne and his wife. La Follette later reported to Belle that "it was a good old fashioned time. Everything seemed all right." [62] Whether Lenroot and La Follette talked of their recent political differences is unclear. But those differences were not so important as they would have been had Hughes won the election in which case Lenroot would have been a valued congressional ally of the administration and La Follette a dangerous enemy.

Lenroot encouraged the Bull Moosers in their effort to return to the Republican party on favorable terms. However, international complications prevented the assembling of a conference. These same complications ulti-

58. *Wisconsin Blue Book*, 1917, p. 291.
59. Lenroot to Wallace S. Sayre, 15 February 1930, Box 4, Lenroot Papers.
60. *Superior Telegram*, 10 November 1916.
61. Ibid.
62. Robert to Belle La Follette, 17 December 1916, Box 19, Series A, La Follette FC.

mately resulted in the organization of the new House of Representatives by the Democrats, but not before the progressive Republicans had won from Mann and his colleagues procedural reforms within the party and elevation of Lenroot to a position of leadership, as one of five on a new steering committee.[63]

These questions and domestic legislative matters suddenly were insignificant when Germany announced all-out submarine warfare, with only a one-month period of grace for neutral ships already in the war zone. The event marked a turning point in American history and in the career of Irvine Lenroot.

Congress and the country anxiously awaited the president's response. After much consideration and a series of conferences, Wilson gave it in an address to a joint session of Congress on 3 February—he was breaking diplomatic relations with Germany. After the cheering that greeted his announcement ended, the president went on to say that he would not believe that Germany would actually take American lives in ruthless submarine war. Wilson asserted the country's hope for peace and desire only to maintain "the undoubted rights of her people." In effect, he had decided to accept a stepped up submarine campaign, so long as Germany did not sink American ships illegally or destroy American lives.

Wilson's address received near-unanimous support in the press. Even the German-language papers felt that he could have done no less. The Senate four days later adopted a resolution of approval by a vote of seventy-eight to five. La Follette was among the five.[64]

Clara Lenroot had a different reaction. She had never seen the president so moved or so impressive and rejoiced in the sense of "a Congress and galleries united in sentiment, and ready to back him up." But afterwards, she wrote Nellie that there had been verbal battles between "pacifists and saner folk, with good red blood in their veins."

"I *dread* war, and *hate* it," she went on, "but to my mind there *is* a limit beyond which the Germans must not go without forcible protest!" There was a general feeling that in any event, the war could not last much longer. Lenroot felt that if the United States became involved, the war would be over before the troops could be sent to Europe. "Still no one can tell," she reflected, "and there is likely to be serious internal disturbance, from German sympathizers, and multiplied Mexican complications, German plotters making things lively for us down there." [65]

In the days that followed Wilson's speech and as the country awaited events, opinion fragmented, and interventionists and peace groups struggled to mold opinion, the latter the more vigorous, open, and strident.

63. Margulies, "Lenroot," pp. 821–26, 852–53.
64. *Superior Telegram*, 1 February 1917; Clara Lenroot to Nellie Nichols, 5 February 1917, Lenroot Papers Addition; Link, *Campaigns for Progressivism and Peace*, pp. 290–302, 347.
65. Clara Lenroot to Nellie Nichols, 5 February 1917, Lenroot Papers Addition.

Peace societies urged La Follette's scheme for an advisory referendum on war and the senator, while looking for a chance to reintroduce his referendum bill of the previous session as an amendment to anything germane, offered a resolution prohibiting owners of American ships from sending them abroad armed.[66] Belle La Follette, active in the cause of peace in Madison, by letter encouraged her husband, as did a great many others.[67]

One constructive suggestion came from the peace forces, in the form of an article by Carlton J. H. Hayes, a history professor at Columbia University and a member of the American Union Against Militarism, with Amos Pinchot, O. G. Villard, and others. The United States, Hayes wrote in "The Survey," had no motive to go to war or to hope for anything but a draw. Short of war, however, the United States might defend her neutral rights by organizing the neutral maritime nations in a league of armed neutrality. The plan, which was presented as being in accord with Wilson's statements, was widely and favorably publicized, and Lenroot found it attractive in some ways. But he did not propose to discuss it in Congress, for he deplored congressional debate on foreign policy as premature and as an inciter of dangerous discord.[68]

Lenroot's hope was vain. With the appropriation bills for the army and navy on the floor for action, it was inevitable that congressmen should discuss the crisis situation. Unhappily, from Lenroot's standpoint, not only did the House debate foreign policy, but it did so in the worst possible way—hearing emotional harangues from the extremists—the interventionists and, more numerous, the pacifists. Angry, Lenroot went home on the night of 16 February and composed a speech of his own, which he hoped to deliver when the opportunity came about. The very next day, he got his chance.[69]

Securing ten minutes, Lenroot set out to present what he believed was the dominant view in Congress, as well as in the White House and the country, to dispel the idea that "if Congress is called upon to act at all it will choose between a general declaration of war against Germany, intervening in the European war, and a position that, whatever the provocation may be, we will under no circumstances defend our rights with force." He went on to say:

> In severing diplomatic relations with Germany the President did only his duty. To have done less would have forfeited any respect the world still had left for us.

66. Link, *Campaigns for Progressivism and Peace,* pp. 503–6; Belle and Fola La Follette, *La Follette,* vol. 1, pp. 597–98.

67. Belle to Robert La Follette, 8, 10 February 1917, La Follette to "Mama and Kids," 7, 18 February 1917, to Belle La Follette, 13 February 1917, Box 20, Series A, La Follette FC.

68. Link, *Campaigns for Progressivism and Peace,* note 10, pp. 293, 306–7; Amos Pinchot to "Dear Sir" (a letter sent to all congressmen), 13 February 1917, Box 40, John J. Esch Papers; *CR* 64:2, 1917, vol. 54, pt. 4, p. 3529.

69. Clara Lenroot to Nellie Nichols, 20 February 1917, Lenroot Papers Addition.

By her own admission Germany has made herself an outlaw. She does not pretend that her act which was the cause of the breach can be justified by international law. . . . Any day may bring the news of destruction of American ships and American lives in admitted violation of international law and of the laws of humanity.

If I understand the views expressed by some gentlemen, . . . if this shall come to pass, we must do nothing; that no matter what the provocation may be, under no circumstances must we defend our rights with force. If this is to be the attitude of Congress and the American people, then the days of this Republic are numbered.

For the fifth time, Lenroot was interrupted by loud applause. Then he continued with words widely noted by the press afterwards. "We will no longer be a nation, for any people too cowardly to fight for their liberty upon the sea, if need be, will be too cowardly to fight for their liberty upon the land. But, Mr. Chairman, that is not the spirit of the American people, and when the time comes that will not be the spirit of this Congress."

Without mentioning Mann, Lenroot answered his warning of entanglement in European affairs and sacrifice of the Monroe Doctrine. Though Congress would, if need be, vote for use of force on the sea,

. . . that does not mean that we will vote a general declaration of war against Germany; it does not mean that we will intervene in the European war; it does not mean that we will send our men to the trenches of Europe; it does not mean that we are to sit in and determine the terms of settlement of European questions. It means only that we are going to settle our difficulty with Germany by compelling her to respect our rights upon the sea. . . . When Germany shall again respect our rights our quarrel with her will be over and we will be ready to make peace with her regardless of European nations or European quarrels.

Fresh waves of applause endorsed these important qualifications.

Lenroot now distinguished between the current situation and that which existed at the time of the McLemore resolution. Then, the issue was one of "doubtful rights"; now "there is no doubt. . . . They are admitted wrongs, and the only question is whether we shall submit to them without any further effort to correct them."

At this point, Lenroot turned to the responsibilities of the representative in the face of crisis and to the domestic aspects of the situation.

If we are called upon to act in this matter, it will be the most solemn responsibility ever laid upon any of us. If any Member in that hour is influenced in the least degree by party politics, by prejudice, by sympathy for either side in the European war, he will be untrue to the oath of office he has taken here. If ever in our lives we should be American citizens only, it will be then.

Lenroot then announced that he was less alarmed about trouble with Germany as "about a divided country here. Divisions now may result in disorder within our own borders, with consequences more serious than war with any foreign power.

"The propaganda now going on throughout the country to avoid war at any cost is a greater peril to the Republic than war with Germany would be." After another round of applause, Lenroot continued:

> The proposition for a war referendum is likewise a great peril. Suppose at this time a referendum was held; suppose 10,000,000 votes were cast, 5,100,000 for war and 4,900,000 against. If war was declared on that vote, does it require a prophet to foresee possible civil war among ourselves? Or suppose 4,900,000 voted for war and 5,100,000 against, and we refuse then to exercise force to maintain our rights, how long would it be before we would have no place upon the seas anywhere—England with impunity shutting us out when to her advantage, and Germany doing likewise when to her profit?
>
>   We each have duties and responsibilities here which we can delegate to no one, . . . chief among which is to do that which will best preserve this Union which we have each sworn to support.[70]

Clara did not exaggerate when she reported to Nellie a few days later that her husband's speech had "excited more comment than any speech made in Congress for a long time," and that the eastern press especially was full of publicity about it and praise for it. She was glad to write, also, that he was getting congratulatory letters and telegrams from all over the country. Many of the larger Wisconsin papers, including the *Superior Telegram,* soon added their praise, some noting that Lenroot did his state a great service.[71]

Not everyone was pleased. La Follette was noticeably cool to Lenroot when they met a day or two after the speech and wrote his family: [72]

> Lenroot came out for "protecting our honour" and against any referendum vote of any kind for the people. He took ground that Congress had some matters too *important to be delegated by it to the people.* It was very plainly gotten up to take a shot at me. I suppose the Milwaukee and Madison Journal & other state papers which I don't see encouraged him to "throw down his mit." I think he lowered his guard at the same time and is due to get some hard bats, before the end comes. Of course nothing will mar our "cordial relations." But easy on that.

To this Belle replied: "Lenroot is building a tight board fence around his small area of progress. His knowledge of parliamentary law is about all he will have to stand on. And Husting too. Perhaps we should not expect more of him." [73]

His heavy antiwar mail encouraged La Follette to think that, despite press opinion, his attitude, not Lenroot's, was a better reflection of public feeling. Although there is no record of Lenroot's constituent correspondence for

70. *CR* 64:2, 1917, vol. 54, pt. 4, p. 3529.

71. Clara Lenroot to Nellie Nichols, 20 February 1917, Lenroot Papers Addition; *Superior Telegram,* 19, 21 February 1917; *Milwaukee Sentinel,* 18–20 February 1917; clippings, *Janesville Gazette,* 21 February 1917, *Kenosha News,* 20 February 1917, *Merrill Herald,* 19 February 1917, Box 15, Lenroot Papers.

72. Clara Lenroot to Nellie Nichols, 20 February 1917, Lenroot Papers Addition.

73. La Follette to "Dear Mamma and Kiddies," 18 February 1917, Belle La Follette to "Dear Ones" (Robert and Robert, Jr.), 21 February 1917, Box 20, Series A, La Follette FC.

the period, it is reasonable to assume that he got some negative criticism from constituents. Earlier in the month, Sweden had rejected Wilson's proposal that she join the United States in breaking diplomatic relations with Germany. And midwesterners generally inclined toward Anglophobia and suspicion that selfish eastern business interests were pushing the country toward war. A mass meeting at Washburn, Wisconsin, petitioned Lenroot for peace. In reply, Lenroot reiterated the stand he had taken in his speech.[74]

The reaction of Roosevelt, expressed to Lenroot in a three-page letter, interested Lenroot especially, as it did Clara.[75] Roosevelt complimented Lenroot on his spirit of patriotism, contrasting him favorably with Mann, and wrote that he looked to Lenroot as one whose leadership in the Republican party could make that party again a suitable vehicle for his own energies. "But my dear Mr. Lenroot," Roosevelt went on, "to advocate that we go to war a little, but not much, is, from the practical standpoint, just as bad as if we refuse to go to war at all; and that is precisely what you advocate when you say that we should have only a naval war." Roosevelt wanted, in the event of war, an expeditionary force of several hundred thousand as soon as possible and compulsory military training for two million more.[76]

Lenroot defended his course. The country was divided—that was the critical fact. Some, a small minority, followed the lead of pacifists and pro-Germans. But the overwhelming majority, he felt, opposed entering a general war or making an alliance with entente powers. The immediate need, he urged, was for "a general awakening of patriotic feeling in this country." Roosevelt, with all his influence, had for two years been trying to develop it but without success. Why? "In my judgement," Lenroot wrote, "it is because the people have believed that you are in favor of intervention in the European War upon the merits of that war, irrespective of any violation of our own rights." This fear and suspicion was not surprising "when we consider the cosmopolitan character of our population." The great need for "a united country with an awakened patriotism" could be met only

. . . by confining ourselves to maintaining our own rights in such a way as will command the support of a practically united country. We must follow such a course as will secure the support, the ungrudging support, of every man in this country, who is really an American first, irrespective of birth or descent. . . . If we shall fail to maintain our rights by the use of our naval forces, then will be the time for us to consider what other steps are necessary. If then we must go farther, we will have a united country back of the Government, and while this policy may mean time lost for preparation, it will be much more than compensated for by the advantage gained through securing in this way the whole hearted support of a united, patriotic people.

74. La Follette to "Mamma and Kids," 7, 18 February 1917, Box 20, Series A, La Follette FC; *Superior Telegram*, 9, 28 February 1917.

75. Clara Lenroot to Nellie Nichols, 26 February 1917, Lenroot Papers Addition.

76. Roosevelt to Lenroot, 20 February 1917, vol. 104, Series 3, Theodore Roosevelt Papers.

He judged, finally, that full assertion of American rights with the use of naval forces would make it unnecessary to send any soldiers to Europe.[77] In follow-up letters, Roosevelt and Lenroot exchanged compliments, while disagreeing still, and made firmer their burgeoning personal and political ties.[78]

On the day in which Lenroot delivered his much noted speech in the House, President Wilson disclosed further plans to a group of Democratic senators. As a necessary complement to the country's break with Germany, he had decided, American-owned merchant ships should be armed to defend themselves; and he, the president, should be given all necessary powers to act swiftly in an emergency while Congress was not in session, after the adjournment on 4 March. Wilson appreciated the risk of war inherent in arming merchant ships, but if America were to insist on her rights, arming ships would be the only reasonable alternative to full belligerency.[79] Though not a full embodiment of the Hayes plan, which required multilateral action, arming merchant ships pleased some of those who had accepted Hayes's idea of armed neutrality.[80]

On 26 February, the president put his proposals to a joint session of Congress in a brief speech. To a reporter that same afternoon, Lenroot expressed the common Republican disinclination to grant the president blanket authority to act in the absence of Congress. But if Wilson simply wanted "the distinct and definite power to arm merchant vessels," he said, "I think there would be no difficulty in getting congress to back him without a dissenting voice." [81]

As a result, discussions followed. The ranking Republican on the House Committee on Foreign Affairs, Henry A. Cooper of Wisconsin, opposed the entire bill as excessively dangerous. In that he spoke for only a small minority, but he had full Republican backing for removal of the blank-check phrase empowering the president to use "other instrumentalities and methods," in addition to arming merchant ships; and he had considerable support for exclusion of arms-bearing ships from the bill's provisions. The president helped to break the logjam in committee when he told newsmen that he regarded the sinking of the armed British liner *Laconia,* with the loss of two American lives, an act of war. Though Cooper still opposed the bill, a majority of the committee, under public pressure for action, agreed to a compromise set of amendments, especially the excision of the blanket authority provision. The legislation now seemed safe. But to assure full public

77. Lenroot to Roosevelt, 26 February 1917, Box 322, Series 1, Roosevelt Papers.

78. Roosevelt to Lenroot, 5 March 1917, letter of introduction written by Roosevelt to five senators and five representatives (one of them Lenroot), 5 March 1917, vol. 105, Series 3, Lenroot to Roosevelt, Box 324, Series 1, Roosevelt Papers.

79. Link, *Campaigns for Progressivism and Peace,* pp. 340, 376.

80. John Esch to Carlton J. H. Hayes, 22 February 1917, to Clara T. Runge, 26 February 1917, to Rev. H. P. Jordan, 27 February 1917, Box 41, Esch Papers; Josephus Daniels to Wilson, 26 February 1917, Box 158, Series 2, Wilson Papers.

81. *Milwaukee Sentinel,* 27 February 1917.

support later, Wilson released to the Associated Press the text of the recently intercepted Zimmermann telegram. As the House began debate on the armed ship bill on 1 March, Washington was in a state of near panic over word of Germany's secret proposal to Mexico, that in the event of war between Germany and the United States, Mexico, with German financial help, should join in and recover her lost territory of Texas, Arizona, and New Mexico.[82]

Early in the debate, Lenroot defended the bill. With the blank-check provision removed, as it would be, the bill simply gave the president power to protect American ships. "From what?" he asked, rhetorically. "From unlawful attacks, and that is all. If war then shall come it will not be the act of the President of the United States, but it will be the act of the foreign power, whatever may be the nation, that made that unlawful attack." Answering a question, Lenroot expressed the opinion that while the bill gave the president the power to protect American citizens on belligerent as well as American ships, from a practical standpoint he could not see how trouble could arise from that source; if the president chose to use the navy for convoying, it would be busy enough protecting American ships. Failure to legislate the limited powers involved, he said, would be to acquiesce in the existing, intolerable conditions.[83]

Hours later, Lenroot joined his Wisconsin colleagues and most midwestern Republicans in support of the Cooper amendment to exclude arms-bearing ships from the bill's provisions. After the amendment failed by a vote of 125 to 293, he voted for the bill, which passed by a vote of 403 to 14. Four Wisconsin men, Cary and Stafford of Milwaukee, Nelson, and Cooper were in the minority.[84]

Publication of the Zimmermann telegram produced widespread feeling for war in the country for the first time. Open talk of war by some advocates of the armed ship bill confirmed the fear of a small group of senators headed by La Follette that the bill would bring war. Encouraged by an outpouring of antiwar mail throughout February and by his wife, La Follette led in an effort to prevent action on the bill prior to expiration of the session. Proponents of the bill found the dilatory tactics of La Follette, Norris, Gronna, Cummins, and their allies inexcusable; tempers heightened and violence seemed a distinct possibility.[85]

82. Link, *Campaigns for Progressivism and Peace*, pp. 343, 349–54.

83. *CR* 64:2, 1917, vol. 54, pt. 5, p. 4638.

84. Ibid., pp. 4691–92. For an analysis of the vote on the Cooper amendment see Cooper, *Vanity of Power*, pp. 179–81, 232–34.

85. Link, *Campaigns for Progressivism and Peace*, pp. 357–61; La Follette to "Mamma, Phil and Mary," 17 February 1917, Belle La Follette to "Dear Ones" (Robert and Robert, Jr.), 21 February 1917, Box 20, Series A, Fola La Follette, interview notes, Irvine L. Lenroot, 27 February 1939, Box 73, Series E, La Follette FC; Belle and Fola La Follette, *La Follette*, vol. 1, pp. 600–625. All Republican senators earlier favored a filibuster to force an extra session, but by 3 March their purpose was accomplished and, as Link notes, they deplored La Follette's efforts.

A year later, Lenroot recalled laboring with La Follette's friends to show them the "folly and unrighteousness" of the senator's position.[86] It is not clear whether Lenroot referred to progressive Republican congressmen like Cooper and Nelson or senators like Norris and Gronna. Whatever the case, the filibusterers proceeded and succeeded. To disassociate themselves and their party from what had happened, Senators Lodge, Brandegee, and Borah drafted a statement for general circulation in the Senate indicating that the signers, if they could, would have voted for the bill. Seventy-five signed; ten were inaccessible; eleven refused to sign. Then, President Wilson, excited and angry, led the country in denouncing the isolated eleven. "A little group of willful men representing no opinion but their own, have rendered the great Government of the United States helpless and contemptible," he said. Where Wilson led, cartoonists, headline writers, and editors quickly followed.[87]

Even before publication of the Zimmermann telegram and the Senate filibuster, a group of Milwaukeeans was organizing a mass petition campaign, supporting the president. After the successful filibuster, the major Wisconsin papers abused La Follette with fury. In the privacy of their homes, however, many citizens from Wisconsin and elsewhere wrote to La Follette, expressing their approval on his course, outnumbering those who wrote critically by a four to one ratio.[88]

By virtue of his 17 February speech, Lenroot had emerged as Wisconsin's most prominent Republican supporter of the president. As such, he was paired with Democratic Sen. Paul Husting and the two were contrasted with La Follette, in the press and other forums of opinion. Stalwart Republican "loyalty" men were entirely willing to praise Lenroot. They had no other good alternative in the Wisconsin delegation, but beyond that, his past association with La Follette made the present contrast the starker. Clearly loyal to his party as well as his country, for stalwarts Lenroot seemed to vindicate Wisconsin Republicanism. And stalwarts had never been reluctant to use the technique of divide and conquer against La Follette, as Lenroot, the victim of that tactic in 1906, had good reason to know.[89]

In Milwaukee, a group led by Willet Spooner, son of the former senator, organized to show patriotism. On 8 March, Spooner wired a message to

86. *Milwaukee Sentinel*, 13 March 1918.

87. Link, *Campaigns for Progressivism and Peace*, pp. 261–65.

88. *Milwaukee Sentinel*, 1, 2, 5 March 1917; *Superior Telegram*, 5, 7, 8 March 1917. The *Superior Telegram* summarized some press opinion on 8 March. La Follette to "Beloved Ones," 8 March 1917, Box 21, Series A, La Follette FC.

89. The *Milwaukee Sentinel* on 28 February commented that Lenroot's "attitude throughout has been patriotic and constitutionally sound." The paper was pleased not only with his support of the armed ship bill but also with his opposition to a blank check that would have allowed the president to act without Congress (and without Republicans). Sixteen state senators, some of them stalwarts, signed a round robin on 8 March disapproving La Follette's course and singled out Husting and Lenroot for special commendation. *Milwaukee Sentinel*, 9 March 1917.

Lenroot, inviting him to join Husting and three local men in addressing the mass meeting they were organizing. After some correspondence, Lenroot accepted, on condition that the meeting confine itself to support of the president. There should be no reference to La Follette.[90]

Seven thousand enthusiastic patriots packed the Milwaukee auditorium on Saturday night of 17 March; stirred by their own flag waving, a band, and several drum corps, they greeted every chance afforded by the five speakers to demonstrate Milwaukee's patriotism. Lenroot, the last of the speakers, using a carefully prepared ten-page manuscript, sought to guide his auditors and those who would read his speech into a long, narrow, and hazardous channel.[91]

"The purpose of this meeting," Lenroot began, "is . . . to make known that whether we be pro-German or pro-ally in our sympathies, we are first of all pro-American." Now, in time of crisis, he went on, was no time for denunciation of the president or those who differed with him. "There are none here who want war to come," he continued. "If war does come it will be begun by some other nation and not by us, for the exercise of the right of self-defense is not war." Then Lenroot drew the familiar distinction between British and German violations of American rights; the one subject to future settlement; the other involving irretrievable loss. In the second case, he said, "the line of patience is crossed, and if we are worthy of the sacrifices made for us by the fathers of the Republic, we will defend by whatever force may be necessary the lives of our people." Whether Wilson had been strictly neutral in the past, he dismissed as irrelevant. "The only question is whether we shall permit any nation, whether England or Germany, to wantonly destroy American lives upon the high seas, where they have a right to be. That is the issue and the only issue." To avert war, Germany need only respect American rights.

As in his speech of a month before, Lenroot made it clear he proposed neither sending troops to Europe nor participating in a European settlement but simply wanted the American rights to be secured. With this accomplishment, America's quarrel would be over, and she would be prepared to make peace.

Returning to his main theme and purpose, Lenroot now said:

We need above all at this time a united people and an awakened patriotism. Is there anything in this policy that should not command the support of every German, of every Englishman, of every citizen, regardless of his birth or ancestry? Wisconsin is made up of people of many lands. You or your forefathers, like mine,

90. Spooner to Lenroot, 8 March 1917, Lenroot to Spooner, n.d. (8 or 9 March 1917), Lenroot to Spooner, n.d. (10 March 1917), Box 1, Lenroot to Spooner, 10 March 1917, Box 4, Spooner and August Vogel to Lenroot, 13 March 1917, Wheeler Bloodgood to Lenroot, 13 March 1917, Lenroot to Bloodgood, n.d. (13 or 14 March 1917), Bloodgood to Lenroot, 14 March 1917, Box 1, Lenroot to Fola La Follette, 14 June 1937, Box 3, Lenroot Papers; *CR* 65:3, 1919, vol. 57, pt. 5, pp. 4815–16.

91. *Milwaukee Sentinel*, 17, 18 March 1917.

emigrated to America because they believed that here the door of opportunity would open a little wider, that liberty would be a little freer, that the pursuit of happiness would be a little easier than in the land from whence they came. They brought with them all that was best from their native land, and here in the great melting pot of the nations, there has come out the best civilization that the world has ever known.

Lenroot paid tribute to the contribution of Germany and other lands and recognized a natural sympathy for one's homeland. He went on to say:

But . . . we are first of all and through all Americans, and we owe allegiance to no land but America. Wherever the interests of America are concerned, we must be one people in thought and in action. We must stand ready to support America against the world. By so doing we will best insure peace. By so doing we will render the highest service, not only to our own country but to any other country whose cause we may believe in, in this war. The best safeguard against war with Germany in this hour is to have Germany understand that we are one people; that every German in America much as he loves his native land, is ready if need be to fight for America even against the land of his fathers.

Lenroot brought forth one of many cheers in clinching the point: "The story of this meeting tonight in the heart of the German population of America will be carried across the sea and will do much to prevent actual conflict. It is still not too late for Germany to withdraw the order that is the cause of this crisis and may we hope that this great meeting tonight will have some influence to bring that about."

But if war should come, Lenroot went on in his closing peroration—borrowed in part from a 1915 Chautauqua speech—regardless of origin Americans would put the liberty, honor, and strength of America first. "Whenever the question shall be asked, 'Where does Wisconsin stand in this crisis?' the reply will be, 'She stands where she has always stood, Ready.' " [92]

Within a matter of days, Lenroot could see that war might be imminent. Newspapers reported that following the news of new sinkings all the cabinet members advised war. When, on 21 March, Wilson advanced the date of the special session from 16 April to 2 April, many conjectured, correctly, that he had decided to ask for a declaration of war. [93]

The new House met in an atmosphere of expectant excitement on Monday of 2 April, to organize and then hear the president. Thomas Schall, the blind Bull Mooser from Minnesota, nominated Champ Clark for Speaker with an emotional appeal to support the president by putting his party in control, but he evoked only perfunctory cheers from Democrats and little

---

92. MS speech, "Loyalty," Milwaukee, March 1917, Box 8, Lenroot Papers; *Superior Telegram*, 19 March 1917; *Milwaukee Sentinel*, 18 March 1917. When the newspaper reports and manuscript differed in instances, I followed the reports of the newspapers.

93. Link, *Campaigns for Progressivism and Peace*, pp. 5, 396, 415–16.

response from Republicans. It remained for Lenroot, in seconding the nomination of Mann, to arouse the first genuine show of enthusiasm. He had not planned to speak but felt impelled to answer Schall. "Mr. Clerk," he said, "as a Republican I can not admit that Republicans are less patriotic than are Democrats." He also added that the country would be more fully united if it knew that there was a Republican House "acting unitedly upon these great questions" with a Democratic president and a Democratic Senate. However, he concluded, notwithstanding any partisanship that House Democrats might show, "there will be no partisanship on the Republican side upon these matters." [94] Clark was duly elected, through the votes of independents.

That night, President Wilson came before the joint session and in a moving thirty-six-minute speech called for a declaration of war against Germany. He explained his rather precipitous abandonment of armed neutrality in several ways. To effectively cope with submarines, he said, one must attack them; but Germany had intimated that she would treat attackers who fell into her hands as beyond the pale of law. To make defense legitimate, one must assume the role of belligerent. Also, he now judged armed neutrality ineffectual and likely to lead swiftly to a condition of war. Under the circumstances, the country would be better off having the privileges and effectiveness of a belligerent at once, unless she proposed to submit and that America would never do. In several ways, Wilson took the conservative approach that Lenroot preferred. He said that Germany was making war on the United States, so it was simply a matter of the United States accepting a situation thrust upon her. He spoke of America's friendship for the German people and appealed for a spirit of tolerance toward Americans of German birth, whose loyalty he did not doubt. At the same time, particularly in his final words, he embraced war aims that went far beyond the limited goals Lenroot had talked of. America would fight, he said, "for democracy, for the right of those who submit to authority to have a voice in their own Governments, for the rights and liberties of small nations, for a universal dominion of right by such a concert of free peoples as shall bring peace and safety to all nations and make the world itself at last free." [95]

La Follette caused a day's delay, which was his prerogative, but late on the night of 4 April, the Senate voted for war by a vote of eighty-two to six. La Follette, who had spoken for four hours against the resolution, was of course one of the six.

Wisconsin sentiment was unmistakably with him.[96] From the letters and

94. *CR* 65:1, 1917, vol. 55, pt. 1, p. 107; *New York Times*, 3 April 1917; *Chicago Tribune*, 3 April 1917.

95. Link, *Campaigns for Progressivism and Peace*, pp. 423–26.

96. Ibid., p. 429; Belle and Fola La Follette, *La Follette*, vol. 1, p. 658; John Esch to Rev. William Crawford, 9 April 1917, Box 41, Esch Papers.

telegrams he received, Lenroot judged about 90 percent of the people in Wisconsin were against the war, especially the Germans and Scandinavians.[97]

Nevertheless, Lenroot decided to vote for war. One of over a hundred speakers to take the floor through the day of 5 April and into the following morning, Lenroot reiterated earlier views. The war had been forced upon the country by Germany. The nation was honor bound to fight. But in so doing, it need not commit itself to grandiose war aims or extensive military operations.[98]

Lenroot's was not the most important speech of the day, but the pro-war *New York Tribune* singled it out as one of the more effective ones. Probably the one speech that made any substantial difference in the voting was an emotional antiwar appeal delivered after much consideration by the able Democratic leader, Kitchin. Early in the day, administration leaders foresaw little opposition, especially since on 2 and 5 April Germany had sunk two more American ships, but after Kitchin's midafternoon speech members were seen scurrying to the correspondents of their hometown papers to change earlier statements that it was time for war. When the vote finally came, after sixteen hours of debate, it turned out that fifty members had decided to vote against war, fewer than the administration had feared in the late afternoon but many more than it expected when debate began that morning. Nine of Wisconsin's eleven members voted against the resolution, and freshman Congressman David Classon from the northeastern ninth district joined Lenroot and the majority.[99]

From Lenroot's standpoint, the situation must have seemed dangerous. Not only was the nation in the war he had hoped it could honorably avoid, but it had entered without the unity of sentiment that he had judged essential. Yet, he did not question the decision for war, so if the tasks ahead were formidable, involving mobilization not only of men and material but also opinion, he could turn to them wholeheartedly.

During the first six months in 1917, Lenroot received more attention and praise from the nation's press and periodicals than in any other period of his lifetime. Mark Sullivan in *Collier's Weekly* described him as one of the three ablest men in the House, the others being Sherley and Fitzgerald, with their ability springing mainly from clear thinking and hard work. *Outlook* contrasted Lenroot and La Follette, praised Lenroot for his courage, and marked him for higher things. *Review of Reviews* pictured him as one of four Republicans who would be especially prominent in the Sixty-fifth Congress,

97. Lenroot to Nellie Nichols, 15 April 1917, Lenroot Papers Addition; "Lenroot and La Follette: A Contrast," *Outlook* 115 (18 April 1917):691.

98. *CR* 65:1, 1917, vol. 55, pt. 1, pp. 353-54.

99. *New York Tribune,* 6 April 1917; *Washington Times,* 5 April 1917; Link, *Campaigns for Progressivism and Peace,* p. 429; *CR* 65:1, 1917, vol. 55, pt. 1, pp. 412-13.

and *Collier's Weekly* agreed. All three magazines were supportive of Roosevelt.[100]

Two newspapers described Lenroot more extensively, affording us, at this turning point in his career, a view of him according to capitol observers. Columnist James B. Morrow likened Lenroot in appearance to President Andrew Johnson, "except that his nose is not so commanding. . . . Brown eyes, deep set, gleam with intelligence and sagacity. And a plain man, noticeably; lean, middling in stature and clothed darkly. A plodding man, also, precise and having the gift for the rhetorical amplification of such thoughts as fill his mind." Theodore Tiller of the *New York Sun* described Lenroot as neither stout nor slender, though

> . . . more inclined toward the latter. His shoulders are a bit stooped. There is firmness in the set of the jaws. His eyes are piercing, yet kindly, and deep wrinkles surround them. The eyebrows are somewhat bushy. His hair is sandy and his teeth somewhat prominent. . . . Lenroot's voice has the ring of the pleader, and is not unpleasing. There is resonance to it when he warms to a subject. His gestures are vigorous and unstilted.

According to Tiller, Lenroot was not inclined to participate in routine debate, but when he spoke, it was with intense earnestness, though "he has always been rather retiring . . . and is essentially modest and unassuming." Lawyer-like in his oratorical style, trying to discount the best arguments of his opponents, a master of parliamentary law, and skilled in rough and tumble debate, Lenroot "obtains a respectful and generally appreciative hearing on both sides of the chamber." Tiller judged him a serious man. Lenroot could enjoy a joke and was companionable to a degree, "but so far as is known he is not the author of any cloak room stories that have brought side splitting laughter. A colleague, asked if he knew any anecdotes about Lenroot, said, 'heavens no! Lenroot is too intense for anecdotes. He is a fine fellow, but awfully intense.' "[101]

Writing for regular Republican papers, Morrow and Tiller gave some indication in their reports why Lenroot was emerging as a leader in the party. He had chided his party, Morrow notes, "but it has been around the hearthstone at home and not at a gloating neighbor's house down the road." Lenroot had started as a La Follette man, but after their 1912 disagreement "he had messed more or less alone." He retained the ideas of the progressive, but "whether he agrees with the statement or not, Mr. Lenroot is an evolutionist. Matters are mending and men are participating in the reformation. Therefore he, unlike many brethren of his cult, is hopeful and cheerful." On the same subject, Tiller wrote that Lenroot had drifted from La

---

100. *Collier's Weekly* 59:13 (9 June 1917):11; *Outlook* 115 (18 April 1917):691; *Review of Reviews* 55 (March 1917):243; *Collier's Weekly* 59:6 (6 April 1917):14.

101. *Cincinnati Enquirer*, 21 January 1917, reprinted in the *Superior Telegram*, 24 January 1917; clipping, *New York Sun*, 1 April 1917, Box 15, Lenroot Papers.

Follette recently, but "he still represents the more radical wing of the Republican party." Yet, "he is radical without being erratic; independent and self-assertive without intolerance for the views of others; progressive without display of demagogy." Tiller felt that there had been some change in Lenroot since he came into the House, partly because of a change in circumstances. First, there had been the Cannon fight. Then, "As he grew accustomed to his new surroundings the Wisconsin man progressed in self-confidence and active participation in the affairs of the House." With Democrats in control, the old insurgent-standpat division became decreasingly visible, so that "there is no militant insurgency today on the Republican side of the House, but Lenroot remains a member of that little group which does not hesitate to vote against the party if conscience dictates." Yet his supporters in the House, though clearly there, could not be readily grouped into one particular faction. His recognition had come because of "constant application to public duty and an increasing ability to say something worthwhile at the right time." [102]

Whatever the accuracy of these analyses, and there are oversimplifications and omissions in them, they are indicative of Lenroot's position of leadership in his party as the war Congress began its work. Disgruntlement among Republicans over Mann's ways enhanced Lenroot's position.[103]

For his part, Wilson, during the first month of American involvement in the war, was willing to accept all the help he could get from House Republicans. The need for bipartisan support for war measures was self-evident under any circumstances, but the slim Democratic hold in the House and the opposition of many House Democrats from the South and West to such measures as conscription, made Republican help all the more necessary. Some of the Republican leaders were disinclined to share responsibility with the Democrats, but Lenroot, while by no means ready to wield a rubber stamp for the president, wanted to cooperate fully. In March of 1918, Lenroot felt justified in claiming that since American entry into the war, he had been called to the White House more than any other Republican.[104]

Most important of the early war measures was the bill on the military draft. For a time the issue was in doubt as the president's proposal encountered stout resistance, especially from the South and West. Pou, who had succeeded as the chairman of the rules committee on the retirement of Robert Henry, on 11 April warned the president that "the sentiment is overwhelmingly in favor of giving the boys a chance to volunteer first," and that if the administration insisted on conscription there would be a bitter fight, though the president would probably win.[105] Some of the opposition

102. Ibid.

103. Clipping, *Chicago Tribune*, 28 July 1917, Scrapbook 23, Mann Papers.

104. Ibid.; *Superior Telegram*, 30 March 1918.

105. Edward W. Pou to Joseph P. Tumulty, 11 April 1917, Box 159, Series 2, Wilson Papers. Tumulty, Wilson's secretary, agreed with Pou. Tumulty to Wilson, 12 April 1917, Box 5, Special Cor., Joseph P. Tumulty Papers, LC.

from the South was due to fear of conscripting and arming Negroes.[106]

Gov. Emanuel Philipp probably expressed the opinion of a majority in Wisconsin when on 10 April he wired a message to the president, urging him to reconsider. He argued, among other things, that "the volunteer system will leave a good feeling at home, while conscription at this time would in my judgment, have a tendency to make the war unpopular." The Wisconsin assembly, by a vote of eighty-one to nine defeated a resolution favoring the draft.[107]

Lenroot, of course, shared Philipp's concern for public opinion, and initially he sympathized with his view "so far as the present exigency is concerned, at least." In response to Philipp's message, he declared himself in favor of compulsory military training but reliance on volunteers for possible service abroad. But to make compulsory military service constitutionally valid, those serving would have to be enrolled in the army and put under the disposal of the commander in chief. Furthermore, Lenroot had to acknowledge the possibility that use of conscripts for service abroad might be necessary at a later date. However, military authorities had given assurance that a year of training would be necessary, and by the end of a year he hoped the war would be over. Five days later, he wrote to James Stone, an advocate of conscription:

> I am very much in favor of compulsory training, and the only question that I am now considering is whether Congress should retain in its hands the determination of such training, or whether full and complete power should be granted the President to be exercised as he sees fit. I have no doubt but that the country is overwhelmingly in favor of compulsory training, and if need be, compulsory service at the end of such training, but to grant to the President authority to send our boys overseas at the end of two or three months when all military authorities hold that they should be trained a year, is a question that we have to face, and I shall come to no conclusion upon that question until I have given the matter further study and investigation.[108]

At five-thirty the following afternoon, Lenroot, accompanied by Mann, visited the president at the White House, responding to Wilson's urgent request. The two Republicans may have found the president in bad humor, for he had just finished an unsatisfactory interview with Stanley Dent of Alabama, chairman of the House Committee on Military Affairs, who, on the eve of a critical vote in committee, remained adamant for trying a volunteer system before resorting to the draft. No less firm, Wilson told Lenroot and Mann that Dent's views must be defeated in order to have a successful prosecution of the war. There is no record of what more he said

---

106. Seward W. Livermore, *Politics Is Adjourned: Woodrow Wilson and the War Congress, 1916–1918* (Middletown, Conn., 1966), p. 17.

107. Robert S. Maxwell, *Emanuel L. Philipp: Wisconsin Stalwart*, pp. 133–34; *Milwaukee Sentinel*, 18 April 1917.

108. Lenroot to Philipp, 11 April 1917, Emanuel L. Philipp Papers, WSHSL; Lenroot to Stone, 16 April 1917, Box 21, Stone Papers.

and with what effect. But after the interview of about an hour, Lenroot and Mann would say only that Republicans would consider the issue without partisanship.[109]

By a thirteen to eight vote, the military affairs committee approved Dent's plan to authorize a volunteer force and permit the president to use conscription if he judged it a failure. Immediately, Secretary Baker began to consult with the ranking Republican, the German-born Julius Kahn of California, who agreed to lead the fight in the House for the general staff's original draft plan.

It is not clear when Lenroot made up his mind, but as the House began eighteen hours of general debate on Monday of 23 April, he was aligned with the administration. In questioning Dent, who opened debate, Lenroot scored what the pro-conscription *New York Times* judged to be a telling point. The following day, on his own time, Lenroot reiterated it, together with other reasons for favoring the draft.

> I might possibly favor the volunteer system if we did not need to conserve every resource we have to win this war, . . . but if we would win within the next 12 months without the loss of American lives, it will be because in that time we will have utilized all possible means of necessary production here. We must feed our own people, we must feed and supply our Army, and in addition we must, in large part, feed and supply the armies of our allies. Food and munitions to our allies now is far more important than sending them additional men to feed and supply. The next twelve months we must devote to production and training an army. Production is the first essential, men the second. Our army should then be selected so as to interfere as little as possible with production and not at all with production absolutely essential to carry on the war.[110]

That could be done only by means of the "selective draft," with its system of exemptions. "Under the volunteer system a large majority of those who will enlist ought not to be spared now for that purpose," he added.

The volunteer system might be restricted, he acknowledged, but if it were it would fail, "for it has always been true that a large majority of volunteers have come from those engaged in productive employment, upon the farm, in the mine and factory." The committee's bill allowed for resort to the draft if the volunteer system did fail, but, Lenroot asked, "What would be the moral effect of such a finding upon Germany—our enemy? Would she not naturally conclude that America is unwilling to fight? And may not the very system that the majority advocates in this bill so prolong the war as to make

109. Ray Stannard Baker, *Woodrow Wilson, Life and Letters: War Leader, 1917–1918,* vol. 7, p. 23; *New York Times,* 18 April 1917; Lenroot to S. D. Slade, 16 December 1918, Box 5, Lenroot Papers; *Milwaukee Sentinel,* 18 April 1917. Perhaps the main purpose of the interview was to have a pro-conscription Republican immediately named to a vacancy on the military affairs committee. James H. Davidson of Wisconsin was appointed and, contrary to the expectations of some, voted against the administration. The matter is unclear and provides no clue to Lenroot's attitude toward the draft following the meeting with Wilson. *New York Times,* 18, 19, 20 April 1917; *Chicago Tribune,* 18, 19 April 1917.

110. *New York Times,* 24, 25 April 1917; *CR* 65:1, 1917, vol. 55, pt. 1, p. 1050.

it necessary to send our men across the sea?" Members applauded when Lenroot said that a show of full determination now would go far toward ending the war without sacrificing American lives.

After talking of the obligations that accompany privileges in a democracy, Lenroot pointed out another of the practical difficulties in the volunteer system. Under a draft system adopted at once, no stigma would be attached to a draftee. But if the draft were resorted to only after the volunteer system had failed, "the finger of scorn and of shame is pointed at the conscript." He concluded by effectively answering a number of relatively weak but common arguments used in opposition.[111]

An amendment designed to permit Roosevelt to raise a volunteer contingent endangered the bill and Lenroot, though friendly to Roosevelt, voted against it. It was defeated, and the House soon acted favorably on the draft bill. Senate adoption of the Roosevelt amendment caused further delay, but eventually conferees reconciled their differences. Appealed to by Roosevelt and realizing that the conscription bill was sound, Lenroot had used his influence to win adoption of the Roosevelt amendment, but the most Roosevelt's supporters could get was a provision making the Roosevelt division permissive but not mandatory. The president declined to use the Roughrider.[112]

While the army bill was in conference, Lenroot served as one of the leaders in what, after a month of struggle, was a successful effort to strike censorship provisions from the espionage bill. The effort, largely conducted by Republicans and praised by newspapers, overcame the objections of the administration and the Senate. The postmaster general retained power to exclude certain matter from the mails, however. In regard to the bill as a whole, Lenroot supported the administration.[113]

On 9 May, Kitchin reported a second war measure, a supplementary revenue bill designed to raise $1.8 billion in taxes to be included with the previously authorized $2 billion of borrowed money for projected war expenditures over the next year. Necessarily, the bill had many unprecedented features and brought about many complaints from various interest groups and from ideologues of left and right. Conservatives complained especially against the heavy income tax and profits tax rates, which broke new ground in the use of these relatively new sources of revenue. But the members of the ways and means committee had settled their differences and produced a report upon which everyone had agreed, so Kitchin had reason to expect the bill to be passed without change in a few days.[114]

111. *CR* 65:1, 1917, vol. 55, pt. 1, pp. 1050–52.

112. Margulies, "Lenroot," pp. 869–72.

113. Livermore, *Politics Is Adjourned*, pp. 32–36; Elisha Hanson to Joseph Medill McCormick, 3 June 1918, Box 2, Joseph Medill McCormick Papers; Frederic L. Paxson, *American Democracy and the World War: America at War, 1917–1918*, vol. 2, pp. 61–65; *CR* 65:1, 1917, vol. 55, pt. 2, pp. 1715, 1718, 1760, 1929–30.

114. Livermore, *Politics Is Adjourned*, p. 58; Charles Gilbert, *American Financing of World War I*, pp. 75–90; *New York Tribune*, 8, 9, 11 May 1917; Paxson, *America at War*, vol. 2, p. 143.

Nevertheless, Lenroot prepared to fight for amendments. The position that he took was simple. Income-tax schedules could be further raised without imposing any hardship on anyone. By increasing them, Congress might eliminate certain consumption taxes that would cause hardship, especially the rates on light, heat, and freight. The public, already paying inflationary prices caused by war, had its fair share of the burden and did not need the additional suffering that might be caused by the consumption taxes, Lenroot argued.[115]

During the preparedness fights of the preceding years, those most fearful of preparedness and of war urged heavier taxes on incomes and profits and inheritances to meet higher costs, partly to discourage the business elements whom they suspected of fostering war preparation in order to line their own pockets. With the war, the large segments of the population thought the wealthy were benefiting from the war. Therefore, progressive taxation, though relatively new, seemed fairest. Reflecting that view, the Wisconsin legislature resolved to meet the state's war costs by higher income-tax rates and urged Congress to tax all incomes in excess of $10,-000.[116] Stressing the need for rates that were equitable, Lenroot had no occasion to make the point that rates should seem equitable, but that was obviously part of his concern.

Lenroot launched his campaign of 16 May, as the House began to consider the bill under the five minute rule. Initially, his fight was for an amendment offered by Sherley, to increase from one percent to two percent the surtax on incomes between $5,000 and $7,500. He was prepared to support other increases that Sherley would propose on incomes above $7,500. However, he made it clear, should the first Sherley amendment fail, which would be a sign of prospective defeat for the rest, he would offer his own more modest schedule of increases, to raise all committee schedules by 25 percent for incomes over $40,000.[117]

Spirited debate ensued. Kitchin charged that various special interest groups such as producers of liquor, jewelry, automobiles, and boats hoped to shift taxes from their products onto incomes, and newspaper and magazine publishers wanted to avoid higher postal rates. Joseph Fordney warned that if taxes were too high, corporations would find ways of avoiding them; and Cannon noted that the revenues that could be derived from "plutocrats" were greatly exaggerated by many. In all likelihood, their arguments were directed less against the Sherley amendment, which was foredoomed, than against the more moderate amendments proposed by Lenroot, which were yet to come.[118]

On a voice vote, which went unchallenged, the House rejected Sherley's amendment. A few minutes later, Lenroot offered his first amendment,

115. CR 65:1, 1917, vol. 55, pt. 3, pp. 2406, 2419, 2611.
116. John Wylie Hillje, "The Progressive Movement and the Graduated Income Tax, 1913–1919" (Ph.D. diss.), pp. 144–45, 189–90, 196; Milwaukee Sentinel, 18 April 1917.
117. CR 65:1, 1917, vol. 55, pt. 3, p. 2406.
118. Ibid., pp. 2406–19.

which would test the viability of his whole 25 percent increase plan. It was to increase the tax on income from $40,000 to $60,000 from 8 percent, the committee figure, to 10 percent. After Lenroot restated the case, the House voted. By a vote of ninety-eight to eighty-seven, it approved his amendment. Kitchin was probably right that those who were primarily concerned about other taxes in the bill supported the proposal of higher income taxes. What had not been foreseeable was that a formula could be found that would make possible a successful coalition. To regroup his own forces, Kitchin immediately stopped consideration of the bill for that day.[119]

The following afternoon, Kitchin had to make an embarrassing admission. Secretary McAdoo had informed him that the government would need not $1.8 billion but $2.245 billion. Nevertheless, committee members continued to oppose changes in the bill, some with the claim that in December the House could enact additional legislation for further revenue. But Lenroot's amendments carried en bloc—146 to 107. However, he failed to win elimination of taxes on light, heat, and freight.[120]

In the Senate, action was delayed by the food bill. Finally, in late summer, the upper House overturned its conservative finance committee and approved the "Lenroot rates," as they were called, and voted higher profits and inheritance taxes than the House had approved. The act in its final form raised $2.5 billion, approximately three-fourths of it coming from taxes on incomes, profits, and inheritances. Lenroot's amendments added only about $60 million, but their initial adoption in the House constituted an identifiable step in the advance of progressive taxation. However, La Follette, Norris, and a few others denounced the act as not going nearly far enough in putting the burden on the "war profiteers," and complaints outweighed praise among the public.[121]

Only a few of the House committees met during the special session. One of them was the rules committee. It considered several matters in which Lenroot had great interest, including changes in House rules and creation of a special House committee on woman suffrage. Prospects for the latter improved materially, when on 16 May President Wilson came out for it in a letter to Chairman Pou. Three weeks later, Lenroot was glad to cast the decisive vote in committee for a favorable report on that long-sought suffrage goal. But at his suggestion, proponents agreed that it not be reported until all war measures were disposed of. A week later, again at Lenroot's suggestion, the committee agreed to postpone consideration of rules reform until the food control and food survey bills were taken care of.[122]

119. Ibid., pp. 2420–21.

120. Ibid., p. 2482; *Washington Post*, 18 May 1917; *CR* 65:1, 1917, vol. 55, pt. 3, pp. 2601–11; *Washington Post*, 20 May 1917.

121. Hillje, "Graduated Income Tax," pp. 191, 262–63; Livermore, *Politics Is Adjourned*, pp. 59–61; Belle and Fola La Follette, *La Follette*, vol. 2, pp. 742–47; Livermore, *Politics Is Adjourned*, p. 61.

122. *Washington Times*, 16 May 1917; Record Group 233, "Committee on Rules, Minutes," 65th Cong., 1st sess., 6, 12 June 1917.

Lenroot participated in the House consideration of the Lever Food Control bill and a number of other war measures. He undertook to ensure the constitutionality of new laws and to limit the extension of federal authority to what was essential. Shocked at evidences of waste and inefficiency, he thought the Republicans could help and supported Sen. John Weeks's proposal for a joint committee to act as watchdog on expenditures. The president opposed the idea and Democratic leaders in the House blocked debate. Lenroot emerged from the session bitter with the president and many of his House colleagues, and in some despair as to the conduct of the war but no less determined than before to assist in its prosecution. The most urgent need, he felt, was for a more favorable public opinion.

VII

THE SENATOR FROM WISCONSIN

Early in August, leaders in Washington discussed a plan that would require every representative and senator to go through his district during the sessional recess to explain the position of the United States in the war and the need for vigorous prosecution of it. Later that month, a group of men in Milwaukee, who were disturbed at the public's lack of enthusiasm for the war, organized the Wisconsin Loyalty Legion, with branches in each congressional district. Lenroot agreed to speak in his district.[1] He had reasons for concern.

Senator La Follette, hoping to organize the country for an early peace settlement, was repeatedly encouraged through the summer by reports from Wisconsin of increasing opposition to the war.[2] Though most extreme in Wisconsin, lack of war enthusiasm was a national problem, the result of the war's remoteness, Allied military reverses, mistakes on the home front, high prices and shortages mingled with rumors of profiteering, and other wartime irritants all superimposed on suspicions surviving from prewar days.[3]

Many of those who worried about Wisconsin opinion were almost as concerned that Wisconsin be thought loyal as that she be loyal. In the face of the open and covert charges against the state, from New York, Washington, and Wisconsin's own superpatriots, Governor Philipp took every opportunity to defend the state's honor.[4] As best they could, many newspapers and private citizens did the same. But the fact of Wisconsin's large German

1. *Superior Telegram*, 9, 30 August, 29 September 1917. On the origins of the Loyalty Legion see Lorin Lee Cary, "The Wisconsin Loyalty Legion, 1917–1918," pp. 33–50.

2. Belle and Fola La Follette, *La Follette*, vol. 2, pp. 737–39; La Follette to "My Beloved Ones," 23 June 1917, to "Dear Mama and Kiddies," 14 July 1917, to "Dear Hearts," 4 August 1917, Box 21, Series A, Robert M. La Follette FC. As farmer support lagged, Wisconsin subscribed only $34 million of a requested $44 million in the first Liberty Loan campaign. Robert S. Maxwell, *Emanuel L. Philipp: Wisconsin Stalwart*, p. 149; Cary, "Loyalty Legion," p. 37.

3. For comments see Medill McCormick to Sir Horace Plunkett, 13 September 1917, Box 2, Joseph Medill McCormick Papers. See also Sen. Henry F. Ashurst's private comment. Henry Fountain Ashurst, *A Many-Colored Toga: The Diary of Henry Fountain Ashurst*, entry for 6 October 1917, p. 72. Some of the sources of discontent are referred to in Seward W. Livermore, *Politics Is Adjourned: Woodrow Wilson and the War Congress, 1916–1918* (Middletown, Conn., 1966), pp. 62–65.

4. *Superior Telegram*, 31 July, 13 September, 19 October 1917; Maxwell, *Philipp*, pp. 138–40.

population and its strong, antiwar social democratic party gave rise to suspicion. And Senator La Follette was a constant source of embarrassment.[5]

Suspect due to his part in blocking the armed ship bill and his vote against the war and by his speeches and votes in the Senate after the war declaration, La Follette worsened his reputation and that of his state among those who supported the war ardently. He was one of six to vote against the espionage bill, one of eight against the conscription bill, one of four against the war revenue bill. La Follette delayed consideration of the aviation bill and sponsored a resolution declaring American war aims in terms that were offensive to the Allies and embarrassing to the administration.[6] Agitating for repeal of the conscription law, he said that most drafted men were protesting; he asserted that the Liberty Loan was possible only because of an "iron hand" inside a soft glove.

Then came press reports of La Follette's speech before the Nonpartisan League in St. Paul on 20 September, which produced numerous severe denunciations of the senior senator. La Follette's troubles were compounded by two noteworthy factors, which were, by no means, the whole source of them. The first was the misquotation by the Associated Press, which stated that America "had no grievances" instead of that America had grievances; the second was his oversimplification of the sinking of the *Lusitania*. Tired and speaking extemporaneously in response to hecklers, La Follette said sarcastically: "We had cause for complaint. They had interfered with the right of American citizens to travel upon the high seas—on ships loaded with munitions for Great Britain." He strongly implied that what was really at stake in the war were the loans made by the House of Morgan and the profits of munitions makers.[7] The Minnesota Public Safety Commission petitioned the Senate to expel him and Roosevelt, on a speaking tour, seconded the idea and called La Follette one of the "Huns within our gates."

While visiting in California on 24 October, Lenroot condemned La Follette's attitude toward the war before the Northern California Alumni Association, as did the other speakers, Congressman Esch, and Richard T. Ely, and Chester Lloyd Jones, both professors at the University of Wisconsin.[8]

By then, perhaps, Lenroot had heard the shocking news from Wisconsin—Sen. Paul Husting had been accidentally killed by his brother while duck hunting. Almost immediately, loyalty advocates called for a special

---

5. In 1910 first- and second-generation German immigrants constituted 28.9 percent of the state's population. Clifford L. Nelson, *German-American Political Behavior in Nebraska and Wisconsin, 1916–1920*, p. 3.

6. Belle and Fola La Follette, *La Follette*, vol. 2, pp. 733, 736, 745, 756–57; *Superior Telegram*, 18 July 1917.

7. Belle and Fola La Follette, *La Follette*, vol. 2, pp. 762–70.

8. Ibid., p. 845; clipping, *Merrill Herald*, 17 November 1917, Box 15, Irvine L. Lenroot Papers; *Superior Telegram*, 31 October 1917.

election on nonpartisan lines, to allow their forces to unite on a single candidate and, by electing him, vindicate the state's honor.[9] While rejecting suggestions from friends that he be a candidate, Lenroot approved the election idea and, with some embellishments, began to urge it after his return to Washington in early November. As he explained the matter to Roosevelt soon afterwards, a special nonpartisan primary to choose two candidates would at worst produce one loyalty candidate and it might possibly produce two. To ensure against dispersal of loyalty strength, Lenroot suggested that the Loyalty Legion hold a pre-primary convention to endorse a single candidate. He hoped that the issue could be confined to "war or anti-war" and believed that if that were done, the election could have a fine effect nationally. "I can think of nothing that would have a better effect throughout the country," he wrote Roosevelt, "than a pronounced victory in Wisconsin in the election of a loyal Senator." [10]

In mid-November, Lenroot spoke at Ashland and, in substantially the same vein, at Merrill, Wisconsin. He cited the events leading to war and noted that Germany's announcement in 31 January of unrestricted submarine warfare was not only a declaration of war on the United States but also "raised the black flag against the world." Lenroot drew the familiar distinction between German and British violation of American rights and referred in passing to the fact that the armed ship bill had been blocked by a filibuster. Then he talked of German efforts to involve Mexico and, something that had become known in September, to bribe congressmen as well as to sabotage factories. Citing German messages of 1916 to prove his point, he drew the moral that in addition to its acts on the high seas, "Germany, through its spies and agents, actually invaded the soil of the United States."

"Why are we at war?" he asked rhetorically.

We are not at war primarily to secure liberty for other peoples, but we are at war to preserve our own liberty, not only upon the sea, but upon the land. The acts of which we complain are not the acts of the German people, but are the acts of the aristocracy of Germany headed by the kaiser, whose mind is seething with ambition, as was Napoleon's to conquer and rule the world.

Lenroot was not just justifying the war but explaining the necessity to do what the government was preparing to do, fight in Europe. He had not expected that it would be necessary, Lenroot admitted, but now saw that it was. The United States would not be safe should Germany win, he argued. Acquiring the Allied navies, and herself insecure in a world half democratic and half autocratic, Germany would have the capacity to bottle up the American navy and invade the Western Hemisphere. Against the threat, the United States would have to become a "military nation" for generations to come.

9. Cary, "Loyalty Legion," p. 42; *Superior Telegram*, 21, 24, 25, 26 October, 3 November 1917.
10. Lenroot to Nellie Nichols, 2 November 1917, Irvine L. Lenroot Papers Addition; to Theodore Roosevelt, 27 December 1917, Box 365, Series 1, Theodore Roosevelt Papers.

Obliquely answering La Follette, Lenroot said that though the United States sought only peace, a peace treaty could not be concluded at once, for one could not make peace with a government "that regards treaties as scraps of paper." Only after a change was effected in the German government could there be a meaningful peace.

Now Lenroot talked of the loyalty of German-Americans and the tragedy of their being held in suspicion, as he had previously distinguished between the German people and the German government. After developing the point with reference to the liberty-loving forty-eighters—German immigrants of 1848—Lenroot turned to the most ticklish but timely phase of his speech, regarding La Follette and the senatorial vacancy.

Without mentioning any names yet, Lenroot developed the theme that the right of free speech is not unlimited. Treason, he said, is a crime, "and treason consists in giving aid and comfort to our enemies. So the right of free speech does not give a man the right to commit treason." He was ready to admit the right of any man to advocate the repeal of any law that Congress has enacted and noted that some were urging the repeal of the conscription law.

> We may admit their right to do this, but it is also the right of every true American citizen to condemn any man who advocates its repeal. Free speech may give him the right to do this, but we may as well understand that by the act he is consciously at the same time advocating the lowering of the stars and stripes and raising the German flag in its place. He is prolonging the war; he would have the rich man's son escape all danger, if he did not volunteer, and if all rich men are as venal as most of the advocates of the repeal of the draft charge them to be, they would make this in fact a "rich man's war and a poor man's fight."

Lenroot then noted that Lincoln was being widely quoted in favor of free speech. So he reminded his listeners of Lincoln's response to protests over sending the Copperhead Clement Vallandigham into the Southern lines: " 'Must I shoot a simple minded soldier boy who deserts, while I must not touch a hair of a wily agitator, who induces him to desert?' "

Lenroot regretted that "all over this land the finger of suspicion is pointed at Wisconsin." Asked about it on the west coast, he had replied that men should not judge "by what Senator La Follette says about the war, but by what Wisconsin does in the war." It was unfortunate for himself and the state, Lenroot declared, that La Follette "has taken the attitude he has regarding the justification for the war but in that attitude he does not represent the people of this great state."

If there were an election to choose a successor to Husting, Lenroot went on, Wisconsin would have a chance to show its loyalty to the government and support for the war. The people must show not only the nation but also Germany that Wisconsin is with the government. "A victory in Wisconsin may mean the shortening of the war. Germany's hope is dissension in the United States." [11]

Back in Washington for the regular session after ten days of hunting, Lenroot reiterated his decision not to be a candidate, but he again urged an election on the loyalty issue and continued to watch the Wisconsin situation closely and anxiously. Governor Philipp, reluctant to see the state plunged into a divisive election campaign and, perhaps, for other reasons, wanted the legislature to empower him to appoint a successor to Husting. To make that proposition as attractive as possible in the legislature, he decided to appoint Lenroot if he would accept. Through friends, he sounded out the congressman, but Lenroot refused to consider it, without even asking to see the fine print that he suspected was there. He still hoped the legislature, when it met, would force a special election, and he urged Roosevelt to advance the cause. Meanwhile, he was occupied with legislative business.[12]

Lenroot voted for both the prohibition and woman suffrage amendments, explaining his reversal of position chiefly on the grounds that the amendments now had a good chance for speedy ratification if put to the states.[13]

The tangled waterpower situation engaged Lenroot's attention again and he contributed substantially. At his suggestion and with help from the president, House leaders agreed that the best approach was to seek a single bill, which would deal with development of waterpower in the national forests, the public lands, and on navigable streams. Waterpower questions would be placed under the jurisdiction of a new commission. They agreed, further, on creation of a single committee to fashion the bill. The committee was approved; Lenroot was named to it; and work began; at the same time a suspect Senate bill was sidetracked by the new committee.[14]

More than anything else during the first three months of the session, Lenroot gave his time and attention to the mineral lands leasing question. He took a moderate position in support of Secretary Lane as against the

11. *Superior Telegram*, 15 November 1917.

12. Maxwell, *Philipp*, pp. 152–53; *Chicago Tribune*, 4 December 1917; Lenroot to Nellie Nichols, 1 January 1917 (1918), Lenroot Papers Addition; *Superior Telegram*, 6 December 1917, 2, 19 February 1918; J. M. Stricker to Lenroot, 21 December 1917, vol. 144, Series 3, Lenroot to Roosevelt, 27 December 1917, Box 365, Series 1, Roosevelt Papers.

13. *CR* 65:1, 1917, vol. 55, pt. 1, p. 768.

14. Record Group 48, "Records of the Office of the Secretary of the Interior," "Historical Summary of Federal Water Power Act, (1931), file, 2–194, pp. 9–26, 233, NA. The narrative consists of footnotes written by O. C. Merrill, accompanying documents. Jerome G. Kerwin, *Federal Water-Power Legislation*, pp. 217–20, 241; Kent to Wilson, 23 November 1917, Lane to Wilson, 31 December 1917, File 1888, Series 4, Woodrow Wilson Papers; Record Group 233, "Committee on Rules, Minutes," 65th Cong., pt. 1, 8 January 1918; *CR* 65:2, 1918, vol. 56, pt. 1, pp. 833, 850–51.

oil lands claimants and the navy people. The latter remained solicitous for naval reserves, even in the face of seeming wartime necessity. Division within the administration contributed to further delay and Lenroot was no longer a member of the House when it adopted a bill on 25 May.[15]

From the start of the regular session in December, no problem loomed so large as that of transportation. Required to move goods to the eastern seaboard as never before, the poorly coordinated, dilapidated, and financially weakened railroad system encountered a shortage of freight cars and other equipment and a congestion snarl in the east that worsened progressively through 1917. A coal shortage, which threatened factories and homes, was not the least of the consequences. Deeply interested in railroad legislation since his days in the Wisconsin legislature and familiar with the topic, Lenroot plunged into it. In mid-December, he introduced a bill that called for the establishment of a new government corporation to construct and lease to the railroads locomotives and cars at reasonable rates, thus relieving the equipment shortage.[16] When, on 26 December, the president announced a government takeover of railroad properties, effective two days later, he rendered obsolete Lenroot's bill but created the need for much broader legislation.

Wilson met a cool reception in Congress as he explained his action on 4 January.[17] Lenroot pinpointed one of the main issues on 14 January, when he said, in his speech, that the president had no authority to supersede the ratemaking powers of the Interstate Commerce Commission and the state commissions, as he presumed to do in his proclamation. He declined to discuss whether such power should be delegated and confined himself to the question of whether the power had been delegated. But it was well known that railroad executives had for a long time wanted to escape from what they considered a narrow-minded and ruinous regulatory regime, while shippers, supported by progressive politicians, upheld the I.C.C. and most of its decisions just as stoutly.[18] By then, the House committee on interstate commerce was busy at work on the Federal Control bill, using as a starting point an administration bill drawn largely by a new member of the Interstate Commerce Commission, George Anderson, at the behest of

15. J. Leonard Bates, *The Origins of Teapot Dome: Progressives, Parties and Petroleum, 1909–1921*, pp. 114–45; Lane's willingness to compromise is noted in Keith Waldemar Olson, "Franklin K. Lane: A Biography," p. 186; U.S., House of Representatives, Committee on Public Lands, *Hearings: Oil Leasing Lands*, pp. 85, 92–95, 98, 157–59, 178, 185–87, 248–54, 286–89, 311–16, 326–29, 364, 370, 416, 420–25, 466–71, 617, 637–39, 797–98, 873, 875, 979, 1010, 1022–26, 1092, 1095, 1097, 1099, 1104, 1119; E. David Cronon, ed., *The Cabinet Diaries of Josephus Daniels* (Lincoln, 1963), entry for 19 January 1918, p. 269.

16. K. Austin Kerr, *American Railroad Politics, 1914–1920: Rates, Wages, and Efficiency*, pp. 39–41, 54–57; *Superior Telegram*, 19 December 1917.

17. Clara Lenroot, Diary, 4 January 1918, Lenroot Papers Addition.

18. *CR* 65:2, 1918, vol. 56, pt. 1, pp. 666–68; Albro Martin, *Enterprise Denied: Origins of the Decline of American Railroads, 1897–1917*, pp. 194–351.

the new director general of the system, William Gibbs McAdoo.[19] The majority on the committee was willing to vest final authority over rates and the like with the president. But Esch of Wisconsin, the ranking Republican, led his party colleagues to the side of the shippers, who were justly suspicious that McAdoo, guided by railroad executives, would seek to sustain the market for railroad securities by raising rates at their expense.[20] The basis for compensation of the railroad companies was largely agreed upon in committee, though room for disagreement remained. More controversial was the duration of federal control. The administration's bill fixed no definite time limit, and Commissioner Anderson hoped government operation would continue after the war. On this question, railroads and shippers were in agreement, and Esch, in his minority report, championed their position and proposed return of the roads within a year of the war's end.[21]

Lenroot agreed with Esch in his major criticisms of the bill and found the measure a poorly crafted thing besides. After preparing a long list of amendments, he was ready for floor debate.

Lenroot won much of what he sought. In addition to technical improvements, he led in gaining amendments to protect the government in its relations with the companies, to protect the state commissions, and to secure workers in rights they had previously enjoyed, such as compensation for on-the-job injuries. In Committee of the Whole, he was successful with respect to final rate determination by the I.C.C. and limiting the duration of government ownership to a year after war's end. The House overturned these decisions, but the conference committee accepted the Senate's strong provision regarding the I.C.C. and compromised the duration of ownership to eighteen months.[22]

If Lenroot had earlier been archaic in his progressivism, he remained so to the extent that he put part of the blame for railroad troubles on the companies themselves, exaggerated their prosperity, and placed continuing reliance on rigid state and federal regulation. But in acknowledging the need for pooling, at least during the war, he was adapting to new economic circumstances.

During the course of debate on the railroad bill, Thetus Sims referred to Lenroot as the "Senator to be from Wisconsin." [23] If Sims presumed a good deal, perhaps he had reason to. The Wisconsin legislature had refused to allow Governor Philipp to make an appointment and Philipp therefore

19. McAdoo subcontracted the work to Anderson and John Barton Payne, a Treasury official who had been a railroad attorney and executive. But in debate congressmen attributed the bill to Anderson. Kerr, *Railroad Politics*, p. 83; *CR* 65:2, 1918, vol. 56, pt. 3, p. 2720.

20. Kerr, *Railroad Politics*, pp. 83–97.

21. Ibid., pp. 74–75, 86; *New York Times*, 15 January 1918.

22. Herbert F. Margulies, "Progressivism, Patriotism, and Politics: The Life and Times of Irvine L. Lenroot," pp. 913–20.

23. *CR* 65:2, 1918, vol. 56, pt. 3, p. 2632.

scheduled a special election.[24] Immediately, Lenroot was strongly pressured by colleagues from Wisconsin and Washington to seek the Republican nomination.

On 24 February, Richard Lloyd Jones, publisher of the *Wisconsin State Journal,* and former state Sen. A. W. Sanborn called Lenroot from Madison, and they, with Andrew Dahl, Walter Houser, and perhaps other veteran progressives, urged him to run. Already, Francis McGovern was in the field as a loyalty candidate, but the abrasive former governor had too many enemies among both progressives and stalwarts to serve the purpose, they all felt. Jones, Sanborn, and the others did not have to argue the importance of defeating whomever the La Follette men might choose, but perhaps they talked of the danger of losing, and certainly they stressed the fact of Lenroot's preeminent strength as a candidate. Either then or later in the day, Lenroot acquiesced but only conditionally. Before he would agree to file nominating papers, he required proof of a genuine demand for his nomination and bi-factional unity behind it.[25]

Before he made his final decision, Lenroot saw the Pinchots and William Kent and was sought out by Sen. Henry Cabot Lodge. His wealthy progressive friends promised financial support if he decided to run, though Kent hoped he would not. Lodge, to Lenroot's surprise and pleasure, was deeply interested. He said his late son-in-law, "Gussie" Gardner, who had enlisted and died in a Georgia army camp, had awakened his enthusiasm for Lenroot.[26] Lodge, of course, saw the special election as important to Republican chances of capturing and organizing the Senate, including the Committee on Foreign Relations, over which he would preside. Will Hays, the new party chairman, was in Washington that week to confer about the November elections, and he may well have encouraged Lenroot, as Congressman Kahn and others did.[27]

Pressure mounted as Wisconsin men flooded Lenroot with telegrams. And the congressman's conditions were promptly and fully met. Jones, Sanborn, and editor Walter Goodland of Racine, Wisconsin, all three active in the Loyalty Legion, engineered a meeting between representatives of McGovern and Lenroot. McGovern came to the meeting and agreed to a conference of loyalty Republicans to meet in Milwaukee on 4 March to decide between himself and Lenroot. Progressives such as James Stone, Otto Bosshard, Goodland, and others circulated Lenroot's petitions and met with speedy success. Stalwarts swung into line, following the lead of Charles Pfister's *Milwaukee Sentinel* and of Philipp. To meet the legal dead-

24. *Milwaukee Sentinel,* 17, 19, 20, 22, 23 February 1917; *Milwaukee Journal,* 19 February 1917.

25. Lenroot, "Memoirs," pp. 135–37, Box 13, Lenroot Papers; *Milwaukee Sentinel,* 25 February 1918.

26. Lenroot, "Memoirs," p. 136, Box 13, Lenroot Papers; Kent to Gifford Pinchot, 26 February 1918, Box 210, Gifford Pinchot Papers; *Milwaukee Sentinel,* 26 October 1920; Clara Lenroot, Diary, 14 February (1 March) 1918, Lenroot Papers Addition.

27. *Milwaukee Sentinel,* 25 February, 26 March 1918.

line, on 28 February Lenroot wired instructions to file his nominating papers.[28]

For Lenroot, the momentous decision must have been difficult. He believed he would one day become Speaker if he remained in the House, and he wanted that office.[29] Even without it, he could exert more influence in the House than in the Senate, at least for some time.

He had other grounds for reluctance. The legislature was under pressure to censure La Follette. He would be called on to comment on that, and on the movement to expel La Follette from the Senate. The last remnant of their once close relationship would surely be a casualty of the contest. And Lenroot could not look forward with much pleasure to service as La Follette's colleague in the Senate.[30]

But the call to duty at such a time was imperious. Wisconsin must show its loyalty, for its own sake and the nation's. Subsurface discontent was great, Lenroot knew, and he, more than any other, could channel it safely away from the La Follette candidate. Farmers complained of inadequate prices for their products, excessive costs, labor shortages, and profiteering—they blamed the government. Lenroot's established reputation as a progressive, indeed, a La Follette man, figured to be useful, especially since the campaign would be short. To counterbalance the heavy German vote of Milwaukee and the lakeshore counties, a strong vote was needed in the north, and Lenroot was best able to get it. When, on 26 February, the La Follette men—Crownhart, Ekern, and John Blaine—disregarding the senator's advice, put aside Lt. Gov. Edward Dithmar and chose as their candidate a popular lawyer of Norwegian background from La Crosse, James Thompson, the need for a man like Lenroot, able to compete successfully among farmers, laborers, Yankees, Scandinavians, and throughout the old La Follette country, increased.[31]

Lenroot was the victim of his own success. By his votes and speeches, he had made himself the champion of those Wisconsin Republicans who supported the war and disapproved La Follette's stand on it. Mindful from the first of the need for unity, he had moved cautiously and successfully toward the common denominator. Now, in the face of seeming emergency, discor-

28. Clipping, *Janesville Gazette*, 25 February 1918, Box 19, Lenroot Papers; Clara Lenroot, Diary, 3 March 1918, Lenroot Papers Addition; *Milwaukee Sentinel*, 25–28 February, 1–3 March 1918; Maxwell, *Philipp*, p. 161.

29. Clara Lenroot, Diary, 14 February (1 March) 1918, Lenroot Papers Addition; Gifford Pinchot, quoted in *Milwaukee Sentinel*, 26 October 1920; Lenroot, "Memoirs," p. 136, Box 13, Lenroot Papers.

30. Lenroot to Wallace Sayre, 15 February 1930, Box 4, Lenroot, "Memoirs," pp. 135–36, Box 13, Lenroot Papers.

31. Herbert F. Margulies, *The Decline of the Progressive Movement in Wisconsin, 1890–1920*, pp. 214–15; *Milwaukee Sentinel*, 25 February, 8 March 1918; La Follette to "My Beloved Ones," 8 March 1919, Box 26, to "My Dear Ones," 25 April 1919, Box 27, Series A, La Follette FC. Thompson had led the ticket for delegate-at-large to the 1916 Republican National Convention.

dant groups could achieve harmony if he would run. That was an achievement, for it required not only that progressives and stalwarts put aside old antagonisms but also that patriot and superpatriot suppress newer differences.

As against running, there was the argument that if Thompson won the primary, he would surely lose the general election to a loyalty Democrat. But a victory for a La Follette surrogate in his party's primary would itself deal a severe blow to Wisconsin's reputation and to the war effort, as Lenroot saw it. Nor could Lenroot ignore a point made by National Chairman Will Hays—that it would be unfortunate for the Republican party if it were represented by a La Follette candidate against a "war Democrat." [32]

Though concerned more about measures than spoils, Lenroot was yet a partisan. Firm in the Rooseveltian view that successful pursuit of the war effort required full Republican participation, Lenroot had to consider party pressures and party interest.

He was sorry that Charles McCarthy, the dynamic head of the Wisconsin Legislative Reference Library on loan to the Food Administration, had little chance to defeat Federal Trade Commissioner Joseph E. Davies for the Democratic nomination.[33] What is not clear is as to whether he feared that Davies would lose to Thompson if the latter were nominated, or simply judged him a poor choice for senator. Certainly, he had no great respect for Davies.[34]

From a party standpoint, of course, even the election of a more capable and independent Democrat would have been less than satisfactory. The winner, Senate Minority Leader Jacob Gallinger and others thought, might cast the decisive vote in determining which party should organize the next Senate. And the outcome could influence later contests around the nation, for the Wisconsin election would get national attention and would stand as the greatest contest between the parties in the war period.[35]

One complication remained. Soon after Governor Philipp came out for Lenroot, McGovern announced that in light of Philipp's action, he would run, regardless of the result of the conference. Lenroot told Hays, Lodge, and perhaps others that only Roosevelt could influence McGovern. Hays, Lodge, and Nicholas Longworth, Roosevelt's son-in-law, appealed to the Roughrider. Lenroot was chosen at the conference, but McGovern persisted, and Roosevelt had to wire a message to him, requesting that

32. Will Hays to Theodore Roosevelt, 4 March 1918, Box 378, Series 1, Roosevelt Papers.

33. William Kent to Gifford Pinchot, 26 February 1918, Box 210, Pinchot Papers.

34. Lenroot, "Memoirs," pp. 136–37, Box 13, Lenroot Papers. For another uncomplimentary view of Davies see William S. Culbertson, Diary, 3 June 1916, 23 April 1917, Box 3, William S. Culbertson Papers.

35. Robert La Follette to Charles Crownhart, 4 January 1918, Box 112, Series B, La Follette FC; Livermore, *Politics Is Adjourned,* pp. 115–17. Livermore notes that of ten senators who died during the war, eight were Democrats, thus making Democratic control precarious.

he withdraw. Disgruntled but hopelessly isolated, McGovern complied.[36]

The names of those who supported Lenroot before and during the conference, and enlisted in his organization afterwards, constitute a virtual "who's who" of prewar Wisconsin politics. Old-time progressives were the most numerous in his ranks, but stalwart leaders were largely for him. Stephenson and Davidson men adhered to his cause, as did many more newly prominent politicians, who were unassociated with old wars.

From the beginning, Lenroot frankly welcomed the support of the stalwarts. There would be time enough after the war to settle the issues of the Republican party, he said—at the present, the only issue was loyalty.[37] He envisioned no permanent realignment, only a temporary expedient. Probably most of his supporters agreed, but it is reasonable to suppose that some among the stalwarts saw lasting rewards in the new alliance against La Follette.

On 6 March, the day after Lenroot's arrival in Madison, the legislature, after two weeks of politicking and sometimes angry debate, adopted the Wilcox resolution that condemned La Follette for impeding the war effort and bringing the state into disrepute. Expressing the common view among Lenroot's supporters, the *Milwaukee Sentinel* warned Lenroot that he would have to speak clearly and strongly on La Follette. "There can be no half way house, no mere dainty deprecation, no semi-neutrality on that issue." [38] Lenroot withheld comment until the start of his campaign.

A terrible snowstorm greeted the six hundred people that gathered at the university gymnasium for Lenroot's opening address. But it was a distinguished and enthusiastic group, including among the platform dignitaries such as professors Commons and Ely, Justice A. J. Vinje, and others. They waited to hear what Lenroot would say about his old friend and political partner. But before getting to that, Lenroot stated the central theme of his campaign. Since he voted for the declaration of war, he said, his only motive had been to help win it. Only that could have induced him to yield his House seat. He began his speech by saying:

> The ballots that fall one week from next Tuesday will not fall silently like the snowflake but they will be heard around the world. . . . Whether they shall en-

---

36. *Milwaukee Sentinel,* 3, 4, 5 March 1918; Will Hays to Roosevelt, 4 March 1918, (two wires), Longworth to Roosevelt, 4 March 1918, Lodge to Roosevelt, 5 March 1918, Box 378, Series 1, Roosevelt to Lenroot, 28 February 1918, vol. 153, Series 3, Hays to Roosevelt, 6 March 1918, Hays to Roosevelt, 7 March 1918, (two wires), Box 378, Series 1, Roosevelt to Hays, 8 March 1918, to McGovern, 8 March 1918, vol. 155, Series 3, McGovern to Roosevelt, 6 March 1918, Box 378, Series 1, Hays to Roosevelt, 9 March 1918, Box 379, Series 1, Roosevelt to Nick Longworth, 16 March 1918, vol. 156, Series 3, McGovern to Roosevelt, 11 March 1918, Box 379, Series 1, Roosevelt Papers; *Milwaukee Sentinel,* 12 March 1918; *New York Times,* 12 March 1918.

37. *Superior Telegram,* 11 March 1918.

38. Belle and Fola La Follette, *La Follette,* vol. 2, pp. 858–65; Margulies, *The Decline of the Progressive Movement,* pp. 211–13; *Milwaukee Sentinel,* 8 March 1918.

courage our enemies abroad and at home or whether they shall cheer the patriotic hearts of this country, our soldier boys in camp, crossing the sea, upon the plains of France; whether they shall serve to prolong or shorten the war is the supreme issue in this campaign. . . . I have but one plank in my platform in this primary campaign and that is LOYALTY.

Elaborating, he talked of the need for "the stamping out of all seditious speech and propaganda." Paraphrasing his November speech in Ashland, as he did throughout, he explained that "the right of free speech does not carry with it the right to give aid and comfort to the enemy." It was not until later into the speech that Lenroot said:

I have been asked whether I condemn Senator La Follette's attitude towards the war. My record in Congress upon the armed neutrality bill, the Declaration of War and the Conscription Act, answers the question, for I could not approve his attitude upon those questions without condemning my own. I do not approve of his attitude and I could not support any man who does approve it.

The applause that greeted these words was the loudest of the night. When it subsided, Lenroot pressed the attack. He knew James Thompson as a man of high character and ability. But his principal support came from two groups, Lenroot said, "those who are pro-German in their sympathies and are against the United States and those who have opposed the war and the administration in carrying on the war." [39]

For the most part, however, Lenroot was defensive and even conciliatory. Discussing the meaning and requirements of loyalty, he laid stress on points that Thompson was already beginning to use—the need for efficiency and economy and to prevent fraud and graft in war contracts; the need to tax excess profits and large incomes before increasing taxes on the masses; price control on products controlled by monopoly; protections for laborers, especially women and children. But he denied that an unjust burden had yet fallen on the poor. He went over the old ground about how Germany had caused the war and by her actions required Americans to fight on land as well as on sea, in their own interest. He distinguished between the German people and their government; he said that the vast majority of German-Americans was loyal. Taking cognizance of attacks on him by Democratic newspapers, which he accused of helping Thompson in order to benefit their candidate in the general election, Lenroot effectively defended in detail his prewar record on the McLemore resolution, the 1916 army bill, and the embargo question.

On the surface, Lenroot's primary prospects were bright following his opening speech and were increasing daily. The *Milwaukee Sentinel* featured his statement on La Follette and expressed satisfaction with it, as did other

39. Clara Lenroot to Nellie Nichols, 12 March 1918, Lenroot Papers Addition; Belle and Fola La Follette, *La Follette*, vol. 2, pp. 865–66; pamphlet, "Loyalty—Address delivered at the University of Wisconsin Gymnasium . . . Friday, March 8, 1918. By Irvine Luther Lenroot," Box 5, Lenroot Papers; *Milwaukee Sentinel*, 9 March 1918.

loyalty advocates, who accepted the argument made for him and later by him that since if elected he would sit in judgment on La Follette, he could not be expected to declare in advance for his expulsion.[40] When such pro-Wilson, out-of-state papers as the *New York Times* and the *New York World* endorsed him, they reinforced the argument that the nation was watching Wisconsin.[41] And Philipp, whose evenhanded administration and earlier opposition to prohibition and woman suffrage made him popular with beleaguered German-Americans, issued a strong statement for Lenroot and introduced him at Sheboygan, Wisconsin.[42]

The candidacy of Victor Berger on the socialist ticket figured to benefit Lenroot by diverting antiwar votes from Thompson. Although Berger was unopposed in his party's primary, he maintained his traditional insistence that socialists should build their own party and vote in its primaries. The effect of McCarthy's candidacy against Davies was more problematical. Afterwards, McCarthy boasted of having helped Lenroot, by drawing labor votes from Thompson and keeping pro-Davies Democrats in their own primary. But Lenroot did not see McCarthy's candidacy as helpful, and it is arguable that both McCarthy and Davies drew votes from Lenroot.[43]

Lenroot gained a surprising advantage from the character of James Thompson's campaign. The La Crosse man contented himself with but two speeches. Sent by La Follette to help with the campaign, John Hannan found Thompson remarkably ill informed on the national issues and agreed with Thompson that he should not take the stump.[44]

Still, Thompson and Hannan were optimistic. Although Hannan judged the La Follette organization in dire need of reconstruction, he reported to the senator on 10 March that "there seems to be the greatest ground swell on for Thompson that we have ever experienced for any candidate other than yourself." Indeed, apart from the war issue itself, many German-Americans were deeply resentful not only over repression by superpatriots but also of the suspicion in which they were held, and of attacks on their press, and the teaching and use of their language. Augmenting others who were cool toward the war or distressed at its conduct on the home front, they offered a potentially great number of votes.[45] Lending his name to the

40. *Milwaukee Sentinel*, 5, 9, 11, 13 March 1918.

41. Ibid., 9, 15, 16, 17 March 1918; *Superior Telegram*, 12, 16 March 1918.

42. *Milwaukee Sentinel*, 15, 17 March 1918; James A. Stone to A. W. Sanborn, 16 March 1918, Box 22, James A. Stone Papers; Clifford L. Nelson, *German-American Political Behavior in Nebraska and Wisconsin, 1916–1920*, pp. 13, 46.

43. McCarthy to Gifford Pinchot, 22 March 1918, Pinchot Papers, cited in James Oliver Robertson, "The Progressives in National Republican Politics, 1916–1921," (Ph.D. diss.), p. 97; Clara Lenroot to Nellie Nichols, 12 March 1918, Lenroot Papers Addition.

44. Belle and Fola La Follette, *La Follette*, vol. 2, p. 867; John Hannan to Robert La Follette, 10 March 1918, wire (17 March 1918), Box 83, Series B, La Follette FC.

45. John Hannan to Robert La Follette, 9, 10, 11 March 1918, to Gilbert Roe, 13, 14, 18 March 1918, Fred Holmes to La Follette, 11 March 1918, Box 83, Series B, La Follette FC; Nelson, *German-American Political Behavior*, pp. 27–30, 33; Belle and Fola La Follette, *La Follette*, vol. 2, p. 867; Stone to Julius T. Dithmar, 14 March 1918, to Frank Moss, 16 March 1918, Box 22, Stone Papers.

cause of the discontented, La Follette came out strongly for Thompson in a form letter and a public statement.[46]

Four days before the primary, Hannan passed on some unexpected good news. "Old stalwarts are to vote for Davies in primary," he wired Gilbert Roe in Washington. "Word going out everywhere." [47] Perhaps related to that, the leaders of the Loyalty Legion declined to endorse anyone until the primary was over. Democrats were prominent in the organization, and the national administration had favored it by channeling Committee on Public Information material through it.[48]

Worried from the start, Lenroot undertook an intensive campaign, giving speeches. He concentrated on populous labor and heavily German areas in south-central Wisconsin, the lakeshore, and the Fox River valley.[49] Hampered by a heavy cold, Lenroot ignored a doctor's advice that he should stop for at least a day, though bad weather limited the size of his crowds.[50]

Lenroot drew heavily on the Ashland and Madison speeches, but by elaborating on some points and meeting opposition arguments as they came, he managed to vary his speeches. His attitude toward La Follette remained a subject of interest to friend and foe alike, and though he never elaborated on the subject, he met the demand to an extent. At Beloit he said that for years he had been La Follette's personal and political friend, but when the existence of the Republic was at stake, duty outweighed personal considerations. Hannan, through Thompson, contended that the armed ship bill had been filibustered by the administration, not La Follette, and that suspicion of La Follette and Wisconsin was the result of false press reports. Lenroot denied both contentions in his Waukesha speech—suspicion was based on La Follette's votes and speeches in Congress—and although administration men occupied the last two hours of debate on the armed ship bill to prevent La Follette from using the time, had La Follette and his friends been willing, a vote could have been taken. Pressed by Thompson regarding expulsion, Lenroot said that on the basis of the facts within his knowledge about La Follette's votes and speeches in Congress, though he disagreed, he could not vote to expel. But the charges, he pointed out, related to the St. Paul speech, and on that he had no facts and would refuse to make a judgment. Thompson had referred to Lenroot's long association with La Follette and what La Follette had done for him, and Lenroot agreed that their relations had been close for years. "Whether Senator La Follette has done more for me than I have done for him, I do not care to discuss at this time," Lenroot said. He regretted that he could

46. Belle and Fola La Follette, *La Follette*, vol. 2, pp. 866–68.

47. Hannan to Roe, 15, March 1918, Box 83, Series B, La Follette FC.

48. Cary, "Loyalty Legion," pp. 40, 43; Livermore, *Politics Is Adjourned*, pp. 43–44.

49. Clara Lenroot to Nellie Nichols, 12 March 1918, Lenroot Papers Addition; John Hannan to Robert La Follette, 10 March 1918, Box 83, Series B, La Follette FC.

50. *Milwaukee Sentinel*, 10, 11, 14, 19 March 1918; *Superior Telegram*, 12, 18, 19 March 1918; John Hannan to Robert La Follette, 10 March 1918, Box 83 Series B, La Follette FC.

not support him any longer and knew "our former relations can never be resumed," but "Mr. Thompson has a strange idea of public duty if he thinks that former personal or political relations should deter me from performing what I believe to be my duty." The following night at Racine, Lenroot answered parts of La Follette's argument for Thompson. He denied that the president could continue the war as long as he wanted to, or that he had been given unconstitutional powers. At Eau Claire, on the eve of the primary election, he again spoke of his separation with La Follette. He had not changed, Lenroot said, it was La Follette who had. And he charged deliberate deception by La Follette and Thompson in saying the burden of the war had fallen on the poor while profiteers reaped great fortunes.[51]

Early returns on primary election night caused men in Thompson headquarters to wire La Follette that they had won. By morning the tide had turned, and that evening Lenroot was able to wire Clara that he had won by approximately 5,000 or 10,000 votes. Official returns, which were published on 27 March, showed Lenroot the winner by a vote of 73,186 to 70,722. With a light vote but a substantial margin, Davies defeated McCarthy, while Victor Berger, uncontested, polled 38,564 votes. The La Follette family was disappointed at the news of Thompson's defeat, but Phil La Follette, the only member on the scene in Madison, took heart at the closeness of the contest. Hannan and other La Follette men looked ahead optimistically.[52]

The votes confirmed what was already evident before—there was a new pattern in the Republican politics of Wisconsin. Lenroot ran strongly in old progressive areas and gained new strength in areas heavily concentrated by stalwarts. But Thompson, bearing La Follette's banner, while holding some of the old La Follette vote, benefited mainly by breaking into entirely new territory, areas that had been largely Democratic before and that were mostly German.[53] It would not be accurate to say that Lenroot had switched sides; instead, the players had chosen new teams. Lenroot now found himself with some old teammates and some who had been on the other side. The same was true of his opponents now. How long the new pattern would last and what effect it would have remained to be seen. But Lenroot had no time to contemplate that, for more immediate problems pressed on him.

At the bottom of the *Chicago Tribune's* election story of 20 March, Lenroot read a dismaying statement made by Davies. "Today the political situation

51. *Milwaukee Sentinel*, 11, 13, 14, 19 March 1918.

52. Rogers to La Follette, 19 March (1918), Box 83, Doug Anderson to La Follette, 19 March 1918, Box 112, Series B, La Follette FC; *Milwaukee Sentinel*, 21 March 1918; *Superior Telegram*, 20 March 1918; Irvine to Clara Lenroot, 20 March 1918, Box 5, Lenroot Papers; Clara Lenroot, Diary, 21 March 1918, Lenroot Papers Addition: *Wisconsin Blue Book*, 1919, p. 45; Belle to Phil La Follette, 20 March 1918, Box 22, Phil to "Dear Ones," 21, 26 March 1918, Box 23, Series A, Hannan to James Thompson, 20 April 1918, Box 83, Series B, La Follette FC.

53. Michael Paul Rogin, *The Intellectuals and McCarthy: The Radical Specter*, pp. 73–74; Margulies, *The Decline of the Progressive Movement*, pp. 222–24; Nelson, *German-American Political Behavior*, pp. 37, 39.

in Wisconsin is exactly what it has been for many months past," Davies said.
Wisconsin's reputation for loyalty still hangs in the balance. The nation
doubted "Wisconsin not because of the acts of any one of her public men.
It is a doubt that can be removed by a clear, unequivocal expression of the
loyal sentiment of Wisconsin registered at the polls. It can be removed by
nothing else." Davies elaborated on this subject for three more paragraphs.
Instead of praise for his part in vindicating Wisconsin and advancing the
war effort, Lenroot's reward for victory in the primaries was to be the
onerous duty of defending his own patriotism in the general election.

Democrats in Milwaukee followed up on the Davies statement by launch-
ing rumors that Lenroot would withdraw in Davies's favor. Lenroot denounced the statement and denied withdrawal reports; Republican leaders
in Milwaukee and Washington supported him strongly.[54] But that same
afternoon, the *Milwaukee Journal* carried a sensational letter from President
Wilson to Davies. Wilson's key paragraph was a not-so-subtle attack on
Lenroot. He wrote: "The McLemore Resolution, the embargo issue and the
armed neutrality measure presented the first opportunities to apply the acid
test to our country to disclose true loyalty and genuine Americanism. It
should always be a source of satisfaction to you that on these crucial proposi-
tions you proved true." [55]

Despite encouragement from state and national leaders, Lenroot took a
dim view of the situation. He wrote Clara that he had a terrible fight on,
with little chance of winning, but that the Democrats had made it practically
impossible for him to withdraw.[56]

After a few days of conferences in Milwaukee, Lenroot felt more sanguine.
What he and other Republicans perceived was that the Wilson appeal could
serve as the vehicle needed to unite Republicans behind him. Not only
would it help him with strong loyalty Republicans, but equally or more
important, with Thompson men. Sanborn found Thompson voters coming
over to Lenroot in droves and explained that: "They blame the President
for not keeping them out of war, as he promised when elected. They also
blame him for being, as they claim, unneutral and not treating the Germans
fairly." Since Lenroot was so strongly attacked by the administration, they
were drawn to him. "They do not want to vote for Berger, because they do
not believe in his doctrines at all." [57]

Not surprisingly, efforts to get Lenroot or Davies to withdraw so loyalty
men would have a single candidate against Berger failed.[58] Lenroot felt no

54. *Milwaukee Sentinel*, 21 March 1918; *Superior Telegram*, 21 March 1918.

55. *Milwaukee Journal*, 20 March 1918.

56. Clara Lenroot, Diary, 23 March 1918, Lenroot Papers Addition.

57. Ibid., 25 March 1918; Will H. Hays, *The Memoirs of Will H. Hays,* p. 160; Lenroot to Henry
Cabot Lodge, 23, 26 March 1918, Henry Cabot Lodge Papers; A. W. Sanborn to Stone, 25
March 1918, Box 22, Stone Papers.

58. James Stone to Richard Lloyd Jones, 21 March 1918, to Sanborn, 21 March 1918, Box
22, Stone Papers; Maxwell, *Philipp*, p. 163; *Milwaukee Sentinel*, 23 March 1918; Sanborn to Stone,
25 March 1918, Box 22, Stone Papers; *New York Times*, 23, 26 March 1918; typewritten statement, no title, n.d., Box 5, Lenroot Papers; Cary, "Loyalty Legion," pp. 43–44.

qualms of conscience, for the prospect that he could win much of the Thompson vote reduced the danger of a Berger victory.

Persuaded by Postmaster General Burleson that he should throw the full weight of his administration behind Davies, a few days before writing his "acid test" letter, the president asked Vice-President Thomas R. Marshall to go to Wisconsin to speak for Davies. On 26 March, before an audience of four or five thousand at the university's livestock pavilion in Madison, Marshall said in part:

> Your state of Wisconsin is under suspicion. You Republicans have made the issue here in Wisconsin. If the vote at the primary is based upon the charges and counter charges you have made each against the other, you are about half for America, half for the kaiser and all against Wilson. Your self appointed leaders are now trying to convince the loyal half that the really important thing is not loyalty or disloyalty, but party success. Having purified the stream in the primary you welcome the sewage to help you over the election.

Lenroot, he said, "is now bidding for the vote of the German sympathizer, the traitor, the seditionist, the pacifist." Wisconsin was on trial before America and the Republicans of Wisconsin were on trial before the world.[59]

Wilson's letter and Marshall's intemperate speech, which set the theme and tone for the brief but furious Democratic campaign, reflected monumental errors of political judgment. Realizing it, Lenroot's first concern was not to negate the advantage by overreacting. Hays had asked Roosevelt to be ready to send a telegram in Lenroot's favor, but Lenroot advised Hays not to get it. There was no just comparison, he later assured Roosevelt, but he feared losing the advantage secured by Wilson's "butting in." How to handle the Wilson issue was a great problem, he explained to the president's enemy. "If I had gone after him in the way that he really deserved it would have been disastrous, for my motives would have been misconstrued." [60]

Instead, Lenroot defended his own record and criticized Wilson's intervention and Marshall's accusations, but he did not join the attack on the administration's conduct of the war that some of his allies put on in the Senate that week.[61]

His eye fixed on the Thompson voters, Lenroot criticized Davies and the Federal Trade Commission for accomplishing nothing against monopoly. He called Marshall's remarks a slander on Wisconsin and the Republican party. And he set out to disprove Berger's charge that it was a capitalist war.[62]

The president's intervention angered and perhaps scared Republican congressmen and they, under direction of a subcommittee composed of Frank Woods, who was head of the Republican Congressional Campaign

59. Livermore, *Politics Is Adjourned*, pp. 117–18; *Milwaukee Sentinel*, 27 March 1918.

60. Roosevelt to Lenroot, 5 April 1918, Lenroot to Roosevelt, 13 April 1918, Box 4, Lenroot Papers.

61. On that attack see Livermore, *Politics Is Adjourned*, pp. 118–19.

62. *Milwaukee Sentinel*, 26, 28 March 1918.

Committee, John Esch, and Simeon Fess, offered to speak on Lenroot's behalf. The subcommittee, meanwhile, cooperating with senators and with Hays, also generated literature and raised funds. Eventually, $7,500 was raised in Washington, the legal limit for the primary and general election.[63]

The senators Lenroot wanted to speak for him—pro-war progressives William Borah, William Kenyon, and Hiram Johnson—failed to come, but most of the representatives Lenroot asked for took the stump. His list was weighted toward progressives, men not vulnerable on the loyalty issue, men who knew Lenroot's record, and men from neighboring states. The only Wisconsin man Lenroot asked for was David Classon, who, besides him, had voted for the war on the delegation. Classon came, along with three Minnesota men, including Sydney Anderson, Good and Woods of Iowa, and five others. Most valuable, perhaps, were trade unionist John Cooper of Ohio, who talked of Lenroot's labor record, and the German-born Kahn, who told of Lenroot's support of the war. In addition, thirty-four Republican senators, including Borah, Johnson, and Norris, signed a letter of endorsement. Nationally circulated magazines pictured and commended him. And Kent, whom the *Milwaukee Sentinel* identified as a Wilson appointee to the Tariff Commission, sent a long and glowing tribute, starting with the statement: "Irvine Lenroot is in my opinion the strongest, cleanest man in either house of congress." [64] Philipp headed the local speakers, while the *Milwaukee Sentinel* continued to give Lenroot his strongest newspaper support.

From the first, Lenroot's campaigners and newspapers set out to unify the Republicans. But during the last days of the campaign and encouraged by Hays, they became less defensive and played down the loyalty issue, while pressing the attack on Wilson's intervention and Marshall's attack, especially his reference to the Thompson voters as "sewage." Lenroot's managers had Marshall's speech translated into German, Swedish, Norwegian, and Polish and mailed through the state, and they quoted Marshall in their ads and editorials.[65]

Following Thompson's defeat in the primary, the La Follette leaders in Madison briefly considered an independent candidacy, but they dismissed the idea as impracticable. Whether because they did not like Berger's radical antiwar platform or did not want to be identified with him, or thought he had no chance, they gave no consideration to supporting him. As between

63. John Esch to Carl Rabenstein, 4 April 1918, to Frank Winter, 9 April 1918, to George W. Andrews, 9 April 1918, to Winter, 25 March 1918, Box 45, to Winter, 30 August 1918, Box 46, John J. Esch Papers; Will Hays to Lenroot, 24 August 1918, Box 5, Lenroot Papers.

64. John Esch to Frank Winter, 25 March 1918, Box 45, Esch Papers; *Milwaukee Sentinel*, 27, 28 March 1918; *The Independent* 93 (2 March 1918):340; *Review of Reviews* 57 (April 1918):358; *The Outlook* 118 (3 April 1918):541. Kent's endorsement was published in the *Milwaukee Sentinel* on 27 March.

65. *New York Times*, 28, 29 March 1918; *Milwaukee Sentinel*, 27–31 March, 1, 2 April 1918; Hays, *The Memoirs*, p. 161; *Superior Telegram*, 30 March 1918; Livermore, *Politics Is Adjourned*, p. 119.

Lenroot and Davies, they preferred the former. Thompson and the recently launched *Capital Times* endorsed Lenroot. La Follette would not go that far, but in an editorial in his magazine he condemned Berger's platform as one that could not be "defended before the American people." [66]

Lenroot won, but by less than many had expected. He polled 163,983 votes to 148,923 for Davies and a surprising tally of 110,487 for Berger. The socialists carried Milwaukee and other heavily German counties that formerly voted Democratic in the main. They reelected the mayor of Milwaukee. Davies made inroads in progressive Republican country in the west and north.[67]

The results attracted widespread national attention. Editorialists deplored the large Berger vote but agreed that the outcome was a victory for loyalty. Republican papers went further. The *New York Sun* hailed Lenroot's victory as lessening the danger that everyone in Congress "would become a mere puppet of the Chief Executive." [68] Lenroot was, incidentally, the first American of recent Swedish ancestry elected to the Senate.[69]

On 17 April, Lenroot resigned his House seat and the next day, as the Senate began its business, Sen. Knute Nelson of Minnesota announced that Senator-elect Lenroot was present and ready to take the oath of office. Senator La Follette had been expected to introduce and accompany the new junior senator. Perhaps it was the continuing illness of Bobby La Follette that spared him and Lenroot mutual embarrassment. Yet the occasion was not devoid of embarrassment. Escorted to the front by Nelson, Lenroot found himself face to face with Vice-President Marshall. But after the amiable Indiana politician administered the oath, he smiled and shook Lenroot's hand warmly, to the amusement of Republican senators. Later in the afternoon, Marshall summoned Lenroot from his desk at the extreme left of the last row on the Republican side to apologize for what he had said in Wisconsin and to explain that the speech came from "higher up." [70]

Lenroot was well received by his party's leadership in the Senate. He was not appointed to the lands committe, as he had hoped to be, but he was assigned to the more important commerce committee, which would deal with shipping, rivers and harbors, and waterpower legislation, among other

---

66. (Gilbert Roe?) to La Follette, 22 March 1918, Box 83, Series B, La Follette FC. Some code was used in the letter. In this as in other letters, Lenroot is referred to as "Black." *Milwaukee Sentinel*, 21 March 1918; *New York Times*, 27, 29 March 1918; Belle and Fola La Follette, *La Follette*, vol. 2, p. 869.

67. *Wisconsin Blue Book*, 1919, p. 46.

68. *Milwaukee Sentinel*, 4 April 1918; *Los Angeles Times*, 4 April 1918; *New York Sun*, 4 April 1918. At least six out-of-state papers sent reporters to cover the campaign. The rest relied on the news services. *Milwaukee Sentinel*, 27 March 1918.

69. Adolph B. Benson and Naboth Hedin, *Americans from Sweden* (Philadelphia and New York, 1950), p. 268.

70. *CR* 65:2, 1918, vol. 57, pt. 1, p. 5236; *Milwaukee Sentinel*, 19 April 1918; Lenroot, "Memoirs," pp. 138–39, Box 13, Lenroot Papers.

things. Freshmen senators rarely received such an assignment. It was understood, moreover, that in the next Congress he would be placed on the lands committee without vacating his commerce post.[71] Lenroot was named also to the Committee on Public Buildings and Grounds, which was especially important in the war and immediate postwar period, and to four lesser committees. The fact of these favorable assignments was gratifying in itself and signified that he might hope to exert influence in party counsels and in the Senate. Jacob Gallinger, the minority leader, had interested himself in Lenroot's election, but it was probably Lodge who was chiefly instrumental in giving Lenroot speedy recognition. Lodge, who on 24 August succeeded to the leadership after Gallinger's death, had personal and political reasons to look with favor on Lenroot and hope to work cooperatively with him on legislative and political matters.

Lodge had been deeply devoted to his late son-in-law, "Gussie" Gardner.[72] He remembered what Gardner said of Lenroot—that he was the ablest man who had come into the House during his time. After Gardner's death, Longworth, trusted and respected by Lodge, endorsed Lenroot to him. The senator had conceived an admiration for Lenroot on the basis of his war stands, even before it became politically and personally advantageous to praise Lenroot and try to get him elected to the Senate.[73]

Though hardly a progressive, Lodge was not the reactionary, as some people thought of him. When Roosevelt recommended his nomination for president to the Progressive party convention in 1916, the proposal was greeted with outrage. But though the two men differed in temperament and style, Lodge was closer to Roosevelt on domestic questions than many believed. To ward off the socialism that both men deplored and feared, Lodge was reluctantly willing to extend federal controls over business; a patrician, with certain sectional and political interests to serve, Lodge sponsored child labor legislation and frequently took the conservationist side in matters relating to public lands and navigable streams in the West and South. Like Roosevelt, too, this scholar in politics was practical and partisan. With critical elections upcoming and the 1920 presidential election in view, when Roosevelt might again take the lead and reunite the party, Lodge was more than ready to make concessions to progressives. Indeed, when it later seemed that one vote might determine which party would organize the next Senate, he even extended the olive branch to the hated La Follette.[74]

71. *Milwaukee Sentinel*, 19 April 1918

72. John A. Garraty, *Henry Cabot Lodge: A Biography*, p. 195; Lodge to William A. Chanler, 7 February 1918, 21 March 1922, to Winthrop Chanler, 28 January 1918, to Robert M. Washburn, 5 March 1920, Lodge Papers.

73. Lodge to Lenroot, 8 September 1920, to Theodore Roosevelt, 5 March 1918, 22 February 1917, Lodge Papers.

74. Lodge to Louis A. Coolidge, 29 June 1921, Lodge Papers; *CR* 65:3, 1918, vol. 57, pt. 1, p. 611; Garraty, *Henry Cabot Lodge*, pp. 225–30, 284–87, 292–93, 324; Robertson, "Progressives in National Republican Politics," p. 108; Belle and Fola La Follette, *La Follette*, vol. 2, pp. 912, 929, 932, 941.

For a time, Lenroot busied himself with routine matters, such as economy measures, but he looked for broader opportunity.[75] The Supreme Court offered a suitable outlet for his energies when, on 3 June, by a five to four vote, in the case of *Hammer* v. *Dagenhart,* it invalidated the Keating-Owen Child Labor Act. The narrowness of the margin, the strong dissenting opinion of Oliver Wendell Holmes, Jr., and the nature of the cause prompted an immediate public clamor for new legislation on the subject. Revelations of new abuses after the decision helped sustain the pitch of public demand.[76] Lenroot took up the cause.

Although Lenroot thought the Court's reasoning was distorted in its refusal to accept the commerce power as basis for child labor legislation, he saw no point in challenging the Court by trying to reenact the law on much the same basis.[77] The constitutional amendment route was open and seemed to be the last resort, but passage and ratification would take a long time. Lenroot decided that there was a more direct and promising approach —use of the tax power. He knew of precedents for successful use of that power as a prohibitory weapon and he was confident these applied. Most notably, in the 1904 case of *McCray* v. *United States,* the Court declined to inquire into the motives of Congress and sustained a prohibitive tax on colored oleomargarine. Subsequent to that decision, Congress used the tax power against dangerous phosphorus matches and against narcotics.[78]

On 11 July, Lenroot introduced his bill. By then Kenyon of Iowa, a progressive Republican, had offered a bill relying on Congress's power over the mails. At the same time, Atlee Pomerene, a progressive Democrat from Ohio, had introduced two bills, one based on the commerce power, the other on the tax power. Recognizing the need for coordinated action, the three senators held a series of meetings in the fall and agreed on a thorough-going measure relying on the tax power, to be introduced as an amendment to the revenue bill, in order to get speedy action. To fortify the amendment's constitutionality, they agreed to put enforcement powers in the Treasury Department rather than with the Children's Bureau in the Department of Labor, though they expected that in practice the Treasury would use the Children's Bureau. To enhance the amendment's political prospects, they agreed that the name of the Democrat, Pomerene, should be attached to it.[79] On 15 November, four days after the armistice, Pomerene

75. Margulies, "Lenroot," pp. 957–60.

76. Stephen B. Wood, *Constitutional Politics in the Progressive Era: Child Labor and the Law,* pp. 178, 203; Walter I. Trattner, *Crusade for the Children: A History of the National Child Labor Committee and Child Labor Reform in America,* p. 138.

77. MS speech, "Child Labor and Federal Taxation," (7 December 1918), Box 10, Lenroot Papers.

78. Ibid.; Alfred H. Kelly and Winfred A. Harbison, *The American Constitution: Its Origins and Development,* pp. 592–98.

79. Irvine L. Lenroot, "Taxing Child Labor Out of Industry," program, Fourteenth National Conference on Child Labor, New York City, 7 December 1918, Box 23, National Child Labor Committee Papers, LC.

introduced the amendment to the revenue bill, which had finally reached the Senate after much delay in the House. More comprehensive than the Keating-Owen Act, it applied to every mine, quarry, mill, cannery, workshop, factory or manufacturing establishment in the nation; included the employment standards of the invalidated act; and placed a 10 percent tax on the net profits of each concern knowingly violating these provisions, over and above all other taxes. (Sixteen was the prescribed minimum age for workers in mines, fourteen for the rest.) [80]

Meanwhile, a coalition of groups spearheaded by the National Child Labor Committee, a group based in New York, and including the A.F.L., the National Consumers League, and the Children's Bureau, was working on its own. The death in April of Alexander McKelway, the Washington lobbyist for the Child Labor Committee, accounted for some floundering and delay. Finally, a distinguished committee drafted a bill based on the tax power but differing, in some respects, from the Pomerene amendment, chiefly in that it gave enforcement powers to the Children's Bureau instead of the Treasury Department. But the senators insisted on their own bill as the safer—constitutionally—and Lenroot and Kenyon assured Owen Lovejoy, executive secretary of the National Child Labor Committee, that their provision would cause no difficulty in practice. Lenroot went to New York to explain the situation in a speech before the organization. The A.F.L.'s legislative representative accepted the Pomerene proposal as the only one likely to pass and advised Lovejoy to do the same. Despite the protests of Grace Abbott of the Children's Bureau, Lovejoy advised in favor of the senators' bill and the executive board acquiesced.[81]

Having long since overcome his own constitutional scruples on such matters, President Wilson gave his support to the Pomerene amendment, leaving Southern opponents isolated, though far from helpless. On 4 December, at the start of the third session of the Sixty-fifth Congress, during the deliberations of the finance committee on the revenue bill, Lodge moved to attach the Pomerene rider. Chairman Furnifold Simmons objected—his state of North Carolina had held out against the Keating–Owen Act and pressed the judicial test that killed it. The committee, nevertheless, adopted Lodge's motion and in effect guaranteed passage of the popular measure in both Houses, so long as the proponents stayed united. When the amendment came up for action in the Senate on 18 December, the outcome was not in doubt, but to make a record for the subsequent use of the Court, senators debated the question rather fully. For the Southern minority, Thomas Hardwick of Georgia took the lead; for the proponents,

80. Wood, *Constitutional Politics,* p. 203; Roy G. and Gladys C. Blakey, "The Revenue Act of 1918," *American Economic Review* 9 (June 1919) :213–43.

81. Minute books, National Child Labor Committee, 7 June 1918–5 March 1919, Box 7, National Child Labor Committee Papers, LC; MS speech, "Child Labor and Federal Taxation," (7 December 1918), Box 10, Lenroot Papers. See also Wood, *Constitutional Politics,* pp. 178–204; and Trattner, *Crusade for the Children,* pp. 138–40.

Lodge and Lenroot were the principal spokesmen. Both sides focused on the issue of constitutionality.[82]

Hardwick and his associates set out to clarify the true purpose of the tax; and Hardwick argued that the tax power could not be used to destroy equally valid constitutional provisions. Prepared for these arguments, Lenroot rehearsed the precedents, including Justice White's admonition for judicial restraint in the McCray case. He contended that under the McCray decision, Congress could destroy by taxation any right that the states could themselves destroy by the exercise of the police power. And of course, the states had the uncontested right to regulate child labor.[83]

Adopted by a fifty to twelve vote that day, the Pomerene amendment was incorporated in the revenue bill when it passed the Senate on 23 December. The amendment was included in the conference committee report, approved overwhelmingly in the House in February, and became law after both Houses approved the report and the president signed the revenue bill. Late in February, Lenroot helped Lodge get money for its enforcement, against the parliamentary objections of Hardwick.[84]

On 15 May 1922, in the case of *Bailey* v. *Drexel* and by an eight to one vote, the Supreme Court ruled the child labor law unconstitutional. Although the new Chief Justice, William Howard Taft, attempted to square the opinion with the McCray precedent, it was a hopeless effort. For the most part, the Court followed the precedent of the Dagenhart case and the argument for the minority in the McCray case. Considering the temper of the judges and of the times, the self-defeating argument offered by Solicitor General James M. Beck, who was an avowed opponent of the law, and other factors, the decision came as no great surprise to many. That Holmes and Brandeis did not join Justice Clarke in dissent remains something of a mystery, although various plausible explanations have been offered.[85] The outcome did not reflect on Lenroot's legal judgment—his precedents and arguments were tenable—and though it was always questionable whether the Court could be brought to go counter to its Dagenhart decision, it was sensible to attempt use of the tax power before turning to the cumbersome constitutional amendment approach.

Midway in the legislative battle over child labor, Lenroot resumed efforts for progressive waterpower legislation. He contributed key wording relating to recapture provisions, which, after acceptance by the president and Gifford Pinchot, won endorsement in the joint conference committee. Unfortunately, Wilson agreed to less popular provisions, perhaps to mollify westerners in his party after the Democrats were defeated in the 1918 elections. Conservationists turned against the measure and it died in the Senate.[86]

82. Wood, *Constitutional Politics*, pp. 205–14; *CR* 65:3, 1918, vol. 57, pt. 1, pp. 610–17.
83. Wood, *Constitutional Politics*, pp. 206–13; *CR* 65:3, 1918, vol. 57, pt. 1, pp. 610–16.
84. Wood, *Constitutional Politics*, pp. 205, 214–16; *CR* 65:3, 1919, vol. 57, pt. 4, pp. 3848–51.
85. Wood, *Constitutional Politics*, pp. 198, 218, 243, 269–84.
86. Margulies, "Lenroot," pp. 964–67.

Lenroot also participated in the national election campaign and was gratified by the result.[87] Despite the president's appeal for a Democratic Congress, the Republicans had won a clear margin in the lower House and a
forty-nine to forty-seven majority in the Senate. News of the election was
followed swiftly by word of an armistice in Europe. Looking to take a larger
role than before in domestic and foreign affairs, the Republicans informally,
almost tacitly, agreed that they would make such little haste in the coming
short session that action would not be completed on some appropriation
bills, thus forcing the president to convene the new Congress in special
session. The president's announcement that he would lead the American
delegation to the peace conference and his subsequent announcement of
the complete delegation, from which he excluded all senators and such
prominent Republican notables as Taft, Root, and Hughes, made it the
more certain that the Republicans would force a special session. Lenroot
had no sympathy with the more extreme responses to Wilson's announce-
ments—proposals to declare Vice-President Marshall to be acting president,
or to send a bipartisan delegation of senators to Paris as "observers," for
he did not want to suggest to the world that his country was divided. But
he did expect the Senate to make known to the president the progress made
during the course of negotiations, and from that standpoint could see the
need for a special session, as he freely asserted. Although his comments on
the floor during the session were always germane, La Follette judged that
some of them represented contributions to the common Republican purpose of delaying appropriations.[88]

Lenroot favored a special session for another reason. He was deeply
concerned over the problems of reconstruction, especially prospective
unemployment.[89] But neither he nor his Republican colleagues were willing
to put reconstruction planning in the hands of a commission appointed by
the president since, in a few months, his own party would assume legislative
responsibility. Instead, he and his colleagues agreed to a plan for six joint
congressional committees, to lay the groundwork for action by the next
Congress.[90]

Apart from Secretary Lane, who had developed a grandiose scheme to
reclaim western land and settle returning veterans on it, the administration
had made no preparation for the transition to peacetime living. Wilson's

87. Lenroot to Walter S. Goodland, 4 October 1918, to George A. West, 25 October 1918,
(printed letter), Box 22, Stone Papers; *Milwaukee Sentinel*, 28, 29 October 1918; *New York Times*,
26 October 1918.

88. Robert M. La Follette to "My Beloved Boy" (Robert, Jr.), 25 November 1918, Box 23,
to "Dear Ones," 3 February 1919, Box 26, Series A, La Follette FC; Frederic L. Paxson,
American Democracy and the World War, Postwar Years: Normalcy, 1918–1923, pp. 9, 12; *Milwaukee
Sentinel*, 2, 3 December 1918; *CR* 65:3, 1919, vol. 57, pt. 5, pp. 4900–4901; La Follette to "My
Loved Ones," 17 February 1919, Box 26, Series A, La Follette FC.

89. Lenroot to James A. Stone, 11 November 1918, Box 22, Stone Papers; to W. D. Conner,
16 November 1918, Box 5, Lenroot Papers.

90. *Milwaukee Sentinel*, 19 November, 3 December 1918.

departure, followed quickly by the resignation of Secretary McAdoo, entailed further delay in the executive branch and among congressional Democrats, who had become habituated to strong executive leadership.[91]

Lenroot favored Lane's scheme and encouraged the Secretary to broaden it so as to utilize cutover lands in northern Michigan, Minnesota, and Wisconsin.[92] Beyond that, however, he was eager for the Republicans to develop a reconstruction program. When resolutions calling for joint reconstruction committees were pigeonholed, early in December Lenroot urged Hays to recruit voluntary planning committees. Hays and others agreed, yet by mid-December no progress had been made, and Lenroot feared that after 4 March his party might have responsibility but be without a program and that the president, resisting a special session, might cause further delay.[93] Events confirmed his fears. Perhaps others convinced Hays that it was no time to arouse dissension in the party with specific proposals. Lenroot put forth a tentative scheme for the railroad system, which he planned to elaborate in detail in the next Congress. It represented an alternative to McAdoo's proposal for a five-year extension of federal control.[94]

On 6 January, while at the Capitol, Lenroot was shocked to learn of the death of Roosevelt. Undoubtedly, Lenroot shared the common view that had he lived, Roosevelt would have been the Republican presidential nominee in 1920. He called his death "a calamity" and explained to an interviewer that, useful as he had been, "his greatest usefulness might have been in the future. No one can now foresee what America must go through in the period of readjustment, and Col. Roosevelt's sterling Americanism, courage, and practical judgment upon domestic questions especially would have been of the greatest value in placing the nation upon the path of true progress in the future." [95]

Viewed from Lenroot's perspective, Roosevelt's death was indeed an unmitigated disaster. Roosevelt was a man who was able to rally the best in people, to bring them to unite their selfish interests and jealousies into a cooperative national interest, and interest that he was able to perceive and explain. As president, he had used the Republican party as a vehicle for

91. Lenroot to Rouget D. Marshall, 16 December 1918, Box 5, Lenroot Papers; Paul A. Samuelson and Everett E. Hagen, *After the War—1918–1920*, p. 6; David Burner, *The Politics of Provincialism: The Democratic Party in Transition, 1918–1932*, p. 50; George Soule, *Prosperity Decade: From War to Depression, 1917–1929*, pp. 81–83; John M. Blum, *Joe Tumulty and the Wilson Era*, p. 89.

92. Lenroot to Stone, 11 November 1918, Lane to Lenroot, 16 November 1918, enclosed in Lenroot to Stone, 19 November 1918, Box 22, Stone Papers.

93. Lenroot to Marshall, 16 December 1918, Box 5, Lenroot Papers.

94. *Superior Telegram*, 14 January 1919.

95. Clara Lenroot, Diary, 6, 7 January 1919, Lenroot Papers Addition; *Chicago Tribune*, 7 January 1919. Robert La Follette noted the common view that Roosevelt, had he lived, would have been the Republican nominee in 1920. La Follette to "My Dear Ones," 6 January 1919, Box 26, Series A, La Follette FC. Lodge later wrote that the nomination would have been beyond doubt. Lodge to Lord Charnwood, 17 November 1923, Lodge Papers.

progressive policies, and progressive Republicans had hoped that he would do the same again. Without him, the progressives would find it hard to unite among themselves, let alone exert a decisive influence within the party.

Meanwhile, Lenroot's relations with La Follette remained personally cold and politically ominous and threatened to get worse before they got better. With the war over and La Follette's vote essential to the Republicans if they were to organize the new Senate, Old Guardsmen made friendly overtures to him and the Committee on Privileges and Elections, in late November agreed by a vote of nine to two to dismiss expulsion proceedings. Even Frank Kellogg of Minnesota, who had presented the charges from his state, was persuaded to vote with the majority. On 16 January, the Senate sustained the committee, with a vote of fifty to twenty-one. The Republicans, including Lenroot, voted almost solidly for the report. But Pomerene, who called for the record vote, had offered a minority report arguing that La Follette had violated the Espionage Act in his speech at St. Paul.[96] Fearing that Pomerene was maneuvering to have the matter reconsidered, La Follette took special note when "Pomerene had quite a long confidential confab with the 'foxy Swede'. . . . They confer quite a good deal. P. always coming over to L's desk." No reconsideration occurred, but La Follette nevertheless replied to Belle's question that "Yes (I) do think Pomerene got a good deal of encouragement on the side from 'Foxy' . . . though of course the latter had to vote with the Republicans on the Dillingham motion. There isn't any doubt about the relations between us." He went on:

> We are courteous and "polite" but it ends there. He proposed a good amendment to increase the appropriation for the Legislative Reference Library today while the Legislative Appropriation bill was pending and I chipped in a suggestion in a single sentence in end of his amendment—so you see I am not fool enough to oppose things he proposes when they are all right.[97]

There is no record indicating how accurate La Follette's suspicions of Lenroot were and how Lenroot felt toward his former friend and leader at the time. Just before the Wisconsin senatorial primary in March 1918, Lodge wrote to Roosevelt that Lenroot "dislikes him (La Follette) excessively." [98] But Lodge's acquaintance with Lenroot was at that time slight, and he had a motive for his comments, which were said in order to please Roosevelt and to influence him on McGovern's withdrawal. Following the Senate's dismissal of charges against La Follette, Lenroot explained to an irate Wisconsin editor that the Senate's action was taken on legalistic grounds with which he and Kellogg agreed—it was in no sense an exon-

---

96. Belle and Fola La Follette, *La Follette,* vol. 2, pp. 901–3, 910–12, 915, 917, 928–29; *CR* 65:2, 1918, vol. 56, pt. 2, p. 1527.

97. Robert to Belle La Follette, 22 January, 3 February 1919, Box 26, Series A, La Follette FC. Family letters dated 17, 18, 19, 20, and 21 January all reflect La Follette's concern over a reconsideration effort.

98. Lodge to Roosevelt, 5 March 1918, Box 378, Series 1, Roosevelt Papers.

eration, and few in the Senate approved La Follette's St. Paul speech.[99]

A historian of the period has remarked that the "lame duck" session did not accomplish much, failing even to pass some of the routine appropriations bills.[100] But for Lenroot the picture was less bleak. He was willing to await Republican control, and the appropriation failures hastened that day. As he saw it, governmental economy was a prime need, and something was accomplished in that direction; Congress adopted the child labor law and took a long step toward construction of the St. Lawrence seaway, for which Lenroot had great hopes; some bad bills were blocked; Congress approved a European relief measure, and Republicans made known their view on the League of Nations, in time for the president to secure essential revisions; and progress was made toward democratization of Senate procedures and resolution of internal differences among Senate Republicans. Lenroot took satisfaction at his own role on each of these matters.

With respect to the dispersal of power within the Senate, Lenroot was accorded a prominent part by Lodge, who was notably agreeable to the progressives throughout the session. Charged by the Republican caucus with naming a committee to propose changes in Senate rules, Lodge selected a representative group composed of Reed Smoot, Warren Harding, Philander Knox, Fred Hale, Lenroot, Cummins, and Norris and named Lenroot chairman. With some difficulty, the committee finally reached agreement on a compromise proposal that was readily accepted by the caucus on 8 February. It specified that no senator can be a member of more than two of the ten principal committees and that chairmen of these committees cannot serve as conferees for another committee merely by virtue of seniority but only by majority vote of the committee.[101]

Near the end of the session, in connection with the conference report on the mineral lands leasing bill, Lenroot weighed the need for economic development against the rights of the public at large, as represented by the government. His decision was against the bill. He must have been keenly disappointed, since the bill as voted in the House and on which he had worked so hard was reasonably satisfactory. But, as with the waterpower bill, the president reversed his stand after the 1918 elections, hoping to consolidate his party for the fight on the League of Nations by conciliating the westerners. When Wilson stopped supporting the navy people, he opened the way for a conference agreement that was favorable to claimants, which he then asked Congress to adopt. To Lenroot, the liberalization of relief provisions, coinciding with the end of the war and the wartime need of oil production, was illogical. But he contented himself with a secondary

99. The letter was to the editor of the *Waupaca Post* and was reprinted in the *Superior Telegram,* 11 February 1919.

100. Paxson, *Postwar Years,* p. 45.

101. Robertson, "Progressives in National Republican Politics," pp. 155–56, 190; Lodge to "My Dear Senator," 22 January 1919, Lodge Papers; *Chicago Tribune,* 8 February 1919; *Milwaukee Sentinel,* 8 February 1919; *New York Times,* 9 February 1919.

role in the opposition, perhaps because he was less enthusiastic about the navy's claims than were some others. He did join in delaying tactics, helping in the formation of the case that the conference report contained matter not in either the House or Senate bill and thus must go back to conference. But it was a subsequent filibuster by La Follette that killed the bill.[102]

Lenroot took a more prominent and satisfying part in connection with the St. Lawrence seaway project. The idea was a very old one in the United States and Canada. For more than a century, its prospects would increase and decrease. With the end of the war, possibilities seemed brighter than ever, especially to an experienced and energetic Charles P. Craig of Duluth, a lawyer and real-estate dealer.[103]

Aided by other veterans of this project, Craig was able to point out to Duluth businessmen and to influential leaders of business and government in Minnesota, Wisconsin, Michigan, and other Midwestern states, that Canada would soon finish the deepening of the Welland Canal, which would connect Lake Ontario to Lake Erie. With that completion and with a canal already available at Sault Sainte Marie connecting Lake Michigan and Lake Superior, all that remained to open the American interior to oceangoing vessels was improvement on the one hundred eighty-one miles of the St. Lawrence River, from Montreal to Lake Ontario. Beyond Montreal to the ocean, the river was adequate. With the prospects for success being bright and the benefits to the lakeshore cities being potentially great, Craig successfully organized a start-up meeting of the Great Lakes-St. Lawrence Tidewater Association in the capital in February 1919, coinciding with the meetings of the powerful National Rivers and Harbors Congress. Official representatives of the states of Wisconsin, Michigan, and Minnesota helped start the Tidewater Association, along with the delegates of Illinois, Indiana, Ohio, and Iowa, with the former states each contributing $12,500 toward initial expenses. These men in turn planned to enlist Great Plains and Rocky Mountain states, whose citizens would benefit as exporters and consumers from the sea line to Europe. Within a year, Craig, who became the executive director, had succeeded in doubling the number of states in the organization.[104]

Before that, however, Craig turned his attention to Congress. Although Sen. Charles Townsend of Michigan had been advocating the seaway idea since 1911, it was Lenroot who, as a member of the Committee on Commerce, could do most immediate good.[105] In 1909, the United States and

102. Bates, *Origins of Teapot Dome*, pp. 151–65; Harry Slattery to Gifford Pinchot, 4 February 1919, Box 1842, Pinchot Papers; Robert La Follette to "My Beloved Ones," 22 February 1919, Box 26, Series A, La Follette FC; *CR* 65:3, 1919, vol. 57, pt. 4, pp. 3824–28, 4045–46; Gifford Pinchot, in *Milwaukee Sentinel*, 30 October 1920.

103. Carleton Mabee, *The Seaway Story*, pp. 1–25, 43–62; William R. Willoughby, *The St. Lawrence Waterway: A Study in Politics and Diplomacy*, pp. 1–91.

104. Mabee, *Seaway Story*, pp. 59–63.

105. Ibid., pp. 58–59.

Canada established an International Joint Commission to deal with boundary water problems, including the portion of the St. Lawrence that was in question. In 1914, in response to a Senate resolution, the State Department had referred the seaway question to that commission, but with the advent of war the project lapsed. Now Craig and his associates wanted from Congress an amendment to the rivers and harbors bill, which requested the commission "to investigate what further improvement of the St. Lawrence River between Montreal and Lake Ontario is necessary to make the same navigable for ocean-going vessels, together with the estimated cost thereof, and report to the Government of the Dominion of Canada and to the Congress of the United States, with its recommendations for cooperation by the United States with the Dominion of Canada in the improvement of the said river." [106] Late in January and in advance of the meetings of the Tidewater Association, Lenroot introduced the amendment and secured its speedy adoption in committee, after several discussions with Senator Nelson of Minnesota. He was aware that the chairman of the joint boundary commission was former Congressman James Tawney of Minnesota, who favored the project.[107] Since Michigan, Wisconsin, and Minnesota were the first and most consistent supporters of the seaway idea, it is hardly surprising that in the Senate its chief defenders, in 1919 and afterwards, were Townsend, Lenroot, and Kellogg.[108] The seaway idea appealed strongly to Lenroot. Superior business leaders had begun to see the possibilities of the project in 1916—regarding shipping and ship building—and in that year Lenroot helped secure an amendment to the rivers and harbors bill providing for a preliminary and partial survey by the army engineers. Immediately after the war, men in Superior renewed their interest and effort.[109] Other Wisconsin ports on Lake Superior and Lake Michigan, especially Milwaukee, would benefit directly, while farmers and others would benefit indirectly. Politically, the issue could be very useful to Lenroot and to the new coalition he was heading, especially in the populous Germanic lakeshore cities of Wisconsin, where he and his friend most needed help. Beyond that, though, Lenroot viewed the seaway as a major step toward national progress and frankly urged those who were pessimistic to take the national approach, as midwesterners had done with respect to the Panama Canal, which diverted traffic from their area.[110] The project was, for him, the kind of "progressive" measure that he found increasingly appealing —one that involved the common interest as he conceived it rather than the advantage of one social class at the expense of another.

106. U.S., Senate, Committee on Commerce, *Report*, No. 665, 65th Cong., 3d sess., quoted in Willoughby, *St. Lawrence Waterway*, p. 91.

107. *Superior Telegram*, 20, 25 January 1919.

108. Mabee, *Seaway Story*, p. 63.

109. *Superior Telegram*, 21 November 1918, 8 January, 1, 2, 7, 19, 26 February, 14, 21 May 1919.

110. *Milwaukee Sentinel*, 28 March 1919.

The seaway question was not a partisan one. President Taft supported a seaway and Wilson soon would; succeeding presidents, whether Republican or Democratic, also backed it. But a powerful bipartisan opposition had long since formed, made itself felt on the Lenroot amendment, and continued active afterwards, It came from eastern economic interests, from patriots fearful of Canadian control of the St. Lawrence, and from those who thought the plan extravagant and impractical.[111] When the amendment came up for Senate action in the face of that kind of opposition, Lenroot, in the course of the three-hour debate, set out to allay fears, to divide in order to conquer, to convince the doubtful and unconcerned, and to rally all those whose constituents stood to directly gain by the project.

James Wadsworth of New York, abetted by Lodge and others—all professing no sectional bias—argued cogently against the amendment. Wadsworth called attention to the operating costs that were involved in sending seagoing vessels into the interior, which would make the route unattractive and the waterway a white elephant.[112] Nevertheless, the Lenroot amendment was adopted by a vote of forty-three to eighteen and approved in the House without a record vote. In the Senate, the favorable votes came mainly from Midwestern, Western, and Southern members, while Easterners supplied the bulk of the opposition.[113]

Lenroot quickly followed up on the victory. He talked to a member of the international commission about procedures for implementing the amendment, sent the information to Frank L. Polk of the State Department, and asked Polk to inform him on what action would be taken. Townsend wrote Polk in similar vein. The State Department acted promptly, while Lenroot began to stir up further interest in the seaway in Wisconsin.[114]

Lenroot's committee assignments permitted him to play an influential role on a variety of questions through the session, in hearings and on the floor. The issues involved the government's program on public buildings, its postwar plans, development of military hospitals, and the new rivers and harbors bill. On the floor, Lenroot also debated on closely related topics reported by other committees, notably the provision on grants to be allotted for road construction, which was included in the bill on post office appropriations, and the matter of equitable cancellation of war contracts.

Certain common themes ran through Lenroot's questions and remarks in connection with these subjects. He continued to stress economy. Related

111. Mabee, *Seaway Story*, p. 48.

112. *Superior Telegram*, 19, 26 February 1919; *CR* 65:3, 1919, vol. 57, pt. 4, pp. 3669–70, 3675–76.

113. Willoughby, *St. Lawrence Waterway*, p. 91. James Elwood Smith of St. Louis, a new convert, and a leader in the Rivers and Harbors Congress and in the movement to improve the Mississippi River and its main tributaries, was credited with influencing Southern senators. *Superior Telegram*, 19, 26 February 1919.

114. Lenroot to Frank L. Polk, 17 March 1919, Townsend to Polk, 17 March 1919, Record Group 59, file, 711.42157, Sa 29/3, NA; Willoughby, *St. Lawrence Waterway*, p. 91; *Milwaukee Sentinel*, 28 March 1919; *Superior Telegram*, 21 May 1919.

to that, he sought to end inefficiency and waste. As the government let new contracts or wound up wartime affairs, Lenroot was on guard to protect the public interest against profiteering. And he fought the pork-barrel principle, whether in connection with public buildings or rivers and harbors.

With other progressives, Lenroot would occasionally subordinate economy. Above all, he wanted to prevent mass unemployment and was willing to spend public money to achieve this end. In a speech given in early February, he noted that unemployment was rising daily. Public spending on post roads was an ideal stopgap measure, since a large part of the money would flow directly to workers. With that in mind, he was not only willing to approve an appropriation of $125 million to the states for construction of roads but would also add another $75 million. Successfully opposing an amendment, he insisted that the states should not delay in spending the money. At the same time, he favored striking from the bill an appropriation of $75 million applicable not to the current or next fiscal year, but years beyond.[115]

Unemployment, which as it turned out increased to three million in February and then abated, contributed to the beginnings of a Red Scare. Strikes began soon after the end of the war, as workers sought to retain wartime gains and cope with inflation, while employers resisted unionization and high-cost labor. On 6 February, a general strike broke out in Seattle, a weapon of revolutionary unionism in a place where the organization of the Industrial Workers of the World was strong. Mayor Ole Hanson promptly called the strike the work of Bolsheviks and the I.W.W. and warned that it marked the beginning of a national uprising. Coinciding with the revival of the I.W.W. in the Mountain and Pacific Coast states, the radical press resumed, and a smattering of socialists, communists, and anarchists received widespread publicity. Indeed, the American socialist movement emerged from the war stronger and more radical than before. Opposed to the war, its ideology of international worker solidarity and class struggle, now given substance by connection with the Soviet Union, tainted it as a dangerous enemy to the American people and their institutions, in the minds of many. Although the Third International, or Comintern, did not meet and pledge itself to world revolution until 2 March 1919, the spread of bolshevism into Germany, Hungary, and elsewhere in Europe augmented fears. It was the fear of bolshevism and its like that lent sinister overtones to industrial disturbance and social unrest.[116]

Lenroot viewed seriously the domestic threat of bolshevism. But he did not share the extreme fears of some of the senators and representatives from the west; he regarded the pro-Bolshevik element as he had the pro-

115. *CR* 65:3, 1919, vol. 57, pt. 3, pp. 2802–6, 2878, 2885.

116. Soule, *Prosperity Decade*, pp. 83–88; Robert K. Murray, *Red Scare: A Study in National Hysteria, 1919–1920* (Minneapolis, 1955), pp. 3–68; James Weinstein, *The Decline of Socialism in America, 1912–1925*, pp. 119–81; Arthur S. Link, *American Epoch: A History of the United States Since the 1890's*, pp. 234–39.

Germans of the war period, a small minority dangerous only to the extent that they could play upon the fears and anxieties of others. He was willing to sanction repressive measures against those he considered truly dangerous, but, as during the war, he preferred positive steps.[117]

The matter took concrete form for senators when on 8 February, Borah asked repeal of three sections of the Espionage Act of 1917 and one in the Sedition Act of 1918 that gave the postmaster general power to exclude matter from the mails. Lenroot asked Borah if he was not seeking to repeal too many features of the Espionage Act, notably Section 2 "declaring letters, writings, and so forth, advocating or urging treason, insurrection, or forcible resistance to any law or the United States to be unmailable, and section 3 providing punishment in the courts for violation of that statute." Borah agreed only in part, but later, to enhance prospects of getting half a loaf, he agreed to leave intact the sections to which Lenroot referred. On a motion to suspend the rules to permit consideration of his modified proposal, Lenroot joined Borah in the minority of twenty-five, twenty-three of them Republicans. But thirty-nine senators defeated the motion.[118]

With others, Lenroot was seriously concerned about the spread of bolshevism in Europe. Despite his preoccupation with economy at this time, he strongly defended an appropriation of $1 hundred million for emergency shipments of food to newly liberated people of the Balkans and Poland. He argued, as did the administration, that the aid might help stem the tide of bolshevism, at least giving the people a chance to stop and think. He spoke of ringing Germany with a set of representative governments. The measure cleared the House with ease but was passed in the Senate only after extended debate, with strong opposition coming mainly from Republicans.[119]

The question that concerned Republican senators more than any other was not before them for action during the last session of the Sixty-fifth Congress—President Wilson's plan for a League of Nations as a foundation stone for the peace settlement. Lenroot did not enter the debate on the League until 28 February, in the final week of the session. But then and later, he played an important part in what developed into a long and perhaps tragic battle.

117. Robert La Follette commented on the extreme fears of western senators at this time in La Follette to "My Beloved Ones," 4 February 1919, Box 26, Series A, La Follette FC.

118. *CR* 65:3, 1919, vol. 57, pt. 3, pp. 2936, 2939–41, 2961, 2968–69. The day before, Lenroot had helped Judson King, the conservationist and direct democracy reformer, insert into the record denial of charges that at a meeting over which he had presided there had been communist propaganda. *CR* 65:3, 1919, vol. 57, pt. 3, p. 2876.

119. *CR* 65:3, 1919, vol. 57, pt. 2, pp. 1805, 1859–60; Gary Dean Best, "Food Relief as Price Support: Hoover and American Pork, January-March 1919," pp. 79–84. The Food Administration could only aid the Allies. See also Arno J. Mayer, *Politics and Diplomacy of Peacemaking: Containment and Counterrevolution at Versailles, 1918–1919*, pp. 267–72.

VIII

THE BATTLE OF
THE LEAGUE OF NATIONS

The idea of developing the League of Nations had surfaced prior to American entry into the war, as a result of the formation of the League to Enforce Peace in 1915, a bipartisan group headed by former President William Howard Taft.[1] President Wilson publicly supported the plan in a speech before that organization in May 1916, discussed it in the election campaign that fall, incorporated it in his celebrated peace notes of 18 December 1916, and gave it new endorsement in his "peace without victory" speech of 22 January 1917. The president made clear his hope that the United States would commit itself to act with other nations to preserve peace by the use of force, if need be.[2]

After the declaration of war, without encumbering it with details that might either weaken it or divide its supporters, Wilson was able to dress the League of Nations idea in the garment of patriotism as one of his Fourteen Points.[3] Lenroot was one of many who, in supporting the war, accepted Wilson's statement of war aims. On one occasion, in the course of his primary election campaign against James Thompson, who endorsed the idea of a congress of nations to settle international disputes, he posed this question to his opponent: "Are you also in favor of an international military and naval force for the purpose of enforcing the decisions of this congress? Do you believe the kaiser of Germany, without such a force, would treat such a decision as anything but a scrap of paper if it was not in his favor?" Lenroot declared himself for a congress of nations armed with the power, by economic and military pressure, to enforce its decisions.[4]

Opposition elements fell silent during the war, but they did not alter their opinions. Even proponents of a League desired something more concrete. When Wilson did not give any specifics in his December 1918 message to Congress and then departed for Europe, he left himself vulnerable to attack.

1. The standard history of the organization is Ruhl J. Bartlett, *The League to Enforce Peace*.
2. Arthur S. Link, *Wilson: Campaigns for Progressivism and Peace, 1916–1917*, pp. 265–68.
3. John Chalmers Vinson, *Referendum for Isolation: Defeat of Article Ten of the League of Nations Covenant*, pp. 32, 35, 46; Leon E. Boothe, "Anglo-American Pro-League Groups Lead Wilson, 1915–1918," pp. 92–107.
4. *Milwaukee Sentinel*, 10 March 1918.

Most Democratic senators were reluctant to criticize Wilson openly, but Republicans felt no such inhibition. Antagonized by what many of them regarded as his blatant partisanship, Republican senators bridled at Wilson's appeal in October for a Democratic Congress and subsequent appointments to the peace delegation. The personal antagonism for Wilson, strong in Lodge and others but absent in Borah,[5] blended easily with a matter of constitutional principle that all senators adhered to, with varying degrees of sincerity and concern—the right of the Senate to advise on as well as consent to treaties.[6]

Borah, a frequent and brilliant speaker within and outside of the Senate, extreme in his opposition, impressive in his bearing and unshakable in his convictions, spearheaded a forceful and effective attack on the League through December and the first half of January; then the subject was dropped for a time. Observers viewed him, then and later, as the most important of those who earned the name *irreconcilables.*[7]

But the most significant remarks in the congressional debate that broke out after Wilson's departure for the peace conference were made by Philander C. Knox of Pennsylvania. Secretary of state under Taft, attorney general under Roosevelt, Knox was respected for his experience and shrewdness; many thought him a great constitutional authority.[8] Only in retrospect was it possible to include Knox among the irreconcilables. Unlike Borah, and his vocal colleagues James A. Reed and Hiram Johnson, he did not espouse traditional isolationism. In his willingness to assume limited international obligations and in other aspects of his thought, Knox articulated views that were widely acceptable, not only among most of those who would become irreconcilables but even in pro-League circles.[9]

Having outlined his position in late October, on 3 December Knox introduced a resolution declaring that at the peace conference the United States should limit its aims to "restitution, reparation, and guarantees against the German menace," and called for postponement of consideration of a League of Nations. In a speech of 18 December, Knox proposed to check Germany with a cordon of new free states, which might require periodic protection. For the most part, the Allies would be able to handle the troubles of Europe, while the United States continued to attend to the Western Hemisphere under the Monroe Doctrine. But, having come to recognize

5. John A. Garraty, *Henry Cabot Lodge: A Biography,* pp. 346, 355; Robert James Maddox, *William E. Borah and American Foreign Policy,* pp. 53–54.

6. Arthur S. Link, *Wilson the Diplomatist,* p. 129. See also Gilbert M. Hitchcock, "Events Leading to the World War . . . ," address before the Nebraska State Historical Society, 13 January 1925, vol. 1, Gilbert M. Hitchcock Papers, LC.

7. Ralph Stone, *The Irreconcilables: The Fight Against the League of Nations* (Lexington, Ky., 1970), pp. 24–25, 42–43, 51, 183; Florence J. Borden Harriman, *From Pinafores to Politics,* p. 358; Maddox, *Borah and American Foreign Policy,* pp. 55–56.

8. Stone, *Irreconcilables,* p. 27; Edward G. Lowry, *Washington Close-Ups: Intimate Views of Some Public Figures,* p. 198.

9. Stone, *Irreconcilables,* pp. 26–27, 41, 44–45.

that "a menace of Europe by the domination of aggressive military power" constituted "a menace also to the safety of this Nation," the United States must now embrace "a new American Doctrine" to supplement the Monroe Doctrine. "I will state this great new doctrine in these words," Knox said. "If a situation should arise in which any power or combination of powers should, directly or indirectly, menace the freedom and peace of Europe, the United States would regard such situation with grave concern as a menace to its own freedom and peace and would consult with other powers affected with a view to concerted action for the removal of such menace." More limited than a universal guarantee, Knox felt his doctrine to be more realistic, for nations could not be expected to act except in pursuance of self-interest, and it seemed unwise to engage in commitments that might not be fulfilled in the future.[10]

Democratic leaders declined to report the Knox resolution. Henry Cabot Lodge, concerned for party unity, made no attempt to force the issue.[11] But he willingly associated himself with all phases of Knox's view.[12] Historians do not agree in the evaluation of Lodge's motives. However, it is clear that, whatever his purposes for a "League of Nations," he shared Knox's view that the matter should be considered separately and subscribed also to Knox's middle ground position of realistic nationalism, in contrast to the more idealistic outlook of Borah or Wilson. That viewpoint, combined with constitutional principles respecting the role of the Senate and personal animus toward Wilson, blended conveniently with a continuing preoccupation with party unity. Lodge had been a party man throughout his long career in politics. Following the disastrous schism of 1912 in which his close friend Roosevelt broke away, he gave constant attention to restoring the party. Now, as minority leader in the Senate and soon to become majority leader if all went well he felt special responsibility to unite divisions and enhance party prospects for the presidential election of 1920.[13]

Knox had lent sophistication, prestige, and respectability to a position that, while critical of Wilson's, was not necessarily against any form of a League. For the time being, at least, Lodge found it a useful unifying vehicle.

News of domestic opposition, far from tempering Wilson's approach at Paris, reinforced him in the unfortunate conviction that he would have to overwhelm his opposition. When negotiations began in January, Wilson insisted successfully that, contrary to the Knox resolution, the League

10. *CR* 65:3, 1918, vol. 57, pt. 1, pp. 603–6. See also his brief comment on 4 December, *CR* 65:3, 1918, vol. 57, pt. 1, p. 78. Stone, *Irreconcilables*, pp. 26–27, 44–45.

11. Stone, *Irreconcilables*, p. 46.

12. Denna Frank Fleming, *The United States and the League of Nations, 1918–1920*, p. 77.

13. Regarding Lodge's motives see especially Garraty, *Henry Cabot Lodge*, pp. 345–46, 354–56. For radically contrasting views, each based on the Henry Cabot Lodge Papers, see James E. Hewes, Jr., "Henry Cabot Lodge and the League of Nations," pp. 245–55; and David Mervin, "Henry Cabot Lodge and the League of Nations," for the British Association for American Studies, pp. 210–14. The latter interprets Lodge's actions as political; Hewes, in agreement with Vinson, stresses Lodge's opposition to a universal commitment.

should be made the first order of business. As chairman of the committee
to draft the covenant, furthermore, he ignored warnings from Lansing and
others on his delegation and demanded a sweeping, positive guarantee of
territorial integrity against aggression—the celebrated Article Ten.[14]

In Wisconsin as elsewhere, the tide of wartime sentiment flowed easily
into pro-League channels, during and immediately after the war. The state
was one of the first to be organized by the League to Enforce Peace.[15] As
debate on the League began to develop in Washington during the first
postwar months, the legislature, echoing the sentiment of a variety of
groups of citizens, including some in which women were prominent, resolved in the League's favor. But the *Milwaukee Sentinel,* perhaps taking a
cue from the national Republican leaders, qualified its endorsement following publication of the covenant.[16]

State and national political considerations undoubtedly influenced Lenroot's course, at this time and afterwards. But these considerations were not
purely personal; they related also to effectiveness in achieving the best
possible result. "The Senate never has had since the beginning of this
Republic a more important responsibility than it will have when the peace
treaty shall finally come before it for ratification, amendment, or rejection,"
Lenroot said at the beginning of his first major speech on the subject on
28 February. Given the importance he attributed to the question, its merits
had to be his first consideration.

"I am not opposed to a League of Nations. I favor it," Lenroot declared.
"I approve the general plan of the formation of the League as proposed.
In my judgment the country will approve the proposed constitution if certain material modifications are made and other provisions simplified and
their interpretation made certain." Reviewing Lenroot's speech ten years
afterwards from a perspective favorable to the League, Denna Frank Fleming concluded that "it was very difficult to deny him any of the amendments
he asked for, even though some of them soon proved in practice to be
unnecessary," and Fleming judged that Lenroot's "was easily the most
impartial criticism of the covenant that had so far been made." [17]

Lenroot considered the covenant article by article. He did not object to
most of it. He did, however, judge the disarmament provision too weak. His
main criticism was directed against Article Ten, that "the Members of the
League undertake to respect and preserve as against external aggression
the territorial integrity and existing political independence of all Members

14. Vinson, *Referendum for Isolation,* pp. 34, 48, 52–57, 61–62; Kurt Wimer, "Woodrow
Wilson's Plan to Enter the League of Nations Through An Executive Agreement," pp. 800–
812.

15. Report of the Field Committee, 15 November 1917, Box 6, League to Enforce Peace
Papers, Harvard University.

16. *Milwaukee Sentinel,* 12, 21, 23 February 1919; Merlin Hull to Woodrow Wilson, 13 February 1919, File 4767, Series 4, Woodrow Wilson Papers.

17. *CR* 65:3, 1919, vol. 57, pt. 5, p. 4569; Fleming, *United States and the League of Nations,*
pp. 140–41.

of the League. In case of any such aggression or in case of any threat or danger of such aggression the Council shall advise upon the means by which this obligation shall be fulfilled." Under that article, according to the understanding of Lenroot and many other officials, the United States could not aid freedom under some circumstances and might be called on to protect despotism. Beyond that, he urged, as Knox had, that the United States should be "primarily responsible for peace in the Western Hemisphere."

If the European nations shall be unable to maintain peace, then they should be free to call upon us for help; but we should be left free to decide for ourselves whether the situation is such as to call for our intervention. If the peace of the world is menaced, we will interfere, as we did in this war, but we should not be obliged to do so. On the other hand, the United States will prevent external aggression against any of the nations in the Western Hemisphere, and will ask no aid from European nations in so doing.

He was willing to see Article Ten amplified to oblige member states not to extend their territory without the consent of the inhabitants of the land affected.

After pointing to some inconsistencies between articles and noting that with respect to League interference with the domestic question of immigration restriction, Wilson's assurances might not prove the last word, Lenroot expressed fear that Article Nineteen, which related to mandates, looked toward the United States becoming responsible for former Turkish territory for all time to come. That proposition alone, he felt, would bring rejection. His final major substantive suggestion was that, since the League would be an experiment, initial membership should be limited to ten years. He concluded that when the people had finally formed their judgment, it would be: "We are for a League of Nations; but in the interest of America, in the interest of liberty, in the interest of mankind, the proposed constitution must be modified." [18]

Lenroot was one of ten Republican senators to speak at length on the League between 14 February, when the text was published, and the last day of the Congress on 4 March, a key period in the development of public opinion respecting specific commitments. Five of the speakers were irreconcilables.[19] Lenroot's speech, though less noted in the press than Lodge's of the same day, was important in initiating a drive for amendments to the covenant, including a watering down of Article Ten.[20]

Within the week, Lenroot signed his name to a round robin declaration prepared by Knox at the suggestion of Lodge and Frank Brandegee, the mercurial Connecticut irreconcilable and Lodge's closest friend in the Senate. The document, which Lodge offered as a resolution, declared it the

18. *CR* 65:3, 1919, vol. 57, pt. 5, pp. 4569–72.
19. W. Stull Holt, *Treaties Defeated by the Senate: A Study of the Struggle Between President and Senate Over the Conduct of Foreign Relations*, pp. 256–57.
20. Vinson, *Referendum for Isolation*, p. 59.

sense of the Senate that "the constitution of the League of Nations in the form now proposed . . . should not be accepted by the United States" and asked that negotiations be directed to peace terms with Germany "and that the proposal for a League of Nations should be then taken up for careful consideration." If voted on, the resolution would have been defeated, but it was clearly out of order and, as Lodge had anticipated, a Democrat blocked unanimous consent for its consideration. Lodge then quietly accomplished his purpose, reading the names of thirty-seven Republican senators and senators-elect who would have voted for it if they could. The following day, two others added their assent. The thirty-nine names constituted six more than would be needed to block ratification.[21]

Of those who signed, only Lenroot had shown any real disposition to improve the covenant, in the view of Fleming. The qualifying words "in the form now proposed" made it possible for him and a few others to join in the resolution.[22]

President Wilson, who had come home for the end of the session, went back to Europe and, with some difficulty, secured four amendments to the covenant. Objections remained, however. Publication of the full treaty, showing the peace terms to be almost Carthaginian, aroused new opposition.[23] Irreconcilables stepped up their campaign and in June capitalized on a "leak" of the treaty to impute sinister influence to "Wall Street bankers." [24] By then, Wilson had been forced to convene the new Republican Congress in special session.

Out of the small tempest over the treaty leak came a Senate resolution to print the text in the *Congressional Record.* On the same day, 10 June, Senator Knox reintroduced his resolution to separate consideration of the League from the treaty. More clearly than before, the resolution reflected the purposes of the irreconcilables. Republican advocates of the League, who opposed it, launched efforts to develop instead a program of reservations. On 11 June, Lenroot was one of a dozen senators to gather at the home of Frank Kellogg to discuss reservations with Nicholas Murray Butler, president of Columbia University, who was an active Republican.

Most of the senators who met with Butler that night came to be called "mild reservationists." They included in addition to Fred Hale and Kellogg, Charles McNary, Arthur Capper, Kenyon and Cummins of Iowa, Selden Spencer of Missouri, Lenroot, and a few others. After dinner, Butler discussed at length the reservations that should be included in the ratification.

21. Fleming, *United States and the League of Nations,* pp. 153–55; Lodge to Frederick H. Gillett, 15 October 1924, Lodge Papers; Garraty, *Henry Cabot Lodge,* pp. 353–54; Henry Cabot Lodge, *The Senate and the League of Nations,* p. 120; Stone, *Irreconcilables,* pp. 70–74.

22. Fleming, *United States and the League of Nations,* p. 156.

23. Thomas A. Bailey, *Woodrow Wilson and the Lost Peace,* p. 306.

24. Jack E. Kendrick, "The League of Nations and the Republican Senate, 1918–1921" (Ph.D. diss.), p. 151; Johnson to Albert J. Beveridge, 3 June 1919, Box 215, Albert J. Beveridge Papers, LC; La Follette to "My Beloved Boys," 11 June 1919, Box 27, Series A, Robert M. La Follette FC; Borah to Rev. T. W. Rainey, 20 June 1919, Box 551, William E. Borah Papers, LC.

He talked about reservations respecting domestic questions and the Monroe Doctrine, but the senators stressed the need for a reservation to Article Ten. Back in New York the following day, Butler sent Hale a draft of mild reservations on each of the three subjects.[25]

If nothing else, the meeting with Butler helped to crystallize sentiment among a sufficient number of Republicans to block the Knox resolution, while directing party effort toward a program of reservations. At a Republican conference, Lenroot voiced the feeling of those who wanted the party to offer positive alternatives instead of unalloyed criticism of the Knox resolution. Lodge, who was increasingly skeptical about the establishment of the League of Nations, had been quite willing to advance the Knox resolution so long as it had a chance of securing wide support among Republicans and occasioning debate about the League, but he was fully prepared to shift to reservationism, and he did.[26]

To this point, and for several months more, Lenroot played only a secondary role. His general attitude, as it was developing, was this: He did not want to impede ratification, felt reservations necessary, and thought that the reservations attached to the instrument of ratification would be not only desirable in themselves but would in fact make it possible to secure the necessary two-thirds majority in the Senate.

Former Secretary of State Elihu Root remained the dominant figure in the minds of Republican senators, and it was he who, after two visits to Washington and after conferences with Lodge, Kellogg, Knox, and others, provided a new basis for Republican unity in the form of a letter on 21 June to Lodge, which the newspapers promptly published. After a bow to the Knox resolution, Root praised the League covenant at length but pointed to defects that he felt should be dealt with in the resolution of ratification. While approving the French security treaty, which would be of limited duration, he condemned Article Ten and proposed that assent to it be refused. Root suggested also that the United States should accept no qualification on the right of withdrawal and that reservations should be added to safeguard the nation from League interference in domestic questions, such as immigration, or with the Monroe Doctrine. The resolution, Root made clear, would take effect unless some of the other signatories expressly objected, but if desired the United States might ask the principal powers to state whether they objected.[27]

Root's suggestions were particularly satisfactory to pro-League Republi-

---

25. Nicholas Murray Butler, *Across the Busy Years: Recollections and Reflections*, vol. 2, pp. 197–201.

26. Hiram Johnson to Albert J. Beveridge, 18 June 1919, Box 215, Beveridge Papers; Gus Karger to William Howard Taft, 14 June 1919, Box 449, Series 3, William Howard Taft Papers; Kendrick, "League of Nations and Republican Senate," pp. 145, 168; *Superior Telegram*, 21 June 1919; Lodge to John T. Morse, Jr., 7 June 1919, to Archibald Hopkins, 23 June 1919, Lodge Papers.

27. Fleming, *United States and the League of Nations*, p. 227; Kellogg to Nicholas Murray Butler, 19 November 1925, Box 11, Frank B. Kellogg Papers; Richard W. Leopold, *Elihu Root and the Conservative Tradition*, p. 138; Philip C. Jessup, *Elihu Root*, p. 401.

cans, who had great confidence in him. The irreconcilables were not over-joyed but not entirely displeased either, for the party was now committed to what they must have regarded as a fortuitously ambiguous program of opposition to the treaty that Wilson would soon present.[28]

The president accepted the advice of Sen. Claude Swanson and Postmaster General Burleson that on his return he should first speak to the Senate, instead of the general public. After presenting the treaty to the Senate on 10 July, Wilson held private conferences at the White House with over twenty Republican senators, from 17 July through 1 August. Initially, he had planned to tour and give speeches for his League starting on 4 August, but he came to believe that he had won over enough senators to control the situation, so he postponed the trip until he could more definitely test sentiment.[29]

The stumbling blocks that remained were greater than Wilson imagined. His speech to the Senate had been vague, disappointing supporters of the treaty and encouraging critics.[30] In his meetings with Republican senators, Wilson merely expounded on the covenant.[31] That approach was useful, but it did not go far toward the achievement of compromise and did not weaken reservationism. Indeed, Wilson felt little need for compromise. Depending on himself, the people, and the righteousness of his cause, he was willingly deluded by overoptimistic and poorly informed reports.[32] Secretary

28. For mild reservationist attitudes toward Root see Charles McNary to Root, 5 May 1919, Box 137, Elihu Root Papers, LC; and Frank B. Kellogg to William Howard Taft, 21 July 1919, Box 5, Kellogg Papers, as well as subsequent correspondence. They were commented on by Lodge in conversation with Chandler P. Anderson. Charles P. Anderson, Diary, 30 July 1919, Box 4, Chandler P. Anderson Papers, LC. On the reaction of irreconcilables see Knox to Beveridge, 21 June 1919, Box 215, Beveridge Papers; and Karger to Taft, 28 June 1919, Box 450, Series 3, Taft Papers.

29. A. S. Burleson to Joseph Tumulty, 25 June 1919, File 4767, Series 4, Wilson Papers; Thomas A. Bailey, *Woodrow Wilson and the Great Betrayal,* p. 376; Kendrick, "League of Nations and Republican Senate," pp. 190–91; Kurt Wimer, "Woodrow Wilson Tries Conciliation: An Effort That Failed," pp. 419–38; Kurt Wimer, "Senator Hitchcock and the League of Nations," pp. 189–204.

30. Henry Fountain Ashurst, *A Many-Colored Toga: The Diary of Henry Fountain Ashurst,* diary entry, 11 July 1919, pp. 98–99; John J. Esch to W. B. Tscharner, 14 July 1919, Box 53, John J. Esch Papers; Fleming, *United States and the League of Nations,* p. 237.

31. Wimer, "Wilson Tries Conciliation," pp. 421–22.

32. Thomas W. Lamont, aboard the *George Washington* en route home, was the only one of Wilson's advisers who was apprehensive of Senate prospects. Thomas W. Lamont, *Across World Frontiers,* pp. 202–13. Gilbert Hitchcock, ranking Democrat on the foreign-relations committee and acting minority leader, was also one who counted on Republican division. Wimer, "Wilson Tries Conciliation," p. 426; Hamilton Holt to A. Lawrence Lowell, 30 June 1919, Box 451, Series 3, Taft Papers; Kendrick, "League of Nations and Republican Senate," pp. 167–68. Other key informants who took overoptimistic views included Key Pittman of the foreign-relations committee, Burleson and Breckinridge Long, an assistant secretary of state. Pittman to Hamilton Holt, 31 July 1919, Box 91, Key Pittman Papers, LC: Burleson to Tumulty, 25 June 1919, File 4767, Series 4, Wilson Papers; Breckinridge Long, Diary, 22 June, 10, 29 July 1919, Box 2, Breckinridge Long Papers, LC. An inaccurate assessment of the views of individual Republican senators was transmitted to Wilson in Joseph Tumulty to Cary T. Grayson, 2 July 1919, Box 1, Special Cor., Joseph P. Tumulty Papers.

of State Robert Lansing took a realistic view. However, he had fallen into disfavor, as had several others.[33] Possibly, his neurological condition, which would weaken him later in the fall, was already upon Wilson, affecting his personal relationships and judgment.[34] He was not wholly intransigent. He publicly stated his willingness to accept "interpretive reservations" separately adopted, and in mid-July he encouraged Thomas Lamont to achieve compromise along those lines.[35] But he rejected anything more. Publicly and privately, he argued that reservations incorporated in the instrument of ratification would require reopening of peace negotiations. In this view, he had the ardent support of Sen. Key Pittman of Nevada, a member of the foreign-relations committee, and other Democratic senators.[36] New negotiations would delay the peace that all nations needed and would permit other great powers, including Germany, to insist on their own conditions, Wilson and others argued. But on 29 July, the solicitor of the State Department disagreed with the view Pittman had expressed in the Senate "that any annex or reservation or addition or qualification" must be submitted to other governments, and by them to their parliaments. American reservations would not be binding, Lester Woolsey acknowledged, but other nations would not have to act on them.[37] Wilson ignored that judgment. He understood that a separate resolution of interpretive reservations would require a two-thirds majority. But if reservations or amendments were added to the instrument of ratification, each one would be attached by a simple majority. Only after that process had been completed would the two-thirds vote be needed. If only a simple majority were required, the Republicans, with some Democratic support, could engraft damaging reservations onto the treaty. The Democrats would then either have to accept the flawed treaty or take the blame for its rejection. If, on the other hand, reservations were kept separate from the treaty, the Republicans would have to assume responsibility for rejection, something they would probably not choose to do. Furthermore, the separate interpretive reservations, requiring a two-thirds majority, could not be adopted without substantial Democratic support and thus would not be offensive.[38]

Behind the problem of form lay matters of substance. Wilson believed ardently in Article Ten. He felt that the other features of the treaty were necessary for peacemaking, such as the Shantung provisions, which trans-

33. Robert Lansing desk books, 1919, 1, 2 August 1919, Robert Lansing Papers, LC; John M. Blum, *Joe Tumulty and the Wilson Era*, p. 201.

34. Edwin A. Weinstein, "Woodrow Wilson's Neurological Illness," pp. 324–51.

35. Bailey, *Great Betrayal*, p. 170; Wimer, "Wilson Tries Conciliation," p. 425.

36. Gus J. Karger to William Howard Taft, 23, 24 June 1919, Box 450, Series 3, Taft Papers; Jessup, *Elihu Root*, p. 403; Fleming, *United States and the League of Nations*, pp. 237, 270–73; Key Pittman to Hamilton Holt, 31 July 1919, Box 91, Pittman Papers; *CR* 66:1, 1919, vol. 58, pt. 3, p. 3096.

37. Lester H. Woolsey, solicitor, Department of State, to "Dear Mr. Secretary," (Robert Lansing), 29 July 1919, Box 190, Series 2, Wilson Papers.

38. Wimer, "Wilson Tries Conciliation," pp. 429–32.

ferred the control of the Shantung peninsula in China from Germany to Japan. Yet, these and other provisions were already under sharp attack and were vulnerable if reservations could be adopted by a simple majority.

Viewed from this standpoint, Wilson's reluctance to accept anything but interpretive reservations, which were separately adopted, and his slowness to negotiate them (for tactical reasons) is readily understandable. He can be blamed only for his failure to fully understand the situation in the Senate and the country. Wilson did not realize that his approach had little chance of success. In unyielding pursuit of it, he sacrificed promising opportunities of compromise, which came about in August.

Pro-League Republicans, even the mildest of them, saw no reason to exclude reservations from the instrument of ratification, believing along with Root, that so long as they were not destructive, they would not require any reopening of the peace conference. If the survival of the League depended on a separation from their party, some would have complied. But if reservations would not result in a resubmission of the treaty, how could they hope to secure enough support from their colleagues to contribute to the Democrats the twenty or so votes needed to make two-thirds? Wadsworth reflected a widespread and well-substantiated view that the mild reservationists shared when he wrote: "Interpretive reservations adopted in a separate resolution would have no force whatsoever; in fact, they would not even be called to the official attention of other governments." And Lodge, who spoke for the largest single faction among the Republicans, those who came to be called "strong reservationists," made it clear to Hays on 19 July that "the best solution would be to carry the reservations by majority vote. We will take no explanatory interpretations such as the President has begun to talk about." [39]

Although the irreconcilables wanted much more, by mid-July the Republicans were unified on at least reservations covering the topics in Root's letter and requiring assent, tacit or explicit, from the principal world powers. Will Hays felt justified in issuing a public statement along those lines.[40] In confidence, Taft submitted reservation proposals to his friends in the Senate, LeBaron Colt of Rhode Island, Charles McNary of Oregon, and Porter J. McCumber of North Dakota, who was second-ranking Republican on the foreign-relations committee. Later, he sent them also to Gilbert Hitchcock of Nebraska, the acting majority leader. Similar to Root's proposal but milder, especially with respect to Article Ten, which he proposed to leave in effect for a limited period of time, Taft was confident they would not require new negotiation. He hoped that at the proper time, these reserva-

39. Fleming, *United States and the League of Nations*, p. 240; Wadsworth to Chancellor Elmer E. Brown, 13 September 1919, Box 11, League to Enforce Peace Papers; Hewes, "Lodge and the League of Nations," p. 251; Kendrick, "League of Nations and Republican Senate," pp. 179–80; Lodge to Hays, 19 July 1919, Lodge Papers.

40. Will H. Hays, *The Memoirs of Will H. Hays*, pp. 211–12; *Superior Telegram*, 16 July 1919.

tions might constitute the basis for compromise with the Democrats, the latter providing most of the votes.[41]

After a series of phone calls and letters, Hays persuaded Taft to allow his proposals to be shown to Lodge in confidence. Apprised of Taft's actions, the officials of the League to Enforce Peace and friends of the former president feared that what Taft recommended as a basis for final settlement would instead become merely a starting point. They were correct. As Taft's letters to Hays moved into wider circulation, newspapers got ahold of them and on 24 July made them public, including remarks critical of Wilson. "Old as I am, I find myself impulsive, earnest and anxious to do things quickly rather than to let time mellow the subject a bit so that it can be seen in its maturer form," Taft wrote ruefully to his friend Charles Hilles. The executive board of the League to Enforce Peace, which included such influential Democrats as William Gibbs McAdoo and Vance McCormick, the party chairman, promptly reaffirmed its stand in favor of unconditional ratification, but the damage had already been done. The organization and the cause of bipartisan unity behind the League had suffered a serious blow. Taken in combination with other things—a reservationist statement by Hughes and rising discontent over the Shantung provision and Great Britain's "six votes" in the Assembly (referring to dominions and colonies), publication of Taft's letters strengthened Republican reservationism. Lodge, who had hoped Taft's position might be made better known to the public, commented that "Taft's performance weakens the attack." He was certain now that reservations could command a majority composed of most or all Republicans and one or two Democrats. After those had been attached, it would be up to the Democrats to accept the resolution or reject it. Such was the general situation when on 24 July Lenroot addressed the Senate on the League.[42]

Lenroot began by deploring the lack of understanding in the country of the situation in the Senate regarding the League. Implicitly alluding to the many speeches delivered by irreconcilables that month, Lenroot said the country should know that most of the Senate and most Republicans favored

---

41. Taft to Colt, 15 July 1919, to Hays, 20 July 1919, Box 452, Series 3, Taft Papers.

42. Relevant correspondence on the Taft proposals is voluminous. See Boxes 452 and 453, Series 3, Taft Papers, for the period 15 July through 31 July. Taft's letter to Hilles, which is cited, is dated 25 July. On League to Enforce Peace and Democratic reaction see McAdoo to Wilson, 31 July 1919, Box 190, Series 2, Wilson Papers. The Hughes statement, solicited by Hays, is in the form of a letter to Hale dated 24 July. Hughes suggested four reservations to be included in the instrument of ratification. Hays to Hughes, 22 July 1919, Box 4A, "The Separate Peace with Germany, the League of Nations, and the Permanent Court of International Justice," (Beerits Memorandum), pp. 9–10, Box 172, Charles Evans Hughes Papers, LC; Betty Glad, *Charles Evans Hughes and the Illusion of Innocence: A Study in American Diplomacy*, p. 171. On the transmittal of Taft's reservations to Lodge, his reaction to publication of the letters, and general strategy at this time, see Hays to Lodge, 17, 22 July 1919, Lodge to Louis A. Coolidge, 15 July 1919, to Hays, 19 July 1919, to Coolidge, 26 July 1919, Lodge Papers. The comment is quoted from the last of these.

the League, with proper reservations, which he proposed to discuss in detail later. But first, he urged the foreign-relations committee, which was in the midst of a two-week reading of the treaty, to make a prompt report, so the people would be informed as soon as possible as to the real issues and realize that the question was not one of joining or not joining but "to what extent . . . the United States shall surrender its rights and independence of action with relation to refraining from war in the future."

Putting aside the question of whether the harsh terms imposed on Germany were more likely to provoke future war than ensure peace, Lenroot turned to the main objections he and others had raised in February and to the changes Wilson had effected in March and April. In his view, several objections had been completely removed. He was not too disturbed over the issues of withdrawal, the Monroe Doctrine, and domestic questions in light of new wording secured by Wilson, but since others, he felt clarifying reservations were in order. "The inequality of voting power still remains and is objectionable," Lenroot said, "but since it has been made clear that unanimous action is required in all cases of disputes between nations, and, indeed, in nearly all of the transactions of the council and the assembly, I do not think the inequality of voting power should be an objection to ratification." He did think, though, that this matter should also be covered in a reservation.

Article Ten was of course the one major substantive problem in Lenroot's mind. But before taking it up, he discussed the main positive contributions the League could make. Lenroot attributed greatest value to Article Twelve under which members agreed not to go to war before submitting international questions to arbitration or to the League and not to make war until three months after the decision of arbitrators or the recommendation of the Executive Council or Assembly of the League. He felt that the cooling-off period would be useful in itself and would give other nations time to provide their good offices. "The next most beneficial article in the League . . . is Article Eleven . . ." Lenroot continued, that "any war or threat of war, whether immediately affecting any of the members of the League or not, is hereby declared a matter of concern to the whole League, and the League shall take any action that may be deemed wise and effectual to safeguard the peace of nations." That article, in Lenroot's judgment, would bring consideration and deliberation respecting war or the threat of war but would not, as some had contended, deprive any member nation of freedom of action. "Nowhere is the League of Nations given power to declare war, nowhere is any force provided to carry out its decisions, nowhere is it given power to command action by any member of the League." The provision, with others, would not prevent all war, but it would prevent some and would help the League to replace the destroyed balance of power system that had helped maintain peace in the late nineteenth century.

But all this would be lost, Lenroot implied, if something were not done about Article Ten, "around which centers the principle contest over the ratification of the covenant in its present form." Unjust and controverted territorial decisions had already been made; treaties with Austria-Hungary, Turkey, and Bulgaria were not yet completed but would surely also result in violations of the Fourteen Points and in territorial disputes. "If we should ratify this treaty now with no reservation as to Article Ten we would guarantee territorial boundaries which are not now in existence and concerning which peoples are to-day actually engaged in war," Lenroot said.

Earlier he had digressed to urge Democratic senators to "forget that President Wilson is the leader of the Democratic party." Now he reiterated his conviction "that if partisanship be forgotten and only Americanism remembered we can agree upon a reservation to this article, now so dangerous to the cause of true liberty, so destructive of American ideals and principles." The wording of such a reservation might take any of several forms. And its adoption would not mean that the United States would be unconcerned about aggression but only that, in future times, those Americans directly involved, through their representatives, would have a voice in the nation's decision.[43]

Five days later, President Wilson invited Lenroot to come to the White House the following afternoon to discuss the treaty. The interview was planned to last forty-five minutes.[44]

Although the meeting was the first between the two men since Wilson had applied the "acid test" to Lenroot, both were so deeply concerned about the situation of the League that the personal difference between them probably caused little embarrassment or constraint. While the other three Republican visitors of the day raised objections to Article Eleven as well as Article Ten, Lenroot confined himself to the latter, which became the main topic of their conversation, although Lenroot also talked of the other reservations he had discussed in his recent speech. When the two men parted, for the last time (as it turned out) they were no closer to agreement on Article Ten than before.[45]

That same afternoon, Lenroot met for a second time with six other reservationist Republicans, Kellogg, Colt, Cummins, McNary, Spencer, and McCumber, to perfect reservations. Each had been working on them individually for at least a week, and Kellogg, assisted by Hale, had secured advice and encouragement from Lodge and Chandler P. Anderson, a distinguished international lawyer. At this final meeting, the seven men tentatively agreed on four reservations that they construed as interpretive and there-

43. *CR* 66:1, 1919, vol. 58, pt. 3, pp. 3090–95. Fleming discusses the speech in *United States and the League of Nations*, pp. 267–69, in the context of mild reservationist efforts.

44. Wilson to Lenroot, 29 July 1919, Box 4, Irvine L. Lenroot Papers; Fleming, *United States and the League of Nations*, p. 296; "Copy of Diary Kept by Head Usher at the White House, March 4, 1913 to March 4, 1921," Box 8, Series 1, Wilson Papers.

45. Fleming, *United States and the League of Nations*, p. 296; Francis Russell, *The Shadow of Blooming Grove: Warren G. Harding in His Times*, p. 320; *New York Times*, 31 July 1919; Lenroot, "Memoirs," p. 144, Box 13, Lenroot Papers; *CR* 66:1, 1919, vol. 58, pt. 6, pp. 5911–12.

fore not requiring resubmission, but which they insisted must be included in the instrument of ratification. The reservations were drawn along lines suggested by Root, but instead of eliminating Article Ten, as Root proposed, the reservationists would declare Congress's freedom of action with respect to advice from the League Council. Lenroot and his cohorts hoped to secure enough Republican support for their proposals to make them the party program and cut off anything more extreme, in substance or form. At the same time, they wanted agreement with the Democrats, so that the program could secure a two-thirds majority on the final vote. On 7 August, Kellogg presented the proposals to the Senate and developed the argument that such reservations would not require resubmission.[46]

Negotiations ensued, but Wilson judged them premature. He looked instead to a meeting with the foreign-relations committee of the Senate at which he would present his case not merely to that largely hostile body but to the country.[47]

In his conference with the foreign-relations committee, transcribed and widely printed, Wilson endangered his cause in a variety of ways. Most important, he failed to remove doubts about Article Ten. On another vital point, the question of whether reservations would require full renegotiation of the treaty, which Wilson asserted was the case, he admitted that authorities were divided and that he had not had time to look them up. He also made the damaging admission that Germany would not have to agree to changes in the League covenant.[48]

The following day, Key Pittman, without consulting the president, introduced the reservations agreed to by the group of seven, but as a resolution separate from the ratification resolution. Each of the seven, together with Knute Nelson, reiterated his disapproval of the idea. Lenroot said: "I have never been for any other programme than that of including strong and clear reservations in the resolution of ratification. So far as I know there is no thought on the Republican side of anything else. The reservations will be adopted as part of the ratifying resolution. The treaty cannot be ratified

46. *New York Times*, 1 August 1919; *New York Tribune*, 1, 2 August 1919; McCumber to William H. Taft, 24, 31 July 1919, Gus Karger to Taft, 31 July 1919, Box 453, Karger to Taft, 4 August 1919, Box 454, Series 3, Taft Papers; Chandler P. Anderson, Diary, 30 July 1919, Box 4, Anderson Papers; Frank Kellogg to Elihu Root, 21 August 1919, Box 137, Root Papers; Oscar S. Straus, *Under Four Administrations, From Cleveland to Taft: Recollections of Oscar S. Straus*, p. 428; Wimer, "Wilson Tries Conciliation," p. 427.

47. Gus Karger to William H. Taft, 11 August 1919, Frank Kellogg to Taft, 11 August 1919, Taft to Porter McCumber, 15 August 1919, Box 454, Hitchcock to Taft, 29 August 1919, Box 455, Series 3, Taft Papers; *New York Tribune*, 16, 17 August 1919; *Superior Telegram*, 15, 16 August 1919; Robert Lansing desk books, 22 November 1919, Lansing Papers; Wimer, "Wilson Tries Conciliation," pp. 428, 433, 436.

48. Garraty, *Henry Cabot Lodge*, pp. 368–69. For other accounts, noting these and other weaknesses in Wilson's presentation, see Bailey, *Great Betrayal*, pp. 86–87, 171; Kendrick, "League of Nations and Republican Senate," pp. 197–98; and Karger to Taft, 21 August 1919, Box 455, Series 3, Taft Papers.

unless such action is taken." Disowned by Hitchcock, the resolution was never voted on.[49]

On 27 August, Wilson announced that he would take his case to the country, in an extensive tour, giving speeches. A week later he set forth. Wilson left behind with Hitchcock a set of four reservations similar to Kellogg's, but the Nebraskan was not empowered to make them known or use them until authorized by the president.[50]

In the Senate, hard-liners gained, partly as the result of damaging admissions by Secretary of State Lansing and angry testimony by representatives of ethnic groups, especially the Irish-Americans.[51] The Committee on Foreign Relations approved reservations on Article Ten and withdrawal that McCumber could not support, along with two other reservations more to his liking. The committee also proposed forty-five amendments to the treaty, including ones on Shantung and the six to one voting question, the latter known as the "Johnson amendment." Lodge also wanted specific assent to reservations by three of the four principal Allied powers, but on that the committee deferred action.[52]

Of the Republicans, only McCumber filed a minority report. Looking past the amendments to the reservations, Lodge and other Republicans speculated that dissident Democrats might give the votes on the Article Ten reservation and perhaps others that McCumber and his friends could withhold.[53] But that was too great a chance for Lodge to take and he therefore persisted in efforts to mend the breach.[54] During late August and early September, the mild reservationists had developed their program and strategy in response to the course of events. They had set out to speed action in the committee and get the treaty onto the floor and block the Knox proposal. Now they were determined to resist amendment, which would require treaty renegotiation, and reach a compromise agreement with Lodge on the Article Ten reservation and perhaps additional ones that might be required as alternatives to amendments, as on the Shantung question and British colonial representation. They expected that once the Democratic program of a separate resolution of reservations was defeated and reservations they could accept were appended to the treaty, the Democrats would vote for ratification. Even if the Democrats entered into immediate

49. Fred L. Israel, *Nevada's Key Pittman*, pp. 39–40; *New York Tribune*, 21 August 1919.

50. Gilbert Hitchcock, "Events Leading to the World War . . . ," vol. 1, Hitchcock Papers.

51. McCumber to Wilson, 29 August 1919, Box 192, Series 2, Wilson Papers. The testimony of Lansing and of the representatives of ethnic groups is summarized in Bailey, *Great Betrayal*, pp. 81–83.

52. Lodge's unyielding position is noted in Kendrick, "League of Nations and Republican Senate," p. 206; and Wimer, "Wilson Tries Conciliation," pp. 432–34.

53. Lodge to James T. Williams, Jr., 6 September 1919, Lodge Papers; *New York Tribune*, 4, 7 September 1919.

54. Newspaper reports and abundant correspondence attest to the negotiations. Lodge placed chief reliance on Elihu Root's influence. Chandler P. Anderson, Diary, 30 July 1919, Box 4, Anderson Papers; Lodge to Root, 15 August, 3 September 1919, Box 161, Root Papers.

negotiations, their canvasses showed that they needed Lodge's help to secure twenty Republican votes for ratification. But they also realized that, in the absence of any early agreement with the Democrats, to attach a Republican slate of reservations to the treaty Lodge would need their help.[55]

For roughly seven weeks, through September and most of October, the mild reservationists took the leading role in preparing what came to be called the "Lodge reservations." [56] Despite the dissatisfaction of individual senators and outside leaders, the Democrats held aloof from reservationist negotiations, following the lead of President Wilson and Hitchcock. Neither were the irreconcilables immediately important in developing reservations.

Much of the negotiation that took place was among the mild reservationists. By mid-September, a nuclear group of six was well defined. It consisted of McCumber, McNary, Colt, Kellogg, Lenroot, and Nelson. Nelson, though staunch in his support of the treaty but less energetic at seventy-six, took little part in the drafting of the reservations, but the other five men conferred with one another frequently.[57] This group, in turn, worked to persuade others who shared their fear of amendments but required reservations that they could defend before their constituents. Spencer and Cummins left the original group of seven that framed the Kellogg reservations of 7 August, but they returned to the fold in opposition to amendments, as did Kenyon, Townsend, Hale, and some others.

The McCumber-McNary group had to negotiate also with Lodge, who continued to command the loyalty of about twenty "strong reservationists," many of them less interested in the complicated issues than in maintaining party unity.[58] Lodge spoke also for the irreconcilables who, though disinterested in reservations, would nevertheless have to vote for them if the Republicans were to put them through without the substantial Democratic help that seemed not to be forthcoming.

Lenroot was the major figure in drafting and later in defending the "Lodge reservations." In addition, increasingly during the seven-week

55. Kellogg to Taft, 20 August 1919, Box 5, Kellogg Papers; League to Enforce Peace press release, 31 August 1919, Box 16, League to Enforce Peace Papers; Kellogg to Elihu Root, 30 August 1919, Box 137, Root Papers; Kendrick, "League of Nations and Republican Senate," pp. 194, 212; *New York Times*, 1 September 1919; Karger to Taft, 21 August 1919, Box 455, Karger to Taft, 3, 5, 8 September 1919, Box 456, Talcott Williams to Taft, 22 September 1919, Box 457, Charles McNary to Taft, 28 October 1919, Box 459, Series 3, Taft Papers; Breckinridge Long to Joseph Tumulty, 22 September 1919, Box 193, Series 2, Wilson Papers; *New York Tribune*, 17 August, 7 September 1919.

56. Lenroot commented on this point in the Senate in November and December. *CR* 66:1, 1919, vol. 58, pt. 7, p. 8799; *CR* 66:2, 1919, vol. 58, pt. 1, p. 535. He made the same point in a speech in Milwaukee in December. *Milwaukee Sentinel*, 2 December 1919. Lodge agreed. *CR* 66:2, 1919, vol. 58, pt. 1, p. 535.

57. Martin W. Odland, *The Life of Knute Nelson*, pp. 288–92.

58. Seven of them said not a word about the treaty in the Senate debate. Mervin, "Lodge and the League of Nations," p. 210.

period and afterwards, he served as the principal representative of the mild reservationists in their continuing negotiations with Lodge. In December, when Hitchcock accused Lodge of having consulted mainly with irreconcilables, it was Lenroot to whom Lodge appealed to refute the charge, for he, more than any other, knew the extent of Lodge's negotiations with the mild reservationists.[59]

The fact of Lenroot's central role, among the mild reservationists, as intermediary to Lodge, and in some things as spokesman for Lodge, is explicable in several ways. He was intensely interested in achieving a satisfactory outcome because of the importance he had attached to the subject from the first. He remained energetic and able in mastering even an intricate subject such as the League question; he was no less facile than before at legislative draftsmanship and compromise. By conviction, he was closer to Lodge than McCumber, Colt, and McNary, and while having the confidence of the McCumber group, with whom he had associated himself since the dinner with Butler in June, he had a better relationship with Lodge than did Colt, Kellogg, McNary, McCumber, or Nelson.[60]

In July 1920, Lodge commented that although Lenroot and Kellogg had represented the "mild reservationists" in January negotiations, "Lenroot was never 'mild'." [61] Above all, in that connection, Lenroot was close to Lodge and Root in resisting obligations under Article Ten.[62] And he quickly recognized the need for strong reservations on other points if amendments were to be defeated and a reservationist program adopted.

Lodge was correct when he said that Lenroot was never really "mild." Yet to the end of his life Lenroot classified himself as a mild reservationist, and he was so regarded by senators and observers in the period after the treaty reached the Senate floor.[63] A major source of confusion lies in the distinction between mild and strong reservationists. While this distinction took on meaning during the course of the battle, in the early stages the mild reservationist group was distinguished not solely because of the character

59. *CR* 66:2, 1919, vol. 58, pt. 7, p. 535.

60. With respect to Lodge's relations with those named see H. Maurice Darling, "Who Kept the United States Out of the League of Nations?," p. 196–211; Colt to Root, 2 September 1919, Box 137, Lodge to Root, 15 August 1919, Box 161, Root Papers; Karger to Taft, 3 September 1919, Box 456, Series 3, Taft Papers; Kendrick, "League of Nations and Republican Senate," p. 215. Lenroot's Republican associates on the commerce and military affairs committees included key figures among mild and strong reservationists, notably James Wadsworth, Joseph Frelinghuysen, Arthur Capper, Wesley Jones, Nelson, Colt, McNary, and Walter Edge. Nelson, Kellogg, and Frelinghuysen were already friendly to him and he soon became good friends with Wadsworth, Capper, McNary, and Edge. Katharine Lenroot to the author, 26 November, 10 December 1968; interview with Katharine Lenroot, 20 November 1968. Lenroot's close friendship with Fred Hale is noteworthy in the same connection.

61. Lodge to Frederick H. Gillett, 26 July 1920, Lodge Papers.

62. Arnold B. Hall to Taft, 7 October 1919, Box 458, Series 3, Taft Papers. Hall's comments, based on conversation with Lenroot, were bourn out by the record Lenroot made in Senate debate and in compromise negotiations.

63. Lenroot to Mary Becker, 31 January 1946, Box 1, Lenroot Papers.

of the reservations they insisted on, although that was a factor; they were more notable for two other factors—their opposition to amendments and their extraordinary concern to secure ratification. In these two respects, Lenroot was very distinctly a leader of the group. Taking the term "mild reservationist" in the more conventional sense, although he was not of the McCumber-McNary-Colt school, neither was he a strong reservationist such as Wadsworth, Joseph Frelinghuysen, and others of the Lodge group.[64]

The floor battle had begun late in August. On 23 August 1919, following damaging testimony, by a nine to eight vote the Senate Committee on Foreign Relations approved the Shantung amendment substituting the word "China" wherever "Japan" appeared. To advocates of the treaty, the first order of business was to defeat this popular amendment, which would clearly require treaty renegotiation.[65] On 26 August, McCumber delivered a speech against the amendment. Afterwards, Lenroot asked a brief question, to reinforce the point that since the other major powers had approved the treaty, the amendment would provide no substantive benefit for China. Perceptive observers recognized the importance of Lenroot's comment, coming at this formative period, and put Lenroot among those who would oppose the amendment.[66] It was widely felt that defeat of the Shantung amendment would presage defeat of all other amendments. Characteristically, Republicans fearful of amendments set about preparing a reservation on the subject. Kellogg asked Root for a suggestion and got one. Meanwhile, Lenroot prepared a reservation of his own that he showed to a number of senators. It was similar to Root's, both merely disclaiming American assent to that phase of the treaty. Lodge hoped the amendment would pass but feared it would not and reconciled himself to a reservation along these lines if the amendment failed.[67]

The order for an amendment on Shantung began to recede following McCumber's speech and the development of possible reservations on the subject. But as it did the Johnson amendment gained favor—that in the Assembly or Council the United States should have votes equal to those of Great Britain and her colonies and dominions.[68] Early in September,

64. Hall to Taft, 7 October 1919, Box 458, Series 3, Taft Papers.

65. *New York Tribune,* 27 August 1919; Talcott Williams to Charles M. Lincoln, 26 August 1919, Rickey to Short, 28 August 1919, Box 17, League to Enforce Peace Papers; Karger to Taft, 21 August 1919, Box 455, Series 3, Taft Papers; Kellogg to Root, 30 August 1919, Box 137, Root Papers. Actually, for technical reasons, more than one amendment was involved.

66. *CR* 66:1, 1919, vol. 58, pt. 5, p. 4349; *New York Tribune,* 27 August 1919; Karger to Taft, 28 August 1919, Box 455, Series 3, Taft Papers.

67. Kellogg to Root, 6 September 1919, Root to Kellogg, 8 September 1919, Kellogg to Root, 11 September 1919, Box 137, Root Papers; Francis McCumber to Taft, 24 October 1919, Box 459, Series 3, Taft Papers; Lodge to James T. Williams, Jr., 5 August 1919, Lodge Papers.

68. Alan J. Ward, *Ireland and Anglo-American Relations, 1899–1921,* pp. 190–210; Fleming, *United States and the League of Nations,* p. 341; Rudolph Foster to Tumulty, 9 September 1919, Box 192, Series 2, Wilson Papers; Short to Rickey, 6 October 1919, Box 17, League to Enforce Peace Papers.

Republican reservationists conferred frequently about the difficult situation. At the same time, Lenroot and his mild reservationist colleagues, hopeful still of speedy ratification, probed for the key to compromise on reservations, especially on the subject of Article Ten.

Lodge was tractable. Perhaps, he was bargaining for votes for the Johnson amendment. In that connection, Lenroot maintained his own bargaining power; he wired the following to a political ally: "No one authorized to give my position upon Johnson amendment(.) Because of its bearing upon other questions will not commit myself until matter comes up." [69]

Lodge had other reasons for conciliating the mild reservationists, even while he encouraged irreconcilables in the development of anti-League sentiment.[70] He could not content himself with preventing the twenty Republican defections that would bring ratification on Democratic terms. Lodge needed to satisfy virtually all of the Republicans in order to attach amendments or, failing that, to get the reservations that he favored. McCumber, in a speech and then in his minority report, condemned Lodge's position on Article Ten and the caustic tone of the majority report. McNary, Colt, Kellogg, Nelson, and Lenroot supported McCumber. Having repeatedly encouraged these men in July and August in the development of reservations and having met their demands in part with the four reservations reported by his committee, Lodge could hardly reverse himself in September without courting disastrous schism. He had to seek a compromise on the Article Ten reservation that would satisfy the McCumber group and also be acceptable to the other Republican senators.

The declaration by Democrat loyalists Furnifold Simmons and Atlee Pomerene that reservations were essential to ratification, together with public and private advocacy of reservations by nine other Democratic senators, confirmed the mild reservationists in their conviction that the Democrats would compromise.[71] At the same time, this strong accretion of Democratic support for reservations lessened the bargaining power of the McCumber group within its own party.[72] Wilson's intemperate and sometimes inaccurate statements on the stump had the same effect.[73]

When Lodge announced the committee's four reservations, Lenroot objected to the second on Article Ten, on the grounds that it would apply against the boycott, a weapon specified in Article Sixteen. The boycott, in

69. Walter Heinemann to L. C. Boyle, n.d. (24 September 1919), Box 550, Borah Papers.

70. Lodge to Beveridge, 9 September 1919, Box 216, Beveridge Papers.

71. *New York Tribune*, 9 September 1919; Fleming, *United States and the League of Nations*, p. 339; William Cochrane to Tumulty, 11 September 1919, Box 192, Series 2, Wilson Papers; Karger to Taft, 21 August 1919, Box 455, Series 3, Taft Papers.

72. Talcott Williams to Short, 9 September 1919, Box 456, Series 3, Taft Papers; *New York Tribune*, 6 September 1919.

73. Bailey, *Great Betrayal*, p. 118; Stone, *Irreconcilables*, pp. 129–30; Fleming, *United States and the League of Nations*, pp. 339, 346–47, 369; *New York Tribune*, 9, 10, 11 September 1919; Lodge to Williams, Jr., 6 September 1919, Lodge Papers; Talcott Williams to Short, 9 September 1919, Box 456, Series 3, Taft Papers; Ashurst, *A Many-Colored Toga*, Diary entry, 12 September 1919, p. 105.

turn, could be used to require arbitration, a cooling-off period, and other non-martial devices that Lenroot had called the most valuable parts of the covenant. In this view, Lenroot was close in his thinking to many of those who had founded the League to Enforce Peace, including Taft. Taft remained solicitous for the boycott and so did his friend Senator Colt.[74]

Mainly because of the boycott question, on 6 September Lenroot joined McNary, McCumber, Colt, and Kellogg when they told Lodge that they could not accept his reservation.[75] Lodge minimized the differences between them and urged his colleagues to develop alternatives that he could accept and recommend to the other Republican senators. Privately, Lodge was confident that an agreement would be reached. By 11 September, Lodge reported to publisher George Harvey that McCumber

> . . . has traveled a long distance. All those so-called mild reservationists have reached a point where they are perfectly content to take the stiffest possible declaration that neither under Article 10 or any other article shall the army or navy of the United States ever be ordered anywhere or any war entered into without action by Congress. It is my principal point. There is a desire on the part of Lenroot, who is very stiff in all other ways . . . that we should not meddle with the economic boycott so far as it relates to putting pressure on a country declining arbitration. I am strongly inclined to yield that point if I can get them all, and I think I can.

Lenroot went briefly to Wisconsin to speak at the state fair confident not only of early agreement on Article Ten but of ratification within two weeks.[76]

Back in Washington, Lenroot plunged into drafting the reservation and into negotiations with his mild reservationist friends and with Lodge. On 18 September, McCormick wired the president the text of a reservation which he understood had been prepared by McCumber, Kellogg, and Lenroot, and which Lodge would accept and urge on his party colleagues.[77] Wilson promptly wired the White House instructions to tell Hitchcock of the confidential information "and say to him that I should regard any such reservation as a practical rejection of the Covenant." [78]

Hitchcock had no occasion for immediate action, since the Republicans had not really reached an agreement. Lenroot still participated but in a more

74. *Milwaukee Sentinel,* 6 September 1919; Taft to Karger, 6 September 1919, Box 457, Series 3, Taft Papers.

75. *Milwaukee Sentinel,* 7 September 1919.

76. Ibid., 9 September 1919; Lodge to George Harvey, 11 September 1919, Lodge Papers; *Milwaukee Sentinel,* 12 September 1919.

77. On reservation negotiations see Kellogg to Root, 11 September 1919, Box 137, Root Papers; Rickey to Short, 15 September 1919, to Tumulty, n.d. (September 1919), Box 17, League to Enforce Peace Papers; Karger to Taft, 13, 17 September 1919, Box 457, Series 3, Taft Papers. McCormick's wire went to both Tumulty and Wilson. It may be found in Box 193, Series 2, Wilson Papers, and vol. 1, Hitchcock Papers.

78. Woodrow Wilson to Rudolph Forster, n.d. (19 September 1919), Box 193, Series 2, Wilson Papers. The wire appeared in vol. 1 of the Hitchcock Papers.

discouraged mood than previously. With others, he felt that every day the president was away added injury to the treaty cause. "It is the greatest mistake he ever made, this tour of his," he said privately.[79]

Though under great pressure, the six mild reservationists remained independent and extracted from Lodge tentative agreement to a reservation that was prepared by McCumber, Lenroot, Kellogg, and possibly McNary, which was more moderate than the draft of 18 September. McCumber, who indiscreetly leaked the latest draft, also said that the six had agreed to stay together on all questions and to block all amendments. In return for his cooperation, the McCumber group was understood to have promised Lodge their full support for the reservations, once finally agreed upon, although McCumber retained the right to first secure votes on the six reservations of his minority report.[80]

Informed of it, President Wilson, in his speech at Salt Lake City, Utah, on 23 September, read the text of the proposed reservation and declared it to constitute rejection of the covenant. The reservation stated the following:

> The United States assumes no obligation under the provisions of Article 10 to preserve the territorial integrity or political independence of any other country or to interfere in controversies between other nations, whether members of the League or not, or to employ military and naval forces of the United States under any article of the treaty for any purpose, unless in any particular case the Congress, which under the Constitution has the sole power to declare war or authorize the employment of the military and naval forces of the United States, shall by act or joint resolution so declare.[81]

Even Joseph Tumulty, who shared Wilson's view, felt that his comments at Salt Lake City lacked specificity and "punch." The following day, at Cheyenne, Wyoming, Wilson added something of the latter, invoking the shade of those who died in France and asserting that the proposed reservation "cuts the heart out of the treaty." [82] Encouraged by cheering crowds and good reports from Washington, the president persisted in his strong stand against reservations at Denver and Pueblo, Colorado.[83]

79. Memo, Charles D. Warner to Rickey, enclosed in Talcott Williams to Taft, 19 September 1919, Box 457, quoting Lenroot, Karger to Taft, 13 September 1919, Box 456, Series 3, Taft Papers.

80. Talcott Williams to Taft, 22 September 1919, Short to Taft, 22 September 1919, Box 457, Series 3, Taft Papers; Anderson, Diary, 2 October 1919, Box 4, Anderson Papers; Breckinridge Long to Tumulty, 22 September 1919, Box 193, Series 2, Wilson Papers; Breckinridge Long, Diary, 24 September 1919, Box 3, Long Papers; *New York Tribune*, 28 September 1919.

81. Fleming, *United States and the League of Nations*, p. 353.

82. Blum, *Tumulty*, p. 212; *New York Tribune*, 28 September 1919.

83. Robert Foster Patterson, "Gilbert M. Hitchcock: A Story of Two Careers" (Ph.D. diss.), p. 444; Earl B. Gaddis (Hitchcock's secretary) to Tumulty, 7 September 1919, File 5191, Series 4, Rudolph Forster to Tumulty, 8 September 1919, Cochrane to Tumulty, 11 September 1919, Box 192, Burleson to Wilson, 13 September 1919, Forster to Tumulty, 23 September 1919, Box 193, Series 2, Wilson Papers; Fleming, *United States and the League of Nations*, pp. 340–41;

Since Wilson's condemnation of the Article Ten reservation had been
directed against the mild reservationists who had drafted it and agreed to
it, it was not inappropriate that one of them responded from the Senate
floor. There is no reason to think that Lenroot required any prodding, but
it is significant that when he spoke, late in the afternoon of 25 September,
it came after extended conferences with his mild reservationist colleagues
and after Lodge and his lieutenant, James Watson of Indiana, had arranged
to have other senators give way to him. Before Lenroot began, word was
passed that he would have an important statement.[84]

"Unless a reservation substantially such as that read by the President is
incorporated as a part of the ratification resolution, this peace treaty is not,
in my judgment, going to be ratified by the Senate," Lenroot said. "And,
Mr. President, when we come to the final consideration of this question, if
I, as one Senator, must choose between voting for the ratification of the
treaty as it is and obligating the people of the country to engage in war
against their will and voting for the rejecting of the treaty, I shall unhesitat-
ingly vote for the rejection of the treaty." Lenroot presumed to speak only
for himself, but his declaration was taken to reflect also the position of his
mild reservationist colleagues.[85]

Compromise and ratification could have been reached if the question
were one of either tactics, emotions, or politics. But in Lenroot's brief
remarks, he made it clear that matters of deep conviction remained to be
resolved, and these would not yield so easily to compromise, at least on the
Republican side. Lenroot pointed to inconsistencies in Wilson's speeches.
At Salt Lake, Wilson had called Article Ten the heart of the covenant. "Since
the President began his transcontinental journey the heart of this covenant
has suffered several displacements. When the President spoke in Indianapolis on September 4 he said: 'The heart of the covenant of the League is that
the nations solemnly covenant not to go to war for nine months after a
controversy becomes acute.' A little later the heart of the covenant was
transferred to article 11." More important, in the same speech in which he
called Article Ten the heart of the covenant, Wilson said, as he had elsewhere, that "nothing can be done without the consent of the United States."
"The President of the United States must take one of the two horns of the
dilemma that he is in," Lenroot went on. "If the United States remains a
free agent under the provisions of the article as it stands, the reservation
that is proposed can not cut the heart out of the covenant. . . . If it is not

---

Bailey, *Great Betrayal,* pp. 109–12; Blum, *Tumulty,* pp. 211–13; Edith Bolling Wilson, *My Memoir,*
p. 283; Hitchcock to J. P. Tumulty, 24 September 1919, Robinson to Wilson, 25 September
1919, Box 193, Series 2, Wilson Papers; David Lawrence, *The True Story of Woodrow Wilson,* pp.
280–81.

84. *New York Tribune,* 26 September 1919; James E. Watson, *As I Knew Them: Memoirs of James
E. Watson,* p. 190; *Milwaukee Sentinel,* 26 September 1919.

85. *CR* 66:1, 1919, vol. 58, pt. 6, p. 5912; *Milwaukee Sentinel,* 26 September 1919; *New York
Tribune,* 26 September 1919; Kellogg to Taft, 25 September 1919, Box 457, Series 3, Taft
Papers.

a free agent, then the President—I do no say intentionally—has been mis-stating to the country the effect of Article 10."

As Lenroot construed it, the United States was not a free agent. Techni-cally, to be sure, under the Constitution the Congress must consent to war. "But the President of the United States is asking us now, . . . to pledge the solemn word of the United States that whenever the occasion arises it will engage in war, if necessary, to preserve the territorial integrity of any mem-ber of the League from external aggression." On another occasion, Lenroot said, Wilson "sought to convey the impression that the United States could only act upon the advice of the council." But he must know

> . . . that the undertaking in article 10 . . . is a promise irrespective of any advice of the council. If we enter into the covenant in its present form and the territorial integrity of any nation is destroyed, the United States must, to the full extent of its last man and its last dollar, in keeping with its promise, restore that integrity or else be in the same position that Germany was in in violating the neutrality of Belgium.[86]

If the Versailles treaty were to be ratified, Wilson would have to compro-mise on matters that he saw as fundamental. Whether or not he would have done so had he retained his good health, no one can say. As it happened, following a breakdown that caused an abrupt return to Washington after the Pueblo speech, on 2 October the president suffered a cerebral thrombo-sis that paralyzed the left side of his face and body. This condition, aug-mented two weeks later by a bladder ailment, endangered his life and ren-dered him almost helpless for several months. During this period, on the advice of one of the consulting physicians, Mrs. Wilson protected her hus-band not only from visitors but also from bad news, counsels of compro-mise, and even a peace overture from Lodge. When, on 7 November, Hitch-cock was finally granted a half-an-hour interview, he was shocked to find that the president had suddenly become an old man, and that Wilson was ill informed as to the situation in the Senate. Until then, and even after-wards, Wilson deluded himself with a mixture of one-sided reports and memories of cheering crowds and reassuring messages.[87]

Wilson's personal physician, Cary Grayson, issued bulletins that were vague and optimistic. In the caldron of Washington gossip, what might have been sympathy for the stricken president boiled off, leaving only a residue of wrath.[88]

At the Capitol, no one took the initiative. Hitchcock offered little leader-

86. *CR* 66:1, 1919, vol. 58, pt. 6, p. 5912.

87. Daniel M. Smith, *The Great Departure: The United States and World War I, 1914–1920*, pp. 190–91; Lawrence, *Story of Woodrow Wilson*, pp. 282, 288; Edith Bolling Wilson, *Memoir*, pp. 289–92; Alden Hatch, *Edith Bolling Wilson: First Lady Extraordinary*, pp. 221–25; Herman H. Kohlsaat, *From McKinley to Harding*, p. 220; Stephen Bonsal, *Unfinished Business*, pp. 276–89; Gilbert Hitchcock, "Wilson's Place in History," Hitchcock Papers, cited in Patterson, "Gilbert M. Hitchcock," p. 445; Blum, *Tumulty*, p. 224.

88. Bailey, *Great Betrayal*, pp. 133–34; Lowry, *Washington Close-Ups*, p. 14; Charles E. Town-send to Taft, 9 October 1919, Box 458, Series 3, Taft Papers.

ship. His position was weakened by the fact that he was only acting minority leader, standing in the shoes of Thomas Martin of Virginia, who died on 13 November, after a long illness. Nor was the Nebraskan recognized as the inevitable successor, for Southern senators favored Underwood. No match for Republican foes in tactics, oratory or parliamentary skill, the unusual petulance that he showed at the end of September betrayed a fateful irresolution. Unable to get new directions from his chief to match the shifting winds, despite belated efforts to do so, Hitchcock pursued a wavering course. As the Committee on Foreign Relations developed a new set of reservations, Hitchcock offered the alternatives secretly supplied to him in August by the president. But he did not disclose their authorship, even to his Democratic colleagues, and made no effort to negotiate with the Republicans. Fellow Democrats voted against most of his reservations, which were all rejected, and as the committee ended its deliberations in late October, he successfully stood against John Shields's proposal for a compromise effort. Underwood might have intervened, but he feared opening a Pandora's box of reservations at that stage of affairs.[89]

For Lenroot, as for the other senators chiefly interested in the controversy on the League, the first order of business in September was the Johnson "six vote" amendment. Lenroot and nine other leaders met on 24 September to consider reservations that might replace the amendment. Kellogg judged Lenroot's the most suitable, and eventually it was his that the Senate adopted. For the moment, however, there was insufficient time to achieve consensus, so on 25 September Lenroot, representing himself, Kellogg, Nelson, McNary, McCumber, Colt, and Hale, called on Lodge and Democrat Claude Swanson to declare that they would vote against any attempt to bring up the Johnson amendment at that time. For different reasons, both men willingly promised delay. Johnson, informed that his amendment could not pass immediately but promised by the mild reservationists that he would be informed four days before the vote, gladly returned to the stump and warned that whatever the outcome of reservationist efforts, he would later force a vote on the amendment. During the course of these negotiations, Lenroot, despite his activity in favor of a reservation and for delay, and his continual association with the mild reservationists, did not commit himself to vote against the Johnson amendment.[90]

89. Patterson, "Gilbert M. Hitchcock," pp. 418, 422; Bailey, *Great Betrayal,* p. 136; Robert La Follette, Jr., to "Dearest Mother and Mary," 30 September 1919, Box 28, Series A, La Follette FC; Ashurst, *A Many-Colored Toga,* entry for 21 October 1919, p. 110; Kendrick, "League of Nations and Republican Senate," pp. 233–35, 238, 241; Stone, *Irreconcilables,* pp. 141–42; Dewey W. Grantham, Jr., "The Southern Senators and the League of Nations, 1918–1920," pp. 187–205; Taft to A. Lawrence Lowell, 5 October 1919, Underwood to Taft, 9 October 1919, Box 458, Series 3, Taft Papers.

90. Karger to Taft, 23 September 1919, Kellogg to Taft, 25 September 1919, Box 457, Series 3, Taft Papers; Edge to Root, 26 September 1919, Box 137, Root Papers; *New York Times,* 26 September 1919; Borah to Heinemann, 22 September, 16 October 1919, Heinemann to Boyle, 23 September 1919, Box 552, Borah Papers.

With the Johnson amendment temporarily shelved, on 27 September, the Senate, in Committee of the Whole, began debate on Albert Fall's thirty-five amendments, which stressed that the United States government be kept off various boards and commissions established under the League. On 2 October, shortly before voting began, Lenroot, joined by Hale, Smoot, and Cummins, spoke against textual amendments. Lenroot spoke twice, on three of the Fall amendments. In each case, he tried to show that the amendment was ineffective and that the subject could better be covered by a reservation. And he quite frankly deplored the idea of sending the treaty back to the peace conference. The Senate soon defeated the first amendment by a vote of thirty to fifty-eight and rejected the rest in swift succession. However, adding the pairs to those who voted favorably, the Fall amendments had from thirty-four to thirty-nine supporters; clearly, relatively strong reservations would be required to secure two-thirds for ratification. Lenroot joined others in an immediate effort to draft reservations to meet Fall's points, as by stipulating that the United States government retained the option to participate or not on a given commission.

By the time Lodge's amendments on Shantung came up for a vote, on 16 October, the Lenroot reservation on Shantung had been widely circulated and accepted by reservationist Republicans. Nevertheless, Lenroot, while condemning the treaty provisions on Shantung, took the occasion to announce publicly the reservation he would offer if no other reservation were proposed. His reservation was this: "The United States withholds its assent to articles 156, 157, and 158, and reserves full liberty of action with respect to any controversy that may arise under said articles." The amendment would accomplish nothing, since the treaty was coming into effect as written, Lenroot said. His reservation, preserving America's freedom of action, might result in some benefit to China. He debated with Borah that Japan could not accept the amendment and those who joined in the 1915 secret treaty were honor bound by that to reject it also. Thus, the amendment would keep the United States out of the Versailles treaty entirely. "I can not give my consent to the position that I am unwilling to make peace with Germany unless Shantung is restored to China." Lodge disagreed, arguing that Great Britain would accept the United States on any terms. But the vote went against him, thirty-five to fifty-five, as had been expected. Fourteen Republicans voted against the amendment and another was announced in opposition. They opposed it with the understanding that a reservation like Lenroot's would later be offered.[91]

With the Shantung amendment disposed of and the reading of the treaty nearing completion, the foreign-relations committee moved quickly to com-

91. George A. Finch, "The Treaty of Peace with Germany in the United States Senate," pp. 155–206; *Milwaukee Sentinel*, 3 October 1919; *CR* 66:1, 1919, vol. 58, pt. 6, pp. 6273, 6280; *New York Tribune*, 3 October 1919, p. 92; *CR* 66:1, 1919, vol. 58, pt. 7, pp. 6951–52; *New York Tribune*, 16 October 1919; *Milwaukee Sentinel*, 17 October 1919; James Oliver Robertson, "The Progressives in National Republican Politics, 1916–1921" (Ph.D. diss.), p. 243.

plete a new program of reservations. The Johnson amendment was yet to be dealt with, as were various amendments that were to be offered by individual senators, but with pressure mounting within the Senate and outside for final treaty action, the committee had no further occasion for delay. If the Johnson amendment were defeated, a reservation could be submitted by the committee or by an individual senator.

Republican senators, occasionally in consultation with individual Democrats but never with authorized party spokesmen, had been working since early September on modification and elaboration of the four reservations initially reported by the foreign-relations committee. The mild reservationists took the largest role, and of these Lenroot and Kellogg were most active. Some pressure from Root and the less subtle efforts of Taft and A. Lawrence Lowell, president of Harvard, helped them.[92] But Lodge, acting for himself and the strong reservationist and irreconcilable Republicans, held high cards and played them.[93] Even some of those Republicans who were called "mild" or "moderate" because they stood against textual amendment insisted on reservations stronger than Taft, McCumber, or McNary approved. On balance, however, the reservations finally reported on 24 October reflected not only the influence but the work of the mild reservationists. On certain points, and to a certain degree, the mildest of the reservationists retained some freedom of action; but to a considerable degree even McCumber and McNary were committed to these reservations and the ratification resolution embodying them. Their obligation was to Lodge and to those he represented, who through Lodge had compromised with them; it was also to those who already had or soon would vote with them against amendments on the promise of satisfactory reservations.[94]

Lenroot was well satisfied with the "Lodge reservations," as they came to be misnamed.[95] Above all, he approved the reservation to Article Ten, although it was not worded precisely as he had suggested. But as he con-

92. Kendrick, "League of Nations and Republican Senate," pp. iv, 241; McNary to Taft, 28 October 1919, Box 459, Series 3, Taft Papers; Lenroot to Nellie Nichols, 16 November 1919, Irvine L. Lenroot Papers Addition; Root to Lodge, 26 September 1919, Box 161, Root Papers.

93. Garraty, *Henry Cabot Lodge*, p. 375; Lodge to Williams, Jr., 15 October 1919, to Mrs. Charles Prince, 16 October 1919, Lodge Papers.

94. Kendrick, "League of Nations and Republican Senate," pp. 235–36, 244; Fleming, *United States and the League of Nations*, p. 393; Colt to Taft, 25 October 1919, McNary to Taft, 28 October 1919, Short to Taft, 23 October 1919, Box 459, Henry to Taft, 7 November 1919, Box 460, "Report of W. H. Short on Treaty Situation in Washington . . . January 8th and 9th," enclosed in Short to Taft, 10 January 1920, Box 465, Series 3, Taft Papers; Stone, *Irreconcilables*, pp. 141–42; Lodge to Hays, 20 October 1919, Lodge Papers; Root to Elbert F. Baldwin, 20 October 1919, Box 137, Root Papers; *Milwaukee Sentinel*, 20–23 October, 18 May 1919. Lenroot was one of Short's informants in January, as to the genesis of the reservations. A Lenroot booster later asserted that Lenroot wrote eight of the fourteen reservations and helped with the other six. *Caspar Daily Tribune* quoted in the *Milwaukee Sentinel*, 21 July 1920. Sen. Arthur Capper said, "It is not going too far to say that he had the largest part in drafting the reservations in their final form. . . ." *Superior Telegram*, 28–29 August 1920, (weekend ed.).

95. Lenroot to Edward A. Ross, 20 October 1919, Box 11, Edward A. Ross Papers.

strued it, the reservation accomplished his two main and somewhat conflicting purposes—it removed the military obligation under Article Ten; and it left the boycott unimpaired, contrary to the wishes of many Republican senators. This last was an achievement that even McCumber saw as great.[96]

With the reservations decided upon among the Republicans, only the Johnson amendment remained to be disposed of before what Lenroot hoped would be the last act in the treaty drama. On the Johnson amendment, Lenroot pursued an intricate and not inconsequential course.

His early position, as of September and the first days of October, was against speedy action and in favor of a reservation on the equal voting question, and he drafted one that met with widespread approval among moderate Republicans. He questioned the effectiveness of the Johnson amendment but left the door open for acceptance of an amendment, Johnson's or someone else's, by distinguishing between amendments to the League covenant and to the treaty proper. Lenroot argued that once the League came into existence, which was imminent, the original members (chiefly or exclusively England, France, and Italy) could amend the covenant as they chose. Amendments to the covenant would not therefore require resubmission to a general peace conference, nor to Germany. Taft returned from a brief trip to Washington with the secondhand impression that Lenroot, among others, had not decided how he would vote on the Johnson amendment. The overall effect of his actions to that point, however, was to weaken Johnson's cause—he had consorted with the resisters and had provided them with the politically most attractive alternative to the amendment.[97]

In mid-October, Lenroot considered abandoning his reservation when its prospects looked hopeless. But after a declaration by Hale against all amendments rallied the forces opposed to the Johnson amendment, Lenroot reverted to his earlier approach. In an extended speech on 23 October, he acknowledged that the Johnson amendment would accomplish some minor purposes his reservation would not, reiterated the distinction between amendments to the covenant and to the treaty, and said he would vote for the Johnson amendment. But he spent most of his time pointing to its limitations, which only his reservation could meet and promised to offer the reservation later. The sophisticated Carter Field of the *New York Tribune,* most astute and well informed of those reporting the battle of the League, wrote that the death of the Johnson amendment, foreseen the previous week, had been clinched that day with the speeches of Colt, Walter

96. *CR* 66:1, 1919, vol. 58, pt. 6, p. 6338; 1919, vol. 58, pt. 8, pp. 7942–50, 66:2, 1920, vol. 59, pt. 4, p. 4214; Francis McCumber to Taft, 24 October, 8 November 1919, Box 460, "Report of W. H. Short on Treaty Situation in Washington . . . January 8th and 9th," enclosed in Short to Taft, Box 465, Series 3, Taft Papers.

97. *CR* 66:1, 1919, vol. 58, pt. 6, p. 6273; 1919, vol. 58, pt. 7, pp. 6445, 6450. Anderson, Diary, 1 October 1919, Box 4, Anderson Papers; Taft to Lowell, 5 October 1919, Townsend to Taft, 9 October 1919, Box 458, Series 3, Taft Papers.

Edge, and Lenroot. Field went on to give the text of Lenroot's reservation.[98]

On 27 October the Senate rejected the Johnson amendment by a vote of thirty-eight to forty. Had every senator been present, however, the margin against it would have been greater. Lenroot voted for the amendment, as he did for two others of similar nature, yet Kellogg, one of nine Republicans to vote in the negative on the first test, freely noted that only the promise of Lenroot's reservation made it possible to marshal so many opposition votes.[99]

Non-committee amendments, none of which were accorded much chance, remained to be acted on before the Senate could take up the reservations. When a group of nine, Lenroot among them, agreed to reject all the amendments, the decision sealed their doom.[100] From 30 October through 6 November, amendments by La Follette, Lodge, and others were defeated or withdrawn. In addition to his votes, Lenroot contributed a long argument against Borah's proposed amendment that Article Ten be stricken from the League charter. He was, in effect, beginning debate on the most important of the reservations. In addition to comments he had made earlier on the same subject, Lenroot took Borah up on the question of whether American participation and acquiescence in a Council decision would not result in a moral obligation on Congress to accept that decision. This was one of the principal arguments of the irreconcilables against the treaty. Lenroot's comment was: "Mr. President, it certainly is a most novel proposition that if a principal sends an agent, and the agent is given authority only to make recommendations back to the principal, . . . the principal feels himself obligated to carry out the recommendations of the agent." To this Borah replied that "if no one were involved except the agent and the principal that would be a very clear proposition but when I send my agent to deal in honor with eight other men and they deal with him as my agent and agree upon a program, he being my agent, I owe something to those eight men." In return, Lenroot said:

> Very well . . . Then I will state the proposition under that situation. A principal sends an agent to meet with a dozen other agents representing a dozen other principals, the agent only having the power to make recommendations, and, acting jointly, they make recommendations, and the principal feels obligated to be bound to carry out the recommendations they make, which is quite as novel as the other proposition to which I referred.[101]

---

98. *Milwaukee Sentinel,* 17 October 1919; *New York Tribune,* 11, 13, 17 October 1919; *CR* 66:1, 1919, vol. 58, pt. 7, pp. 7362–66. See also *CR* 66:1, 1919, vol. 58, pt. 8, pp. 7685–86 for a 29 October reiteration.

99. Finch, "Treaty of Peace with Germany," pp. 171–72; *New York Tribune,* 28, 30 October 1919; Colt to Taft, 25 October [*sic*] 1919, Kellogg to Taft, 27 October 1919, Box 459, Series 3, Taft Papers.

100. Memo, 29 October 1919, Talcott Williams to Taft, 31 October 1919, Box 459, Series 3, Taft Papers.

101. *CR* 66:1, 1919, vol. 58, pt. 8, pp. 7948–50.

While Lenroot denied that the obligation to go to war was the result of American participation in Council decisions, he continued to believe that Article Ten, nevertheless, involved an unacceptable obligation to defend members against aggression, devolving directly on member states irrespective of Council or Assembly action. For this reason, he insisted on a reservation and considered the committee's not perfect but adequate. He took pains, however, to distinguish between Article Ten and other articles that he had long judged beneficial. In defense of these, he argued that in several instances Council recommendations would not be binding; in other cases, the obligation assumed, as to acceptance of arbitration and the submission of international questions to inquiry by the League, were obligations that should be assumed.[102]

While the amendments were being debated on the floor, the Democrats planned the battle strategy in their offices and committee rooms. Pending new word from the president, Hitchcock, supported by Underwood and Pomerene, secured the acquiescence of his colleagues in an updated version of the strategy that he had pursued somewhat erratically since July. The Democrats would seek to improve the reservations as they came up but without expecting much or any success. Then they would vote against the resolution of ratification with the "Lodge reservations." Afterwards, they thought the parliamentary situation would permit not only a vote on ratification without reservations but, presuming defeat of that by the votes of Democrats and irreconcilables, on a new set of milder reservations, which would be drawn up in consultation with the Republican mild reservationists. They had the promise of favorable rulings from Vice-President Marshall, but in the event the Republicans remained sufficiently unified to override these and to restrict the options and turn the Senate to other matters, the Democrats thought they could keep raising the treaty question and thus show the country which party was obstructing action. Underwood had assured Taft early in October that a two-thirds majority was required to postpone action on a treaty indefinitely.[103]

Although Lenroot was one of those with whom the Democrats hoped to deal directly before the end of November, in his mind the time for such negotiations had passed. He was willing to make minor concessions to the Democrats, but he realized that now, more than ever—in light of the pledges

102. Ibid., pp. 7946–49.

103. *New York Tribune*, 18, 25 October, 2 November 1919; *Milwaukee Sentinel*, 22, 23 October 1919; memo, 29 October, Talcott Williams to Taft, 31 October 1919, Gus Karger to Taft, 29 October 1919, Box 459, confidential memo, Talcott Williams, n.d., enclosed in William H. Short to Taft, 6 November 1919, Box 460, Series 3, Taft Papers; Ashurst, *A Many-Colored Toga*, diary entries, 1, 7 November 1919, pp. 111–13; Rickey to Short, 1 November 1919, Box 17, League to Enforce Peace Papers; Taft to A. Lawrence Lowell, 5 October 1919, Box 459, Series 3, Taft Papers. Hitchcock may have been heartened by several private polls indicating that more than twenty Republicans favored only mild reservations. "Treaty Poll as per 'g' " and "Favorable to Treaty with mild reservations as per 'K'," n.d. (late October or early November 1919), vol. 2, Hitchcock Papers.

made and the drift of national opinion—no considerable number of Republicans could be detached from their party. Thus, compromise, if it were to occur at all, must be through Lodge. And he had reason to believe that Lodge would listen. Meanwhile, prospects for ratification would improve if Democrats could be made to see that the Republicans were unified behind the "Lodge reservations," and compromise would have to be on the basis of those.[104]

On the morning of 7 November, Hitchcock was at last permitted to see the president. The senator had become pessimistic and dubious of his own strategy, but under the watchful eyes of Mrs. Wilson and Doctor Grayson, who monitored the interview, he could not present the situation fully. The fact that Lodge's name was attached to the Republican reservations made it inexpedient if not impossible to state the case in unvarnished form. Furthermore, Hitchcock did not foresee all that would occur after the Lodge resolution has been voted on. He did realize that it might be necessary to shift course but found consolation in an agreement by which he would keep the president informed through Mrs. Wilson. For his part, following the interview Wilson remained content in the belief that in one way or another the treaty and covenant could gain ratification without destructive concessions.[105]

All that Hitchcock really got from the interview was authorization to use his own judgment to a limited extent in the battle that would ensue. But he was not authorized to accept the Lodge reservations and so stated to the press.[106] He put the best possible face on it, suggesting that the president was open to compromise on reservations. But when the time came, all he offered were the four reservations Wilson had given him prior to his tour and a fifth of his own based on conversation with the president.[107] These had already proved unacceptable, and, more important, they were not to be part of the instrument of ratification.[108] In his own mind, there lingered

104. Kendrick, "League of Nations and Republican Senate," pp. 253–56, 260; McNary to Taft, 28 October 1919, Box 459, Talcott Williams to Taft, 4 November 1919, Box 460, Series 3, Taft Papers; Ashurst, *A Many-Colored Toga,* diary entry, 7 November 1919, p. 119; *New York Tribune,* 6 November 1919; Bonsal, *Unfinished Business,* pp. 272–89; Garraty, *Henry Cabot Lodge,* pp. 375–76, note 8. The modifications of the Lodge reservations were to be transmitted to Wilson by Edward House, but the president, who perhaps had not seen them, made no response.

105. *New York Tribune,* 4 November 1919; Talcott Williams to Taft, 4 November 1919, Box 460, Series 3, Taft Papers; Bailey, *Great Betrayal,* pp. 177–78; Bonsal, *Unfinished Business,* p. 290; Josephus Daniels, *The Wilson Era: Years of War and After, 1917–1923,* p. 481. The recollections of Hitchcock, Mrs. Wilson, and Grayson have been widely used in reconstructing the interview, but, while useful for certain purposes, they must be used with great caution since it was easy, years later, to confuse the interviews of 7 and 17 November with one another and with meetings in January and March 1920.

106. *New York Tribune,* 8 November 1919; *Milwaukee Sentinel,* 7 November 1919.

107. Hitchcock to Mrs. Edith Bolling Wilson, 5 January 1920, vol. 2, Hitchcock Papers.

108. Stone, *Irreconcilables,* p. 141; Fleming, *United States and the League of Nations,* p. 494.

a fatal residue of misplaced hope for compromise between twenty to thirty Republicans after defeat of the Lodge resolution.[109]

From 7 November through 18 November, the Senate, in Committee of the Whole, approved the program to which virtually all Republicans had committed themselves, consisting of the preamble, twelve committee reservations, and two "from outside," on equal voting and on participation in the International Labor Organization. Committee reservations framed by Reed and Shields to which reservationists had not been committed were rejected, as were those offered by Hitchcock and others. Except for McCumber and Nelson in a few instances, Republican lines held solidly. By contrast, from four to twelve Democrats deserted their leaders on certain reservations.[110]

Lenroot's following reservation on equal voting was also adopted:

> The United States assumes no obligation to be bound by any election, decision, report, or finding of the council or assembly in which any member of the League and its self-governing dominions, colonies, or parts of empire, in the aggregate have cast more than one vote, and assumes no obligation to be bound by any decision, report, or finding of the council or assembly arising out of any dispute between the United States and any member of the League if such a member, or any self-governing dominion, colony, empire or part of empire united with it politically has voted.[111]

Some considered this reservation harsh, but it was milder than Johnson's alternative, which lost by only two votes. Denna Frank Fleming, pro-League historian, later concluded that it "was perhaps as mild as any statement could be, after the months of protest against the Dominion votes." In debate, Lenroot showed that it was not so drastic as many thought. As he construed the covenant, there were not many articles that provided for binding action by the Council or Assembly, when his reservation would take force. In those instances, if Britain wanted the United States to be bound, she could arrange to have but one vote cast.[112]

With the adoption of the Lenroot reservation, final action on the treaty was possible the following day. Already, Hitchcock had received his instructions from the president. On the morning of 17 November, the Nebraskan was granted an hour at the president's bedside. Wilson made it clear that if the Lodge resolution were adopted, he would pocket the treaty rather than complete its ratification. He felt the nation's honor was at stake; that the

109. Hitchcock to Mrs. Wilson, 13, 15, 17 November 1919, Box 193, Series 3, Wilson Papers; to Taft, 12 November 1919, Box 460, Karger to Taft, 17 November 1919, Box 461, Series 3, Taft Papers; Bailey, *Great Betrayal*, pp. 177–79.

110. Lodge to Robert M. Washburn, 15 November 1919, Lodge Papers; Kendrick, "League of Nations and Republican Senate," pp. 247–51; Finch, "Treaty of Peace with Germany," pp. 182–85; *Milwaukee Sentinel*, 16 November 1919.

111. Bailey, *Great Betrayal*, p. 392.

112. Fleming, *United States and the League of Nations*, p. 431; *CR* 66:1, 1919, vol. 58, pt. 9, p. 8739.

reservations would seriously weaken the treaty; and that they would require that all other powers, including Germany, be permitted similar privileges. Hitchcock, accepting the president's decision, still hoped for compromise following the deadlock. For the moment, what he wanted was a strong letter from the president that he could show his colleagues, to hold them in line. Wilson, ignoring counsels of compromise, complied.[113]

The evening papers of 17 November carried word of Wilson's attitude, as announced by Hitchcock. The president would not deposit the instrument of ratification based on the Lodge reservations. At the least, the preamble must be omitted and the reservation to Article Ten changed. In this last, mild reservationists found an opening for compromise, and they met together the following morning to plan common action.[114]

Lenroot agreed with Root and the others that the preamble could well be modified to the extent of eliminating the demand for affirmative notes of acceptance by three of the great powers. He thought that the change, to permit silent acquiescence, could be effected in the Senate and would pave the way for ratification. Outside observers agreed, after the fact.[115]

The mild reservationists further agreed that if Hitchcock insisted on additional concessions, he would have to propose them through Lodge. Lenroot conveyed the message to the Democrats.[116]

At their 18 November conference, the mild reservationists also agreed that, if the Lodge resolution were defeated, they would support a motion to reconsider. But they would not vote with the Democrats to sustain anticipated rulings by Marshall that would open the door to reservationist resolutions other than Lodge's.[117]

Despite the caucuses, speeches, parliamentary maneuvers, and frantic conferences by senators on 19 November, for that day at least the treaty was expected to be defeated. The Republican position was already firm and the Democratic position became so after Hitchcock read the president's letter to the caucus that morning. Nevertheless, Lenroot participated in the day's business. To some degree, he acted on the vain hope that Democrats

113. On the attitude of Hitchcock and Wilson see especially Hitchcock to Mrs. Wilson, 17, 18 November 1919, Box 193, Series 2, Wilson Papers; Wimer, "Senator Hitchcock and the League of Nations," pp. 196–97; and Smith, *Great Departure*. Regarding compromise advice see Blum, *Tumulty*, p. 224; Edith Bolling Wilson, *Memoir*, pp. 296–97; Bailey, *Great Betrayal*, pp. 182–83; Frank I. Cobb to Taft, 12 November 1919, Box 460, E. A. Grozier to Taft, 17 November 1919, Clark Howell to Taft, 17 November 1919, Box 461, Series 3, Taft Papers. The genesis of the Wilson letter is discussed in Blum, *Tumulty*, pp. 226–27; and Wimer, "Senator Hitchcock and the League of Nations," p. 196.

114. Wimer, "Senator Hitchcock and the League of Nations," p. 203; *Milwaukee Sentinel*, 18 November 1919.

115. *New York Tribune*, 18 November 1919; *Milwaukee Sentinel*, 2 December 1919; Root to Kellogg, 12 November 1919, Box 137, Root Papers; *CR* 66:2, 1919, vol. 59, pt. 1, p. 401; Cobb to Taft, 20 November 1919, William to Horace Taft, 26 November 1919, Box 461, Series 3, Taft Papers.

116. *New York Tribune*, 18 November 1919; Lodge to Frederick Gillett, 26 July 1920, Lodge Papers.

117. *Milwaukee Sentinel*, 19 November 1919; *Superior Telegram*, 18 November 1919.

who earlier had been prepared to accept the Lodge reservations might still be induced to do so, despite the president's letter. More important, he acted as spokesman at once for Lodge and for the mild reservationists, preparing the way, he hoped, for ratification in the near future.

Lenroot reviewed the covenant article by article, arguing that most articles had remained unchanged by any reservation and that none had suffered improper harm. When he came to Article Ten Lenroot said: "I would resign my seat in the Senate, Mr. President, before I would vote to ratify this treaty with the obligation imposed by article 10 as the president of the United States asks us to accept it." Article Eleven had been unaffected by reservations, and Wilson had once called it his "favorite article," Lenroot noted. He praised articles relating to arbitration, compulsory inquiry, the cooling-off period, and the boycott, and noted that these useful articles had been affected by reservations only slightly. "The heart of it, so denominated by President Wilson, will be left. The beneficial articles, in so far as settling disputes is concerned, will be left intact," Lenroot said. "What is it that will be taken away? Obligations only, Mr. President." Then Lenroot considered each reservation, explaining and defending each one. He concluded with the hope that the treaty would not be left for the 1920 campaign and the warning that if it were, "we will welcome the issue." The treaty had not been widely read, but the fourteen reservations would be, and they would be approved by the people.[118]

Historian Jack Kendrick later judged that Lenroot had given "a very sound and well-balanced analysis." [119] Contemporary observers, noting that Hays had been conferring with Republican senators that afternoon, thought that when Lenroot issued the political warning to the Democrats, "he was speaking by the book." Who wrote the book remained undetermined, but the view gained further credence when, a few days later, Lodge issued a statement using almost the exact words Lenroot had. It was announced that millions of copies of the reservations, together with Lenroot's speech defending them, would be printed and distributed.[120]

Not long after Lenroot's speech, debate finally came to a close, with a last-minute appeal by McCumber to the Democrats. But the ensuing vote on the Lodge resolution showed that mild reservationist pleas were far less effective with Democrats than Wilson's letter, reinforced by Burleson's lobbying. The vote was thirty-nine to fifty-five against the resolution. Four Democrats voted for Lodge's resolution, but the rest joined the irreconcilables in defeating it.[121]

When a motion was made to reconsider, Lenroot and other Republican reservationists broke from Lodge to pass it.[122] Had Hitchcock even then

118. *CR* 66:1, 1919, vol. 58, pt. 9, pp. 8771–73.

119. Kendrick, "League of Nations and Republican Senate," pp. 262–63.

120. *Milwaukee Sentinel,* 22 November 1919; *New York Tribune,* 22 November 1919.

121. Stone, *Irreconcilables,* p. 145.

122. Kendrick, "League of Nations and Republican Senate," p. 265; *CR* 66:1, 1919, vol. 58, pt. 9, pp. 8786–87.

promised compromise on the basis of a change in the preamble, as Lenroot proposed, he might have secured ratification.[123] But he did not and instead attempted to get a vote on his own reservations. The vice-president ruled such a motion in order, but with the sole exception of McCumber, the mild reservationists voted solidly with their party in overturning the ruling. Lenroot contributed to the discussion of the difficult parliamentary point at issue and served as parliamentary watchdog for his party.[124] Finally, Pomerene proposed a conciliation committee of six, including Lodge and Hitchcock. Again, the Republicans stood virtually united in opposition. Lenroot condemned the idea on two related grounds—on Article Ten there could be no negotiation and the obligation, which remained in Hitchcock's proposal, could not be accepted. Furthermore, none of the reservations had been written by irreconcilables, as Democratic spokesmen had suggested; they were the work of the supporters of the treaty and wholly defensible.[125]

Finally the Senate voted again on the Lodge reservation, which was defeated, but the reservationists gained three new Democratic recruits, Pomerene, Robert Owen, and Henry Myers, to go with the four who had already bolted. Now, to the surprise of many, Lodge permitted a vote on a resolution offered by Underwood for ratification without reservations. The motion lost by a vote of thirty-eight to fifty-three—seven Democrats voting against and of the Republicans only McCumber voting in favor.[126]

Lodge admitted that the treaty had been disposed of and, thus, might be withdrawn and resubmitted by the president. At the same time, he introduced a resolution declaring that peace existed with Germany, in effect reviving the old Knox resolution. That done, and minor business disposed of, the Senate voted to adjourn sine die.[127]

Although their attitudes toward the League and ratification differed markedly, when Lenroot returned from Wisconsin on 9 December, he felt that he could and should work through Lodge. Lenroot still shared a number of Lodge's views, saw Lodge's assistance as vital, and believed that he could nudge Lodge in the right direction.

Lenroot told a newsman that there would be no modification of the Lodge reservations, but privately he remained willing to compromise on the preamble and on minor verbal changes in other reservations.[128]

On 11 and 13 December, Lenroot participated in the session's first open

123. *New York Tribune,* 20 November 1919; Karger to Taft, 20 November 1919, Box 461, Series 3, Taft Papers; Raymond Clapper in *Washington Evening Post,* 20 November 1919, Box 6, Raymond Clapper Papers, LC.

124. Kendrick, "League of Nations and Republican Senate," pp. 265–66; *CR* 66:1, 1919, vol. 58, pt. 9, pp. 8787–90; *Milwaukee Sentinel,* 4 November 1919.

125. *CR* 66:1, 1919, vol. 58, pt. 9, p. 8788; *CR* 66:2, 1919, vol. 59, pt. 1, p. 539.

126. Bailey, *Great Betrayal,* p. 191.

127. *New York Tribune,* 20 November 1919; *Milwaukee Sentinel,* 20 November 1919.

128. *New York Tribune,* 10 December 1919; Rickey to Short, n.d. (December 1919), enclosed in Short to Taft, 12 December 1919, Box 462, Series 3, Taft Papers.

discussion of the treaty situation in the Senate. Much of the debate was political, turning on which party was responsible for the impasse, and Lenroot rallied to the defense of Lodge and the Republicans. With Lodge, also, he said that it was up to the Democrats to make an offer of compromise, since only they, following the wishes of the president, could supply votes enough for ratification. More positively, however, when Hitchcock pointed to Lodge's statement about refusal to compromise, Lenroot said: "Does the Senator from Nebraska believe that is the position of the Senators on this side of the aisle?" A moment later, he added that Lodge and others had stated their willingness to consider proposals of compromise. Lodge quickly confirmed Lenroot's comment. Some believed that Lenroot's bid for compromise had been made with the consent of Lodge, but that is not certain. In any case, Lenroot had not moved himself or Lodge far from Lodge's initial position. When Hitchcock approached Lenroot and asked him to submit compromise proposals, Lenroot said he would not—the Lodge resolution embodied compromise—now it was up to the Democrats to say what they would accept. Hitchcock insisted, at least, that the Republicans must abandon the position that any Democratic proposal must have the endorsement of the president. As one who constantly urged the Democrats to act on their own, Lenroot could not very well refuse that overture. In fact, after the president announced the next day that he would make no concessions, Lenroot urged the Democrats to act independently.[129] He quickly saw signs of such effort that on 15 December he announced that he would not at that time support a resolution for separate peace, predicting that ratification would soon make it unnecessary.[130]

Three days later, as compromise efforts among the senatorial rank and file accelerated, Lenroot and the mild reservationists learned that the foreign-relations committee, without prior consultation with any of the mild reservationists, voted out the revised Knox resolution. The action reflected Lodge's current inclination, which was to keep the United States free of the obligations of the League and the Versailles treaty.[131]

The majority leader had gone too far. With pressure mounting for treaty ratification in some form and with reservationism developing strongly among the Democrats, the mild reservationists had no reason to abandon hope for the treaty and every reason to take offense at Lodge's action.[132]

A group of them met on the morning of Sunday, 21 December, and that evening called on Lodge to notify him of their strong opposition to the Knox

129. *CR* 66:2, 1919, vol. 59, pt. 1, pp. 401, 535, 539–40; *Milwaukee Sentinel*, 12, 14 December 1919; *New York Tribune*, 15, 17 December 1919.

130. *Milwaukee Sentinel*, 16 December 1919.

131. Fleming, *United States and the League of Nations*, p. 403; Lodge to Brooks Adams, 17 December 1919, to Williams, Jr., 20 December 1919, Lodge Papers.

132. *Milwaukee Sentinel*, 18, 19, 23 December 1919; Rickey to Short, 22 December 1919, Box 463, Series 3, Taft Papers; Grantham, "Southern Senators and the League," p. 196; Bailey, *Great Betrayal*, pp. 225–26.

resolution and to urge the need for compromise and speedy ratification. Lenroot was not among them, but in a statement to the press Kellogg named him and McNary as among those who would not support the Knox resolution until shown that ratification with reservations was impossible.[133]

The Knox resolution was checked for the time, but on the subject of reservations the party leaders remained in disagreement. Individual senators, less constrained than Lodge or Hitchcock, soon became involved in drafting and discussing reservation modifications. Among the Democrats, Bryanites such as Kenneth McKellar of Tennessee took the lead; the mild reservationists acted for the Republicans in looking for a package that could command sixty-four votes. While observers doubted that, if forced to choose, Lenroot would part company with Lodge, he was nevertheless "more active in the interests of a compromise than any other Republican senator" in this period.[134] But Article Ten remained the major problem, and Democrats also complained about Lenroot's reservation on equal voting, the preamble, and some other features of the Lodge reservations. With a Jackson Day statement from the president imminent, the negotiators agreed for the moment to disagree but with the intention of resuming their efforts whatever Wilson might say.[135]

The president, still ill and utterly deluded, urged on the Jackson Day celebrants only interpretive reservations. Perhaps casting himself as the League's prospective champion again, he proposed that if need be the Democrats convert the 1920 presidential election into a "solemn referendum" on the League issue. But Bryan, alerted in advance to Wilson's message, spoke afterwards and derided it as impractical on all counts. Bryan called for compromise.[136] Recognizing the temporary confusion of the Democrats, Lenroot postponed a 9 January meeting between mild reservationists and Lodge that he had arranged. By way of preliminary to the critical negotiations ahead, he decried the president's talk of interpretive reservations and warned that "the reservations must be vital." Privately, he helped

133. McNary to Taft, 22 December 1919, Box 463, Series 3, Taft Papers; *New York Tribune,* 21 December 1919.

134. Ashurst, *A Many-Colored Toga,* diary entry, 4 January 1920, p. 120; *New York Tribune,* 1, 4, 5, 7, 8 January 1920; Taft to Karger, 1 January 1920, Karger to Taft, 3 January 1920, Charles D. Warner to Short, 5 January 1920, enclosed in Short to Taft, 6 January 1920, Box 465, Series 3, Taft Papers; Edna Huber Church in the *Milwaukee Sentinel,* 28 March 1920; *New York Tribune,* 4, 9 January 1920.

135. *Milwaukee Sentinel,* 30 December 1919; *New York Journal,* 3 January 1920; Root to Theodore Marburg, 6 January 1920, in John H. Latane, ed., *The Development of the League of Nations Idea: Documents and Correspondence of Theodore Marburg,* vol. 2 of 2 vols., p. 665; McNary to Taft, 8 January 1920, Box 465, Series 3, Taft Papers.

136. On Wilson's health and his misconceptions about the immediate situation and the future prospects see Lawrence, *Woodrow Wilson,* p. 290; Herbert C. Hoover, *The Ordeal of Woodrow Wilson,* p. 275; David F. Houston, *Eight Years with Wilson's Cabinet, 1913–1920,* pp. 47–48, 92; Daniels, *Years of War and After,* p. 481; Cary T. Grayson, *Woodrow Wilson: An Intimate Portrait,* pp. 106, 114–17.

to convince William Short, executive secretary of the League to Enforce Peace, that the Lodge reservations were justifiable and reflected extensive compromise.[137]

Although Democratic opinion varied widely following the president's letter, a welter of conferences ensued, involving factions within each party, the factions and the party leaders, and bipartisan groups. Lenroot was never more active. At an early stage of informal bipartisan negotiations initiated by McKellar and Colt, the latter brought in Lenroot. He came only on the condition that Lodge soon be included, although a number of senators of both parties hoped to secure agreement without reference to the party leaders. But among the Democrats, Hitchcock had already succeeded in getting acceptance of the premise that any reservation agreed upon must be acceptable to the president. Given that stringent prerequisite, which in effect restored the old game of a united Democracy acting as siren to individual Republicans, Lenroot's approach made good sense. It accorded not only with his view of the kind of reservations that were needed but with the continuing realities of the situation on the Republican side, where twenty votes still had to be obtained.[138]

On 15 January, the long-sought bipartisan conference began in Lodge's office, where with some interruptions it continued for two weeks. Hitchcock, whose continuance as acting minority leader hindered the conference, brought with him a representative group of Democratic negotiators who, on balance, figured to be more conciliatory than he—there was McKellar of the Bryan group; Owen, a leader among those who had acted without consulting the president; Simmons, who had been in McKellar's bipartisan conference and who would take compromise as the price for ratification; and Thomas Walsh, who was opposed to strong reservations but understood the need for compromise and had urged it on the president. Afterwards, Pomerene occasionally substituted for Owen. These were men of ability, and ones who commanded respect in the Senate.[139]

The Democrats were met by Lodge; Harry New of Indiana, a member of the foreign-relations committee who represented Lodge's followers; Kellogg, representing the mild reservationists, who had been negotiating with Democrats on the basis of very substantial Republican compromises; and Lenroot, whom Carter Field described as representing the "middle ground" Republicans and "who had been working for a compromise on the basis of making a few concessions on the Lodge reservations." [140] This group, too,

137. *New York Tribune,* 10 January 1920; "Report of W. H. Short on Treaty Situation in Washington . . . January 8th and 9th," enclosed in Short to William H. Taft, 10 January 1920, Box 465, Series 3, Taft Papers.

138. H. Maurice Darling, "Who Kept the United States Out of the League of Nations?," pp. 200, 211; *New York Journal,* 15 January 1920; *New York Times,* 16 January 1920; *New York Tribune,* 13 January 1920.

139. Carter Field, writing in the *New York Journal,* 16 January 1920, characterized them in general terms. Lodge refers to Pomerene in Lodge to Gillett, 26 July 1920, Lodge Papers.

140. *New York Journal,* 16 January 1920.

possessed more than average ability for the task at hand. But Democrats criticized Lodge's choice of associates, regarding only Kellogg as conciliatory.[141]

The Democrats were correct in this judgment of Lenroot. Like Lodge and New, he was eager to consider and revise Democratic proposals but was reluctant to initiate compromise. The Lodge reservations were already acceptable to him, and he would not consider substantial changes in the major ones, notably the second on Article Ten. From the standpoint of tactics, too, he shied from major concessions. The president might at any time exert his influence against a proposal for even a tentative agreement. For the Republicans to commit themselves prematurely, courting further division in their own ranks, only to fall short of the necessary two-thirds in the Senate, seemed foolhardy from every standpoint. By requiring that the Democrats initiate proposals, Lenroot, Lodge, and New risked less and gained more, in the sense that the Democratic negotiators would have to secure substantial party support for whatever was agreed upon, with the president's consent or without it. Precautions were warranted, for Mrs. Wilson was protecting her husband from all proposals of compromise,[142] and Hitchcock himself entered negotiations with the intention of proposing, after agreement had been reached and the Republicans had committed themselves fully, that any reservations adopted "should be put in the form of interpretations and understandings." [143]

For Lenroot to insist that the Democrats initiate proposals, he had to believe that Lodge would, in good faith, consider such proposals. Lenroot had conferred frequently with Lodge in the days preceding the bipartisan conference and had good reason to think that Lodge did indeed seek agreement.[144] Lenroot was not mistaken. Lodge understood the need to conciliate McNary and his associates, who kept threatening to join the Democrats in bringing the treaty to the floor; and he was pressured from outside groups clamoring for ratification in some form. Furthermore, Lodge wanted to change certain reservations and found the conference an occasion to do so gracefully. While unwilling to yield on what he considered matters of principle, he was now anxious to test the possibilities of verbal compromise and even relished the idea of securing adoption in the Senate and putting the final ratification decision to Wilson.[145]

Meanwhile, Lenroot made preparations for the conferences and participated in them. Encouraged by early signs of progress, he initiated some

141. *New York Times,* 17 January 1920; *New York Journal,* 17 January 1920; Hitchcock to Tumulty, 16 January 1920, Box 195, Series 2, Wilson Papers.

142. Blum, *Tumulty,* pp. 232–36.

143. Hitchcock to Tumulty, 16 January 1920, Box 195, Series 2, Wilson Papers.

144. In addition to the conferences referred to above, others are mentioned in the *Milwaukee Sentinel,* 11, 15 January 1920.

145. Garraty, *Henry Cabot Lodge,* p. 284; Stone, *Irreconcilables,* pp. 148, 154; Lodge to W. S. Bigelow, 15 January 1920, to George Harvey, 16 January 1920, to Williams, Jr., 2 February 1920, to Gillett, 26 July 1920, Lodge Papers.

revisions on his equal voting reservation, which met with general, though tentative, approval and got the conference over a major sandbar. The conferees passed over the issues that were most controversial, and by the evening of 21 January, Lodge was able to write: "I think we could come to agreement except on two of the absolutely vital things, on which we will not yield because principles are involved. How it will finally come out I do not know." Lodge blamed Wilson for the difficulty that remained respecting the Monroe Doctrine and Article Ten, and Lenroot agreed that "it all depends on the democrats." [146]

Whether in response to renewed pressure from mild reservationists, or by coincidence, when the conferees turned again to Article Ten on 22 January, they made such progress that Hitchcock afterwards reported to the president that "both sides are seriously considering a proposition," which he enclosed.[147] "We resume consideration of it tomorrow afternoon," he informed Wilson, perhaps ruefully.[148] The Republican conferees agreed that the situation now looked more favorable than previously.[149]

The events of the following day have become legendary. Before the conferees could resume their deliberations, Lodge was summoned to the office of Knox, where he encountered eight angry irreconcilables. By phone, he soon informed the bipartisan group that they would have to postpone their meeting; then, for two hours alone and a third joined by New, he heard out Borah and his colleagues. They quoted Lodge's words back to him, that the Lodge reservations were an "irreducible minimum," and negotiation over verbal changes was "silly." The irreconcilables also threatened an immediate bolt, which would result in a third party. And they warned Lodge that thirty-eight senators would vote against ratification if he consummated the prospective agreement with the Democrats.[150]

The political threat, which has been viewed as decisive, was real enough. Borah, Johnson, Lawrence Sherman, and others were in dead earnest. Already there was talk of a third party supported by William Randolph Hearst and his press. Borah and Johnson were magnetic, compelling speakers, as

146. *Milwaukee Sentinel,* 17 January 1920; Lodge to Williams, Jr., 2 February 1920, to Gillett, 26 July 1920, to J. D. H. Luce, 21 January 1920, Lodge Papers; Hitchcock to Tumulty, 16, 17 January 1920, Box 195, Series 2, Wilson Papers. On the importance and difficulty of the equal voting questions see the *New York Tribune,* 1 January 1920, Taft to George M. Wrong, 14 January 1920, Letterbook, vol. 93, Part 1, Series 8, Taft Papers; and *New York Times,* 20 January 1920.

147. Taft to Karger, 21 January 1920, to McCumber, 21 January 1920, Box 466, Series 3, Taft Papers; Darling, "Who Kept the United States Out of the League?," p. 203; *New York Times,* 21 January 1920; Grace Lynch to Robert M. La Follette, Jr., 23 January 1920, Box 112, Series B, La Follette FC.

148. Hitchcock to Wilson, 22 January 1920, Box 195, Series 2, Wilson Papers.

149. *New York Times,* 23 January 1920; Stone, *Irreconcilables,* p. 155.

150. Bailey, *Great Betrayal,* p. 230; Garraty, *Henry Cabot Lodge,* pp. 385–87; Fleming, *United States and the League of Nations,* p. 408; Stone, *Irreconcilables,* pp. 156–57; *New York Times,* 24 January 1920.

was La Follette, who under some circumstances might join them. Undoubt-edly, the threat influenced Lodge.[151]

Not much attention has been given to other factors. The statement by the irreconcilables that thirty-eight senators would vote against the treaty if Lodge yielded was entirely credible. Frelinghuysen and then Howard Sutherland of West Virginia, who were both reservationists, issued strong public warnings. A week earlier, all but three or four Republicans had told their party's conferees that they would not consent to substantive changes in the Article Ten reservation. Hale reiterated the warning to Lodge.[152] Lenroot and Kellogg also opposed any reservation to Article Ten that would leave an obligation; that being so, the conferees were farther from reaching an agreement on 22 January than some hoped and others feared.[153] Lodge was influenced by word from Sir Edward Grey that he would explain to his countrymen the historical and constitutional aspects of the reservationist movement and in effect make publicly clear what he had come to tell the president privately, had he been permitted an audience, that Great Britain would accept the reservations.[154] Furthermore, it was with some seriousness that negotiations resumed the following week, despite the irreconcilables' effort of 23 January.

The four Republicans stood together on Monday of 26 January. They insisted that two-thirds of the Senate could not be secured if there were any change in the reservations on the Monroe Doctrine or Article Ten. Although the Democrats declined to yield on the following day, the conferees agreed to try again. On Friday, 30 January, they met for the last time. The Republicans rejected several alternative reservations to Article Ten, one fashioned by Taft, as suggesting an obligation. They offered none of their own. Thus, the group dispersed, knowing that they would soon discuss the treaty again on the Senate floor.[155]

For Lenroot, word of a public statement by Lord Grey came as good news. Grey's lengthy letter to the *London Times* explained and in effect accepted

151. Borah to Heinemann, 16 January 1920, Box 552, to Lodge, 24 January 1920, Box 550, Borah Papers; Stone, *Irreconcilables,* pp. 187–88 (regarding Sherman); Clifford B. Liljekvist, "Senator Hiram Johnson" (Ph.D. diss.), pp. 206–7; William A. Swanberg, *Citizen Hearst: A Biography of William Randolph Hearst,* pp. 333–35; *New York Tribune,* 28 January 1920; Garraty, *Henry Cabot Lodge,* p. 387.

152. *New York Times,* 21, 24 January 1920; *New York Journal,* 17 January 1920; Taft to Karger, 2 February 1920, Box 467, Series 3, Taft Papers.

153. Darling, "Who Kept the United States Out of the League?," p. 210; Stone, *Irreconcilables,* p. 156; *CR* 66:2, 1920, vol. 59, pt. 5, pp. 4323–24.

154. Kenneth McKellar to Hitchcock, 26 June 1920, vol. 2, Hitchcock Papers; Lodge to Lord Charnwood, 24 January 1920, Lodge Papers; Stone, *Irreconcilables,* pp. 160–61.

155. Newspaper reports may be supplemented by Lodge to Louis A. Coolidge, 28 January 1920, and to J. Otis Wardell, 29 January 1920, to Coolidge, 2 February 1920, and to Gillett, 26 July, 21 October 1920, Lodge Papers. Lenroot expressed his judgment of the Taft reservation in conversation with Short. "Substance of an Interview with Senator Lenroot, Sunday, Feb. 29, 1920," in Short to Lowell, League to Enforce Peace, Box 11, A. Lawrence Lowell Papers, Widener Library.

all the reservations except the one on equal voting. Though he wrote as a private citizen, it was reasonable to presume that Grey spoke also for his government. Lenroot told newsmen that the letter "should make it very much easier to reach an agreement when the treaty again comes up on the floor." Lodge, seizing the initiative from Hitchcock, announced that he would call up the treaty.[156]

As the Senate began its second consideration of the treaty, in mid-February, mild reservationists were surprisingly optimistic, while irreconcilables despondently predicted ratification. Hays urged ratification before the 1920 campaign; New and other reservationists not of the mild group echoed the thought; many Democrats evinced a desire to compromise; and Lodge was conciliatory. While McCumber preferred to deal directly with the Democrats, Lenroot and the other mild reservationists still saw no reason not to work through Lodge, nor any alternative to that course, and so assured Lodge. In conference with them, Lodge consented to offer many of the reservations tentatively agreed to at the bipartisan conference, all of them more moderate than their November counterparts, and expressed willingness to submit to Republicans and then the Democrats new proposals on Article Ten and the Monroe Doctrine. Lenroot and Kellogg prepared three new versions of the Article Ten reservation, and Lodge accepted one of them. Although Hitchcock promptly rejected it, the increasing restiveness of the Democracy augured well for some form of compromise.[157]

The president remained intransigent. He would not have accepted the bipartisan conference's Article Ten reservation, and in early February he rejected compromise suggestions from Carter Glass, who was until recently his secretary of the treasury and now a senator from Virginia.[158] Despite the president's view, which was elaborated in a favorable tone by Hitchcock at a 7 February caucus, many Democratic senators continued to agitate for meaningful compromise.[159]

In late February and the first days of March, as senators began voting on reservations and conferring on the more difficult ones to come later, Lenroot thought there was a chance of success. According to his analysis, whatever his earlier desires, Lodge now definitely wanted to ratify and keep the issue out of the political campaign. With that in view, he was willing to make verbal, though not substantive changes in Article Ten, a position that Len-

156. *New York Tribune,* 2, 3 February 1920.

157. Karger to Taft, 5, 6, 11 February 1920, Taft to Karger, 7 February 1920, Box 467, Series 3, Taft Papers; Beveridge to Coolidge, 6 February 1920, Coolidge to Beveridge, 11 February 1920, Box 219, Beveridge Papers; *New York Tribune,* 7–12 February 1920; *Milwaukee Sentinel,* 7–12 February 1920; Stone, *Irreconcilables,* p. 163; *CR* 66:2, 1920, vol. 59, pt. 5, p. 4321.

158. Wilson to Hitchcock, 26 January 1920, Box 195, Series 2, Wilson Papers; Wimer, "Senator Hitchcock and the League of Nations," pp. 200–201; Patterson, "Gilbert M. Hitchcock," pp. 463–64; Ashurst, *A Many-Colored Toga,* diary entry, 7 February 1920, pp. 122–23; Rixey Smith and Norman Beasley, *Carter Glass: A Biography,* pp. 201–3.

159. *New York Tribune,* 8 February 1920; Breckinridge Long, Diary, 11 February 1920, Box 2, Long Papers.

root approved and shared. The chief difficulty lay with Wilson and Hitch-cock, both of whom wanted the issue in the campaign, he thought. Lenroot pointed to Hitchcock's efforts to scuttle modification of reservations by voting with the Republicans and noted his frequent conferences with Borah. But he hoped, with the help of other mild reservationists, to expose the Hitchcock-Borah alliance "so fully as to make it impossible for Hitchcock to hold the Democratic Senators together in opposition to ratification of the amended Lodge reservations." [160]

Lenroot's actions on the Senate floor and in the conference rooms in February and March comported with that strategy. His most consistent theme in debate was criticism of Wilson and Hitchcock. As he had so often since 1913, Lenroot combined insurgent doctrine with the interests of Republican unity. In so doing, he was trying to be effective legislatively not just politically. Lenroot wanted no separation in Republican reservationist lines and foresaw no possibility of a massive Republican break toward as-sumption of obligations under Article Ten. Only on the basis of the Lodge reservations, modified as necessary to allow Democrats to save face, was ratification possible. "Middle grounders" such as Capper, Kenyon, Spencer, Cummins, and others had made that clear when treaty consideration resumed.[161] Underlying Lenroot's criticisms was the purpose of either forc-ing Hitchcock to ignore the president's wishes or to encourage rebellion among the Democrats by demonstrating the weakness, political and other-wise, in the position of supine acquiescence that Wilson and Hitchcock seemed to force on them.

Lenroot's approach was not entirely negative. He drafted and argued for changed reservations and was instrumental in the adoption of the new reservations on Shantung, equal voting, and other questions, often over the opposition of irreconcilable Republicans.[162] He also joined with other mild reservationists in pressuring Lodge to remain open-minded toward com-promise, despite threats from irreconcilables, while at the same time dis-couraging talk of rebellion from Lodge's leadership.[163] As "chief adviser to Senator Lodge in the treaty fight," as described by the New York Tribune, he exerted more than ordinary influence.[164]

On 8 March, the president dashed the hopes of mild reservationists. Irritated at constant pressure (he refused to see Senator Simmons to discuss a reservation to Article Ten), Wilson gave Hitchcock a written statement that he could use with recalcitrant Democrats. Wilson wrote that practically

160. "Substance of an Interview with Senator Lenroot, Sunday, Feb. 29, 1920," enclosed in Short to Lowell, 9 March 1920, League to Enforce Peace, Box 11, Lowell Papers.
161. New York Tribune, 15, 22 February 1920; Milwaukee Sentinel, 24 February 1920; Clapper, Diary, 21 February 1920, Box 6, Clapper Papers; Albert B. Cummins to Beveridge, 6 March 1920, Box 219, Beveridge Papers.
162. CR 66:2, 1920, vol. 59, pt. 4, pp. 3231, 3515–20, 3795–96, 3801–2, 3840–41, 3849–50, 3857–63, 4011–16, 4055–58, 4065.
163. New York Tribune, 2, 5, 7, 8 March 1920; Milwaukee Sentinel, 1 March 1920.
164. New York Tribune, 2, 5, 7, 8 March 1920; Milwaukee Sentinel, 1 March 1920.

all of the Lodge reservations in effect nullified treaty terms and he stressed the critical value of Article Ten. He went on to say, "I hear of reservationists and mild reservationists, but I cannot understand the difference between a nullifier and a mild nullifier." [165]

Wilson's letter had some immediate effect on wavering Democrats. It also infuriated mild reservationists. But it by no means ended either the hopes or the efforts of Lenroot and his colleagues. If only to keep their loyalty, Lodge also persisted in efforts to secure agreement. He consoled irreconcilables with the thought that Wilson would not complete ratification. Many Democrats continued to believe, to the contrary, that despite his letter the president would finally accept mild reservations and the influential Owen declared that he would not follow Wilson's lead. Republican reservationists, therefore, had grounds for continued hope of a two-thirds majority.[166]

During the final week of treaty consideration, Hitchcock solicited the president's views on a compromise proposal. Wilson scrawled a terse rejection and wrote Simmons to reiterate his position and urged his continued loyalty. Hitchcock, meanwhile, made the president's position known to Democrats.[167]

The continued intransigence of Wilson and Hitchcock made ratification unlikely but not impossible. Lenroot knew that most of the reservations being voted were milder than those of November and that ratification pressure was developing from outside opinion leaders like Bryan, Hoover, and from editors of a number of staunch Democratic newspapers, including the *New York World.* Lenroot counted on twenty-nine or thirty Democrats to disregard Wilson's advice. But Lenroot's own party would still have to supply thirty-four or thirty-five votes.[168] To get them, Lenroot had to keep the support of all or almost all Republicans other than the irreconcilable fourteen. At the same time, he could not alienate those Democrats on whom he counted. More specifically, as Lenroot saw it, the Republicans would have to put through a reservation to Article Ten that would leave no doubt that all obligation had been removed. To mollify the Democrats, the reservation

165. With respect to the pressure on Wilson and his attitude in this period see Ray Stannard Baker, *American Chronicle: The Autobiography of Ray Stannard Baker,* p. 474; Oscar S. Straus to Wilson, 4 March 1920, in the Oscar S. Straus Diaries, Box 24, Oscar Straus Papers, LC; *Milwaukee Sentinel,* 5, 7 March 1920; Albert Burleson to Tumulty, 5 March 1920, Box 3, Special Cor., Tumulty Papers; and Bailey, *Great Betrayal,* p. 258. On Hitchcock's role see Blum, *Tumulty,* pp. 238–39; and Wimer, "Senator Hitchcock and the League of Nations," p. 202.

166. Lawrence, *Woodrow Wilson,* p. 294; *New York Tribune,* 9, 19 March 1920; Karger to Taft, 9 March 1920, Box 468, Series 3, Taft Papers; Lodge to Brooks Adams, 12 March 1920, to Williams, Jr., 13 March 1920, to Coolidge, 13 March 1920, Lodge Papers; Wimer, "Senator Hitchcock and the League of Nations," p. 201; *Milwaukee Sentinel,* 9 March 1920.

167. Allan Nevins, *Henry White: Thirty Years of American Diplomacy,* p. 482; Patterson, "Gilbert M. Hitchcock," p. 468; Wilson to Simmons, 11 March 1920, Box 196, Series 2, Wilson Papers; *Milwaukee Sentinel,* 13, 16 March 1920.

168. Bailey, *Great Betrayal,* pp. 265–66; *New York Tribune,* 12, 13 March 1920; Kellogg to Root, 12 March 1920, Box 138, Root Papers.

must be worded differently from that adopted on 19 November. But strong reservationists like Frelinghuysen, Wadsworth, Howard Sutherland, and Lewis Ball of Delaware agreed with the irreconcilables in objecting to any change, and Root saw no need for any.[169] The senators would have to be somehow satisfied. And the Democrats would have to be made content with the slender morsel reserved for them in the form of the verbal change, plus any other tidbit that would not cost Republican votes.

The mild reservationists had won a tactical victory on 26 February when the Senate voted to put off consideration of the Article Ten reservation to the last. Taking advantage of the time, as the Senate acted on lesser reservations, Lenroot helped draft the Article Ten reservation that Lodge offered on 12 March. He suggested to Kellogg that he phone Root and Charles Evans Hughes to explain the situation and solicit their help with Wadsworth, chiefly. Then, on 12 March and again on the thirteenth, Lenroot took the floor to act as principal defender of the new wording, mainly against attacks from Frelinghuysen and Wadsworth.[170]

On 13 March, Lenroot received help from an unexpected official. Borah, no less irreconcilable than before, was determined to protect his country against any obligation under Article Ten in the event the treaty was ratified. Finding an ambiguity in the wording of the Lodge reservation, he proposed a minor amendment. Lenroot thought the proposed amendment redundant, but he readily agreed to it, for himself and his mild reservationist colleagues. Borah, McCormick, Wadsworth, and Frelinghuysen left the floor and soon returned with wording that Lenroot and Lodge accepted. It added after reference to controversies between nations the words: "meaning, as well, controversies over territorial integrity and political independence." This made the denial of obligation entirely clear and removed the danger that several strong reservationists would go over to the irreconcilables.[171] On 15 March, the Senate in Committee of the Whole considered Democratic alternatives. Lenroot, debating with Simmons, set out to show that Simmons's proposal suggested obligation. After it and some other substitutes were rejected, the Senate approved the Lodge reservation by a vote of fifty-six to twenty-six. No Republican opposed it and fourteen Democrats supported it.[172] But, of course, the irreconcilables would not vote aye later, so many more Democratic votes had to be found.

Lenroot did what he could. Walsh of Montana had offered as an amendment to the Article Ten reservation a paraphrase of Knox's so-called "New

169. *New York Tribune*, 12–15 March 1920; Root to Lodge, 11 March 1920, Box 161, Root Papers.

170. *Milwaukee Sentinel*, 10 March 1920; *New York Tribune*, 11 March 1920; Kellogg to Root, 18 March 1920, Box 138, Root Papers; Kendrick, "League of Nations and Republican Senate," pp. 306–8; *CR* 66:2, 1920, vol. 59, pt. 4, pp. 4212–16, 4262–64.

171. *Milwaukee Sentinel*, 14 March 1920; *New York Tribune*, 15 March 1920; *CR* 66:2, 1920, vol. 59, pt. 4, pp. 4262–64; Lodge to Coolidge, 13–17 March 1920, to Williams, Jr., 13 March 1920, Lodge Papers.

172. *CR* 66:2, 1920, vol. 59, pt. 5, pp. 4325–27, 4329–30; *New York Tribune*, 16 March 1920.

American Doctrine," which dated to December 1918. Walsh would declare the nation's intention to act with other nations against any aggressions that it judged a threat to world peace. Lenroot opposed attaching it to the reservation, and it was voted down, but two days later he offered substantially the same thing as a separate reservation.[173] John Sharp Williams, a fervent Wilsonian, delivered a long speech against such a halfway measure and soon afterwards the reservation was rejected by a vote of twenty-five to thirty-nine, with Democrats and irreconcilables in the majority.[174]

Beyond that, there was little Lenroot could do. He did attempt to ward off destructive and frivolous reservations, such as one by the irreconcilable James Reed that would have the League act to free subject peoples. This reservation was tabled on Lenroot's motion, after he had strongly objected to it. But on 18 March, which was the last day of consideration before the final vote, the Senate adopted a reservation sponsored by Democrat Peter Gerry of Rhode Island. Gerry's proposal, declaring for Irish freedom and independence and for the self-determination of peoples, was accepted by a vote of thirty-eight to thirty-six, despite objections from Lenroot and Kellogg. Party and factional lines broke on this reservation, but it was significant that Hitchcock and his followers gave it ardent support.[175]

It was almost eleven o'clock at night when Lodge asked unanimous consent for a vote on ratification with the new reservations at two the following afternoon. Lenroot, however, objected to a definite time. The odds remained against the treaty, but he still entertained some hope for last-minute defections among the Democrats.[176]

Early the next day, by prearrangement Lodge offered a more conciliatory preamble requiring only tacit assent to the reservations by three of the four great powers. After adoption of this change, senators began to discuss the new Lodge resolution. Though much of their oratory was dull, it was far from perfunctory. No Republican votes were in doubt, so everything depended on the Democrats. Joseph Ransdell of Louisiana delivered an impassioned speech for ratification with the Lodge reservations, and other Democrats, including Pomerene, William King, and Myers, advocated the same course. But it was Thomas Walsh who won closest attention when he delivered an able and emotional address decrying some of the reservations but advocating their acceptance as by far the lesser of evils. Walsh had been western manager for Wilson's 1916 campaign and had always been considered an administration leader. Following his departure, rumors swept the floor that only four more votes were needed for ratification, and the administration forces became worried. Cabinet officers Burleson and Daniels

173. *CR* 66:2, 1920, vol. 59, pt. 5, pp. 4330–31.
174. Ibid., pp. 4458–63.
175. Ibid., pp. 4517, 4576; *New York Tribune*, 19 March 1920; Fleming, *United States and the League of Nations*, p. 432; Kendrick, "League of Nations and Republican Senate," p. 310.
176. *Milwaukee Sentinel*, 19 March 1920.

and Senator Glass circulated among the Democrats, reiterating the president's wishes.[177]

For the Republicans, Lenroot delivered the fullest and ablest address. His speech paralleled the one he had made on 19 November, which was actually an analysis of the reservations and their impact on the treaty. In part, it was a document for party use in the 1920 campaign, and, indeed, Lodge later recommended it along with Lenroot's other three speeches made in 1919 for that purpose.[178] But in addition, and more important, it was an effort to win Democratic votes for ratification by showing, as no Democratic senator could, that if the issue went into the campaign the Republicans would be in control. After arguing at length the reasonableness of each reservation and the good that remained unimpaired in the League structure, Lenroot warned that if the treaty became a campaign issue: "We will meet you as Americans. You must meet us as internationalists. We will meet you as being for America first. You must meet us as advocates of the surrender of Americanism." [179]

At last came the vote. For a moment, at the start of the roll call, it seemed that the treaty might carry. But after all the votes were cast, it lacked seven of the necessary two-thirds, the tally being forty-nine for, thirty-five against. Except for Hitchcock and Edwin Johnson of South Dakota, all the Democrats who united with the irreconcilables against the treaty were from the South, where loyalty to the League, the president, and the Democratic party was strong and election prospects were not frightening. Western Democrats, by contrast, were angered by the administration favoritism to the South and were not satisfied with the League.[180]

Following the vote, Lenroot supported Lodge's resolution to return the treaty to the president. It was clear, Lenroot said, that it could not be approved without his consent, and Wilson could resubmit it at any time. The Senate approved the motion.[181]

But a motion to reconsider the vote on the Lodge resolution of ratification remained in order, and Democrat Joseph Robinson of Arkansas so moved. Watson moved to table, but Lenroot and six other mild reservationists opposed. Brandegee asserted that the Robinson motion was not in order, and Cummins, presiding, upheld the point of order though admitting doubt. Meanwhile, the mild reservationists and Robinson had reached an impasse. Robinson and his friends wanted delay, presumably to charm reservationists with new proposals. Lenroot and others conferred hurriedly

177. *New York Tribune*, 20 March 1920; Stone, *Irreconcilables*, p. 169; Kendrick, "League of Nations and Republican Senate," p. 311; Lodge to F. H. Gillett, 26 July 1920, Lodge Papers.

178. Charles F. Redmond to Samuel McCune Lindsay, 30 July 1920, Lodge Papers.

179. *CR* 66:2, 1920, vol. 59, pt. 5, pp. 4574–78.

180. Grantham, "Southern Senators and the League," pp. 200–201; Garraty, *Henry Cabot Lodge*, p. 389; J. Leonard Bates, "Senator Walsh of Montana, 1918–1924: A Liberal Under Pressure" (Ph.D. diss.), pp. 157–58.

181. *CR* 66:2, 1920, vol. 59, pt. 5, p. 4600.

and decided to insist on an immediate vote. Under the circumstances, it was pointless even to challenge Cummins's ruling, and no one did.[182]

Knox now moved his resolution, which declared the state of war between the United States and Germany at an end. In January, most of the mild reservationists had committed themselves to that approach should the second ratification effort fail, but Lenroot objected to precipitous action and Lodge, therefore, moved to adjourn.[183]

"I am of course sorry that the treaty was defeated with the reservations," Lenroot wrote James Stone a few days later, "but I am glad it is out of the way. It has been a long and hard pull for me, as I have been giving it my entire time." Lenroot went on to write of his confidence that national sentiment was with the reservationists. "It will be fortunate indeed for the country when the next 4th of March comes and Wilson is no longer President," he concluded.[184]

Wilson took the news calmly and awaited with confidence the people's verdict. For him, as for Lenroot, the fight was far from over.

As it turned out, despite the Republican landslide in November 1920, the Senate never again had occasion to consider the Treaty of Versailles, and the United States remained stiffly aloof from the League of Nations. What can be said of Lenroot's part in the prolonged Senate phase of the fight that concluded on 19 March? A historian has written: "Republican moderates, lacking real leadership or direction, muddled about, wavering between devotion to ideals and loyalty to party; in the end they counted for little. The outcome might have been different had the mild reservationists exerted anywhere near the grit and cohesiveness exhibited by the irreconcilables." [185] If this judgment is correct, Lenroot counted for little and failed in courage and leadership capacity.

It is true that none of the mild reservationists threatened to bolt the party, as Borah and Johnson and Sherman did for the irreconcilables. But the mild reservationists, a smaller group than the irreconcilables, did use to good advantage a comparable threat—to join with the Democrats in the framing of reservations. On occasion, as in the reconsideration votes of November and March, they did vote with the Democrats. More often, however, they were able to get satisfactory terms from Lodge. Thus, for instance, they took the leading role in the framing of the November reservations, after first defeating amendments. They forced new consideration in January, and, when that effort failed, they again used their bargaining power to bring the treaty to the floor and to write reservations that were, on the whole, milder than those of November. In all of this, Lenroot played a leading part. He

182. *New York Times*, 20 March 1920; *Milwaukee Sentinel*, 17 March 1920; Kendrick, "League of Nations and Republican Senate," pp. 313–14.

183. *Milwaukee Sentinel*, 17–21 March 1920; *CR* 66:2, 1920, vol. 59, pt. 5, p. 4604.

184. Lenroot to Stone, 22 March 1920, James A. Stone Papers.

185. Maddox, *Borah and American Foreign Policy*, p. 70.

did more than his share in writing the reservations, and it was he who insisted among the mild reservationists on working through Lodge while implicitly and occasionally explicitly pressuring Lodge to accommodate to mild reservationist demands.

Was Lenroot mistaken in taking this approach? Did he place too much faith in Lodge? The evidence suggests not. Lodge was determined to keep his party together. He accorded the mild reservationists fair treatment and left it up to Wilson, Hitchcock, and the Democratic senators to accept or reject ratification.

In any case, Lenroot had no other alternative. The mild reservationists, acting without Lodge's followers, could never deliver to the Democrats enough votes to accomplish ratification. And they could not win the supporters of Lodge so long as he did not discredit himself by joining the irreconcilables. Lodge, whatever his inclinations, was too shrewd to do that and thus bring the schism he so much wanted to avoid. Under the circumstances, Lenroot did well in bringing from and through Lodge the concessions that were made.

These concessions were enough to make the reservationist program tolerable to most friends of the League, inside the Senate and in the country. And, particularly after the modification of the preamble in March, the terms were almost certainly acceptable to the other great powers. It was the extraordinary intransigence of President Wilson that rendered all of Lenroot's efforts useless.[186] During and immediately following World War II, Wilson and the idea of collective security were lionized. But even in that period the distinguished diplomatic historian Thomas Bailey, reviewing the November reservations, judged them inconsequential, or useless, or repetitious, or tactless, but not so offensive as to warrant the Wilsonian veto. Moreover they may have been necessary, Bailey noted, to pacify public opinion or save senatorial face.[187]

Many of Lenroot's actions in connection with the treaty were tactical, designed to bring ratification. But in developing and supporting a reservationist program, he was moved also by conviction. He was particularly concerned about the guarantees in Article Ten. Half a century later, influenced by the experience of the Vietnam War, Americans became more sympathetic with those who wished to place limits on the extent of the nation's military commitments. But the present-day perspective, whether it results in a favorable or an unfavorable judgment, skews our image of the past. In his time, Lenroot's position was relatively advanced. He favored international consultation, adjudication, and arbitration; was willing to engage in limited collective security through use of the boycott; and agreed that the United States should undertake a liberal share of the burdens of peace, within the Western Hemisphere and, on extraordinary occasions,

186. For one example of this view see Bailey, *Great Betrayal*, pp. 240, 271.
187. Ibid., pp. 154–57.

elsewhere. Before the president went to Paris, few members of the League to Enforce Peace would have gone further in negotiating.

The spread-eagle Americanism presented in Lenroot's views on Article Ten and, to a lesser extent, the other reservations seemed archaic decades later, as it already did in Lenroot's own day to intellectuals like H. L. Mencken. But for the vast majority, including the leaders of opinion, patriotism was altogether laudable. Lenroot's concern for the nation's autonomy, his refusal to commit future generations to war without their consent, resulted from a profound respect for his country as one that was uniquely blessed.

In summary, Lenroot did far more than his share to bring the nation to ratification of the treaty and entry into the League of Nations. Unusual factors such as the health of the president, the circumstances of his illness, and the unfortunate feeling of Wilson toward Lodge, combined with the loyalty of the Southern Democrats to their party and president, deprived Lenroot of the credit he deserved and, more important, kept the country aloof from the League while hampering recovery in Europe.

IX

THE PERIOD
OF RECONSTRUCTION

During the first two sessions of the Sixty-sixth Congress from May 1919 into June 1920, which involved the battle of the League of Nations, Lenroot managed to participate in other legislative activities, visited Wisconsin occasionally, and gave speeches outside his home state.[1]

He was not able to devote much time to Wisconsin politics, but the situation worried him. The new alignment of wartime, cutting across old factional lines, persisted into the postwar period. In the first test between the new factions, Lenroot's group opposed La Follette's candidates for delegate to the Republican National Convention with a slate of their own. To maximize the vote-getting capacity of this group, it was necessary to present them as unpledged.[2]

Lenroot had reason to be wary of the situation in his home state. Working from a formidable base of wartime discontent, the La Follette group now capitalized on feelings against the League of Nations, the fears and suspicions of workers who were concerned to preserve wartime gains, anxiety among farmers and others about the continually increasing cost of living, and much else. The I.W.W. was a negligible factor, but by early 1920 the radical Nonpartisan League had spread from North Dakota and Minnesota into Wisconsin, where in March 1920, it united all other dissident elements in support of La Follette's delegate ticket. Victor Berger, though under sentence for violation of the Espionage Act and denied his seat in Congress, nevertheless won a special election in December. For the time being at least, he too was willing to back the La Follette group. The La Follette men, in turn, deferred to these and worked closely with the editor of Hearst's *Wisconsin News* in the selection of delegate candidates.[3]

1. *Milwaukee Sentinel,* 15 January, 6 March, 15 May 1920; Ben B. Felt to Henry Cabot Lodge, 19 April 1920, Henry Cabot Lodge Papers; Clara Lenroot to Nellie Nichols, 5 April 1920, Irvine L. Lenroot Papers Addition.

2. *New York Tribune,* 28 January 1920; *Milwaukee Sentinel,* 25 December 1919, 6 January, 1 February, 1–29 March 1920; Lenroot to James A. Stone, 3 February 1920, Box 22, James A. Stone Papers.

3. Herbert F. Margulies, *The Decline of the Progressive Movement in Wisconsin,* 1890–1920, pp. 244–57; Ernst Kronshage to Alfred T. Rogers, 17 February 1920, Box 85, Series B, Robert M. La Follette FC.

As election day neared, Lenroot understood that the uninstructed delegates would win "unless the Socialists go over to La Follette, which I have some indication is possible." The socialists did vote in the Republican primary, as did many Democrats, helping the La Follette forces achieve victory. They won the four delegate-at-large positions by wide margins and elected twenty-four of the twenty-six member delegation. Lenroot found the loss discouraging, not only because of the result but also because of its magnitude. But analysis of the vote left hope for the future. The turnout of voters had been minimal, and the socialist voters would normally return to their own party in the fall.[4]

To some extent, national and state politics influenced Lenroot's outlook and his public and private actions in the reconstruction period.

Lenroot remained the insurgent, the progressive, the moderate. But the temper of the times contrasted markedly with prewar days. Radicalism and reaction, which were symbiotic elements, combined, minimizing the chances of a middle ground. Lenroot had witnessed such a movement during the war. But now the challenge was greater, partly because the end of the war removed the greatest force for unity, whether genuine or enforced. Lenroot looked for constructive answers, to ameliorate conditions and calm feelings. At the same time, he approved the repression of those few who seemed hopelessly beyond redemption, the anarchists, communists, and revolutionists. But when the cost of living began to increase intolerably, he called for the conviction of "profiteers."[5]

Speaking on some of the problems on reconstruction in the spring of 1919, Lenroot became involved with the burgeoning "industrial democracy" movement. He exhorted businessmen and laborers to settle their problems by understanding one another's viewpoint, and by agreements according minimum wage and minimum return on capital guarantees, and by division of remaining profits between the two groups. Having consulted with the entire commerce committee and the general manager of the Emergency Fleet Corporation, he now condemned the Seattle shipyard strikers who, he said, broke their contract with the government, refused wage increases, and made great demands, even though the government was losing money on all the ships being built. America was fortunate in that "Seattle had a real American as its Mayor in Ole Hanson, and the revolution there ended very quickly." But though he was unsympathetic to the general strike in Seattle or to the mailing of bombs to prominent leaders, he urged that in addition to profit sharing, employers should include in their arrangements with blue-collar workers at least a two-week paid vacation per year, as was already the practice with white-collar workers. In more general terms,

4. Margulies, *The Decline of the Progressive Movement,* pp. 252, 258–59; Stone to Lenroot, 15 April 1920, Lenroot to Stone, 14, 20, 27 April 1920, Box 22, Stone Papers; Clara Lenroot to Nellie Nichols, 14 April 1920, Lenroot Papers Addition.

5. *CR* 66:2, 1920, vol. 59, pt. 6, p. 6111.

the spirit of cooperation and self-sacrifice of the war should persist, brother-hood cutting across all lines; Americans had learned the value of service, "not only to our country and to our fellows, but to ourselves," he said. Turning to things government could do, Lenroot gave attention to the alien, whom many people associated with radical lawlessness. He advocated a law requiring that every foreign-born resident between the ages of eighteen and forty-five become literate in English and "receive instruction as to the form of our government and its principles." The federal government, moreover, should aid the states not only in providing elementary education but voca-tional training and, through extension and correspondence courses, college training.

With the end of the war, Lenroot feared an influx of immigrants that would menace unskilled American laborers. He proposed to limit immigra-tion, and in the process ban Bolsheviks, "and any others who carry with them the idea that some other form of government is better than ours." Aliens with such beliefs should be deported. Such problems he considered of prime importance, "because their solution affects the character of our citizenship."

Lenroot thought the railroad situation was another important problem with which the government would have to deal. Unemployment worried him, and he advocated public works, especially the construction of roads, "but in view of the present condition of the Treasury, only to the extent necessary to relieve unemployment." In other areas, the government should practice strict economy, in the interest of the taxpayer.[6]

By autumn, the hazard of unemployment had abated, only to be replaced as a source of general concern with the cost of living. The cause of postwar inflation was not deferred demand but continued heavy spending by gov-ernment, deficit financing, easy credit, speculative excess, and an overac-cumulation of inventories.[7] The strikes, accompanied by radical agitation and acts of violence, had meanwhile accelerated.

Lenroot related the rise in living costs to the growth of class conscious-ness, and it caused him much concern. When at Gifford Pinchot's country home in August, Harry Slattery broached the subject of a "natural resources monopoly" and the unusual increase in lumber prices, Lenroot evinced great interest. Soon afterwards, he gave a speech on "The High Cost of Living." He put the blame on undue profits by some and the governmental policy that allowed too much purchasing for Europe. The main problem, he said, was that "men not actually engaged either in manufacture or distri-bution, have thru manipulation, hoarding and combination, been able to

6. MS speech, "Some Reconstruction Problems," n.d. (March or April 1919), Box 10, Irvine L. Lenroot Papers. He told of the Seattle strike consultation in testimony before the House Committee on Interstate and Foreign Commerce, *Hearings: Return of Railroads to Private Owner-ship*, p. 2129.

7. John D. Hicks, *Rehearsal for Disaster*, pp. 17–23, 37. See also Paul A. Samuelson and Everett E. Hagen, *After the War—1918–1920*, pp. 30–34, 38–39.

control the supply of many necessaries." He was wary of a heavy tax on excess profits as dangerous to incentive but thought the government might have to resort to it. In any case, he felt, much would depend on the spirit and action of individuals. Lenroot urged businessmen to curb profiteering in their own ranks and called for a new order in the relations of capital and labor. Commending the attitude of cooperation instead of antagonism, he reverted to the increasingly popular idea of profit sharing and suggested that if widely applied it would do so much for efficiency in production as to curb the rise in living costs.[8] He also advocated farm cooperatives as a means of cutting costs for the consumer while also benefiting the farmer, whose labor was the foundation of prosperity.[9]

By November, in the face of steel, coal, and railroad strikes, continually mounting prices, further acts of violence, and increasing unrest in all quarters, Lenroot wrote James Stone:

> With monopolies of capital upon one side, and coercion by labor upon the other, it seems as if we are between two millstones. I am not at all sure but that the time has come when we ought to amend our Constitution so as to give to the Federal Government unquestioned power to deal with both capital and labor. There can be no permanent solution that is not advantageous to both.
>
> We hear a great deal about the law of supply and demand . . . but when that law is artificially interfered with it cannot function. If capital does not realize that exorbitant prices will be its own undoing I believe we will have to pass a law that will tax as excess profits all of the income beyond a certain liberal percentage.

He had in the past opposed such a step "because its tendency would be to prevent expansion in business and industry."

Now, however, he thought that "we had better suffer somewhat from lack of expansion than to suffer indefinitely the incessant grab for profits being made on every hand." He hoped to touch on some of those problems in Wisconsin speeches in December, he wrote Stone, for "I feel that we are at a greater crisis at this time than at any time during the war, and that the present situation calls for the highest patriotism." [10]

Inside the Senate, Lenroot spread himself thin but acted with a sure hand. He helped win approval of the amendment on woman suffrage; battled to regain for Congress powers lost to the executive during the war; took the leading role in the adoption of a more liberal code of military justice; defended economy; and tried to protect the government as it ended wartime contracts with corporations.[11]

8. Harry Slattery to Gifford Pinchot, 21 August 1919, Box 1842, Gifford Pinchot Papers; MS speech, "The High Cost of Living," n.d. (September 1919), Box 10, Lenroot Papers. See also the *Milwaukee Sentinel*, 29 August, 13 September 1919.

9. *Superior Telegram*, 13–14 September 1919, (weekend ed.).

10. Lenroot to Stone, 4 November 1919, Box 22, Stone Papers.

11. Herbert F. Margulies, "Progressivism, Patriotism, and Politics: The Life and Times of Irvine L. Lenroot," pp. 1110–18.

Protection of the government was a major consideration for Lenroot in his approach to the three measures to which he gave the greatest attention in the reconstruction days—the railroad bill, the mineral lands leasing bill, and the waterpower bill. In that respect and in some others, he acted as a progressive on these questions. But he was a moderate progressive, a "semi-conservative" according to Harry Slattery, a "sane progressive" in the jargon current in Wisconsin at the time.[12] He wanted the positive results that could only come from legislation, so he was not content merely to block legislation, though he was prepared to do that if the public interest were not protected to a reasonable degree.

Lenroot regarded the railroad question as the major domestic issue of the time, and many of his contemporaries would have agreed.[13] He did not favor returning to the prewar system, partly because the railroad companies were not strong enough. But he also opposed the administration's proposal for a five-year extension of government operation, which carried with it the possibility of nationalization. His chief objection to national ownership was that it would put a vast number of jobs under political control, subject to political abuse. Even worse than government ownership, in Lenroot's view, was the Plumb Plan, which was conceived by an attorney for the railroad unions and strongly supported by those unions. Under that plan, as Lenroot understood it, the railroad employees would have effective control, which they might use at the expense of the general public.[14]

Lenroot offered an alternative. He proposed federal incorporation of "one or more railway companies to acquire all the roads of the country through a unified operation." This would give the benefits of government ownership and operation without the attendant evils. On a basis fixed by law, one corporation or a number of regional corporations would be able to acquire the existing railroad property. The capital stock would be sold to the public or issued to present owners in exchange for their property on a guaranteed return of a minimum percentage, "probably 3.5 or 4%"; the majority on the board or boards would be appointed by the president and confirmed by the Senate, with the remainder chosen by the stockholders and the railroad employees. There would be no issuance of stock or other securities without the approval of the I.C.C., and that agency would continue to regulate rates and service and act against discrimination. State railroad commissions would likewise continue in coordination with the I.C.C.

Any return on capital beyond a specified maximum, perhaps 6 percent, would be divided between the stockholders, the employees, and the government. The government recoveries would be used first to reimburse the government for "any deficiency that the Government may be called upon

12. Slattery to Pinchot, 21 August 1919, Box 1842, Pinchot Papers.

13. *Milwaukee Sentinel,* 5 December 1919.

14. Lenroot to Rouget D. Marshall, 16 December 1918, Box 5, Lenroot Papers; to Stone, 21 December 1919, Box 22, Stone Papers; *CR* 66:2, 1919, vol. 59, pt. 1, pp. 566–69.

to pay in fulfillment of its guarantee." The remainder would be loaned to the corporation without interest for extension and improvement. There would be heavy penalties for use of political influences in the making of appointments.[15]

Although Lenroot's plan coincided with the views of a Bostonian named Nathan Amster, who headed an organization of noninstitutional railroad investors, its chance of adoption was minimal. Reconciling to that fact, Lenroot was willing to support something less grandiose, at least in the short run. But he could not approve the bill that Albert Cummins reported, chiefly because of its no-strike provision. The House bill, reported by John Esch, was more to his liking. After the conferees adopted most of the provisions of that bill and eliminated the no-strike clause of the Cummins bill, Lenroot spoke and voted for the conference report. The Esch-Cummins Act stressed consolidation of the railroad system under strong I.C.C. control and was, to Lenroot and others, representative of an updating of the progressive tradition to meet present-day circumstances.[16]

Lenroot took no less interest and exerted considerably greater influence in the Congress's effort to, at last, enact a mineral lands leasing bill and waterpower legislation. He was as familiar with these subjects as with the railroad question and had two additional advantages as well—the cooperation of a much more powerful lobby (that of Gifford Pinchot) than Nathan Amster's and membership on the key Senate committees, public lands and commerce. Good relations with such members of the House as Esch and Nicholas Sinnott (chairman of the lands committee) and with certain members of the administration, including Secretary Lane, further strengthened his position.[17]

It was natural that the National Conservation Association coterie should look to Lenroot as the one to introduce their bills and serve as their principal ally in the Senate. He was, after all, a knowledgeable, trusted, and influential friend of long standing. Therefore, in the spring of 1919, Philip Wells and George Woodruff prepared the mineral lands leasing and waterpower bills for Lenroot to introduce in the new Congress, with whatever alterations he

15. *Superior Telegram,* 14 January 1919; MS speech, "The Railway Problem," 22 March 1919, Box 8, Lenroot Papers.

16. U.S., House of Representatives, Committee on Interstate and Foreign Commerce, *Hearings: Return of Railroads to Private Ownership,* pp. 2114, 2128, 2131; E. Marshall Young to Mark Sullivan, 17 September 1919, Amster to Sullivan, 11 November 1919, Box 19, Mark Sullivan Papers, Hoover Institution of War, Revolution and Peace; *CR* 66:2, 1919, vol. 59, pt. 1, pp. 570, 576; 1920, vol. 59, pt. 4, pp. 3340–42; *Milwaukee Sentinel,* 22–24 February 1920; K. Austin Kerr, *American Railroad Politics, 1914–1920: Rates, Wages, and Efficiency,* pp. 218–21.

17. On Lenroot's continuing friendship with Lane see Lane to Lenroot, 16 September, 5 November 1920, Box 3, Lenroot Papers. Sen. Pat Harrison of Mississippi, himself a former member of the House and its rules committee, commented on Lenroot's "powerful influences in the House of Representatives" in May 1920. *CR* 66:2, 1920, vol. 59, pt. 7, p. 7216. Lenroot saw Esch almost daily. John J. Esch to Judge James O'Neill, 23 August 1919, Box 54, John J. Esch Papers.

might insist on.[18] There was a complication, however. The group had worked with La Follette in the previous Congress, ignoring the La Follette-Pinchot break of 1912, and Wells had promised to keep La Follette supplied with ammunition in the future. Moreover, both Slattery and Pinchot saw government ownership and operation as the best long-run method of resource development, in this respect leaning toward La Follette and away from Lenroot. But the leasing principle was the one for which the group had been contending for a decade, and now, with victory seemingly at hand, it would not do to abandon either leasing or Lenroot. Wells asked Woodruff and Pinchot "to consider our situation with respect to La Follette carefully in order that we may not get the wires crossed between him and Lenroot." [19]

The Pinchot coterie met the problem skillfully. Pinchot's aides gave Lenroot their most consistent cooperation, especially in his committee work. At the same time, they supplied La Follette with material for such floor debates as might develop. Through Lenroot, on the mineral lands leasing bill especially, they were in a position to extract what concessions they could from the westerners. But to the extent that Lenroot got less than all they wanted, they could rely on La Follette, unencumbered by any commitments to committee associates, to raise a hubbub in the Senate.[20]

Lenroot introduced the association's waterpower bill, but contrary to the expectations of Pinchot and his friends, he decided not to introduce a leasing bill. Slattery became alarmed with the situation, but Lenroot was wise in his judgment.[21] In committee in July and August, he was able to use the influence of the Pinchot group without disassociating himself from his colleagues.

The key to the situation was Reed Smoot, the lands committee's new chairman. Smoot had not theretofore supported the leasing principle, but he was impatient at the continuing delay; appalled at the vast resources still being withheld by the government; aware that only a leasing bill could pass both Houses; and fearful that the administration, aided by others, would pressure for government ownership and operation.[22]

Of the other westerners on the lands committee, only Thomas Walsh was

18. Pinchot to Slattery, 18 May 1919, Nellie D. McSherry to Slattery, 19 May 1919, Box 1842, Philip P. Wells to Lenroot, 21 May 1919, Box 1700, Pinchot Papers; Pinchot to James R. Garfield, 27 May 1919, Box 118, James R. Garfield Papers.

19. Wells to George Woodruff, 22 May 1919, Slattery to Pinchot, 21 March 1919, to Carl D. Thompson, 24 October 1919, Box 1700, Pinchot to Matthew Hale, 14 December 1916, Box 194, Pinchot Papers; Belle La Follette to "My Dear Ones," 26 February 1920, Box 28, Series A, La Follette FC; Wells to Woodruff, 22 May 1919, Box 1700, Pinchot Papers.

20. The skillful coordination of the attack is noted in J. Leonard Bates, *The Origins of Teapot Dome: Progressives, Parties and Petroleum, 1909–1921*, p. 184.

21. Pinchot to Will Hays, 7 June 1919, Box 2050, Slattery to Pinchot, 1 July 1919, Box 1842, Pinchot Papers.

22. Thomas G. Alexander, "Senator Reed Smoot and Western Land Policy, 1905–1920," pp. 245–64; Elmo R. Richardson, *The Politics of Conservation: Crusades and Controversies, 1897–1913*, p. 26; Paul Gates, *History of Public Land Law Development*, p. 741.

committed to the leasing idea. But the others, including even Albert Fall of New Mexico, by now agreed with Smoot that leasing was the price of development and the resolution of dispute over title and that the threat of government operation was a real one. "It is not a question of what we want but what we can get," Key Pittman wrote.[23] Pittman and the other westerners reflected the chastened attitude of the claimants.

Instead of offering a separate bill, Lenroot argued in committee for amendments to the Smoot bill, the amendments however drawn from the bill Wells had prepared or suggested in Pinchot's letter to Smoot. Lenroot found Smoot and the others remarkably conciliatory, though on some questions he had to argue strongly for his amendments. Lenroot won most of what he sought and much more than he had expected. He emerged from the committee's deliberations delighted at the results and justly proud of his own efforts. Slattery, after inquiring into the details of the situation, was surprised and pleased at how much Lenroot had gotten, as was Pinchot.[24] Above all, Lenroot was pleased that he won his fight to make the bill a pure leasing measure not one providing for patent, even as a reward for discovery, as in previous bills. He was pleased also to win what was the hardest fight in the committee, which was to remove maximum royalties on new leases and subject them to competitive bidding, though a maximum remained for old claims being converted to leases.[25]

In the Senate, Lenroot took the lead in successfully defending the bill against critics on the left and right.[26] On 3 September, the Senate approved the bill without a record vote. As he had anticipated, the conference committee improved the final product.[27]

The bill was quickly passed in both Houses and the president, on the recommendation of Secretary Daniels, Scott Ferris, Pinchot, and others,

23. John Ise, *The United States Oil Policy*, pp. 343–44; Gates, *Public Land Law Development*, p. 741; Key Pittman to James D. Finch, 1 September 1919, Key Pittman Papers, quoted in Bates, *Origins of Teapot Dome*, p. 182.

24. Pinchot to Slattery, 12 August 1919, Slattery to Pinchot, 14 August 1919, Box 1842, Lenroot to Pinchot, 19 September 1919, Box 2050, Slattery to Pinchot, 14 August 1919, Box 1842, to Woodruff, 21 August 1919, Box 1843, Pinchot to Lenroot, 8 September 1919, Box 2050, Pinchot Papers; Bates, *Origins of Teapot Dome*, pp. 185–87.

25. "Lenroot's Record," n.d. (1920), Box 1948, Pinchot Papers; *CR* 66:1, 1919, vol. 58, pt. 4, pp. 4172, 4175.

26. Pinchot to Lenroot, 8 September 1919, Box 2050, Slattery to Pinchot, 23, 27, 30 August, 3 September 1919, Box 1842, Pinchot Papers; Bates, *Origins of Teapot Dome*, pp. 189–92; Alexander, "Senator Reed Smoot," p. 258; Gates, *Public Land Law Development*, p. 743; Bates, *Origins of Teapot Dome*, pp. 192–93; "Lenroot's Record," n.d. (1920), Box 1948, Pinchot Papers; *CR* 66:1, 1919, vol. 58, pt. 4, pp. 4168, 4271; 1919, vol. 58, pt. 5, pp. 4447, 4733–35, 4761–64. At the time, Lenroot was correct about Midwest Oil but soon afterwards it fell under the control of Standard Oil (Indiana). Harold D. Roberts, *Salt Creek, Wyoming: The Story of a Great Oil Field*, pp. 144–45, 148. *CR* 66:1, 1919, vol. 58, pt. 4, pp. 3734, 4172; 1919, vol. 58, pt. 5, pp. 4275–79, 4579, 4586, 4737–38, 4761–64.

27. Lenroot to Pinchot, 17 February 1920, Box 2050, Pinchot Papers. For a summary of the provisions of the report see Gates, *Public Land Law Development*, pp. 743–45. See also Roberts, *Salt Creek, Wyoming*, pp. 135–39.

promptly signed it into law on 25 February 1920.[28] Within a few years, the naval reserve provisions were grossly misused under a new administration and the celebrated Teapot Dome scandal resulted. But even in the heated atmosphere of 1924, the law was not judged to be faulty. A belated effort to bring rational control to the development of the mineral resources on the remaining public lands, the Mineral Lands Leasing Act provided a full and equitable framework. Amended periodically, it remains the basic charter in its field.[29]

Typically, Lenroot's contribution was not widely visible and was not confined to the period when legislation was finally enacted. Though his role in committee, on the Senate floor, and in the joint conference during 1919 and 1920 was of significance, what he had done to uphold the leasing principle in the House through the decade was even more important. Before the Navy Department began to exert a counter-influence, it was chiefly Lenroot, abetted mainly by Ferris and James R. Mann, who held the House firm in its insistence on the leasing principle, even at the cost of delay. Slattery, concluding a fifteen-point statement of Lenroot's contributions to conservation through the years, summarized:

> Lenroot because of his influence in House and Senate, because of his legal abilities as recognized by men in Congress regardless of party; and because of his untiring efforts for the conservation principle, and to protect the great National resources, stands out as the most potent cause in Congress for conservation winning out.[30]

Part of Slattery's bill of particulars related to Lenroot's role in the waterpower fight over the years, and one feature of the triumph of conservation to which he referred was adoption of the Federal Waterpower Act of 1920. For Lenroot, however, the culminating phase of the waterpower battle differed substantially from that of the mineral lands leasing bill. As he viewed it, from the start of the session through to the end, there was less prospect of getting what he could regard as a really good bill. Part of the difficulty was that, in dealing with waterpower sites on all navigable streams not just those on the public lands, Congress was under greater pressure than when acting on the mineral lands leasing legislation. Another important factor was the complexity of the subject, which made it extremely difficult to define a progressive position and to secure any considerable agreement on it.

Lenroot approved many features of the bill that emerged from the commerce committee. But he objected to several provisions, chiefly those relating to recapture on the expiration of the lease. The issue was quite technical, but though Lenroot mastered and expounded the technicalities, he failed

---

28. Joseph P. Tumulty to Mrs. Wilson, 25 February 1920, Special Cor., Box 3, Joseph P. Tumulty Papers.

29. Even after Teapot Dome, Professor Ise judged the law a conservationist victory. Ise, *United States Oil Policy*, p. 352.

30. "Lenroot's Record Briefly on Conservation" (penciled: "from Slattery"), October 1920, Box 1948, Pinchot Papers.

to win the amendments he wanted and reluctantly voted against the bill when it passed the Senate.[31]

The conference committee revised the bill to be more acceptable, but certain provisions remained that Lenroot construed as opening the way to perpetual leases.[32] Although the Pinchot group was pleased with the conference report, Lenroot voted against it. The bill, nevertheless, passed in both Houses and was signed by the president.[33]

Historians favoring the conservationist position have given the act qualified endorsement. They have not discussed whether something better could have or should have been developed at the price of further delay.[34] Lenroot deserved the credit Slattery and Pinchot gave him, despite his negative votes. He helped to improve the final bill; but more important, as with the Mineral Lands Leasing Act, he played a large part in the decade-long struggle for federal control. Although the act of 1920 was not entirely to his liking, Lenroot would have been the first to admit that it was superior to anything obtainable ten or six or even four years earlier.

His heavy legislative schedule did not prevent Lenroot from becoming involved in Republican pre-platform deliberations.

The efforts of erstwhile Bull Moosers to organize in advance of the 1920 Republican National Convention failed, largely because the issue of the League of Nations remained too divisive.[35] But progressive stirrings perhaps encouraged Hays in his idea of creating a broadly based committee to advise on the platform, and giving progressives such as Pinchot, William Allen White, and Garfield full scope on such a committee.[36]

Advisory committees were not unusual, but Hays carried the practice to an extreme in naming a hundred seventy-one members, who were divided into twenty-four subcommittees. Senators and representatives, Hays knew, would be sensitive to advice from "outsiders," so he saw to it that they were given ample representation and more than their numerical share of influence. In December 1919, Hays asked Lodge to recommend three senators

31. Margulies, "Lenroot," pp. 1136–42.

32. *CR* 66:2, 1920, vol. 59, pt. 7, pp. 7723–24.

33. M. Nelson McGeary, *Gifford Pinchot: Forester-Politician*, pp. 204–5; Jerome G. Kerwin, *Federal Water-Power Legislation*, pp. 259–61; Judson King, *The Conservation Fight from Theodore Roosevelt to the Tennessee Valley Authority*, pp. 57–58.

34. Roy M. Robbins, *Our Landed Heritage: The Public Domain, 1776–1936*, p. 393; Keith Waldemar Olson, "Franklin K. Lane: A Biography" (Ph.D. diss.), pp. 174–75; James C. Malin, *The United States After the World War*, p. 260; King, *The Conservation Fight*, p. 58.

35. Correspondence is voluminous but see especially Harold Ickes to Pinchot, 16 January, 20 February 1920, Box 229, Pinchot Papers.

36. Ickes to Hays, 12 December 1919, Box 218, Hays to Pinchot, 6 January 1920, Box 228, Ickes to Pinchot, 7 April 1920, Box 229, Pinchot to Slattery, 4 January 1920, Box 1841, Pinchot Papers; William Allen White to Hays, 3 March 1920, enclosed in White to Garfield, 3 March 1920, Box 162, Garfield Papers; Hays to John C. O'Laughlin, 5 April 1920, Box 19, John C. O'Laughlin Papers, LC; Harold Ickes, *The Autobiography of a Curmudgeon* (New York, 1943), pp. 223–25.

"representative of the different lines of thought," who would serve in addition to himself and to three senatorial members of the National Committee. Lodge recommended George Moses, Lenroot, and Watson as "most admirable men" and Lenroot accepted Hays's offer. Soon, he served on the subcommittee on international relations headed by Lodge, and on the executive committee, which on 18 and 19 May attempted to finalize its work, based on the reports of the subcommittee chairmen. Later Lenroot was selected as one of three to represent the advisory committee at the national convention.[37]

Hays and Advisory Committee Chairman Ogden Mills were chiefly responsible for Lenroot's continuing preferment. He was willing, able, and brought to the platform a degree of progressivism that was acceptable. Lodge, too, viewed Lenroot favorably.[38]

The only recorded account respecting Lenroot's specific work on domestic planks is that of reporter Fred Sheasby, who stated in his article for the *Milwaukee Sentinel* that Lenroot wrote the plank on the St. Lawrence Seaway project. This and other domestic matters were generally agreed to at the meetings of 18 and 19 May; afterwards Lenroot participated in drafting the final wording of all other domestic planks. But despite extensive preliminary efforts, in which Lenroot played a part, the executive committee could not agree on a League of Nations plank.[39]

Lodge, intimidated by continuing threats from Borah and Johnson that they might bolt, would not support a plank favoring ratification, even with the reservations named after himself. Instead, he helped to draft a plank that the Indiana Republicans adopted that dodged the issue by endorsing the actions of Republican senators in opposing the League as presented by President Wilson. Lenroot and Kellogg, however, backed from the outside by a group led by former Sen. Murray Crane of Massachusetts, insisted on endorsement of reservations. Nor were all the irreconcilables happy with the Indiana plank, for it left the door open to ratification and also promised that if freedom and peace were threatened in Europe, the United States would consult with other powers. Lodge persisted in efforts to compromise the differences, but in a series of meetings at the end of May Lenroot and his associates continued to advocate endorsement of the Lodge reservations. By the time Congress adjourned on 5 June, the conferees had reached a vague understanding that the action of Republican senators would be endorsed, but no definite wording had been agreed to and it was not clear

37. Marie Chatham, "The Role of the National Party Chairman from Hanna to Farley" (Ph.D. diss.), p. 54; James Oliver Robertson, "The Progressives in National Republican Politics, 1916–1921," pp. 261–62; Hays to Lodge, 17 December 1919, Lodge to Hays, 18 December 1919, Ogden L. Mills to Lodge, 20 April 1920, Henry Cabot Lodge Papers; *Milwaukee Sentinel,* 7 June 1920.

38. Ben F. Felt to Lodge, 19 April 1920, Louis A. Coolidge to Lodge, 20 April 1920, Lodge to Felt, 22 April 1920, to Coolidge, 22 April 1920, Lodge Papers.

39. *Milwaukee Sentinel,* 8 June, 20 May 1920; Clara Lenroot to Nellie Nichols, 20 May 1919 (1920), Lenroot Papers Addition; Lenroot, "Memoirs," p. 156, Box 13, Lenroot Papers.

that the plank would stop there.[40] Lenroot, Lodge, Watson, and other draftsmen of the platform left Washington for Chicago with much left to settle. For Lenroot, the convention would be the most fateful of his life.

Sen. Medill McCormick, one of the irreconcilables, thought the question of the League plank had been settled in Washington by gentleman's agreement. But no definite wording had been accepted, and in Chicago a dispute resulted, lasting for several days. The official platform committee, under Senator Watson, remanded drafting duties to a subcommittee of thirteen, which Watson also headed, while it became involved in taking testimony and hearing the recommendations of the advisory committee. Paralleling and occasionally meeting with the subcommittee, or a segment thereof, a group of others, with semiofficial or unofficial status, also conferred. Lenroot, representing the advisory committee, participated in some of these conferences. He and Kellogg, abetted by Hale, McCumber, and others, drafted and contended for a plank specifically endorsing the Lodge reservations. Murray Crane gave aggressive leadership to the group. Initially, influential Old Guardsmen who were moderate on the League question agreed to support such a plank, but when Borah, Brandegee, McCormick, and Johnson, supported in the background by William Randolph Hearst, threatened a floor fight and a bolt, they reconsidered. Lodge determined the outcome when he threatened to vacate the chair and take the floor in opposition to a plank endorsing reservations. Mills produced a plank drafted earlier by Root; Watson, Smoot, and Lodge urged its acceptance as a basis for compromise. As finally worded, the plan criticized the covenant but declared for "agreement among nations to preserve the peace of the world." Such an international association should "maintain the rule of public right by development of law and the decision of impartial courts." It should, moreover, "secure instant and general conference whenever peace shall be threatened by political action, so that the nations pledged to do and insist upon what is just and fair may exercise their influence and power for the prevention of war." The irreconcilables were not entirely satisfied with the ambiguous plank, much preferring a flat repudiation of the League, but Borah and McCormick, their spokesmen, acquiesced because of their partial victory, out of concern for the party, and the potential candidacy of Hiram Johnson. Then and later, pro- and anti-League elements within the party interpreted the Root plank according to its own lights.[41]

40. John A. Garraty, *Henry Cabot Lodge: A Biography*, pp. 392–93; Philip C. Jessup, *Elihu Root*, pp. 409–10; Lodge to Hays, 9, 12 May 1920, Lodge Papers; John Hannan to La Follette, 20 May 1920, Box 85, Series B, La Follette FC; *Milwaukee Sentinel*, 15 May 1920; Clara Lenroot to Nellie Nichols, 26 May 1919 (1920), Lenroot Papers Addition; W. Murray Crane to A. Lawrence Lowell, 21 May 1920, Box 4, League to Enforce Peace, A. Lawrence Lowell Papers; *Washington Evening Star*, 28, 30 May 1920; *New York Tribune*, 9 June 1920; *Chicago Daily News*, 10 June 1920; Lodge to Robert Winsor, 4 June 1920, Lodge Papers.

41. *Chicago Daily News*, 10 June 1920; *The Sun and New York Herald*, 11 June 1920; Lodge to Winsor, 4 June 1920, Lodge Papers; *Milwaukee Sentinel*, 7–10 June 1920; *New York Tribune*, 9–10 June 1920; *Washington Herald*, 6, 10, 11 June 1920; *Washington Evening Star*, 9–11 June 1920;

On balance, Lenroot had reason to be satisfied with the platform, for as finally reported it embodied most of the recommendations of the advisory committee. It was brief and casual about tariff protection, pensions for Civil War veterans, and the party heroes of the past; it asked prevention of unreasonable profits; it was moderate on labor, supporting collective bargaining while distinguishing between classes of industries in which strikes were tolerable or not; it called for opening trade relations with all nations, by implication including Soviet Russia. The platform gave attention to protection of women in industry, prevention of child labor, federal highways, conservation, and farm questions. With respect to the last, in adopting a plank largely drawn by farm editor Henry C. Wallace, the Republicans produced a program more advanced than the Democrats would adopt at San Francisco in July. The call for rigid economy and a more businesslike government appealed to conservative elements but was hardly objectionable to Lenroot. Nor could he disapprove planks that called for free speech and assembly but warned that advocacy of violent overthrow of government or resistance to law would not be tolerated and urged registration of aliens. The cheering and flag-waving that greeted the reading of this plank and the one opposing strikes against the government showed the mood of the delegates.[42]

While the platform committee completed its work and the convention marked time impatiently, Lenroot took a short trip to Oregon, near Madison, to help dedicate a war memorial.[43] If he had arrived in Chicago in time to hear the presentation of the platform that evening, he would have been embarrassed by the position his home state took and the reception accorded its spokesman, Edwin J. Gross. Again, as in 1908, 1912, and 1916, Wisconsin's representative on the platform committee offered a minority report. Only with difficulty was Chairman Lodge able to maintain order as Gross

---

Portland Oregonian, 17 June 1920; James E. Watson, As I Knew Them: Memoirs of James E. Watson, pp. 213–15; Crane to Lowell, 17 June 1920, League to Enforce Peace, Box 1, Lowell Papers; Carolyn W. Johnson, Winthrop Murray Crane: A Study in Republican Leadership, 1892–1920, pp. 69–72; Joseph Medill McCormick to Arthur W. Page, 12 August 1921, Box 3, Joseph Medill McCormick Papers; Chicago Daily News, 11 June 1920; Denna Frank Fleming, The United States and the League of Nations, 1918–1920, pp. 451–52; Richard W. Leopold, Elihu Root and the Conservative Tradition, pp. 144–45; Jack E. Kendrick, "The League of Nations and Republican Senate, 1918–1921" (Ph.D. diss.), pp. 325–26; Edwin J. Gross, "A Political Grab Bag," Edwin J. Gross Papers; Isaac M. Ullman to William H. Taft, 11 June 1920, Taft to Lowell, 19 June 1920, to Caspar S. Yost, 19 June 1920, Box 471, Series 3, William Howard Taft Papers; Ralph Stone, The Irreconcilables: The Fight Against the League of Nations, p. 172.

42. Lenroot, "Memoirs," p. 156, Box 13, Lenroot Papers; Milwaukee Sentinel, 11 June 1920; White in the Chicago Daily News, 11 June 1920; Robert H. Zieger, Republicans and Labor, 1919–1929, pp. 32–34; James H. Shideler, Farm Crisis, 1919–1923, p. 34; Francis Russell, The Shadow of Blooming Grove: Warren G. Harding in His Times, p. 367; Boston Herald, 11 June 1920; Watson, As I Knew Them, p. 218; Wesley M. Bagby, The Road to Normalcy: The Presidential Campaign and Election of 1920, p. 81.

43. Wisconsin Week-End, 3 August 1967. I am grateful to Frieda Lease for bringing the incident to my attention.

read his report. When he read planks calling for government ownership of railroads and stockyards, delegates hooted and jeered; when, midway in his reading, Gross said, "Don't be afraid to applaud—it won't hurt you," the overheated and tired delegates and observers hissed until Lodge threatened to clear the galleries. In due course, Gross finished and the delegates greeted his motion to substitute the Wisconsin platform for the committee's with a deafening roar on no. Then, they approved the platform with a great shout, and only the La Follette group dissented. None of this dismayed those of the La Follette inner circle, for the senator was merely making a record for use if he decided to lead a third party.[44]

On Friday, 11 June, the already weary delegates turned to their main task—the nomination of a presidential candidate. Nominating and seconding speeches, punctuated by demonstrations, consumed the better part of the day, but the delegates finally managed four inconclusive ballots before adjourning for the night. The conference in the Blackstone Hotel suite shared by Hays and publicist George Harvey—widely known afterwards as the smoke-filled room where Sen. Warren Harding was chosen to be president—was less consequential than many have thought through the years, but it was not insignificant. It was less a conference than an open house, presided over by Harvey, and attended at one time or another by many party leaders, most of them senators. Lenroot did not appear. If the conclave, which lasted from eight in the evening until two in the morning, produced no large working force in Harding's behalf, it resulted in general agreement that Harding was likely to get the nomination, and that he deserved the first chance among the dark horses. Word of that conviction, when it spread through the convention on Saturday, assisted Harding.[45]

Through the week, while Lenroot steadfastly refused to become a candidate, a large number of newsmen considered him among the more likely dark horse possibilities. They wrote of his ability, his prominence in the battle of the League, the blessing that Roosevelt had placed upon him, the strength that his progressivism would bring the ticket in the west, and the fact that he had powerful friends in the east.[46]

44. *Milwaukee Sentinel*, 11 June 1920; *Boston Herald*, 11 June 1920; *Washington Herald*, 11 June 1920; Belle and Fola La Follette, *La Follette*, vol. 2, pp. 996–1010.

45. Robert K. Murray, *The Harding Era: Warren G. Harding and His Administration*, p. 39; Lenroot to Sullivan, 2 March 1935, Box 22A, Sullivan Papers; Randolph C. Downes, *The Rise of Warren Gamaliel Harding, 1865–1920*, p. 416; Bagby, *Road to Normalcy*, p. 91.

46. *Milwaukee Sentinel*, 1, 2, 6 June 1920; *Wisconsin State Journal*, 9, 10 June 1920; *Superior Telegram*, 11 June 1920, (Wisconsin papers cited out-of-state comment); *The Sun and New York Herald*, 8 June 1920; *Washington Herald*, 5, 11 June 1920; Walter Lippmann, "Our Next President?," pp. 9, 49; John M. Whitehead to E. B. Goodell, 3 August 1923, John M. Whitehead Papers. Charles McNary supplied testimonials for himself, Wesley Jones, and Democrat John Kendrick of Wyoming, and wished Lenroot political success "wherever your ambition may lie." McNary to Lenroot, 5 June 1920, Box 3, Lenroot Papers. A list of Lenroot's eastern friends would include Senators Calder and Hale and probably Lodge, Edge, Frelinghuysen, and Knox; it would include former Congressmen Fiorello La Guardia and Herbert Parsons, and might include former Senators Weeks and Crane, and publisher Frank Munsey.

When the senatorial clique gathered at the Blackstone, the prospect of a dark-horse nominee was great. It could not be said yet that Leonard Wood and Frank Lowden were in hopeless deadlock, but each of the two front-runners was greatly flawed as a prospective candidate. A recent senatorial investigation had revealed vast spending by both candidates, especially Wood. And some of the Lowden money had been used to bribe two delegates from Missouri.[47]

During the course of the long evening, the senatorial conferees considered all the possible nominees, Lenroot among him. The chief objection to him was that he was from Wisconsin, and that name connoted La Follette, Berger, "and who not else that is obnoxious."[48] Connotations aside, non-support from his home state was a crippling obstacle. Even so, Lenroot was evidently not dismissed entirely. One feature of the smoke-filled room legend is true—in the early morning hours Harding appeared in the suite and was asked whether he knew of any reason why he should not be nominated. After some minutes of private deliberation during which Harding surely considered the false rumors of his Negro ancestry and the facts of his illicit romances, the handsome Ohio senator replied in the negative—his record was clean. Meanwhile, however, Congressman James Frear of Wisconsin, who still admired Lenroot though he was uncomfortably located in La Follette's camp, was interviewed and told "from what seemed the highest available authority that instead of being the foremost Republican candidate for Vice President, as generally supposed, Lenroot was a presidential possibility, and the nomination was understood to be hanging on assurances first to be given by the successful candidate." When Harding became the nominee, Frear concluded that it was he who had given the assurances.[49] The purpose of the interview with Frear was undoubtedly to determine Lenroot's prospects for support from Wisconsin's twenty-four pro-La Follette delegates. Frear could not give any encouragement. Nevertheless, the next morning an uncertain number of leaders from New York and other large states met at the Congress hotel and agreed on Lenroot as a compromise candidate. But their emissaries failed to persuade General Wood and his manager, Col. William Procter, that Wood's cause was hopeless. Meanwhile, the swing toward Harding had begun.[50] On the seventh ballot, Harding passed Johnson and moved into third place. Following the eighth ballot on which he scored further gains, Harding's nomination seemed assured.

At that point, at 1:40 P.M., Lodge, who had been made permanent chair-

47. William T. Hutchinson, *Lowden of Illinois, The Life of Frank O. Lowden: Nation and Country-side*, p. 462; Downes, *Rise of Warren Gamaliel Harding*, pp. 406–8; Bagby, *Road to Normalcy*, p. 85; Mayer, *Republican Party*, p. 371.

48. Russell, *Shadow of Blooming Grove*, p. 379; Willis Fletcher Johnson, *George Harvey: "A Passionate Patriot,"* p. 277.

49. James A. Frear, *Forty Years of Progressive Public Service*, pp. 124–25.

50. *Superior Telegram*, 25 June 1920. The source for the *Superior Telegram*'s story was Luther W. Mott, dean of the New York Republican delegation in Congress.

man, engineered a recess. At first, Harding's managers protested, but Lodge explained that the recess would permit Harding to ensure fullest harmony by offering the vice-presidential nomination to Johnson.[51]

Johnson rejected second place, for the same reasons he had turned down Harding's previous proffer and that of other candidates, all of whom recognized his vote-getting power and the danger of his enmity. As a presidential candidate, Johnson was publicly committed not to barter his popularity in the primaries for the vice-presidency. To break that commitment now and to be a running mate with the man who had called him a "blackguard" and who was widely known as reactionary was out of the question.[52]

During the recess, which lasted for three hours, several efforts to combine against Harding aborted. Soon after the convention began its ninth ballot, the delegates from Connecticut, Kansas, and Kentucky made Harding's nomination sure. On the tenth ballot, Pennsylvania put Harding over the top and in due course the customary motion was put to make the nomination unanimous. Wisconsin, which had antagonized delegates by consistently casting twenty-four votes for La Follette, in effect disdaining participation in the nominating process, now led the minority that shouted loud but ineffectual noes to a chorus of boos and hisses.[53]

All that remained was the choice of a running mate for Harding. To the hot and tired delegates, many of whom were at the end of their patience and some nearing the end of their resources and chiefly concerned to check out of their hotels and keep their train reservations, the matter was of no great consequence.[54] But for the nation, the decision that would soon be made was of the highest consequence, for the man to be nominated was to become president of the United States.

Lenroot had been talked of as a vice-presidential prospect before the convention met, but nothing could be decided until the first place was filled.

51. Downes, *Rise of Warren Gamaliel Harding*, pp. 421–22; Bagby, *Road to Normalcy*, pp. 92–93; Harry M. Daugherty, *The Inside Story of the Harding Tragedy*, p. 48.

52. *Washington Evening Star*, 13 June 1920; Daugherty, *The Inside Story*, p. 50; Henry L. Stoddard, *It Costs to be President*, p. 71; Cora M. Fremont Older, *William Randolph Hearst: American*, p. 429; Henry J. Allen to Herman Hagedorn, 18 February 1929, Box 23, Herman Hagedorn Papers, LC; *Milwaukee Sentinel*, 13, 24 May 1920; Clifford B. Liljekvist, "Senator Hiram Johnson" (Ph.D. diss.), pp. 252–55.

53. Downes, *Rise of Warren Gamaliel Harding*, pp. 422–25; Hutchinson, *Lowden of Illinois*, pp. 465–68; Bagby, *Road to Normalcy*, pp. 93–96; *Washington Herald*, 13 June 1920; *The Sun and New York Herald*, 13, 14 June 1920; *New York Times*, 13, 14 June 1920; *Milwaukee Sentinel*, 12, 13 June 1920; *Portland Oregonian*, 15 June 1920; Daugherty, *The Inside Story*, p. 55; Mark Sullivan, *Our Times: The United States, 1900–1925*, vol. 6, p. 80; Republican Party, *Official Report of the Proceedings of the Seventeenth Republican National Convention* (New York, 1920), p. 224. From the seventh through the tenth ballots, Lenroot received one vote, that of La Guardia, a progressive Republican who had served with Lenroot in the House and had supported the League of Nations. *New York Times*, 13 June 1920; Elbridge L. Adams to League to Enforce Peace, 20 January 1919, Box 11, League to Enforce Peace Papers.

54. Donald R. McCoy, *Calvin Coolidge: The Quiet President*, pp. 119–20; Daugherty, *The Inside Story*, p. 45; *Washington Herald*, 14 June 1920.

Even those in Harvey's smoke-filled room deferred consideration of the matter.[55]

Not until Saturday afternoon did any substantial group of leaders discuss the question. Gathered initially to consider the presidency, the conferees, eighteen or twenty in total, were sure of Harding's nomination when Alvin T. Hert, one of Lowden's managers, appeared and announced at 3 P.M. that Lowden was withdrawing. Then or very shortly after, as they discussed prospective candidates for vice-president, they learned that Johnson was unavailable.[56]

The slate makers considered and eliminated the possibilities one by one. The governor of Kentucky was too close to Harding geographically; Gov. Calvin Coolidge of Massachusetts was talked of and put aside, perhaps because he was too close to the Harding ideology. What was needed to balance the ticket was a western progressive. Herbert Parsons, as Charles Hilles later recalled it, suggested Lenroot. (Parsons, the outgoing national committeeman from New York, had once been a congressional insurgent in the Cannon fight; more recently, he was committed to the cause of the League of Nations.) Lenroot was popular and respected among his senatorial colleagues, who were more than adequately represented at the conference. The Wisconsin onus would not matter if Lenroot were advertised as Harding's choice. He would do. Medill McCormick, still a friend and co-worker with Lenroot despite their differences over the League, asked the privilege of nominating him. First, however, Lenroot would have to agree to accept. McCormick went to get him.[57]

Lenroot declined the offer;[58] he said he preferred to remain in the Senate, and if he could not do that would rather resume private life than "be shut up in the vice president's chair."[59] Lenroot's decision was not surprising, for senators wielded far greater power than vice-presidents and Lenroot

55. Thomas A. Bailey, *Woodrow Wilson and the Great Betrayal*, p. 374; Charles Willis Thompson, *Presidents I've Known and Two Near Presidents*, p. 327; James W. Wadsworth to Sullivan, 5 March 1935, Box 17, James W. Wadsworth Family Papers, LC. Thompson claimed the matter had been settled in advance but it was patently impossible to do so with any finality.

56. Charles D. Hilles to Sullivan, 2 March 1935, to Wadsworth, 9 March 1935, Box 17, Wadsworth Papers; Lenroot, "Memoirs," p. 157, Box 13, Lenroot Papers. The *Washington Herald*, 13 June 1920, refers to the conference, though, as Hilles noted in his letter to Wadsworth, an effort was made to keep it secret. Among those certainly present were Hilles, Parsons, and McCormick. Others mentioned either by Hilles, the *Wasington Herald*, or Lenroot, were Crane, Smoot, Borah, New, Wadsworth, Warren, Hert, and Hays. Lenroot referred to Hays in Lenroot to Sullivan, 18 April 1935, Box 4, Lenroot Papers.

57. Hilles to Sullivan, 2 March 1935, to Wadsworth, 9 March 1935, Box 17, Wadsworth Papers; McGeorge Bundy and Henry L. Stimson, *On Active Service in Peace and War* (New York, 1948), p. 105; *The Sun and New York Herald*, 13 June 1920; *Chicago Daily News*, 14 June 1920; *Boston Herald*, 13 June 1920; Lenroot, "Memoirs," p. 156, Box 13, Lenroot Papers.

58. Lenroot to Sullivan, 18 April 1935, Box 4, to Cyril Clemens, 22 August 1939, Box 1, Lenroot Papers.

59. Lenroot to E. Mont Reily, 21 August 1945, to Sullivan, 18 April 1935, Box 4, Lenroot, "Memoirs," p. 157, Box 13, Lenroot Papers; *Superior Telegram*, 15 June 1920.

now thought he could win reelection.[60] Perhaps he thought, too, of the onerous social burdens the vice-presidency would impose on Clara, who agreed with him—whether before or after the conference is not clear—that he should not take the nomination.[61] And the office, though far surer of attainment than reelection, was a political deadend. Nor could he forget his political obligations in Wisconsin—it would not do to leave the polyglot anti-radical element without strong and progressive leadership. Finally, the prospect of political defeat was not intolerable. He was fifty-one; Clara was sixty-three. It was time to earn some money toward retirement. The conferees, for want of further time, dispersed without having reached a decision.[62]

McCormick, who for years had attempted to reunite the Republican party on a basis that was fair to progressives, continued to view Lenroot as the ideal man. When, as the expected Harding shift proceeded, he and Borah learned from Watson that he had promised to nominate Gov. Henry Allen of Kansas for vice-president, they objected. Although the delegates from Kansas switched from Wood to Harding at a critical moment during the ninth ballot in the expectation of Allen's nomination, McCormick and Borah persuaded Watson that the Kansas industrial court law was anathema to organized labor and that a Harding-Allen ticket would lose much of the labor vote.[63]

Hastily the energetic McCormick led in assembling a group of party elders in a little cubicle beneath the stage; there he pressured them for a quick decision, which was of necessity, and urged the name of Lenroot. The need for a progressive to balance the ticket remained obvious; Lenroot was well liked and he came from the right region, if not the ideal state. The others— Hert of Kentucky, Borah, Weeks, Harry Daugherty, Harding's manager, Wadsworth, Watson, Sen. Lawrence Phipps of Colorado, perhaps Smoot, and Sen. William Calder—agreed on him.[64]

60. Esch to Homer C. Denison, 14 June 1920, Box 58, Esch Papers.

61. Lenroot to Sullivan, 18 April 1935, Box 4, Lenroot Papers.

62. In his letter to Wadsworth of 9 March 1935, Hilles recalled that Lenroot had been present throughout the conference and had acquiesced in its decision. Events showed, however, that he had not acquiesced, and that no decision had been reached. It is possible, but not likely, that he had been present throughout. If he were, his refusal would have been more quickly registered, leaving time for a decision favoring someone else. Moreover, the facts of this incident, which Lenroot had many occasions to rehearse over the years, were more likely to have remained in his memory than in Hilles's.

63. Watson, *As I Knew Them*, p. 223; White in the *Chicago Daily News*, 14 June 1920; Bagby, *Road to Normalcy*, pp. 95, 100.

64. *Portland Oregonian*, 14 June 1920; Bagby, *Road to Normalcy*, p. 100; McCoy, *Calvin Coolidge*, p. 119; Sullivan, *Our Times*, vol. 6, p. 78; Wadsworth to Hilles, 6 March 1935, Box 17, Wadsworth Papers; James W. Wadsworth, "The Smoke-Filled Room," pp. 109–10, (from a 1952 Columbia University Oral History Research Office interview); Wadsworth to Ray Baker Harris, 27 June 1938, Reel 257, Harry Daugherty to Harris, 9 October 1939, Reel 259, Ray Baker Harris Deposit, Warren G. Harding Papers; Raymond Clapper, "The Dark Horse Wins," n.d. (June 1920), Box 66, Raymond Clapper Papers.

Quickly Watson explained the situation to Allen, who accepted it with good grace, although his friends in the delegation later put forth his name on their own.[65] McCormick, meanwhile, got the cooperation of Chairman Hays, who continued to think well of Lenroot and who had made a career of unifying the party.[66]

Watson saw Harding about the vice-presidency and found the prospective presidential nominee willing to give his senatorial friends carte blanche. But Hays, in conferring with Lenroot in a corridor below the stage to which he had summoned the senator, said that Harding wanted Lenroot. Although Hays was seeking to persuade, there is reason to think that Harding was, indeed, pleased with the choice of his colleagues.[67]

Hays, who had been present when Lenroot earlier rejected the offer, now tried to make it as attractive as possible. He quoted Harding as saying that the office would be more than honorary—Lenroot would sit with the Cabinet and help to make policy. And he appealed to Lenroot's party loyalty—the nomination would be made in a few minutes, it would be a fait accompli, and one on whose wisdom the leaders agreed. Would Lenroot go before the convention and reject the nomination? Lenroot restated his objections, Hays urged further consideration, and finally, after the two had consumed a good deal of time, Lenroot said he would consult with his wife and their friends General and Mrs. William Crozier, who were seated adjacent to the platform and would return with his answer.[68]

By this time, Harding had been nominated, and McCormick, in a state of high excitement, immediately nominated Lenroot for vice-president in a brief speech, calling him a man of exceptional ability, experience, and magnetic force.[69] Others hastened onto the floor to pass the word.[70] In swift succession, speeches that seconded the nomination were made by Hert; H. L. Remmel of Arkansas, well known for conveying the wishes of the party leaders; Myron T. Herrick of Ohio, a spokesman for Harding; and Senator Calder of the powerful New York delegation. But during McCormick's speech, someone shouted "Coolidge! Coolidge!" and after Calder uttered

65. Watson, *As I Knew Them,* pp. 233–36; Bagby, *Road to Normalcy,* p. 100.

66. Hays to Sullivan, 3 July 1935, Box 22A, Sullivan Papers. In this letter Hays admits that he thought well of Lenroot but does not discuss the part he played. See note below.

67. Watson, *As I Knew Them,* p. 224; Lenroot, "Memoirs," p. 157, Box 13, Reily to Lenroot, 10 August 1945, Box 4, Lenroot Papers; *Milwaukee Sentinel,* 20 October 1920. Reily, Harding's western manager in 1920, asserted that prior to the convention Harding said that if he were nominated he wanted Lenroot as running mate. The story is not inconsistent with his expediential offers to Johnson prior to the nomination. Harding later endorsed Lenroot for senator in more than perfunctory terms. *Milwaukee Sentinel,* 20 October–2 November 1920.

68. Lenroot to Sullivan, 18 April 1935, Box 4, Lenroot, "Memoirs," p. 157, Box 13, Lenroot Papers.

69. Lenroot to Sullivan, 18 April 1935, Box 4, Lenroot Papers; Stoddard, *It Costs to be President,* p. 71; Hilles to Wadsworth, 9 March 1935, Box 17, Wadsworth Papers; *The Sun and New York Herald,* 13 June 1920.

70. Clapper, "The Dark Horse Wins," n.d. (June 1920), Box 66, Clapper Papers.

the words "of Wisconsin" following Lenroot's name, another voice shouted "Not on your life." [71]

A man of small stature with a strong voice stood on a chair in the rear of the hall and demanded to be recognized. Frank Willis, evidently expecting another seconding motion for Lenroot, recognized him. Amidst the general turmoil, few of the conventioneers heard all the words the man said, but the delegates heard the name "Coolidge" and greeted it with applause and cheers. Seconding motions came from all over the hall, and even Remmel, sensing the temper of the convention, withdrew his second for Lenroot and switched to Coolidge.[72] Back at his seat by then, Lenroot could see that there was no occasion to respond to Hays.[73] Two other names were put in nomination but the enthusiasm for Governor Coolidge did not wane; he was promptly nominated by the somewhat depleted convention, getting $674\frac{1}{2}$ votes to Lenroot's $146\frac{1}{2}$. Lenroot received just two votes from Wisconsin; the other twenty-four were given to Gronna.[74]

Afterwards, reporters and politicians had a chance to sort out what had happened. Many delegates associated Lenroot with Wisconsin, whose delegates each day held themselves righteously apart; voted for La Follette when no one else would; and within the hour had refused to make unanimous the nomination of Harding. Coolidge, on the other hand, represented law and order against the excesses of labor. It was he who had wired Samuel Gompers after the police strike in Boston was broken: "There is no right to strike against the public safety by anybody, anywhere, anytime." He had been pushed for the presidency earlier and in the course of that campaign his managers distributed a felicitous collection of his speeches and pronouncements; later, they saw to it that each delegate and alternate had a copy.[75]

Wallace McCamant, the Oregon delegate who had nominated Coolidge, was one of those who had approved Coolidge's words. McCamant was not so obscure a figure as some historians have thought. A former judge on the

71. Republican Party, *Proceedings of the Seventeenth Republican National Convention*, p. 225; Sullivan, *Our Times*, vol. 6, p. 78; McCoy, *Calvin Coolidge*, p. 120.

72. McCoy, *Calvin Coolidge*, pp. 120–21; William Allen White, *A Puritan in Babylon: The Story of Calvin Coolidge*, pp. 108–9; Sullivan, *Our Times*, vol. 6, p. 79; Republican Party, *Proceedings of the Seventeenth Republican National Convention*, p. 226.

73. Lenroot to Sullivan, 18 April 1935, Box 4, Lenroot Papers; *Superior Telegram*, 15 June 1920; Lenroot, "Memoirs," pp. 157–58, Box 13, Lenroot Papers. In his letter to Sullivan, Lenroot wrote that he returned from his conversation with Hays in time to hear McCormick finish his nomination speech. He told a reporter days after the event that he did not know his name would be presented until five minutes before he was nominated. In his "Memoirs" he wrote that the Coolidge stampede was practically over when he returned. Even presuming the account to Sullivan accurate, there would have been little time for consultation with Clara, and, as Lenroot maintained, no occasion to reply to Hays.

74. John Whitehead, one of the uninstructed delegates, urged John Blaine, head of the delegation, to support Lenroot, but Blaine scorned the idea. Whitehead to Goodell, 4 August 1923, Whitehead Papers.

75. Sullivan, *Our Times*, vol. 6, p. 80; McCoy, *Calvin Coolidge*, pp. 94, 102–21.

supreme court of Oregon and head of the Sons of the American Revolution, McCamant was elected as a delegate at large. At the convention, he served not only on the platform committee but on the thirteen-member subcommittee that did the actual platform drafting. Although Johnson won Oregon's preferential primary, McCamant, a conservative Rooseveltian in his politics, voted for Wood on every ballot. He was a strong law-and-order man whose thinking accorded with all of the Oregon delegates and with most of the others in the convention. Informed in advance of nominations that Lenroot had been decided on, McCamant and his Oregon colleagues, for a variety of reasons, disapproved and decided to nominate Coolidge. But first, McCamant sought out Lodge to get permission to put him in nomination, in accordance with the results of the Oregon primary. When Lodge declined, McCamant secured his assent to the nomination of Coolidge; Lodge had no reason to think that Coolidge would actually win.[76]

Due in large part to their resentment against dictation by senators, most delegates supported Coolidge's nomination. The senatorial contingent, they believed, made their own men temporary and permanent chairman and head of the resolutions committee. They had dictated the nomination of Harding, another of their own; Senator Penrose, rumor had it, gave the word by telephone from his sick bed in Philadelphia. Now the senators were demanding even the second place. The delegates, mainly supporters of Lowden, Wood, or Johnson, had been denied their first choice on the presidency; tired and resentful, they would not again accept senatorial dictation.[77]

The *New York Times*'s reporter doubted that the leaders really wanted Lenroot as a nominee for the vice-presidency. It seemed inconceivable that they could not effect their complete program if they really wanted to. The reporter's conjecture was inaccurate in doubting the sincerity of the effort for Lenroot but was correct in judging it strange that the leaders had been unable to control the situation. Later, Hays told Lenroot that if he had accepted the offer of the earlier conference, during the recess, there would have been enough time to get the word to the delegates. The name of Lenroot would have gone out not as the choice of a Senate clique, but the selection of the presidential nominee, which was quite another matter. As it was, some delegates were in doubt to the last as to whom the leaders had chosen or what Harding wanted. Coolidge noted that night that had McCamant not nominated him, some one else would have. But if Harding's

76. Claude M. Fuess, *Calvin Coolidge: The Man From Vermont,* p. 261; *Washington Evening Star,* 1 February 1926, 8 June 1920; *The Sun and New York Herald,* 11 June 1920; Joseph W. Martin, Jr., *My First Fifty Years in Politics,* p. 143; McCoy, *Calvin Coolidge,* pp. 119–20; *Portland Oregonian,* 13 June 1920.

77. *Washington Evening Star,* 6 June 1920; *The Sun and New York Herald,* 8 June 1920; *Washington Herald,* 10 June 1920; *Chicago Daily News,* 14 June 1920; Murray, *The Harding Era,* pp. 39–40; White, *A Puritan in Babylon,* pp. 208–9; Martin, *My First Fifty Years,* p. 143; *Portland Oregonian,* 14 June 1920.

preference had been made forcefully clear, nothing else would have mattered—neither Wisconsin's unpopularity nor the conservatism of the delegates and the popularity of Coolidge nor the smoldering resentment against the senators.[78]

Ultimately, then, it was Lenroot who determined the outcome. What answer he would have given Hays had he been nominated we do not know. Perhaps he himself never knew. But chatting with friends in the Palmer House after the convention he appeared in good spirits. In later life, knowing that he had denied himself the presidency, Lenroot always said he had no regrets. But in 1935, after reviewing Mark Sullivan's account of the convention, he asked Sullivan to make clear that he had declined the prospective nomination in the afternoon.[79]

Before Lenroot could begin his reelection campaign, he had to say something about his party's national ticket, whose leader he knew well through association on the commerce committee. On 15 June, he made a public statement in Superior:

> I frankly regret the choice of the Republican convention as I believe a man who had been allied with the liberal wing of the party should have been selected. . . . However, Senator Harding is a most lovable man, of the McKinley type, and makes friends easily. . . . There is dissatisfaction upon the part of progressives but they must choose between supporting the Republican ticket and having another four years of Democratic rule and all it implies. In this situation . . . there can be but one choice . . . and that is heartily to support the republican ticket.

In regard to talk of a third party, he replied:

> . . . this, if supported by progressives, would only insure a democratic victory. . . . If, when elected president, Harding shall adopt reactionary policies and be controlled by the old guard, I shall be among the first to join a new political party with policies that are constructively liberal and not destructively radical. The fact is that there is a struggle going on today between predatory wealth and certain branches of labor, each seeking special privilege, to the injury of the general public. We must oppose both, and both must be given to understand that the interests of all the people are paramount to those of any class. No man, no corporation, no organization, has any right to anything but a square deal, and that all should have.

However cool the endorsement, having declared himself for Harding, Lenroot wired a pledge of support and offered his services in the campaign.[80]

It must have been comforting to Lenroot when progressives such as Kent,

78. *New York Times*, 14 June 1920; Lenroot, "Memoirs," p. 158, Box 13, Lenroot Papers; *Milwaukee Journal*, 27 January 1949; *Boston Herald*, 13 June 1920.

79. *Milwaukee Journal*, 27 January 1949; Lenroot to Sullivan, 18 April 1935, Box 4, Lenroot Papers.

80. Lenroot to Sullivan, 2 March 1935, Box 4, Lenroot Papers; *The Sun and New York Herald*, 16 June 1920; *Milwaukee Sentinel*, 16 June 1920; *Superior Telegram*, 15 June 1920; Lenroot to Harding, 19 July 1920, Harding to Lenroot, 26 July 1920, Reel 75, Harding Papers.

Norris, Gifford Pinchot, White, and many others succumbed to Harding's good-natured conciliation and endorsed him as against the Democratic nominee, Gov. James Cox of Ohio.[81]

After issuing his statement on Harding, Lenroot took a few days of rest, then he began a semi-campaign, making frequent trips outside of his base in Superior. Despite his earlier optimism, by 21 July, as he was about to start an intensive and extended tour of Wisconsin, he saw only "*a bare possibility of winning out*," as Clara reported to the Croziers.[82] Clara and Irvine remained pessimistic until nearly the end of the primary campaign. Others, friend and foe alike, assessed the situation as the Lenroots did.[83]

The roadblocks to reelection, which Lenroot had not fully perceived earlier, were many and formidable. Discontent remained rife in the state, and those who proposed to exploit it were well organized. In midsummer, farm prices began declining, thus worsening the situation for Wisconsin farmers. With a decrease in exports, in federal spending, and in credit came the beginning of a business slump. Laborers, who constituted over a third of the state's gainfully employed, suffered from high prices and feared the efforts of employers to lower wages, break strikes, and block or destroy unionism. Railroad workers were especially unhappy following the termination of federal operation, and they, with others, tended to misconstrue the Esch-Cummins law. A middle-class group that organized into the Wisconsin branch of the Committee of 48 pressed the issue of individual liberty. They found a receptive audience among the Germans in the state. That was the nub of the matter. "The fact that one third of our population is of German blood is what makes the fight so hard," Lenroot wrote Herbert Hoover, and with some justification.[84]

On the state level, the Nonpartisan League was not as wealthy as the La Follette men hoped and Lenroot feared, but it did have over twenty-three

81. Downes, *Rise of Warren Gamaliel Harding*, pp. 425–47; Robertson, "Progressives In National Republican Politics," pp. 301–8; George W. Norris, *Fighting Liberal: The Autobiography of George W. Norris*, p. 214; Oscar S. Straus, Diary, 8–24 June 1920, Box 24, Oscar S. Straus Papers; Slattery to Pinchot, 23, 29 June 1920, Box 141, Pinchot Papers; Bates, *Origins of Teapot Dome*, pp. 210–11.

82. Clara Lenroot to Mrs. William Crozier, 21 July 1920, Mary William Crozier Papers, Connecticut College.

83. Clara Lenroot to Mr. and Mrs. William Crozier, 13 September 1920, Crozier Papers; *Milwaukee Sentinel*, 9 September 1920; Henry G. Teigan, to W. C. Zumach, 19 July 1920, Teigan to Thomas Amlie, 12 July 1920, W. C. Zumach to Teigan, 3, 19 August 1920, Reel 1, Henry G. Teigan Papers; Robert M. La Follette, Jr., to Charles Crownhart, 20 August 1920, Box 113, Series B, La Follette FC; W. B. Tscharner to Esch, 17 July 1920, Box 59, Esch Papers.

84. Margulies, *The Decline of the Progressive Movement*, pp. 248–50; Shideler, *Farm Crisis*, p. 46; Hicks, *Rehearsal for Disaster*, pp. 24–26, 77; Samuelson and Hagen, *After the War*, pp. 34–37; Esch to Fred A. Holden, 20 July 1920, A. P. Nelson to Esch, 9 July 1920, Box 59, Esch Papers; Lenroot to Herbert Hoover, 4 August 1920, Pre-Commerce Papers, 1920 Campaign, Herbert Hoover Papers, Herbert Hoover Presidential Library (hereafter referred to as HHPL). With respect to the German vote see also Lenroot to Pinchot, 23 August 1920, Box 229, Pinchot Papers; George M. Sheldon to La Follette, 19 August 1920, Box 87, Series B, La Follette FC; Esch to Tscharner, 19 July 1920, Box 59, Esch Papers; and Michael Paul Rogin, *The Intellectuals and McCarthy: The Radical Specter*, pp. 73–75.

thousand members, had eighty or more organizers in the field, and distributed its own newspaper and other literature. Appealing to farmers and laborers against the "Plunderbund," the league had its largest membership among normally conservative German farmers in the southern and eastern parts of the state, despite its radical program of government ownership.[85] The State Federation of Labor and the powerful railroad brotherhoods willingly allied with the Nonpartisan League for the 1920 campaign. Under the leadership of Attorney General John Blaine and of La Follette, La Follette's lieutenants at a convention in June coalesced with the league behind a full slate of candidates representing both elements. The convention endorsed James Thompson for senator and Blaine for governor, but three of the other four on the state ticket were Nonpartisan Leaguers.[86]

So far as national issues were concerned, the Esch-Cummins Act offered the most convenient target for the radical coalition. By alleging that the act raised costs for all, by requiring higher rates to ensure profits on watered stock, the La Follette men and the Nonpartisan Leaguers were able to appeal to farmers and other producers and consumers. In so doing, they cemented their alliance with the aggressive railroad unions. With their weekly paper *Labor* and their many officials and organizers, they were determined to defeat congressmen and senators who had supported the new law.[87]

The coalition against Lenroot was not as complete as it might have been. Berger, angry that Nonpartisan Leaguers in Congress had voted not to seat him and eager to advance the fortunes of the social democratic party, held aloof from the radical coalition.[88] Equally important, in June, Mayor A. C. McHenry of Oshkosh, Wisconsin, could not be dissuaded in announcing himself as a Republican candidate for the Senate on a "wet" platform. He figured to draw most of his support from Thompson's natural constituency.[89]

Because of a recent operation, La Follette was unable to take the stump,

85. Theodore Saloutos, "The Non-Partisan League in the Western Middle West," *Agricultural History* 20 (October 1946):235–51; financial summary, 1 January 1920 to 29 February 1921, Wisconsin Nonpartisan League Papers, WSHSL, both cited in Margulies, *The Decline of the Progressive Movement*, p. 251; *Milwaukee Sentinel*, 17 June 1920; Lenroot to Pinchot, 15 July 1920, Box 229, Pinchot Papers; Zumach to Teigan, 5 January 1920, 27 September 1920, Reel 1, Teigan Papers; Esch to Tscharner, 17 July 1920, Box 59, Esch Papers.

86. Margulies, *The Decline of the Progressive Movement*, pp. 251–52; *Milwaukee Sentinel*, 17 June 1920. On the background of the Nonpartisan League see especially Robert L. Morlan, *Political Prairie Fire: The Non-Partisan League, 1915–1922* (Minneapolis, 1955).

87. Margulies, *The Decline of the Progressive Movement*, pp. 253, 264; leaflet, "To Americans Ready for the American Nonpartisan League," n.d. (1920), Reel 7, National Nonpartisan League Papers, Minnesota Historical Society; Edward Keating, *The Gentleman from Colorado: A Memoir*, pp. 477–80, 487, 491, 493, 501; Philip Taft, *The A. F. of L. in the Time of Gompers*, pp. 467–68; Edward Keating to La Follette, 29 June 1920, Box 85, Series B, La Follette FC.

88. Margulies, *The Decline of the Progressive Movement*, pp. 259–61; Teigan to Zumach, 19 July 1920, Zumach to Teigan, 3 August 1920, Teigan to Zumach, 23 August 1920, Zumach to Teigan, 27 September, 14 November 1920, Reel 1, Teigan Papers.

89. Margulies, *The Decline of the Progressive Movement*, pp. 267–68.

but he endorsed Thompson. On 24 August, in the pages of his magazine, he provided a roll call against Lenroot and a signed editorial denouncing the Esch-Cummins Act and noting Lenroot's support of it. The League of Nations issue was not the most prominent in the anti-Lenroot campaign, but La Follette and his friends gave it some attention.[90]

The roll call on Lenroot stressed his votes for treaty ratification and against various La Follette amendments. It referred to his vote for the 1918 amendments to the Espionage Act and said "Lenroot voted AGAINST taxing war profits to pay the cost of the war, as provided in the La Follette substitute to the War Revenue Bill." The article used similar phrasing with reference to Lenroot's vote against La Follette amendments to the mineral lands leasing bill. The roll call claimed he switched positions overnight on the no-strike provision of the Cummins bill, "without explanation." On 29 July, the I.C.C. had approved substantial rate increases, which were to take effect on 26 August. The roll call asserted that extension of government operation, which La Follette proposed and Lenroot voted against, would have made unnecessary the increase. As to the Esch-Cummins law, La Follette asserted that it "guaranteed fabulous profits to the private owners, regardless of whether they moved the freight or squandered millions in wasteful management. LENROOT CAST HIS VOTE IN THE FACE OF THE ASSURANCE THAT UNDER THIS LAW RATES WOULD BE IM-MEDIATELY ADVANCED." The rate increase would cost each family a dollar a day, on the average. Furthermore, according to the roll call, Lenroot had voted against a reservation "recognizing Ireland's right of self determination, and urging Ireland's admission to the League of Nations." And he voted for the Army Reorganization bill, a costly and militaristic one.[91] Newspaper advertisements and pamphlets spread the word.[92] At the last, Lenroot's position on the leasing bill and more particularly the Esch-Cummins Act became the big issues of the Thompson campaign.

Two weeks before the end of the campaign, Lenroot wrote Gifford Pinchot: "Our old-time friend, La Follette, is conducting the most unscrupulous campaign, so far as misrepresentation of public questions is concerned, that I have ever known in my more than twenty years of political life." Afterwards, Clara wrote the Croziers that against Irvine "was opposed a desperate campaign of lying and misrepresentations, growing worse and worse daily as the situation grew more and more desperate for La Follette's candidate." Her husband had stayed away from personalities "just as long as the enemy made it at all possible. When the lies came too thick and fast and vicious to be longer ignored he was forced to take notice of them." [93]

90. La Follette, Jr., to Paul C. Olson, 25 August 1920, to Sullivan, 27 August 1920, Box 113, Series B, La Follette FC; *Milwaukee Sentinel,* 21 July 1920; *La Follette's Magazine* 12:8 (August 1920): 115; *Superior Telegram,* 24 August 1920.

91. *La Follette's Magazine* 12:8 (August 1920):115.

92. J. D. Beck to La Follette, 17 August 1920, Box 85, Series B, La Follette, Jr., to Gilbert Roe, 30 August 1920, Box 6, Series H, La Follette FC.

93. Lenroot to Pinchot, 23 August 1920, Box 229, Pinchot Papers; Clara Lenroot to Mr. and Mrs. William Crozier, 13 September 1920, Crozier Papers.

It is true that Lenroot referred to La Follette by name only in the last stages of the campaign. But the misrepresentations of which he complained had been circulating for some time, especially with respect to the Esch-Cummins Act. From the first, he had attempted not only to correct these but to denounce those responsible. At Janesville, Wisconsin, a city of conservative outlook, Lenroot stressed the dangers of class government and then offered a test of a demagogue. It is easy to fight organized wealth or an organization that does not command a large number of votes; but will the politician fight an organization that does have large numbers (such as the Nonpartisan League). "If we are not, then we are nothing but political profiteers, counting upon the indifference of the unorganized masses and gathering to ourselves the support of organizations that menace a government of, by and for the people." At Fond du Lac, Wisconsin, the next day he corrected misrepresentations about the guarantee in the Esch-Cummins Act and said he was impatient with those who would use the party without intending to support the party's candidates, reminding the crowd of the actions of the twenty-four La Follette delegates at the national convention.[94]

In mid-August, at La Crosse, Wisconsin, after denouncing "political profiteers" as being as bad as economic profiteers, Lenroot defended his record on oil leasing and contrasted it with La Follette's inaction through the years. The next day he promised that if elected he would "not be a rubber stamp for any man living." Then, at Richland Center, he offered to withdraw as a candidate if Thompson could prove that the railroad law guaranteed a 6 percent return on $8 billion of watered stock and challenged Thompson to withdraw if he could not. In his final speech at Madison, Lenroot answered all the charges in La Follette's roll call and tried to show that they were misleading. He again contrasted his own record on mineral leasing over the years with that of La Follette, whom he depicted as a Johnny-come-lately.[95]

On the morning of the primaries, Sheasby's lead article in the *Milwaukee Sentinel* began: "The great issue of progressivism against Townleyism and extreme radicalism will be fought out . . . at the primary election." [96] If that was the case, then the electorate gave an inconclusive verdict. Blaine was nominated for governor, and two other state candidates of the radical coalition also won nomination. Esch lost, after eleven terms in Congress. But in the senatorial contest, Lenroot won. The tally stood Lenroot, 169,296; Thompson, 149,442; McHenry, 46,952. La Follette was able to make a good case when he ascribed Lenroot's victory to McHenry's candidacy.

94. *Milwaukee Sentinel*, 29, 30 July, 4 August 1920. With respect to the Esch-Cummins Act, Lenroot pointed out that under terms of the act for six months the railway companies would receive no less than the amount of rental paid them during the period of federal operation. After 1 September, the law provided no guarantee at all. The I.C.C. would fix rates designed to yield 5.5 or 6 percent return on the value of property, but if a company did not earn that much it would get nothing from the Treasury.

95. Ibid., 18, 19, 20, 26, 28 August, 4 September 1920.

96. Ibid., 7 September 1920.

Thompson had foreseen the danger but he had hedged on his answers to the questionnaire from the Order of the Camels, hoping that the anti-prohibition organization would support him nevertheless. But the Camels thought McHenry could win and refused to deviate from their established standards for endorsement. On the other side, the Anti-Saloon League, regarding Lenroot's candidacy as of great importance, put on a quiet but effective campaign for him. A week before the end, the head of the Wisconsin branch made known the League's position in a letter to ministers around the state.[97]

The Lenroots felt relatively comfortable about the general election as they traveled to California to visit Dorothy. Dr. Paul Reinsch, the Democratic candidate, was an admirable man, a political scientist from the University of Wisconsin, and more recently minister to China. But clearly, it was a Republican year, so extreme and diffuse was the public reaction against the Wilson administration. If La Follette's backers bolted to Reinsch, they might make a hard fight of it, but they would thereby jeopardize the prospects of Blaine and others on the state ticket.

By 10 October, when Lenroot established campaign headquarters in Milwaukee, he knew his confidence had been misplaced. Immediately after the primary, La Follette began arranging to put James Thompson into the field as an independent candidate. He successfully negotiated for continuing support from the railroad brotherhoods in the form of money, men, and literature; he renewed his alliance with the Nonpartisan League; in a signed editorial in his magazine he established the League of Nations as the main issue of the campaign, although he granted the Esch-Cummins Act co-billing, perhaps for the edification of the railroad men; on the basis of the League issue, he got from Hearst the support of his newspapers in Chicago and Milwaukee; on the same basis, Senator Reed, though a Democrat, promised to make speeches. La Follette made it clear to his allies that the fight for Thompson meant a great deal to him personally and that he would not only organize but speak against Lenroot.[98]

The situation was in many ways dangerous to Lenroot. At the platform convention, his own manager, Alvin Peterson, had been chosen state chairman over Blaine's man, but the fact was not comforting for the rejection

97. *Wisconsin Blue Book*, 1921, p. 75; La Follette to Stone, W. G. Lee, and W. S. Carter, 19 September 1920, to S. H. Gruenheck, 30 September 1920, to William Borah, 2 October 1920, to James Reed, 8 October 1920, Box 113, Christian Doerfler to La Follette, 3 August 1920, Box 85, Series B, La Follette FC; Peter D. Odegard, *Pressure Politics: The Story of the Anti-Saloon League*, p. 93; Margulies, *The Decline of the Progressive Movement*, p. 268.

98. *Milwaukee Sentinel*, 11 October 1920; Margulies, *The Decline of the Progressive Movement*, p. 273; La Follette to Stone, Lee, Carter, 10 September 1920, Box 113, Stone to La Follette, 15, 23 September, 9 October 1920, Box 87, La Follette to Kronshage, Box 113, to Frederic C. Howe, 19 October 1920, Box 87, La Follette FC; Zumach to Teigan, 24, 27 September 1920, Reel 1, Teigan Papers; *La Follette's Magazine* 12:9 (September 1920):129; La Follette to Reed, 8 October 1920, Reed to La Follette, 5, 17 October 1920, Box 86, La Follette FC; Zumach to Teigan, 13 October 1920, Reel 1, Teigan Papers.

of the gubernatorial candidate's choice was unusual and signaled a polarization of forces outside of party lines. The platform adopted was largely progressive, but at the insistence of a group led by William J. Morgan, candidate for attorney general, it denounced the Nonpartisan League and withheld endorsement of Blaine. In short order, Morgan called on the Republican State Central Committee to give no help to any candidate who would not support the platform, including Blaine, and a number of Republican newspapers and politicians came out for the Democratic nominee, Col. R. B. McCoy. To many, this was to be the showdown, carrying over from the war period and intensified by postwar grievances; it had strong ethnic as well as economic overtones, and in many communities feeling became intense. There could be but two sides not three. Lenroot could count on the support of the State Central Committee, the business community, most of the city newspapers, and those of Yankee stock. But to win he would have to make some inroads among Germans and among farmers and workers of whatever extraction.[99]

Thompson took the widespread bolt against Blaine as justification for his own candidacy. In announcing it on 6 October, he willingly embraced the League issue and warned that if the United States entered the League "our soldiers will continue to police the Rhine and act as debt collectors for foreign nations. The league will almost certainly embroil us in foreign wars. Two times," he went on, "Lenroot deliberately voted to get this country into the League. If elected he will do so again." He also stressed the Esch-Cummins Act as the source of high prices in the face of declining farm income, an argument that struck home with farmers as they felt the impact of rate increases.[100] But despite intensive negotiations and an endorsement from Mayor McHenry, he failed to convince the Order of Camels. Nor would the social democrats give way in his favor, and the Camels endorsed their candidate, Frank Weber.[101] Even so, Thompson's prospects were bright as Lenroot launched his campaign in Milwaukee on 14 October.[102]

Lenroot took up a defensive position. Ostensibly talking Republican doctrine against Cox and Reinsch, he called the League as offered by Wilson the paramount issue. A vote for any of the minor parties for president is half a vote for Cox and Franklin Roosevelt, "and a vote for their Senatorial candidate or any Independent candidate for Senate is half a vote for Dr. Reinsch." Lenroot elaborated on his objections to Article Ten while ignoring other parts of the covenant; he endorsed the vague position taken by Harding in favor of an association of nations under which the United States

99. Margulies, *The Decline of the Progressive Movement*, pp. 272–76; A. O. Barton to James M. Pierce, 22 September 1920, Box 1, Albert O. Barton Papers.

100. *Milwaukee Sentinel*, 6 October 1920.

101. Thompson to La Follette, 7 October 1920, Box 87, Walter Corrigan to La Follette, 11 October 1920, Box 85, La Follette to A. C. McHenry, 4 November 1920, Box 113, Series B, La Follette FC; *Milwaukee Sentinel*, 30 October 1920.

102. *Milwaukee Sentinel*, 19 October 1920.

would use its moral force against war. But he did not renew his fight for ratification with reservations.[103]

On 21 October, La Follette took center stage before a turn away audience in excess of seven thousand at the Milwaukee auditorium. For nearly two hours, he gave his interpretation of public measures and read the roll call against Lenroot along the lines of his magazine article published in August. Chiefly, La Follette stressed the Treaty of Versailles, with its "diabolic league of nations," and the Transportation Act of 1920. Behind both, he said, "are the great exploiting interest of the United States and the world— the international bankers with their deposit boxes full of worthless foreign securities and bonds which they seek to have the United States guarantee by dragging us into the league of nations, and of watered railroad securities which they have already had the government guarantee by the iniquitous terms of the Esch-Cummins railroad law." Once a progressive, Lenroot had "deserted the progressive ranks under fire" and become a tool of such special interests, La Follette charged.[104]

After reading an account of La Follette's speech, Lenroot sent him an angry challenge, which the pro-Lenroot press gave front-page coverage. He accused his former friend of uttering "plain unvarnished falsehoods."

> In your vindictive hate of one who would not be your willing tool you have lost all regard for truth, all sense of honor. . . . You parade in your Magazine the motto "Ye shall know the truth and the truth shall make you free." The people of Wisconsin desire to know the truth in this campaign and to assist them in learning it I invite you to discuss with me the issues of the campaign, as outlined by you, at the same place in Milwaukee that you delivered your speech, or any other place that you may desire. I concede your superior eloquence, I realize your disregard of facts, but I shall rely upon the truth to secure a verdict from any audience in the State of Wisconsin.[105]

La Follette dismissed the challenge. The intemperate language of Lenroot's letter "shows that he is incapable of presenting a fair discussion of any subject before an intelligent audience at the present time," La Follette said. He went on to reiterate his charges, as he did in two other speeches.[106] Thompson offered to defend La Follette's position but Lenroot immediately wired him, care of La Follette: "Your invitation declined. This controversy brought on by your principal and no one can take his place. Please urge him to accept my invitation." [107]

In the remaining days of the campaign, Lenroot defended the progressiv-

103. Ibid., 15 October 1920; "Wisconsin Speech, 1920," Box 8, Lenroot Papers.

104. *Milwaukee Sentinel*, 22 October 1920; Belle and Fola La Follette, *La Follette*, vol. 2, pp. 1016–17.

105. Lenroot, "Memoirs," pp. 159–60, Lenroot Papers; *Milwaukee Sentinel*, 25 October 1920.

106. Belle and Fola La Follette, *La Follette*, vol. 2, p. 1017; *Milwaukee Sentinel*, 29, 31 October 1920.

107. *Milwaukee Sentinel*, 25, 26 October 1920.

ism of his record and charged that it was La Follette who had changed not he. In recent years, Lenroot said, La Follette had been unwilling to work with anyone and preferred "that conditions shall not be improved in order that he may use discontent for political purposes."[108]

Lenroot got some help from outside. Poindexter came and Townsend endorsed Lenroot in an interview. Gifford Pinchot spent a full week in Wisconsin, stumping vigorously and enthusiastically for Lenroot. He called Lenroot "the ablest man in either house of congress." La Follette by contrast, he depicted as an autocrat. Garfield, too, contrasted La Follette and Lenroot, to the latter's advantage.[109] Endorsements from Beveridge and Hoover received press attention,[110] but by far the largest amount of space was reserved for a strong endorsement from Harding.[111] Though hardly a progressive, Harding was the man who would replace Wilson in the White House; for most Wisconsin voters, as for voters throughout the northern and western states, that was enough to commend him, the *Milwaukee Sentinel* and other papers realized.

The Anti-Saloon League focused its attention on about thirty contests throughout the country. One of these was Lenroot's, which the League considered second in importance only to the reelection of Andrew Volstead, chairman of the House judiciary committee and author of the act defining the permissible alcoholic content of drinks at one-half of one percent. The League spent $70,103 in Wisconsin, but a portion of that was used in the primary.[112]

Lenroot won the election. He received 281,576 votes; to 235,029 for Thompson; 89,265 for Reinsch; and 66,172 for Weber.[113] Clara saw in La Follette's refusal to debate the turning point; she also credited the women. But the La Follettes were closer to the mark in attributing Lenroot's victory to the Harding landslide. In Wisconsin, where the anti-administration reaction from all quarters was greater than elsewhere, Harding carried every county and amassed a total of 498,576 votes; to 113,442 for Cox; and 80,635 for Eugene V. Debs.[114]

108. Ibid., 26, 28, 29 October 1920; Lenroot, "Memoirs," pp. 160–61, Box 13, Lenroot Papers.

109. *Superior Telegram*, 21 October 1920; *Milwaukee Sentinel*, 18, 26 October 1920; Frank B. Kellogg to Frederick Hale, 23 September 1920, Box 1, Frederick Hale Papers; *Milwaukee Sentinel*, 17, 24–30 October 1920.

110. *Milwaukee Sentinel*, 16 October, 2 November 1920.

111. Ibid., 20 October–2 November 1920.

112. Justin Steuart, *Wayne Wheeler: Dry Boss*, pp. 164, 167; Odegard, *Pressure Politics*, pp. 93, 201.

113. *Wisconsin Blue Book*, 1921, p. 209.

114. Clara Lenroot to General and Mrs. William Crozier, 10 November 1920, Crozier Papers; *Milwaukee Sentinel*, 30 October 1920; La Follette, Jr., to Slattery, 26 November 1920, Box 1840, Pinchot Papers; *La Follette's Magazine* 12:11 (November 1920): 162; *Wisconsin Blue Book*, 1921, p. 209.

In his victory statement Lenroot promised to work for reconstruction measures "along true progressive lines" and to seek the confidence "of all those who desire constructive policies and not destructive radicalism." A few days later, in acknowledging Lodge's congratulations, Lenroot reported that it had been the hardest fight in his life, "owing to my colleague." Taking note of the twenty-two vote majority the Republicans would have in the Senate, instead of the two votes in the Sixty-sixth Congress, Lenroot suggested that La Follette be no longer regarded as a Republican. Not only had he bolted the ticket in the senatorial race, Lenroot pointed out, but he had attacked Harding throughout. "In fact," Lenroot wrote, "he has not supported a Republican candidate for President for twelve years and he is a Republican only when running for office himself." Clara, meanwhile, took a hopeful view respecting the president-elect, on the basis of his campaign. He had said some unwise things, she acknowledged, but he had never lost his dignity and had "impressed himself upon the American people as being a man of great conscientiousness, and of high ideal coupled with a modesty which will lead him to consult others upon the great questions which will confront him. So we really hope and expect good—perhaps *great* things of him." [115]

Although Lenroot's attitude toward Harding would change somewhat in the light of experience, it was La Follette who was his enemy. Lenroot and La Follette did not speak for several years, and when they resumed relations, after finding themselves seated next to one another at the opening of the Washington conference, it was only on a formal basis of courteous greeting.[116]

On 6 December, the senators began their business by giving a warm and unanimous ovation to Harding. The event served as an appropriate keynote for the session. Everyone looked ahead to the new administration that would assume authority in March and expected little of the "lame duck" session of Congress beyond the adoption of routine measures.[117]

The collapse of speculation, coinciding with a lessened supply of credit, contributed to a belated postwar deflation. By the end of 1920, the estimate of unemployed "employables" was four million. The farmer was affected the most by price declines. By the end of 1920, using 1913 as the base year, the price of what the farmer had to sell was down to 116, while what he had to buy stood at 156. The chief difficulty was a dollar decline in exports, as a bumper crop entered into competition on the world market with the products of Australia and Argentina (now back into export competition with the increased supply of shipping) and the products of a reviving Europe.

115. *Milwaukee Sentinel,* 5 November 1920; Lenroot to Lodge, 8 November 1920, Lodge Papers; Clara Lenroot to General and Mrs. William Crozier, 10 November 1920, Crozier Papers.

116. *Milwaukee Journal,* 27 January 1949.

117. *Milwaukee Sentinel,* 4, 6, 8 December 1921.

Many farmers faced the specter of foreclosure.[118] Dairying was relatively better off than other agricultural enterprises and remained so through the twenties, but Lenroot could not and would not ignore the economic situation either in Wisconsin or in other states.[119]

Shortly before the start of the session, Franklin K. Lane, no longer secretary of interior, wrote bleakly: "I see no evidence of constructive statesmanship on this side of the water, excepting Hoover. The best man in Congress is Lenroot, and he writes me that unless the Republicans do something more than fail to make mistakes that the Democrats will take the power from them in another four years." [120] At Janesville, Lenroot indicated what he had in mind. For the farmer, Lenroot wanted legislation to promote cooperative marketing, so farmers might gain some control over prices. He wanted also to improve credit facilities available to the farmer and give him tariff protection. To reduce the burden on all Americans, Lenroot hoped for strict economy in government and, pending substantial curtailment of the national debt, tax revision if not reduction. He called for action against profiteering, such as he believed to exist in the coal industry; immigration laws "dealing with distribution as well as admission of immigrants"; and a quick end to the war with Germany.[121] In other speeches, in Wisconsin and elsewhere, Lenroot indicated concern for the country's economic position in the world; he proposed that the United States enter some kind of association of nations; and he suggested that the country use the European debt as a lever to get for itself equal access to oil reserves and markets; and to promote disarmament. He viewed disarmament as being desirable and conducive to economy, which he saw as a key to renewed prosperity. Not everything could be accomplished by legislation, however, and Lenroot urged businessmen to resume a higher ethical standard than he believed prevalent in postwar society.[122]

In advance of the short session, farm organizations strengthened their Washington offices and prepared legislation. In response to pressure from their constituents and to the deteriorating farm situation, an informal farm bloc was organized in Congress.[123] Though never a member of that group —indeed, he deplored narrowly conceived blocs—Lenroot gave support to the various farm measures that reached the floor during the "lame duck" session. In particular, he supported legislation to create a federal livestock

118. George Soule, *Prosperity Decade: From War to Depression, 1917–1929*, pp. 99–103; Frederic L. Paxson, *American Democracy and the World War, Postwar Years: Normalcy, 1918–1923*, vol. 3, pp. 175–77.

119. Shideler, *Farm Crisis*, p. 46.

120. Lane to Benjamin Ide Wheeler, 18 November 1920, in Franklin K. Lane, *The Letters of Franklin K. Lane*, p. 370.

121. *Milwaukee Sentinel*, 6 January 1921; MS, "Janesville Speech," 13 January 1921, Box 9, Lenroot Papers.

122. *Milwaukee Sentinel*, 3, 11 December 1920, 14, 18, 19 January, 27 February 1921; *New York Times*, 11 December 1920, 11 February 1921.

123. Shideler, *Farm Crisis*, pp. 68–69.

commission to regulate the meat-packing industry, a subject in which he had taken an interest for several years; spoke for the Capper-Volstead bill to exempt farm cooperatives from antitrust prosecution; and voted for other farm measures. Extension of the War Finance Corporation, designed to assist farm exports, was accomplished over a presidential veto, but the House failed to override Wilson's veto of an emergency tariff bill and the other farm measures remained to be acted on when the session ended.[124]

The main business before the Congress was adoption of appropriation bills and Lenroot's chief preoccupation, from the start of the session to its finish, was with effecting economies. He did not exaggerate when he wrote Nils Haugen in mid-February: "I am putting in all my time from morning until late at night in appropriation bills on the floor of the Senate." [125]

When Harding took office in March, Lenroot was less optimistic than before.[126] But the appointment of Hoover as secretary of commerce encouraged him. Hoover had accepted on condition that he might construe his functions broadly, and that was entirely satisfactory to Lenroot, for he strongly admired Hoover. Already, the two men were well on the way toward development of a close personal and political friendship.[127]

Hoover was Lenroot's kind of progressive. He was practical and constructive; he deplored classes and class consciousness and preached a doctrine of equal opportunity and individualism. But his was a modernized individualism. Hoover recognized the fact of interdependence and urged voluntary cooperation among individuals and groups. Such a spirit of cooperation, he admitted, depended upon a measure of public spirit such as existed in wartime. He relied also on the dispassionate talents of the expert, the engineer.

An enemy to socialism and radicalism as to reaction, Hoover deplored repression; he believed in unionism, various forms of industrial cooperation, and cooperative marketing by farmers. He believed strongly in individual initiative but remained staunchly humanitarian and raised no ideo-

124. *CR* 66:3, 1920, vol. 60, pt. 1, pp. 82–83, 324; William Kent to Walter L. Fisher, 30 December 1918, Box 4, Walter L. Fisher Papers; *CR* 66:3, 1920, vol. 60, pt. 1, pp. 365–69, 679; Paxson, *Postwar Years,* vol. 3, p. 190.

125. Lenroot to Hugh P. Baker, 14 December 1920, attached to Lenroot to Pinchot, 15 December 1920, Box 229, Pinchot Papers; Lenroot to Nils P. Haugen, 18 February 1921, Box 60, Nils P. Haugen Papers.

126. Clara Lenroot to Mrs. William Crozier, 15 March 1921, Crozier Papers; Edward G. Lowry, *Washington Close-Ups: Intimate Views of Some Public Figures,* pp. 13, 16–17; Murray, *The Harding Era,* p. 113.

127. Hoover to Harris, 2 December 1935, Reel 258, Harris Deposit, Harding Papers; Ellis W. Hawley, "Herbert Hoover, the Commerce Secretariat, and the Vision of an 'Associative State,' 1921–1928," pp. 116–40; clipping, Bascom Timmons in the *Milwaukee Sentinel,* n.d., Box 20, A. B. Cargill to Katharine Lenroot, 28 January 1949, Box 1, Lenroot, "Memoirs," p. 188, Box 13, Lenroot Papers.

logical objection to government intervention in economic life when conditions, social or technical, warranted it.

With Lenroot, Hoover was concerned to promote economy and efficiency in government and opposed the pork barrel; he favored the St. Lawrence Seaway, federal aid to farmers in the promotion of cooperatives, tax reform, prohibition, and certain federal credit measures. During the battle of the League, he urged ratification with reservations hoping that through the League, and through other expedients, the tide of destructive radicalism might be stemmed in Europe. He saw European recovery as vital to America's postwar economic adjustment.[128]

Personally, Hoover was shy, sensitive, retiring. He had few habits of relaxation other than work and was not notably sociable. He knew little of politics and, having blundered into endorsement of the Democrats in the 1918 elections, only to blossom forth as a Republican presidential aspirant in 1920, he was disliked and distrusted by many Republican politicians, particularly those of the Old Guard. Lenroot was like Hoover in some ways, but unlike Hoover he understood politics. He was, moreover, in a position to exert some influence in Congress. The collaboration that developed between the two men was not one sided, therefore.[129]

In advance of the special session called for April 1921, President Harding promised Lenroot all the Wisconsin senatorial patronage, his own and La Follette's as well.[130] Very soon, La Follette established a pattern of opposition to administration proposals. Naturally then, Lenroot searched for areas of agreement with the administration.[131] He was pleased to be in accord with Harding and Secretary of State Charles Evans Hughes on most of the questions on foreign policy.

Lenroot, like Secretary of State Hughes, acquiesced in the political reality that entry into the League of Nations was out of the question. As alternatives, he favored, along with Harding and Hughes, adherence to the Permanent Court of International Justice then being created under the League auspices; codification of international law; "a league or association of nations for the purpose of conference and counsel only"; and efforts by the great powers to achieve an agreement on disarmament or arms reduction.[132]

Lenroot soon found the administration apathetic to domestic problems,

128. Gary Dean Best, "Herbert Clark Hoover in Transition, 1919–1921" (Ph.D. diss.), pp. 152–69; Hawley, "Herbert Hoover," pp. 117–19.

129. Lewis L. Strauss, *Men and Decision* (Garden City, N.Y., 1962), p. 51; Lowry, *Washington Close-Ups*, p. 206; Edward A. Fitzpatrick, *McCarthy of Wisconsin* (New York, 1944), pp. 216–17; John Hays Hammond, *The Autobiography of John Hays Hammond* (New York, 1935), vol. 2 of 2 vols., p. 711; Murray, *The Harding Era*, pp. 98–100.

130. *Milwaukee Sentinel*, 17 March 1921; Lenroot, "Memoirs," pp. 163–64, Box 13, Lenroot Papers.

131. Lenroot to J. L. Sturtevant, 8 August 1921, Box 4, Lenroot Papers.

132. *Milwaukee Sentinel*, 15 May 1921; Irvine L. Lenroot, "The Essentials of World Organization," pp. 1–4.

and he judged that lack of leadership in the Senate worsened the situation, as Lodge, in his seventy-first year, increasingly turned his limited energies away from Senate routine.[133] Thus, Lenroot prepared to pursue an independent course, but in practice he found acceptable the approach used by the president and by Secretaries Hoover and Wallace in dealing with the difficult farm problem, which continued to plague the nation in the summer of 1921.

In April, Charles Barrett, president of the National Farmers Union, representing himself and leaders of other farm organizations, asked Lenroot and Congressman James G. Strong of Kansas to introduce a resolution calling for a congressional investigation of the farm situation by a special joint committee. Lenroot and Strong agreed to do so, and on 25 April, they offered the concurrent resolution calling for a "joint commission of agricultural inquiry," to report within ninety days on the causes and remedies of the farm crisis. With little difficulty, Lenroot steered the resolution through the Senate after only slight modifications in the agriculture committee. Lenroot declined to head the commission because of the time involved, but he accepted membership on it and his friend Sydney Anderson became the chairman.[134]

The recently formed farm bloc was not prepared to wait for completion of the commission hearings and investigations, which, as it turned out, required an extension of time. It had already secured adoption of an emergency tariff bill to protect farm products. With the further cooperation of the administration, the farm bloc went on to get two amendments to the Farm Loan Act bearing on long-term rural credits; the Packers and Stockyards Act, vesting the secretary of agriculture with supervisory powers over the packers; and the Capper-Tincher Act, which sought to curtail gambling in grain futures. The latter act was struck down by the Supreme Court but was reenacted in a more acceptable form, under the commerce clause, the following year. The Capper-Volstead bill, which would exempt farm cooperatives from antitrust action, was set on course of adoption. Lenroot approved and supported all of these bills.[135]

As the disparity between farm and other prices persisted, bankruptcy and foreclosure proliferated. Wheat farmers and cattle and hog raisers in Nebraska were among those who suffered severely, and their senator, George Norris, who was the new chairman of the Committee on Agriculture and

133. Clara Lenroot to General and Mrs. William Crozier, 3 August 1921, Crozier Papers; Sturtevant to Lenroot, 4 August 1921, Lenroot to Sturtevant, 8 August 1921, Box 4, Lenroot Papers; George Rothwell Brown, *The Leadership of Congress* (Indianapolis, 1922), pp. 260–62, 272; Clinton Wallace Gilbert, *Behind the Mirrors: The Psychology of Disintegration at Washington*, pp. 157–58; Russell, *Shadow of Blooming Grove*, pp. 456–57; Garraty, *Henry Cabot Lodge*, p. 419.

134. Shideler, *Farm Crisis*, p. 157; Charles S. Barrett, *Uncle Reuben in Washington*, pp. 126–28; *CR* 67:1, 1921, vol. 61, pt. 1, p. 595; 1921, vol. 61, pt. 2, pp. 1346, 1629, 1899–1900; 1921, vol. 61, pt. 3, p. 2373; 1921, vol. 61, pt. 5, p. 4644.

135. Shideler, *Farm Crisis*, pp. 113–14, 120–21, 157–59; *Milwaukee Sentinel*, 16, 17 June 1921; *CR* 67:1, 1921, vol. 61, pt. 3, pp. 2669, 2673.

Forestry, presented a radical solution. Moved by the realization of overproduction in America and hunger in Europe, Norris proposed to bridge the gap by means of a government corporation empowered to buy American farm products and sell them on generous terms abroad. The corporation would be provided with capital amounting to $1 hundred million from the Treasury and would be empowered to borrow ten times that with a government guarantee on the bonds. Later, Norris reduced the amount that might be borrowed to $5 hundred million.[136]

Supported by the Farm Bureau, the Farmers National Council, and many farmers, Norris's bill was favorably reported by his agriculture committee on 30 June. But strong opposition quickly developed in the country, within the administration, and in the Senate. Lenroot joined that opposition. He doubted that Norris's bill would pass, doubted its efficacy, and most important, he disapproved the principle of it. Not only would the government be overstepping its proper bounds by becoming the principal buyer and seller of farm products, but it would be using and losing the money of all the taxpayers for the benefit of one segment of the population. He saw little prospect that the proposed corporation would recover its investment.[137]

Looking for an alternative, Lenroot consulted with other senators. After securing a good deal of agreement, Lenroot and Kellogg met with Hoover and Eugene Meyer, head of the War Finance Corporation. These two, along with Secretary Wallace, opposed the Norris bill and agreed that the best alternative was to authorize Meyer's organization to provide temporary help to the agricultural credit institutions. Meyer and Hoover proceeded to prepare the legislation, in consultation with Lenroot and other senators, including members of the farm bloc and the agriculture committee, but not with Norris, who was understood to oppose any such compromise. Meyer hoped Harding could smooth over "the Norris situation" in a personal interview with the Nebraskan. To the last, Hoover hoped to include a railroad relief provision in the bill. But the senators, notably Charles Curtis, Wadsworth, Kellogg, Lenroot, and Capper, saw political trouble in the proposal and rejected it. The amendment to the War Finance Corporation Act that they finally agreed upon gave the War Finance Corporation powers to advance up to a billion dollars at any one time to distressed local banks on the security of farm paper.[138]

136. Richard Lowitt, *George W. Norris: The Making of a Progressive, 1861–1912*, vol. 2, pp. 165, 168–69.

137. Shideler, *Farm Crisis*, p. 160; Gary Harlan Koerselman, "Herbert Hoover and the Farm Crisis of the Twenties: A Study of the Commerce Department's Efforts to Solve the Agricultural Depression, 1921–1928" (Ph.D. diss.), pp. 123–28; *CR* 67:1, 1921, vol. 61, pt. 5, pp. 4303, 4306, 4385, 4393–95, 4580.

138. *CR* 67:1, 1921, vol. 61, pt. 5, p. 4393; Shideler, *Farm Crisis*, pp. 160–62; Meyer to Harding, 26 July 1921, Hoover to Harding, 25 July 1921, Reel 182, Harding Papers; Frieda Baird and Claude L. Benner, *Ten Years of Federal Intermediate Credits*, pp. 44–45. See also Koerselman, "Hoover and the Farm Crisis," pp. 128–31.

Whether or not the measure would go far toward solving the farm problem was debatable, but none could deny the need for some such legislation. From 1915 to 1920, despite and partly because of prosperity, farm debt more than doubled. When farm prices suddenly decreased, farmers were unable to maintain deposits, which made it difficult for the country banks to renew loans. Overextended, these banks also were unable to borrow and thus collapsed. The more optimistic proponents of the new credit plan thought the condition of farm prices as being temporary and believed that temporary credit relief would save the farmers and their lenders. Even the less sanguine admitted the need for some legislation to permit loan renewals.[139]

Kellogg, a member of the farm bloc, agreed to introduce the bill as a substitute for Norris's. He informed Norris of his purpose, but the Nebraskan was not reconciled to the idea, and when the Senate met at noon on 26 July, he hoped that debate would continue on his bill. But by obvious prearrangement Vice-President Coolidge, who had promised to recognize a backer of the Norris plan, Joseph E. Ransdell, vacated the chair in favor of Curtis, and Curtis recognized Kellogg to introduce the substitute. The following day, in a stormy session, a majority of the farm bloc senators agreed to endorse the substitute, and on the morning of 28 July, by a vote of ten to two, with Norris and Edwin Ladd of North Dakota dissenting, the agriculture committee approved the substitute with slight modifications.[140]

Meanwhile, overheated, overtired, and furious at the treatment accorded him, on 27 July, Norris began a tirade against the progenitors of the substitute and those of his former allies who had been induced to support it; he continued the next day until he had to leave the floor. In the cloakroom he collapsed in exhaustion. Lenroot, meanwhile, responded; he defended Hoover, Kellogg, and the War Finance Corporation, explained the genesis of the substitute, and compared it in some detail with the Norris bill. By then the outcome was determined. The Senate approved the substitute without a record vote, and on 24 August, just before the beginning of a much needed recess of a month, it became law.[141]

The act provided some relief.[142] But it could not and did not arrest the collapse of markets and prices. Norris, who late in life called the defeat of his bill the greatest single disappointment of his public career, returned to the Senate in October and judged the Kellogg bill a failure.[143]

139. Baird and Benner, *Federal Intermediate Credits*, pp. 25–43.

140. *CR* 67:1, 1921, vol. 61, pt. 5, p. 4378; McCoy, *Calvin Coolidge*, pp. 135–36; *Milwaukee Sentinel*, 28 July 1921; Lowitt, *Norris*, vol. 2, p. 172.

141. Lowitt, *Norris*, vol. 2, p. 171; Alfred Lief, *Democracy's Norris: The Biography of a Lonely Crusader*, pp. 230–35; *CR* 67:1, 1921, vol. 61, pt. 5, pp. 4392–97.

142. Koerselman, "Hoover and the Farm Crisis," pp. 134–42; Baird and Benner, *Federal Intermediate Credits*, pp. 47–52.

143. Norris, *Fighting Liberal*, p. 279; George W. Norris to J. T. James, 14 November 1921, Tray 5, Box 1, George W. Norris Papers, LC.

The act, though extended several times, was a temporary measure. And the War Finance Corporation was not adapted to serve as a permanent part of the rural credit structure.[144] The Joint Commission of Agricultural Inquiry therefore recommended further legislation respecting farm credits. In four reports delivered to Congress between 14 December 1921 and 20 June 1922, it also recommended encouragement to farm cooperatives, reduction in freight rates, more agricultural research, improved terminal facilities for perishables, and better roads from farm to market. But it did not endorse the popular theory of a bankers' conspiracy to constrict farm credit, nor did it recommend anything approximating the Norris plan. As a result, Barrett, the man who had initially approached Lenroot on the subject of a congressional inquiry, became bitterly disillusioned with Lenroot and Anderson.[145] His anger, like Norris's, was a sign of the times and a harbinger of future events. Lenroot remained concerned for the good opinion of farm leaders but he would go only so far to secure it.[146]

After much delay, in late September the Senate finally took up the tax bill. Lenroot opposed both the House and Senate bills, which had the support of Secretary of the Treasury Andrew Mellon and the president, and were very similar to one another. He wanted legislation more equitable and more easily defensible politically than the party leadership offered. Lenroot had no complaint over the higher exemptions on income tax that the House had conceded to the farm bloc nor to the repeal of the tax on excess profits, a tax he had for some time considered undesirable from various standpoints. But he objected to other provisions, especially the reduction in the maximum surtax from 65 to 32 percent. And he realized that the Democrats, with farm bloc help, would capitalize on widespread criticism of what was being called a "rich man's bill" and would seek to retain the tax on excess profits and the existing rates on income tax. When the bill reached the Senate floor, he promptly introduced two amendments, one to set the surtax at 50 percent on incomes between $100,000 and $300,000, the other to tax incomes over $300,000 at 60 percent.[147]

Lenroot and McCormick took the lead in seeking compromise. Lodge, aware of the widespread criticism of the bills and of difficulties in the Senate, reluctantly promised to support a compromise proposal if the westerners could agree on one. Some of them did, and Lenroot and McCormick were authorized to prepare the proposal in detail during a meeting in October at Capper's home, which was also attended by Lodge, Kellogg, McNary, and four others. Then Lenroot tried to win Democratic support for the compro-

144. Baird and Benner, *Federal Intermediate Credits*, pp. 44, 52.

145. Murray, *The Harding Era*, p. 212; *CR* 67:2, 1921, vol. 62, pt. 1, p. 340; 1922, vol. 62, pt. 2, p. 1494; Barrett, *Uncle Reuben*, pp. 129–35.

146. Clara Lenroot to Nellie Nichols, 2 December (1921), Lenroot Papers Addition.

147. Benjamin G. Rader, "Federal Taxation in the 1920s: A Re-examination," pp. 415–35; Roy G. Blakey, "The Revenue Act of 1921," pp. 75–108; Murray, *Harding Era*, pp. 185, 188; *Milwaukee Sentinel*, 3 August, 28 September, 3 October 1921.

mise through Simmons, the ranking Democrat on the finance committee. Simmons agreed on some aspects of the proposal but not on all of them. Nor were conservative eastern Republicans prepared to acquiesce. Nevertheless, Penrose used his power and prestige in securing support for the compromise in his committee, perhaps with a view toward retreat from radical provisions in the conference committee. The finance committee agreed to change the bill by increasing the surtax to a 50 percent maximum; to repeal all transportation taxes, as farmers wanted; to increase the estate tax to a 50 percent maximum; to restore the tax on capital stock; to eliminate a number of nuisance taxes, as on chewing gum; and to increase the tax on distilled spirits withdrawn from bond. The compromise, in comparison with the House and Senate bills, reduced surtaxes on the middle incomes while increasing rates on the higher brackets.[148]

The compromise bill still had to be approved by the full Senate. Democrats and independent Republicans like Norris, La Follette, and Ladd were prepared to back alternatives, as were the eastern Republicans. Even supporters of the compromise, including Lenroot, retained freedom of action with respect to provisions of the committee bill not touched on in the compromise.

The eastern Republicans, strong advocates of repealing the tax on excess profits, favored a sales tax to make up for the lost revenue and opposed high income and corporate taxes. With Mellon, they warned that such taxes would destroy incentive and would drive men of wealth to tax-exempt securities instead of job-producing investments. The hard-working and painstaking Smoot, third-ranked Republican on the finance committee, offered the substitute they liked, chief feature of which was a one percent tax on manufacturers' gross income—a form of sales tax. Smoot's proposal had the backing of prominent bankers, the American Legion, the National Association of Manufacturers, and the Business Men's National Tax Committee, which was formed to lead the movement and put forth massive publicity in its behalf. In the Senate, Lenroot took the lead in opposition. He argued that the proposed tax was regressive, would often be passed on, and when not would be burdensome to manufacturers, constituting a large part of their net income. Some manufacturers would be able to pass the burden to the producers of raw materials, further hurting the farmer. He also thought it would be hard to administer. Following Lenroot's long speech of 3 November, the Senate rejected Smoot's amendment by a vote of forty-three to twenty-five. Seventeen Republicans voted against it. One senator, whose name was not recorded, credited Lenroot with swaying eight votes.

148. "Medill McCormick's Years in the United States Senate," n.d., attached to "Proposed letter to be mailed to all political writers," n.d. (1924), Box 8, McCormick Papers; Lodge to Charles Curtis, 15 September 1921, to Edward Channing, 11 March 1922, to C. B. Wetherby, 7 July 1922, Lodge Papers; *Milwaukee Sentinel*, 6–11 October 1921, 3 January 1922; *New York Times*, 9 October 1921; CR 67:1, 1921, vol. 61, pt. 7, p. 6538.

The estimate was probably exaggerated, but it is true that the day before some proponents of the sales tax had counted on forty-five votes.[149]

Lenroot also participated in the Senate's consideration of other amendments, some of them his own. For the most part, he defended the compromise agreement and maintained that it was not the work of any bloc. But he did not hesitate to work with progressive Democrat David I. Walsh of Massachusetts to tighten the provisions on capital gains and for a more steeply graduated scale of corporation taxes. Lenroot's main effort was used in defending the compromise on the rates of income tax against those who wanted a 32 percent maximum and others who favored the 65 percent maximum of the existing law. On this and on most other questions, the compromise survived challenges from left and right.[150]

The conference committee approved most of the changes made in the Senate. But the Senate conferees willingly accepted a compromise proposed by President Harding, setting the surtax maximum at 40 percent. Unexpectedly, however, the House instructed its conferees to accept the Senate's 50 percent provision.[151] On the whole, contrary to the widespread view that Mellon's conservative policies were embodied in the tax legislation of the twenties, the Revenue Act of 1921 was a victory for the moderate Republicans. Working with their own party leaders and with the Democrats, they yielded completely to neither. They warded off the sales tax on the one hand, and on the other, the continuation of the tax on excess profits along with prohibitive wartime rates. For Lenroot, who with McCormick had more to do with the outcome than anyone else, it was a satisfying way to end a congressional session.

During the early days of the regular session, Lenroot was in accord with the administration and the party leaders of the Senate. On the first major issue, the long-term political cost in Wisconsin was considerable. In 1918, Truman Newberry, a Roosevelt man, while serving in the navy in New York, had been elected to the Senate in Michigan over Henry Ford. Charges of huge spending, contrary to Michigan law, were immediately made against Newberry in the Michigan courts and in the Senate. Although an initial conviction was dismissed by the Supreme Court, the battle persisted in the Senate, with the Democrats making a party issue of it. Norris and Borah rallied to their cause, and in the farm states, particularly, "Newberryism" represented all that was evil and corrupt in politics. At the insistence of wavering Republicans, as the Senate prepared to vote on a report exonerat-

149. Rader, "Federal Taxation in the 1920s," p. 420; Blakey, "Revenue Act of 1921," p. 93; *CR* 67:1, vol. 12, pp. 6076–77, 7241–46; *New York Times*, 4 November 1923; *Milwaukee Sentinel*, 2, 4 November 1921, 17 February 1922.

150. *CR* 67:1, 1921, vol. 61, pt. 7, pp. 6538, 6575, 6641–43, 7477, 7515; *Milwaukee Sentinel*, 21, 23 October, 1, 8 November 1921.

151. Murray, *The Harding Era*, p. 189.

ing the senator, Newberry spoke in his own defense. Even so, the situation was touch and go and the Democrats countenanced no pairs.

Lenroot returned to Washington just days before the vote. On 12 January 1922, in advance of the vote, he explained his position. Senators should vote against Newberry if they thought he was aware of the spending or that the heavy use of money had caused his election. But Newberry had not known of it, and in Lenroot's judgment the high spending had lost him more votes than it had gained. Lenroot acknowledged that the cold record left room for doubt, but he argued that the character of the senator had bearing on his credibility, and he gave Newberry credit for his behavior throughout the protracted battle and in his speech before the Senate.

Soon afterwards, the Senate adopted a resolution exonerating Newberry but deploring the heavy spending, which was estimated close to $200,000. The vote was forty-six to forty-one—nine Republicans voting with the Democrats. Lenroot said a month later that had the Democrats not made a party issue of it, over half of them would have voted for Newberry.[152] Within the year, Newberry resigned.

On the issues that confronted Lenroot following the Newberry vote, it was not hard for him to act with his party's leadership, at least until the tariff bill reached the Senate in April. On the subject of refunding the European debt, Lenroot was satisfied with a bill setting up a commission composed of the secretaries of state, treasury, and commerce, and a representative from each House of Congress.[153] With the great bulk of the public and the Senate, Lenroot wanted the debt collected, but he was inclined to extend liberal terms so long as the nations in debt used their resources for their own reconstruction and not for foreign exploitation.[154]

While Congress acted on the debt bill, the Washington Conference drew to a close. It was already clear that there would be some controversy in the Senate, particularly over the Four Power Treaty, and Lenroot planned to take an active part in its defense.[155]

The Four Power Treaty, which was between the United States, Britain, Japan, and France, was an agreement by which the signatories promised to respect each other's possessions in the Pacific and to confer together in the event of threats to peace resulting from quarrels among themselves or aggression by a non-signatory power. The treaty provided also for the

152. Ibid., pp. 306–8; *CR* 67:2, 1922, vol. 62, pt. 2, pp. 1109–10; MS speech, "Lincoln Day Address," Maine, 12 February 1922, Box 10, Lenroot Papers.

153. *CR* 67:2, 1922, vol. 62, pt. 2, p. 1801.

154. L. Ethan Ellis, *Republican Foreign Policy, 1921–1933*, pp. 193, 196–97; MS speech, "American Club Pittsburgh," n.d. (27 April 1922), MS speech, "Lincoln Day Address," Maine, 12 February 1922, Box 10, Lenroot Papers; *CR* 67:2, 1922, vol. 62, pt. 2, pp. 1798–99, 1896–97, 1899, 1904.

155. John Chalmers Vinson, *The Parchment Peace: The United States Senate and the Washington Conference, 1921–1922*, p. 189; *Milwaukee Sentinel*, 19 November, 13, 18 December 1921; Lenroot to Kent, 21 January 1922, Box 62, Kent Papers.

abrogation of the Anglo-Japanese alliance, which was then up for renewal.[156]

Although the Washington agreements as a whole, and especially the disarmament agreement, were generally popular in the country, the Four Power Treaty had powerful enemies among Democrats, such Republican irreconcilables as Borah, Johnson, and La Follette, the Irish, and the Hearst press. The terms of the treaty had been worked out secretly and mainly between Japan and Great Britain, since abrogation of their alliance was at issue. These facts opened the way for suspicion and criticism.[157] During the early stages of debate, the opponents held center stage, and Lenroot remained contented with comments and questions.[158] But on 14 March, before packed galleries and a chamber full of senators ready for the first test vote on an amendment, Lenroot led the pro-treaty counterattack with a frequently interrupted speech that occupied two hours.[159]

Early on, Lenroot warned that failure to ratify the Four Power Treaty might result in the death of the other treaties, contrary to the argument of some. Destruction of the work of the Washington Conference, Lenroot went on, might well mean war. "No conference looking to the maintenance of peace would be possible during this generation. Friendly understanding would be replaced by hate and suspicion." [160]

Lenroot's main point was that, contrary to the charges of some, the obligation to confer when a contracting party was threatened with aggression involved no moral obligation to fight. Congress would be free to decide. Furthermore, the United States would benefit by the termination of the Anglo-Japanese alliance, "which makes possible and safe the reduction of our Navy to the point provided in the limitation of naval armament treaty."

On 24 March, by a vote of sixty-seven to twenty-seven, the Senate ratified the treaty. Fifty-five Republicans and twelve Democrats voted for it, while twenty-three Democrats and four Republicans voted against. The margin of victory was four votes.[161]

As Lenroot turned his attention to other questions, more often than not he continued in accord with the administration and the party leaders in the Senate. Harding, with the support of Lodge and others, consistently plumped for economy and debt reduction and managed to achieve surpluses in each year of his administration. For his part, Lenroot worked for

---

156. Arthur S. Link, *American Epoch: A History of the United States Since the 1890's,* pp. 343–45.

157. Vinson, *Parchment Peace,* pp. 149–89; Selig Adler, *The Uncertain Giant, 1921–1941: American Foreign Policy Between the Wars,* p. 66.

158. Vinson, *Parchment Peace,* p. 196; *CR* 67:2, 1922, vol. 62, pt. 4, pp. 3236–37, 3599, 3616, 3792–93, 3796–99.

159. *Milwaukee Sentinel,* 15 March 1922; *New York Times,* 15 March 1922; *Chicago Tribune,* 15 March 1922.

160. *CR* 67:2, 1922, vol. 62, pt. 4, pp. 3839–48.

161. Vinson, *Parchment Peace,* p. 192.

economy on a number of appropriations bills. Beyond that, he argued for a structural reform by which all appropriation functions would be centralized in the appropriations committee, in accord with a change in procedure recently adopted in the House. When named to a vacancy on that committee (he gave up his post on the military affairs committee), Lenroot stood staunchly for economy, even in connection with a forest land item that both he and Pinchot in principal favored.[162]

Lenroot supported the St. Lawrence Seaway project, as he had in 1920 and 1921. Hughes was entirely cooperative, as was Harding, who endorsed the project. But Canada, not ready for the expenditure, shelved it.[163]

The Commission of Agricultural Inquiry viewed the farm crisis as temporary, as did Harding, and opposed federal intervention to sustain prices. Instead, it recommended additional credit facilities to meet the need for credit of intermediate duration, six months to three years, legalization of agricultural cooperatives, reduction of freight rates, and certain other moderate measures. Lenroot introduced the credit bill, and Herbert Hoover, alarmed as farm conditions worsened, urged its prompt enactment. But at the behest of the farm bloc Lenroot caused delay, while a farm bloc committee studied the subject. However, Lenroot, acting with Kellogg, Capper, and representatives of farm organizations, secured adoption of a cooperative marketing law that met the specifications of the farm bloc.[164]

Lenroot's close relationship with the administration, and with the Senate leadership, survived his opposition to many features of his party's tariff bill and his stand in opposition to the president on the soldiers' bonus measure. Perhaps the explanation lies in the fact that on each of these important questions he was manifestly working not only for the public interest but for what he conceived to be the welfare of the Republican party. With respect to the tariff, furthermore, Lenroot worked through finance committee leaders McCumber and Smoot to achieve compromise to the extent possible and whenever he conscientiously could, he accommodated to them. On the so-called flexible tariff provisions, Lenroot was in general accord with Harding. With respect to the soldiers' bonus measure, Lenroot had

162. Lewis H. Kimmel, *Federal Budget and Fiscal Policy, 1789–1958*, pp. 89–90, 318; Lodge to Fred C. Shattuck, 10 August 1923, Lodge Papers; *CR* 67:2, 1921, vol. 62, pt. 1, p. 293; 1922, vol. 62, pt. 4, pp. 3338, 4192; 1922, vol. 62, pt. 5, pp. 5393, 5482, 8893; Lenroot to Pinchot, 6 April 1922, Box 4, Lenroot Papers.

163. *Superior Telegram*, 18–19 December 1920 (weekend ed.); *Milwaukee Sentinel*, 8, 11 July, 21 August, 6 December 1921; Lenroot to Reed, 13 January 1926, Box 11, Lenroot Papers; *Milwaukee Sentinel*, 4, 29 April 1922; Shideler, *Farm Crisis*, p. 175; *Boston Herald*, 27 May 1922; Carleton Mabee, *The Seaway Story*, p. 74.

164. Shideler, *Farm Crisis*, pp. 112–13, 167–69; *CR* 67:2, 1921, vol. 62, pt. 1, p. 1494; *CR* 67:4, 1923, vol. 64, pt. 3, pp. 2666, 2813; 1923, vol. 64, pt. 4, p. 4182; U.S., Senate, Committee on Banking and Currency, *Hearings: Discounts and Loans by Federal Land Banks for Farming Purposes*, pp. 3–7; Hoover to Lenroot, 5 March 1922, Box 2, Lenroot Papers; *Milwaukee Sentinel*, 30 March, 22 September 1923; MS speech, "Campaign Speech, 1922, Minnesota," Box 5, Lenroot Papers; *CR* 67:2, 1921, vol. 62, pt. 1, p. 1494; *CR* 67:4, 1923, vol. 64, pt. 3, pp. 2666, 2813; 1923, vol. 64, pt. 4, p. 4182; *Milwaukee Sentinel*, 9 February 1922.

ample company among Republican senators in opposing the president's wishes.

Although the House adopted the Fordney tariff bill on 21 July 1921, it was not until 20 April of the following year that the Senate began to take action. Delayed initially by the illness and death of Chairman Penrose, the finance committee had worked on the tariff for eight months and had produced what amounted to a new bill. The committee bill showed the influence of Tariff Commissioner Culbertson, the progressive Republican economist from Kansas. It included provisions permitting the president to raise or lower rates on his own initiative, presumably on the advice of the Tariff Commission, to meet changed conditions. This flexible tariff provision, advocated by Harding in his December message and embraced by committee member Smoot, embodied the old progressive dream of removing the tariff from politics and making it on a scientific basis.[165] On the subject of greatest controversy, the bill abandoned the system of American valuation incorporated in the House bill by which the value of goods would be determined on the basis of selling price in the United States of a similar article of domestic production. American valuation, everyone understood, would increase rates. On the other hand, the Senate bill, though requiring foreign valuation, specified exceptionally high duties, especially on farm products.

The committee's bill reflected not only the traditional desire of Eastern manufacturers for protection but the influence of a determined group of about twenty senators representing the West and the Mountain States who were concerned to protect such products as wool, hides, and meat, and willing to barter their votes to get that protection. This farm tariff bloc, as it came to be called, to distinguish it from the larger but less cohesive farm bloc, was led by Frank Gooding of Idaho, a vociferous man with a violent temper. A less conspicuous yet important element in the protectionist coalition was a group of Democrats, Southern as well as Northern, who though still in principle dedicated to the revenue tariff, were anxious for protection of their own states' products.[166]

By the time the bill reached the floor, Lenroot's general opinions were well formed. In 1921, he said in various speeches that the tariff must not be too high lest American trade be ruined. The United States, he noted, had become a creditor nation, had a favorable balance of trade, and possessed about a third of the world's gold supply. Unless she bought foreign goods, she would have no market for surpluses of agricultural or manufac-

---

165. Murray, *The Harding Era*, p. 273; William S. Culbertson, Diary, 7 December 1921, 28 May, 31 August 1922, Box 4, Culbertson to White, 27 February, 12 April 1922, Records, 1922–1928, Box 48, William S. Culbertson Papers.

166. Frank W. Taussig, *The Tariff History of the United States*, 8th rev. ed., pp. 449, 454; Shideler, *Farm Crisis*, p. 184; Culbertson to White, 29 March 1922, Records, 1922–1928, Box 48, Culbertson Papers; Charles M. Dollar, "The South and the Fordney-McCumber Tariff of 1922: A Study in Regional Politics," pp. 45–66.

tured goods.[167] In Senate debate, Lenroot stressed something else. The average farmer, as consumer, had more to lose from high duties on the things he bought than he could hope to gain from protection of his products.[168] Yet Lenroot remained a protectionist, willing to levy rates on the basis of difference in cost of production at home and abroad on those products that Americans could produce with reasonable efficiency. And he shared Culbertson's enthusiasm for foreign as against American valuation and for the idea of the flexible tariff. Moreover, he wanted protection for Wisconsin products to the extent that such protection was justified under his general tariff views.[169] Therefore, Lenroot became involved in a long and bitter tariff fight, hoping to be able to support his party's bill, but also determined to win lower rates.[170]

The high tariff lineup was formidable, but Lenroot had some bargaining power and he was willing to use it. Depending on the schedule at issue, Lenroot could expect voting help in a floor fight from enough Republicans to make the outcome doubtful and to cause embarrassment to the committee. With that bargaining power and at the very outset of the Senate action, Lenroot consulted privately with the committee leaders, McCumber and Smoot, and through them succeeded in getting the committee to reduce some recommended rates. But he was under no illusion that when the Senate reached the major schedules the committee would continue to retreat without a fight.[171]

Lenroot gave public notice of his intentions on 17 May, in connection with a relatively minor item, a duty on barite ore, a mineral used largely for bleaching and found in Missouri and Georgia. Not having discussed rates on the floor to that time, he undertook to set forth his position in general terms. He thought a protectionist tariff necessary and was inclined to give the committee the benefit of the doubt. But senators should not assume that the committee was infallible, and when an error was clearly shown, he felt it "the duty of every Republican to do what he can to rectify the mistake." Lenroot went on to demonstrate that the proposed rate, three times that in the Payne-Aldrich Act and five times above the Underwood tariff rate, was not defensible. After some debate, McCumber admitted a miscalculation in setting the rate and agreed that the item be passed over. The *New York Evening Post,* taking editorial note of the incident, judged that the tariff battle had begun and declared that "Lenroot's vigorous and successful onslaught changes the whole aspect of the struggle." Lenroot was not alone

167. *Milwaukee Sentinel,* 14 May 1921; MS speech, "Watertown Chamber of Commerce, May 26, 1921," MS speech, "West Virginia Bankers Association, Sept. 14, 1921," Box 9, Lenroot Papers.

168. See for example *CR* 67:2, 1922, vol. 62, pt. 11, pp. 1117–20.

169. *Milwaukee Sentinel,* 25 March, 12 April 1922; *CR* 67:2, 1922, vol. 62, pt. 7, p. 11215.

170. *CR* 67:2, 1922, vol. 62, pt. 7, p. 7093.

171. Lenroot to Kent, 27 May 1922, Box 63, Kent Papers; *Boston Herald,* 20 August 1922.

among Republican dissidents, the *New York Evening Post* noted, for Capper had given a speech against American valuation.[172]

Lenroot again attacked a committee rate and further developed his overall position on 6 June, in connection with a proposed 30 percent ad valorem duty on saws. After voting against a Democratic proposal to reduce the rate to 12 percent, Lenroot offered an amendment to set it at 20 percent. He noted that the volume of imports was small while exports were great. Watson pointed out that the committee was acting in a time of instability and uncertainty and therefore looked not just to the immediate situation but to the future. Lenroot refused to accept that standard. It would result in prohibitive duties on articles in common use. "The test," he said, "is what are the imports under present conditions." The flexible tariff provisions, Lenroot argued, could be relied on to meet future contingencies. By a vote of twenty-two to twenty-seven, the Senate rejected Lenroot's amendment.[173]

At this point, Lenroot began to vote fairly regularly against committee rates. In connection with the tariff on printing presses, Lenroot again disparaged the argument about future contingencies and referred to the flexible tariff provisions. In this instance, with the aid of six other Republicans who joined him in voting with the Democrats, Lenroot won his battle by a vote of twenty-eight to twenty-seven. It was the fourth time the committee had been overturned on the floor.[174]

In July, as the Senate began to consider some of the more important schedules, Lenroot took the lead against what he considered excessive rates. By way of preliminary, he warned that he had not yet decided what he would do on the final vote. "I want to resolve all doubts in favor of the bill," he said, "but if such rates as this are to be voted into this bill to any considerable extent, I want to say very frankly that I shall not support the bill when it comes to final passage." [175]

When the Senate came to the very important cotton schedule, the high protectionist element was at a disadvantage since the raw-material producers were as interested in export as in domestic production. At the outset, the committee submitted thirty-four amendments, most of them reducing rates below those previously agreed upon. Lenroot was still not satisfied; he pointed out that most rates in the Senate bill were higher than those in the House measure and warned that the Democrats would be the gainers in November. On the first test vote, Lenroot won by a vote of twenty-four to thirty-two. Lenroot pressed his advantage and the Senate rejected other committee amendments. When the Senate resumed action on the cotton schedule two days later, the committee, through Smoot, modified amend-

172. *CR* 67:2, 1922, vol. 62, pt. 7, pp. 7091–95; Clipping, *New York Evening Post*, 19 May 1922, Box 11, Lenroot Papers.
173. *CR* 67:2, 1922, vol. 62, pt. 8, pp. 8262, 8267–68.
174. Ibid., p. 8389; *Milwaukee Sentinel*, 9 June 1922.
175. *CR* 67:2, 1922, vol. 62, pt. 10, p. 9936.

ments to accommodate Lenroot. The *Boston Herald,* an influential Republican newspaper favorable to moderate protectionism, labeled the result as a major blow to the "Old Guard," noting not only the result but the fact that thirteen Republicans had broken with their party's leadership to support Lenroot's position. The thirteen were Borah, Capper, Cummins, Jones, McCormick, Nelson, Norbeck, Kellogg, Thomas Sterling, Townsend, McNary, Willis, and Wadsworth. La Follette and Norris were not present.[176] On the same day, fourteen Republican rebels caused defeat of a committee amendment to extend for a year the embargo on foreign-made dyes, a very controversial subject.[177]

By 17 July, two days later, the leadership had regrouped. Lenroot resumed his attack on committee rates, but on the first test vote he lost by a vote of twenty-four to thirty-three, with only Borah, Capper, Kellogg, and Nelson remaining with him of the original thirteen. Lenroot won slight concessions on several rates that day and the next, but in other instances he was outvoted.[178] Finally, after losing a twenty-six to twenty-nine vote, Lenroot took advantage of the temporary presence of many senators who had come into the chamber only to vote and delivered an angry lecture. He expressed doubt that as many as 10 percent of those who had just voted on the underwear schedule "had any knowledge concerning, or apparent care" about it.

> Is it any wonder that this bill is being criticized the country over, when Republican Senators take the attitude with reference to it which they have taken, when Republican Senators do not take the pains to try to inform themselves as to the correctness of the rates? One more word. Last week there was a very considerable break on this side in the beginning of the consideration of the cotton schedule, and the committee was defeated in a number of instances. Immediately word went around the Republican side of this Chamber that there would be retaliation if that were continued; that if these cotton rates were disturbed, and if the committee was not blindly followed with reference to them, the agricultural schedule would suffer when the bill came into the Senate. Whether or not those threats have had any effect is not for me to say . . . but the way these amendments are being voted upon is not to the credit of the Republican side.

Minutes later, Lenroot moved a second amendment, setting the duty on cotton-knit underwear at 45 percent ad valorem instead of the committee's 50 percent or the 40 percent that he had originally proposed. On this vote, to the chagrin of the party leaders, Lenroot won by a vote of twenty-eight to twenty-seven. The *New York Evening Post* again commented editorially on the outcome, and other papers remarked on the sensational turn of events.[179]

176. Ibid., pp. 10219–20, 10229, 10232–39, 10315, 10320–21; *Boston Herald,* 14 July 1922.
177. *Milwaukee Sentinel,* 16 July 1922.
178. *CR* 67:2, 1922, vol. 62, pt. 10, pp. 10337–56, 10361–71.
179. Ibid., p. 10372; clipping, *New York Evening Post,* 19 July 1922, Box 15, Lenroot Papers; *Boston Herald,* 19 July 1922; *Milwaukee Sentinel,* 19 July 1922.

The following day, Lenroot and McCormick lunched with Culbertson and discussed with him the possibility of organizing a progressive bloc to oppose high rates and press for a flexible tariff along lines that would give a decisive role to the Tariff Commission in the raising or lowering of rates. The day after that, Lenroot and McCormick met with Capper and four or five others to discuss the same subject. McCormick, and probably the others as well, were fearful of the political consequences for the Republican party if rates were not substantially cut. The defeat of New and McCumber in primary contests and the primary victory in Iowa of administration critic Smith Brookhart signaled the mood of the country and gave point to the warnings Lenroot had already voiced in the Senate. Culbertson was more than willing to offer his help with respect to drafting proper flexible tariff provisions, and Lenroot, at a second meeting with Culbertson, agreed to sponsor them if the finance committee would not. Lenroot also secured from Culbertson the promise of technical help in connection with the schedules yet to be acted on.[180]

Republican leaders like Senator Lodge recognized the tide of public sentiment and yielded to it with respect to the products of flax, hemp, and jute. Lenroot was successful, also, in securing an amendment to the paragraph on cotton gloves.[181]

Then came the long-awaited fight on the wool rates. Now Lenroot was in enemy country, dealing with a schedule that was strongly supported by the powerful, hyper-protective farm tariff bloc led by Gooding, who reminded Lenroot privately that there were half a million sheep in Wisconsin. Failing to get concessions from the finance committee, on the floor Lenroot led a week-long attack on the schedule, particularly on paragraphs relating to coarse wool and to manufactured wool products. Lenroot warned direly of the impact on consumers and on the Republican party if the committee rates became law. After losing the early votes, Lenroot despaired of winning any, but he nevertheless proposed amendments and insisted on roll calls, only for the record. Smoot acceded to him on one set of amendments, but he lost all the rest, though, in some instances, the votes were close. Simmons undoubtedly was correct when he charged that high rates on raw wool were the keystone to a Republican bargain; if they fell, no tariffs on manufactured goods were safe.[182]

Lenroot voted against a compromise on the sugar rate, which nevertheless passed by two votes, and he voted with a majority of two that defeated a bounty on potash.[183] Then the Senate turned to the schedule on hides,

180. Culbertson, Diary, 19, 20, 24, 25 July 1922, Box 4, Culbertson Papers; Dollar, "The South and the Tariff," p. 61; Taussig, *Tariff History*, 8th rev. ed., p. 488; "Memorandum for Mr. Comer," 11 August 1922, Records, 1922, Box 47, Culbertson Papers.

181. Lodge to Alexander H. Bullock, 22 July 1922, Lodge Papers; *Milwaukee Sentinel*, 22 July 1922; *CR* 67:2, 1922, vol. 62, pt. 10, pp. 10465–66, 10473, 10481.

182. *CR* 67:2, 1922, vol. 62, pt. 10, pp. 10596, 10601, 10652–55, 10670–71, 10719, 10756, 10759, 10776; 1922, vol. 62, pt. 11, pp. 10804, 11215; *Milwaukee Sentinel*, 29 July 1922.

183. *Boston Herald*, 9 August 1922.

boots, and shoes. The farm tariff bloc felt no less strongly about protection for hides as for wool, but its position was weaker, for a majority of the manufacturers of boots and shoes preferred free hides and the Farm Bureau Federation wanted hides, leather, and leather products to be on the free list. As early as April, Lenroot had begun to receive information from a leader in the industry and veteran reformer, Charles H. Jones of Boston, and when the subject came before the Senate he was ready to again take the lead. The group that Jones represented was willing to have boots and shoes on the free list along with hides, so Lenroot's position was strong. In the course of a long and acrimonious debate, Lenroot argued that protection would cost the farmer, as consumer, far more than he would get for his few hides. Also, he claimed that the chief beneficiaries of a tariff on hides would be the meat packers, who controlled most of the industry and exerted decisive influence over independent tanners. With many eastern Republicans at last on his side along with some senators from the Midwest, Lenroot won his fight against the committee schedule by a vote of twenty-six to thirty-nine.[184]

The Senate, still in Committee of the Whole, next took up the flexible tariff provision. Again, Lenroot took a leading part. He defended the constitutionality of the provisions but urged some modifications. One was to substitute the words "cost of production" in place of "conditions of competition" wherever the latter words occurred. The proposal, which had Culbertson's approval though it did not arise at his suggestion, was designed to make more definite and constitutional the standard for rate adjustment. It was calculated also to work against excessive rates. Lenroot also proposed to limit the president's authority to invoke American valuation. Finally, he wanted to do as Culbertson had suggested and make specific reference to the Tariff Commission in Section 315. Under Lenroot's proposal, the president would not be empowered to make upward or downward adjustments until he had received a report from the Tariff Commission. Culbertson got the president to intervene in favor of the latter provision in a letter to McCumber, but it was not necessary, for Smoot and McCumber had already agreed to accept Lenroot's proposal, which had strong support in the Senate. They acceded also to his other suggestions and Lenroot did not have to force the major issues with amendments. Gooding and others of his bloc, dissatisfied with the changes, did push through an amendment offered by Olaf Bursum of New Mexico, setting 1 July 1924 as a terminal date for key portions of the flexible provisions, which many regarded as temporary expedients to meet the unsettled conditions of the time. Culbertson, who

184. Charles H. Jones to Lenroot, 25 April, 6 June, 10 August 1922, Commonwealth Shoe and Leather Company Papers, Baker Library; Henry Fountain Ashurst, *A Many-Colored Toga: The Diary of Henry Fountain Ashurst,* diary entry, 9 August 1922, p. 172; Taussig, *Tariff History,* 8th rev. ed., p. 471; *Boston Herald,* 10 August 1922. Jones had been a close associate of Louis Brandeis in his reforming days. Alpheus T. Mason, *Brandeis: A Free Man's Life,* pp. 158, 163–65, 176, 391, 394.

probably mirrored Lenroot's sentiments, was generally pleased at the outcome and hoped that the Bursum amendment might be eliminated in conference.[185]

In the last days of debate preceding the 19 August vote, as tempers flared, Lenroot led an unsuccessful attack on the cutlery schedule and voted with the minority in new efforts to lower duties on wool, sugar, and chemicals.[186] Then, with some reservations, Lenroot voted for the bill. He did so, he told the Senate, because of the flexible provisions and in the hope that the conference would effect rate reductions. If it did not, however, he would vote against the conference report. Jones of Washington said he took the same view as Lenroot. The bill passed the Senate by a vote of forty-eight to twenty-five. Borah was the only Republican voting against it. Had La Follette and Norris been present, they too would have voted no.[187]

The conference report, as finally agreed to, eliminated the time limit on the flexible tariff and retained the so-called scientific tariff features. It was based also on foreign rather than American valuation. But the rate cuts were disappointingly small. Average rates were only slightly less than those of the Payne-Aldrich bill. Without explanation, Lenroot voted against the report, which nevertheless passed the Senate, with a vote of forty-three to twenty-eight. He was one of five Republicans to vote no. It had already cleared the House.[188]

The Fordney-McCumber Act did the average farmer more harm than good. Insofar as it protected manufactured goods, moreover, it ignored America's new position in the world economy. Politically, it further eroded confidence in the Republican party. Lenroot had warned of each of these consequences during the long Senate debate. Although frustrated in many of his efforts, such improvements as were made in the bill in the Senate were due more largely to Lenroot than to any other senator. Some called him the Dolliver of the 1922 tariff debate (referring to the hero of the Payne-Aldrich tariff battle of 1909). In the judgment of Culbertson, "he was the most resourceful and effective man on the floor of the Senate. He had his facts well in hand and proved to be a powerful debater." [189]

The tariff disposed of, the Senate turned at last to the soldier bonus question. Lenroot had taken a great interest in the issue from the first. At a Senate Republican caucus in April, he urged his colleagues to take a

185. *CR* 67:2, 1922, vol. 62, pt. 11, pp. 11186–95, 11208–18, 11228–48; Culbertson to White, 12 August 1922, Records, 1922–1928, Box 48, "Memorandum for the President," 11 August 1922, "Memorandum for the President," 5 September 1922, Records, 1922, Box 47, Culbertson Papers.

186. *CR* 67:2, 1922, vol. 62, pt. 11, pp. 11466–79, 11485, 11605; *Boston Herald,* 18 August 1922.

187. *CR* 67:2, 1922, vol. 62, pt. 11, p. 11597; *Boston Herald,* 20 August 1922.

188. Culbertson, Diary, 5 September 1922, Box 4, Culbertson Papers; Murray, *The Harding Era,* p. 279; *Milwaukee Sentinel,* 16, 20 September 1922.

189. Culbertson to White, 19 September 1922, Records, 1922–1928, Box 48, Culbertson Papers.

definite position and to pass the bill that session. Although the measure was popular not only among the veterans but with the public generally, there were major stumbling blocks. The president, prodded by Secretary Mellon and supported by business organizations and most of the press, insisted that there be no bonus without an accompanying tax to finance it. But the sales tax, which the administration had in mind, was a political impossibility. Lenroot hoped to meet the objection by keeping the early costs of the bonus down and financing it by interest on the foreign debt and by bonds. On 31 May, the finance committee voted to report a bonus bill and Chairman McCumber was willing to have it temporarily displace the tariff on the calendar. When Harding raised violent objection to that, only Lenroot and a few others stuck to the idea. They were reassured, however, that the Senate would act on the bill before it adjourned.[190]

When the bill reached the Senate, Lenroot opposed amendments that he felt would make more likely a presidential veto or would jeopardize the bill's constitutionality. Arguing for the bill, he noted that the money commitment would be less than $80 million in each of the first two years of operation.[191] On 31 August, the Senate passed it by a vote of forty-seven to twenty-two and sent it to conference. The conference committee eliminated features to which the president might object, and the two Houses promptly passed the report. Veterans might secure certificates worth $1.00 a day for home service and $1.25 a day for overseas service beyond sixty days. If held for twenty years, the value of a certificate would increase threefold through compound interest.[192] The president disappointed the hopes of Lenroot and others. In a veto message that Mellon helped to prepare, he objected to adding substantially to the public debt, and thus impairing confidence in the government's credit, for the benefit of a small minority of the population. The House overrode the veto without difficulty, but in the Senate the supporters of the bill were four votes short.[193]

On 22 September, a dispirited Congress finally adjourned, and the Republicans had to deal with an unhappy electorate. Internal bickering, legislative delay, a heavy-handed labor policy featured by a sweeping injunction against the railroad strikers, and, above all, continued unemployment, and agricultural distress, combined to antagonize the public toward the Republican Congress. The administration called on prominent speakers, including Cabinet officers, to uphold the party's candidates. Lenroot, after a two-week vacation in Wisconsin, took the stump in Minnesota, Indiana, Ohio, New Jersey, New York, and Massachusetts.[194]

190. *Milwaukee Sentinel*, 19, 20 April 1920; Murray, *The Harding Era*, pp. 308–12; *Milwaukee Sentinel*, 21, 22, 25, 26, 27 February 1922; *CR* 67:2, 1922, vol. 62, pt. 9, pp. 8908, 9019.

191. *CR* 67:2, 1922, vol. 62, pt. 9, pp. 11900–11901, 11912–49, 11961–64.

192. Murray, *The Harding Era*, p. 312.

193. Ibid., p. 313.

194. Ibid., pp. 315–16; *Milwaukee Sentinel*, 21 September, 16 October 1922; *Superior Telegram*, 26 September, 28–29 October 1922 (weekend ed.).

He was able to leave his home state at election time because there the battle was already fought and lost. Though prevented by Senate business from campaigning during the summer, Lenroot had done what he could to stem the tide that swept La Follette, Blaine, and the rest of their ticket to easy renomination in September.[195] But the cause was hopeless, as Lenroot realized in advance of the election.[196] More important than the support of state officeholders, La Follette and his cohorts benefited from the disturbed economic conditions and the still strong reaction against the war, especially among the Germans.

Lenroot had tried to present the anti-La Follette group as a moderate, progressive coalition, opposed not only to arch-radicalism but to reaction.[197] But the conference that put forth the anti-La Follette ticket came to be seen by many as akin to the old stalwart Eleventh Story League, as one of its nominees ruefully acknowledged.[198]

To Lenroot, the Wisconsin situation only mirrored the national picture. Prior to his campaign tour, during the last month of the regular session, he viewed events despondently and came home each night "discouraged, disgusted, and full of wrath," as Clara reported to Mary Crozier in China. "The tension between labor and capital is very menacing," she wrote. Clara reported her husband's belief that

> . . . all sides responsible for this industrial warfare are criminally to blame. With proposals of perfectly fair commissions, or Boards of Arbitration offered them, to make the fullest investigation of grievances on both sides, and to impartially arbitrate between them, and to have first one faction and then another scorn all such efforts to assist them towards an amicable settlement and *peace,* is disheartening! . . . This situation is taken advantage of by all extreme radicals and demagogues everywhere.[199]

Election returns did nothing to improve Lenroot's spirits. Despite his five days of campaigning in Minnesota, Kellogg was defeated.[200] He was one of seven Republican senators to be defeated, along with seventy congressmen.[201] To be sure, the results might jolt the party toward a more vigorous and progressive posture. But the more obvious result of the election was to advance what in Lenroot's view of things La Follette represented—irresponsible, self-seeking, demagogic radicalism. Moving from his base as chairman of the People's Legislative Service, and the more substantial fact of his backing by the railroad brotherhoods, the A.F.L., and certain farm

195. *Milwaukee Sentinel,* 9 May, 1 June, 29 August 1922; Lenroot to William Morgan, 4 August 1922, Box 3, Lenroot Papers.

196. Clara Lenroot to Mrs. William Crozier, 28 August 1922, Crozier Papers.

197. Whitehead to Charles L. Alvord, 19 March 1923, to Daugherty, 27 March 1923, Whitehead Papers; *Milwaukee Sentinel,* 1 June 1922.

198. Morgan to Lenroot, 16 September 1922, Box 3, Lenroot Papers.

199. Clara Lenroot to Mrs. William Crozier, 22 August 1922, Crozier Papers.

200. *Superior Telegram,* 28–29 October (weekend ed.), 6 November 1922; MS speech, "1922, Minnesota," Box 5, Lenroot Papers.

201. Murray, *The Harding Era,* p. 319.

groups, on 1 December La Follette was able to organize a congressional bloc that included Norris, Ladd, Borah, and Brookhart, as well as Democrats Morris Sheppard, Henry Ashurst, and Robert Owen.[202] The group could expect support from such others as Lynn Frazier, the Nonpartisan Leaguer who had defeated McCumber, Norbeck, Johnson, James Couzens, replacement for Newberry, Henrik Shipstead of Minnesota, and Robert Howell, who had defeated Hitchcock in Nebraska. Democratic newcomers Burton K. Wheeler of Montana and Clarence Dill of Washington, victor over Poindexter, could also be counted on, together with some Democratic holdovers. Thus, in the Sixty-eighth Congress, the balance of power within the Senate might well fall to La Follette's independents.[203]

Following up on the 1 December meeting of congressmen, La Follette sponsored a second meeting to organize a non-congressional group to work in the states. Then in mid-December, the Conference for Progressive Political Action, an organization formed in 1921 with the backing of the railroad brotherhoods, convened in Cleveland. It was obviously pointing toward a third party effort in 1924, under the leadership of La Follette. While such a candidacy was not calculated to succeed, unless the Republicans could counter it well in advance it might weaken the party and leave it entirely to conservatives and reactionaries. Moreover, the buildup for a third party campaign, and the campaign itself, promised to be highly divisive and destructive.

As early as October, in the wake of La Follette's renomination, rumors circulated in Wisconsin that Lenroot would resign from the Senate. In February, Clara wrote in her diary: "Irvine offered $15,000 job with Milwaukee lawyer today. Didn't think it right to accept and leave Wisconsin to La Follette." [204] But the task ahead was literally a lonely one—the 1922 election would remove from Washington many of Lenroot's good friends.[205]

The new Congress would not meet for thirteen months, however, and much could happen in that time. Difficult and important business remained to be dealt with. Above all, the last session of the Sixty-seventh Congress might again attempt solution of the farm problem. If farm prosperity could be restored, the specter of angry radicalism would surely recede. Lenroot welcomed the challenge and the opportunity, ready to take the leading part in the Senate.

202. George Huddleston, announcement, n.d. (December 1922), Box 93, Series B, La Follette FC.

203. Some of those mentioned above were named by La Follette's office as sympathizing but unable to attend the 1 December meeting. *Milwaukee Sentinel,* 30 November 1922; Belle and Fola La Follette, *La Follette,* vol. 2, pp. 1066–67.

204. A. J. Myrland to Haugen, 22 February 1923, Box 62, Haugen Papers; Clara Lenroot, Diary, 20 February 1923, Lenroot Papers Addition.

205. Clara Lenroot to General and Mrs. William Crozier, 7 August 1923, Crozier Papers.

X

THE COOLIDGE DAYS
AND AFTER

Although a bill on ship subsidy was at the top of the president's agenda, when Lenroot returned to Washington in December he was mainly concerned about farm credits. As previously mentioned, Lenroot had introduced the Joint Commission of Agricultural Inquiry's bill on rural credits in the second session but had asked the Committee on Banking and Currency to delay action pending a study by the farm bloc. A farm bloc subcommittee finally concluded in favor of the Lenroot-Anderson bill, while recommending some liberalization of its terms. The Agriculture Department also supported the plan and suggested a few modifications. Now Lenroot introduced the modified bill and then met with the full farm bloc, seeking its endorsement. That amorphous body, swiftly disintegrating, could come to no conclusion as between the Lenroot bill and a number of rivals, although many individuals within the bloc supported the Lenroot bill. Thereupon, Lenroot urged George McLean, chairman of the banking and currency committee, to proceed with hearings on the bill. President Harding and Republican leaders in the Senate gave general endorsement to the legislation on rural credits along the lines of the Lenroot plan, and the bill met only sparse objection in committee, where Hoover and Wallace spoke for it. Lenroot and Arthur Capper, author of another credit plan, each stressed that their bills were complementary. Lenroot incorporated minor committee changes in a new bill, and on 9 January the committee, having already approved the Capper bill, reported the Lenroot bill favorably.[1]

The Lenroot-Anderson bill set out to plug a gap in the farm credit system. Long-term credit, on the security of land, was available, and so was short-term credit, for periods of up to six months. But personal credit to synchronize with the farmers' turnover period, from six months to three years, was not, except on a temporary, makeshift basis through the War Finance Corporation. And the intermediate credit that was available was costly. The bill

1. *CR* 67:4, 1923, vol. 64, pt. 3, pp. 2368, 2687–88; 1923, vol. 64, pt. 4, p. 4178; Lawrence H. Chamberlain, *The President, Congress and Legislation*, p. 284; *Milwaukee Sentinel*, 1 December 1922; *CR* 67:4, 1923, vol. 64, pt. 3, p. 2813; *Milwaukee Sentinel*, 11 December 1922; James H. Shideler, *Farm Crisis: 1919–1923*, p. 170; Warren G. Harding to Sydney Anderson, 1 February 1923, Reel 191, Warren G. Harding Papers; U.S., Senate, Committee on Banking and Currency, *Hearings: Rural Credits*, pp. 1–19.

undertook to meet the problem by authorizing establishment of twelve intermediate credit banks, each associated with a Federal Farm Land Bank and under the overall supervision of the Federal Farm Loan Board, which had charge of long-term farm credit. The federal government would subscribe $5 million of initial capital for each intermediate credit bank, and under extraordinary circumstances each bank might secure an additional $5 million. The banks were authorized to issue debentures equal to ten times their capital, and because these debentures would be tax free, interest costs to the ultimate credit consumer—the farmer—would be kept down. Lenroot was aware of demands from within the farm community, subscribed to by Sen. Peter Norbeck of South Dakota, a member of the banking and currency committee, that a completely separate intermediate credit structure be established. But he and his colleagues preferred to use existing machinery to the extent possible to minimize costs and to hasten the start of the system. The intermediate credit banks would not loan directly to farmers but would rediscount a farmer's notes of indebtedness to banks and other credit institutions and would loan directly to cooperative marketing associations. The private credit institutions, in turn, were limited in the markup they might charge. Finally, among the more important provisions of the bill, there was a section extending the rediscounting authority of the Federal Reserve banks from six months to nine months, to better accommodate the farmer.[2]

The Capper bill contained similar provisions respecting the Federal Reserve system. In addition, it extended the life of the War Finance Corporation. To this extent, it was an alternative to the Lenroot bill. But the main feature of the Capper bill was to give federal supervision to private credit corporations with a minimum capital of $250,000. In practice, livestock raisers were the ones who would benefit, by the greater security such supervision would provide.

Andrew Mellon had testified against the Lenroot bill, but Senate Republican leaders nevertheless accorded it the status of an administration measure and agreed to temporarily set aside the ship subsidy bill in favor of the Capper and Lenroot bills.[3]

In the Senate, the real challenge to the Capper and Lenroot bills came not from the right but the left. On 15 January, George Norris attempted to displace the subsidy bill with his bill calling for a government corporation to handle farm products. Lenroot, still opposed to the principle of the Norris bill and fearful that its consideration would preclude action on credits legislation, opposed the motion. Its defeat, by a vote of fifty-three to nineteen, paved the way for credit legislation, and the Senate, by unanimous consent, immediately took up the Capper bill.[4]

2. *CR* 67:4, 1923, vol. 64, pt. 3, pp. 2366–69; Frieda Baird and Claude L. Benner, *Ten Years of Federal Intermediate Credits*, pp. 70–71.

3. *Milwaukee Sentinel*, 14 December 1922.

4. Ibid., 15, 19 December 1922; *CR* 67:4, 1923, vol. 64, pt. 2, p. 1735; *New York Times*, 16 January 1923.

After the Capper bill had been approved, on 25 January, the Senate, again by unanimous consent, put aside the ship subsidy bill in favor of the Lenroot bill. As Lenroot prepared to explain and defend it, Claude Swanson, a member of the farm bloc subcommittee that had approved the Lenroot-Anderson bill, called for a quorum so that more senators might hear Lenroot's exposition.[5] In a two-hour speech, which was interrupted in the latter part with questions and comments, Lenroot proceeded to detail the history of the bill, tell of the need for it and the main provisions in it, and distinguish it from the Capper bill. Then he took up some of the criticisms of the bill, including those in Norbeck's minority report. The capital provided was ample, he said. He defended the principle of loaning to banks instead of farmers, noting that to do the latter would be vastly expensive in overhead and the farmer would have to bear the cost. After meeting some other criticisms lodged by Norbeck, Brookhart, and others, Lenroot concluded with the point that the bill's value would not be measured by the sum of the capital and the debentures but rather by the bank loans that would ensue, once the banks were secure in the knowledge that if need be they could borrow on their agricultural paper.[6]

In the following week, much heated debate resulted as the Senate in Committee of the Whole acted on the Lenroot bill. Norbeck and Brookhart strongly criticized the bill and, they, with others, condemned efforts to a quick consideration of it.[7]

Virtually all the senators favored some credit legislation, and a majority thought it was Lenroot's bill or nothing, except, perhaps, for the extremely limited Capper bill. Thus, Lenroot controlled the situation. He welcomed a vote on a motion to recommit and saw the motion defeated by a vote of four to fifty-one. The vote on Norbeck's substitute, which would have centralized administration under a new agency, increased the initial capital, and made the system's funds more mobile, was a better index of opinion. The substitute motion was defeated with a vote of twenty-one to fifty-three. Lenroot was able to defeat other amendments that he opposed, but he accepted amendments by Swanson and Sterling, to achieve greater mobility of funds within the system. Finally, on 2 February, Lenroot had the satisfaction of seeing his bill approved by the unanimous vote of sixty-nine senators.[8]

Sydney Anderson knew, however, that the majority in the House Committee on Banking and Currency was unfavorable to the legislation and that presidential intervention might be needed. Harding responded to Anderson's appeal by saying that he favored the bill but hoped that it would be

5. *CR* 67:4, 1923, vol. 64, pt. 2, p. 1735; 1923, vol. 64, pt. 3, p. 2366; 1923, vol. 64, pt. 4, p. 4178.

6. Ibid., pp. 2366–71.

7. Ibid., pp. 2660–65, 2761–64, 2814–15; *New York Times*, 30 January 1923; *Milwaukee Sentinel*, 2 February 1923.

8. *Milwaukee Sentinel*, 1 February 1923; *CR* 67:4, 1923, vol. 64, pt. 3, pp. 2779, 2822, 2882, 2894.

possible "to compose the differences in Congress." Mellon made that more difficult when, three weeks later, he wrote Chairman Louis McFadden reiterating his opposition. Secretary Mellon stated various reasons for his objection, but Lenroot thought the main one was the cost to the Treasury. While rebutting Mellon's contentions on the Senate floor, he was asked by Atlee Pomerene how he felt about the ship subsidy bill. He frankly voiced opposition to subsidizing passenger liners. Then Swanson asked him if he believed the rumor that if the ship subsidy bill were not passed in the Senate, the legislation on credits would not pass in the House. Lenroot chose to reverse it, saying that if there were no legislation on credits, there would be no subsidy law. Since there now seemed little hope for legislation on credits and since something should be done for the farmers, Lenroot announced his intention to vote for the pending motion to take up the "filled milk" bill in place of the subsidy bill. The press picked up Lenroot's undisguised ultimatum and, presumably, it was not kept from the president.[9]

Two days later on 23 February, Secretary Wallace gave the press an open letter in effect backing the Lenroot-Anderson bill. He said that the Capper bill to which Mellon raised no objection would help only the cattle industry and cooperative marketing associations. In a letter to Anderson, Herbert Hoover also endorsed the bill. On the same day, President Harding issued a statement saying that the Lenroot bill was part of the administration's program and inviting House leaders to confer with him. The House committee took the hint and promptly set to work drafting a composite bill.[10]

With insufficient time to mold the several bills into a coherent whole, the House committee attached a slightly modified version of the Lenroot bill to the Capper bill and added to both of them the Strong bill, which liberalized terms of the farm loan act to permit larger loans on land mortgages. The mongrel bill passed the House on 1 March, was accepted by conferees on 3 March, and in the last hours of the Congress was passed in both Houses. Lenroot took a hand at the last to get Southerners concerned about a different measure to permit a vote on the credit bill. On 4 March, President Harding signed it into law.[11]

The Agricultural Credits Act of 1923 was the capstone of the farm program of the administration and of the major farm organizations, notably the Grange and the Farm Bureau Federation. In the years that followed, it

9. Anderson to Harding, 30 January 1923, Harding to Anderson, 1 February 1923, Reel 191, Harding Papers; *Milwaukee Sentinel*, 21 February 1923; *CR* 67:4, 1923, vol. 64, pt. 4, pp. 4178–80; *Milwaukee Sentinel*, 22 February 1923.

10. Donald L. Winters, *Henry Cantwell Wallace as Secretary of Agriculture, 1921–1924*, p. 105; Baird and Benner, *Federal Intermediate Credits*, p. 81; *Milwaukee Sentinel*, 23, 24 February 1923; Robert K. Murray, *The Harding Era: Warren G. Harding and His Administration*, p. 384.

11. *Milwaukee Sentinel*, 24, 25 February, 1, 3 March 1923; Baird and Benner, *Federal Intermediate Credits*, p. 82; *Milwaukee Sentinel*, 4 March 1923.

was updated by amendments and remained useful. But under the circumstances in the twenties, it was not a complete answer to the problems of the farmer, who continued to suffer from surplus, depressed prices, and high costs. Already, with the failure of many cooperatives on which it had staked its hopes, the Farm Bureau was beginning to give attention to some form of farm subsidy and Secretary Wallace was considering some subsidy schemes.[12]

Lenroot was not supportive, as some of his colleagues were, of the McNary-Haugen bill, which was introduced in January 1924. As of the fourth session of the Sixty-seventh Congress, however, he did not have to face that issue. Instead, as the Congress drew to a close, he gave his attention and support to a more modest proposal and one that was of direct concern to his constituents, the "filled milk" bill. Despite Harding's belated intervention in favor of the credit bill, Lenroot followed through on his threat to push the "filled milk" bill in place of the ship subsidy bill in the Senate during the last week of February. On 3 March, both Houses approved the measure, outlawing in interstate commerce the shipment of milk whose fat content had been replaced in part or whole with vegetable oil. In supporting the bill, Lenroot asserted that the subsidy bill was dead for the session, and finally, in face of a Senate filibuster, Harding bitterly acquiesced in that judgment. Whether because of the ship subsidy issue or for some other reason, William Culbertson judged that Lenroot was "not as popular at the White House as he once was." [13]

But Culbertson went on to write: "I do not think that his difference with the President is at all fundamental." During the late stages of the farm credit battle, Bascom Timmons, the astute Washington correspondent for the *Milwaukee Sentinel,* called Lenroot "the leader of the administration wing of the progressive forces in the Senate." That was, indeed, Lenroot's position. But there were ambiguities about it, fuzziness at the edges, room for disagreement and misunderstanding.[14]

Lenroot was drawn toward the administration not only by his habitual inclination to cooperate with those who could help achieve constructive measures but also by his continuing hostility toward those whom he considered destructive radicals, who were headed by La Follette. That his friend turned enemy had gained measurably by the 1922 election meant for Lenroot that there was greater need than before to counter him. He took up the gage on the issue of the Constitution and the sanctity of judicial review,

12. Shideler, *Farm Crisis,* pp. 188, 241; Murray, *The Harding Era,* pp. 384–86.

13. *CR* 67:4, 1923, vol. 64, pt. 5, pp. 4470–71, 4751, 4851, 4983–84; Murray, *The Harding Era,* p. 324; Culbertson to Homer Hoch, 2 April 1923, Records, 1923, Box 49, William S. Culbertson Papers.

14. Culbertson to Hoch, 2 April 1923, Records, 1923, Box 49, Culbertson Papers; *Milwaukee Sentinel,* 22 February 1923.

after La Follette proposed a constitutional amendment to curb the conservative federal courts.[15]

On important foreign economic questions, Lenroot was in accord with the administration and served as one of its main spokesmen in the Senate. He argued for a conference to cope with problems arising from the unrealistic reparations burden that had been imposed on Germany.[16] And he defended against La Follette, Borah, and others an agreement with Great Britain by which her war debts might be paid over a long term at low interest.[17]

Lenroot sometimes served as party defender, particularly against the partisan jibes of Pat Harrison. Occasionally, too, he held heated confrontations with the independent George Norris, who felt that he and his bills were ignored by such party leaders as Lenroot.[18]

But if Lenroot was a regular, it was within the context of a loosely defined regularity that left scope for a wide range of differences. Given the power of the western wing of the party and the conciliatory character of Harding, Lodge, Curtis, and Watson, progressive regulars, men like Lenroot, Capper, McCormick, and McNary, could get as much as they gave.

Lenroot continued to believe that the Republican party could be the vehicle for disinterested, constructive progressivism. On one occasion in February, he worked long into the night with Hoover, Assistant Secretary of the Navy Theodore Roosevelt, Jr., and the new senator from Pennsylvania, George Wharton Pepper, on the outlines of a progressive program that they hoped Harding would enunciate during his tour that summer. He worked with Tariff Commissioner Culbertson and Secretary Hoover for vigorous implementation of the flexible tariff provisions, and when Congress adjourned he remained hopeful that Harding would give the Tariff Commission authority to launch investigations on its own, a hope that proved vain.[19]

Although he believed in and used the methods of conciliation and compromise, Lenroot remained firm in regard to the procedures of government. Through the session, he persistently risked his popularity by insisting on

15. Philip Taft, *The A. F. of L. in the Time of Gompers*, pp. 403–4; Belle and Fola La Follette, *La Follette*, vol. 2, pp. 1055–57; Clara Lenroot to Nellie Nichols, 28 January (1923), Clara Lenroot, Diary, 10, 13 February 1923, Irvine L. Lenroot Papers Addition; *CR* 67:4, 1923, vol. 64, pt. 4, pp. 3819–21.

16. *CR* 67:4, 1922, vol. 64, pt. 1, pp. 936–37; *Milwaukee Sentinel*, 26–30 December 1922; *New York Times*, 31 December 1922; Murray, *The Harding Era*, pp. 365–67; L. Ethan Ellis, *Republican Foreign Policy, 1921–1933*, p. 137.

17. Murray, *The Harding Era*, pp. 362–63; *CR* 67:4, 1923, vol. 64, pt. 3, pp. 2823–24; 1923, vol. 64, pt. 4, pp. 3766, 3772.

18. *CR* 67:4, 1923, vol. 64, pt. 3, pp. 2692–93, 5070–73.

19. Theodore Roosevelt, Jr., Diary, 5 February 1923, Box 1, Theodore Roosevelt, Jr., Papers, LC; William S. Culbertson to Lenroot, 9 February 1923, Box 49, Culbertson, Diary, 4 March 1923, Box 4, Lenroot to Culbertson, 21 March 1923, Records, 1923, Box 49, Culbertson Papers; J. Richard Snyder, "William S. Culbertson and the Formation of Modern American Commercial Policy, 1917–1925," pp. 397–410.

observation of the rules and adherence to the new appropriations system. Similarly, he continued to oppose excessive rivers and harbors appropriations, even when they might benefit Wisconsin. In the last days of the session he decried useless delay and failure to act on bills already passed in the House. And on 3 March, when he detected former Sen. Hoke Smith misusing his privilege of the floor by blatant lobbying, Lenroot threatened to call the matter to the attention of the Senate if Smith did not leave immediately.[20]

Lenroot was in Iowa for the start of a Chautauqua tour when newspapers reported that the president had been taken ill on the west coast, the apparent victim of food poisoning. On 3 August, the newspapers stated that the president's death was due—the doctors now diagnosed—to apoplexy. Lenroot wrote Clara:

> I have been and still am awfully depressed over the situation. It is a good thing the country doesn't know how weak Coolidge is although I am surprised to find a general opinion that there isn't much to him. Oh I am so glad I wasn't elected Vice President. To go in and try to fill a dead man's shoes, especially at this time, is an awful task.

He went on to say that his political friend Walter Heinemann proposed to launch a presidential boom for him but that he had wired Heinemann not to, that he would see him in Chicago on 20 August. "I haven't the slightest ambition to be President," Lenroot wrote.

> I'm afraid if elected it would be disastrous for you and probably for me, and I'd rather have a few more years of happiness with you than be President of the United States. If a situation should arise where it would seem to be a duty to let my friends start something that would be different, but I haven't any idea that would be the case. In fact I don't think they would get very far anyway for I am too conservative for the radicals and too radical for the conservatives. But I can't bear to think of Johnson as President. Oh if Hoover only had a different temperament, for I don't suppose he could get very far as it is—There's one thing about Coolidge, he won't make any bad breaks in talking.[21]

Despite private doubts and dissatisfaction, with the start of the Sixty-eighth Congress, Lenroot accepted the role of a Coolidge man. A Coolidge boom had developed steadily since the quiet New Englander was sworn in as president by his father. His first message to Congress clinched matters, so far as regulars were concerned. "On the whole," Clara wrote afterwards, *"he* and *it* made a very good impression. Better than some of us expected."

20. *CR* 67:4, 1923, vol. 64, pt. 2, pp. 1525–33, 1584–86, 1640–42, 2176; 1923, vol. 64, pt. 3, pp. 3199–3202; 1923, vol. 64, pt. 5, pp. 5070–73; *Milwaukee Sentinel,* 4 March 1923.
21. Murray, *The Harding Era,* pp. 448–51; Dorothy Black to Irvine L. Lenroot, 1 August 1923, Box 1, Irvine L. Lenroot Papers; Clara Lenroot, Diary, 1 August 1923, Clara Lenroot to Nellie Nichols, 1 August 1923, Lenroot Papers Addition; Irvine to Clara Lenroot, 3, 4 August 1923, Box 1, Lenroot Papers.

Lenroot expressed some qualifications, notably with respect to the bill on the soldier .bonus that was coming up before the tax cuts, which Coolidge had made the keystone of his program. But Lenroot praised the seaway endorsement, the proposal to consolidate the railroad system, and the passages on foreign policy, which included advocacy of the World Court. With Johnson already a candidate and La Follette a prospective one, in the primaries or on a third party ticket, Lenroot had little option but to accept the leadership of Coolidge.[22]

While the Lenroots enjoyed the hospitality of the new president and his gracious wife, the La Follette forces were demonstrating their newfound strength in both the House and the Senate.[23] In the House, insurgents held up the election of Frederick Gillett as Speaker for three days and eight ballots, until they gained a minor concession. In the Senate, where there were fifty-one Republicans, forty-three Democrats, and two Farmer-Laborites, La Follette, Norris, Ladd, Brookhart, Frazier, Shipstead, and Magnus Johnson formed the nucleus of a group that, with the help of some others, successfully blocked the reelection of Cummins to the post of chairman of the Committee on Interstate Commerce, the honor finally going to Democrat Ellison Smith of South Carolina after thirty-two ballots and over a month of conflict. At issue in the symbolic struggle was the Esch-Cummins Act. Meanwhile, Norris and eight others voted against the nomination of Kellogg for ambassador to Britain.[24] Presidential politics were not far below the surface.[25]

Lenroot saw little prospect of capturing the Wisconsin delegation for the president but gave thought to putting up an uninstructed delegate slate and declared his opposition to Johnson and La Follette.[26]

Hoover's position in the administration made it much easier for Lenroot to accept Coolidge's leadership. Furthermore, he knew he would have the same degree of independence as he had in Harding's time.

In the Senate, Lenroot's ties with the regular Republicans and their leaders were at once evidenced and strengthened when he was named to one of the vacancies on the foreign-relations committee.[27]

Lenroot's main concern at the start of the session was with the World

22. William Allen White, *A Puritan in Babylon: The Story of Calvin Coolidge*, pp. 295–96; Clara Lenroot, Diary, 6 December 1923, Lenroot Papers Addition; Donald R. McCoy, *Calvin Coolidge: The Quiet President*, pp. 199–201; *Milwaukee Sentinel*, 7 December 1923.

23. Clara Lenroot, Diary, 11, 14, 15, 19, 20, 24 December 1923, Lenroot Papers Addition.

24. McCoy, *Calvin Coolidge*, pp. 203–4; Ralph Mills Sayre, "Albert Baird Cummins and the Progressive Movement in Iowa," pp. 531–32; *Milwaukee Sentinel*, 19 November 1923, 10 January 1924; Richard Lowitt, *George W. Norris: The Making of a Progressive, 1861–1912*, vol. 2, p. 140.

25. Robert La Follette, Jr., to W. T. Rawleigh, 19 December 1923, Box 118, Series B, Phil La Follette to "Dear Ones," 26, 28 January 1924, Robert La Follette to "Dear Boys," 20 January 1924, Box 31, Series A, Robert M. La Follette FC.

26. Lenroot to James Good, 22 December 1923, Good to Lenroot, 7 February 1924, Lenroot to Good, 12 February 1924, Box 5, Lenroot Papers.

27. Henry Cabot Lodge to Walter Edge, 9 December 1923, Henry Cabot Lodge Papers.

Court. On 10 December, he introduced a resolution on the subject and had it referred to the foreign-relations committee. While declaring for American adherence, it set up elaborate new procedures for electing judges and prescribed thoroughgoing separation from the League of Nations, which had established it. Though similar to a plan drafted by George Harvey, and at one point endorsed by Harding during his summer tour, and calculated to appeal to those who in the battle of the League had been reservationists, Lenroot's scheme was not favored by the irreconcilables and was promptly condemned by such World Court proponents as Manley O. Hudson of the Harvard Law School. Lenroot might nevertheless have pushed for action on his plan in committee had not he and the Senate been diverted by the burgeoning Teapot Dome scandal.[28]

On 31 May 1921 President Harding had signed an order transferring administration of the naval oil reserves from the Department of Navy to the Department of Interior. Subsequently, Secretary of Interior Albert Fall, with some secrecy, leased Naval Reserve No. 1, the Elks Hill Reserve in California, to his old friend Edward Doheny and Naval Reserve No. 3, Teapot Dome, in Wyoming, to a newer friend Harry Sinclair. In mid-April 1922, the Senate adopted a resolution offered by John B. Kendrick of Wyoming calling on the secretaries of the Navy and Interior departments to inform the Senate about the rumored Teapot Dome lease. At the end of the month, the Senate unanimously adopted La Follette's resolution calling on Fall to supply full information about all naval reserve leases and authorizing an investigation by the Committee on Public Lands and Surveys. La Follette and Kendrick prevailed on a Democratic member of the committee, Thomas J. Walsh, to play the role of prosecutor.[29]

After considerable delay, hearings at last began on 22 October 1923. Lenroot, the second-ranking Republican to Chairman Smoot, was one of five committee members present.

A year before, Lenroot expressed some sympathy for the projected investigation. He understood that the Teapot formation was "practically closed in without danger of it being drained." He also wondered whether the government was to receive ample compensation.[30] But when the investigation began, and for some time afterwards, until he became convinced of fraud, Lenroot was sympathetic to the leasing policy, though not necessarily convinced of its full legality. Walsh later complained that Smoot and Lenroot had made no preparation for the hearings but left all of the work of ferreting out the facts and assembling witnesses to him, and that in their

---

28. *CR* 68:1, 1923, vol. 65, pt. 1, p. 151; Denna F. Fleming, *The United States and the World Court*, pp. 44–45; Robert D. Accinelli, "The Harding Administration and the World Court," pp. 11–12; Accinelli, "The United States and the World Court, 1920–1927" (Ph.D. diss.), pp. 119–30, 154–55; *New York Times*, 26 December 1923. See also the *New York Times*, 27 December 1923, and 3 January 1924.

29. Thomas J. Walsh, "The True History of Teapot Dome," pp. 1–12.

30. Lenroot to William Kent, 8 July 1922, Box 64, William Kent Papers.

questions and remarks they revealed "a decidedly hostile attitude in which they persisted until the sensational and corrupt features were developed and the whole country was up in arms." [31] Peter Norbeck, a member of the committee, agreed, as have several historians.[32]

Lenroot's attitude is readily explicable. Reports of government geologists and two geologists hired by the committee indicated that there was, indeed, a good deal of drainage from Teapot Dome and the danger of more. Also, there was much to be said for the leases and pursuant contracts on other grounds. Doheny and Sinclair had agreed to provide payment to the government not only of royalty oil but of refined oil and storage facilities on the seacoasts and in Hawaii, so the navy would have ready access to oil in usable form if it needed it. Even dredging, and other construction work, was provided for under a contract with Doheny. The facilities to be made available to the navy in this way were valued in excess of $1 hundred million.[33] As previously stated, Lenroot had not sympathized with the attitude of the Navy Department during the last five years of the battle for leasing legislation. Not a preservationist but a conservationist himself, he could approve a policy of use such as Fall outlined in an earlier letter to Harding and now in his testimony before the committee. Furthermore, with respect to the transfer of authority, it made good sense administratively to consolidate control in the department that had the machinery for the task, namely, the Department of Interior. Lenroot had reservations with respect to the extent of the leasing and the method of bypassing Congress to get storage facilities, an expedient that he attributed to navy people, yet he saw good arguments for the basic policy embodied in the agreements.[34]

Furthermore, Lenroot had reason to suspect the motives of Walsh. High-minded, persevering, and able, Walsh nevertheless had not been a consistent defender of conservationism; he was, however, well known as an intense partisan.[35] And a presidential election was just ahead. A partisan himself, Lenroot was naturally inclined to parry Walsh's thrusts rather than to abet either the Democrats or La Follette, the prospective candidate of a third party.

31. Walsh to David F. Pugh, 13 December 1927, Box 213, Thomas J. Walsh Papers, LC.

32. Norbeck to Harry King, 2 February 1924, Peter Norbeck Papers, quoted in Gilbert C. Fite, *Peter Norbeck: Prairie Statesman*, p. 113; David H. Stratton, "Albert B. Fall and the Teapot Dome Affair" (Ph.D. diss.), pp. 237–38; Burl Noggle, *Teapot Dome: Oil and Politics in the 1920's*, p. 66. For examples of questions and comments by Lenroot that, during the first phase of the hearing, suggested sympathy for Fall's position see U.S., Congress, Senate, Committee on Public Lands and Surveys, *Hearings: Leases Upon Naval Oil Reserves*, pp. 172, 174, 278–79, 308–9, 315–16, 403, 510–16, 663–64, 704–10.

33. Stratton, "Albert B. Fall," pp. 145–74; Gerald D. Nash, *United States Oil Policy, 1890–1964: Business and Government in Twentieth Century America*, pp. 78–79.

34. *CR* 68:1, 1924, vol. 65, pt. 2, pp. 1593–95.

35. J. Leonard Bates, *The Origins of Teapot Dome: Progressives, Parties and Petroleum, 1909–1921*, p. 241; J. Leonard Bates, "Senator Walsh of Montana, 1918–1924: A Liberal Under Pressure" (Ph.D. diss.), pp. 213, 272–73, 291, 418; Thomas R. Marshall, *Recollections of Thomas R. Marshall, Vice-President and Hoosier Philosopher: A Hoosier Salad*, p. 314.

But for the fact that Fall had accepted loans from Doheny and Sinclair, his actions were defensible.[36] And corruption had not yet been cast over the hearings. Even under suspicious circumstances, colleagues thought Fall a man of courage and honor.[37]

Walsh, however, was already suspicious.[38] During November, while the hearings were adjourned, Walsh gathered new information and prepared to attack Fall on his weakest ground, his personal financial situation and transactions.[39]

When the hearings resumed on 30 November, Carl C. Magee, an Albuquerque editor, was the star witness. He testified that while in 1920 Fall had been impecunious, soon after a visit from Sinclair and prior to the execution of the Teapot Dome lease to Sinclair, Fall had shown sudden opulence, improving his ranch and buying another. Other witnesses from New Mexico corroborated the testimony. In his questioning, Lenroot attempted to prove that Magee was Fall's political enemy and that he exaggerated the extent of Fall's change of fortune. In questioning the director of the Bureau of Mines on 5 December, he continued to show the advantages of the Teapot Dome leases.[40] But when Fall wired the committee that he would send his son-in-law to explain, Lenroot was not at all satisfied with a surrogate and again insisted, as he had earlier, that Chairman Smoot should make certain that Fall appears.[41]

Chiefly at issue was the source of the $91,500 Fall had used in buying a new ranch. In fact the money came from Doheny. In accepting this money and other gratuities from Doheny and Sinclair, which in the aggregate exceeded $4 hundred thousand, Fall acted foolishly. It is not clear that his intent was criminal, however. Probably Doheny would have loaned his friend the money in any case, and Fall would have executed the lease as a matter of policy even without the loan. Had he wanted to accept a bribe, he might have insisted on $2 million, considering the value of the leased property. Be that as it may, during the course of a tortuous trip north, which was partly prolonged by illness, Fall saw Doheny and found him unwilling to have the $100,000 loan revealed, for business and political reasons.[42] But Fall's wealthy friend in Washington, Edward McLean, publisher of the *Washington Post,* agreed that he should be named as source of the money.

As Fall wended his way toward Washington, Lenroot succeeded Smoot as chairman. Smoot retained a place on the committee. On 14 and 15 December, Lenroot wired Fall at Atlantic City, where he was purportedly

36. Francis Russell, *The Shadow of Blooming Grove: Warren G. Harding in His Times,* p 499.

37. Mark Sullivan, *Our Times: The United States, 1900–1925,* vol. 6, p. 288.

38. Bates, "Senator Walsh," pp. 324–25, 328–29; *St. Louis Post-Dispatch,* 27 February 1924.

39. Bates, "Senator Walsh," p. 328; Walsh, "True History of Teapot Dome," p. 8; Stratton, "Albert B. Fall," p. 229.

40. U.S., Senate, Committee on Public Lands and Surveys, *Hearings: Leases on Naval Reserves,* pp. 840–41, 886, 1100–1105, 1218–20.

41. Walsh, "True History of Teapot Dome," p. 9; *CR* 68:1, 1924, vol. 65, pt. 4, p. 3230.

42. Stratton, "Albert B. Fall," pp. 510–11.

ill, urging him to testify as soon as possible.[43] Finally, a day or two before Christmas, Lenroot learned that though still unwell, Fall was in Washington at the Wardman Park Inn. Together with Smoot, Lenroot visited Fall in the afternoon and urged him to tell the committee where he got the money for the new ranch. Fall was reluctant, but near the end of the half-hour conversation Lenroot understood Fall to name McLean as the source. Smoot did not hear McLean's name mentioned. When the senators left their former colleague, Lenroot expected him to testify promptly.[44]

On the night of 26 December, Will Hays visited Fall. Sinclair was also present. Sinclair had recently provided Hays with $185,000 in Liberty Bonds to make up for the 1920 campaign deficit. Hays, though no longer chairman of the Republican National Committee or postmaster general, retained a great interest in party affairs. In all likelihood, he wanted to end the investigation before Sinclair's munificence was known. Hays urged Fall to write a letter to the committee naming McLean as the source of the money. According to Fall's later recollection, Hays told him that he had talked to some members of the committee and was assured that such a letter of explanation would end the hearings. Hays had seen Lenroot on the evening of 23 December. He later admitted talking to other senators in search of a deciding vote to end the hearings. Hays's interview with Fall was prolonged, but finally Fall dictated a letter naming McLean and declaring that he had received nothing from Sinclair or Doheny. The following morning before leaving Washington, Hays called on Lenroot, possibly to give him Fall's letter, which Lenroot presented to the committee.[45]

McLean wired a message from Florida, which corroborated Fall's testimony, but Walsh privately thought the only source of the money was Sinclair and insisted that McLean be asked to testify. Lenroot and Smoot, who were anxious to end the hearings, agreed. Thereupon, Walsh said that in light of McLean's prospective testimony and since Fall was reluctant to appear, he would not insist on Fall testifying at that time. Lenroot said that since Fall had named the source of the money, he saw no need for him to appear.[46]

McLean, through various Washington agents, struggled to avoid returning to Washington. He and his physician wired the committee that return to the chilly capital might aggravate an acute sinus infection. But his representative, aware that some cooperation was essential, suggested that a deposition might be taken. Smoot suggested that Walsh send written questions or go to Florida to take testimony. Walsh rejected these proposals, but Lenroot argued that unless some such scheme were adopted the committee

43. Ibid., p. 289.

44. *Milwaukee Sentinel*, 27 February 1924; *CR* 68:1, 1924, vol. 65, pt. 4, p. 3230.

45. Stratton, "Albert B. Fall," p. 291; Clara Lenroot, Diary, 23 December 1923, Lenroot Papers Addition; *Washington Herald*, 5 April 1928; Clara Lenroot to Nellie Nichols, 28 December 1923, Lenroot Papers Addition; U.S., Senate, Committee on Public Lands and Surveys, *Hearings: Leases Upon Naval Oil Reserves*, pp. 1429–33.

46. Walsh, "True History of Teapot Dome," p. 11; U.S., Senate, Committee on Public Lands and Surveys, *Hearings: Leases Upon Naval Reserves*, pp. 1453–55.

might have to wait all winter for McLean to appear. He moved that McLean be required to make a full statement under oath, with the understanding that after receiving it the committee could decide what further steps, if any, might be needed. Walsh, who deprecated the seriousness of McLean's illness, called for a record vote, which he lost, by a vote of five to two. He asked if he might submit questions and Lenroot said he could. But four days later, Walsh told the committee he had changed his mind and would go to Palm Beach after all, as a subcommittee of one.[47]

Within days, the newspapers printed the sensational news of McLean's testimony. He had given Fall two or three checks, but Fall had returned them, saying he had gotten the money from another source. McLean was unable to produce Fall's note or the stubs for the checks. Fall was present at Palm Beach, but he declined to be examined on the grounds of his physical condition. In a letter to Walsh, he reiterated his denial that the money had come from Sinclair or had anything to do with any oil leases. Further than that he would not go. Then he moved on to New Orleans. On 18 January, Lenroot and Walsh wired the governor of Louisiana asking that Fall be kept under surveillance, in case he attempted to leave the country.[48]

Whatever faith Lenroot now had in Fall was destroyed on Sunday, 20 January, when one of Theodore Roosevelt's sons, Archie, accompanied by his brother Theodore, made startling disclosures to Lenroot and Walsh in Lenroot's apartment. Roosevelt, who was employed by Sinclair, told Walsh and Lenroot, as he did the full committee on the following day, that Sinclair had departed secretly for Europe after the Palm Springs revelations and that later Sinclair's secretary had said Sinclair had paid the foreman of Fall's ranch $68,000. The secretary, Gustav Wahlberg, had advised Roosevelt to sever his connections with Sinclair to protect the Roosevelt name. Lenroot and Walsh issued subpoenas for witnesses, and Lenroot informed the president of the turn of events.[49]

Wahlberg told the committee he had been misunderstood, but Sinclair's lawyers revealed that Fall had received from Sinclair $25,000 in Liberty Bonds, allegedly for services unconnected with the Teapot Dome lease. More sensational still, on 24 January, Doheny admitted to the committee that he was the source of the $100,000, which was delivered by his son in cash in a black satchel. By then, Lenroot had gone into action "with a ferocity which made Senator Walsh's tactics seem mild by comparison," in the view of a hostile reporter.[50] But it was already too late, in some respects. In the weeks that followed, Lenroot attempted to defend the national inter-

47. U.S., Senate, Committee on Public Lands and Surveys, *Hearings: Leases Upon Naval Reserves*, pp. 1545–49, 1649.

48. M. R. Werner and John Starr, *Teapot Dome*, pp. 123–26.

49. Ibid., pp. 128–31; Clara Lenroot, Diary, 20 January 1924, Lenroot Papers Addition; Theodore Roosevelt, Jr., to William W. Campbell, 15 February 1924, Box 23, Roosevelt, Jr., Papers; *CR* 68:1, 1924, vol. 65, pt. 2, p. 1592.

50. Werner and Starr, *Teapot Dome*, pp. 131–36; Paul Y. Anderson, "The Scandal in Oil," pp. 277–79.

est while, at the same time, protecting the interests of his party. Increasingly, as suspicion spread wider and Democratic charges became stronger, he found that he had to defend himself, particularly about the Wardman Park meeting with Fall. Thus, Lenroot suffered a physical breakdown due to his responsibilities. This occasioned his resignation from membership on the lands committee.[51]

Not until mid-May was Lenroot in condition to resume work, and then only so much as was necessary.[52] Of the various matters to which he attended, the most important related to the World Court. In the foreign-relations committee, Lenroot voted with the Democrats to report a World Court resolution embodying Harding-Hughes reservations, which Coolidge now supported. But when that was defeated by a vote of ten to eight, Lenroot voted with most of his Republican colleagues for the Pepper plan, a scheme that supporters of the World Court, including the Democrats, found unacceptable.[53] It stood no chance and was not brought to a vote in the Senate. The hostility of Lodge to what he often called the "League Court" was a major stumbling block to constructive action.[54]

En route home to Superior after adjournment, the Lenroots stopped at Cleveland to attend the Republican National Convention. Concomitant with the Teapot Dome disclosures, other iniquities of the Harding years had come to light—surreptitious sale of war supplies, larceny in the operation of the Shipping Board, graft in the Veterans Bureau, irregularities in prohibition enforcement, and more. But Coolidge was not blamed, and he emerged from the Teapot Dome investigation unscathed.[55]

Lenroot was not close to Coolidge. The president was cordial, but during the winter he consulted Lenroot only on the oil investigation.[56] But Lenroot accepted Coolidge's renomination as a matter of course. The platform offered concessions to labor and agriculture, included a tariff plank that was satisfactory to Culbertson, and endorsed the World Court. But, to Lenroot's disgust, it straddled on child labor.[57]

Spearheaded by the railroad brotherhoods, the liberals, socialists, and

51. Herbert F. Margulies, "Progressivism, Patriotism, and Politics: The Life and Times of Irvine L. Lenroot," pp. 1269–81.

52. Lenroot to Nellie Nichols, 24 April 1924, Clara Lenroot, Diary, 26, 27 April, 17 May 1924, Louis Lenroot, Diary, 30 April, 16 May 1924, Lenroot to Nellie Nichols, 25 May 1924, Lenroot Papers Addition.

53. Accinelli, "United States and the World Court," pp. 172–76; *Milwaukee Sentinel*, 24 May 1924.

54. On Lodge's attitude see for example Lodge to Elihu Root, 27 April 1923, to Arthur M. Hyde, 28 April 1923, to Louis A. Coolidge, 3 May 1923, to David Jayne Hill, 7 December 1923, to John H. Finley, 23 February 1924, to Medill McCormick, 19 May 1924, Lodge Papers.

55. McCoy, *Calvin Coolidge*, p. 244; Stratton, "Albert B. Fall," p. 244.

56. Lenroot to William Kent, 21 February 1924, Box 71, Kent Papers.

57. Robert H. Zieger, *Republicans and Labor, 1919–1929*, pp. 179–80; Culbertson to William Allen White, 12 June 1924, Records, 1922–1928, Box 48, Culbertson Papers; McCoy, *Calvin Coolidge*, p. 244; Lenroot to C. B. Slemp, 22 July 1924, Box 5, Lenroot Papers.

other labor elements formed the Progressive party and nominated La Follette for president. The Democrats deadlocked and finally chose a compromise ticket of John W. Davis and Charles Bryan, brother of William Jennings Bryan. Fifty-three of Theodore Roosevelt's supporters in 1912 denounced La Follette's candidacy as based on radicalism and endorsed Coolidge. The latter cultivated the likes of Norbeck, Pinchot, William Allen White, and even Norris, in an effort to limit the extent of progressive defection.[58]

Lenroot feared that La Follette might succeed in throwing the election into the House, which might deadlock, and that in the Senate La Follette would lend his strength to Charles Bryan who would become vice-president and would serve as acting president. He was not alone in envisioning such a possibility.[59] At the same time, Lenroot was unhappy with his party's leadership and the political situation generally. "It looks to me as if some of us were in a fair way to be ground between the upper millstone of standpattism and the nether one of radicalism," he wrote William Kent late in July. Two months later, he felt no better about politics, and to Kent he reaffirmed his determination to retire from it when his term ended. There was no political middle ground for a politician who was neither reactionary nor radical. He expressed sorrow that Kent had decided to support La Follette—in his view the government was in the hands of minorities and interest groups and La Follette would merely substitute one set for another. The only solution, Lenroot felt, was an aroused public opinion and the organization of the majority. In private life, he hoped to be able to speak along those lines for a year or two if he could afford it.[60]

Blaine won reelection and La Follette carried Wisconsin, but contrary to earlier expectations he won in no other state. Some improvement in farm prices and defection in labor's ranks worked against La Follette. The return of industrial prosperity, Democratic disarray, and other factors helped Coolidge score an overwhelming victory while his party made moderate gains in both House and Senate. Lenroot was happy at the results.[61]

Days after the election, Henry Cabot Lodge died. At the end of the month, in preparation for the "lame duck" session, Republican senators made Charles Curtis majority leader and James E. Watson assistant leader and whip. At the same time, in a surprise move that was spearheaded by younger senators, the party conference resolved that La Follette and three senators who had supported him, Frazier, Brookhart, and Ladd, "be not invited to future Republican conferences, and be not named to fill any Republican vacancies on Senate committees." Lenroot was not in Washington at the

58. Belle and Fola La Follette, *La Follette*, vol. 2, pp. 1120–21; McCoy, *Calvin Coolidge*, p. 254.
59. Clara Lenroot to Mrs. William Crozier, 22 July 1924, Mary Williams Crozier Papers; Frank B. Kellogg to Elbert H. Gary, 25 September 1924, to C. A. Severance, 6 October 1924, Box 9, Frank B. Kellogg Papers.
60. Lenroot to William Kent, 30 July, 25 September 1924, Box 72, Kent Papers.
61. Clara Lenroot, Diary, 4 November 1924, Lenroot Papers Addition.

time, but he surely would have approved the action. Subsequently, after a bitter fight, the four senators were deprived of their seniority on committees but not of all committee assignments.[62]

Early in the summer, Clara became seriously ill. Since the doctors at the university hospital in Madison were unable to determine the nature of her ailment after several weeks, Lenroot transferred Clara to the Mayo Clinic at Rochester, Minnesota, at the end of November. There the doctors concluded that Clara had a thyroid malfunction, diagnosed as myxedema. But she did not quickly respond to treatment and instead suffered from crippled limbs, extreme weakness, and other disorders. For a time, her life was in danger. For a longer time, it did not seem that she would recover her physical mobility. At last, she improved to the point that on 27 March she was permitted to go to Washington, where an ambulance met her train. For about a year after that, however, she required painful physical therapy before she finally regained full use of her body.[63]

While Clara was at the Mayo Clinic, the "lame duck" session of the Sixty-eighth Congress and a special two-week session of the new Senate were in progress. Occasionally, in periods when Clara was feeling better and Katharine or Dorothy was with her, Lenroot went to Washington.

His most significant action during the "lame duck" session was a form of inaction. He declined to be paired to sustain a veto of a bill that granted postal wage increase, despite the president's use of strong pressure.[64] But during the special session, he voted to confirm the nomination of Charles Beecher Warren for attorney general, though Warren was under attack for association with the "sugar trust." The nomination failed.[65]

The Lenroots were in Washington when they received word that Emanuel Philipp had died. Lenroot issued a statement praising Philipp as "one of the outstanding governors of Wisconsin, serving during one of its most trying periods with conspicuous ability and judgment." [66]

Three days later, a reporter of the *Milwaukee Sentinel* told Lenroot of the death of Robert M. La Follette. Although La Follette had been seriously ill during the winter and gravely ill for the previous several days, news of his

62. *Milwaukee Sentinel*, 29 November, 17, 20, 23 December 1924; *New York Times*, 30 November 1924, quoted in Belle and Fola La Follette, *La Follette*, vol. 2, p. 1150; McCoy, *Calvin Coolidge*, p. 267; Walter E. Edge, *A Jerseyman's Journal: Fifty Years of American Business and Politics*, pp. 134–35; Belle and Fola La Follette, *La Follette*, vol. 2, pp. 1159–60.

63. See the extensive family correspondence for the period in the Lenroot Papers Addition. Irvine made entries in Clara's diary that Katharine later summarized. The summaries, also in the Lenroot Papers Addition, likewise trace the course of Clara's illness.

64. C. B. Slemp to Lenroot, 23 December 1924, Box 5, Coolidge to Lenroot, 23 December 1924, Box 5, Coolidge to Lenroot, 24 December 1924, Lenroot to Coolidge, n.d. (December 1924), Coolidge to Lenroot, 3 January 1925, Box 2, Lenroot Papers.

65. McCoy, *Calvin Coolidge*, pp. 278–80; Lenroot to Nellie Nichols, 4 March 1925, Lenroot Papers Addition; *CR* 69th Cong., Special session of the Senate, 1925, vol. 67, pt. 1, pp. 101, 275.

66. *Milwaukee Sentinel*, 16 June 1925.

death came as a great shock to Lenroot and he cried. After waiting for an hour, he went to the La Follette home to offer his services. The two sons, Robert and Phil, and La Follette's son-in-law, George Middleton, were glad to see him and said they had told the sergeant at arms in the Senate that they would like him to be chairman of the Senate Funeral Committee, as was customary in such cases. He readily agreed and made the necessary arrangements for the special train to Madison. During the afternoon, Irvine, Clara, and Katharine talked of the intimacy that had once existed between themselves and the La Follettes, "and" as Lenroot wrote his sister, "the really splendid qualities that La Follette had." That evening, Lenroot returned to the La Follette home bearing a graceful letter of condolence from Clara to Belle La Follette.[67]

Despite the genuineness of his sorrow, Lenroot gave thought to the political consequences of La Follette's death. He wrote Nellie: "This is going to cause more political turmoil in Wisconsin right away, and between us I am very strongly inclined to get out of politics altogether. While superficially what has happened might seem to clear the political atmosphere, I am afraid both factions will now split up, and the situation is going to be anything but pleasant." [68] With the removal of the common enemy, La Follette, it would be doubly difficult, Lenroot foresaw, to keep together the heterogeneous alliance of conservatives and ex-La Follette men, "wets" and "drys," and those for whom matters of religion made a difference. But Lenroot was not ready for the political sidelines just yet.

Within ten days of La Follette's death, the La Follette family and a few close friends decided that Robert La Follette, Jr., should succeed his father. Despite great pressure, Belle La Follette had decided against running, and Phil, the more natural politician of the brothers, was twenty-eight, two years too young for the office. A number of other politicians were willing to run, but that only made it more imperative that a La Follette should do so, to prevent a factional fight. Even so, Governor Blaine had to be pacified, and in late July Robert La Follette, Jr., made a treaty of friendship with him.[69]

As Lenroot had foreseen, the anti-La Follette element found it difficult to unify, despite his best efforts. He addressed their convention at Oshkosh and supported the conventional nominee, Roy Wilcox, but he was not surprised when La Follette, Jr., won in the Republican primary. Lenroot then supported the independent candidacy of Edward Dithmar, but La Follette, Jr., more than doubled Dithmar's vote.[70]

---

67. Ibid., 19 June 1925; Lenroot to Nellie Nichols, 18 June 1925, Lenroot Papers Addition; Clara Lenroot to Mrs. La Follette, 18 June 1925, Lenroot to Mrs. La Follette, 18 June 1925, Box 18, Series D, La Follette FC; *Milwaukee Sentinel*, 19 June 1925.

68. Lenroot to Nellie Nichols, 18 June 1925, Lenroot Papers Addition.

69. Robert La Follette, Jr., to Dante Pierce, 28 June 1925, Box 2, Series C, La Follette FC; Roger T. Johnson, *Robert M. La Follette, Jr., and the Decline of the Progressive Party in Wisconsin*, pp. 4–9. The *Milwaukee Sentinel* for the period offers informative details.

70. Margulies, "Lenroot," pp. 1295–98.

With Wisconsin unredeemed and the national scene still blighted by radicalism and reaction, Lenroot had reasons for pessimism. But foreign affairs offered an outlet for constructive activity. Already, during the summer of 1925, Lenroot was preparing to lead the Senate Republicans in an all-out effort to bring the United States into the World Court.

During the summer and fall of 1925, Clara's illness kept Lenroot in Washington for the most part.[71] His presence there made him available for consultation with President Coolidge and Kellogg, who had become secretary of state in January 1925.

The president was concerned at this time that when the new Congress met, it should promptly vote for American adherence to the World Court. He was committed to it by his own prior statements and the platform of his party; he believed in it; and he was under strong pressure from a wide variety of organizations, especially influential church and peace groups. Strong opposition existed, headed by the Hearst newspapers. The Ku Klux Klan called the Court a back door to the League of Nations, a tool of the Vatican, and a threat to American immigration policy. And a segment of the peace movement opposed it in the interest of a more thoroughgoing approach to peace—the outlawry of war. But the House of Representatives reflected majority opinion as of March 1925, when it resolved 301 members to 28 in favor of adherence. The matter had languished for almost three years, but during the special session the Senate had set 17 December for the start of debate on the matter and Coolidge, together with Kellogg, Hughes, and Root, spoke forcefully for it in the summer and fall. Among other things, they were able to point to the American origins of the Court, for the United States had advocated some such court since 1899, and Root had helped to draft the statute of the Court in 1920. John Bassett Moore was one of the eleven judges on it.[72]

Coolidge was open to whatever reservations the Senate might approve. But in advance of the session, on the advice of Kellogg, Hughes, and others, he avoided committing himself to anything that might alienate the Democrats. At issue, in particular, was a proposal drafted by Moore and supported by the prestigious Sen. George W. Pepper to seriously limit the World Court with respect to rendering advisory opinions. The ranking Democrat on the foreign-relations committee, Claude Swanson, and the most forceful of the Democrats on that committee, Thomas J. Walsh, while favoring a limitation on advisory opinions that Walsh had proposed in 1924, were unwilling to go so far as Moore and Pepper wanted. Coolidge was determined to avoid a repetition of the Versailles treaty fiasco and, therefore, gave an effective veto power to the Democrats to ensure bipartisan support for the Court

71. Lenroot to Nellie Nichols, 4 November 1925, Lenroot Papers Addition; *Milwaukee Sentinel,* 7 April 1926.

72. McCoy, *Calvin Coolidge,* pp. 266, 359–60; Fleming, *United States and the World Court,* pp. 49–51; Accinelli, "United States and the World Court," pp. 96–98, 203, 262–63, 291.

resolution. The Republicans, even if united and enthusiastic for the World Court, which they were not, did not have votes enough to ratify without Democratic help.[73]

Although the administration could not and would not ignore Pepper, who had chaired the subcommittee proceedings on the World Court in 1924, it entrusted Lenroot with the task of leading the Senate Republicans in the upcoming fight. He would have the assistance of Pepper and Majority Leader Curtis and would work with Swanson, Walsh, and Joseph Robinson, who had succeeded Oscar Underwood as minority leader.[74] Lenroot was a logical choice for several reasons. On the foreign-relations committee, he was the highest-ranked Republican favorable to the World Court. Borah, the chairman following the death of Lodge, and those ranked just behind him, Johnson and Moses, opposed adherence, as they had opposed entry into the League of Nations. Moreover, in 1924, Lenroot, alone among the Republicans, had voted in committee for the Swanson resolution, which remained the basis for bipartisan action. Also, Lenroot was a close friend of Secretary Kellogg.[75]

Lenroot understood and endorsed the administration's strategy. After he and Swanson saw the president on 4 August, he told the press that there was no need to compromise with the opponents of adherence, as Republican reservationists had compromised with irreconcilables during the battle of the League. He spoke of an organized effort to misrepresent the situation and make it seem that such a compromise was necessary.

> Their hope is that republican senators will agree to such compromises upon reservations, and that on the final vote the democrats will vote against the resolution and thus defeat it. I am satisfied . . . that there are at least seventy-five senators who will vote for ratification of the protocol with the Hughes-Harding-Coolidge reservations and the only danger lies in compromise upon reservations that may defeat it.

Lenroot went on to cite the platform pledge of the Republican party and to say that those who were silent on the issue at the convention or in the campaign were bound to support adherence without additional reservations.[76]

73. Kellogg to Coolidge, 26 October 1925, Record Group 59, file, 500, C 114 Advisory Opinions, S/39, NA; Coolidge to Hughes, 3, 4 November 1925, Hughes to Coolidge, 5 November 1925, Box 5a, Charles Evans Hughes Papers; John Bassett Moore to Harlan Fiske Stone, 28 January 1926, Box 172, John Bassett Moore Papers, LC; "Proceedings of the Committee on Foreign Relations, printed for the use of the Committee on Foreign Relations, 1934," 22 May 1924, Box 545, William E. Borah Papers; Accinelli, "United States and the World Court," pp. 157, 175, 292–93, 309–10.

74. Accinelli, "United States and the World Court," pp. 316–17.

75. Frank Kellogg to Lenroot, 10 March 1924, Charlotte Kellogg to Lenroot, 21 August 1937, Box 3, Lenroot Papers; R. J. McNeil to Kellogg, 24 November 1924, Box 9, Kellogg Papers.

76. *Milwaukee Sentinel*, 5 August 1925; Coolidge to Lenroot, 12 August 1925, Box 2, Lenroot Papers.

While eschewing compromises with the enemies of the protocol, he left the door open for additional reservations that might mollify lukewarm friends. In a speech on the Court at Princeton, a week before Senate debate began, he showed sensitivity to the major opposition charge against it—that it was an instrumentality of the League of Nations. Lenroot argued that though the judges were chosen by the League Assembly and Council through concurrent votes and were paid by the League, and though the League might ask advisory opinions of the Court, yet the Court's powers and duties were defined by the statute creating it and it was essentially independent of the League. Lenroot surely did not hope to win over Borah or his followers, but he saw the need to keep the support of Pepper, a onetime irreconcilable and to arm regular Republicans so they might defend pro-Court votes among anti-League constituents.[77]

Lenroot's sensitivity to anti-League opinions of some Republicans—a sensitivity shared by Collidge and Kellogg—made him vulnerable to a hazard that he had guarded against during the battle of the League. In 1919 and 1920, Lenroot had sought to avoid amendments, because they would have to be accepted by the other great powers. But the reservations being proposed to the resolution of adherence to the Court protocol were themselves amendments, in effect, for the proposals, such as that the United States must participate in the election of judges, would require the assent of other countries. It was essential, therefore, that Lenroot was certain not only of approval in the Senate but also of acceptance by the Court members. Concessions to lukewarm proponents endangered that assent.

Hughes had secured prior acceptance of his four reservations, which were now embodied in the Swanson resolution. Nor was there any danger in Swanson's fifth reservation, bearing on advisory opinions. It read: "That the United States shall be in no manner bound by any advisory opinion of the Permanent Court of International Justice not rendered pursuant to a request in which it, the United States, shall expressly join." [78] But Moore, the American judge on the Court, a man of extensive learning, charm, and experience, and one who had the confidence of the administration, considered it "worse than worthless." Moore, whose ideas were similar to those of Pepper, was deeply concerned to preserve the independence and integrity of the Court. He distrusted the League of Nations, which he condemned for its emphasis on force, its subordination of judicial institutions, and for other reasons. He saw the League as nothing more than an alliance based on national interest and power. He wished above all to preserve the Court's

77. *Milwaukee Sentinel,* 22 November 1925; Lenroot to Frank Kellogg, 4 June 1925, Box 3, Lenroot Papers; Kellogg to John Bassett Moore, 1 October 1925, Box 11, Kellogg Papers; to Lenroot, 19 October 1925, Record Group 59, file, 500, C114/420, NA; "Speech of Honorable I. L. Lenroot, Princeton, New Jersey, Dec. 11, 1925," Box 12, Lenroot Papers; *Washington Evening Post,* 12 December 1925; Accinelli, "United States and the World Court," pp. 154, 293, commenting on Republican Senate opinion. Accinelli also notes the various connections between the League and the Court, p. 21.

78. Fleming, *United States and the World Court,* p. 56.

independence of the League and to enhance its prestige as a molder and expounder of international law.[79]

Moore was pleased at the outcome of the Eastern Karelia case in 1923. The League Council asked the Court for an advisory opinion respecting a controversy between Russia and Finland. Russia, not a member of the League or the Court, declined to participate, and by a seven to four vote the Court refused to render an opinion. But Moore realized that the composition of the Court would change and the decision might be reversed. He was further alarmed when the League Council's subsequent report contained a thinly veiled admonition of the Court. At about the same time, a Spanish judge moved to empower the Court with the authority to amend its rules so that it might give advisory opinions without public sittings or even notification to interested parties and might communicate opinions to the League Council without public notice. In November 1925, without Moore's participation, in the Mosul case the Court seemed to water down the Eastern Karelia precedent by giving an opinion to the Council in a case in which Turkey, a nonmember of the League, objected to the request for an opinion. But even before that, Moore had made his objections known to Pepper and the administration and had proposed an alternative fifth reservation:[80]

> That, in acting upon requests for Advisory Opinions, the Court, as an independent judicial tribunal, shall itself determine, in each instance, in the exercise of its uncontrolled judgment, whether it will or will not give an opinion upon the question presented to it; that in no event shall the Court give any secret or confidential opinion or advice; that the Court will not give an opinion on any question to which the United States is a party, without the consent of the United States; and that the United States disclaims all responsibility for any opinion on any question to the submission of which the United States was not a party.

Deferring to the Democrats, Coolidge, Kellogg, and Lenroot did not press for Moore's proposal in advance of the session. But they did not foreclose on the possibility of compromise along Moore's lines should the Democrats prove amenable. As early as June 1925, Lenroot had submitted to Kellogg a draft reservation.[81] By leaving the matter somewhat in abeyance, the pro-Court forces retained the ability to adjust to unforeseen circumstances in the Senate. But they sacrificed the opportunity to obtain prior assent from the Court members to a compromise reservation.[82]

Kellogg and Coolidge, busy with other things and respecting the sensitivi-

79. Moore to Harlan F. Stone, 4 January 1926, Box 172, Moore Papers; Richard Megargee, "The Diplomacy of John Bassett Moore: Realism in American Foreign Policy" (Ph.D. diss.), pp. 319–32; Accinelli, "United States and the World Court," pp. 298–300.

80. Megargee, "John Bassett Moore," pp. 333–35; Moore to Francis Colt de Wolf, 23 December 1930, to Arthur Vandenberg, 20 February 1930, Box 172, Moore Papers; Accinelli, "United States and the World Court," p. 346; Moore, "Suggestions . . . as to clauses to follow the first two paragraphs . . . of the Draft Resolution," 31 July 1925, Box 172, Moore Papers.

81. Lenroot to Kellogg, 4 June 1925, Box 3, Lenroot Papers.

82. Accinelli, "United States and the World Court," pp. 308–10.

ties of senators, took little part in the debate on the World Court in the Senate. But the president's wishes were well known and had influenced many Republican senators who were otherwise indifferent. Even so, the outcome was rendered doubtful when the Ku Klux Klan and Irish groups mounted a strenuous campaign against adherence by writing letters.[83]

Swanson led off for his resolution on 17 December, and the next day Lenroot presented his opening argument, before packed galleries and most senators. His job was to keep the lukewarm Republicans in line. To that end, he stressed the American origins of the Court and its independence of the League of Nations. Lenroot did not claim that the Court could or would guarantee peace, but he saw it as a short step in that direction. If national animosities exist, Lenroot said, the Court could not prevent war. But sometimes such hatreds were bred by fermenting disputes that might have been adjudicated at the outset.[84]

Lenroot was anxious to expedite consideration of the Swanson resolution, for when the tax bill was ready, embodying new reductions, there would be strong pressure to displace the Court measure in its favor, so that tax cuts might be effected in time for the 15 March returns. Accordingly, on 21 December he told the Senate that, after the holiday recess, he would try to keep the Court proposal before the Senate and push it to final disposition.[85]

During the recess, Lenroot made several speeches in Milwaukee in favor of the Court proposal. He also prepared for the upcoming Senate debates by getting information and advice from the State Department and from Philip Jessup, then a young lawyer whose services were provided to Lenroot by one of the peace organizations.[86]

After Congress reconvened, Lenroot participated in debate, attempting to refute the arguments of the increasingly vocal opponents.[87] In order to expedite proceedings, on 7 January he announced that proponents would make no prearranged speeches and voting would begin when the opponents of the Court ended their speechmaking. This they showed no inclination to do, as Cole Blease of South Carolina launched an obvious filibuster on 15 January. Lenroot had warned before of cloture, but he continued to hope that it would not be necessary.[88]

83. William to Robert Taft, 20 December 1925, Box 590, to Col. I. M. Ullman, 9 January 1926, Box 591, Series 3, William Howard Taft Papers; *Washington Evening Star*, 29 January 1926; Peter Norbeck to Leslie Jensen, 8 February 1926, Norbeck Papers, cited in Fite, *Peter Norbeck*, pp. 118–19; *Washington Evening Star*, 9, 10 January 1926; Samuel Colcord to Elihu Root, 19 January 1926, Box 141, Elihu Root Papers.

84. *Milwaukee Sentinel*, 19 December 1925; *CR* 69:1, 1926, vol. 67, pt. 2, pp. 1067–70.

85. Ibid., p. 1249; *Washington Evening Star*, 25 December 1925, 10, 11 January 1926.

86. *Milwaukee Sentinel*, 30, 31 December 1925; Robert E. Olds to Lenroot, 30 December 1925, Record Group 59, file, 500, C114/428a, NA; Philip C. Jessup to Lenroot, 2 January 1926, Box 12, Lenroot Papers; Accinelli, "United States and the World Court," p. 317.

87. *CR* 69:1, 1926, vol. 67, pt. 2, pp. 1424, 1427, 1565, 1567, 2027–30, 2035–36, 2103–5, 2194–95.

88. Accinelli, "United States and the World Court," p. 321.

In retrospect, it is evident that the more serious challenge was substantive not procedural. Increasing pressure from the outside, and from senators led by Borah, endangered ratification. The central issue was the question of advisory opinions. In Senate debate, Lenroot sought to refute some arguments against advisory opinions but he also made it clear that a compromise would be effected by the supporters of the Court.[89]

Even before Senate debate began, Lenroot and Pepper worked behind the scenes with a small group of Democrats and Republicans on a compromise. Pepper and Walsh were deputized to seek agreement among themselves with the presumption that the others would find it acceptable. Walsh was willing to adopt a reservation requiring that the Eastern Karelia decision be made permanent policy, but he balked at the other suggestions made by Pepper. Pepper wanted to ban secret opinions to the Council or Assembly of the League and to tighten the wording to ensure that there be no opinion directly affecting the United States without her assent.[90]

Lenroot and Pepper continued negotiations with Swanson and Robinson, but the two Democrats would agree to nothing to which Walsh would not assent. To persuade Walsh, Lenroot and Pepper urged Moore to come to Washington from his home at Rye, New York. Through a misunderstanding, Swanson failed to issue the requisite invitation, but finally, on Lenroot's suggestions, Walsh asked Moore to come. Considering Moore's position as the American judge on the World Court, it is hardly surprising to find that proponents of adherence asked him for advice. With respect to Lenroot's opinion of Moore, it may be significant that the legal adviser provided for him by the pro-Court American Foundation, Jessup, was a former student of Moore and one of his enduring correspondents.[91]

Moore was more than willing to press his arguments. Indeed, he took the initiative in objecting to the Swanson reservations in correspondence with Pepper and with Supreme Court Justice Harlan Fiske Stone, a friend and colleague of long standing. To Stone, he sent an elaborate memo and the judge soon assured his friend that he was "lodging the ideas embodied in your memorandum where possibly they may do good." [92]

On 14 January, Moore conferred in Washington with Walsh and Swanson.[93] No doubt he reminded them that such opinions could only be requested by the League Council acting unanimously and that, therefore, the great powers had a veto on requesting advisory opinions that the United

89. Harlan F. Stone to John B. Moore, 21 January 1926, Box 172, Moore Papers; *CR* 69:1, 1926, vol. 67, pt. 2, pp. 2043–45, 2290–91, 2294–97; 1926, vol. 67, pt. 3, pp. 2354, 2435, 2437.

90. Pepper to John Bassett Moore, 17 December 1925, Box 172, Moore Papers.

91. Pepper to Moore, 23 December 1925, 4, 6, 28 January 1926, to George Wickersham, 22 July 1929, enclosed in Pepper to Moore, 30 July 1929, Walsh to Moore, 7 January 1926, Box 172, Moore Papers; Megargee, "John Bassett Moore," p. 310.

92. Moore to Pepper, 14, 21 December 1925, 5 January 1926, to Stone, 28 December 1925, Box 172, Moore Papers; Megargee, "John Bassett Moore," p. 310; Stone to Moore, 6 January 1926, Box 172, Moore Papers.

93. Moore to Hope K. Thompson, 1 August 1933, Box 172, Moore Papers.

States, a nonmember, would not have.[94] Although no agreement was reached, Moore impressed Walsh, who on the following day sent the judge a proposal of his own.[95]

Justice Stone, meanwhile, supplemented persuasion with power when he entrusted Borah with a copy of Moore's memorandum. Without attributing it to Moore by name but leaving little doubt of its source, on 18 January Borah presented it to the Senate. Moore was not displeased, for the public recital of his views brought Walsh and Swanson to accept them in large part after Moore replied in detail to Walsh's proposal of 15 January. Lenroot, who helped to modify the reservations, raised no objections, nor did Frank Willis or others who were shown the revised draft. On 20 January, Lenroot secured the assent of Kellogg and Coolidge.[96]

Swanson introduced his modified reservations on 23 January. They altered the four noncontroversial Harding-Hughes reservations only slightly. Two "understandings" not requiring the assent of other powers were attached, reaffirming America's tradition of nonentanglement and stating that recourse by the United States to the Court would only come through treaty with the party or parties in question. The latter statement ensured the Senate's continuing role and allayed fears of Southerners that the Court might hear a case involving defaulted Confederate war debts.[97] The critical reservation was the fifth. It stated in part:

> That the court shall not render any advisory opinion except publicly after due notice to all states adhering to the court and to all interested states and after public hearing or opportunity for hearing given to any state concerned, nor shall it without the consent of the United States entertain any request for an advisory opinion touching any dispute or question in which the United States has or claims an interest.[98]

As it turned out, the words "or claims" were the major stumbling block to acceptance by the members of the Court.

The announcement of the new Swanson reservations came a day after Lenroot filed a cloture petition. He resorted to that extreme measure, which was used but once before by the Senate during the battle of the League of Nations, only after some of the new irreconcilables refused to set a date for a vote. Continuing pressure for action on the tax bill was another factor.

94. Moore to Pepper, 21 December 1925, to Stone, 26 December 1926, to Francis de Wolf, 23 December 1930, Box 172, Moore Papers; Accinelli, "United States and the World Court," pp. 351–56.

95. Frederick H. Gillett to Elihu Root, 27 January 1926, Box 141, Root Papers; Pepper to Moore, 28 January 1926, Walsh to Moore, 15 January 1926, Box 172, Moore Papers.

96. Stone to Moore, 25 January 1926, Moore to Stone, 28 January 1926, Box 172, Moore Papers; Fleming, *United States and the World Court;* Moore to Walsh, 19 January 1926, to Stone, 28 January 1926, Box 172, Moore Papers; L. Ethan Ellis, *Frank B. Kellogg and American Foreign Relations, 1925–1929,* p. 226; *New York Times,* 28 January 1926; memo by W. H. B., 20 January 1926, Record Group 59, "Office of the Secretary," file 500, C 114/437, NA.

97. Accinelli, "United States and the World Court," pp. 326–27.

98. *CR* 69:1, 1926, vol. 67, pt. 3, pp. 2656–57.

On 25 January, the Senate voted cloture by a vote of sixty-eight to twenty-six. Thereafter, the Court was the unfinished business before the Senate, excluding all else, and no senator could speak for more than an hour. Clara recorded the Senate vote as "a victory for Irvine." On the basis of it, she judged correctly that the World Court would soon be approved. James Reed attempted dilatory tactics, but Lenroot successfully repelled them, and on 27 January, following overwhelming approval of the reservations and understandings and rejections of alternatives, the Senate adopted the Swanson resolution by a vote of seventy-six to seventeen.[99] Most of the opposition came from states in which the Ku Klux Klan was strong.

Proponents of adherence, inside the government and out, expressed gratification at the outcome. Prof. Manley Hudson of Harvard was among the few proponents that saw difficulties ahead but, nevertheless, presumed that the United States would soon be in the World Court. For their part, the opponents of adherence were dissatisfied with the outcome.[100]

On 18 March, the League Council took up the reservations of the United States. For several reasons, including doubt as to the meaning of the fifth reservation, the Council called for a conference between a United States representative and members of the Court at Geneva on 1 September. Council members had not consulted with the State Department in advance and knew the invitation might cause embarrassment in the United States but, nevertheless, felt impelled to issue the invitation.[101]

Lenroot, in a series of speeches in February and March, defended the decision to adhere to the World Court. Continuing to emphasize the Court's independence of the League and realizing that acceptance of the Council's invitation would seem to belie that argument, he took the legally correct position, which Moore also espoused, that no representative could interpret the Senate's actions. The reservations would have to speak for themselves.[102] Kellogg and Coolidge soon accepted that position, which Hughes and Root promptly endorsed.[103]

99. Accinelli, "United States and the World Court," pp. 325–26; *Washington Evening Star,* 16–28 January 1926; *Milwaukee Sentinel,* 19–28 January 1926; *CR* 69:1, 1926, vol. 67, pt. 3, pp. 2569, 2678–79; Clara Lenroot, Diary, 25 January 1926, Lenroot Papers Addition; *CR* 69:1, 1926, vol. 67, pt. 3, pp. 2680–82, 2756–59, 2825.

100. Accinelli, "United States and the World Court," pp. 349–51, 358–59; Frank Kellogg to Silas Strawn, 2 February 1926, Box 12, Kellogg Papers; Samuel Colcord to Elihu Root, 1 February 1926, Box 141, Root Papers; Casper S. Yost to William H. Taft, 30 January 1926, Taft to Yost, 30 January 1926, Box 592, Series 3, Taft Papers; *Washington Evening Star,* 4 February 1926; Hiram Johnson to Harold Ickes, 1 February 1926, Box 2, Harold Ickes Papers, LC.

101. Fleming, *United States and the World Court,* p. 70; Accinelli, "United States and the World Court," pp. 360–62.

102. *Washington Evening Star,* 14, 23 February, 21 March 1926; *Milwaukee Sentinel,* 24 February, 2, 20, 29 March 1926; MS, "Speech of Hon. I. L. Lenroot, Philadelphia, Pennsylvania, March 16, 1926," MS, "Chicago Bar Association, March 30, 1926," Box 12, Lenroot Papers; Moore to Harlan F. Stone, 22 March 1926, Box 172, Moore Papers.

103. Accinelli, "United States and the World Court," pp. 364, 368.

There were many difficulties associated with the fifth reservation. A major one was that it rested on a questionable assumption—that only by unanimous action could the League Council request an advisory opinion. Of course if that were not the case, then the American request for a veto was asking for more than Council members could agree to. Though anxious for American entry, those at the Geneva conference in September were not disposed to put obstacles in the way of advisory opinions. In the brief history of the Court, advisory opinions had been more numerous and more important than judicial decisions. Many supporters of the Court felt its jurisdiction would most easily grow through its advisory role.[104]

After three weeks of deliberation as a group and in committee, the members of the Court offered the United States a compromise. Without deciding whether unanimity was in fact required, or remanding that question to the Court itself, they offered the United States rights equal to those of the major powers, whatever those might be.[105] Coolidge told a press conference that he would have to consult with senators before giving an answer. Walsh, Swanson, and others advised him not to accept the offer, for it might have the effect of contravening the fifth reservation and assurances that they also had given in the Senate and outside. Coolidge followed that advice. Nor did he judge it useful to go back to the Senate for a revision of the fifth reservation. So the question of American entry into the World Court remained undetermined by the end of 1926 despite the apparent victory for the Court when the year began.[106]

During and after the World Court debate, Lenroot pondered on whether to seek reelection. As Lenroot worried over the decision he would have to make, he did not renew his complaint about the situation in the Senate as grounds for retiring to private life. That is not to say that he was entirely content with things. A firmer believer in party government than earlier in life, he disapproved the effort of some party leaders to mollify the independent radicals of the west and unsuccessfully fought against recognizing young La Follette as a Republican. Yet, he found some comfort even in this decision, for, as he informed Curtis, he would now feel somewhat freer of party discipline not only on matters of principle, on which he would follow his own conscience in any case, but on matters of policy. More important, perhaps, the coalition of radical Republicans and Democrats that had dominated the previous Congress had collapsed. The Republican margin in the Senate had grown from six to sixteen. Norris declined to replace La Follette as leader of a distinctive radical group of Republicans, and, most important, the Democrats drew apart from the radical Republicans. The atmosphere

104. Ibid., pp. 357–58, 370–71, 389.
105. Ibid., pp. 389, 397, 399, 403.
106. Ibid., pp. 405–9; Walsh to Charles C. Bauer, 9 November 1926, Box 15, Thomas J. Walsh—John E. Erickson Papers, LC; *New York Herald Tribune*, 12 November 1926; Samuel Colcord to Elihu Root, 20 December 1926, Box 141, Root Papers.

in the Senate, while far from harmonious, was less tense than previously.[107]

This point should not be overemphasized, for the situation in the Senate was far from ideal, from Lenroot's standpoint. Among those gone from the Senate was McCormick, who was defeated in the primaries of 1924, and his departure left Lenroot more isolated than before. Heightened prosperity outside the agricultural sections, the increased number of conservative Republicans in the Senate, and the effort of the Democrats to show that they too were friends of business made it difficult for Lenroot to exert moderating leadership, as events were to demonstrate in connection with the tax and farm bills. But from an emotional standpoint, Lenroot could live with the present situation far more easily than before.

Lenroot's own inclination was to retire when his term expired. At the age of fifty-seven, Lenroot much preferred a summer on the Brule instead of a grueling campaign. Realizing his lack of savings, he felt the need to earn more money than he could as a senator, and reelection would add little to his glory. Clara, perhaps supported by Katharine, hoped he would not run.[108]

Under great pressure from friends and supporters who argued that he alone could defeat Blaine and redeem the state, Lenroot began to reconsider and to think that with a strong campaign he might win. But of more importance was another factor, which is evident in his correspondence to Heinemann.

> Confidentially, there is only one thing that is troubling me now, from a personal standpoint, and that is whether hereafter I shall feel quite contented in my own mind with Blaine in the Senate and all that it implies, without having made a fight. While I do not feel that I am under any obligations whatever to make the fight, I am thinking about how I, myself, may feel about it in the years to come.[109]

Reluctantly, he decided to run. "I think I will feel better for having made the fight," he wrote Nellie, "and I shant [sic] worry a bit about being

107. Lenroot to William J. Campbell, 11 December 1925, to Gerhard Moe, 15 December 1925, to Walter B. Heinemann, 17 December 1925, Box 6, Lenroot Papers; McCoy, *Calvin Coolidge*, p. 274; Lowitt, *Norris*, vol. 2, p. 288; David Burner, *The Politics of Provincialism: The Democratic Party in Transition, 1918–1932*, pp. 161–74.

108. Lenroot to Nellie Nichols, 7 February, 14 March 1926, Lenroot Papers Addition; to T. P. Abel, 3 April 1926, to James R. Hile, 3 March 1926, Box 6, Lenroot Papers; to Nils P. Haugen, 16 March 1926, Box 63, Nils P. Haugen Papers; to Leathem D. Smith, 13 March 1926, Box 6, Lenroot Papers; Clara Lenroot, Diary, 8 February, 1 April 1926, Lenroot Papers Addition.

109. Edward Dithmar to Lenroot, 2 March 1926, J. W. Jackson to Lenroot, 28 November 1925, Leathem Smith to Lenroot, 10 March 1926, Thorwald P. Abel to Lenroot, 29 March 1926, Box 6, Lenroot to Stephen Bolles, 2 March 1927, Box 1, to William J. Campbell, 27 March 1926, to Walter Heinemann, 5 March 1926, to Edward Dithmar, 8 March 1926, to John E. Fitzgibbon, 3 April 1926, to Walter Heinemann, 12 March 1926, Box 6, Lenroot Papers. To another correspondent he wrote, "I am frank to say that the prospect of Governor Blaine going to the Senate is the only consideration that would impel me to again be a candidate." Lenroot to Robert Caldwell, 12 March 1926, Box 6, Lenroot Papers.

whipped. Nearly everybody expects that so there will be no surprise or disgrace if it turns out that way—but I will be glad when September comes." [110]

Much of Lenroot's activity in Washington that winter related directly to the welfare of Wisconsin and indirectly to his own reelection prospects. Habitually, he paid close attention to the interests of his constituents, and his efforts in 1926 cannot, therefore, be attributed solely to political exigencies.

Lenroot again gave attention to the St. Lawrence Seaway project. He first prevented administration endorsement of an alternate route, which would be through New York,[111] and then succeeded in getting some reduction in the amount of water being diverted from Lake Michigan by a canal in Chicago and improvements on the Illinois River.[112] The matter was of concern to Canada, America's partner in the seaway project.

Lenroot also acted in behalf of dairymen. He persuaded the president to increase the tariff on butter under the flexible tariff provisions of the Fordney-McCumber Act.[113] Then he directed efforts toward legislative protection for American milk and cream against Canadian imports, by means of health inspection requirements that would raise Canadian costs to the American level. The bill passed in the House, but in the Senate it was blocked by Norris. Lenroot expected it to pass the following session.[114]

On a variety of issues, Lenroot established a moderately progressive record, though his efforts were not notably successful. Young Robert La Follette attributed Lenroot's votes to his concern for reelection, but one need not accept that verdict, for his positions were generally consistent with his previous record.[115]

On taxation—the prime issue of the session—Lenroot proposed amendments for a higher surtax than the bipartisan bill called for and for retention of the estate tax. He lost on both counts.[116]

110. Lenroot to Nellie Nichols, 4 April 1926, Lenroot Papers Addition.

111. Lenroot to Walter Heinemann, 11 March 1926, Lenroot Papers; *Milwaukee Sentinel,* 11 March 1926; *CR* 69:1, 1926, vol. 67, pt. 6, pp. 6153–55; William R. Willoughby, *The St. Lawrence Waterway: A Study in Politics and Diplomacy,* pp. 109–10.

112. Willoughby, *St. Lawrence Waterway,* pp. 100–102, 107; U.S., Senate, Committee on Commerce, *Hearings: Improvement of Rivers and Harbors* (Washington, 1926), 69th Cong., 1st sess., pp. 384–99; *Milwaukee Sentinel,* 11, 22, 28 June, 13 August 1926.

113. *Milwaukee Sentinel,* 1 July 1926; Lenroot to Walter Heinemann, 11 March 1926, Box 6, Lenroot Papers.

114. *CR* 69:1, 1926, vol. 67, pt. 4, pp. 4120, 4122; 1926, vol. 67, pt. 5, p. 5267; 1926, vol. 67, pt. 6, p. 5988; Lenroot to A. J. Glover, 26 April 1926, Box 6, Lenroot Papers; to James A. Stone, 7 October 1926, Box 25, James A. Stone Papers. For Lenroot's argument in favor of his bill see *CR* 69:1, 1926, vol. 67, pt. 8, pp. 8408–9.

115. Robert La Follette, Jr., to Fola and Robert Middleton, 10 April 1926, Box 34, Series A, to W. T. Rawleigh, 22 April 1926, Box 5, Series C, La Follette FC.

116. *CR* 69:1, 1926, vol. 67, pt. 3, pp. 3219–24, 3268; 1926, vol. 67, pt. 4, pp. 3595, 3598, 3601–2, 3620–24, 3670, 3684–85, 3703, 3834.

No less important, though unpublicized, Lenroot tried his best to improve the actions of the Federal Reserve system in respect to the stock market. It was Hoover who aroused Lenroot to action and who helped to formulate the pointed questions he directed to key Federal Reserve officials, by correspondence and in a personal interview. Lenroot exchanged letters with Daniel R. Crissinger, chairman of the Federal Reserve Board, in November and December; as a result of this correspondence, Benjamin Strong, the governor of the Federal Reserve Bank in New York, came to Washington and conferred with him for about two hours.[117]

Lenroot asked about the relationship between the easy money policy of the Board and the rise of speculation on Wall Street and suggested that the matter might come up for discussion in the Senate. Perhaps Lenroot's threat contributed to a tightening of policy for a time, according to the beliefs of Hoover's friends. But for a variety of reasons, the Board, in 1927, reverted to an easy money policy regarding the rediscount rate and open market operations and again contributed to the stock market speculation that reached its disastrous crescendo in 1929.[118]

Lenroot devoted much of his time during the session to a federal building bill, which was the first since 1913. The bill, emanating from the Committee on Public Buildings and Grounds on which he ranked third among Republicans, proposed to scrap the old pork-barrel system and to vest large discretionary authority with the secretary of the treasury. Those who feared Mellon and those who wanted to be sure of at least some construction in their own states each year joined to force a compromise in which Lenroot, who was in charge of the bill, acquiesced. He steered the bill to Senate adoption that session.[119]

On the farm question, Lenroot stood uncomfortably between the administration and the major farm organizations, which were supporting the

117. Lenroot to Mark Sullivan, 6 November 1947, Box 4, Lenroot, "Memoirs," pp. 188–89, Box 13, Lenroot Papers. Hoover, because of his position in the executive branch, was unwilling to take an open part in the negotiations.

118. The relevant correspondence is Lenroot to Crissinger, 23 November, 23 December 1925, Secretary of Commerce Papers, Box AG 3a/275, Herbert Hoover Papers; Lenroot to Crissinger, 14 December 1925, 4 January 1926, Box 2, to Benjamin Strong, 13 January 1926, Box 4, Lenroot Papers. Favorable judgment on the Hoover-Lenroot effort is given in Edward Eyre Hunt to Lawrence Richey, 1 May 1935, Edward Eyre Hunt Papers, Hoover Institution, Stanford. Federal Reserve policy is referred to in George Soule, *Prosperity Decade: From War to Depression, 1917–1929*, pp. 279–80. In April 1926, Lenroot warned brokers of speculative excesses. Pamphlet, "Address delivered by Hon. Irvine L. Lenroot . . . at the Thirteenth Annual Dinner of the Association of Stock Exchange Firms," Hotel Astor, New York City, 16 April 1926, Box 9, Lenroot Papers. The continuing close relationship between Lenroot and Hoover is evident in Clara Lenroot, Diary, 24 January, 3 February, 7 March, 25 April, 27 June 1926; *CR* 69:1, 1926, vol. 67, pt. 11, pp. 11859–61; Hoover to Lenroot, 8 December 1925, Secretary of Commerce Papers, AG 3a/310, Hoover to Lenroot, 9 April 1926, Box AG 3a/275, Hoover Papers.

119. *CR* 69:1, 1926, vol. 67, pt. 8, pp. 8356–64, 8490–91, 8569–70, 8588–91, 8602, 8667, 8678–80, 8736–40; 1926, vol. 67, pt. 9, pp. 9495–9501.

McNary-Haugen plan. The McNary bill proposed a government board that directly or indirectly would buy the entirety of specified crops at relatively high prices, that is, the international price plus the American tariff rate. The board would assist in selling the produce on the domestic market at the artificially increased price while dumping the surplus abroad at the world price. The government's loss was to be made up by an equalization fee paid by the farmer to the processor.[120]

In the Senate, Lenroot argued that the equalization fee in effect took money from A and gave it to B and would surely fail the test of constitutionality. He objected to the fee also because it guaranteed the profits of such unpopular middlemen as the packers and millers.[121]

Lenroot introduced a proposal of his own, which was a modified and watered-down version of the McNary plan. Classified by Lenroot as a temporary, one-year experiment, the plan would provide a sounder solution to the problem and would aid cooperatives on a fuller and more progressive basis than the administration proposed, an idea that Lenroot discussed with Hoover, who might well have influenced him. The main emphasis, however, was on furnishing capital—a loan of $150 million without security—for federation of cooperatives so they could exert some control over marketing. In this way, the cooperatives would be able to buy the surplus of some crop or crops and hold the surplus until it could be marketed without breaking price levels. Lenroot argued that this one-shot experiment would not encourage new production, since the planting season was over.[122]

As the session came to an end, the opposing forces found themselves in a stalemate, and Congress passed only a minor bill setting up a cooperative marketing division in the Department of Agriculture.[123]

On 29 June, with the course of agricultural legislation determined, Lenroot returned to Wisconsin, to begin what he knew would be an uphill fight. Before the primary election defeats of McKinley in Illinois and then Cummins in Iowa, Lenroot thought he could win the fight. After those events, the situation looked less promising, but Lenroot was determined to make an all-out campaign.[124]

By the end of June, the campaign was already well begun. In Lenroot's

120. Arthur S. Link, *American Epoch: A History of the United States Since the 1890's*, pp. 328–29; Murray R. Benedict, *Farm Policies of the United States, 1790–1950* (New York, 1953), pp. 224–25; Gilbert C. Fite, *George N. Peek and the Fight for Farm Parity*, pp. 152–53, 166.

121. *CR* 69:1, 1926, vol. 67, pt. 10, pp. 10905, 11000, 11130–31, 11210–16, 11628.

122. Ibid., pp. 11136, 11216–18, 11447, 11515, 11869, 11879–81, 11939–40; Charles Frederick Williams, "William M. Jardine and the Development of Republican Farm Policy, 1925–1929" (Ph.D. diss.), p. 148. See also James H. Shideler, "Herbert Hoover and the Federal Farm Board Project, 1921–1925," pp. 710–29.

123. *CR* 69:1, 1926, vol. 67, pt. 10, pp. 11869, 11940–42, 11949, 12105, 12184; *Washington Evening Star*, 25–30 June 1926.

124. Lenroot to Richard Lloyd Jones, 13 April 1926, Box 6, Lenroot Papers; Clara Lenroot, Diary, 14 April, 8 June 1926, Lenroot Papers Addition.

favor was the fact that there was some disarray among the opposition. While the name La Follette retained its old-time magic, Blaine had made many enemies among the La Follette men. The three-time governor was vain, arbitrary, and highly political. As he developed a machine of his own and pushed his own policies strongly, he had antagonized some of those most loyal to the La Follettes.

Even the La Follettes were not in complete control, and their choice of Attorney General Ekern for governor was not universally popular. Although the La Follettes and Blaine had attempted in 1925 to compose their differences in preparation for the 1926 campaign, it was impossible for them to secure full unity behind a slate. Fred Zimmerman, the gregarious secretary of state and a Milwaukeean, came out for governor as a progressive Republican and bade fair to defeat the scholarly but lackluster Ekern.

Blaine remained loyal to Ekern and retained the support of the La Follettes, and a progressive slate, though not unrivaled, was put into the field. Blaine had a strong personal organization based on state patronage, and with the assistance of La Follette, Jr., he was able to get favorable publicity from Hearst's *Milwaukee News*, largely because he stressed issues in which Hearst had great interest.[125] Those issues were calculated to keep him strong among the numerous Germans in Wisconsin.

The issue of the World Court was Blaine's initial theme in his campaign, which was underway on 23 June. The Court, he said, was inseparable from the League of Nations; the reservations written by the Senate offered no protection. Once in the Court, the United States would be legally and morally obligated to enforce Court decisions by war, if the League so decided.[126]

Blaine developed other themes. He appealed against militarism; called for a referendum on war; asked for a cut in appropriations for the army and navy; denounced the debt settlements as being unfair to the American taxpayer; and attacked the prohibition amendment. He also talked of debauchery in government and attacked Lenroot for voting to seat Newberry, for his role in the Teapot Dome investigation, including his visit to Fall, and for the positions he had taken in 1919 and 1920 in favor of the League of Nations.[127]

Although senatorial business had delayed Lenroot in the start of his full-scale campaign during May and June, Lenroot had managed to make several brief visits to Wisconsin. At the same time, others were working in

125. Ira Lorenz to Robert La Follette, Jr., 14 May 1926, La Follette to Lorenz, 17 May 1926, Lorenz to La Follette, 14, 24 June 1926, Box 4, La Follette to William Randolph Hearst, 23 June 1926, Box 3, Series C, La Follette FC; Blaine to E. H. Kronshage, 9 September 1926, Box 58, John J. Blaine Papers, WSHSL.

126. "Announcement of Governor John J. Blaine as Candidate for United States Senator," 25 May 1926, "Excerpts from Address of Governor John J. Blaine," Clintonville, Wis., 23 June 1926, Box 56, Blaine Papers; *Milwaukee Sentinel*, 23 June 1926.

127. Press releases, 23–29 June 1926, John B. Page to Blaine, 26 June 1926, Box 56, Blaine Papers; *Milwaukee Sentinel*, 24–30 June 1926.

his behalf, trying to develop an organization and avoid factional pitfalls, with
the latter bringing some difficulties. The conservatives were divided between Oshkosh and Milwaukee factions and between supporting Zimmerman or backing an outright conservative for governor. Lenroot's supporters
stayed aloof from the organizational efforts of the Oshkosh group, and
despite Lenroot's reassurances of good will, he incurred some animosity.
But he managed to bring the conservatives to confine their convention
nominations to a state ticket while he set up several organizations of his
own.[128]

"I think Lenroot will win," Andrew Dahl wrote to Haugen, "but it will
require a lot of work to combat the false rumors and charges that are and
have been made against him." Lenroot recognized the problem. He also
hoped to dispel the pervasive pessimism of his forces that worked against
effective organization.[129]

From the very start, Lenroot's campaign was aggressively defensive. He
realized that the liquor question was the major issue to the voters and
among powerful and wealthy pressure groups. At Ripon, Wisconsin, in his
opening speech, he established his position on the issue. Admitting that the
amendment had not worked as well as many had hoped because of lack of
sentiment for observance and enforcement, he agreed to support modification of the Volstead Act to permit beer with up to 2.75 percent alcohol if
Wisconsin voters supported it in a scheduled referendum. The opposition
was seeking to block the referendum in the courts and this he regretted.
He called for a special session of the legislature to meet the difficulty.
Earlier, Lenroot and his managers had given a good deal of thought to the
liquor question. Presently, they were trying to play down the backing of the
Anti-Saloon League.[130]

In his Ripon speech, Lenroot said:

The citizen is injuriously affected by congress in two ways—the passage of unjust
laws, and the failure to pass laws which are just. This involves both protest and

128. Stephen Bolles to James A. Stone, 17 June 1926, Box 25, Stone Papers; William J.
Campbell, *History of the Republican Party in Wisconsin: Under Convention Plan, 1924–1940*, pp.
10–11; Fred Holmes to Robert La Follette, Jr., 17 May 1926, Box 3, Series C, La Follette FC;
Lenroot to John Fitzgibbon, 6 April 1926, W. O. Wipperman to Lenroot, 6 May 1926, Lenroot
to Wipperman, 6 May 1926, John Fitzgibbon to Lenroot, 6 May 1926, Lenroot to Fitzgibbon,
7 May 1926, Box 6, William J. Campbell to Lenroot, 11 May 1926, Lenroot to Campbell, 20
May 1926, W. B. Heinemann to Campbell, 16 June 1926, enclosed in Campbell to Lenroot,
1 July 1926, Box 1, Campbell to Lenroot, 7 October 1926, Box 6, Roy Reed to Lenroot, 6
June 1926, Lenroot to Reed, 10 June 1926, Box 11, Lenroot Papers; *Milwaukee Sentinel*, 11
May–25 June 1926; *Superior Telegram*, 25, 28, 29, 31 May, 14 June 1926.
129. Dahl to Haugen, 13 July 1926, Box 63, Haugen Papers; Fred Holmes to Robert La
Follette, Jr., 17 May 1926, Box 3, Series C, La Follette FC; T. J. Cunningham to Blaine, 10
June 1926, Box 55, *The Lenrooter*, 17 May 1926, Box 54, Blaine Papers.
130. *Milwaukee Sentinel*, 1 July 1926; Lenroot to John Fitzgibbon, 6, 12 April 1926, Fitzgibbon
to Lenroot, 15 April 1926, Lenroot to Paul C. Burchard, 26 April 1926, to Fitzgibbon, 15 May
1926, Box 6, Lenroot Papers; J. F. Hartman to James A. Stone, 28 July 1926, Box 25, Stone
Papers.

constructive action. Protest is often necessary and highly beneficial, but one who merely protests, though he calls himself progressive, is really reactionary. The reactionary worships the god of things as they are, he desires no change, and his most valuable allies are those who oppose everything, decline to cooperate with others, and are content with being merely in opposition.

Lenroot declared his belief in parties and party responsibility, to produce the majorities needed for legislation.

He called the St. Lawrence Seaway the most important question before the Wisconsin people, so far as their prosperity was concerned, recited his record on the issue, and pointed out that while La Follette, Jr., could work among the "so-called insurgent republicans," he, better than Blaine, could influence regular Republicans and Democrats to ratify a treaty with Canada for the seaway.

At some length, Lenroot reviewed his farm record. He also discussed the stands he had taken on the 1926 tax bill and contrasted the federal and state tax laws to the advantage of the former, with respect to income exempted from taxation. He defended his labor record and gave the scorecard the A. F. L. had compiled on his labor votes. Lenroot was relatively vague respecting foreign affairs but pointed out that the United States had an economic stake in European peace and could promote it with no loss of independence. Taking cognizance of the uses to which Blaine was putting the World Court issue, Lenroot invited the governor to debate the matter with him while doubting that he would.[131]

Blaine did decline to debate with Lenroot. Lenroot, on the other hand, used Blaine's refusal as one of his few offensive weapons and kept issuing the invitation, with some effect. He also renewed his offensive on the tax front. For the most part, however, during the grueling days of July and August, when he spoke five, six, and even seven times a day, Lenroot continued to defend his own record.[132]

Lenroot and his supporters became more confident as the campaign progressed.[133] Legitimate ideological issues could have been used against Lenroot and some were, but for the most part the Blaine campaign was based on talk of Wall Street and the like and misrepresentation of Lenroot's record. To a degree, that stratagem redounded to Lenroot's favor, for he had the facts to meet the charges of Blaine and his friends.

But Lenroot's campaign had too many obstacles to overcome. There was

131. *Superior Telegram*, 1 July 1926; *Milwaukee Sentinel*, 1 July 1926.

132. Several men supporting Blaine testified to the effectiveness of Lenroot's debate challenge. J. D. Dwyer to F. M. Wylie, 15 July 1926, Box 56, Lawrence W. Hevey to Blaine, 8 August 1926, Box 57, Blaine Papers. Fred Sheasby agreed in a balanced appraisal for the *Milwaukee Journal.* Clipping, *Milwaukee Journal,* 24 August 1926, Box 17, Lenroot Papers. On Lenroot's busy schedule see the *Superior Telegram,* 20, 26 July 1926.

133. M. H. Fisher to Orland S. Loomis, 26 July 1926, Box 1, Orland S. Loomis Papers, WSHSL; James Stone to Dorothy L. Black, 7 August 1926, Dorothy Black to Stone, 9 August 1926, George M. Sheldon to Stone, 24 August 1926, Robert Caldwell to Stone, 27 August 1926, Box 25, Stone Papers; Clara to Katharine Lenroot, 10 August 1926, Lenroot Papers Addition; Nils P. Haugen to Andrew Dahl, 22 August 1926, Box 63, Haugen Papers.

continuing disaffection among die-hard conservatives, since the Lenroot men favored Zimmerman and ignored the convention's nominee, Charles Perry.[134] And defeatism persisted among potential Lenroot workers, as the result of repeated failure since 1922.[135] Blaine's emphasis on corruption and conspiracy gained credence from the fact that Fall, Sinclair, and Doheny remained at large and that recent elections in Illinois and Pennsylvania had been marred by excessive spending reminiscent of the Newberry campaign.[136] Partly through the intervention of La Follette, Jr., the railroad brotherhoods flooded the state with a special issue of their paper *Labor* directed largely against Lenroot.[137] But of more importance, in Lenroot's own judgment and that of his friends, was the liquor question. Wisconsin sentiment was heavily against the Volstead Act, as the general election referendum later showed, and probably was against the prohibition amendment as well. Although Lenroot hedged his approach late in the campaign, saying that if no referendum were held he would, nevertheless, support modification of the law to permit 2.75 percent beer, to the dissatisfaction of the president of the Association Opposed to Prohibition. In the final week of the campaign, the "wet" interests put on a massive advertising campaign against Lenroot.[138] The World Court issue also hurt Lenroot. Many Wisconsin people continued to lump together the Court and the unpopular League of Nations. Especially adamant against the Court were the members of the Ku Klux Klan, which in Wisconsin was devoted more to fraternal activity than to the acts of violence and intimidation that characterized it elsewhere. Although Blaine had antagonized the Klan, on the basis of the League issue the organization surreptitiously threw its support to the governor.[139]

134. Elizabeth L. Cushing to Fred Wylie, 17 August 1926, Box 58, Blaine Papers; Walter Heinemann to Lenroot, 10 December 1927, Box 4, clipping, *Milwaukee Journal,* 25 August 1926, Box 17, Lenroot Papers; *Milwaukee Sentinel,* 28 August 1926.

135. Bascom Timmons to Lenroot, 17 September 1926, Bill Dougherty to Lenroot, 13 September 1926, W. D. Connor to Lenroot, 25 October 1926, Box 6, Lenroot Papers.

136. James Stone to Francis E. McGovern, 8 September 1926, Box 25, Stone Papers.

137. Robert La Follette, Jr., to Edward Keating, Basil Manly, Ralph Sucher, 19 July 1926, to Keating, 31 August 1926, Box 3, Series C, La Follette FC; Philip F. La Follette, *Adventures in Politics: The Memoirs of Philip La Follette,* p. 129; Edward Keating, *The Gentleman from Colorado: A Memoir,* p. 490; E. F. Dithmar to James A. Stone, 26 August 1926, Box 25, Stone Papers.

138. *Wisconsin Blue Book,* 1927, pp. 592–93; Lenroot, "Memoirs," pp. 184–85, Box 13, E. F. Kileen to Lenroot, 17 September 1926, Edward J. Gehl to Lenroot, 6 December 1926, H. L. Hoard to Lenroot, 13 September 1926, Box 6, Lenroot Papers; Campbell, *Republican Party in Wisconsin,* p. 12; *Milwaukee Sentinel,* 26 August, 4 September 1926; clippings, *Milwaukee Journal,* 24, 26 August 1926, Box 17, J. J. Seelman to Otto Falk, 1 October 1926, Box 6, Lenroot Papers.

139. *Superior Telegram,* 24 September 1926; H. L. Hoard to Lenroot, 13 September 1926, W. D. Connor to Lenroot, 28 September 1926, Bill Dougherty to Lenroot, n.d. (September 1926), Box 6, Orland S. Loomis to Lenroot, 7 June 1926, Box 1, Lenroot Papers; Norman Frederick Weaver, "The Knights of the Ku Klux Klan in Wisconsin, Indiana, Ohio and Michigan" (Ph.D. diss.), pp. 40–144; E. F. Kileen to Lenroot, 17 September 1926, Edward J. Gehl to Lenroot, 6 December 1926, Box 6, clipping, *Milwaukee Journal,* 12 April 1928, Box 15, Lenroot "Memoirs," p. 185, Box 13, Lenroot Papers.

The election results were closer than some had anticipated, but before the evening was over, the Lenroots realized that they had lost. When all votes were tabulated, Blaine had defeated Lenroot by a vote of 233,803 to 208,738. Blaine's strength was drawn from much the same sources as Thompson's in 1920, primarily the heavily concentrated German counties. Lenroot was not surprised at the result, and he and his family bore up well under defeat. Zimmerman's victory in the gubernatorial primaries gave some encouragement. And Lenroot felt that his efforts in the primary election had brought a "moral victory" for it had "put heart and confidence in our people . . . for the future." [140]

Many of his friends urged Lenroot to run as an independent, and he investigated the possibility but decided against it due to uncertain prospects. He explained to a conservative leader that he did not want to risk the moral victory of the primary campaign.[141]

In December Lenroot began his final session in the Senate. He was busier than he had expected to be.[142]

The administration policy regarding Nicaragua and Mexico was severely criticized in Congress and outside. Lenroot emerged as the prime congressional defender of that policy.

The situation in Nicaragua was complicated. Due to revolutionary upheaval, in 1925 the United States landed troops. Borah, chairman of the Senate foreign-relations committee, charged imperialism, as did others. Lenroot denied that any American economic interests were involved and insisted on the right, indeed the necessity, of protecting the lives and property of American and European nationals.[143]

In Mexico, two 1925 laws threatened the property rights of Americans. The Senate foreign-relations committee put forth a resolution calling for arbitration, but Lenroot, while giving it *pro forma* support, sought to limit its applicability. Arbitration was inapplicable respecting confiscation, he

140. Clara Lenroot, Diary, 7 September 1926, Lenroot Papers Addition; *Superior Telegram,* 13 October 1926; Wisconsin, Secretary of State, Elections and Records, Election Return Statements, Series No. 2/3/2–15, Box 100, Wisconsin State Archives, WSHSL; Rogin, *The Intellectuals and McCarthy,* p. 74; Clara Lenroot, Diary, 29 August, 8, 9 September 1926, Lenroot Papers Addition; Lenroot to Arthur Capper, 12 October 1926, Box 1, Lenroot Papers.

141. Lenroot to James A. Stone, 12 September 1926, Box 25, Stone Papers; W. B. Heinemann to Lenroot, 9 September 1926, John Fitzgibbon to Lenroot, n.d. (September 1926), Oscar Morris to Lenroot, 10 September 1926, Lenroot to Emil Vinter, 11 September 1926, to W. J. Campbell, 11 September 1926, W. B. Heinemann to Lenroot, 13 September 1926, Lillian Wilkinson to Lenroot, 17 September 1926, Box 6, Lenroot Papers; Clara Lenroot, Diary, 19 September 1926, Clara to Katharine Lenroot, 16 September 1926, Lenroot Papers Addition; Lenroot, "Memoirs," Box 13, Lenroot to Walter Heinemann, 6 October 1926, to William J. Campbell, 13 October 1926, Box 6, Lenroot Papers; Clara Lenroot, Diary, 23 September, 1 October 1926, Lenroot Papers Addition.

142. Clara Lenroot to Nellie Nichols, 27 February 1927, Lenroot Papers Addition.

143. William Kamman, *A Search for Stability: United States Diplomacy Toward Nicaragua, 1925–1933,* pp. 1–80; McCoy, *Calvin Coolidge,* pp. 351–54; Ellis, *Kellogg and American Foreign Relations,* pp. 59–71; *CR* 69:2, 1926, vol. 68, pt. 1, pp. 1563–69.

said, and "an international right can not be so swept away." What was chiefly involved, he explained, was not oil rights but land claims, and many of these were held by small operators.[144]

Ultimately, the administration settled both disputes peacefully, using the skilled services of Henry Stimson and Dwight Morrow.

Although a defender of administration policy, Lenroot was no jingo. The administration was not itself jingoistic, though sometimes it was maladroit. Basically, however, its Nicaraguan policy was designed to bring removal of troops and the Mexican policy to avoid war, while at the same time protecting the rights of American nationals. In connection with the naval appropriations bill, Lenroot opposed appropriation for three cruisers partly on the grounds that it would advance the accusation that the United States was imperialistic.[145]

Lenroot's attitude respecting Central American policy may be likened to his views preceding and during World War I. He saw need for national unity in foreign policy. And he would not go so far as some progressives in suspecting that private financial interests manipulated governmental policy. Since he identified the government with the nation, to some extent, that sort of suspicion ran counter to his deeply felt patriotism. And again he felt the necessity of protecting international rights.

Lenroot continued to agree with the administration respecting the McNary-Haugen bill, and he again was a major opponent of it, despite modifications in the bill that were designed to meet earlier objections. He regarded it as a special privilege legislation.[146] The bill, nevertheless, passed both Houses but was vetoed by the president.

Of equal importance to Lenroot was his milk importation bill, the companion to the bill passed in the House the previous session. The bill had the support of the National Milk Producers Association, the National Grange, and the Farm Bureau Federation. In short, it required inspection of Canadian cows and dairies as well as the Canadian milk itself. Lenroot presented it as a health measure but frankly admitted that he also wanted to equalize production costs as between American and Canadian milk producers.[147] At the end of the session, it passed the Senate, as it had the House earlier, and the president signed it.

Nevertheless, as Lenroot ended his legislative career, he viewed future prospects more pessimistically than in the past. In February, he assured an audience in Newark, New Jersey, that morality among public officials was

144. John D. Hicks, *Republican Ascendancy, 1921–1933*, pp. 154–56; Ellis, *Kellogg and American Foreign Relations*, pp. 29–40; "Proceedings of the Committee on Foreign Relations, printed for use of the Committee . . . 1934," 21 January 1927, Box 545, Borah Papers; *CR* 69:2, 1927, vol. 68, pt. 2, pp. 2201–6.

145. *CR* 69:2, 1927, vol. 68, pt. 2, pp. 2540–41.

146. MS speech, "Masonic banquet, Newark, N. J., Feb. (19), 1927," MS speech, "Milwaukee Rotary Club, March 17, 1927," Box 9, Lenroot Papers.

147. *Milwaukee Sentinel*, 23 December 1926.

high, "but there is also a greater fear of punishment at the polls than ever before, destroying in large part the independence of thought and action of members of Congress." That would be all right if the public took the interest in affairs that it should; but instead "more and more we are becoming a Government by minorities, seeking selfish ends." He used the McNary-Haugen bill as an example. Propaganda was compounding the difficulty, according to Lenroot's views, making it harder for the public to recognize the truth. And the age was marked by greater disrespect for law and the Constitution than he had known at any time before. In this connection, he commented on demagogic attacks on the government's Central American policy.[148]

Yet, with respect to his own legislative career, he had written journalist William Hard soon after his primary defeat that he had no regrets, "for I have always fought for my convictions, mistaken though some of them may have been." It is hard to believe other than that Lenroot still saw his public career as part of an ongoing pattern of human progress. Although he wrote in December that he would retire from politics, he qualified the declaration by adding, "at least until I have a little money laid aside." [149]

Lenroot remained in Washington as head of a law firm created by the merger of two existing firms. The firm would practice before government departments and in international law, but Lenroot would do no personal lobbying and would not represent liquor interests.[150]

Lenroot's most important case, and one that brought him back to public attention in an unfavorable light, was as counsel for the Joint Committee of National Utility Associations. The organization, which was sustained by contributions from the larger utilities, retained Lenroot to represent it in opposition to a resolution by Walsh calling for a Senate investigation. After a month of extensive preparation, on 16 January 1928, Lenroot began to present his witnesses before the Committee on Interstate Commerce. Two days later, Lenroot also testified. He argued that the committee should go into the merits of the matter enough to determine whether an investigation was needed. Any investigation should be on the basis of specific charges against a particular company, and even then such an investigation should be by a nonpolitical agency, such as the Federal Trade Commission. The proposed investigation, he thought, would be one of great complication and

148. MS speech, "Milwaukee Rotary Club, March 17, 1927," MS speech, "Masonic banquet, Newark, N. J., Feb. (19), 1927," Box 9, Lenroot Papers.

149. Lenroot to Hard, 6 October 1926, to Gilbert E. Vandercook, 16 December 1926, Box 6, Lenroot Papers.

150. Lenroot to John Fitzgibbon, 30 December 1926, to Walter B. Heinemann, 7 February 1927, Box 6, to Stephen Bolles, 2 March 1927, Box 1, Lenroot Papers; to Nellie Nichols, 21 November 1926, Clara Lenroot, Diary, 1 March 1927, Lenroot Papers Addition; printed card, 4 March 1927, Box 35, Stone Papers; Lenroot to George Morton, 21 February 1927, Box 7, to Fitzgibbon, 30 December 1926, Box 6, to Frank H. Keefer, 8 January 1927, Box 11, Lenroot Papers.

beyond federal jurisdiction. In addition to the legal question, there was a policy question, Lenroot pointed out. There is a dual field in this industry, he said, in which the state has full powers in the absence of federal legislation. "But in that dual field the moment that the Federal Government puts its hand upon the subject all the power of the States is destroyed over that particular subject." He defended the securities of the companies as sound and defended the holding company device as not unique to the utility field and one that had proved useful to the growth of the industry.[151]

Lenroot lost his case in committee, but, to his pleasure, the Senate referred the matter to the Federal Trade Commission.

The sentiment against the power trust, which was stimulated partly by the Hearst press, was strong. It was widely believed to be exploiting investors and consumers and engaging in massive propaganda efforts against public power. Soon after the Senate action on the Walsh resolution and after Lenroot came to the defense of presidential candidate Hoover, he was attacked with a series of charges that he had misused the privilege of the Senate floor to lobby against the Walsh resolution. The charges were untrue, as Walsh explained to the editor of the *Boston Herald,* but they were believed nevertheless.[152]

At about the same time, Lenroot was burdened by two phases of the lingering Teapot Dome scandal. In connection with a new trial of Sinclair, newspapers reported that Fall had deposed that Lenroot, Smoot, and Hays pressured him to conceal the Doheny connection and urged him to name McLean instead. Lenroot promptly appeared before the lands committee to give his version of the Wardman Park visit, and a few days later a newsman interviewed Fall and discovered that his deposition was not as initially reported.[153]

In Lenroot's view, his defense of the utilities made it clear that he would not again seek elective office.[154] The brief revival of Teapot Dome unpleasantness could only have reinforced the determination. But during the years of his law practice, Lenroot continued to be active politically and in public affairs.

He saw little of the president but maintained close and frequent contact

151. *Washington Evening Star,* 24 April 1928; Clara Lenroot, Diary, 15 December 1927–1 February 1928, Lenroot Papers Addition; U.S., Senate, Committee on Interstate Commerce, *Hearings: Investigation of Public Utility Corporations,* 16, 17, 18, 20, 21, 24, 25, 26 January 1928, pp. 58–88.

152. Older, *William Randolph Hearst,* pp. 482–589; James C. Malin, *The United States After the World War,* p. 265; Clara Lenroot, Diary 5, 10 March 1928, Lenroot Papers Addition; *Boston Herald,* 7 March 1928; Walsh to Lenroot, 10 April 1928, Lenroot to Walsh, 12 April 1928, Box 1, Lenroot Papers; Silas Bent, *Strange Bedfellows* (New York, 1928), pp. 21, 279; *Washington Evening Star,* 24 April 1928; Arthur to Irvine L. Lenroot, 25 April 1928, Box 1, Irvine L. Lenroot to P. B. Fontaine, 3 May 1928, Box 2, Lenroot Papers.

153. *Boston Herald,* 3 April 1928; U.S., Senate, Committee on Public Lands and Surveys, *Hearings: Leases Upon Reserves,* pp. 880–85; *Washington Herald,* 5 April 1928.

154. Lenroot to W. H. Dougherty, 7 February 1928, Box 7, Lenroot Papers.

with Kellogg. Lenroot made speeches in defense of administration foreign policy and advised Kellogg in the outlawry of war proposal and particularly in the World Court question.[155]

The American Foundation, leader of the World Court movement, accepted the outlawry of war idea. On this matter and on the question of the World Court, Esther Everett Lape, the dynamic executive secretary of the organization, corresponded extensively with Lenroot, continuing an association that had begun during the 1926 battle for the Court. As Lape noted at one point, Lenroot's defeat in Wisconsin had left the Republican side in the Senate void of leadership in matters of foreign policy, and she evidently hoped that Lenroot might continue to exert influence within the administration and in the Senate.[156] While there is no evidence that Lenroot attempted to influence senators, he did occasionally serve as liaison with the State Department. With respect to the World Court, he also advised Lape as to what he thought could or could not be accomplished within the Senate and freely indicated his own inclinations.

On balance, Lenroot took a cautious view as to what the Senate would accept.[157] When in 1929, Root negotiated a new proposal respecting advisory opinions Lenroot was willing to accept the modification but doubted that the Senate would.[158] After many postponements, in 1935 the Senate rejected adherence by seven votes.

Lenroot's primary political concern in 1927 and 1928 was for the nomination and election of Hoover as president. He even subordinated Wisconsin political considerations to that end. Lenroot approached the question of state patronage, for example, from the standpoint of its impact on the makeup of the Wisconsin delegation to the 1928 Republican convention.[159]

At the national level, Lenroot served Hoover's cause in a variety of ways. Among other things, he acted as attorney for his friend. Hoover took cognizance of charges that he had acted improperly in a dispute over Chinese mining claims twenty-eight years before, a matter that had been adjudicated in England in 1905. Supplied with written statements fetched from England by Hoover's secretary, Lawrence Richey, Lenroot prepared a convincing

155. Lenroot to Mrs. E. A. Harriman, 18 March 1927, Thomas H. Healy to Lenroot, 13 April 1927, George A. Finch to Lenroot, 17 May 1927, Box 2, MS speech, "Our Foreign Relations," Syracuse, N. Y., 5 April 1927, Box 9, Lenroot Papers.

156. Accinelli, "United States and the World Court," p. 381; Esther Everett Lape to Lenroot, 2 February 1932, Box 12, Lenroot Papers.

157. Lenroot to Lape, 14 April 1927, Lape to Lenroot, 18 April 1927, Lenroot to Lape, 20 April 1927, Box 12, MS speech, "American Society of International Law," Washington, D. C., 30 April 1927, Box 9, Lenroot Papers.

158. Fleming, *United States and the World Court*, pp. 85–87; Megargee, "John Bassett Moore," p. 340; Esther Everett Lape to Lenroot, 14 May 1929, Lenroot to Lape, 20 May 1929, Box 12, Lenroot Papers.

159. Lenroot to A. H. Wilkinson, 2 January 1927, to Walter Heinemann, 7 February 1927, Box 6, Lenroot Papers; to James A. Stone, 14 July 1927, Box 26, Stone Papers.

refutation, which he offered with accompanying documents in a letter to Congressman Arthur Free, who inserted the defense of Hoover in the *Congressional Record*.[160]

Lenroot also helped substantiate the claim that Hoover had always regarded himself as a resident of the United States, despite long absences.[161]

As the convention approached, Hoover asked Lenroot to take charge of the delegate contests before the Republican National Committee. Seventy-three seats were in dispute, mainly from the South. Lenroot prepared his cases carefully and won most of them.[162]

As it turned out, even though there was much opposition to Hoover, mainly from professional politicians, the opposition was divided and he won nomination on a first ballot.[163]

Starting on 13 October in New York City, Lenroot campaigned for Hoover into November. In all, he made seventeen speeches. The titles of some of the manuscripts he used indicate his main thrust. He talked of "Farm Relief," "The St. Lawrence Seaway," "Mr. Hoover and European Relief," "Qualifications Required by the Next President," and "The Two Parties." Corruption and prohibition he presented as non-issues. Lenroot branded Fall as a Judas and said the liquor question crossed party lines. In discussing Hoover personally, he asserted that "no party in the last fifty years has offered a candidate for the Presidency better qualified than Mr. Hoover." [164]

After Hoover's victory, newspapers speculated that Lenroot would be appointed to the Cabinet, perhaps as secretary of the treasury or secretary of state. But Lenroot disclaimed such ambitions. "For the first time in my life I am getting on my feet financially," he explained to a close political friend, "and I can't afford to take any political appointment which would put me on the rocks again." Soon afterwards Hoover offered him a Cabinet post but Lenroot declined. However he was free with advice and later judged himself responsible for the appointments of Stimson as secretary of state, William D. Mitchell as attorney general, and Good as secretary of war.[165]

While unwilling to enter the Cabinet, during the summer Lenroot had

160. Herbert C. Hoover, *The Memoirs of Herbert Hoover: The Cabinet and the Presidency, 1920–1933*, p. 191; *CR* 70:1, 1928, vol. 69, pt. 4, pp. 3825–27; *New York Times*, 1 March 1928.

161. Hoover to Lenroot, 31 March 1928, Box 2, Lenroot Papers.

162. Clara Lenroot, Diary, 18 May 1928, Lenroot Papers Addition; Lenroot to Miller Hughes, 26 May 1928, to Arthur H. Bartlett, 25 June 1928, Box 7, Lenroot Papers; *Duluth News Tribune*, 4, 5 June 1928.

163. William T. Hutchinson, *Lowden of Illinois, The Life of Frank O. Lowden: Nation and Countryside*, vol. 2, pp. 584–94; McCoy, *Calvin Coolidge*, pp. 327–28.

164. Manuscripts in Box 7, Lenroot Papers; *Duluth News Tribune*, 20 October 1928; MS, "Qualifications Required by the Next President," Box 7, Lenroot Papers.

165. Clippings, *Washington Post*, 25 November 1928, *Atlanta Journal*, 12 November 1928, Box 20, Lenroot to William H. Dougherty, 12 November 1928, Box 7, Lenroot, "Memoirs," p. 191, Box 13, Lenroot Papers.

suggested to Coolidge that he would accept a vacancy on the Court of Customs Appeals. Coolidge said that he had practically promised the vacancy to someone else, but in February 1929, after a second vacancy opened on that court the outgoing president offered the post. Coolidge's secretary, who served as intermediary, told Lenroot that the judgeship carried a salary of $12,500 a year and was a lifetime appointment with the privilege of retiring at the age of seventy, after ten years service, at full pay. If Lenroot proved hesitant, Coolidge wanted him to appreciate that, as Lenroot later recorded it, "$12,500 per year for life was five per cent on $250,000 and that sum was a good deal of money for any lawyer to save for his old age." [166]

At the time, Lenroot's law practice was economically promising. In addition, the American Paper and Pulp Association, through Frank Sensenbrenner of Wisconsin and others, was negotiating with Lenroot to become president of their association with headquarters in New York, at a salary of $50,000 a year. Acceptance of the judgeship, moreover, would make it ethically impossible for Lenroot to serve as adviser to Hoover. Nevertheless, he decided to accept. Apart from the financial security, the post offered Lenroot the chance to be with Clara on the Brule during the summers. Her health was not good and he wanted to take care of her. Moreover, he treasured his Wisconsin vacations. Since he had participated in enacting three tariff measures he felt fully equal to the work of the court, which took appeals from the United States Customs Court on tariff matters.[167] At the same time, Lenroot left the door open to Sensenbrenner, in the event the nomination failed to win Senate approval.[168]

Lenroot had reasons for doubt, for the chairman of the judiciary committee, which would consider the nomination, was Norris, by then Lenroot's implacable enemy. Other considerations aside, and there were many other considerations, Norris was engaged in a war on the power trust and associated Lenroot with that trust. And Norris was not hesitant in opposing presidential nominations. He had fought the appointment of Stone to the Supreme Court, seeing him as a representative of organized wealth, and was to oppose appointment of Hughes as chief justice on similar grounds.[169]

Not content with the adverse written testimony of the People's Legislative Service and of *Denver Post* publisher F. G. Bonfils, Norris solicited informa-

166. Clara Lenroot, Diary 25, 28 August 1928, Lenroot Papers Addition; Lenroot, "Memoirs," p. 195, Box 13, Lenroot Papers.

167. Lenroot, "Memoirs," pp. 195–96, Box 13, Lenroot to Lewis Alstead, 22 February 1929, to F. J. Sensenbrenner, 4 May 1929, Box 1, Lenroot Papers.

168. Lenroot to F. J. Sensenbrenner, 21 February 1929, Box 4, Lenroot Papers.

169. Lowitt, *Norris*, vol. 2, pp. 250, 444–47; Jonathan Daniels, *Frontier on the Potomac*, p. 90; Manus J. Clancy, III, "Senator George W. Norris: An Analysis and Evaluation of His Role of Insurgency During the Hoover Years" (Ph.D. diss.), pp. 132–33. See also Tray 80, Box 12, and Tray 81, Box 6, George W. Norris Papers, for evidence of his war on the "power trust" at this time.

tion as to the Fall deposition with respect to the Wardman Park visit.[170] He also secured other matter relating to Lenroot's role in the Teapot Dome investigation.[171]

Borah, the second-ranked Republican on the committee, also had doubts, asking for some information about Lenroot's connection with the power companies when they opposed the Walsh resolution. Lenroot appeared before Borah, the only member of a subcommittee to attend, and denied that he had ever been a lobbyist. He said he considered his appearance before the committee similar to appearance before a court and asserted that he had consistently turned down lobbying work.[172]

Guy Goff, a Republican from West Virginia and formerly a politician in Wisconsin, took the task of defending Lenroot. At Goff's solicitation, Lenroot reviewed the Wardman Park incident and went again into his activity for the National Utility Associations. He added that he had taken cases from poorer folks as well.[173]

The subcommittee recommended favorably on Lenroot and the full committee did likewise. The committee's vote was eleven to four. But with the Congress drawing to a close. Norris held up the nomination of nine judges, Lenroot among them.[174]

After much thought, Lenroot decided to permit Hoover to resubmit his name. In addition to his initial reasons, he did not want to create the impression that he had backed off from a fight. And he was confident of confirmation.[175]

Norris required the committee to reconsider the nomination, but again it won committee approval by an eleven to four vote. Lenroot again supplied Goff with answers to anticipated charges, but when the Senate met in executive session on the afternoon of 16 May, Norris raised a new one during the course of a bitter debate that turned in part on whether the session should be open. Norris charged that, as Clara summarized in her diary, "Hanson would never on his own account have gotten the Standard Oil case, and that Irvine must have been in collusion with him and shared the fee a year and a half before he left the Senate!" As the confirmation awaited

170. Record Group 46, "Committee on the Judiciary, Papers Re Nominations, Irvine L. Lenroot," Sen. 70B–A4, NA.

171. Norris to Atlee Pomerene, 18 February 1929, Tray 42, Box 1, copy of telegram, Warren F. Austin to Harry N. Daugherty, 4 February 1924, Tray 7, Box 7, Norris Papers.

172. *New York Times,* 18 February 1929; clipping, *Washington Post,* 20 February 1929, Box 15, Lenroot Papers.

173. Lenroot to Goff, 23 February 1929, Box 2, Lenroot Papers.

174. *New York Times,* 26 February 1929; Record Group 46, "Committee on the Judiciary, Minutes," 70th Cong., Senate, 1927–1929, NA; clipping, *Lincoln Herald,* 9 March 1929, Tray 7, Box 7, Norris Papers.

175. Lenroot to W. H. Dougherty, 9 March 1929, to C. A. Fowler, 29 March 1929, Box 2, to John T. Murphy, 1 April 1929, Box 3, Otto Bosshard to Lenroot, 17 April 1929, Lenroot to Bosshard, 22 April 1929, Box 1, Lenroot Papers.

action the following day, Hanson called on the Lenroots that evening and told them how he had secured employment with Standard Oil. When Lenroot entered partnership with Hanson, it was expressly agreed that he should not share in fees from Standard Oil. This agreement Lenroot clarified in a memorandum for Goff's use. The Lenroots anticipated that Norris's effort would draw some votes and it did. But by a margin of forty-two to twenty-six, Lenroot won confirmation. Almost to the last he was not sure he would take the appointment, but just days before the Senate fight he busied himself with plans for a new lodge on his Brule property. Perhaps it was the thought of summers there that caused him to accept.[176]

This event almost marked the end of Lenroot's career in legislation and politics. He had anticipated the end when he first broached the matter of a court appointment to Coolidge, but the break was more abrupt than he had expected. He continued to advise Hoover on several legislative matters in January and February, but the incoming president was quite apparently hurt at Lenroot's decision to go on the bench.[177] Perhaps it was because he had not been consulted initially, Lenroot thought. The Lenroots saw less and less of the Hoovers thereafter, although Lenroot did in November advise Hoover on his message to Congress and as late as 1931 and 1932 was helping him with speeches. He volunteered only one Wisconsin patronage recommendation during Hoover's presidency.[178]

The court to which Lenroot had been appointed was something of a sanctuary for lame ducks. However, the work was more difficult than Lenroot had expected due to the enlargement of the court's jurisdiction to include appeals from decisions of the Patent Office. Nevertheless, Lenroot enjoyed the work of the court, and he did more than his share of it. But he remained preoccupied with the problems of society and in late 1932 gave thought to resigning his position "to be free to get into active participation in the new adjustments." Clara wrote in her diary that she was amazed that "Irvine really longs to get into some new movement." It was not until 1944, however, that he left the court. When he did so, it was by resignation rather

176. Record Group 46, "Committee on the Judiciary, Minutes," 71st Cong., 1929–1930, 29 April 1929, NA; *New York Times*, 17 May 1929, Box 2, Lenroot Papers; U.S., Senate, *Journal of the Executive Proceedings of the Senate of the United States of America*, vol. 28, pt. 1, pp. 83–88; *New York Times*, 18 May 1929; Clara Lenroot, Diary, 11, 13, 15 May 1929, Lenroot Papers Addition; Lenroot to A. M. Brayton, 17 May 1929, Box 1, Lenroot Papers.

177. Lenroot to Hoover, 12 January, 2, 8 February 1929, Box 2, Lenroot Papers.

178. Clara Lenroot, Diary, 11 May 1929, Lenroot Papers Addition; Lenroot to E. A. Gilmore, 1 March 1929, Box 2, A. M. Brayton to Lenroot, 10 January 1944, Lenroot to Brayton, 24 January 1944, Box 1, Lenroot Papers; Clara Lenroot, Diary, 10 November 1932, 16, 27 February 1933, Lenroot Papers Addition; "Hoover's draft message, Nov. 27, 1929, suggested changes by Lenroot," Box 11, Lenroot Papers; Clara Lenroot, Diary, 19 February 1931, 19 September 1932, Lenroot Papers Addition; Lenroot to John T. Murphy, 6 October 1931, Box 3, Lenroot Papers.

than retirement, so that he could freely express his opinions on public questions.[179]

Even before his resignation, he had occasionally voiced his views at meetings of the Superior Kiwanis and Rotary clubs. And he confided them to his family and correspondents.

During economic crisis, Lenroot rallied to the government, and, in October 1933, he delivered a radio address to the nation urging adherence to the codes of the National Recovery Administration.[180] Soon, however, Lenroot turned against the New Deal. He was repelled by deficit financing and was fearful that the millions of people going onto the government payroll would be used for political ends. The sit-down strikes of 1937 also alarmed him. He saw the division of people into classes as the greatest domestic danger. In this connection, Lenroot expressed concern over abuses by capital as well as by labor. His abiding theme was the need for an awakened, disinterested, educated citizenry. In 1946, he urged creation of a national organization that would promote forums in every community for discussion and debate, get out the vote, and encourage friendship between capital and labor. "The time is short. The urgency was never greater. The issue is the life or death of democracy." [181]

During the thirties, Lenroot feared European developments and was inclined toward isolationism. By 1940, however, he supported preparedness, and when war came he gave the government ardent support. But early on, he became leery of Russian intentions, and he remained so after the war was over. He proposed a hard line.

Lenroot experienced both sadness and joy in his last years. Dorothy had been divorced and remarried, had obtained a law degree, and fashioned a brilliant career as an assistant United States attorney. But in 1933, she suddenly contracted an obscure disease known as agranulocytosis, a depletion of the corpuscles in the blood. She died before her parents could reach her.[182]

Clara fell victim to angina pectoris in 1936 and as a result, became an invalid. On 4 April 1942 she died.[183]

In February 1943 Lenroot married Clara's vivacious niece Eleonore von

179. Lenroot, "Memoirs," p. 197, Box 13, Lenroot Papers; interview with Frederick W. Smith, 30 January 1969; Clara Lenroot, Diary, 1 January 1932, Lenroot Papers Addition; Lenroot to Monte Appel, 30 November 1934, 7 January 1943, to William H. Dougherty, 21 January 1935, Box 1, Lenroot Papers; interview with Katharine Lenroot, 20 November 1968; interview with Irvine L. Nichols, 28 June 1971; Clara Lenroot, Diary, 6 December 1932, Lenroot Papers Addition; clipping, *Milwaukee Journal,* 15 August 1944, Box 13, Lenroot Papers.

180. MS speech, "Doing our part," Saturday, 21 October 1933, printed as N. R. A. release, No. 1232, Box 10, Lenroot Papers.

181. The manuscript speeches are in Box 10, Lenroot Papers. The quotation is from an unpublished article, "Can Democracy live?," Box 10, Lenroot Papers.

182. Lenroot, "Memoirs," p. 200, Box 13, Lenroot Papers; Clara Lenroot, Diary, 12, 16, 18, 19, 20, 22 September 1933, Lenroot Papers Addition.

183. Lenroot, "Memoirs," p. 201, Box 13, Lenroot Papers.

Eltz, who was then in her late forties. The Lenroots had known "Daughto" since her childhood. She was a cheerful and devoted companion to Lenroot in his last years. Katharine also was a continuing source of pride and comfort to Lenroot. In 1934, she became head of the Children's Bureau. It was partly through her that the Lenroots effected a rapprochement with the La Follettes. She worked with La Follette, Jr., on legislation and in the late thirties arranged for Mary to be employed in the Children's Bureau. In 1937, Lenroot willingly assisted Fola La Follette with her biography of her father, whom he praised as "the ablest of the progressives and the most far sighted." [184] By correspondence, Lenroot also resumed friendly relations with Rogers and Hannan.[185]

To Clough Gates, it seemed that Lenroot enjoyed serenity and satisfaction in later life. Yet, he was concerned for his place in history and as early as 1942 was thinking of writing an autobiography. In the summer of 1944, following his resignation from the court, he began work on it and continued doggedly at it through the summer of 1948 when it was completed. During the summer of 1948, afflicted with terminal cancer of the stomach, "he fairly drove himself to making a typed copy from the hand-written manuscript." In his two-hundred-eight-page "Memoirs," which is unpublished, Lenroot told of his role in major events and tried to demonstrate the consistency of his career.[186]

On 26 January 1949, Lenroot died, five days before his eightieth birthday. Wisconsin newspapers in particular noted the event, and Alexander Wiley of Wisconsin delivered a eulogy in the Senate.[187] But to history, Lenroot was already almost forgotten.

Lenroot might easily have been president in place of Coolidge, for in 1920 the Republican vice-presidential nomination was his for the taking. Perhaps the course of American history would have been substantially different had Lenroot succeeded Harding to the presidency. Among Lenroot's differences from Coolidge was a greater awareness of the economic hazards that underlay the prosperity of the late twenties.

Beyond that, Lenroot had been a highly effective legislator for almost three decades. The value one places on his accomplishments depends on one's own outlook, but certainly he had achieved much of what he undertook. Lenroot's role in development of such Wisconsin legislation as the

184. Interview with Katharine Lenroot, 2 April 1969; Katharine Lenroot to the author, 8 January 1969; Irvine to Clara Lenroot, 17 June 1937, Lenroot Papers Addition. See also Clara Lenroot, Diary, 12 January 1932, 3, 23 March, 29 May 1933, and Fola La Follette to Clara Lenroot, 6 April 1938, Lenroot Papers Addition.

185. Lenroot to Rogers, 9 March 1934, Rogers to Lenroot, 16 March 1934, Box 4, Lenroot to Grace Lynch, 16 March 1939, Hannan to Lenroot, 23 March 1939, Box 2, Lenroot Papers.

186. *Superior Telegram*, 4 February 1949; Edward P. Alexander to Lenroot, 4 March 1942, Box 1, Lenroot Papers; Dorothy Ganfield Fowler to the author, 27 January 1970; Mrs. Irvine L. Lenroot to the author, 28 August 1970; Lenroot, "Memoirs," Box 13, Lenroot Papers.

187. *CR* 81:1, 1949, vol. 96, pt. 1, p. 699.

direct primary and railroad commission laws comes to mind. On the national level, he helped to mold the Mann-Elkins Act, the second child labor law, the mineral lands and waterpower acts, the Fordney-McCumber tariff, and the Agricultural Credits Act, and helped lay the groundwork for the St. Lawrence Seaway. Conscientious and able, he left his mark on countless other laws as well.

On many questions of great concern, Lenroot was disappointed in the outcome. But the large role he played in such things as the battle of the League of Nations and ratification of the World Court protocol should not be ignored.

Politically, too, Lenroot was important. It was he, more than any other, who helped La Follette win election to the Senate in 1905, and who led the congressional insurgents in the period 1911 to 1918. His election to the Senate allowed the Republicans to organize that body in 1919. As much as any Senate Republican, he offered a middle ground during the administrations of Harding and Coolidge. And in Wisconsin he rallied the anti-La Follette forces during and after World War I.

History has reserved more than a fair share of its attention for reformers. Had Lenroot remained a "progressive" throughout his life, he might have received greater recognition. But the erstwhile insurgent Republican yielded some of his claims to attention when he became a regular. The transition warrants explanation, partly because it is suggestive of the history of the Progressive movement itself.

The transition was more factional than philosophical. Lenroot's basic assumptions stayed remarkably constant. He venerated America as uniquely blessed, a land of liberty and human dignity. Though not belligerent, Lenroot always felt it important that the nation's honor be upheld. Equality of opportunity he saw as among the country's most precious treasures. Given a fair chance and America's natural bounty, the individual could benefit within the capitalistic framework with only limited assistance from government. He saw need for regulation and looked to the dispassionate services of reason and science for assistance, but he was never an advocate of the welfare state. Instead, he always stressed economy in government. Radical only in unswerving insistence on honesty and fair play, Lenroot consistently believed in progress through compromise. Even during his insurgent days, he considered the Republican party the most likely vehicle for progress.

Lenroot's hopes for America rested with the people. They must control their government, but that alone never seemed enough. Above all, they must be of good character. The citizen must be independent and responsible in his actions. Special privilege was the enemy, but the good citizen must seek no more than fair treatment. And the spirit of patriotism and community must prevail, as against ethnic, class, or other loyalties.

Lenroot was relatively constant not only in thought but in action. His consistency was hidden by changes in label, but in his policies respecting railroads, natural resources, agriculture, tariffs, and internal taxation, the

Lenroot of the postwar years was the moderate progressive still. Fearful of radicalism, he saw reform not reaction as the proper antidote.

In sum, the change in Lenroot was less severe than the contrast between insurgent and regular might suggest. But there was a change and an important one. It resulted from a combination of circumstances.

The separation with La Follette after 1912 caused Lenroot to stand on his own in the House more than he otherwise might have. Part of a minority during the Wilson years, it was easier than in the days of Taft to work with and through his party, and Mann encouraged his cooperation. No sacrifice of principle was demanded, and in the undemocratic procedures of Democrats Lenroot found a constant basis for adherence to Republicanism without sacrifice of progressive credentials. Even when his party resumed the presidency and majority status in Congress, Lenroot was not politically suppressed. Still seeking progress through compromise, he worked with Harding and Coolidge, Lodge, and Curtis, but often to get as much as he could for moderate policies. Slowly, subtly, he became a regular, and more than before he defended government by party.

World War I was for Lenroot the decisive turning point. It brought a change in the emphasis of his thought and a major change in his factional affiliation. The war, more than any experience in his life, did not create but reinforced in Lenroot the desire for consensus. Then and thereafter, the goal of consensus underlay his judgment of men and measures. If anything, this concern enhanced his desire for moderate reforms. But it also increased his fear of demagoguery, and this he found on the left. To him, conservatives were less guilty of stirring class and ethnic animosities.

The factional shifts resulting from the war were profound and long lived. Such was the antagonism between supporters and opponents of American involvement that no speedy reconciliation was possible, especially under the disturbed economic circumstances that followed and flowed from the war. The wartime realignment in Wisconsin politics remained an abiding fixture. Associated now with conservatives as well as progressives and bitterly opposed by La Follette and his more radical associates, Lenroot quite naturally accommodated to the new situation and his new friends. As Lenroot found that his Wisconsin enemies—the Nonpartisan League, the socialists, the railroad unions, the La Follette men—had their counterparts in national affairs, he drifted closer to his conservative colleagues in the administration and the Senate, in action and emotion, becoming a rather irregular regular.

In earlier times, corporations sought special privilege and corrupted democracy in the process. After the war, big business often was selfish and shortsighted. But in Lenroot's view, the greater menace now lay with certain labor and farm groups that asked for more than equal opportunity. Thus, Lenroot found further reason to act with the regular Republicans.

On the political spectrum, the Lenroot of the twenties and afterwards was further to the right than before, but essentially he remained the moderate progressive. Due to radically changed circumstances, the progressive movement had fragmented and was no longer vital. For a time during the postwar years, the challenge of the left gave moderates like Lenroot some bargaining power in dealing with conservative Republicans. But Lenroot's base in the middle was slender to begin with and became weaker still with the onset of Coolidge prosperity. After 1923, especially, Lenroot's progressivism was mainly ritualistic.

Increasingly frustrated in domestic policy, Lenroot devoted more time to foreign affairs during his last years in the Senate. In that area, he was in full accord with the administration, and the opportunity for constructive work remained open still.

The election of Hoover in 1928 stirred Lenroot's hopes, but the depression of 1929 and then the New Deal again polarized political forces.

Even in the last decades of his life, however, Lenroot withstood despair. Indeed, the goals of equal opportunity; fair play to the consumer and taxpayer as against special interests; greater democracy and honesty and openness in government; a responsible citizenry; community; and much else that was integral to Lenroot's thought were far from dead in the American political tradition. Lenroot retained faith in this tradition, took comfort in that faith, felt pride in the contributions he had made, and yearned for further action.

BIBLIOGRAPHY

Primary Sources

National Archives of the United States, Washington, D. C.

Record Group 46, "Records of the United States Senate"
"Committee on the Judiciary, Papers Re Nominations, Irvine L. Lenroot"
"Committee on the Judiciary, Minutes," 70th Cong.
Record Group 48, "General Records of the Department of the Interior"
"Records of the Office of the Secretary of the Interior"
Record Group 59, "General Records of the Department of State"
Record Group 165, "Records of the War Department General Staff"
Record Group 233, "Records of the United States House of Representatives"
"Committee on Rules, Minutes," 62d–65th Cong.

Autobiographies, Memoirs, and Published Letters

Ashurst, Henry Fountain. *A Many-Colored Toga: The Diary of Henry Fountain Ashurst.* Edited by George F. Sparks. Tucson, 1962.
Baker, Ray Stannard. *American Chronicle: The Autobiography of Ray Stannard Baker.* New York, 1945.
Bonsal, Stephen. *Unfinished Business.* New York, 1944.
Butler, Nicholas Murray. *Across the Busy Years: Recollections and Reflections.* 2 vols. New York, 1939–1940.
Clark, Champ. *My Quarter Century of American Politics.* 2 vols. New York, 1920.
Cox, James M. *Journey Through My Years.* New York, 1946.
Daniels, Jonathan. *Frontier on the Potomac.* New York, 1946.
Daniels, Josephus. *The Cabinet Diaries of Josephus Daniels, 1913–1921.* Edited by E. David Cronon. Lincoln, Nebr., 1963.
Edge, Walter E. *A Jerseyman's Journal: Fifty Years of American Business and Politics.* New York, 1972 (1948).
Frear, James A. *Forty Years of Progressive Public Service.* Washington, 1937.
Gardner, Augustus Peabody. *Some Letters of Augustus Peabody Gardner.* Edited by Constance Gardner. Cambridge, Mass., 1920.
Harriman, Florence J. Borden. *From Pinafores to Politics.* New York, 1923.
Hays, Will H. *The Memoirs of Will H. Hays.* Garden City, N. Y., 1955.
Hoover, Herbert C. *The Memoirs of Herbert Hoover: The Cabinet and the Presidency, 1920–1933.* New York, 1952.
Houston, David F. *Eight Years With Wilson's Cabinet, 1913 to 1920.* Vol. 2. New York, 1926.
Keating, Edward. *The Gentleman from Colorado: A Memoir.* Denver, 1964.
Kohlsaat, Herman H. *From McKinley to Harding.* New York, 1923.
La Follette, Philip F. *Adventures in Politics: The Memoirs of Philip La Follette.* Edited by Donald Young. New York, 1970.

La Follette, Robert M. *La Follette's Autobiography: A Personal Narrative of Political Experiences.* Madison, Wis., 1960 (1913).

Lamont, Thomas W. *Across World Frontiers.* New York, 1951.

Lane, Franklin K. *The Letters of Franklin K. Lane.* Edited by Anne W. Lane and Louise H. Wall. Cambridge, Mass., 1922.

Lenroot, Clara Clough. *Long, Long Ago.* U. S. A., 1929.

Longworth, Alice Roosevelt. *Crowded Hours.* New York, 1933.

Marburg, Theodore. *The Development of the League of Nations Idea: Documents and Correspondence of Theodore Marburg.* Edited by John H. Latane. Vol. 2. New York, 1932.

Marshall, Thomas R. *Recollections of Thomas R. Marshall, Vice-President and Hoosier Philosopher: A Hoosier Salad.* Indianapolis, 1925.

Martin, Joseph W., Jr. *My First Fifty Years in Politics.* New York, 1960.

Norris, George W. *Fighting Liberal: The Autobiography of George W. Norris.* New York, 1961 (1945).

Pepper, George Wharton. *In the Senate.* Philadelphia and London, 1930.

Roosevelt, Theodore. *The Letters of Theodore Roosevelt.* Edited by Elting E. Morison. 8 vols. Cambridge, Mass., 1951–1954.

Stephenson, Isaac. *Recollections of a Long Life, 1829–1915.* Chicago, 1915.

Stewart, Lillian K. *A Pioneer of Old Superior.* Boston, 1930.

Straus, Oscar S. *Under Four Administrations, From Cleveland to Taft: Recollections of Oscar S. Straus.* Boston and New York, 1922.

Thompson, Charles Willis. *Presidents I've Known and Two Near Presidents.* Indianapolis, 1929.

Watson, James E. *As I Knew Them: Memoirs of James E. Watson.* Indianapolis, 1936.

White, William Allen. *The Autobiography of William Allen White.* New York, 1946.

Wilson, Edith Bolling. *My Memoir.* Indianapolis, 1938.

Government Documents

Congressional Record. 1909–1927.

Legislature of Wisconsin. *Assembly Journal,* 46th sess.–48th sess.

Flower, Frank A. *The Eye of the North-West.* First annual report of the statistician of Superior, Wis., Milwaukee, 1890.

United States Census Reports. Nos. 8 (1860), 9 (1870), 10 (1880), 11 (1890), 12 (1900).

U.S., Congress. *Biographical Directory of the American Congress, 1774–1961.* Washington, 1961.

U.S., House of Representatives, Committee on Interstate and Foreign Commerce. *Hearings: Return of Railroads to Private Ownership.* 66th. Cong., 1st. sess., Washington, 1919.

U.S., House of Representatives, Committee on Public Lands. *Hearings: Alaska Coal Leasing Bill.* 63d Cong., 2d sess., Washington, 1914.

———. *Hearings: Exploration for and Disposition of Oil, Gas, Etc.* 63d Cong., 2d sess., Washington, 1914.

———. *Hearings: Hetch Hetchy Dam Site.* 63d Cong., 1st. sess., Washington, 1913.

———. *Hearings: Imperial Valley.* 63d Cong., 3d sess., Washington, 1915.

———. *Hearings: Land in Alaska, Certain Purchase Of.* 63d Cong., 2d sess., Washington, 1914.

———. *Hearings: Oil Leasing Lands.* 65th Cong., 2d sess., Washington, 1918.

———. *Hearings: Rocky Mountain National Park.* 63d Cong., 3d sess., Washington, 1915.

U.S., House of Representatives, Committee on Rules. *Hearings: Committee on Woman Suffrage.* 63d Cong., 2d sess., Washington, 1913.

———. *Hearings: Grain Exchanges.* 63d Cong., 2d sess., Washington, 1914.

———. *Hearings: Industrial Disputes in Colorado and Michigan.* 63d Cong., 2d sess., Washington, 1913.

———. *Hearings: International Harvester Co.* 62d Cong., 1st sess., Washington, 1912.

———. *Hearings: Investigation of Shipping Trust.* 62d Cong., 2d sess., Washington, 1912.

———. *Hearings: The Strike at Lawrence, Mass.* 62d Cong., 2d sess., Washington, 1912.

U.S., House of Representatives. *Reports,* Nos. 352, 668, 695. 63d Cong., 2d sess., Washington, 1913–1914.

———. *Report,* No. 1037. 65th Cong., 3d sess., Washington, 1919.

U.S., Senate, Committee on Banking and Currency. *Hearings: Discounts and Loans by Federal Land Banks for Farming Purposes.* 67th Cong., 2d sess., Washington, 1922.

———. *Hearings: Rural Credits.* 67th Cong., 4th sess., Washington, 1923.

U.S., Senate, Committee on Interstate Commerce. *Hearings: Investigation of Public Utility Corporations.* 70th Cong., 1st sess., Washington, 1928.

U.S., Senate, Committee on Public Lands and Surveys. *Hearings: Leases Upon Naval Oil Reserves.* 68th Cong., 1st sess., Washington, 1924.

———. *Hearings: Leases Upon Reserves.* 70th Cong., 1st sess., Washington, 1928.

U.S., Senate. *Reports,* Nos. 443, 535. 65th Cong., 2d sess., Washington, 1918.

———. *Report,* No. 823. 66th Cong., 3d sess., Washington, 1921.

———. *Journal of the Executive Proceedings of the Senate of the United States of America.* Vol. 67. 71st Cong., Washington, 1931.

Wisconsin Blue Book, Madison, Wis., 1901–1927.

Interviews

Columbia University Oral History Project, "The Reminiscences of William S. Bennet," 1972 (1949–1950)

———. Social Security Project. Katharine Lenroot, 2 February 1965

Helen Hobbs, 15 February 1969

Mrs. Irvine L. Lenroot, 7 October 1968

Katharine Lenroot, 20 November 1968; 2 April 1969; 19 June 1971

John Lenroot, 28 June 1970

Robert Lenroot, 27 June 1970

Irvine L. Nichols, 28 June 1970

Frederick W. Smith, 30 January 1969

Letters to the Author

Jay C. Halls, 4 February 1969

Dorothy Ganfield Fowler, 27 January 1970

Frieda M. Lease, 17 July 1970

Mrs. Irvine L. Lenroot, 27 January 1969; 28 August 1970

Katharine F. Lenroot, 26 November, 5, 10, 11 December 1968; 8, 29 January, 10, 19 April, 1 May, 10 June, 7 August, 9 October 1969; 15 March 1970; 25 June, 15 September, 18 October 1971; 17 February 1972; 19 April 1976

Hayden M. Pickering, 11 February 1969

Arthur Roberts, 10 July 1970

Manuscript Collections

Library of Congress, Manuscript Division, Washington, D. C.

Chandler P. Anderson Papers; Ray Stannard Baker Papers; Albert J. Beveridge Papers; William E. Borah Papers; Albert S. Burleson Papers; William E. Chandler Papers; Raymond Clapper Papers; William S. Culbertson Papers; Walter L. Fisher Papers; James R. Garfield Papers; Francis Burton Harrison Papers (Burton Harrison Collection); Gilbert M. Hitchcock Papers; Charles Evans Hughes Papers; Harold L. Ickes Papers; Philander C. Knox Papers; Robert M. La Follette Papers (La Follette Family Collection, including the Alfred T. Rogers Papers and Gilbert Roe Papers); Robert Lansing Papers; Irvine L. Lenroot Papers (Lenroot Papers Addition); Breckinridge Long Papers; James R. Mann Papers; William G. McAdoo

Papers; Joseph Medill McCormick Papers (McCormick Family Papers); Ogden L. Mills Papers; John Bassett Moore Papers; Victor Murdock Papers; National Child Labor Committee Papers; George W. Norris Papers; John C. O'Laughlin Papers; Amos Pinchot Papers; Gifford Pinchot Papers; Theodore Roosevelt Papers; Theodore Roosevelt, Jr., Papers; Elihu Root Papers; John C. Spooner Papers; Oscar S. Straus Papers; William Howard Taft Papers; Joseph P. Tumulty Papers; James W. Wadsworth Papers (Wadsworth Family Collection); Thomas J. Walsh Papers; Woodrow Wilson Papers.

State Historical Society of Wisconsin, Madison
Albert O. Barton Papers; John J. Blaine Papers; James O. Davidson Papers; Herman L. Ekern Papers; John J. Esch Papers; Edwin J. Gross Papers; Nils P. Haugen Papers; Robert M. La Follette Papers; John M. Nelson Papers; Emanuel L. Philipp Papers; Edward A. Ross Papers; James A. S'one Papers; John Strange Papers; John M. Whitehead Papers.

Minnesota State Historical Society, St. Paul
Ethan C. Clarke Papers (Ethan C. Clarke Family Papers); Frank B. Kellogg Papers; National Nonpartisan League Papers; Henry G. Teigan Papers.

Harvard University, Cambridge, Mass.
Commonwealth Shoe and Leather Company Papers (Baker Library); League to Enforce Peace Papers (Houghton Library); A. Lawrence Lowell Papers (Widener Library).

Connecticut College, New London
Mary Williams Crozier Papers.

Syracuse University, N.Y.
Frederick Hale Papers.

Ohio Historical Society, Columbus
Warren G. Harding Papers.

Herbert Hoover Presidential Library, West Bend, Iowa
Herbert Hoover Papers.

Hoover Institution, Stanford University, Calif.
Edward Eyre Hunt Papers; Mark Sullivan Papers.

Yale University, New Haven, Conn.
William Kent Papers.

Massachusetts Historical Society, Boston
Henry Cabot Lodge Papers.

University of Virginia, Charlottesville
Miles Poindexter Papers.

Newspapers

Boston Herald, 1918, 1920, 1922, 1928
Chicago News, June 1920
Chicago Record-Herald, March 1910
Chicago Tribune, 1910, 1911, 1915, 1917
Duluth News Tribune, 1890–1906, 1910, 1914–1917, 1928
Los Angeles Times, 1918
Milwaukee Journal, 1901, 1917, 1920, 1926, 1949
Milwaukee News, 1901, 1904–1905
Milwaukee Sentinel, 1916–1926
Minneapolis Tribune, 1909
New York American, 1924
New York Herald Tribune, 1926
New York Journal, 1919–1920
New York Post, 1909
New York Sun, 1918, 1920

New York Times, 1909–1912, 1914–1929
New York Tribune, 1917, 1919–1920
Portland Oregonian, 1920
Spokane Spokesman-Review, 1909
St. *Louis Post-Dispatch,* 1924
The Sun and New York Herald, 1920
Superior Leader, 1891–1897
Superior Telegram, 1891, 1896–1927, 1949
Washington Evening Star, 1916–1920, 1926, 1928
Washington Herald, 1910, 1916, 1920, 1924
Washington Post, 1916–1918
Washington Times, 1910, 1917, 1920
Wisconsin State Journal (Madison), 1901–1907, 1910–1913, 1920

Pamphlets

Bertrand, Achille H. "Recollections of Old Superior." Indexed by W.P.A. Project 6227. Superior, Wis., 1938.
Gates, Clough. "Superior: An Outline of History." Reprint from the *Superior Telegram* Centennial Edition. 15 July 1954.
Republican Party. *Official Report of the Seventeenth Republican National Convention held in Chicago, Illinois, June 8, 9, 10, 11 and 12, 1920.* New York, 1920.

Periodicals

Collier's Weekly, 16 May 1908; 6 April, 9 June 1917
The Forum, June 1918
La Follette's Magazine (Madison, Wis.), 1915–1926
La Follette's Weekly Magazine (Madison, Wis.), 1909–1914
New Republic, 14 April 1920
Outlook, 18 April 1917; 3 April 1918
Review of Reviews, March 1917; April 1918

Secondary Sources

Unpublished Materials

Accinelli, Robert D. "The Harding Administration and the World Court." Paper delivered before the Association of American Historians (Spring 1971).
_____. "The United States and the World Court, 1920–1927." Ph.D. diss., University of California, Berkeley, 1968.
Acrea, Kenneth Claire, Jr. "Wisconsin Progressivism: Legislative Response to Social Change, 1891–1909." Ph.D. diss., University of Wisconsin, 1968.
Allen, Howard W. "Miles Poindexter: A Political Biography." Ph.D. diss., University of Washington, 1959.
Atkinson, Charles R. "The Committee on Rules and the Overthrow of Speaker Cannon." Ph.D. diss., Columbia University, 1911.
Barfield, Claude E. "The Democratic Party in Congress, 1909–1913." Ph.D. diss., Northwestern University, 1965.
Bates, J. Leonard. "Senator Walsh of Montana, 1918–1924: A Liberal Under Pressure." Ph.D. diss., University of North Carolina, 1952.
Best, Gary Dean. "Herbert Clark Hoover in Transition, 1919–1921." Ph.D. diss., University of Hawaii, 1973.
Birr, Kendall. "Social Ideas of Superior Business Men, 1880–1898." M.A. thesis, University of Wisconsin, 1948.
Bocage, Leo Joseph. "The Public Career of Charles R. Crane." Ph.D. diss., Fordham University, 1962.

Caine, Stanley P. "Railroad Regulation in Wisconsin, 1903–1910: An Assessment of a Progressive Reform." Ph.D. diss., University of Wisconsin, 1967.

Chatham, Marie. "The Role of the National Party Chairman from Hanna to Farley." Ph.D. diss., University of Maryland, 1953.

Clancy, Manus J., III. "Senator George W. Norris: An Analysis and Evaluation of His Role of Insurgency During the Hoover Years." Ph.D. diss., Johns Hopkins University, 1965.

Clubb, Jerome Martin. "Congressional Opponents of Reform, 1901–1913." Ph.D. diss., University of Washington, 1963.

Detzer, David W. "The Politics of the Payne-Aldrich Tariff of 1909." Ph.D. diss., University of Connecticut, 1970.

Erlebacher, Albert. "Herman L. Ekern, the Quiet Progressive." Ph.D. diss., University of Wisconsin, 1965.

Greenlee, Howard Scott. "The Republican Party in Division and Reunion, 1913–1920." Ph.D. diss., University of Chicago, 1950.

Havig, Alan Rolf. "The Poverty of Insurgency: The Movement to Progressivize the Republican Party, 1916–1924." Ph.D. diss., University of Missouri, 1966.

Hillje, John Wylie. "The Progressive Movement and the Graduated Income Tax, 1913–1919." Ph.D. diss., University of Texas, 1966.

Kendrick, Jack E. "The League of Nations and the Republican Senate, 1918–1921." Ph.D. diss., University of North Carolina, 1952.

Kenkel, Joseph Frederick. "The Tariff Commission Movement: The Search for a Nonpartisan Solution of the Tariff Question." Ph.D. diss., University of Maryland, 1962.

Koerselman, Gary Harlan. "Herbert Hoover and the Farm Crisis of the Twenties: A Study of the Commerce Department's Efforts to Solve the Agricultural Depression, 1921–1928." Ph.D. diss., Northern Illinois University, 1971.

Liljekvist, Clifford B. "Senator Hiram Johnson." Ph.D. diss., University of Southern California, 1953.

Margulies, Herbert F. "Issues and Politics of Wisconsin Progressivism, 1906–1920." Ph.D. diss., University of Wisconsin, 1955.

———. "Progressivism, Patriotism, and Politics: The Life and Times of Irvine L. Lenroot." State Historical Society of Wisconsin and Lenroot Papers Addition, Library of Congress.

McKnight, Gerald D. "A Party Against Itself—The Grand Old Party in the New Freedom Era, 1913–1916." Ph.D. diss., University of Maryland, 1972.

Megargee, Richard. "The Diplomacy of John Bassett Moore: Realism in American Foreign Policy." Ph.D. diss., Northwestern University, 1963.

Olson, Keith Waldemar. "Franklin K. Lane: A Biography." Ph.D. diss., University of Wisconsin, 1964.

Patterson, Robert Foster. "Gilbert M. Hitchcock: A Story of Two Careers." Ph.D. diss., University of Colorado, 1940.

Pike, Albert H., Jr. "Jonathan Bourne, Jr., Progressive." Ph.D. diss., University of Oregon, 1957.

Roady, Elston Edward. "Party Regularity in the Sixty-third Congress." Ph.D. diss., University of Illinois, 1951.

Robertson, James Oliver. "The Progressives in National Republican Politics, 1916–1921." Ph.D. diss., Harvard University, 1964.

Roots, John McCook. "The Treaty of Versailles in the United States Senate." B.A. (honors thesis), Harvard University, 1925.

Sayre, Ralph Mills. "Albert Baird Cummins and the Progressive Movement in Iowa." Ph.D. diss., Columbia University, 1958.

Shaw, Reginald Mathison. "Historical Geography of Superior, Wisconsin." Ph.D. diss., University of Wisconsin, 1938.

Stratton, David H. "Albert B. Fall and the Teapot Dome Affair." Ph.D. diss., University of Colorado, 1955.

Thompson, Jack T. "James R. Garfield: The Career of a Rooseveltian Progressive, 1895–1915." Ph.D. diss., University of South Carolina, 1958.

Weaver, Norman Frederick. "The Knights of the Ku Klux Klan in Wisconsin, Indiana, Ohio and Michigan." Ph.D. diss., University of Wisconsin, 1954.

Williams, Charles Frederick. "William M. Jardine and the Development of Republican Farm Policy, 1925–1929." Ph.D. diss., University of Oklahoma, 1970.

Wolner, Helen Marie. "The History of Superior, Wisconsin, to 1900." M.A. thesis, University of Wisconsin, 1939.

Wyman, Roger E. "Voting Behavior in the Progressive Era: Wisconsin as a Case Study." Ph.D. diss., University of Wisconsin, 1970.

Articles

Alexander, Thomas G. "Senator Reed Smoot and Western Land Policy, 1905–1920." *Arizona and the West* 13:3 (1971).

Allen, Howard W. "Miles Poindexter and the Progressive Movement." *Pacific Northwest Quarterly* (July 1962).

Anderson, Paul Y. "The Scandal in Oil." *New Republic* 37 (6 February 1924).

Baker, John D. "The Character of the Congressional Revolution of 1910." *Journal of American History* 60:3 (December 1973).

Berdahl, Clarence A. "Myths about the Peace Treaties of 1919–1920." *American Scholar* (Winter 1941–1942).

Best, Gary Dean. "Food Relief as Price Support: Hoover and American Pork, January-March 1919." *Agricultural History* 45 (April 1971).

Blakey, Roy G. "The Revenue Act of 1921." *American Economic Review* 12:1 (March 1922).

Boothe, Leon E. "Anglo-American Pro-League Groups Lead Wilson, 1915–1918." *Mid-America* 51:2 (April 1969).

Cary, Lorin Lee. "The Wisconsin Loyalty Legion, 1917–1918." *Wisconsin Magazine of History* 53:1 (Autumn 1969).

Darling, H. Maurice. "Who Kept the United States Out of the League of Nations?" *Canadian Historical Review* 10 (September 1969).

Dixon, Frank H. "The Mann-Elkins Act." *Quarterly Journal of Economics* (August 1910).

Dollar, Charles M. "The South and the Fordney-McCumber Tariff of 1922: A Study in Regional Politics." *Journal of Southern History* 39:1 (February 1973).

Finch, George A. "The Treaty of Peace with Germany in the United States Senate." *American Journal of International Law* 14 (1920).

Fleming, James S. "Re-Establishing Leadership in the House of Representatives: The Case of Oscar W. Underwood." *Mid-America* 54:4 (October 1972).

Gould, Lewis L. "Western Range Senators and the Payne-Aldrich Tariff." *Pacific Northwest Quarterly* 64:2 (April 1973).

Grantham, Dewey W., Jr. "The Southern Senators and the League of Nations, 1918–1920." *North Carolina Historical Review* 33 (April 1949).

Griffith, Robert. "Prelude to Insurgency: Irvine L. Lenroot and the Republican Primary of 1908." *Wisconsin Magazine of History* 49:1 (Autumn 1965).

Harbison, Robert W. "Railroads and Regulation, 1877–1916: Conspiracy or Public Interest?" *Journal of Economic History* 27:2 (June 1967).

Hawley, Ellis W. "Herbert Hoover, the Commerce Secretariat, and the Vision of an 'Associative State,' 1921–1928." *Journal of American History* 61:1 (June 1974).

Hewes, James E., Jr. "Henry Cabot Lodge and the League of Nations." *Proceedings of the American Philosophical Society* 114:4 (August 1970).

Kennedy, Padraic C. "Lenroot, La Follette and the Campaign of 1906." *Wisconsin Magazine of History* 43:3 (Spring 1959).

Lenroot, Irvine L. Review of *La Follette and the Direct Primary in Wisconsin,* by Allen
 P. Lovejoy, *Wisconsin Magazine of History* 26:2 (December 1942).
────. "The Essentials of World Organization." *The Annals of the American Academy
 of Political and Social Science* No. 1525 (July 1921).
Lippmann, Walter. "Our Next President?" *World Outlook* 6 (June 1920).
Margulies, Herbert F. "Robert La Follette Goes to the Senate, 1905." *Wisconsin
 Magazine of History* 59:3 (Spring 1976).
Mervin, David. "Henry Cabot Lodge and the League of Nations." *Journal of American
 Studies* 4:2 (February 1971).
Rader, Benjamin G. "Federal Taxation in the 1920s: A Re-Examination." *The His-
 torian* 33:3 (May 1971).
Shideler, James H. "Herbert Hoover and the Federal Farm Board Project, 1921–
 1925." *Mississippi Valley Historical Review* 42:4 (March 1956).
Snyder, J. Richard. "William S. Culbertson and the Formation of Modern American
 Commercial Policy, 1917–1925." *Kansas Historical Quarterly* 35 (Winter 1969).
Solvick, Stanley D. "The Conservative as Progressive: William Howard Taft and the
 Politics of the Square Deal." *Northwest Ohio Quarterly* (Summer 1967).
────. "William Howard Taft and Cannonism." *Wisconsin Magazine of History* 48:1
 (August 1964).
────. "William Howard Taft and the Insurgents." *Papers of the Michigan Academy
 of Science, Arts and Letters* 45, 1963 (1962 meeting).
────. "William Howard Taft and the Payne-Aldrich Tariff." *Mississippi Valley His-
 torical Review* 50:3 (December 1963).
Stephenson, George M. "The Attitude of the Swedish-Americans Toward the World
 War." *Mississippi Valley Historical Association Proceedings* 10 (1918–1921).
────. "When America Was the Land of Canaan." *Minnesota History* 10:3 (Septem-
 ber 1929).
Wadsworth, James W. "The Smoke-Filled Room." *American Heritage* 23:3 (June
 1972).
Walsh, Thomas J. "The True History of Teapot Dome." *The Forum* 2 (July 1924).
Weibull, Jorgen. "The Wisconsin Progressives, 1900–1914." *Mid-America* 1:47 (July
 1965).
Weinstein, Edwin A. "Woodrow Wilson's Neurological Illness." *Journal of American
 History* 17:2 (September 1970).
Wimer, Kurt. "Senator Hitchcock and the League of Nations." *Nebraska History* 45:4
 (September 1963).
────. "Woodrow Wilson's Plan to Enter the League of Nations through an Execu-
 tive Agreement." *Western Political Quarterly* 11:4 (December 1958).
────. "Woodrow Wilson Tries Conciliation: An Effort That Failed." *The Historian*
 25:4 (August 1963).

Books

Adler, Selig. *The Uncertain Giant, 1921–1941: American Foreign Policy Between the Wars.*
 New York, 1971 (1965).
Alexander, DeAlva Stanwood. *History and Procedure of the House of Representatives.*
 Boston and New York, 1916.
Anderson, Donald F. *William Howard Taft: A Conservative's Conception of the Presidency.*
 Ithaca, N. Y., 1973.
Arnett, Alex M. *Claude Kitchin and the Wilson War Policies.* Boston, 1937.
Ashby, LeRoy. *The Spearless Leader: Senator Borah and the Progressive Movement in the
 1920's.* Urbana, Ill., 1972.
Bagby, Wesley M. *The Road to Normalcy: The Presidential Campaign and Election of 1920.*
 Baltimore, 1968 (1962).

Bailey, Thomas A. *Woodrow Wilson and the Great Betrayal.* New York, 1947.
_____. *Woodrow Wilson and the Lost Peace.* New York, 1947.
Baird, Frieda, and Benner, Claude L. *Ten Years of Federal Intermediate Credits.* Washington, 1933.
Baker, Ray Stannard. *Woodrow Wilson, Life and Letters: War Leader, 1917–1918.* Vol. 7. New York, 1939.
_____. *Woodrow Wilson, Life and Letters: Armistice March 1–November 11, 1918.* Vol. 8. New York, 1939.
Baker, Richard C. *The Tariff Under Roosevelt and Taft.* Hastings, Nebr., 1941.
Barrett, Charles S. *Uncle Reuben in Washington.* Washington, 1923.
Bartlett, Ruhl J. *The League to Enforce Peace.* Chapel Hill, N. C., 1944.
Barton, Albert O. *La Follette's Winning of Wisconsin.* Des Moines, 1922.
Bates, J. Leonard. *The Origins of Teapot Dome: Progressives, Parties and Petroleum, 1909–1921.* Urbana, Ill., 1963.
Beers, J. H. and Co. *Commemorative Biographical Record of the Upper Lake Region.* Chicago, 1905.
Best, Gary Dean. *The Politics of American Individualism: Herbert Hoover in Transition, 1918–1921.* Westport, Conn., and London, Eng., 1975.
Billington, Monroe Lee. *Thomas P. Gore: The Blind Senator from Oklahoma.* Lawrence, Kans., 1967.
Blum, John M. *Joe Tumulty and the Wilson Era.* Boston, 1951.
Bolles, Blair. *Tyrant from Illinois: Uncle Joe Cannon's Experiment with Personal Power.* New York, 1951.
Bowers, Claude G. *Beveridge and the Progressive Era.* Cambridge, Mass., 1932.
Braeman, John. *Albert J. Beveridge: American Nationalist.* Chicago and London, 1971.
Bryn-Jones, David. *Frank B. Kellogg: A Biography.* New York, 1937.
Burner, David. *The Politics of Provincialism: The Democratic Party in Transition, 1918–1932.* New York, 1968.
Busbey, L. White. *Uncle Joe Cannon.* New York, 1927.
Caine, Stanley P. *The Myth of a Progressive Reform: Railroad Regulation in Wisconsin, 1903–1910.* Madison, 1970.
Campbell, William J. *History of the Republican Party in Wisconsin: Under Convention Plan, 1924–1940.* Oshkosh, 1942.
Capps, Finis Herbert. *From Isolationism to Involvement: The Swedish Immigrant Press in America, 1914–1945.* Chicago, 1966.
Chamberlain, Lawrence H. *The President, Congress and Legislation.* New York, 1946.
Coben, Stanley. *A. Mitchell Palmer: Politician.* New York, 1963.
Cohen, Naomi W. *A Dual Heritage: The Public Career of Oscar Straus.* Philadelphia, 1969.
Coletta, Paolo E. *The Presidency of William Howard Taft.* Lawrence, Manhattan, Wichita, Kans., 1973.
Cooper, John Milton, Jr. *The Vanity of Power: American Isolationism and the First World War, 1914–1917.* Westport, Conn., 1969.
Daniels, Josephus. *The Wilson Era: Years of War and After, 1917–1923.* Vol. 2. Chapel Hill, N. C., 1946.
Daugherty, Harry M. in collaboration with Thomas Dixon. *The Inside Story of the Harding Tragedy.* New York, 1932.
Downes, Randolph C. *The Rise of Warren Gamaliel Harding, 1865–1920.* Columbus, Ohio, 1970.
Ellis, L. Ethan. *Frank B. Kellogg and American Foreign Relations, 1925–1929.* New Brunswick, 1961.
_____. *Republican Foreign Policy, 1921–1933.* New Brunswick, 1968.
Fausold, Martin L. *Gifford Pinchot: Bull Moose Progressive.* Binghamton, N. Y., 1961.
Fite, Gilbert C. *George N. Peek and the Fight for Farm Parity.* Norman, Okla., 1954.
_____. *Peter Norbeck: Prairie Statesman.* Columbia, Mo., 1948.

Fleming, Denna Frank. *The United States and the League of Nations, 1918–1920.* New York and London, 1932.

———. *The United States and the World Court.* Garden City, N. Y., 1945.

Flexner, Eleanor. *Century of Struggle: The Woman's Rights Movement in the United States.* U. S. A., 1968.

Fowler, Dorothy Ganfield. *John Coit Spooner: Defender of Presidents.* New York, 1961.

Fuess, Claude M. *Calvin Coolidge: The Man from Vermont.* Hamden, Conn., 1965.

Galloway, George B. *History of the House of Representatives.* New York, 1961.

Garraty, John A. *Henry Cabot Lodge: A Biography.* New York, 1953.

Gates, Paul. *History of Public Land Law Development.* Washington, 1968.

Gilbert, Charles. *American Financing of World War I.* Westport, Conn., 1970.

Gilbert, Clinton Wallace. *Behind the Mirrors: The Psychology of Disintegration at Washington.* New York, 1922.

Glad, Betty. *Charles Evans Hughes and the Illusion of Innocence: A Study in American Diplomacy.* Urbana, Ill., 1966.

Grayson, Cary T. *Woodrow Wilson: An Intimate Portrait.* New York, 1960.

Gwinn, William Rea. *Uncle Joe Cannon, Archfoe of Insurgency: A History of the Rise and Fall of Cannonism.* U. S. A., 1957.

Hasbrouck, Paul DeWitt. *Party Government in the House of Representatives.* New York, 1927.

Hatch, Alden. *Edith Bolling Wilson: First Lady Extraordinary.* New York, 1961.

Hays, Samuel P. *Conservation and the Gospel of Efficiency: The Progressive Conservation Movement, 1890–1920.* Cambridge, Mass., 1959.

Hechler, Kenneth. *Insurgency: Personalities and Politics of the Taft Era.* New York, 1964 (1940).

Hicks, John D. *Rehearsal for Disaster.* Gainesville, Fla., 1961.

———. *Republican Ascendancy, 1921–1933.* New York, 1942.

Hinton, Harold B. *Cordell Hull: A Biography.* New York, 1942.

Holt, James. *Congressional Insurgents and the Party System, 1909–1916.* Cambridge, Mass., 1967.

Holt, W. Stull. *Treaties Defeated by the Senate: A Study of the Struggle Between President and Senate Over the Conduct of Foreign Relations.* Baltimore, 1933.

Hoover, Herbert C. *The Ordeal of Woodrow Wilson.* New York, 1958.

Hutchinson, William T. *Lowden of Illinois, The Life of Frank O. Lowden: Nation and Countryside.* Vol. 2. Chicago, 1957.

Ise, John. *The United States Oil Policy.* New Haven, 1926.

Israel, Fred L. *Nevada's Key Pittman.* Lincoln, Nebr., 1963.

Janson, Florence Edith. *The Background of Swedish Immigration, 1840–1930.* Chicago, 1931.

Jensen, Richard. *The Winning of the Midwest: Social and Political Conflict, 1888–1896.* Chicago, 1971.

Jessup, Philip C. *Elihu Root.* Vol. 2. New York, 1938.

Johnson, Carolyn W. *Winthrop Murray Crane: A Study in Republican Leadership, 1892–1920.* Northhampton, Mass., 1967.

Johnson, Claudius O. *Borah of Idaho.* Seattle and London, 1967 (1936).

Johnson, Roger T. *Robert M. La Follette, Jr., and the Decline of the Progressive Party in Wisconsin.* Madison, 1964.

Johnson, Willis Fletcher. *George Harvey: "A Passionate Patriot."* Boston and New York, 1929.

Kamman, William. *A Search for Stability: United States Diplomacy Toward Nicaragua, 1925–1933.* South Bend, 1968.

Karson, Mark. *American Labor Unions and Politics, 1900–1918.* Carbondale, Ill., 1958.

Kelly, Alfred H., and Harbison, Winfred A. *The American Constitution: Its Origin and Development.* 4th ed. New York, 1970.

Kent, Elizabeth. *William Kent, Independent: A Biography.* U. S. A., 1951.
Kerr, K. Austin. *American Railroad Politics, 1914–1920: Rates, Wages, and Efficiency.* Pittsburgh, 1968.
Kerwin, Jerome G. *Federal Water-Power Legislation.* New York, 1926.
Kimmel, Lewis H. *Federal Budget and Fiscal Policy, 1789–1958.* Washington, 1959.
King, Judson. *The Conservation Fight from Theodore Roosevelt to the Tennessee Valley Authority.* Washington, 1959.
Kleppner, Paul. *The Cross of Culture: A Social Analysis of Midwestern Politics, 1850–1900.* New York, 1970.
La Follette, Belle Case, and Fola. *Robert M. La Follette, 1855–1925.* 2 vols. New York, 1953.
Lawrence, David. *The True Story of Woodrow Wilson.* New York, 1924.
Leopold, Richard W. *Elihu Root and the Conservative Tradition.* Boston, 1954.
Lief, Alfred. *Democracy's Norris: The Biography of a Lonely Crusader.* New York, 1939.
Link, Arthur S. *American Epoch: A History of the United States Since 1890's.* 2d rev. ed. New York, 1965.
———. *Wilson: Campaigns for Progressivism and Peace, 1916–1917.* Princeton, 1965.
———. *Wilson: Confusions and Crises, 1915–1916.* Princeton, 1964.
———. *Wilson the Diplomatist.* Baltimore, 1957.
———. *Wilson: The New Freedom.* Princeton, 1956.
———. *Wilson: The Struggle for Neutrality, 1914–1915.* Princeton, 1960.
———. *Woodrow Wilson and the Progressive Era, 1900–1917.* New York, 1954.
Lodge, Henry Cabot. *The Senate and the League of Nations.* New York and London, 1925.
Lovejoy, Allan Fraser. *La Follette and the Establishment of the Direct Primary in Wisconsin, 1890–1904.* New Haven, 1941.
Lowitt, Richard. *George W. Norris: The Making of a Progressive, 1861–1912.* Clinton, Mass., 1963.
———. *George W. Norris: The Persistence of a Progressive, 1913–1933.* Urbana, Ill., 1971.
Lowry, Edward G. *Washington Close-Ups: Intimate Views of Some Public Figures.* Cambridge, Mass., 1921.
Mabee, Carleton. *The Seaway Story.* New York, 1961.
Maddox, Robert James. *William E. Borah and American Foreign Policy.* Baton Rouge, 1969.
Malin, James C. *The United States After the World War.* Boston, 1930.
Margulies, Herbert F. *The Decline of the Progressive Movement in Wisconsin, 1890–1920.* Madison, 1968.
Martin, Albro. *Enterprise Denied: Origins of the Decline of American Railroads, 1897–1917.* New York, 1971.
Mason, Alpheus T. *Brandeis: A Free Man's Life.* New York, 1946.
———. *Bureaucracy Convicts Itself: The Ballinger-Pinchot Controversy of 1910.* New York, 1941.
Maxwell, Robert S. *Emanuel L. Philipp: Wisconsin Stalwart.* Madison, 1959.
———. *La Follette and the Rise of the Progressives in Wisconsin.* Madison, 1956.
Mayer, Arno J. *Politics and Diplomacy of Peacemaking: Containment and Counterrevolution at Versailles, 1918–1919.* New York, 1967.
McCoy, Donald R. *Calvin Coolidge: The Quiet President.* New York, 1967.
McGeary, M. Nelson. *Gifford Pinchot: Forester-Politician.* Princeton, 1960.
Merk, Frederick. *Economic History of Wisconsin During the Civil War Decade.* Madison, 1916.
Merrill, Horace S., and Marion G. *The Republican Command, 1897–1913.* Lexington, Ky., 1971.
Meyer, Ernst C. *Nominating Systems: Direct Primaries Versus Conventions in the United States.* Madison, 1902.

Meyers, William Starr. *The Republican Party: A History*. New York, 1931.

Morgan, H. Wayne. *From Hayes to McKinley: National Party Politics, 1877–1896*. Syracuse, 1969.

Mowry, George E. *The Era of Theodore Roosevelt, 1900–1912*. New York, 1958.

———. *Theodore Roosevelt and the Progressive Movement*. Madison, 1947.

Murray, Robert K. *The Harding Era: Warren G. Harding and His Administration*. Minneapolis, 1969.

Nash, Gerald D. *United States Oil Policy, 1890–1964: Business and Government in Twentieth Century America*. Pittsburgh, 1968.

Nelson, Clifford L. *German-American Political Behavior in Nebraska and Wisconsin, 1916–1920*. Lincoln, Nebr., 1972.

Nevins, Allan. *Henry White: Thirty Years of American Diplomacy*. New York, 1930.

Noggle, Burl. *Teapot Dome: Oil and Politics in the 1920's*. Baton Rouge, 1962.

Odegard, Peter D. *Pressure Politics: The Story of the Anti-Saloon League*. New York, 1928.

Odland, Martin W. *The Life of Knute Nelson*. Minneapolis, 1926.

Older, Cora M. *William Randolph Hearst: American*. New York and London, 1936.

Paxson, Frederic L. *American Democracy and the World War: Pre-War Years, 1913–1917*. Vol. 1. Boston, 1936.

———. *American Democracy and the World War: America at War, 1917–1918*. Vol. 2. Boston, 1939.

———. *American Democracy and the World War, Postwar Years: Normalcy, 1918–1923*. Vol. 3. Berkeley and Los Angeles, 1948.

Penick, James, Jr. *Progressive Politics and Conservation: The Ballinger-Pinchot Affair*. Chicago, 1968.

Pinchot, Amos. *The History of the Progressive Party, 1912–1916*. Edited by Helene Hooker. New York, 1958.

Pringle, Henry F. *The Life and Times of William Howard Taft*. 2 vols. New York, 1939.

Pusey, Merlo J. *Charles Evans Hughes*. 2 vols. New York, 1951.

Ratner, Sidney. *American Taxation: Its History as a Social Force in Democracy*. New York, 1942.

Richardson, Elmo R. *The Politics of Conservation: Crusades and Controversies, 1897–1913*. Berkeley and Los Angeles, 1962.

Robbins, Roy M. *Our Landed Heritage: The Public Domain, 1776–1936*. Princeton, 1942.

Roberts, Harold D. *Salt Creek, Wyoming: The Story of a Great Oil Field*. Denver, 1956.

Rogin, Michael Paul. *The Intellectuals and McCarthy: The Radical Specter*. Cambridge, Mass., 1967.

Ross, Thomas R. *Jonathan Prentice Dolliver: A Study in Political Integrity and Independence*. Iowa City, 1958.

Russell, Francis. *The Shadow of Blooming Grove: Warren G. Harding in His Times*. New York and Toronto, 1968.

Samuelson, Paul A., and Hagen, Everett E. *After the War—1918–1920*. Washington, 1943.

Shideler, James H. *Farm Crisis, 1919–1923*. Berkeley and Los Angeles, 1957.

Smith, Daniel M. *The Great Departure: The United States and World War I, 1914–1920*. New York, 1965.

Smith, Rixey, and Beasley, Norman. *Carter Glass: A Biography*. Freeport, N. Y., 1970.

Soule, George. *Prosperity Decade: From War to Depression, 1917–1929*. New York and Toronto, 1947.

Sprout, Harold and Margaret. *The Rise of American Naval Power, 1776–1918*. Princeton, 1946.

Stephenson, George M. *The Religious Aspects of Swedish Immigration: A Study of Immigrant Churches*. Minneapolis, 1932.

Steuart, Justin. *Wayne Wheeler: Dry Boss*. U. S. A., 1928.

Stoddard, Henry L. *It Costs to Be President*. New York, 1938.

Sullivan, Mark. *Our Times: The United States, 1900–1925.* 6 vols. New York, 1926–1935.

Swanberg, William A. *Citizen Hearst: A Biography of William Randolph Hearst.* New York, 1961.

Taft, Philip. *The A. F. of L. in the Time of Gompers.* New York, 1957.

Taussig, Frank W. *The Tariff History of the United States.* 6th ed. New York and London, 1914; 8th ed. New York, 1964 (1931).

Thelen, David P. *The Early Life of Robert M. La Follette, 1855–1884.* Chicago, 1966.

––––––. *The New Citizenship: Origins of Progressivism in Wisconsin, 1885–1900.* Columbia, Mo., 1972.

Timmons, Bascom N. *Garner of Texas: A Personal History.* New York, 1948.

Trattner, Walter I. *Crusade for the Children: A History of the National Child Labor Committee and Child Labor Reform in America.* Chicago, 1970.

Vinson, John Chalmers. *The Parchment Peace: The United States Senate and the Washington Conference, 1921–1922.* Athens, Ga., 1955.

––––––. *Referendum for Isolation: Defeat of Article Ten of the League of Nations Covenant.* Athens, Ga., 1961.

Viorst, Milton. *Fall From Grace: The Republican Party and the Puritan Ethic.* New York, 1971 (1968).

Ward, Alan J. *Ireland and Anglo-American Relations, 1899–1921.* Toronto, 1969.

Weinstein, James. *The Decline of Socialism in America, 1912–1925.* New York, 1969 (1967).

Welch, Richard E., Jr. *George Frisbee: Hoar and the Half-Breed Republicans.* Cambridge, Mass., 1971.

Werner, M. R., and Starr, John. *Teapot Dome.* New York, 1959.

White, Gerald T. *Formative Years in the Far West: A History of Standard Oil Company of California and Predecessors Through 1919.* New York, 1962.

White, William Allen. *A Puritan in Babylon: The Story of Calvin Coolidge.* New York, 1938.

Wilensky, Norman M. *Conservatives in the Progressive Era: The Taft Republicans of 1912.* Tallahassee, 1965.

Willoughby, William R. *The St. Lawrence Waterway: A Study in Politics and Diplomacy.* Madison, 1961.

Winters, Donald L. *Henry Cantwell Wallace as Secretary of Agriculture, 1921–1924.* Urbana, Ill., 1970.

Wood, Stephen B. *Constitutional Politics in the Progressive Era: Child Labor and the Law.* Chicago and London, 1968.

Zieger, Robert H. *Republicans and Labor, 1919–1929.* Lexington, Ky., 1969.

INDEX